Rough Daddy Erotic Short Stories

Izzie Vee

Published by Izzie Vee, 2023.

Table of Contents

Rough Daddy Erotic Short Stories & Novels 10 Stories Collection

Age-Gap, Sexy Taboo Men, Raunchy Virgin Women, Dirty Explicit Sex

Izzie Vee

Erotic & Forbidden[1]

IZZIE VEE[2]

1. https://www.amazon.com/s?k=izzie+vee&i=digital-text&crid=31LQJTEQYT2EE&sprefix=izzie+vee%2Cdigital-text%2C121&ref=nb_sb_noss
2. https://www.amazon.com/s?k=izzie+vee&i=digital-text&crid=31LQJTEQYT2EE&sprefix=izzie+vee%2Cdigital-text%2C121&ref=nb_sb_noss

Cover Design by Izzie Vee
Cover Photo by VitalikRadko on Depositphotos.com

Important Readers' Note

Happy greetings!
Go follow me on Amazon with only 2 quick clicks. CLICK **THE FOLLOW BUTTON**[1] below to be notified about my hot new releases weekly. Then it'll take you to my Amazon's author page, where *you'll need to click the follow button on amazon's site as well*. It's that simple! Two quick seconds and you're all done!

2

Thanks for joining and be ready to be notified about the hottest releases sent straight to your inbox. Cheers!

1. **https://www.amazon.com/-/e/B09VZQM39S**

2. https://www.amazon.com/-/e/B09VZQM39S

Daddy's Taboo Family-Friend

Izzie Vee

Erotic & Forbidden[1]

IZZIE VEE[2]

1. https://www.amazon.com/s?k=izzie+vee&i=digital-text&crid=31LQJTEQYT2EE&sprefix=izzie+vee%2Cdigital-text%2C121&ref=nb_sb_noss
2. https://www.amazon.com/s?k=izzie+vee&i=digital-text&crid=31LQJTEQYT2EE&sprefix=izzie+vee%2Cdigital-text%2C121&ref=nb_sb_noss

All characters in this book are fictious and figments of the author's imagination.

Cover Design by Izzie Vee
Cover Photo by VitalikRadko on Depositphotos.com

Table of Content

Chapter 1

Kat

"Mom, I'm a college student; I can handle myself perfectly fine," I say to my mother even though I'm inwardly rejoicing.

"We know, honey, but we would feel a lot better if you stayed with Grayson. It will only be for a week," my mom says as she makes a face at me that reminds me of sad little puppies.

I glance at dad, who has that silent plea in his eyes, while he momentarily glances at his watch. I know he's just dying to leave and get this over with.

I huff and slump my shoulders. "Fine. If you insist."

Mom immediately sighs and looks to my dad with a smile on her face. They think they've won, but it's really a win-win situation for all of us.

"You're such a sweetheart," she says as she kisses me on the cheeks and then proceeds to grab her bag. "We'll talk more on this later tonight, sweetie. Have a good one."

I nod. "Bye, guys."

I watch as they leave before I grab my phone and text my best friend, telling her the news. I couldn't be happier minutes ago when my parents broke the news to me, telling me they had business to take care of and would be gone for the week. I had just come back for summer break the previous night, and imagine my surprise when they told me that the man I had had a crush on for years would be my 'babysitter' for a week. I didn't want to push their buttons to the point that makes them reconsider, but I wanted to seem believable at the time. Of course, I suggested staying with my best friend Amy, but they said it wouldn't be convenient seeing that Amy shared a room with her little sister.

And of course, I had suggested staying alone, but my parents are too over-protective and are especially cautious with the rise in robbery in the area lately. Their next best option was dad's best friend, Grayson, whom they had no idea I had a crush on.

As I text Amy, my mind begins to race with possibilities. I have always looked for the perfect opportunity to flirt and shoot my shot, but I don't think Grayson ever considers me as anything other than a kid. Being under his roof would be different. I will show him just how much I can offer him – or at least I will try to – being a virgin and all.

Half an hour later, I'm face to face with my best friend, who's finding it hard to believe that this is actually happening. She's staring at me with big hazel eyes – amusement clear as day as she awaits what I have to say next.

"It'll only be for a week, but I plan to make the best of it," I say to her.

"So you're planning to seduce him?" she asks with an excited pitch to her voice.

I bite my lips. "Or at least try..."

Amy chokes a laugh as she stares at me. "You're actually serious," she realizes.

"Yeah... Grayson is the only guy I'm attracted to Ames, and you know that. I have loved him for a long time," I casually say. Anyone apart from my best friend would think I'm crazy, but after harboring a crush for so long, I came to realize it is more than that. I am in love with a guy that I possibly can't even have.

"I know, I know," she sighs. "But what if this goes south Kat... you can end up hurt," she says as her eyes and voice soften.

I swallow, not even wanting to think of the possibility. "No negative thinking, okay. This is going to happen. I'm gonna convince Grayson that I'm a desirable woman and not a kid that he probably thinks I am," I say, trying to convince myself more than my best friend.

She smiles at me, but I can still see the bit of doubt in her eyes that tells me she isn't as confident. But I totally understand; Amy has been there every step with me and my crisis into getting Grayson to see me. No matter what I wore in the past or how much I tried to do to get his attention, it never seemed to work. He barely saw me. Whenever he ended a fling, I would rejoice, and when he was back on track again, I would break down. Amy was there through all of it, and now I figure she probably knows better than to get her hopes up this time around.

She sighs again. "Well, this time, things might actually change for real. I mean, you actually gained a few flattering pounds since last semester." Her eyes settle on my boobs, and I grin, knowing that to be true.

I no longer look like stick and bones but have actually gained a few pounds in areas that have seemingly caught the attention of numerous guys back on campus. Still, I have no interest in anyone but Grayson Tuck.

"If this pulls through, just make sure you have protection on standby," she winks and I can't help but giggle.

I am too excited to think of anything other than the possibilities of Grayson and I being together. I want to start packing but know that my mom will probably find it weird if I do it too soon. So instead, I wait on them to arrive that following evening. It's a Saturday so I order pizza and wait for it to arrive just in time when my parents actually does.

We're sitting at the dining table eating and chatting when a thought comes to me and I freeze.

I swallow the bite in my mouth and lift my gaze up to my parents. "Er – Is Grayson actually on board with this?"

"Of course he is honey. I mean, how else would we be sending you there?" she laughs heartily and shakes her head. My heart's bubbling with joy but I can't actually make them see it.

"So he doesn't mind me in the way. I know he can be strict and all that stuff," I say.

"Honey, he's fine with it plus, he will be at work throughout the day anyway, and when night comes, you'd both have retired to your rooms," she smiles.

The idea of him constantly working puts me on edge, but I know that if I'm smart, I can actually seduce him between times.

"We're really sorry to be running off on your break, honey, but I promise we will be back before you know it and will have plenty of time before your summer ends anyway," she smiles.

I nod, picking at the pizza on my plate. "It's fine mom, I totally understand."

I understood ever since I was ten and finally realized that my parents were art dealers who were always going to be away at sometimes the most inopportune times. Sometimes they missed pageants, school meetings and lunch dates but I'm still eternally grateful for them and the fact that they never allowed me to be short of anything.

Guilt suddenly courses through me at the realisation that I'm planning to seduce a family friend they have known for almost a decade. The thought of them finding out, almost cripples me on spot and I immediately have half the mind to cancel my ridiculous plan and find some ways to get over Grayson; but I can't. I've been wanting this for so long. He has now occupied every part of me and to not have him – or at least try to, would possibly ruin me. I don't know how this will eventually end, but I'm prepared for anything as long as I get Grayson to want me.

I FALL ASLEEP THAT night with him on my mind and wake up with him being a constant thought. I stretch, turning to the side to grab my phone. It's six, and it takes me a minute to realize that it's raining cats and dogs outside.

I mutter a curse and head to my closet to start packing a bag. I already planned what I would be bringing for the week, but once in my underwear drawer, my hand lingers, and my heart starts to race. I don't have a single pair of sexy underwear in sight. It's a bit sad, really, seeing I want to seduce a man, yet I have nothing sexy... just cotton panties with unmatched bras.

"Fuck Kat... way to be a plain Jane," I mutter, grabbing up a handful of what I have and throwing them in the case.

When I am finally done about twenty minutes later, I stare at myself and wonder if I'm actually capable of doing this. Yes, I'm not that bad looking, but surely I had to have more to actually pull this off. I can't dirty talk, I can't flirt... I've never even kissed someone before. Like a real kiss. With my experience, I belong in a fucking convent. There's no way a sexy, God-like bachelor like Grayson will want me. He's passed through many girlfriends and probably has enough experience up his belt to last him a lifetime. I don't have anything but desire.

My phone buzzes on the bed. I look down to realize its Amy who's sending me a message.

Today is the day. Break a leg ... or your hymen rather, lol.

I can't help but giggle, instantly putting me in a better mood.

It's still raining when I get dressed in long sleeves and shorts and head downstairs with my suitcase in hand. Mom and dad have already packed for their trip and are around the kitchen counter, having breakfast.

"Where did this rain come from?" I ask as I look outside and then sit around the table. "Gosh, I hate rainy summers."

"Yeah, it might be a thing this time around. I haven't seen the weather reports, but this type of rain always means there's more to come," mom shrugs as she sips on her coffee.

"Yeah, I mean, we're in the hurricane season after all, and this is Florida," my dad chuckles.

I huff out a breath. "What time do you guys plan on leaving?" I ask.

"In the next thirty minutes. Our flight is at eleven, and plus we have to drop you off at Grayson's first. The earlier the better," dad says.

"Do you have everything, honey?"

"Yeah, I'm all set."

"OK well I'm gonna send off an email and be right back," she says as she leaves the room.

I try to eat some breakfast but I'm too nervous, so I drink some coffee instead and hope that settles me for a bit.

Twenty minutes later, we are inside the car, driving to Grayson's place, a fifteen-minute drive from where we live, in a neighborhood that's way better than the one we live in. Dad definitely doesn't have to worry about anyone getting robbed there. The closer we get to his house, the more nervous I become. My stomach churns, and I feel sweaty all over despite the air condition in the car and the rain outside.

When we actually park in his driveway, I'm a mess who can't seem to get her emotions in check. This is it.

"Shoot, Oh honey, we forgot to bring an umbrella," mom says, almost startling me.

I swallow. "It's fine, I guess. I can make a run for it," I say as I pull at my coat.

Mom sighs. "Are you sure?"

"Of course, don't worry. I'll change into something warm as soon as I get inside," I assure her, reaching for my over-the-shoulder bag.

"Ok, sweetheart. Call us if you need anything and try to have fun," she smiles.

Not the type of fun you're thinking, but sure.

"I will. I love you guys," I exclaim as I reach forward to kiss them both on the cheeks.

"We love you too, honey," they say in unison before I finally push the car door open and make a run for it.

The front door seems miles away as the cold rain beats against my skin. I am soaked and panting when I finally arrive at his doorstep. I look back to wave my parents goodbye and watch them drive away before I finally ring the doorbell on the huge mahogany door. There's a small porch, but the rain is still blowing in and making me even wetter. I become antsy the longer I wait, no longer nervous – but impatient, as I wait for Grayson to open the door.

As I begin to wonder if he's actually at home, the door bursts open, and he stands in front of me. I immediately go weak in the knees.

Chapter 2

Grayson

I'm hopping out of the shower when the ringing of my doorbell puts me at a standstill. I don't usually get visitors so early in the morning, but then it dawns on me that today is the day that Kat will be coming over. Shit, I had remembered up to last night but had forgotten entirely this morning. It's pouring outside, so I quickly grab a robe and throw it on before I dash downstairs to open up. When I pull the door, open, Kat is on the other side. I half expect to see her parents as well, but with it raining, I figure that they wouldn't bother.

I stare at Kat, soaked with a coat draped over her that's drenched. I don't waste any time; I quickly reach for her bag and usher her inside before closing the door behind her.

I return to find her shrugging off her coat and kicking off her shoes. As I watch her, I freeze in the spot, and lust suddenly overrides me. The rain has plastered her clothes against her skin, and the white long sleeve top is almost see-through as it clings to her. She drops the coat to the floor and rakes her fingers through her hair as she turns to me.

I swallow hard and feel the blood rush to my crotch as she stands there, practically naked from the top half with pointy nipples sticking out her chest. Her breasts are stiff, and so is my cock the longer I stand staring at her.

But fuck, this is Kat, my best friend's kid – a girl that's twelve years my junior.

I clear my throat. "Sorry I couldn't come down earlier. I was er – just getting out of the shower," I say, watching as her gaze skims over me.

I can't help it, but I'm staring at her and not in the way a man should stare at his friend's kid. But I can't help it – I actually cannot believe that this is the same Kat who was by my house on New Year's. She was scrawny then – a tiny little thing – but the Kat standing before me now is the one from a literal wet dream. She definitely filled out in the right areas, namely her hips, breast and her ass. My gaze trail down her legs, and they are wet... beads of water trailing down each slender column. I am suddenly filled with dirty thoughts, but in my mind, it isn't water that has gotten her all wet.

I can feel my loin responding to the imagery I have created in my head, so I quickly tear my gaze away and bring it to her face instead, holding her bag in front of me to hide any possible erection. She's still beautiful – that certainly hasn't changed. But her stunning blue eyes seem even brighter now that her dark hair is clamped down on her head. Her skin has a beautiful tan that almost glistens beneath the glaze of the water.

"It's okay. Sorry for making a mess, by the way," she says as she inspects the puddle forming around her feet.

"Oh, that's fine. You may want to change out of those before you catch a cold."

The thought of her nakedness fills me with longing, and at this point, if I don't control myself, Kat will catch me with a boner, and that's the last thing I want.

"Yeah,... good thing my bag is leather, or everything would've been soaked as well," she exclaims with a short laugh. I smile and our eyes meet. It's like my heart has stopped and the intensity of her gaze freezes me.

Fuck, this shouldn't be happening; I shouldn't be having these thoughts towards Kat. I begin to blame it on the rain; I always get horny when it rains, so maybe that's the reason, but it's not a fucking excuse.

"Well, er – you know where the guest bedroom is. Everything you need is there," I tell her as I manage a smile. "I'm gonna make some coffee while you get settled in."

She quickly nods and reaches for her bag that I hand her and then promptly turn towards the kitchen before she catches sight of my growing erection. Kat escapes up the stairs; I mutter a curse, unable to believe that this is actually happening.

I've known the Wellingtons for years, and never once have I looked at their daughter in a manner that wasn't respect and admiration. But today, for the first time, I'm no longer seeing Kat as a kid but a grown woman who is as tempting as ever. I can't help but wonder what it would feel like to sink my manhood into –.

"Fuck Grayson, what the heck are you doing?" I mutter to myself, trying to let anything other than Kat occupy my brain.

I should be thinking about work and the fact that I should be getting ready to leave, but here I am, thinking about the last person I should even be thinking about. But it's like I'm suddenly plagued, and then a thought strikes me. Kat will be staying over for an entire week. If I'm already tempted by her within a day of her being here, what will it be like days from now when she will be all that I see when I come home, tired, sexually frustrated and hornier than ever? I won't be able to call anyone over with her here. I can, but I don't want to make her uncomfortable – which is stupid because I'm a grown man and this is my house.

I pour myself a cup of coffee and gulp it down, feeling as it warms my inside. Just as I'm finally able to get my mind off Kat, she enters the kitchen with a smile. She is dry for the most part. Her hair wrapped in a towel, and she is in fresh clothes. A sweater hides the wonders I had witnessed earlier and baggy pants that don't show an inch of her shape.

I should be grateful. I am, but a part of me wants more, as stupid as it may sound.

"Coffee?" I ask, gesturing towards the cup I filled earlier.

"Thanks," she says with a smile as she reaches for it and takes a sip. She watches me from over the rim as she drinks, and I know that the screws are turning in her head. I just want to know what she's thinking.

When she has had her fill, she sets the cup on the counter and licks her lips, drawing my attention to them. They are a bright pink, looking incredibly soft and juicy.

"Thanks for letting me stay here, by the way. I told mom and dad that I would've been fine home alone, but you know how they are," she shrugs.

I smile despite myself. "Yeah, your father is very overprotective, and your mother has learned to be the same."

She laughs and somehow it manages to warm all my insides. "I see you redecorated. It's really nice," she says as she looks around the all-white kitchen.

Nice of her to notice. "Yeah, a friend of mine helped me with the redesign. Apparently, the pop of colors is much more welcoming than the black."

Her smile broadens. "It certainly is."

There's a bit of silence, but it isn't the awkward type. It's like an electrical field has been charged around us and is pulling us together. My body is heating up, my cock is starting to respond again and fuck, I want to kiss her so bad.

But my cell phone shrills, breaking the silence like ice around us, and I don't know whether to be thankful or a little disappointed. My gaze travels to the device, and I suddenly realize that it's my work alarm, letting me know that I should be leaving right about now.

I sigh as I switch it off. "Duty calls," I say as I look towards her. She manages a smile and fondles with the handle of her mug. "I er – I will be back later this evening. Make yourself at home and if there's anything you need, just call me. The pantry and the fridge are stocked by the way, and there's a number for a delivery service on the coffee table in the living room." I know I'm blabbering, which is unlike me, but I can't seem to help it.

It seems to get a giggle out of Kat. "Yeah, noted. Thanks, Grayson."

I nod and move past her, heading upstairs to get dressed. I have half a mind to take a cold shower before I leave, but time won't allow it. I'm already late, and the faster I leave this house, the better.

Chapter 3

Kat

I watch as his car leaves the driveway, and it's like the oxygen has finally returned to my lungs. I take a deep breath and skip to my room which is like a master in itself with how nicely put it is. But that's the least of my worries, considering the handsome beast that just left its lair.

Grayson is even more handsome than I remembered – which is strange considering he has a face that you can't likely forget. But at thirty-two, he has a wrinkle-free face, tanned skin and green eyes that remind me of the forest. He's just as ripped as I remembered but has certainly gained a few more muscle mass in certain areas despite the unflattering robe he was wearing at the time.

I try to relay that encounter over and over in my head, and each time, it rustles my insides. If I'm not mistaken, I could have sworn he was checking me out at one point. Though I don't know what to make of it. Maybe he was just checking me out considering the fact that he hasn't seen me in a while, but if that's not the case, then he must've been pleased with what he saw.

My cheeks warm with a blush at the idea of him being attracted to me. It would definitely make seducing him a lot easier, but if I'm mistaken, then things would be a bit difficult.

For the rest of the day, all I can think about is how I will be going about my first attempt. Should I be blunt about it? Should I just approach him and tell him what's going on, or should I try to tease him a little first? How far would teasing get me, how long will it be, considering I only have a week to make it all happen.

I huff and take a shower that evening and prepare dinner which is highly unlike me, but I do it anyway. I am in his dining area, eating, when I hear his car drive-in. my heart immediately begins to flutter, and I am instantly filled with nervousness. My eyes drop to the clothes I'm wearing and luckily for me I had decided on a crop top and sweats. That should get his attention, at least, with my nipples standing like shoulders in my chest. But as the keys jingle from outside, my heart pounces faster, and I get too jittery. I dash across the room and head upstairs to mine, locking myself in as I quickly dial Amy's number.

"Hey, what's happening?" she asks.

"What should I do? The whole seduction only seemed plausible in my head," I almost whisper.

Amy giggles on the other end. “Figured. Listen, just go for it; we both know you’re not a tease, so you’ll probably fail at that anyway...”

I frown. “So what are you saying? That I just throw myself at him?” I ask beneath my breath.

There’s a slight pause. “Yeah.”

I scoff. “I can’t believe I’m taking advice from a lesbian about men.”

Amy laughs heartily. “There’s no difference really when it comes to lust. The goal is the same.”

Sighing, I ease up from the bed. “Okay, well, wish me luck. I’m about to shoot my shot.”

“Good luck; I hope you’re sore tomorrow when I call.”

I can feel a blush coming on. “We’ll see. Bye Ames.”

The call ends, and I’m still pondering over what Amy said. For so long, I’ve been the shy, timid girl and now that I am finally getting the opportunity to come out of my shell, will I blow it?

I can’t.

Getting up, I adjust myself in the large wall mirror beside my bed and muster a sigh before I decide to head back downstairs. But as I open my door, I almost bump into Grayson who’s just outside my door. He looks me over, a smile on his face.

“Hey, is everything okay?”

“Yeah, I heard your car and decided to come say hi,” I lie, forcing a smile.

He’s smiling too, still looking fresh in his dark suit and white undershirt with a few buttons loose. I can see a small glimpse of his bare chest that makes me wonder just where else is bare. I can feel my cheeks going warm and immediately clear my throat to distract from it.

“I er – I made dinner; I left you some in the microwave.”

“You didn’t have to do that, but thank you nonetheless. I’m gonna take a quick shower and then maybe you can join me?”

My heart skips a beat, my mouth dropping open as I stare into his dark green eyes. “J-join you?”

“For dinner,” he quickly says, and I suddenly feel like an idiot. *Of course, for dinner Kat, what else?*

“Oh, I – I had mine earlier, sorry.”

“A glass of wine then?” he adds with a tight smile.

“Yeah, sure, sounds good.”

He nods before giving me one final once-over and leaving for his room. Sighing heavily, I head downstairs to clear the plate I left on the counter, and warm Grayson’s in the meantime. When he comes down, he’s wearing sweats and a t-shirt that emphasizes every bit of muscle. It surprises me how he manages to be this fit having an office job and working all the time. His arms are bulky, shoulders are broad, and even his legs seem massive in the shorts. It makes me wonder if his manhood is just as big.

Grayson's brows furrow as he catches me staring at him. I quickly rush towards the microwave to get his food out and set it before him.

He raises a brow and looks up at me. "This looks tasty. I haven't had alfredo in a while."

He gets up and walks towards the wine cabinet, where he inspects the bottles and ultimately decides on one. He places it on the table and moves around me towards the cupboards for glasses. His scent fills me, makes me weak in the knees and clenching between the legs. It's that sweet musky scent that sticks, and I can bet his pillows smell the same, his coats... everywhere.

I almost gasp when he comes beside me and sets a glass in front of me as he pours red wine into it.

"Should you even be drinking, by the way?" he asks me, pausing.

"Well, I'll be twenty-one in a couple of months," I confess.

He seems hesitant, but then he offers me a polite smile and continues to pour. "Well, I won't tell if you don't."

I'm grinning. "Thanks."

After a few minutes, he is at the other side of the counter, eating his dinner and complimenting me on creating a tasty meal. I sip my wine as I watch him, unable to take my eyes off him, especially when the cream dangles on his lips before catching it with his tongue and swoops it in his mouth. I'm hot all over, and I know my panties are drenched with the impure thoughts of him that take permanent residence in my mind.

I am itching to get up and head over to his side, trap myself between him and the table and see how he would react, but then my heart starts to beat so fast, I fear I'd have a heart attack before anything actually happens. But the way he is looking at me is almost an invite in itself – or am I imagining things? His gaze seems hungry and animalistic, and I'm starting to notice the way he shifts on his seat when his eyes trail from my face to my chest.

I bite my lips as a theory comes to me. Deciding to test it, I lean over with my hands below my tits, pushing it up, even more, causing it to almost spill out of the top.

I clear my throat. "So, how's work been?" I ask, deciding to start a casual conversation while trying to see if I am getting his attention.

He swallows, eyes quickly going back and forth from my face to my cleavage. I can see he's flustered. His ears are red, and he can't seem to meet my gaze. I may be a virgin, but I've watched enough movies and read enough books to know what this is.

"Er... work is fine. We are actually planning on expanding in the coming months."

"Really, where?"

"New York," he says, his eyes now trained on the plate in front of him instead of me.

I perk up. "That's awesome. Maybe I'll see you around sometime when I head back to college."

He looks up at me. "How long do you have left?"

"A year." I take my glass of wine and take a sip, my eyes not leaving his. With him looking at me, I take a chance and allow the wine to spill on me, crashing against my tits and slipping through the middle. Grayson's eyes follow every bit of it, though at this point, I don't think he can help himself. I'm rejoicing inwardly, but I want to push his buttons a little more.

"Oh shoot, I'm such a klutz; can you pass me a napkin, please?" I ask, looking down on my wet chest and then at him.

He visibly swallows, and it seemingly takes a second for him to process before he nods and gets up. "Yeah, sure," he says, racing over to the sink area to get me a piece. As he returns and hands it to me, I bite the inside of my lips, a bit hesitant, and reach for his hands. He seems taken by surprise, even more so when I place his hand on my chest.

Heat courses through every fiber in my body, and I can feel my panties pooling with wetness at his simple touch and close proximity. His eyes darken, and the breath hitches in my throat with the intensity of his lethal gaze.

"Kat, what are you doing?" he asks, voice steely and gruff – quite a stark contrast from what it was just moments ago.

I swallow, now overcome with fear. I lick my lips and try to think of something, already regretting my choices, but it's already done. I have gotten this far. Of course, I can't just chicken out without knowing the outcome.

"What does it look like?" I hear myself asking, my voice gone soft and somehow sultry.

"A mistake. You shouldn't be doing this," he says sharply, yet his hand remains in place. He can pull away, but he doesn't, which gives me a reason to continue with this.

"Don't you find me attractive, Grayson?" I ask. At this point, my heart is hammering in my chest, and I am sure he can feel it too.

"Kat, what is going on with you?"

"I just want to know if you desire me as much as I desire you," I say.

He swallows, tears his gaze away for a second and shakes his head. "What does it matter; you are young, small, and most importantly, you're my friend's kid. Whatever this is, Kat, don't let it happen again." He finally pulls away, and it tugs at my heart as tears threaten to spill from me. In the next second, he is gone, and I'm all alone in the empty room with regret crashing into me like a tidal wave.

My lips start to tremble, and before I know it, my face is swimming in my tears. I completely read the signals wrong, and now I am embarrassed more than ever. How can I even continue living in his house after all that? How can I even look him in the eyes again?

After a few minutes of wallowing in my self-pity and blaming myself for even deciding to do this in the first place, I run towards my room and throw myself under my covers as sobs wrack my body. I cry for what seems like hours, even though it's a few minutes, and decide to use the bathroom down the hall before I head to bed. I can't even call Amy as yet to let her know what's happening. I am too ashamed to mutter a word of this to anyone.

I am about to open the bathroom door when I pause after hearing a sound. Curious, I press my face against the door and hear him mutter a curse. The longer I listen, the more I realize he isn't talking to himself or anyone for that matter.

He is moaning and grunting, and though I am inexperienced, I am well aware that he is pleasuring himself. I am frozen in shock, unable to believe my ears but the realization sends heat cascading throughout my body, making me wetter than ever and ecstatic that I am the cause of it. I have to be. Less than five minutes ago, he was downstairs with his hand on my chest. I could see the lust in his eyes then, but I would never have imagined that it affected him to this degree.

I can't help but smile as I continue to listen to his moans that set me ablaze. I can feel the wetness on the top of my thighs and feel an intense need to stroke myself as well. But then his moans become louder, and he almost grunts before he settles, breathing heavily. I can hear a muffled 'Fuck," and that's enough to let me know he came. I immediately dash back to my room, thinking it would be way too awkward if I got caught. For the entire night, all I can think about is him nestled deep within me and not in his hands. It fills me with lewd thoughts, and I know I will have to up my game in the morning to get Grayson to admit his desire for me or at least act on it.

Chapter 4

Grayson

My sudden need for Kat is unlike anything I've ever felt for a woman. No woman has ever had me so confused and certainly never so sexually frustrated. If a couple of days ago someone came to me and told me I'd be lusting after my best friend's kid, I would have laughed in their face or even punched them across the face for saying such a thing, but here I am, in a predicament that's greater than anything I've ever had to overcome.

Last night took me by surprise; I didn't expect Kat to make such a move, but there she was, admitting that she wanted me, which was a dick-hardening statement in itself. I can still feel her soft flesh against the pad of my fingers, I can still see the creamy contours of her chest and how her beady nipples stuck out from her chest. Even now, I am itching to squeeze them, to wrap them in my mouth and then suck on each perky, ripe tit like a succulent fruit.

Even now while thinking about it, I can feel my desires stirring in my loin despite the speed on the treadmill. Exercising always does the trick, but I am still tainted with thoughts of the desirous little minx. I lack sleep because apart from stroking myself, all I could have thought about was her and the possibilities of plunging into her soft, young flesh, over and over again.

But Fuck, this is Kat, who I shouldn't even be having such feelings towards. I would ruin her with a single thrust. She would fall for me, no doubt, because she's young and evidently has a crush on me. I know this pattern – you fuck them, they want more than a good time. They want a relationship that I can't give – heck, I certainly can't give Kat that no matter the outcome. There are too many risks, too many things at stake.

But suddenly, all thoughts of that seem like a needle in a haystack when she appears at the door, dressed in a mini-skirt and a crop top. She's braless, her hair is down, spilling over her shoulders in beautiful dark waves, and her skin is flawless – ivory and as smooth as an old renaissance painting. Her cheeks have a blush, and from where I stand, I can see her biting the inside of her lips.

"I didn't know you have an in-house gym," she says, and even her soft little innocent voice alone puts me on edge.

I stop the treadmill and reach for a towel to dry my face. "Yeah, I had it installed a few months ago. It's more convenient," I say, trying to be as casual as I can.

She nods as her gaze skims over me. "I see it's working in your favor."

In my mind, I would have liked to give her the benefit of the doubt and pass off last night as a moment of insanity. Maybe the sip of wine had charred her brain and made her act like that. That's what a part of me wants to believe in all this. Maybe this morning, she would forget, apologize for being so bold even, and save both of us the torture of sexual chemistry and awkwardness. But clearly, with that statement, I know her goal is the same, and so are her intentions.

"Thanks," I smile as I step off.

This can't go any further, no matter what desire I feel towards her. Kat is forbidden. And being the bigger adult here, I should set things straight.

I turn towards her and meet her fiery gaze. I have half a mind to forget my pep talk and damn this all to hell, but I know I must do this.

"Listen Kat, I'm sorry if I came off a little too harsh last night..." I sigh. "That wasn't my intention, but you have to stop whatever this is," I say, making a gesture over her entire body.

Her cheeks get pinker. "You are a kid, and I –

Something flashes across her eyes before she cuts me off. "I'm not a kid." Her voice is firmer than usual, and I know she's angry.

"You aren't; true, but that's how I see you," I lie. Maybe anger is best. Perhaps she can hate me after insinuating such a thing and finally stop.

"Do you usually get hard for kids, Grayson?" she asks me with a dangerous glint in her eyes.

I freeze, my eyes widening as I stare at her.

"I know you want me just as much as I want you, Grayson, and there's no point in denying it. I heard you in the bathroom last night. You want me."

I swallow hard, feeling my cock stir even though I am embarrassed and shocked – to say the least. I knew I should have used the bathroom in my room, but that one was nearer, and I needed a quick release. Fuck! What do I even say to that?

"That was a mistake," are the words that come out of my mouth.

"So if I kiss you right now, you wouldn't feel anything?"

Before I get the chance to respond, her lips have crashed against mine, and I can feel their softness against me. Her tongue pushes out, and stakes claim, her body presses against mine. No matter how I will myself to resist her and push her away, the sweet, inviting feel of her mouth tells me otherwise. I can't help myself. Katherine has come to damn me to hell, and in this moment, I don't mind eternal damnation.

My tongue dabbles with her, explores her mouth in the most sensual fashion before my hunger takes course. The longer I kiss her, the longer her body is pressed against mine, the more my body aches with need. My hand circles her waist, and I pull her even harder against me. She is soft, and welcoming. Her kiss is sweet and innocent, but it drives me insane. Her perfume is like fresh fruits, the shampoo in her hair like vanilla. Her sweetness overwhelms me, her body drives me insane, and her lips are like heaven – each lip like a soft cloud. I take all she gives as her soft little whimpers fill my sex with hardness.

Desire pumps through my veins like fire, my brain has gone to mush, and the only thing I can make sense of is Kat's body against mine. Needily, my hands begin to explore her body, trailing over her round little ass, skimming at her smooth flesh before I realize she isn't wearing any panties. I freeze, but she continues to kiss me while I think about how easy it might be to turn her over, hoist her skirt and fuck her senseless. My cock hardens against her tummy, and I am seconds away from going through with it when my cell phone rings.

I pull away from her as if I've been burned and look her in the eyes.

"Kat, please. This isn't a good idea," I almost plead with her even though every inch of my body calls for her.

I shake my head to clear the fog as I contemplate answering the phone that continues to shrill in the background. I should, but I don't, Kat pins me with her beauty and the sensation still buzzing against my skin. I am torn between right and wrong. The need to fuck her and the need to push her away.

But I'm needy, she's beautiful and as tempting as ever with doe-y blue eyes that shatter my resolve. I am ruined with a single kiss. My body is dying to have more – taste more of her sweet flesh. To give her exactly what she wants.

"I want you so much," she whispers, inching closer towards me.

I swallow. "You're killing me here, Kat. This isn't right."

She licks her lips, still flushed from the intense kissing session. "What's wrong about it?"

She's so near again that I can feel the heat radiating from her skin on me. Her stomach is grazing my cock again, and fuck, it almost hurts.

"We don't have to have sex right away. We can work our way towards it," she softly says. "I'm not giving up until I have you inside me, Grayson."

My heart races. I open my mouth to speak, and she's right there, collecting every breath. "My cock would ruin you, little girl."

She pauses, but the slyest smile forms on her peachy pink lips. "One way to find out...daddy."

My breath hitch, and my cock swell to a painful degree as I process her words. The single word in particular. Damn it all!

I reach for her and pull her against me, loving the little gasp that leaves her mouth in return. I kiss her hard, and she kisses me back just as greedily. My hands then start to roam over her. Over her sides, her breast and her ass. With each contact, she moans against me, getting louder when my strong hands cup her ass cheek and greet it with a hard squeeze. I am reminded that she isn't wearing any panties and push my hand further down to graze her intimate flesh. The wetness that greets me sends a moan bubbling from my throat. She is bare, warm and incredibly wet. For me. This beauty could have anyone she wants, yet she is dripping for me.

She shimmies a bit closer, and I can feel her stomach rubbing against my erection. If she keeps it up, it will be inside it in a matter of seconds. But I know I have to take it fucking slow – if not for me, then definitely for Kat. Despite the tease she seems to be, she deserves so much more. She deserves everything.

I lift her legs and my buckle from all the pent-up sexual tension. I want to lay her down in a bed and make sweet love to her, but the futon is closest I get to that.

I lay her glorious body down, and she smiles at me, spreading her legs and giving me an eyeful of her exquisite, wet snatch.

"Jesus fucking Christ," I mutter under my breath as I study her welcoming flesh.

"All yours, daddy," she says, her hands reaching down to spread her flesh. The imagery sends signals to my cock, and it twitches in my pants, letting me know what time it is. If I look at her any longer, I will combust in my pants.

Kat is a treasure; she is magic.

I get on my knees, unlike I have done to any other woman and come face to face with her dripping pussy. She smells magnificent, her arousal seducing me like a pheromone in the atmosphere.

As eager as I am, I look up to her and study her face. She looks a tad bit nervous, but the need on her face is crystal clear.

"Are you sure about this?" I ask, hoping she will say yes but know I will respect her all the same even if she changes her mind.

"Yes, please."

It's all the answer I want. Without hesitating a second longer, I push her skirt up a little higher and lower my mouth to her succulent flesh. She tastes as expected, sweet and intensely intoxicating as I feast on her. She whimpers; she writhes a little as my tongue feasts on the perimeter of her flesh, lapping up the sweet nectar she produced for me. I hum against her skin, watching as her lips part with each lick and then regain their position again. My tongue juts inside her tiny hole and fucks her repeatedly, my saliva draining down her flesh as she begins to writhe even more.

"Ohhh, oh ... yes," she exclaims, her legs closing up. I reach for them and press them to the side, opening her even more as I continue to tongue fuck her. Her pussy looks like it's never been used before, but I know that can't be true. There's no way a virgin can be such an incredible tease. Still, I give it little thought as I stray from her tiny hole to suck her hardened clit, which moves along my tongue like silk.

She trembles as I suck hard, now watching her and the way she arches her neck, her mouth wide open and her eyes closed. She is the perfect vision of endless wet dreams – a picture of perfection, and I know I'm already hooked.

I begin to suck on her clit even faster before moving a finger inside her sopping quim. She gasps, her walls instantly clamping down on the single-digit as it welcomes the unfamiliar object. She's all feathery and soft, and I know I would be in heaven when I finally take her. After this, I know I have to. I drive my middle finger back and forth, my tongue fanning against her clit as I gradually increase my pace.

I know she's near; her moans have gotten louder, and her fingers are now running through my hair as she urges me on.

"Cum for me, princess," I rasp against her, and she shivers.

I start to take her even faster, her walls now clenching and unclenching as her ass lifts from the sofa. Juices ooze from her, and I know I have her just where I want her. She starts to bucks, and I drill her even harder and faster, my mouth still on her clit as I drive her insane.

"Grayson!" she shouts and grips my fingers so tight even I can't resist a moan. Her orgasm is the most beautiful thing I have ever seen as she starts to tremble like a leaf in the wind, her body writhing, her eyes rolling to the back of her head as she groans and grunts breathlessly.

I stop to watch her, my finger still curling inside her as she climbs her mountain and comes back down again. Sweat glistens on her ivory skin, and from thrashing around so much, I can see a glimpse of her pink nipples peeking out from her crop top.

I am tempted to fill her again but not with my finger this time. Her eyes slowly flutter open, and she has a glow that tugs at my heart. She smiles, blushes, and says something that surprises me completely.

She licks her lips and meets my gaze. "I- I want your hot cum all over me... please," she softly says.

I am stiff everywhere but I need a release, and Kat is begging to see that happen. She pushes her crop top to either side of her tits, leaving them to point at me as I push down my pants and straddle her stomach with one leg up on the futon and the other on the floor. I am rock hard – literally pulsing for a release. When Kat sees its size, her eyes widen, and a blush warms her cheeks. She must be wondering if it can even fit in her small pussy. I doubt it.

Wordlessly, she reaches for it and starts to stroke it. I moan, loving the way her small hands massage me. She does this for a while, but then she reaches beneath me, rubs her palm over her core and brings it back to my manhood. It's glistening with her juices as she uses it as lube to stroke me. I clench my teeth so hard I fear it will shatter in my mouth. The pleasure is too good. Me perched above her is surreal.

"Faster princess," I barely make out, baring my teeth as her hand tightens around my hardened length.

A couple of strokes later and I'm grunting loudly while Kat continues to jerk me off. I bust and I bust hard, bucking and trembling as spurts of my semen shoot out from my cock and land across her chest.

"Yes, I want it all!" she exclaims, and she continues to stroke me.

It seems I now have an endless supply as cum plasters across her chest, some even hitting her chin. Her breasts are creamy with it... her nipples glazed like a freshly baked donut. Cum drains down her fingers, which is wrapped around my head, squeezing out every drop that renders me weak and useless.

I collapse beside her on the small piece of furniture, our bodies smashed together as we come down from our high. I still can't believe it. I can't believe it's Kat who has given me the most glorious hand job of my life. I can't believe that despite the orgasm I just had, I still need her as badly as I need oxygen.

I am fucked.

Chapter 5

Kat

I am buzzing; my entire body feels euphoric as I bask in the aftermath of my orgasm and the one I just gave Grayson. His warmth is plastered all over me and is now liquefying as it warms against my skin. Grayson is still beside me, breathing heavily while I'm still finding it hard to believe that he just ate me out – that his mouth was on me.

I still don't know where I got the courage from to be teasing him in such a manner earlier but when I'm around Grayson, it's like I'm a new person. He brings out my wild side, and I want to explore every bit of it with him. I want him again. Regardless of the orgasm I just had that leaves me exhausted, I want this to last a little longer. I need him inside me.

But then he eases up, unable to meet my gaze and pulls on his pants. He still doesn't look at me as he reaches across for his phone to maybe check who was calling him. His face hardens immediately, and I can see him visibly clench his teeth as he looks down on it.

"It was your dad," he manages to say in a husky tone. I can see the guilt on his face and can tell that he's regretting what happened. My heart tugs painfully. "I should have answered earlier."

I swallow, afraid of what I'm about to ask. "Would it have changed anything?" I croak.

He finally looks at me with his intense green eyes, a slight frown on his face. "It would. I'm sorry, Kat, but this should never have happened," he says, and I instantly feel like crying.

"Quit saying that!" I snap. "It did."

"Have you ever even considered the shit storm this could cause? What if your parents find out?" he exclaims a tad bit louder.

"Then so be it! We are both adults," I exclaim as I get up. His cum slips between my boobs, and I watch as his eyes follow the movement before he seemingly catches himself and shakes his head.

He licks across his lips. "Kat, I just don't want you to get hurt."

"I won't," I say with as much confidence as I can muster.

He doesn't seem convinced. His mouth opens and closes before he finally says. "Are you sure that you can keep your heart out of this? You already know that no one lasts for a long time with me," he says.

I know that much, but I can't let him know that my heart is already involved – have been from the very start. But I already want everything Grayson has to offer, and honesty won't give me that.

"I understand casual, Grayson; don't worry," I say as I drop my gaze to adjust my top.

I look up after to find him nodding. "Good, but your parents can't ever know about this..." he warns.

"I get it." There's an edge to my voice, and I quickly clear my throat, smiling at him. "I'm gonna take a shower," I say as I get up, my knees feeling wobbly, but I stand my ground and head upstairs, sighing heavily when I get to the bathroom.

I feel sad somehow and know it's based on the fact that all this is just possibly sex to him. He doesn't want me for the long haul – I don't arouse any other part of him other than his cock. I will be a notch on his huge, decorated bedpost. That should be enough to have me running for the hills and forgetting him, but my heart is already involved. I'm growing to love this man even more after finding out that we are sexually compatible in every way.

The following day, I'm expecting him to be at work, but it's raining heavily outside and he's in the kitchen making breakfast in his sweat shorts and a sleeveless shirt that's got his muscles on full display.

"Good morning," he says as if sensing my presence. He doesn't look up; just continues to do what he's doing in the sexiest way possible.

"Good morning."

"I remembered you saying that you like omelets," he says, looking up at me with a smile on his face. His eyes rove over my body before it's on the task at hand again.

"Correct," I smile, happy that he even remembered.

Feeling a bit more comfortable, I walk to the counter and take a seat. "Want any help?"

"I've got it covered," he smiles. "I have all the time on my hands anyway." His eyes shift to the windows. "Weather forecast says the rain will continue throughout the day. A storm's passing."

"Oh wow," I perk up. "So, no work today?"

"Well yeah, but I just won't be going in. That's one of the perks of being your own boss," he winks.

I bite my lips as I think about the possibility of being stuck inside all day with Grayson on a rainy day. I don't want to push him anymore just yet, but I feel the mood has already set itself for any possible outcome.

"Have your parents called?" he asks, cutting into my thoughts.

"Yeah, mom called me last night to ask if I was okay. Spain is all sunshine and rainbows, apparently."

He nods, smiling, but I can still see that any mention of my parents will forever make him feel guilty.

I swallow. "Grayson, are we good?"

His gaze settles on me. "Yeah, why wouldn't we be?"

I resist a snort. "Because any mention of my parents and guilt takes over..."

He sighs and presses his palms to the counter. "Can you blame me? I'm torn between wanting you and not wanting to betray my friends," he exclaims, and my heart starts to thud in my chest.

Our gazes meet and that heat returns to my body full force, settling between my legs. I want to leap forward and kiss him – to experience something similar to what happened the other day and I can see he wants it too, but instead, he shakes his head and sigh, moving to the cupboard.

"I'm just about done with breakfast. We can maybe sit in and watch a movie or something," he shrugs.

I nod. "Sounds great."

Ten minutes later, we are in the living room having breakfast and scrolling through movies to watch.

"Any suggestions?" he asks.

"Well, the proposal is my all-time favorite, so I'd say that." I smile, and he nods while proceeding to search.

A few minutes later, the movie starts. The rain is still pouring, and I can't concentrate on the movie. I only see Grayson. I can't do anything but think about him. I don't want his attention on the movie; I want it on me.

"Have you ever been with someone like me?" I ask him. He looks to me a little confused. "My age."

He swallows. "Never."

I bite my lips. "Oh, well, it's your turn to ask me a question," I say.

He looks at the tv and then at me. "I guess we're putting the movie on pause then...." I nod, and he shifts in his seat and turns to me.

"What's the most adventurous thing you've ever done?" he asks me, genuine curiosity in his eyes which makes me feel comfortable.

I want to tell him that the most adventurous thing I've ever done was what we did together on his futon, but I don't want to scare him off so easily.

"Amy and I went Skydiving on our eighteenth birthday. It was insane, and I really wanna do it again."

He nods. "Sounds fun but do you wanna hear a secret?"

I perk up. "Yeah, sure."

"I'm afraid of heights, so that's something I'll never do."

"Wow, well, never say never."

He smiles, his gaze pinned on me in a way that makes me all warm on the inside. "Your turn."

"Have you ever had your heart broken?"

He immediately shifts in his seat and rubs his jaw. "Um... this one time, a few years back. I was in love with this girl; I thought she was the one..." Grayson trails off and rakes his fingers through his hair before he sighs. "I was planning to propose, so I made sure everything was perfect. I popped the question, she said no, and I later found out she was cheating on me all along."

"Wow, that must've sucked. I'm sorry to hear that."

Shrugging, he says. "Yeah; if it were meant to be, it would have been. My turn...Tell me something most people would've been shocked to find out about you."

It takes me a minute to process because I am still processing his reply to the heartbreak question. I want to understand the root of the problem and try to figure out if that's why he is the way he is now – afraid of commitment. I want to think on it, but I guess I must have spaced because I am pushed from my thoughts when I hear Grayson calling my name.

He looks a little worried as he awaits my answer. I blurt the only reply I know. "That I'm a virgin."

His face suddenly pales and I can see he is more shocked than anything else. I want to kick myself for saying such a thing. Trying to get Grayson to want me is hard enough, but now I can see the screws turning in his head. There's no way he will want me now as a virgin – it would make things more complicated, I am sure, but he'd find out eventually. Better now than to have him regretting mid-penetration.

"Fuck, Kat," he hisses, raking his fingers through his hair again, the tousled look making him look even hotter.

"I just thought you should know," I exclaim softly.

"You said you can do casual, but there's no way you can being a virgin and all." His voice raises an octave and I can feel my heart thudding in my chest.

"I can!" I exclaim, glad that my voice is actually firm in all this. "I'm not an idiot, Grayson. I know you don't want a relationship from me, and I don't want one from you either," I lie. "But neither of us can ignore the chemistry that we have."

His eyes soften, and I'm sweaty all over. "Kat, I don't want to hurt you – I've made that clear – so I think the best thing we can both do, is try to stay our separate ways until your parents get back. After that, we can forget any of this ever happened."

He gets up, and just like that, he's gone again. My eyes burn, it feels like I'm carrying a bolder in my throat, and as soon as he disappears up the stairs, I can't help the sob that breaks free.

Chapter 6

Grayson

A *virgin.*

I can't believe it but yet, I probably should have seen it coming. There was an unforgettable innocence in the way she kissed me and jerked me off but I had shrugged it off as her being nervous. Hearing her say the words earlier, allowed me to gain more clarity. I am now a hundred percent sure that nothing can happen between Kat and me. Virgins always get attached – they always want more, and I can't give her that. No matter how much I want her, I cant.

And yet, the thought of being her first intrigues me in a way that I can't explain. I can't help but picture her face as I enter her for the first time, I want to know how her body responds, and most of all, since she's a virgin, I am curious to see if she'll be able to take all of me. My fingers still remember her tightness, and my cock responds to the thought. Resisting Kat will be torture, and quite frankly, I know that if she pushes a little harder, I may not be able to control myself again.

The rain is still falling later that night, and I'm lying restless in my bed with one thing on my mind; Kat. This type of weather has always managed to get me horny but I'm the horniest I've ever been in my entire life. All for a woman I can't even have. My manhood is like a pole in my pants, and I'm tempted to stroke myself to an orgasm but I know that it'll only be for a few minutes until I'm hard again.

Thunder blares, and I can see streaks of light flash through my window as the rain continues to pour. I am tempted to check in on Kat. Ever since the whole ordeal this morning, I haven't seen or said a word to her, wanting to uphold my earlier statement to avoid her. But for courtesy's sake, I know I have to.

I get up and head to her bedroom, knocking on the door.

"It's open," her soft voice greets me.

I am a bit hesitant to answer, but I do so. She's all cuddled up in bed with the covers drawn over her head but when she hears me enter, she pulls it down and peeks up at me.

"I er... I was just checking in to see if you're okay," I say.

Thunder rumbles, and she flinches. "Yeah, just not a fan of this type of weather. I just prefer the rain without all this drama," she smiles, and I chuckle. "Could you stay with me for a while, until I fall asleep?" she asks.

I am taken aback by her request, my dirty mind starting to conjure up pictures of her petite body pressed against mine. My cock stirs, and I know no is the best answer, but I also want to comfort her and give some type of reassurance that she will be fine.

"I promise, I won't do anything."

Her short statement should reassure me, but it doesn't. I nod nonetheless and move towards her on the tiny bed, sitting beside her. She smiles – the perfect picture of innocence and beauty and snuggles closer in her blanket. I'm expecting her to try something – a part of me wants her to – but instead, she closes her eyes, willing herself to sleep.

She is asleep minutes later. I know I should leave now, but I can't bring myself to do so. So instead, I move beneath her covers and try to do the same but my body grazes Kat's and I can feel everything awaken inside me. She stirs, and I freeze, muttering a soft curse beneath my breath. I expect her to be asleep, but her eyes flutter open, and she stares up at me with dreamy eyes, a timid smile on her face.

"Do you want to leave?" she asks.

I swallow. Of course, I don't, but I have to. "Do you want me to?" I ask.

She bites her lips and shakes her head, easing up a bit. "What if I lied earlier...Would you be upset?"

I stiffen. "Lied about what?"

"Saying I won't try anything."

"I'm not upset." My voice is husky.

Our gazes lock before mine trail down to her juicy lips, which I've been dying to taste again. I know that resisting Kat will only make me want her even more. We have days to go before she leaves, but I know I can't make it to tomorrow without kissing her again. When her lips touch mine, the fire in my body starts to blaze even hotter, and I know that I'm fucked.

I kiss her hard, exploring every bit of her sweet mouth with my tongue. There's no hesitation from her – just pure desire that I can taste on her warm tongue. It stirs my insides and increases the need that rages inside.

Kat eases and hovers over me, our lips still joined. Holding her by the hips, I settle her on the hard erection that is throbbing through my pants. She whimpers, kissing me deeper as she starts to grind on me.

"Tell me this is what you want, Kat," I rasp against her lips, and she moans before slightly pulling apart and looking deep into my eyes.

"More than anything," she says, capturing my mouth again and taking me by surprise. My hands run up her side and under her tiny crop top. Fingers grazing across the swell of her breast and all the way up until I am pulling it over her head. Her hair falls back in a tousled mess, and my breath catches in my throat as I look at her and how beautiful she is. My hands find her tits, and mold each one while she continues to grind on me, looking straight into my eyes. I'm painfully hard and becomes even harder with her crotch rubbing against me.

I am desperate, needy, and I want nothing else but to feel her naked pussy on me. Flipping her over, I make her lay on her back before moving down her body and pulling off her little cotton shorts. I am surprised to find that she isn't wearing any panties, and when I look at her, she smiles.

"You little minx," I chuckle, kissing between her tits, licking her soft skin until I reach her belly button. The fast rise and fall of her stomach tell me that she is enjoying this – that she is aroused and in need of me. I move down and lick over her pussy, loving the whimper that leaves her mouth. My tongue probes deeper, immediately drenched by her wetness which still tastes like the sweet nectar from succulent fruit.

But it's only a tease; today, it's all about my entire length deep into her. Kat is like an angel, all sprawled out on the bed with her legs spread for me. I want to fuck her senseless, but I'm reminded that she is a virgin and will have to take it slow.

She watches me until I strip, eyeing below my waist, which is at full attention, large and hard. She swallows and licks her lips, and fuck, the last thing I want to do is take it slow.

But I kiss her again and bask in the feeling of her hand on my skin – her fingers entwined around my neck as she traps me in a kiss. I want to do this forever. To relish in the feeling of my body pressed against hers, her warm skin and the way her hard nipples rub against me as we kiss. I shift, the smooth head of my erection settling at her warm entrance. Kat instantly moves down, rolling her hips against me and moaning against my mouth as her body begs for penetration.

My body is buzzing, each nerve responding to Kat. I want to take her now, but instead my hands move between us, my fingers finding her cunt. I slip a finger inside, and she gasps, deepening the kiss as I test her readiness. She meets my fingers with each thrust, pushing down her body so I can enter her deeper. Her wetness bathes my fingers, the heat from her core increasing my passion.

I add another finger and her moans increase as I drive them back and forth. She starts to writhe, pulling me further on her as I finger fuck her. She clenches around my digits, and the more I push them inside her, the more she slackens and pools with wetness.

"Oh God, Grayson... I'm gonna come!" she exclaims as the first shiver jolts her body. I hook my fingers inside her, and she stiffens, but before she can ride the waves of her orgasm, I pull my fingers out and watch the shock that takes over her face. Her legs move to tighten around me, but I push them apart and ease up.

"I want you inside me... please." She blushes at the request, and I smile.

"Tell me everything you'd like, princess," I rasp.

She licks her lips. "I want you to fuck me like this, and then I want to ride you," she says in a soft tone.

I smile and reach for Kat's lips with the fingers that had just fucked her. They are doused in her juices, but she collects every drop with the twirl of her tongue as she sucks on them.

"Do you like the way your pussy tastes, Kat?" I ask her.

"Mmhmm," she says with my fingers still in her mouth.

When she has licked off every drop, I settle myself between her legs and push her legs apart. Her bald flesh is soaked. I guide my cock towards it and watch as her lips slowly part to grant me access. Her mouth is open as she awaits the intrusion with bated breath. I'm so huge against her and for a sec I think it won't fit. The head gains access and she moans but that isn't even the hardest part. She still has the beefier parts to take in.

I press further into her, and she gasps, grabbing onto my arms, and she clamps her eyes shut. Her walls contract around the head, and I know there's no fucking way she can take me.

"Fuck," I hiss.

She looks at me and before I can say a word, she shuffles from beneath me and lies on her stomach. The glistening tip of me is mere inches from her mouth before it dawns on me what she is about to do.

"Kat..."

She holds onto the base of it and takes me into her mouth. She licks around the head and sucks hard while I close my eyes, unable to believe this is true. I have my fucking cock in Kat's mouth, and she is doing a damn good job of blowing me off. She gradually takes me in deeper, and I watch in amazement as her small mouth stretches to take me further in, her saliva running down the column of my cock. It is sloppy, and I love it. She gags when she takes me too far, but being the fucking firecracker that she is that never fails to amaze me, she goes again until I am halfway in her mouth.

I want to feel her throat but know that'll only happen with some practice. She continues to slobber on my length, moaning as she moves back and forth with her sweet lips massaging me. I close my eyes to bask in the feeling and know that I won't last another minute. So instead, I pull her up and kiss her, tasting myself on her while I clean her mouth with my own.

"I think we can try again...daddy," she smiles, licking at her lips.

There she goes again with that word that brings me more pleasure than I could ever imagine. The thought of being a daddy dom to Kat and her being my little submissive gives me a high I can't explain.

I push her down on her back and she giggles while spreading her legs again. She glistens with her wetness and without a bit of hesitance, I position my cock towards her opening again. I push in and she gasps, but as I continue, I realize I am gaining much more leeway than before. I stroke her insides with my manhood until I feel some amount of resistance that gives me confirmation that she is a virgin.

I look into her eyes, and she nods, urging me to go further. I push in and feel her narrow passage parts to accept me. She gasps, her face reddens, and her hold on me tightens, but I don't stop. I penetrate her until half my length is buried inside her small cunt. She starts to involuntarily clench around me while I remain still, allowing her to get accustomed to my size. When I begin to move back and forth, her gasps fill the air with each stroke.

"Are you okay?"

"Yes... don't stop, please."

I move slowly until I see the tension fade from her face and know that she isn't in as much pain as before. She is like heaven, and I have to muster up every restraint possible not to fuck her senseless. The slowness, the intimacy and the emotional and physical connection are driving me crazy. I almost want to get up and run to my room, but the sheer euphoria of having her under me – of being inside her, is all I need to continue. All I need to know is that one time with Kat definitely won't be enough.

I reach down to suck on a nipple, and she screams, her inner walls tightening around my cock.

"Faster...I want more," she begs me, her breath fanning against my skin, sweat beading on our bodies.

I oblige, pushing further into her as I fuck her faster. She clings to me tighter, her legs widening as she accepts each hard thrust. The contact of flesh and flesh creates slapping sounds in the room, and with the way my cock has started to glide more effortlessly back and forth, I know she is drenched slippery with desire.

Her slick body rolls against mine as she tries to meet each of my thrusts. I sink deeper, and her core convulses around me again, soft moans leaving her mouth.

"Oh, Kat, you are so perfect... so fucking perfect," I exclaim as I fuck her without holding back. Her nails dig into my back, and her whimpers tell me she is near. I am too.

"I want to be on top," she whispers.

I reach for her and flip her on top of me without withdrawing from her core. She scrapes her hair to the back and starts to bounce on top of me. I can't believe she has me buried inside of her and seems to be enjoying it. My entire shaft is slick with our juices, some settling in a creamy white ring around the base.

Her tits bounce with each stroke, and her body is glistening with sweat.

"Oh my gosh... oh my gosh!" she exclaims as she starts to grind on me, hips rolling back and forth, side to side with all of my length inside her. I mutter a curse under my breath and grab her hips as she starts to move wildly on me. Her eyes roll over, she shrieks, does a final roll and then she stiffens, her walls convulsing around me, growing tight like the first time I entered her.

My cock twitches inside her, and I grab onto her and have her on her back again, rutting into her as hard as I can while collecting her screams against my mouth. Her legs wrap around me and pin me in place, her walls clenching and unclenching as her orgasm takes course.

"Ohhh Ahhggn! Yess!" she exclaims, body trembling. "I want to feel your cum inside me."

That wasn't my initial plan, but as soon as I hear the words, I buck inside her, twitching as I pump gouts of semen inside her. I press my forehead against hers, my ass flexing as I fill her up. My heart is hammering against my chest, and I bask in the bliss, making a mental statement for this being the best sex of my life.

Chapter 7

Kat

My heart is pounding in my chest as I descend from the high of my orgasm. I am happy, and it feels like my heart is about to explode in my chest. Prior to this, there were many ways I tried to imagine how I would feel my first time, but no amount of thought, porn or masturbation can compare to the feeling that I had when Grayson was inside me. Admittedly, it was painful and uncomfortable at first, but the more he moved inside me, the more the pain faded, and pleasure took its course.

Even now, in the aftermath, my body still thrums from the reminder of him, though I know the ache between my legs won't leave anytime soon. I am sore I know; Grayson is huge, and for a while, I feared I wouldn't take him but was glad when I did. I can feel his essence between my legs, slick against my thighs as it slowly trickles from me.

He is beside me, still breathing heavily and drenched in sweat that smells like body wash and cologne. My eyes lower to his groin and I can feel my face heating with a blush. He's still surprisingly hard and is glistening with my juices. Though I am exhausted, I want him again. I don't think I will ever stop wanting him.

I look up to him and our gazes meet. I'm glad to see that there isn't any regret there – just pure desire for me.

"What are you thinking?" I ask, huddling up to him.

"That you're the most beautiful woman I've ever seen. You are perfect, Kat." He reaches in and brushes a lock of hair from my face. I smile. I'm even more in love with this man than before. God help me.

"What's in that pretty little head of yours?" he asks, smiling down at me.

I bite my lips. "I want you again," I whisper.

His eyes darken but he chuckles. "Someone's a little greedy."

I blush, looking down at his crotch. "Makes two of us."

He knows he's guilty and only smiles as he captures my mouth for a kiss. This time it isn't primal or hungry; it's soft and feathery and makes my heart soar. He turns me on my side and settles behind me with his erection poking in my back. But then he shifts further down, his hands clasped around my breast and enters me from behind.

I WAKE UP THE FOLLOWING morning with the sun bright on my face. My eyes shift to the clock on the nightstand and I realize its minutes to ten. It suddenly dawns on me that Grayson is gone, and I'm alone. Apart of me wanting to wake up in his arms like in the movies, but as I look around, the clearer my reality becomes. My stomach churns as I ease up from the bed, wincing at the discomfort between my legs and the soreness in my limbs. Having sex with Grayson was already too good to be true; expecting him to still be here is a reach.

But as I sling my legs out of bed, he enters the room with a smile on his face and two mugs in hand. A robe is draped around his lean body, and my stomach flutters as I feel the heat rise to my cheeks.

"Good morning, beautiful. Coffee?" he asks, handing me a cup.

I take it with a grin. "Thank you," I say as I take a sip. "I thought you left for work or something."

"Yeah, I'll be leaving a little late today. About noon," he says as she sits beside me. "How do you feel?"

I bite my lips. "Just a little sore but I'll be fine."

Something flashes across his gaze before he gets up and places his mug on the side table. "I'm gonna run you a warm bath."

I'm cheesing and have no idea when I will stop. "You're sweet but you don't have to do that," I assure.

He only smiles. "I want to."

He leaves the room, and in less than ten minutes' time, he returns. "All ready."

I get up, and my knees almost buck together with the bliss still floating through my body. Grayson comes over, and I almost gasp when he takes me into his arms and carries me to the bathroom. I'm stunned at his sweetness. I'd expected him to be a little cold – to have some form of regret based on the conversations we've had about this, but he's being such a gentleman. Is it because he feels some type of responsibility for taking my virginity?

He sets me on the floor and looks to the filled tub. "I put some things in there that should help you relax."

The water looks a bit creamy, and I can smell a few essential oils. I step in, and the warmth sends shivers up my spine. When I finally settle in, I smile up at him. "Join me?"

He shakes his head. "This is all for you, Kat."

"I want to enjoy it with you," I insist.

He seems a bit hesitant but wordlessly peels off his robe and stands before me in all his naked glory. His muscular body makes me more heated in the warm bath. He steps in and settles behind me. I lean against him and almost sigh with the flurry that his presence brings me. I feel small against him as I lean into his chest and feel his warmth radiate on me. I never want to leave his side. I want to know everything about this man – I want to spend each day wrapped up in his arms.

But even as he holds me, as he pours handfuls of water all over my body, I can sense the elephant in the room and can't help but ask;

"Do you regret anything, Grayson?" My voice is so low, I doubt he hears a word that I say, but he pauses, and I know that he does.

"I don't," he admits, and I smile. "Last night was amazing, and that's all I'm trying to focus on. The now."

I guess that's better than regrets. After all this, he's going to walk away unscathed, while I will definitely have a broken heart. Might as well enjoy it while it lasts.

"Could we go out on Friday?" I ask, biting my lips. "It'll be my last night and I want to make it memorable."

"Ok, where do you have in mind?"

"There's a club that I really want to go but it's not really Amy's style, so I haven't gone because I have no one to go with."

"A club?"

"Yeah. It's about twenty minutes away."

He pulls me closer to him and kisses me along my neck. "Ok, sure. We can do that."

I smile and turn to kiss him. We make out until I feel him growing hard against me and know that he is ready as much as I am. My body slides against his like butter as we kiss, and somehow I am wetter despite being drenched in water.

"We should take this to the bedroom," he growls against my lips. We both get up and step outside of the tub, still kissing while we tumble to the bedroom. But we don't reach the bed. I slip, and Grayson comes crashing with me to the floor.

I burst into a giggle, and so does he, but he obviously has no plans of getting back up. He leaves my mouth and trail down my wet body to my breast, where he sucks hard, earning a gasp from me. The sheer intimacy has me pooling with wetness even more and I realize that in less than a day, my need for this stallion has increased.

His cock rubs up against my thighs and finally settles between my thighs where I am wet the most. There isn't any foreplay this time – just an animalistic need that overpowers both of us. I claw at him needily and he responds by plunging into me. I gasp and cling to him as he starts to drive in and out of me. My aching core accepts him, massaging his hardness with every stroke as he goes back and forth.

Grayson suddenly eases up, bracing my legs against my chest as he inspects my pussy and watches his cock going in and out. I feel more exposed than ever before but realize that he's getting more excited as he watches his length drill into my opening.

"Oh, God... Kat. What are you doing to me!" he exclaims in a guttural tone that causes my lady-bits to clench. I'm already getting closer and closer with each stroke especially since this time around, there isn't any pain, just pure pleasure.

He pulls me up, his cock slipping out as he kisses me long and hard as if staking his claim on me. I am weak in the knees – weak all over.

"Get on your knees, princess."

My heart flutters but I do so nonetheless, arching my back and spreading my legs for him. I feel dirty and exposed, but I love every second of it. I love the feeling of sluttiness that comes out when I'm with Grayson.

He grabs onto my hips and thrusts into me. I can't help but gasp at the new feeling this angle brings. He feels bigger, and somehow it's like my core starts to ache again, but yet it feels so good. An overwhelming type of good that has me whimpering with each thrust. Grayson doesn't hold back, he fucks me like a dog in heat, digging into my flesh with his fingers, grunting as he bucks into me. My mouth is gaped open, trying to make sense of all this pleasure, and for a second, I feel as if I want to cry.

He fills me with so much more than his cock. I feel renewed, I feel alive, and my heart is flooding with a type of happiness that I cannot describe. Desperate to cum, I start to push back onto him as he thrusts into me. The loud slaps of skin-to-skin echo in my ears. I can feel liquid trailing down the sides of my legs.

It's all too much. I tremble, shiver, and scream his name as I cum hard. He holds me up, steadies my shaking body and continues to fuck me until he moans and bucks, twitching inside me as he fills me with his cum.

I am breathing hard, I am salivating, and my body is in a state of bliss as his warm cum floods me. When he pulls out, it all rushes to the front, falling to the carpet in a plop. I think Grayson is done with me now, but I'm highly mistaken.

He rubs his still-hard cock against my drenched pussy, and I quiver from the overstimulation. He is slick against me, yet hard. When he inserts again, I am surprised to find he still has more up his sleeves.

"Ohhhh," he moans as he slides back and forth inside me while I double over in pleasure at the immense lubrication that makes this feel like heaven on earth.

I leak to the floor as he fills me with slow, agonizing strokes, rocking my body against him to meet everyone. One of his hands leaves my hips to move beneath me and presses onto my overly sensitive clit. He smears his cum all over my pussy, and I shiver as he starts playing with my clit – all the while still thrusting into me.

I am on the verge of losing my mind. One more stroke, and I know I will bawl my eyes out, so I beg him to fuck me faster.

"Please," I say below my breath, my body on fire.

He does as asked and fucks me until I am screaming his name and clenching hard around him. With my knees now too weak to support me, I fall to the floor and Grayson comes along with me. I am flat on my stomach, and he is still above me, fucking me like crazy.

"Daddy, please come for me!" I exclaim, unable to take another minute of his sweet cock.

His grip tightens, and he drills into me faster but not for long. He quickly pulls out and shoots his cum onto my ass while I continue to writhe beneath him.

God, I love this man.

Chapter 8

Grayson

I leave the house feeling more alive than I've ever felt in my life. Kat makes me want to take on the world. Being with her makes me feel like I can conquer anything. I don't know what it is but she makes me happy. I feel complete. Even leaving her to head to work was hard. I wanted to make her cum over and over again – I wanted to enjoy the feel of her body pressed against mine.

But then it dawns on me like a dark cloud that Kat will be leaving in a couple of days and I'll be all alone again. The feeling fills me with dread, but I know there's nothing I can do about it. As good as we are in bed, too many things are at stake. Relationships would be ruined, gossip would escalate, and I can't risk any of that. Kat is too young. She may think this is what she wants but later, she will look back and regret everything. She will find someone younger, hotter and smarter – someone who is well-deserving of her.

I want that for her – I want her to be happy – yet, I can't help the anger that bubbles up inside me when I think about Kat being with another man.

I want to be her first and her last.

"Snap out of it, Grayson. This is ridiculous." I know it is. This is Kat, for Christ's sake. The sex was good and that's it.

Yet, for the rest of the day, all I can think about is her and going home to her. I want to be inside her again, and the thought stirs me to the point of discomfort. For the first time in a long while, I can't even concentrate on work. All I can think about is a woman I promised myself I'd never touch, yet I've touched her in all the right places countless times.

My phone rings, and I am jolted from my thoughts. I look at the caller ID and feel myself going pale at the contact on the screen. I clear my throat as I pick it up.

"Hey Steven, what's up?"

"Hey man, just checking in as usual. How's everything going?"

I scratch my neck. "Everything is great; how's Spain?"

"Great, and it's really good for business too. I can definitely see myself spending my retirement here."

I smile. "That sounds awesome, man."

"Yeah, so how's everything with Kat?"

I swallow the guilt that threatens to choke me. "Kat's a sweetheart as always. I left her at the house when I left for work this morning. She should be fine." Of course, she is. She is probably sound asleep after the fuck session we had before I left.

"Thanks again, buddy for taking care of her. I know she's an adult and all, but it's nice to have her around someone we trust who can also keep her safe."

Guilt eats at me, and I want to kick myself for being such a fucking dick. How can I betray my friend like that?

I clear my throat. "Hey, it's not a problem. Listen, enjoy the rest of your trip, and I'll see you on the weekend." I say.

"We might arrive on Thursday instead. During our stay here, a dealer called Emily wants to show her a few pieces in person. He'll be out of town after Friday. He really has some great propositions, and we don't want to pass that up."

"I wouldn't either; that sounds amazing, man. I understand."

"Yeah, so I'll let you know what's happening tomorrow. I'm gonna call Kat afterward. She should be excited to have us home," Steven chuckles.

"Definitely. Well, I better get back to work. Talk to you soon."

I hang up and manage a sigh, riddled by guilt once again. Steven has always been a good friend to me from the very day we met until now. I had said once that I wouldn't let anything get in the way of our friendship, and here I am, allowing his own daughter to do just that. It's not right; this is betrayal on so many levels, but Kat is an irresistible young woman – even more so now that I've explored every inch of her.

It dawns on me that our time together will be limited. I'd hoped to have her for a few more days but with her parents coming back, I only have her for one night. Somehow that fills me with dread and I can't explain why. I should be happy; the sooner she leaves, the quicker things can get back to normal, but I'm not.

That evening when I leave to head home, she's there in the living room in her little cotton shorts and crop top. Her legs seem endless, her skin like butter as she walks toward me. Her scent fills my nostrils, her smile making me weak in the knees. She excites me, plain and simple, in a way that no woman ever has. I just wish things weren't so complicated.

She reaches up to kiss me, and it seems all the stress from today has faded with the simple caress. It feels like no one else matters when I'm with her. I kiss her back with all I've got, and she eases off a little to smile against my mouth.

"You seemed to have missed me," she teases.

"Really? What gave it away?" I chuckle, and she blushes a bright red. "Did your parents call?" I ask her and watch as the smile falls from her face.

"Yeah, they're coming back tomorrow. We won't even be able to go to that club I was telling you about," she pouts.

I use my thumb to caress her cheeks, admiring her beauty. "We can go some other time." I know that false hope is the last thing I should be giving her, but I don't want to ruin this moment. "I just want to spend all of tonight with you."

Admiration fills her eyes, and she reaches up to kiss me again. This time it's soft and sweet and passionate, taking a piece of my heart second by second. I'm already hard for her – every inch of my body recognizes hers and I want to dive right in. As she kisses me, she starts to fumble with my belt, her kiss getting needier and needier. I reach for her crop top and push it just above her tits so I can see them – feel them pressed against me. I then reach into her shorts and cup her sodden flesh. I like the fact that Kat has learned to be panty-less around me in the short space of time she's been here. It's definitely something a guy can get used to.

I quickly pull off my pants while she kicks her shorts to the side and pulls me in for another kiss. My hard erection rubs against her stomach, her tits against my chest as desire heightens tenfold. I want her so fucking bad, and I can't wait. I've already waited hours to get to this point, and I can't do it any longer.

I turn her around and lift one of her legs so her knee is resting on the armrest of the sofa. She juts out her ass, and I swipe my hand across her aroused flesh; it's wet, my fingers parting her soft folds. Kat whimpers and grinds on my flattened fingers until they are soaked with her juices.

"I want you now," she says softly, looking back at me with lust evident in her eyes. I rub my cock against her opening, smearing it with her juices before pushing it inside her. She gasps the way she always does when she takes me for the first time, and it motivates me to push a little deeper until I at least have half my length inside her. She's tight and fucking creamy. I can feel every bit of her walls massaging my cock, expanding for deeper reach.

Kat starts to moan endlessly for a few minutes in, her cunt hugging me tighter. The feeling is blissful. I don't want to stop but know I'll have to soon. Kat is a cum buster. The need to fuck her harder grows more intense with each passing second. I reach for her and pull her against me, clasping her tits with my face on her neck, kissing her subtle flesh. I continue to plunge into her, pinching her nipples before my hands slide to her neck. I hold her there, her neck arched back against me while I fuck her.

"Yes, Oh my gosh, yes! Harder, please," she begs, and I do just that, collecting her shivers and holding her against me while I give her all that I've got.

She starts to clench around me, her body shivering as her orgasm approaches. I don't stop, even when her moans have heightened and she finally reaches the peak.

"Oh, Grayson yes! I love you!" she blurts as she cums around me.

I stiffen as my own orgasm takes course and at the fact that she really just said those words. I let her loose and she immediately seems to realize her mistake as she looks to me. Fucking hell, this can't be happening.

"Kat," I say to her while she scurries to put on her clothes.

She doesn't answer me, she doesn't look at me, and it lets me know her words are true. She does. I know her declaration should bring me joy, but it doesn't. I already told her from the very beginning that this could only be casual, but I should have known better. She was a virgin, for Christ's sake and nine times out of ten, they always get attached.

She finally looks toward me with tears brimming in her eyes. "I'm sorry. I know that this isn't what you wanted to hear, but I can't control what I feel."

"Kat, we agreed this would be casual. I made myself clear and you said you wouldn't get your feeling involved—"

"My feelings were already involved before I got here," she sniffs, using her small crop top to cover her chest.

I freeze in that spot and just stare at her. She licks her lips. "I've loved you for a long time, Grayson and being here just made it all clearer. I just wanted you, and I'm sorry if I lied to you when I said I'd keep my feelings out of it. I just wanted you so much."

I just stare at her. I don't know what to say. This is a mess that I never anticipated. Yes, I was kinda expecting shit to hit the fan but I never imagined Kat confessing her love to me during sex.

It is inevitable now. Her heart would be broken at the end of this. I can't be the man she wants, and I can't give her what she needs.

"I think it's time to call it a night," I say as I move past her and head upstairs.

Chapter 9

Kat

I don't know what I was thinking blurting out such a thing to Grayson, but I was so caught up in my feelings that I couldn't help myself—added with the fact that it was our last night. I couldn't control the burst of emotions that overcame me.

But I want to kick myself. It was evident on Grayson's face that he didn't return those feelings. I didn't expect him to, but the sudden disappointment that had marred his features was unforgettable. I feel like an idiot – a complete fool for falling so deep for a man I knew from the very beginning wouldn't love me back. He made that clear and I appreciated that, but a tiny piece of me had hope that his mind would change during our time together.

I cry myself to sleep for the rest of the night, knowing I will be going back to a sad reality without Grayson in it.

That morning when I get up, I hear him shuffling around the house, but I don't leave my room. I can't meet his gaze; I don't want to be embarrassed all over again, knowing I am the only one in love. I pack my bags and wait in my room for my parents to come and pick me up. Hours later, I hear a car in the driveway, and I know it's them. I head downstairs, trying to seem as calm and collective as I can muster but I'm quaking on the inside. Grayson is in the living room with my family, talking and laughing about their trip, and I'm scared to enter.

But I do. I make an appearance with a practiced smile on my face and watch as my parents bound from the sofa to hug me. I hug them and almost resist the urge to cry.

"Oh, sweetheart, we are so happy to be back. We missed you so much!" Mom hugs me and then dad follows.

"I missed you guys too." My eyes shift to Grayson to find that he isn't even looking my way. He's finding every excuse not to, and it tugs at my heart. "Are you guys ready to go?" I ask.

Mom seems shocked and a little taken aback as she looks between Grayson and me, but she doesn't say anything about it. She nods instead and reaches for her purse. "Grayson, we'll talk. Thanks again for allowing Kat to stay here," she says with a smile.

"Don't mention it," he says, smiling at her. I expect him to look at me even once but he doesn't.

We're gone from his house in a matter of minutes. Just like that, it's over, and it feels like my world is crumbling around me. Mom keeps asking me if everything is okay, and I tell her it is, even though that's the furthest from the truth.

When we finally arrive at my house, I head to my room and lock myself in as I cry.

A MONTH PASSES, AND I am packing for my flight the following day with Amy there to help me. The feeling is bittersweet but more bitter than sweet. For the past month, I haven't heard a word from Grayson. I haven't seen him either. When my parents chose to visit, I always stayed behind. That is the reality now. I had been waiting for him to say something but the last words that's were spoken were when I told him I loved him. Ever since, he has made it a point of duty to avoid me. It shouldn't hurt me the way it does but I can't help it. The fact that he's been acting like this has torn at every part of my heart.

"You're still thinking about him, aren't you?" she asks.

"I can't help it," I admit.

"Listen, something amazing happened to you this summer, and now it's over. Don't beat yourself up over it; just be grateful for the experience. This is life, Kat... we get heartbreaks, we fall in love, and sometimes it works out, and sometimes it doesn't. You'll be fine at the end of the day," she reassures, patting my back.

"I know... I just.... I just wish things were different. He's not even talking to me."

"I just think he needs more time to come to terms with this. I mean, you kinda really did drop a huge bomb on him, Kat."

I huff. "I know, but I'm leaving tomorrow. Even a goodbye would suffice."

Amy reaches for me and pulls me in for a hug. "I'm sorry, babe."

I'm packing my things into my dad's car the next afternoon, saddened to the point of tears. There's still no Grayson, and at this point, I've given up hope.

"Sweetheart, are you okay? You seem a little bit down," my mom says.

"I'm fine, mom. Don't worry," I reassure her, and she doesn't push any further.

I throw the last bag in and am about to head to the house when I hear a voice behind me.

"Kat...?"

I think maybe I'm hallucinating, but when I turn around, Grayson is standing there. He still looks fresh and handsome, but his hair has grown out a little, making him look a little rugged. As I stare at him, shocked, all the feelings I have for him leap forward – all the memories back at his house. I want to run in his arms, but I want to be angry too. It's been a month. What does he even have to say?

He approaches me, my parents look a little confused as they pause what they're doing to see what's happening.

"I'm sorry," he simply says to me. His eyes are genuine, and I can feel the tears pricking the back of my eyes. But he then turns to my parents and surprises me. "Steven... Emily, you can disown me after this or punch me in the face however many times you want, but that won't change the fact that I'm in love with your daughter," he exclaims, and I gasp, along with my mom.

My heart is about to burst in my chest, and my eyes are burning with impending tears when I play over the words in my head. This can't be true; this has to be a joke.

"Grayson, what are you doing?" I choke.

He reaches for my hand. "I was a coward for allowing you to leave. A coward for refusing to love you because of what happened in my past, but I realize that now. I've realized that it's now hard to wake up without you being there. I didn't realize I was empty before but after you came and left, I knew that you were the missing piece in my life. You fill the gap, Kat and I'm sorry it took me so fucking long to realize it... Please forgive me."

At this point, I'm a sobbing mess. Tears are streaming down my face, and my heart is full with his declaration. I can't believe it. Grayson Tuck is actually in love with me. Me!

"There's nothing to forgive. I love you so much!" I cry as I lunge into his arms, kissing him hard on the lips. All this feels like a fairy tale, and I'm the luckiest princess alive. It seems surreal. But then I am pulled from Grayson abruptly, and before I can process what's happening, he's on the ground with my dad hovering over him.

I DAB AT HIS BUSTED lip while he smiles at me. I smile back, my heart doing a double flip with the joy that radiates through me.

"I can't believe you said all that before my parents," I say to him.

"I couldn't hold it in any longer, and they deserved to know," he says, wincing when I apply more peroxide to the cotton pad and place it on his mouth.

"My dad hates you."

He frowns, but his smile quickly takes its place again. "I can live with that, but I can't live without you. You win some, you lose some, princess."

"He'll come around eventually. He's just hurt now, but at the end of the day, my dad only wants what's best for me."

"And you think that's me?" he grins.

"I know so. I love you, Grayson."

"I love you. I'm sorry I was such an asshole to you when you said it the first time," he says as he hangs his head. I reach for his face and kiss him softly against the bruise.

"Don't feel bad. I understand."

He smiles. "How did I get so lucky?"

"I ask myself the same thing when I think about you."

He laughs, and fuck, I am on cloud nine. My parents don't want anything to do with Grayson, they are disappointed in me and yet I'm the happiest I've ever been. As long as I have Grayson, I know that everything else will work out fine in time.

"How will we make this work, Kat?"

I bite my lips as I ponder his question. I never really gave that much thought before. "I'm not sure, but we have to. I can come during my breaks, and you can visit me every now and then. It'll only be for a year until I'm done with college," I remind.

He nods. "Yeah, and I will be taking plenty trips to New York to sort out business anyway. I can see you for weeks on end," he grins.

I blush. "We will make this work, won't we?"

"Most definitely. This is the beginning of forever, princess. I hope you're ready for the ride."

"There's one particular ride I have in mind," I blush, and he knows right away what I'm talking about. He chuckles, reaches for me and kisses me hard and passionately. I am weak in the knees, completely head over heels in love with this man.

Epilogue

A year has passed and I can say I'm at my happiest. Ever since I decided to look past my fears and truly open myself to love again, life has been great. Kat completes me in every single way and though it seems almost impossible to love her more than I already have, I love her more with each passing day.

I smile as I dig into my pocket and retrieve the box that has been tucked there all afternoon. My hands are shaky as I open it up and gaze at the diamond ring that sparkles under the glow of the light. My heart swells and a nervous jolt moves through me, but I know I have to do this. I have never been this certain. I've wanted to for so long but have held back because I wanted her to finish college first. And now that she has, I want her to enter this new chapter of life with me as her husband. It feels only right.

I know she loves me, but my only fear in asking is her readiness. What if she isn't ready to make such a big commitment. What if she is still feeling out this whole relationship between me and her and would want to explore some more? I can't help all these questions as I look at the piece of jewelry and try to envision her reaction as I ask her.

With a sigh, I wipe a bead of sweat from my brows and clear my throat before grabbing up my car keys. I glance at my watch as I step outside and realize I have some time to spare before Kat gets home. She's out now celebrating with her friends for finally being done with college. And tonight I'll have her all to myself as planned.

I drive to Kat's parents house and muster a sigh as I park into their driveway. Ever since our falling out a year ago, they've barely said a word to me even though I've tried countless times to get them to see my side. They hate me – which is understandable from their point of view. It's like I swooped in like a predator and snatched their only daughter from them. The betrayal that I inflicted still leaves my mouth a bit sour, but I'd gladly sacrifice anything if it meant having Kat.

I get out and walk towards the door, my steps feeling heavy as I do so. I know they're home because their cars are parked outside and Kat had mentioned that they would be. I pull at my shirt and rake my hand through my hair before I knock and wait for someone to open up.

It seems like I'm standing there forever before the door finally swings open and Steven appears on the other side. His expression falls as soon as he sees it's me, his face gone completely blank as his gaze roams my face.

"What are you doing here?" He asks, hand planted on the door as if he just can't wait to close it in my face.

"I wanted to talk to you – both of you," I say, glancing over his shoulder to see Mrs. Wellington in the back, her arms crossed and brows furrowed.

"I can't imagine what you might have to say to us," Steven quips and I clear my throat.

"Can we maybe take this inside? I won't be long," I say, knowing this wasn't the ideal place for a proper conversation.

Stevens thinks on it for a second, his mouth twisting derisively before he turns to his wife. Their gazes hold before she offers a small nod. Steven turns back to me, pulling the door further open as he steps to the side and allow me room to enter.

"Thank you," I say as I walk behind Mrs. Wellington to the living room. There, we all take a seat – both of them sitting on one end while I am forced to sit at the other, facing them while they stare back at me with judgement in their eyes.

"I er – I know that the relationship that we had in the past will never exist again..." I begin.

"Damn right about that," Steven exclaims.

"Can you blame us?" Mrs Wellington put in. "We trusted you and so much so that we placed her in your care for some time and what did you do ... you seduced our little girl!" She croaked.

"Kat's an adult and she was more than capable of making her own decisions," I say before quickly continuing. "Anyway, I didn't come here to fight – there's no point in it. Kat and I are happy and I haven't regretted a single thing since meeting her. I love her and she loves me and as long as we're together, nothing else matters to me, but now, I think it's time for our relationship to grow and that's why I'm here..."

They both glance at each other before looking back at me with a quizzical expression on their faces.

"I'm sorry that I betrayed your trust, I'm sorry that I didn't go about telling you in a different manner but I can't change what happened. I can tell you a thousand times that I love Kat but I don't know if it'll make any difference to you, but I wanna marry her – she's everything to me – and I've come here to ask for your blessings before I do so," I say, watching as their faces pale, their mouths falling open.

"I love your daughter and I would do anything to see her happy; I believe I can do that. I want to make her my wife."

Steven's mouth opens and closes as he sits there completely flabbergasted. He looks to his wife whose eyes starts to well with tears and then he clears his throat, looking at me.

"Despite our differences, I know you know that I love Kat and I'm here because I still respect you both and I don't want to do this without letting you know first."

Mrs. Wellington sniffs and quickly blink back the tears as she stares back at me. There is silence for a while before she finally says. "We know you love her, Grayson and me know she loves you too. We've seen it for ourselves but you've got to understand that this hasn't been easy for us."

I nod and then she continues after a pregnant silence fills the room again. "But this isn't about us, is it? Kat is happy and that's all that matters to me and as long as you're the source of her happiness, I really can't get in the way of it," she says before wiping the tears that had finally managed to spill from her face.

I manage a smile and look to Steven who grinds his teeth together and looks at the floor. He's there in deep thought and I give him the time to come to whatever conclusion he wants. A yes or no wouldn't change the fact that I want to marry Kat; I just know that if he says no, it will break her heart and that's the last thing I want.

Stevens looks up after an eternity and steadies his gaze on me. "I can't deny that you make her happy and that's all I ever want for my baby girl, but if she ever comes over with a single tear on her face, that's where we're gonna have a problem, Grayson."

I nod, feeling some relief override me. "I would never hurt Kat."

"See, that's a promise you can't keep," he cut in. "But if she does say yes, I won't get in the way."

I pull in a breath, feeling the full effect of my relief. "Thank you, thank you both." I can't help my laugh as joy spurs within my heart.

For a couple minutes more we engage in light chatter before I decide it's time to go home and prepare for my evening with Kat. She doesn't know that I have an evening planned for us but that's exactly the way I wanted it.

After I'm finished setting up a table for us and checking with the two private chefs that I've hired, I take a shower before heading back downstairs. As soon as I descend the stairs, Kat enters through the front door and closes it behind her. My heart flutters in my chest as I look at her and try to envision the rest of the evening together. I've missed her so much even though it's been a couple of hours but for the past months, it's like Kat has become a part of me and I simply can't live without her constantly by my side.

When she turns and spots me at the foot of the stairs, her eyes light up and a hundred-watt smile brightens her face. I can't help my own, knowing that I have such an effect on her. Her joy is infectious and I crave for it.

She bounds toward me and stares into my eyes as I stare into hers. Without any more hesitation, she captures my lips and my entire body awakens. She's soft and sweet as usual and I can't get enough. My manhood stirs and my heart swells as I grow more desirous.

"I've missed you," she says, kissing me again, needier this time. I can tell what she wants and want so much to give it to her but I know I have to hold out until later – no matter how hard. No pun intended.

“I missed you too,” I say as I break our kiss and look down at her. “And I have something special planned for us.”

She raises a brow and looks around the house, her nose twitching a bit. “Is that food I smell?” She muses, her voice raising a pitch.

“That’s right. I have the garden set up for just us two,” I inform.

Her mouth widens. “What? What is all this about?”

“Do you really have to ask?” I tease. “My baby just completed college and was the valedictorian. Of course more celebrations are in order.”

Her cheeks redden. “Aww babe... you didn’t have to...”

“Of course I had to,” I say before I kiss her again.

“Okay, but can I just go freshen up first?”

“Of course.”

She smiles, give me a quick peck on the lips before she dashes up the stairs and to our bedroom. It then dawns on me that within the hour I’ll ask her to be my wife. With a huff, I wipe my now sweaty palms against my pants and move to see if everything’s in place.

I’m waiting for Kat downstairs, feeling like time had gone at a standstill despite the fact that it wasn’t even thirty minutes yet. But when she finally rejoins me, my breath catches in my throat as my gaze roam over her.

She’s in a silk peach dress that does wonders to her ivory skin. It skims past her knees, a narrow split at the side, hinting at her creamy thighs. The cleavage area is slightly snug but the material falls between her breasts, showing just a hint of the creamy mounds. I know she’s bra-less from the way her tight nipples protrudes and how her full breasts bounce slightly with each movement. I swallow the saliva that pools in my mouth, now completely hungry for her. She’s beautiful and has managed to take my breath away on every occasion.

“I know that look,” she teases.

I try not to grin. “Don’t be a tease; I’m already trying extra hard to get through dinner.”

She giggles as she reached for my hand. “Alright then; I promise to be a good little girl for daddy tonight,” she whispers.

Blood rushes to my cock. “Not for the entire night,” I whisper against her ear and she shivers.

She flashes me a look that tells me she’s up for the challenge before we both head outside. It’s a bit chilly, but not cold. Either way, I don’t think Kat realizes with how entranced she is at the setup. The dinner table sits in the middle of the garden – a table for two – with lights lining the pathway, highlighting every single flower that it’s wrapped around. There’s a bouquet for her right in the center of the table with a wild assortment because she always said she could never really pick one.

The expression on her face brings me joy and it makes me realize I’ve done a good job.

"Babe, this is lovely," she says, looking from me to the décor.

I smile as I usher her towards the chair and pull one out for her. She takes a seat as her gaze continues to inspect the place.

Just then the two chefs enter; one with a bottle of chilled wine and the other with some appetizers.

"Wha–" Kat soaks everything up, looking at me with so much adoration, I feel like hopping around like a kid.

It makes me anxious because now I feel like I can't wait until the end of this to ask her the big question. I'm too on edge – too desperate for an answer.

But I wait – at least until she has completed the main course as she might have been hungry. As we eat, she tells me about her day and I tell her about mine – cropping out certain details of course.

After the main course we decide on dessert and I'm glad I ordered her favorite – tiramisu. Her mouth falls open as soon as she sees it and she digs in right away, making me laugh.

"I love you," I tell her and she looks up at me with a bright blush on her face.

"I love you too."

"And that's how I know that what I'm about to ask you is probably the best decision I've made in my entire life," I say and her brows furrow.

I clear my throat. "I've loved you for a long time, Kat and now that you're constantly by my side, it seems like loving you and making you happy is my only priority. You've given me so much joy over the past year and I can't explain how much I appreciate you; I just know that I want to wake up to you every single morning and go to bed with you every single night. I'm the happiest I've been with you in my life..."

"Grayson..." she begins to say, her eyes welling with tears.

I move off the chair and pluck the small box from my pocket before I approach her and bend on one knee. Kat's hand is already over her mouth as soon as she sees the box and freezes in that spot when she realizes what's about to happen.

I look up to her once I'm settled and pop the small velvet box open. She gasps when she sees the ring and the tears finally spills from her eyes.

"Katherine Wellington, will you make me the luckiest man alive by becoming my wife?" I ask her, my heart galloping in my chest as I await her answer.

Fortunately for me, I don't have to wait long because her resounding "Yes!" comes as quickly as the words leave my mouth. She bounds off the chair and plunges herself into my arms, almost knocking both of us to the floor. I am quick to steady her as I cling to her and get us to our feet. I smash my lips against her, tasting her salty tears mixed with her sweet, wine-stained breath.

We kiss for a long time until my cock grows hard against her, so much so that I know she feels it. But she only breaks apart to grin at me as she stretches out her hand for me to place the ring on. More tears continue to tumble down her unblemished skin as I slip on the diamond ring that fits her slender finger perfectly.

She chokes out a sob as she looks at me and throws her hands around me. "A thousand times yes! I love you so much Grayson!"

"I love you too, baby girl," I say, hugging her tight and not wanting to ever let her go.

I know it. I know that I'm the luckiest man alive and that's all because I have Kat by my side. Nothing else have ever been so certain, so right and I know that I'll spend the rest of our lives, showing her why she made the right choice.

Possessive Alpha-Daddy & Virgin

Izzie Vee

Erotic & Forbidden

IZZIE VEE[1]

1. https://www.amazon.com/s?k=izzie+vee&i=digital-text&crid=31LQJTEQYT2EE&sprefix=izzie+vee%2Cdigital-text%2C121&ref=nb_sb_noss

Cover Design by Izzie Vee
Cover Photo by VitalikRadko on Depositphotos.com

Table of Content

Chapter 1

Mike

My knuckles hurt and are bruised, but the adrenaline rushing through me is insane. I feel refreshed and renewed and know there's only one thing that could have made me feel like that, and that's fighting. To top it off, I have a stack of money from doing it, so win-win. It was only once per week until I got attached and decided I'd add two more days to it. It was a type of high that I found myself indulging in time and time again, plus people loved me for it.

There's no better way to quell the anger – to soothe the beast inside me that always wants an out.

Stretching my fingers, I make my way inside the bar that isn't far from my apartment. This is my sanctuary – the place I go to cool off after crushing it in the pit. After two glasses of whiskey and a hamburger, I know I will be good for the night and heck, I might even find a woman to bring home and pump my balls dry. The thought excites me for some reason, and I am more enthusiastic about making that a reality.

As I step inside, the familiar scent of liquor greets me, along with the hearty ruckus from those inside. Some country music is playing, the smell from the kitchen is making my mouth water, and I know the night will be perfect. I take a seat by the counter, and Cherry pops up immediately with a smile on her wide, red lips. She's had a crush on me that's longer than time, and even after fucking her a few times, she still can't seem to get me out of her system. Still, she is good for keeping my bed warm on lonely nights, but I've made it clear time and time again that it would just be for a couple of fucks and nothing else.

"Having the usual?" she asks me as she wipes at a glass, eyeing me in that seductive way that lets me know she may want me in her sack tonight.

"Yeah, neat, please..." I say as I rub my hands together. Cherry seems to notice the bruises and shakes her head as she goes to pour me my drink.

"That looks like it needs some tending to," she says as she places a glass in front of me and meets my gaze. She's attractive; I've got to give her that. She has a straight face and curly, big blonde hair, that's probably her most attractive feature, but she just doesn't bring out the hot-blooded male in me.

"It's fine," I say as I grind my teeth, knowing what's coming next.

"You planning on doing that for the rest of your life?" she quips.

"Maybe," I say as I down the glass in one go, baring my teeth at the harshness.

"I'm getting off soon; what do you say about me coming over?" she smiles, incredibly seductive. "I can make you forget about the pain," she says as she glances at my raw knuckles.

Tapping my glass against the counter, I signal for another round while she awaits an answer. Cherry fits the bill for a good lay, but she isn't the type for continuous repeats. Over time, she begins to get overbearing and demanding, and I'd rather fuck without that type of baggage. As much as I'd like to release all this sexual pent-up I have, I'm gonna have to pass on this one.

Plus, at thirty-five, I think it's time to finally find me a woman to settle down with. Trouble is, I can't find the woman who can give me that spark, and at this point, I no longer have hope that I will. Maybe I should just give in to Cherry after all... learn to adjust to her ways.

Just as I'm about to answer, I hear chuckling and teasing in the back, which grabs my attention. I turn my head to see what's causing the ruckus. A big, bulky guy a bit smaller than me sits with his friends as they chat with a petite waitress I'm seeing for the first time. Her back is turned to me, but I can make out her slender form, the flare to her waist, her long legs, and the healthy ponytail that swings down her back.

I've been to this place enough times to know the staff to a T, yet she isn't familiar. I'd know someone like her. I glance to Cherry who seems more interested in getting an answer from me than anything else.

"Who's the new girl?"

"Amanda, she started this morning," she says.

I look back at her, somehow drawn to her, despite not knowing what the fuck she looks like. But I'm interested more than anything to know. Suddenly, the man grabs her hand and pulls her into his lap. A gasp escapes her, and I finally get a chance to see her face. She's beautiful with a tiny face, a narrow nose, and by the looks of it, blue eyes that could touch my soul. But her face is as pale as paper, and I can see the fear in her eyes. She's like a doll in the hands of the big man, and I can see that her heart is in her mouth.

He brings his mouth to her ear and says something to her that makes her shiver as he clutches her tighter. An overwhelming amount of anger rises inside me, and it's like my vision turns red as I watch the interaction. Setting my glass down, I ease from my stool and hear a protest from Cherry, which I ignore. With hands balled into fists, I approach the table of big men and watch as their gazes turned to me. I can see the fear that flashes across one of their gazes, but it quickly fades when he realizes that though I am bigger than them, I am outnumbered. Dumb fuck.

Her face becomes clearer, and the big, bright eyes filled with fear and amusement tell me that what I'm about to do is the right thing. For a moment, I'm captivated, and it seems all is right in the world if I continue to stare at her, but then I remember what the fuck I'm here for.

"You assholes take pleasure in scaring and assaulting innocent women?" I ask, my voice grabbing their attention even more.

The girl pulls out of the big guy's grasp after realizing she has a savior and stands at my side. The crew of three stands as well, but I can see the disappointment and the small ounce of fear when they have to look up at me.

"Next time, how about you mind your own business, motherfucker?" the captor seethes.

My blood boils with anger the longer I stare at them and that sweet rush to beat their face in overpowers me.

"Thank you, but they're not worth the time," the petite waitress announces by my side.

"You fucking bitch-"

He attempts to grab at her, but I quickly block his path and piston my fists across his jaw. Blood immediately spurts from his mouth from the impact as he launches back into the table, sending the beer bottles to the floor. The others charge at me, one managing to land a punch across my jaw. The unexpectedness of it and the sudden pain that takes residence sends me over the edge, and I become angrier than ever. I pull one by the collar and punch him squarely across the jaw; he swings at me but misses, and I take the opportunity to punch him again. When all three are down, I grab the closest one and start to beat in his face. My hands ache, but the adrenaline inside me is insane. His face is covered in blood, and I can hear the repeated crunching of his face each time I pound into it, but I don't stop, even when my knuckles feel bare on the skin.

"Fucking Christ, Mike, stop!" I can hear Cherry's voice, but I don't stop. I can feel people gathered around me, their gasps echoing in my head, but I can't seem to stop. Assholes like these always get away with doing shit they aren't supposed to do because of the fear factor they pack with them but not this time around.

"I think that's enough...please," I hear a familiar, not-so-familiar voice, and my heart skips a beat; still, I continue. But when a hand is placed on my shoulder, every nerve in my body acknowledges it, and I pause in my tracks, my fist mid-air.

I turn to look who it is and realize it's the pretty little damsel with the fucking prettiest face I've ever seen. It still amazes me how pretty she is. But that's not what shocks me the most. It's the fact that her simple touch can calm me; the beast inside me relaxes, and I can see every other color again apart from red. She gives me a gentle, appreciative smile, and it's like the block of ice around my heart thaws completely.

"Fucking shit, Mike, get out of here!" I am torn from my trance when Cherry shoves at me. I immediately realize the difference each touch has on me. How different they are and how they affect me on both different levels.

I get up from my stupor, stare at the grunting men on the floor that can barely move, and then I turn to Cherry.

"Leave before someone calls the cops," she hisses.

I flash my hands. I don't care about the fucking cops. I've been around them enough times to know not to be afraid. This sense of responsibility overtakes me, and I can only think about the little lady beside me. I stand before her and run my gaze over her. She's in a tight little shirt that pushes up her bra and hints at her creamy cleavage. An apron snugly fits around her tiny waist that flares into hips I wouldn't mind exploring. Her skin is flawless and looks as soft as cotton. My fingers itch to touch. As my eyes travel to her face, I can feel my body reacting to her mere presence, her tiny pink mouth that I can't help but imagine wrapped around my manhood while she sucks me dry.

My cock twitches, and thoughts of this beautiful little minx fill me to the brim. Despite the grime and the people that surround us, she is the only one I see, and I feel this sense of duty to protect her forever and keep her safe and away from assholes like these.

"Thank you," she says, her voice like a lullaby that brings me a sense of peace that I can't ignore. That I crave more of.

"Fuck, Mike, go!" Cherry interrupts a-fucking-gain, and I grit my teeth.

I reach for her hand and pull her along with me and am happy that there's not a protest from her, but Cherry, on the other hand, is flabbergasted and spitting fire.

"Where are you going with her?!" she blares. "She still has all this to clean up. Her shift isn't over as yet!"

I continue to walk with her, not saying a word until I am near the door. "She's not coming back," I say, watching Cherry's face whiten a little, her eyes going wide.

Amanda gasps when she reaches the outside and tugs at my hand. "What do you think you're doing?"

I stop to face her – well, not exactly since I have to look down at her. "You're not safe there..." I say.

"And you think I'm safe with you...a complete stranger," she argues.

"Who saved your ass back there..." I add, taken aback by her tone but unable to ignore the fire that looms in her eyes.

She clasps her arms and stands defiantly, the action causing her breast to push out even more. I wet my lips with the tip of my tongue, trying to ignore the way my fucking body is responding to her, but I can't help it. She's too fucking perfect.

"The fact still remains..."

I sigh, feeling my anger begin to rise, but not the type that allowed me to beat the shit out of those guys.

"Listen, those assholes will be back, and I might not be around to protect you the second time around. You can't be here."

"I have nowhere else to go... this job is all I have. It comes with a spare room upstairs, and that's the best deal I can get for now," she says as her eyes flicker to the ground.

My resolve softens yet again – this woman is like a fucking pacifier to my anger. "Come with me," I insist.

"I don't know you," she argues.

"That's how every friendship starts isn't it?" I ask, but friendship is the furthest thing from my mind right now. I want her beneath me, screaming my name while I plunge into her repeatedly. She's mine; I can feel it in every fiber of my being, see it as I stand before her. There's no explaining how I know it, I just know, and there's no fucking way I'm letting her out of my sight.

She swallows and looks back to the bar and then at me again. "I think it's pretty obvious I won't hurt you, princess; I've got a place to stay, and you don't. I'd say that's a catch."

Indecision clouds her gaze, and she bites those juicy lips as she stares at me as if trying to see within my deep, dark soul. Finally, she says, "I'll have to get my things."

"I'll have them brought over to you. Let's go," I say, gesturing toward my car.

She hesitates, and for a second, I think she will run, but then she moves toward me. "Ok, big guy... lead the way."

I only smile.

Chapter 2

Amanda

I don't know what the hell got into me to be saying this to this complete stranger–a man as big and bulky as the hulk, a man who took down three huge guys with barely a scratch. I should be running for the hills, but instead, I'm inside his car, watching how he fills out the tiny space with his big frame. Every single part of him has a muscle that prints through his clothes, but he is incredibly handsome with the darkest eyes I've ever seen on a person. Despite him being a walking red flag for a girl like me, I can't forget how he stood up for me. It was like my own personal knight in shining armor, but he wears leather instead.

I felt safe – the safest I've felt in all my life, and I loved the feeling it brought me. Still, I know I shouldn't have agreed to come with him – he is still a stranger, after all. But he is right; I can't stay at the bar for another day to be pounced on by the same men who might come back and take revenge, and I have nowhere else to go.

I watch how silently he drives, his eyes fixed on the road like he doesn't even remember I'm here. He adjusts his hands on the steering wheel occasionally, bringing my eyes to his hands. I gulp when I see his raw knuckles and the blood on his hands. He's hurt, and guilt suddenly tugs at me for being the reason. I should have fought back on my own and given them some sass, but in that moment, fear overcame me and brought me back to my past, which made my blood run cold.

I swallow hard and ignore my churning gut. "I can help you with that," I say, my voice sounding barely a whisper.

He spares a glance at me and then his bruised hand. "It's fine."

"You make a habit of saving damsels, Mike," I ask, emphasizing the name I learned back at the bar.

"Just the pretty ones," he says, and before I can even reply, we stop outside an apartment building. He gets out and then looks at me, still seated, wondering if I'm gonna do the same.

There's something about his eyes on me that makes me feel exposed and warm all over, a feeling that I've never experienced before. Despite the danger this man defines in every single aspect, I hold onto the door handle and push it open. The night wind whips against my skin and sends a shiver down my spine. A part of me tells me to just leave and figure it out like I've done many times before, but deep down, a part of me wants this. Strangely enough, I'm not scared as I should be.

I make my way to him, and we go inside, the warmth in the building attending to my chills. After climbing a flight of stairs, we settle at a door with the number 9 on it. His keys cling, and in no time, he is inside, waiting for me to do the same.

I timidly step in, my eyes traveling around the space. I didn't expect it to be so clean – coming here, I somehow expected a sort of dump, but I'm amazed at the clean wooden-type floors and the crisp, black sofa set that surrounds a wooden coffee table as soon as you enter. The walls are exposed brick with black and white portraits of motorcycles and a boxing ring. Everything smells fresh with a hint of cigarette.

He turns to me after peeling off his jacket and throwing it over the edge of the sofa. My breath hitches when I see bulky hands that are probably the size of my legs. He is ripped, and if I thought he looked strapping in that leather jacket, I was clearly mistaken. I imagine this man does weightlifting with people instead of actual weights. His shoulders are broad, his neck is thick, and I can see how hard his stomach is even with a shirt on. My eyes travel to his narrow waist and his thick, muscular legs, and somehow, I can't help my thoughts as my eyes settle at his crotch.

Anyone would think I'm a creep for thinking like this, but I can't help but wonder if his manhood is just as big as the rest of him. The thoughts cause a sensation to settle between my legs and my stomach to churn, but I quickly tear my gaze away and bring it to his face, realizing the smirk that it holds. Heat instantly rises to my cheeks. He knows I was checking him out, and the dark lust in his eyes tells me he doesn't mind.

My face warms, and my gaze drops to his hand, the guilt pulling at me again. I move closer toward him and can feel the heat radiate from his body on me, his musky cologne filling my senses.

"Do you have a first aid kit?" I ask as I reach for his hand. Heat floods me as I take him in my grasp. I examine his huge hands and imagine how calloused they would feel against me.

"It's fine..." he insists and pins me with his gaze with those sexy, dark eyes and long lashes. My heart starts to thud faster in my chest, and I'm somehow breathless despite standing so still.

"I want to help," I say, watching his features soften as he concedes. The closer I stare at him, I realize that what I thought was a slit in his thick arched brows is actually a scar that separates the hair. I want to touch it – enquire about the injury – because part of me wants to know everything about this man.

"I'll get the peroxide and the gauze... that's all I have," he says as he pulls away and moves inside his room.

My gaze continues to take in his apartment, and I find myself at ease. Despite the fear that should be bolting through me, I feel completely safe and at home, which is strange considering the complete giant of a stranger that's nearby.

He returns with the items in his hand and moves toward the sofa, where the small furniture sinks with his weight. I approach him, and seeing that he is seated on the single recliner, I wonder where I should sit. Biting my lips, I straddle him, sitting on his lap. I can see that my actions catch him by surprise, and his eyes darken even more. However, he doesn't say anything, and I smile inwardly while I busy myself dabbing the cotton with peroxide and placing it against the bruises. He doesn't even flinch, and I wonder if this happens often.

But I have no time to think on it with being so close to him. I can tell I have an effect on him, and part of me wants to explore that in its entirety. I am small against him, my crotch just inches away from his manhood, which I can tell is blossoming beneath his denim pants.

"How can I repay you for what you did for me earlier?" I ask.

"You don't have to," he exclaims, his breath against my skin, sending shivers throughout my body. I look at him, but his gaze is trained on the task at hand. His lips catch my eyes – wide and full – and I lick my own.

"I want to," I insist, and he looks up at me, holding my gaze while I shift on his lap. His Adam's apple visibly bobs, and I know with just a little more teasing I will have him under my thumb.

"You have no idea what you're doing to me right now, Amanda," he says under his breath, his voice like a soft growl.

"Oh, I have an idea," I say as a smile curves my lips. He twitches between me, and heat sears through my body in full waves.

There's an attraction to this beast that I can't quite understand. I've never done this before – I've never teased a man to this degree, but somehow, I want everything this giant has to offer. Maybe it's the adrenaline still rushing through me from what happened at the bar; maybe it's my sex finally telling me that it's ready to take on life by the balls – literally. Is it because he saved my ass back there? Is it because he was a gentleman to me when nobody else was? Or is it the peace that his presence brings me?

"I want to repay you... tell me what you want me to do," I say in what sounds like a mere whisper.

His eyes study my face, and I can feel his manhood twitching even more beneath me, telling me this beast wants me as much as I want him. I can feel it, I can see it, and I even want to taste it. My eyes suddenly drop to his lips again, and I swear my heart will soon leave my chest with how fast it's beating. I'm done for. I want to kiss him so bad!

I move my head closer to him, and his breath blows against my face. I can smell the faint scent of whiskey on his breath as they gently part to receive what I have to offer. I know my panties are sodden from the close proximity and the way his body seems to set me on fire. I am intoxicated by his warmth, his scent, and his seeming callousness; when my lips touch his, I know I'm a goner.

Fuck.

Chapter 3

Mike

I wasn't expecting any of this. The kindness, the warmth, and the gentleness, and definitely not an offer to repay me. But as the words leave her lips, I can think of only one thing, and that's to make her mine. Mine only. She is irresistible, attractive and she sets my heart and body on fire. I want to rip off her clothes, bend her over and have my way with her – give her a life she can't refuse – which includes my cock. But she is too small, too fragile, and I know my size will split her into halves.

As she grinds herself purposely on me, I know she's just too tiny. My cock would destroy her, and that's the last thing I want to do. Yet, my body screams against every bit of control I have. I should be pushing her away – heck, I should have left her at the bar because I know that one real touch from her would ruin me.

Her lips move towards mine – I can see it coming, and there's nothing I want to do to stop it. I await my glorious fate and almost come in my pants when her soft, feathery lips touch mine. They are like cotton that brushes against me and awaken me to the hardness of steel. Her lips part for me, and I welcome her as her sweet tongue probes within my mouth, sending fire all over my body. I fucking knew it – knew that she would be the death of me from the very first time I laid eyes on her. And here it is; I am one foot in a glorious grave. But if this is heaven, I don't mind dying.

Her tongue courses through my mouth and the hunger there ignites my own. She is warm – her mouth is warm and soft, and I imagine between her legs is the same, but one fucking step at a time, Mike. She sucks on my tongue, and our tongues dance together in a needy caress. She moans against me, which sends vibrations straight through my body and settles at my cock. Her small hands lace around my neck, and her chest is now almost pressed against mine, her nipples rubbing against me, making me harder than steel itself. She's sweet, almost like a drug that I know will get me addicted, but I don't stop. I take all she gives and give some of my own – making it clear in every caress that I need her more than oxygen itself.

My hands find her back and trail beneath her blouse and up her spine. When the pad of my fingers touches her bare skin, she shivers and moans, grinding a little on my erection and making the lump even more painful. But that seems to set her off as she continues to grind her clothed cunt on me. She moans as she does so, eyes closed as she enjoys her actions.

I can barely believe that I have it within me to arouse a fragile beauty like her, but I can see it as well as I can feel it thrumming through every fiber of my being. The feeling gets so intense, my mind is so hazy that I can't help myself. The fucking dry humping sets me off, and before I can hold back, I can feel the pressure ease from my testicles as my semen shoots and fills my pants.

I shudder, closing my eyes in an attempt to hide the embarrassment. This has never happened before. I have a hard time coming from penetration, much less fucking dry humping, but here I am, having one of the best orgasms of my life.

"I've never felt this way before, Mike," she says in barely a whisper. Her voice brings me back to life. I open my eyes to find her staring up at me with a pleased smile on her face.

"How do you feel?" I ask her. I hold my breath for an answer, still hard as a rock despite cumming just seconds ago. Fuck.

"Alive," she smiles, and my heart skips a beat. "I want you."

I have never considered myself lucky, but at this moment, I am the happiest man alive just by her mere words. My body is on fire, I am overwhelmed by this woman and in the best possible way.

But she's so fucking tiny, and I am a beast. "You can't handle my cock, princess. Let's get that out from now."

She swallows and folds her lips. "Says who?"

I grit my teeth. "Almost every fucking woman I've been with."

"Well, maybe I'm the exception."

Somehow that gives me hope, but I know better than to do that. I'm always disappointed in the end, and so are a lot of women.

I scoff and shake my head, reaching for her hips to peel her from me, so I can leave and think about anything apart from her pussy, which is still seated on me. But she surprises me and holds my hand still, meeting my gaze with the lust still clear in her blue eyes.

"I don't know what it is about you, but I know in my heart that I want you more than anything..." she says, and her words alone are enough to make me harder. Damn this woman.

I want her so much, it aches, but I know if I have her, it will pain her more than it's doing me right now.

"How old are you?" I can't help but ask. It's a question I should have asked before it reached this far, but I know she's an adult. After all, she was working at a bar.

"Twenty-one," she says.

Even younger than I thought. Fuck.

"Have you ever been with a man like me, princess?" I ask her, still cognizant of her on me and how my body is responding to her every movement.

She hesitates. "I've never been with anyone."

I stiffen at her reply, waiting for her to laugh and tell me she's joking, but the seriousness on her face tells me she's not. An unexpected feeling suddenly overwhelms me that I can't explain. There's this sudden urge to lock her away for myself and myself alone – away from the gazes of any man who would take even a glimpse of her. It surprises me beyond measure that a fairy like this would find attractiveness in me – almost begging me to have her – take her virginity–her most prized possession. I want to honor that immediately – do as she asks, but I can't. I can't fucking do it – not tonight or any other night, for that matter.

"I can't," I develop the courage to say as I peel her away from me and sit her on the armrest of the chair. I glance at her wide eyes and her furrowed brows. She's just as confused as I am. "There's a spare bedroom that has all you might need. Good night, Amanda," I say as I leave the room and leave her there, still shocked from my denial.

I head to my bedroom and flop down on the king-sized bed, staring at the blank ceiling for God knows how long. I can hear her shuffling around in the bedroom that's next door. I want to know what she's doing – I don't even want to take my eyes off her. I want that sense of peace again whenever her blue eyes trap me and make me feel like I can accomplish anything. I can't figure out how I got so lucky to have her – to have such a beautiful woman want me, and yet I feel unlucky too because what's the point if I can't have her in the end? I wouldn't dare. Amanda is a fragile beauty meant for endless pampering and princess treatment. I can't give her that. One stroke in her glorious heat, and I'd lose my mind. I fuck hard and doubt a woman like Amanda could handle it.

But when have I ever been a man to care in the first place? I could be buried deep inside her right now if I wanted to, but instead, I am here, basically pining over a woman I could have if I wanted to. When had I ever given propriety a thought? I question myself with a mounting surge of annoyance for my actions.

I am allowing a woman to get under my skin, which has never happened. But I knew from the very moment back at the bar that Amanda was different. Unlike all the others, she spoke to my soul on a level I couldn't quite understand.

I lay there, pondering for what seemed like hours until the apartment was quiet, and I knew she was probably asleep. I take the opportunity to get up and head to the bathroom for a quick shower, seeing that my pants are still icky from cumming inside them. The thought and the memory of her body against mine – the euphoric feeling of her cunt on mine – gets me hard again. I mutter a curse and stroke myself to an orgasm before I take a cold shower and head to bed with the pretty little minx on my mind.

I WOKE UP EARLIER THAN usual the following morning because I was restless all night, plagued with sweet dreams of the minx in the other room. I have never practiced control as much as I did last night. Every single nerve in my body told me to get up and sneak into her room – convince her that my earlier decision was a mistake and I'd like nothing else than to bury my length inside her. I was tempted – fighting demons I didn't even know I had, but I had clung onto every bit of control I could muster and stopped myself from doing something insane. She's twenty-one – way younger than the women I'd go for, and that, too, was another factor that had grated my conscience.

A pot of coffee is already made when I enter the kitchen, and Amanda is sitting by the counter having a cup. Her dark hair is down, and for the first time, I catch a streak of blue towards the back I hadn't noticed before. It makes her eyes seem more attractive and makes her more alluring than before. Damn.

"Good morning," I say as I move past her to pour myself a cup. "You didn't have to do all this," I say when I realize there are also eggs and toast beside the stove.

"I wanted to," she manages a tight smile and hangs her head, obviously trying her hardest to avoid my gaze.

I pull in a breath as I approach her. "Listen, if I came off a little too harsh last night, I'm sorry. That wasn't my intention."

"It's fine. I admire what you did, Mike. Not many men would pass up such an opportunity, but I respect you for it," she smiles at me.

Respect is the last fucking thing I want from her, but heck, I caused this on myself.

"How was your sleep?" she asks me, and I pause, seeing that all too familiar glint in her eyes again.

"I've had better," I confess. "You?"

"I slept like a baby. It's the best sleep I've had in a while, Mike. Thanks to you."

Great. Good to know I was the only one affected by last night. I nod my head and take a sip of the coffee while we settle into silence. There seems to be a forcefield around, which seems tangible.

"I'll be back soon. Don't leave the house," I say as I place my mug down.

"What? Why?"

I approach her, standing dangerously close to her, which may or may not prove to be a mistake.

"Because you are mine, and I don't want you alone on those crazy streets," I say as I cup her face in the palms of my hands because I can't help myself. I ache for the feel of her soft skin against the pads of my calloused hands.

She stares up at me, and her throat bobs as she swallows. "How can you claim I am yours, and yet you don't want to have me?"

"I don't want to hurt you."

"You're killing me now."

My cock stirs at her statement. I grit my teeth so hard I fear they will shatter in my mouth. Fuck, this is hard. But maybe not as hard as I am right now. I press my mouth to her forehead, fighting for control.

"What does it matter if we have sex a week or a year from now?" she says under her breath. "Your cock will still be the same, and I will still be a virgin."

I lick across my lips and stare down at her. "It's harder than you think. Stay here until I get back," I say as I tear myself away from her and reach for my keys.

"On one condition," she challenges.

"You'll fuck me when you get back."

Chapter 4

Mike

I hate afternoon fights for some reason, and even more now, seeing that I have to leave Amanda's side.

As I enter the ring with my opponent, I'm expecting to have this overwhelming urge that usually takes control, but it doesn't come. Instead, when he charges at me, I quickly shift from his path of destruction and send an uppercut up his face. My head isn't in it, though, regardless of the chairs and the bets I know will be in my favor at the end of this. The adrenaline is gone, and I only can think about Amanda at my house, waiting for me to come home and fuck her. I said I would because, at that moment, there was nothing else I could say.

What was the point in denying it? I want her as much as I want oxygen, and it isn't only primal or sexual. I want endless nights with her. I want her in my bed even when I'm not. I want to be a constant on her mind- someone she never ever forgets, even when she wants to. I want to be that man for her. I want to explore every inch of her young flesh and savor the feeling and the taste. The desire for her is so strong that the task at hand seems meaningless.

What will she think of me anyway, knowing this is how I make a living? Will she think I'm a monster? Would it make her want me less? All of these things start to plague my mind. A passion I've had since I was a kid seems irrelevant because of a woman I've known for just mere hours. I want to be a better man for a woman I haven't even explored – a woman who hasn't even felt the full length of my manhood. This is bullshit; I am stark-raving mad.

I jolt back when a strike across my face sends me crashing to the ground. There's an incessant ringing and the blurred image of my opponent who hovers over me. Before I can react, his fist throws my head to the side with another blow. The metallic taste of blood starts to pool in my mouth, and pain races through my head like a bolt of lightning.

I know I'm in a losing battle, but the encouraging shouts put me back on course and remind me where I am and what I'm about. A punch in his side sends him tumbling over and gives me the upper hand once again – one which I use to my full advantage.

At the end of it, I'm sorer than I've ever been and have attracted an angry manager – Paul.

"What the hell was that all about?" he exclaims, following behind me as I venture into the small changing room.

I sigh as I wipe at my sweat. "Sorry, my head wasn't in it," I mumble, taking a seat on a bench.

The man who I've known for years – a short, stocky man with a bald head that he usually covers with a baseball cap – scoffs and shakes his head.

"It was like you weren't even trying."

"I won, didn't I?" I snapped, getting irritated by his tone.

"Barely," he hisses back. "What do you think people will do when they see you start to look weak? You can kiss this fighting thing goodbye if you plan on keeping up this behavior."

Something I have never considered comes to mind. Maybe that's exactly what I should do! I could do better – be better for Amanda. I couldn't spend the rest of my life in the pits anyway. I needed a backup plan.

"When is my next fight?" I ask, pulling on a shirt.

"Tomorrow night at the warehouse, and then you're out till next week. Why?" he says casually, not having a clue what I planned on saying next.

I stand before him. "It'll be my last. Spread the word," I say as I grab my bag from the bench.

Paul's mouth falls open as he stares at me. He then shakes his head and adjusts his hat. "What?"

"I'm done with the fighting. Tomorrow night will be my last," I clarify, sidestepping him.

"Mike, what are you talking about? What has gotten into you? You love this!"

"Something else has gotten my attention." I continue to walk until I am outside the building.

"Mike, I know you are usually impulsive but think about what you're saying for a sec, please. You've been boxing all your life."

"Boxing?" I scoff. "Whatever you tell yourself, Paul."

He catches up to me and stands in front of me, blocking my entrance to the car. "Sure, none of it is legal, but we both get to live the way we want at the end of the day."

"Yeah, and now I don't want to do it anymore. Move."

Paul wipes his hand across his face and sighs. "Just think about this, please," he says as he steps to the side.

"I have. Saturday is the last time." I pull the door open and step inside my car. "After that, I'm done." I drive off, leaving Paul in the dust. He peels off his baseball cap and throws it to the ground as he stomps his feet and sweeps his hand over his bald head.

I have one thing on my mind as I head home, and that's being between Amanda's legs. Every single thought is of her, and for the first time in forever, I feel free – like a weight has been lifted off my shoulders.

I enter the apartment to find her on the couch, watching T.V. She's in one of my t-shirts that swallow her whole form, but fuck, it's the sexiest thing I have ever seen. It also reminds me that I never stopped at Cherry's to get her clothes, but what do I give a fuck about her clothes when all I want to do is take them all off? She looks better in mine, anyway.

"Mike, I didn't think you'd be back so early," she says as she stands.

"I couldn't keep away. I couldn't stop thinking about you."

She smiles at me. "Same. I couldn't wait for you to get back."

I slowly move towards her. "And now that I'm back, what do you plan on doing?" I challenge.

"Take you by force if you try to resist me again." Her sweet smile causes my heart to flutter. I move toward her, and her eyes widen as she gets a clearer view of my face and the bruises on it. "What happened?"

"A fight, but it's all good... don't worry about it."

Her hands move towards my face, and I almost close my eyes in pure bliss when her touch warms my skin. She caresses every bruise with the feathery light movements of her small hands making me forget that they ached in the first place.

I should be running as far away from this woman as I can, but here I am, with an ache I only have for her. She's young and fragile – far from the women I'd go for, but she entered my life in the least expected manner, and I am entranced – so fucking marveled by a woman I know nothing about. But I want to know her – I want to know every single thing about Amanda as early as her childhood. But right now, in this moment, I crave to know the feel of her cunt. I can't help it, and there's nothing I want to do to stop it.

I crash my lips to hers and feel the fire spread throughout my body. She kisses me back with just as much fierceness, latching her hands around my neck while her sweet mouth sends me into euphoria. I know I am fucking doomed as I kiss her, as I feel her body being pressed against mine. There's nothing in this world that can keep me away from this woman after this. She's mine, and I plan on showing her just how much she is.

I wrap my hands around her waist and stand. She wraps her legs around me and still continues to kiss me while we walk to my room. I'm painfully hard in my pants, acknowledging that the sweetest temptation is just mere inches away from my erection.

I toss her on the bed, and she giggles a little as she stares up at me, drinking in every inch of my body, propped up on her elbows. Her gaze settles on the bulge in my pants, and I can see the way her eyes darken with lust. She licks her lips, her cheeks redden, and I know that all will be fucking right in the world after this.

I give her a show, peeling off my clothes and tossing them to the side with my eyes remaining fixed on her. When I am completely naked, her eyes roam over my entire body, and she swallows, shifting a little on the bed. My cock points at her, smeared with a bit of my pre-cum as it patiently waits to have her.

Wordlessly, she starts to strip as well, taking her time to peel her blouse over her head and welcoming perky breasts, which makes me instantly salivate for a taste. They are perfect and ripe – a slight slope before hard, pointy nipples. Her skin is creamy, smooth like velvet, and incredibly flawless. My manhood pulses the longer I look at her, and I hold onto every bit of restraint I have while I fill my eyes with a memory that will live with me forever.

She rests back on her shoulders and raises her hips as she pulls off the shirt and her panties in one go. I swallow hard as my eyes travel up her long creamy legs only to rest between them at the treasure that lies between them. When she parts her legs for me, it's glistening – wet and ready for me and only me.

"You are fucking perfect," my voice is husky as I study her body one last time before I approach the bed to join her.

My mouth is mere inches away from hers before I say, "Tell me this is what you want, princess. I need to hear you say it."

She presses her forehead to mine. "I want you, Mike... every inch." Her breath fans against my skin and I almost shiver. She then kisses me again, and the world suddenly no longer exists.

As I kiss her, my hands trail along her body, memorizing every curve, feeling every inch of softness – the warmth that radiates from her skin onto mine. She smells sweet; she tastes sweet – she is a drug that will become more intoxicating every single time I touch her.

I lay her on her back and kiss her for a few seconds before my mouth trails along her neck, and I suckle on her flesh. She whimpers softly, her fingers pressing into me tighter as I take my time to explore her. When I reach her tits, my mouth almost waters as I stare at them and then take each supple nipple into my mouth. I suck on them feverishly, and she writhes beneath me, soft moans escaping her sweet lips that I start to miss.

"Please... I can't stand another second. I want you inside me now...please," she begs me.

I look up at her and see the impatience, the look in her eyes that tells me every word she speaks is true. I move back up and kiss her, my hands trailing along her body – squeezing her breasts occasionally and rubbing her hips.

"After tonight, you do know that you're mine, right? No other man will ever look at you or touch you. Your body will belong to me to have whenever I want, and mine will be yours," I say to her just as my fingers find her heated flesh.

She sucks in a breath as she stares up at me as my fingers part her flesh and find her tiny hole. She doesn't say anything as I continue to tease her flesh with featherlike strokes. She rolls her hips to meet them, but I don't give her more.

"Tell me you understand," I exclaim.

Her breath hitches as I push a finger in. "I do...please," she says, eyes momentarily closing as she soaks in the bliss.

I smile, still unable to believe that she is this wet for me – soaking really. My single finger enters with ease, and so I enter another and stroke her flesh until she starts to clench against my digits. I then pull them out, watch the dismay on her face and smile.

Smearing her wetness across my tip, I position myself between her legs and kiss her as I guide my thickening cock to her entrance. Her mouth parts open when it presses against her soft folds and gently parts them for access. At this point, it's already agony to hold back and not ram into her with a single thrust. I keep her innocence in mind and slowly push my way in, feeling my cock sear with heat as it gains access to her tight little snatch. I feel the resistance and pause, looking into her eyes, which have become glassy.

"I won't hurt you... I never will, but you will feel some discomfort for the first time. After that, I promise to make you feel heaven on earth." I don't know how true that is with my size, but for Amanda, I will go to the end of the earth to make her happy. I see that now – I feel it as I cruise deeper into her and break the barrier of her innocence. I know that I am done for when she winces and pulls me closer to her – as her pussy welcomes me with unending pleasure.

I pause a bit, and our eyes meet while she gets accustomed to a man being inside her for the first time. Me. I can see the admiration in her eyes as I start to move inside her, and my heart swells bigger in my chest, as does my manhood in her narrowness. She's wet, tight, and warm, and though I only have half my length inside her, I know it will be more than enough to get me off.

Her fingers ease into my back and slide to my ass, where she grabs it and urges me on a little further. But as I release another inch, she gasps, and I know that she can't take it. So I give her all with what she can take, moving faster as her pussy smacks against me.

"Oh, Daddy... yes!" she cries out, her cunt clenching against me with each stroke that I give her. The sound of her sweet voice calling me Daddy sets me on fire.

Sweat has started to bead on my forehead, and there's this urge to fuck her recklessly, but I'd die if I hurt her. She must've seen the look on my face because she reaches for it and gently caresses my cheeks while I fuck her.

The affection almost sets me off, and I buck inside her, sending my cock deeper. Amanda screams, but it isn't pained – more like pleasure as her heat starts to convulse around me. I kiss her hard and increase my pace a little as she clings to me.

She's like silk and tastes just like honey. Her sweet cunt hugging me repeatedly is all I need.

I growl. "You are my woman, Amanda. This sweet little pussy is mine and only mine! You were made for me!"

"Yes, Daddy, I am yours... completely!" her words are affirmations that immediately set me off. I grunt, and I buckle, shooting streams of semen into her. She cums with me, writhing and moaning as she basks in the sensation. Even when her body peaks and settles, I am still pumping cum inside her while she lies completely exhausted, collecting every drop.

When I pull out, she gasps while a steady stream races to the front and spills from her. The imagery is enough to make me hard again, but I flop back onto the bed beside her and pull her into my arms.

"That was incredible," she says after a few seconds when she finally manages to catch her breath.

"You are incredible, princess," I say, tracing circles around her belly button.

She smiles as her eyes flutter open and close. She's asleep in a matter of minutes while I am lying there, still struck by disbelief that a beautiful woman such as this was willing to give her virginity up to me. I want to believe that the attraction is mutual. There's no way it isn't. We are soulmates, and I am the happiest man alive. I feel weightless – completely at ease – with a sense of peace that I have searched for, for years and never had until now.

I am never letting Amanda go – she's mine forever, and nothing will ever get in the way of that. No man will look at her but me, no man will touch her, and if they do, they will suffer the consequences. She is mine and mine only. I go to bed with that thought in mind and a smile on my face.

Chapter 5

Amanda

I wake up with butterflies in my belly and a warm glow of sunshine settling on my face. A smile immediately forms on my face when I realize where I am and who I am with. Last night dawns on me fully, and heat sears through my body when I remember Mike kissing all over my body, caressing me, entering me, then proceeding to give me the best orgasm of my life.

When I got up yesterday, I didn't have the slightest thought that a man like Mike would swoop in and take me under his wings. The thought of losing my virginity didn't even cross my mind as I had given up hope that good men actually existed. I was willing to vow on that after being harassed, but then Mike came in and changed everything completely.

I knew that I wanted him – knew that I couldn't give my virginity to anyone else but him. Last night, I craved every inch of him, and when I didn't have him, it felt like torture. Watching him leave was even harder, but I experienced the best feeling ever when he returned. The thought makes me warm all over, the memory still throbs between my legs and makes me want him even now. I can't get enough.

His words still echo in my head – his claim on me. I should be scared that he meant every word, but I don't. I share the same sentiments. The thought of another woman eyeing my man, lusting after him... it puts me on edge. Mike is mine and mine alone, and fuck, it is insane. This is insane, but here I am, completely captivated and in love with a man I met hours ago. It has only been a day, yet I can't imagine life moving forward without him.

I shift in the bed and am surprised to find him hard. He isn't even fully awake, and yet he is hard. I smile, feeling a fire between my legs and a dirty thought in mind. Mike's manhood looks and feels good enough to taste, and at this moment, I am practically salivating to do just that.

I throw the sheet from my naked body and move down on him. His eyes pop open, and he seems confused for a second before it dawns on him. He smiles and adjusts a little while I get comfortable, ready to taste.

It's huge and a complete wonder how I managed to fit him last night, but I'm glad I did. It sits in the palm of my hand, hard as a rock, and yet it feels soft when I glide my hand along it. The purple-pinkish head is welcoming and oozing white pre-cum while thick veins streak the entire shaft. I can't help myself; I am wetter than ever before, and my mouth is pooling with saliva. I open my mouth as wide as I can and take him in. I bask in the soft moan he releases upon contact and the sweet-salty taste of his shaft in my mouth, filling it to maximum capacity. But the feeling is thrilling, and I can feel the need all the way in my gut – I want more.

I start to suck him, twirling my tongue around the bulbous head, flicking my tongue along the small hole. He moans, his hand coming down to grip my hair as he urges me on. My core tightens, and I begin to get more enthusiastic as I trail my tongue along his shaft to the base. I take him in my mouth again and move down on him, trying to capture as much of him as I can. I only manage to get a few inches in before I feel a sudden urge to gag.

I pull back, and he massages my scalp as if to reassure me. I look up at him and see the agony marked all over it. I can tell he wants to cum badly, and I want to make that happen, so I go at it again, loving his moans as I go back and forth on him.

"Fuck," he growls through his teeth, his grip tightening, hips slightly thrusting as my mouth consumes more of him. I start to move faster, my saliva draining down his shaft before I scoop it between my lips and continue with my rhythm. I can feel him swell inside my mouth, his thrusting more erratic. I almost gag again, but this time, I hold my breath and can feel when the tip touches the back of my throat.

He mutters another curse, his hips bucking, and before I know it, I feel hot cum blasting against my throat. I quickly withdraw, allowing the rest to splatter against my lips and drain down my chin.

Taken off guard, I can only giggle as I swallow timidly and look up at him to see that the tension has eased from his face. He looks completely satisfied, and I feel happy with myself for being the one to make that happen.

I wipe my mouth with the back of my hand, and he pulls me up to him. Our eyes meet, and his is the most captivating and intense. My heart starts to flutter, my body seemingly hotter. I want so much to kiss him, and he does just that, leaving me tingly all over.

"You are perfect," he says when he pulls away to stare at me again.

My heart's so full I want to burst. The emotions overpowering me are like no other, and I allow myself to bask in every second. I straddle him, he's still hard. Fuck, I don't think he's capable of not being. As my legs stretch over his body, I can feel the small aches still present – a constant reminder of last night.

"Keep this up, and I might not let you leave the house ever, princess. For my eyes only, my body only... completely mine," he says as I take his shaft in hand and position myself over its shiny head.

"Who says I'd have a problem with that?" I tease as I lower myself on him and impale myself on his thick length.

My mouth falls open as inch after inch disappears inside me. I'm halfway there like I was last night, but I want all of him this time. I press myself lower, ignoring the dull ache between my legs while I focus solely on his girth and length, stretching and filling me. He watches me with intense eyes and looks between us at my tiny lady-bits swallowing his monstrous cock inch after inch. I almost orgasm on the spot when I manage to take all of him in and look down to see my lips squeezing around him like a vice grip. His girth stretches me thin, making him too big to fit inside me.

"Fuck Amanda, I will spend every day of my life fucking this sweet thing.... Filling you over and over again." Mike says huskily as he grips my hips and starts to roll them against him.

I lick my lips, but they drop open again when his thickness massages my insides and sends pleasure rippling through me. If I experience this feeling every day, I know that I will be the happiest woman alive. I am now. Mike makes me happy... him deep inside me, brings out something strange and almost unreal. The pleasure is numbing.

Mike reaches for my tits and squeezes them, pulling at my nipples. Simultaneously, I start to bounce on him, whimpering at the small withdrawals before I am filled again, harder and somehow deeper. It gets more intense the longer I do it, and I start to ride him harder the longer I stay. My cream has completely coated him and lubricates me in a way that can only guarantee pure pleasure.

"Yes, baby girl... use this cock however you want. It's yours!" he growls as he lifts my hips, only to slam them down on him again.

"Yes, Oh, yes!" I exclaim, resting my palms on his muscular chest as I start to grind now. My movements are almost frantic as I bask in the feel of his cock on my insides. I can't get enough of him. My mouth remains open for so long that I don't even realize I am literally salivating until a drop of saliva lands on his chest.

Mike's eyes darken as he pulls me to him and kisses me hard, his hands wrapped around my back. I can feel the greed, the need, the power in his kiss and almost begin to cry as he starts to thrust inside me from below, still holding me to him – still kissing me as he gives me every inch of his cock. I moan, my mouth opens up over his, and he licks across my open mouth while he continues to fuck me with all he's got.

My orgasm hits me like a boulder, but it's pleasure that's swimming throughout my body. My legs almost clamp up, but Mike holds them apart as he continues to rut inside me like a wild animal. I collapse completely on him – wrecked by the orgasm that storms through me, speechless as I glorify in the high.

He grips me tighter as he cums, his grunts and moans filling me as he fills me with his hot seed that sets off another orgasm from me. I am shaking like a leaf in the wind, fulfilled beyond measure as he finishes off inside me. When he finally pulls out, I feel empty.

"You are a miracle, Amanda... my greatest joy, and I will show you that every single day."

I smile against his warm skin. "I have no doubt."

As I adjust to snuggle closer to him, the moistness between my thighs informs me with a knowledge that I hadn't even thought about. "We didn't use protection," I whisper.

There's a bit of silence before Mike says. "Would it be such a horrible thing if you become pregnant?"

It should scare me, but it doesn't. I already know Mike is the man of my dreams, and nothing will change that. "No, I always wanted a family – a big one with a dog," I smile up at him.

He rubs my hips. "And I will make sure you have all of that. Anything for you."

I smile and revel in the warmth of the moment.

Chapter 6

Amanda

I don't know when I fell asleep, but I awakened in Mike's arms for the second time. He's awake and is on his phone with a small frown on his face.

"Is everything okay?" I ask him, shuffling up closer, trailing my hands across the broad expanse of his chest.

He looks down at me and manages a smile. "Yeah, I just have a few things to take care of. I'll be back tonight." Kissing me on the forehead, he swings his feet over the bed and stands naked in front of me. I stare at him unabashedly, feeling the heat overtake my body once again.

He chuckles. "I promise to make it up to you."

I smile and move toward him. "Don't worry about it," I say as I tiptoe to kiss him.

"Keep this up, and I might not leave at all."

"That's kinda the plan," I say, smiling against his mouth.

He chuckles and palms my face with his hands, staring down at me with his lovely dark eyes. "I promise that after today, you will get me whenever you want me; no questions."

I smile. "Okay."

He finally manages to get to the bathroom after a few more kisses. I sigh dreamily because that seems to be what I'm still in. Part of me can't believe I got so lucky finding the man of my dreams without even trying. And he is that. No doubt. It seems like a fairy-tale really, and I have found my rugged prince charming, ready to take on forever after. Being with Mike makes me feel like a heavy weight has been lifted off my shoulders – like I have a purpose now.

My heart feels so full I can't keep myself from smiling. Even after making the bed and hopping to the kitchen to make lunch.

He comes out just as I am done pouring him a cup. My eyes settle on his pants as I watch the way he buckles his belt – wishing he was taking it off instead. When my eyes go back to his face, he has a smirk there, which tells me I've been caught staring.

"You're an insatiable woman," he laughs, and I do too.

"Blame yourself for being a capable lover."

His brows shot up, but his eyes are filled with mirth. "Capable? That's the best word you could find?" he challenges as he approaches me, and just like that, I'm burning for him again.

"My bad; I should have said amazing, otherworldly..."

"That sounds more like it," he grins as he kisses me softly on the lips. Mike has no idea how handsome he is – how his eyes light up when he smiles or how the simple act makes me fall deeper in love with him.

"That's more like it," he says as he reaches behind me to get his cup of coffee, taking a few sips. "Same rules apply for today...you don't leave the house, and I will fuck you later when I get back. We can even do dinner." His eyes roam over my body, and I can see the lust that takes over.

I lick my lips and nod, completely submissive to his demands because I am entranced with this man and how he makes me feel. He kisses me again, and my knees almost buckle with the sensation that rushes through me.

"I'm gonna spend hours fucking you and making up for the time I should have been here doing just that." It's a promise that makes me weak in the knees and needier more than ever.

"Yes." It comes out more like a moan than anything else.

He clenches his jaw, and I can see the way his face tightens. There's this look in his eyes that resembles the one when he's about to fuck me, and I know that that is exactly what he wants to do. I want him to... I want to feel every inch of him in me before he leaves, but part of me knows I'll have to wait until tonight.

"I'll see you later, princess. Lock the doors, and if you need anything, call me." He hands me a small piece of paper with a number scribbled on it.

I nod, and he kisses me one last time, adjusts his clothes, gets his keys, and then he is out of the house. I sigh dreamily and plop back on the sofa as I replay the events in my head. Even now, I can feel the dampness between my thighs. I ache to touch myself and get myself off, but that's Mike's job from here onward. I want all that pent-up energy for later when he comes home.

After thirty minutes of sitting there, I sigh and reach for my phone and see a missed call from Cherry and a message demanding to talk to me. I swallow hard; somehow, in this craziness, I had forgotten that I worked and was an employee to someone. My things are still there, and even though Mike said he would bring them over, I still needed to let Cherry know what was up.

I read her last text again and pondered over it.

Where are you?

I don't want to say, but from the looks of it, she was already familiar with Mike back at the bar. Maybe they knew each other well. So deciding to go with my instinct, I tell her that I am at Mike's place.

An immediate text comes in seconds later, *Ok, I'm coming over.*

My brows furrow; I'm somehow taken aback that she knows where he lives. Maybe they are closer than I thought, I can't help but think. Jealousy consumes me at the idea. The thought of Mike and Cherry doesn't really sit well with me, even though I knew that though Mike is my first,

I'm not his. I try not to think about a relationship with them, but it's all I can think about until a knock sounds at the door.

I move to unlock it and realize it's Cherry, but she doesn't have the most pleasant expression on her face. Her eyes roam over me in disgust, and she shoves past me and moves behind me to stand, taking me by surprise.

She crosses her arms under her breast and frowns. "What the hell are you doing?"

"Mike offered me a place to stay, and I agreed."

Cherry scoffs. "You don't know Mike, and you already have a place at the bar," she quips.

"Who knows when those looneys will be back? I can't take that chance."

Cherry seems taken aback. "But you want to with a complete stranger. Listen, Amanda, those guys are cowards who won't be coming back to do anything insane. I know them."

I sigh as I ponder her words. How can I even take her word for it when she seemed more upset at Mike for protecting me rather than the actual bad guys back at the bar?

"Maybe the job wasn't for me after all," I say, lifting my chin a little. "Mike will be by to pick up my things soon, so don't worry about that."

Cherry is silent for a while as she stares at me. "Mike isn't the knight in shining armor you peg him to be. He can be cold and ruthless; I'm guessing that's the last thing you want right now. The job is still yours, but if you stay here, it won't be."

I can see the challenge in her eyes, and the small frown on her face, which tells me she doesn't agree with any of this. Maybe I should listen to what she is saying since she obviously knows Mike better than I do. But I want to stay for two reasons: I want Mike, and I feel safe with him more than I have ever felt in all my life. I love him, but I don't tell Cherry because I know that she'll freak out.

"I'll admit, he is a good lay, and I get that maybe that's the reason you want to stay." There she goes, giving me confirmation that they in fact know each other too well. My heart tugs a little, but I try to tell myself I'm the one Mike wants now. I'm his and he has told me that over and over.

"But," she continues, "he has anger issues, which he may or may not take out on you eventually. You don't want to be on his wrong side," she says, staring deep within my soul.

"Mike wouldn't hurt me," I am quick to say, but to my chagrin, Cherry doesn't seem too convinced.

She scoffs. "You barely know the guy. It's only been a day, and here you are shacked up with a man that's more than twice your size!" she snaps, green eyes blazing.

I swallow. "Mike makes me feel alive...he makes me feel safe!"

Cherry swallows as she inspects me. "You don't want to believe me, fine. You can see for yourself tonight at eight at the old warehouse that's a block away from the bar." With that, she moves past me and is gone within the next second. I'm left to ponder her words and what she means by them. What's happening at eight, and why does it have anything to do with Mike? Part of me wants to forget Cherry's visit altogether, but I can't help but be curious about what this is all about.

So I wait patiently for the entire day and started to get ready in my old work clothes for eight.

IT DOESN'T TAKE ME long to get there, but the whole thing strikes me as odd when I see the number of people and the fact that you have to pay to enter a building that's literally falling apart. I can hear the noises inside, though, and know it'll be some kind of contest, but I still don't know what it has to do with Mike.

I look around, but there's still no sign of him. I don't even see Cherry, who I at least expected to be here since she orchestrated the whole thing. When I enter, I immediately know what's going on. There's a fighting pit in the center of the room that's fenced, and people are obviously betting on who they want to win.

My mind is still reeling, and I don't know what's going on, but then a man enters the ring and announces two names, which makes me pause. Mike! He's one of the contestants, and the crowd is in a ruckus at the mention of his name. I hug my shoulders and watch through an uncrowded opening as Mike and another man who's just as tall but not as bulky – enter with their game faces on. The announcer holds both their hands in the air, and another round of celebration echoes through the building.

I silently watch as they get into position. They are both shirtless, but Mike wears shorts while the other guy sports tight jeans. I hold my breath as I watch it transpire before me. The other guy is the first one to throw a punch, but Mike dodges it. I bite my lips and watch the scene. Not one punch lands, but they play around each other almost as if they are studying each other's moves.

This continues for a few minutes until the other guy punches Mike square across the jaw. I gasp, and he topples back, hand on the wound, quickly realizing that his mouth is busted. The crowd seems disappointed; only a few cheers on the other guy while they obviously wait for Mike to make a comeback.

I'm heartbroken at the idea of him being hurt; I want to shout and tell him to stop. I want to comfort him. But before I can do any of that, the guy charges at him again. I hold my breath, preparing for a more violent blow to land on Mike, but he dodges and punches the guy instead. He stumbles backward, squinting a few times, but before he can recover, Mike is on top of him, riddling his face with punches while the guy lays there, accepting every last one.

The crowd is in a frenzy, shouts so boisterous I know my ears will be ringing after this. The man's face is covered with blood within minutes, but Mike doesn't stop. It's like he doesn't want to – it's almost like he gains a high off acts like this. The crowd cheering him on is no better; it's like they want him to kill the guy.

There's no remorse on Mike's face; he just keeps going and going. My eyes sting, I can feel the tears coming. The whole thing reminds me of my past, and my stomach churns at the memories. The tears roll down my eyes, and the referee or whoever it is comes and peels Mike off the obviously unconscious guy. He immediately raises his hands in the air – a sign of victory – and the crowd goes crazy once again.

The coldness had fallen from Mike's face, and the pride is evident there while the other man lays seemingly lifeless in the back, bloody and defeated. Mike's eyes scan the crowd, and our eyes meet.

The smile fades from his face and is replaced by horror as he stares at me. I can see him mouthing my name, but I can't hear it with the noise around us. My heart breaks, and I immediately run from the building.

Maybe Cherry was right, and maybe I was too much of an idiot and a love-struck virgin to see what was really in front of me.

A monster?

Chapter 7

Mike

Amanda is the only thing I can think about for the entire day. I ache to touch her, to feel her soft skin against mine... to plunge into her until she has had her fill. She occupies every piece of me... every memory I now have is of her, and I can't wait to get home and create more. She's the sweetest drug, the most intoxicating and fuels my body with such inexplicit need that I can't explain. She's my everything – I know that now. I know that I can't live without her. She's part of me – my other half and today just gives me confirmation.

I don't want to spend another day without her by my side. Yesterday was torture, and today is even worse. But before I go home, there's one thing I have to do. One final thing that I haven't swayed from. The thought still remains solid. This is my last fight.

With Amanda in my life, I don't need it anymore. She calms me and makes me feel alive, which is all I've been searching for my entire life. But I promised one final fight, and it's going to be tonight. However, unlike the other nights, I realise something is the same as it was the day before. There's no rush – no great need to fight. There's only one thing I want, to go home to Amanda and follow through on my promise from this morning.

I was wrapping my hands when Cherry entered the room. No one should enter, but since she knows Paul very well, I'm guessing he is the one who gave her access.

"What are you doing here?" I immediately ask.

"Here to wish you luck, of course," she smiles in a way that gives me an ick.

"Thanks, but I should be getting on any minute now."

She moves towards me, one step at a time, looking up at me with her seductive eyes. She's attractive but doesn't hold a candle to Amanda.

"I can show you a good time after this y'know. My place?" She's in front of me, palms on my exposed pecs as she trails long fingers across my skin.

I feel nothing but disgust for having another woman other than Amanda touch me. I immediately reach for her hands and peel them off me, dropping them to her sides.

"I'm gonna have to pass on that one."

Her smile falters to a frown as she huffs. "This is about Amanda, isn't it?"

I pause at the mention of my woman's name. "And what if it is?"

"Mike, she isn't the woman for you –"

"And you are?" I abruptly cut in, feeling as the anger rises within me.

Cherry stands defiantly, raising her chin as she holds my gaze. "I am. I have been there for you on cold nights – when you were at your worst!" she blares.

What a way to throw kindness in your face. "I made it clear from the very beginning that we wouldn't be anything other than fuck buddies. I didn't mislead you in any way."

She swallows and takes a step back as if I struck her. "You men are all the same, aren't you? I was good enough for a few fucks, but as soon as a younger, beautiful woman comes along, I am forgotten."

"I'm sorry, Cherry, but I felt nothing for you, and you knew that," I can't help but clarify.

She scoffs as her lips tremble. "And you do for Amanda?"

"Yes. I love her," I confess.

Cherry snorts, her eyes glistening as she stares up at me with cloudy eyes. "You're so pathetic. That little slut is gonna leave you as soon as she finds someone better. I found her on the streets, and that's exactly where she belongs!" she hisses.

I take a step towards Cherry and fill the space between us. My hands are balled into fists as I stare down at her with tightly clenched teeth. "You should be fucking lucky that you're a woman right now, Cherry. Don't you dare talk about my woman like that again," I say through my teeth.

She doesn't back down, but her throat bobs, and I know she's scared. She continues to stare at me, lips drawn in a thin line, tears hanging on her lids before she turns and moves towards the door.

"You're gonna regret meeting her soon enough. Mark my words, Mike." With that measly threat, she opens the door and leaves. I don't even have a chance to collect my thoughts before Paul pokes his head around and says, "We're ready."

I can't wait for this to be over with.

As I enter the ring, that's all I want. My supporters cheer me on, and I'm thankful, but the thrill I normally have isn't there anymore. My opponent and I start skipping around the ring for a while, trying to figure each other out. He's new ... they mostly are. There's always someone new thinking they can beat me, and I have proven them wrong over and over again. This place is what it is because of me.

I must've been lost in thought because I am taken aback when something crashes against my cheeks, sending pain jolting throughout my face. And just like that, it's like the switch that had been turned off is back on again, and all I see is red. I need to make this fucking quick, so I can go home to get what I actually want. I do what I do best. I beat his face in until my hands started to hurt with every punch. The crowd in the back gives me more motivation to continue, and I do just that until I feel myself being dragged away from the unconscious body.

The victory is sweet as it always is, but this time, I take a moment to soak it all in and appreciate the love these people have for me. After all, it will be my last time. As my eyes scan the crowd, taking note of everyone who's cheering me on, I see a familiar face that halts me. It's Amanda, and she is crying. She has that look of disappointment and disgust on her face... fear even? And I can feel the blood drain from my face as what she just witnessed dawns on me. The last thing I wanted was for her to see this – this side of me. In her eyes, I should always be a protector; her savior... not a fucking beast. "Amanda!" I call, but she moves off and is swallowed by the big crowd.

"Fuck!" I mutter, running out of the pit and grabbing my bags. A few people try to stop me, but all that's on my mind is getting Amanda back.

I don't fucking know what I'll do if she decides to leave my life. I can't really stop her, but I'll be damned if I don't try. I catch up to her and call her name once again. This time she stops, face still wet with tears.

"Amanda, I'm sorry. I didn't mean for you to see any of that!"

She stops in her tracks and stares at me. The look is still there, and fuck, I'd do anything to make it go away.

"Obviously," she sneers, shaking her head. "Maybe we aren't meant for each other after all," she croaks, sniffing.

My heart breaks a little. "That isn't who I am!" I defend.

"It's exactly who you are, Mike!" she snaps. "And I can't be with someone like that."

"I would never hurt you!" I say between clenched teeth, hurt that she would even assume something like that. "I'd rather die than lay a finger on you."

Our eyes meet, she swallows. "The way you kept beating that guy, I..." She trails off and shakes her head as another stream of tears falls down her face.

"This is what I do," I say, and she looks up at me. "I fight for a living, and it isn't exactly conventional, but it pays the bills. After meeting you, I was willing to give it all up – and I have. Tonight is the last night you'll see me in the ring." I see some hope there and know that she'll give in if I just push a little bit harder.

"Please... let me buy you something to eat, and then I can explain all this," I plea.

She seems to ponder on it before she nods. I sigh in relief.

WE ORDER BURGERS AND fries at a small diner and start to eat when I decide to resume the conversation.

"I grew up in foster care," I begin, watching as she pauses to look up at me. "My mom was an addict who gave me up, and I didn't know my dad. I was picked on for years until I decided to do something about it. I didn't know where to channel my anger, so I got in fights and realized that did the trick. It always made me feel better, especially when I got good at it. That's why I started to join fight clubs – even the illegal ones. Then I met you, and you became my peace right that very moment. I knew you were the one for me..."

Her lips tremble. "Why didn't you tell me?"

"I was afraid of this – that you might see the monster there and not want me anymore. I hated the thought of that, so I decided to stop before that happened. I'm sorry it did." I explain, reaching for her hand.

"The way you kept hitting him, I-"

"I got carried away, but I promise you, that pit was the last time. It's over."

She nods and manages a tight smile that makes me feel light again, but I know there's something else there.

"I'm not from New York..." she begins. "I came here because I was running from the life I had back in New Jersey. My dad was an abusive asshole who pounced on my mom every chance he got. When he couldn't get to her, he took it out all on me." My grip tightens on her hand, my lips now drawn in a thin line. "I told her we could leave – get away and start a new life without him, but she wouldn't listen. She was too scared, and I couldn't leave her. She never pressed charges, she never fought back, she just took it all. If I did, he would beat her even more... to teach me a lesson." her voice cracked, and her lips quivered while her blue eyes became glossy.

"Baby, you don't have to-"

"I want to," she sniffs. "I never really talked to anyone about it."

I nod, allowing her to continue while I silently seethe beside her, wanting to rip her father to shreds for causing her so much pain.

"It continued for a while until she finally developed the courage to leave – for my sake. They got into a fight the day before and...he shoved her, and she hit her head." She couldn't contain it anymore. Amanda started sobbing uncontrollably. I move closer to her and take her into my arms, holding her to me.

"You are safe now, and I will never let anything happen to you. I wish I were there to rip that bastard's throat out, but any man who dares to do the same will meet the same fate. They'll have me to deal with princess; believe that."

She nods against me as she continues to cry, but soon after, her cries subside, and she is resting peacefully on my shoulder.

"How did you find me?"

"Cherry came by the apartment and kinda warned me you had a temper."

I grit my teeth, remembering the confrontation earlier. "Nothing or nobody should come between us, Amanda. My heart is bare with you; I'll tell you everything, and if there's anything you want to know, you ask me. All I'll ever give is the truth."

She smiles. "Likewise."

We continue to eat until she asks, "Were you and Cherry a thing?"

I shift in my seat. "We hooked up a few times – nothing serious. I only wish you were my first."

"Luckily, there's not more to go from here. I'll settle with being your last."

I grin. "And only."

Her smile is so sweet, she is sweet, and every part of my body aches to have her. It has been too long. Too fucking long. "Gosh, I want to fuck you right now," I mutter in her ear, my hand finding her leg. She's wearing the clothes she had on at the bar that night, which reminds me that I need to get her things, but her creamy thighs are exposed, and I can feel myself burning to touch her further.

"If we leave now, we can get to the apartment in no time."

"I don't think I can make it that far, princess." Her eyes light up as my fingers trickle further up, pausing right at her crotch. "Are you wet for me?"

"Always." I touch her and prove that to be true. Her panties are soaked, and her pussy is hot... waiting eagerly for me.

I smile at her, and her cheeks redden. "Something tells me you can't make it that far either."

She licks her lips. "I'll leave for the bathroom first, and then you follow?"

"No. Whoever here will know that I want to fuck my woman. There's no shame in it." I stand, holding my hand out to her.

Her cheeks get redder as she scans her surroundings and then stands, leading the way to the back. A few eyes follow us, and I know that my raging boner is probably visible, but I don't give a fuck, I just want to.

My mouth immediately meets hers as we get inside the small bathroom. I don't bother to lock the door behind us because I don't care who sees me loving my woman. Mine. Not anyone else. I savor in her sweetness, sucking her tongue, licking across her lips, and feel the need that matches my own.

But I'm too eager; as sweet as her lips are, I want to feel my cock inside her. I want to give her my all. So I hastily bunch her skirt up around her hips and peel her panties off while she pulls down my shorts and boxers. She is already panting, and so am I.

I hoist her up and place her against the small sink, her back arched against the wall, blocking the mirror that's hung there. Her legs part, I move closer and guide my dick into her opening. It sheaths me like a cloak, warm but wet. I almost sigh against her as I drive my cock further and further until I'm at the hilt. Her open mouth warms my face as she clings onto me and parts her legs even wider apart.

I ram into her, filling her to the hilt each time before I pull back and fill her again. I glide back and forth effortlessly, working up a sweat as I take her and bask in her tiny moans. If only the entire diner could hear.

"Yes, please... harder..." she moans against me, and I almost smile as I increase my pace, still amazed that this tiny person could stretch to take my cock... all of it. But I give her, her wish and take her hard, holding her hips in place, so she doesn't slip off the sink. She creams my cock even more as I stroke deep into her. Not an orgasm. Just her wetness that drips between us – evidence of how much she wants me. The thought, the sight – all of it empowers me and urges me to go faster. Her cries increase – she is loud, but I do nothing to stop her, and she doesn't either. When her narrow walls clench and squeeze around me, I know she is near, but then I catch a glimpse of us in the small mirror, and a thought comes to me.

Chapter 8

Amanda

THE THRILL THAT COMES with being caught and the way Mike is fucking me is driving me insane. I feel like I'm losing my mind to pleasure, and I want to do nothing to stop it. He feels amazing – it feels amazing like this. I can feel him all the way inside me, hitting the right spot, massaging my insides with his glorious cock over and over again, which sets me on edge. Each amazing thrust pulls me closer and closer... I get even wetter and know that I'm near.

But just as I'm about to have the most amazing orgasm, Mike pulls out. I gasp as he flips me around so I am facing the mirror. My mind is racing; I can't even think straight, but in the next instant, he is entering me from behind. I tiptoe a little, and he stoops a bit to fit against me comfortably. This position is new and possibly the most overwhelming, but it feels so good. Too damn good. I close my eyes to bask in it.

"Open your eyes, baby, I want you to watch me fuck you – I want you to watch us fuck!" he growls in my ears, somehow managing to get me even wetter.

My eyes flutter open to see the reflection of both of us in the mirror. Mike seems like a giant behind me as he pushes in and out, his muscles bulging and flexing. He's so big that it's a wonder I can manage him, but I do, even with my flushed face and sweat beading on my forehead. He grabs my breasts with one hand and squeezes them as he continues to fuck me hard.

"We might've only known each other for a day, princess, but I'm gonna spend the rest of my life showing you why it was worth it," he pants, sucking my neck. I mewl like a helpless kitten as heat engulfs my body.

I know Mike means every word – I just know it, and I can't wait to see our future play out before our very eyes.

"I'll always fuck you raw like this until I breed you and even after, I'll do the fucking same. I want a houseful of kids, and I want to be in you every single day for the rest of our lives. That's all I ask," he growls, and I clench around him.

"Yes! Yes... yes, Daddy!" I exclaim, my hands wrapping around the edge of the sink as his pace increases. My core is burning at a fever pitch, and I can feel my wetness trailing down my legs.

I can't help my cries or the loud moans which leave my lips. I can't hold back – not with Mike drilling me like this.

I scream, almost crying when he slams into me, and my orgasm takes course like a tidal wave. I shake, my knees buckle, but Mike holds me up with his strong arms as his thrusting slows, and his hot seed welcomes my womb. He grunts and kisses me against the neck, pumping his cum inside me. At this point, I think I am already pregnant, but nothing brings me greater joy.

I am over the moon. It's times like these that make me know Mike is my person, and I will never leave his side.

"I love you," I mutter.

He pulls out, turns me to face him, and smiles down at me. "My heart is yours, Amanda."

Half an hour later, we are walking back to the apartment. I'm so happy I can't even put it into words. Mike is my man, and I can feel it as much as I can see it. I didn't know how tonight would have ended after seeing him in that pit, but he was so transparent and vulnerable in telling me about his past that I couldn't help but love him even more.

We are both pieces of a broken puzzle that have found their way to each other and fully completed each other. I didn't need six months to see that or even a year. I know now that Mike is my soul mate, my knight in shining armor – my future husband. I can't wait for our future.

"Now that you're no longer gonna do the fights, what do you plan on doing?" I ask him, hands entwined in his as we walk.

He shrugs. "I haven't given it much thought as yet, but I'll figure something out soon. Until then, I have enough savings to get us by."

I smile at him. "I'll help you."

"I have no doubt you will," he says as he smiles down at me.

Tonight seems perfect, but the smile falls off my face, and an acidic feeling stirs on my tongue as I stare ahead. Mike stiffens as well and glances down at me.

"Head straight to the apartment and call the cops. I'll take care of this," he says in a firm tone.

"Mike-"

"Don't worry about me; I'll be fine, I promise. Just do as I say, princess."

"There are more of them this time," I whisper under my breath, feeling a lump rise in my throat.

He turns to me and palms my face, kissing me on the forehead. "Nothing I can't handle. Promise you'll head upstairs and call the cops immediately."

"How do they even know where to find you?" I choke.

"I have an idea," he says as he shakes his head and grits his teeth. "Cherry, of course."

"Why-"

"Do as I say, please. Go now!" he exclaims an octave higher. I almost jump as I look up at him with tears trailing down my face. I then look at the group of five men who stand waiting near the door of the apartment. Of course, I recognize three from the other day, but there are two new ones who are almost the size of Mike. My heart is plummeting in my chest, and my limbs seem to have frozen up.

"Scared now, big boy?" the ring leader from the bar exclaims, clearly spotting us and waiting for Mike to make a move.

"Not in the least, asshole," Mike says as he moves towards them, holding onto my hand. "Apparently, one beat down wasn't enough."

He scoffs, chewing his mouth as he eyes the others. "Nah, we just came to have some fun, is all," he snarls. "And maybe when we're done with you, we can have a go at your little bitch." I shudder, and his wide mouth stretches into a smile, but before it's in full effect, it disappears with a punch across his jaw.

I gasp as he goes tumbling backward, caught by his friends, who are taken by surprise.

"Go!" he tells me, and I take the opportunity to run past them and into the building.

But I don't go all the way up. I stay to the side, fumbling with my phone as I dial 911. I can hear the grunts, the howls, the pained cries, and with my brain being so fogged, I can't even tell which is Mike's. I wish I wasn't so useless – I wish I could do something to help him rather than hide. If he hadn't met me in the bar that night, he would have been fine – having nothing to worry about. But I don't even want to fathom the idea of not knowing Mike. He is already so important to me; I can't even stand the idea of losing him.

Standing here feels like forever, hearing all that ruckus and not knowing whether or not Mike is on the losing side. It was torturous. Of course, I feel confident in his skills, but there're five people this time, and he's probably exhausted from earlier.

It quiets down to just moans, and I hold my breath as a shadow appears. My heart is going a mile a second, but when I see that it's Mike, I quickly rush into his arms. He has a few evident bruises but looks fine overall. I cling to him like my life depends on it and kiss the side of his face, feeling the happiness bubble up inside me.

"Thank God, you're okay," I whisper, pulling apart to examine him thoroughly.

"Nobody threatens my woman and gets away with it."

I can't help but smile. "I'm sorry I put you in trouble."

He cupped my jaw with a single hand and used his thumb to caress my skin. "Hey, you didn't do anything wrong. I'd go to the ends of the earth to protect you – you know that, right?"

"I know that as much as I know that I love you," I smile. "But I want to help myself, too...when you're not around."

His brows furrow. "What are you saying?"

I lick my lips. "I want you to teach me self-defense."

"Amanda-"

"Please Mike. I've lived in fear all my life and that changed when I met you, but I want to take back some control – feel less powerless."

He sighs and lowers his forehead to mine. "Ok, anything for you, princess."

Epilogue

Amanda

I can't believe we made it to five years. Five glorious years with Mike by my side. Admittedly, we had a few hiccups here and there, but we always found our way back to each other. We got married three months after our first encounter, and ever since it has been an uphill ride. We bring out the best in each other, and when the twins Dylan and Lylah came along a year later, it only got better. After years of wanting something like this and running from the one I had, I have finally found my happy home. It isn't a structure – just the people in it... my little family.

"What are you here thinking about?" Large hands wrap around me, making me feel all fuzzy and warm. It's the 'Mike effect' that has not faded a bit since day one.

I smile as I continue to stare out the window of the apartment we had moved to a little before the twins were born. "You," I tell him. "Always you."

He pulls me tighter to him, and I can feel his boner poking at me. Typical Mike. "About how far we've come," I tell him, turning to face him. "Was there ever a doubt in your mind that we would make it this far?"

"Never," he quickly says. "You've been the most certain thing in my life, Amanda. You're my anchor, my biggest pride and achievement. Not a single day goes by that I don't thank God for having you in my life."

Every single day, he proves to me that everything he says is true, and every day, I try my best to reciprocate. I reach up to kiss him, knowing that nine out of ten times, it never just ends in a kiss. He gropes my ass and presses me against him, wanting me to feel just how much he wants me. We tumble towards the bed, and he sits on the edge. He pulls his hard cock out, and I straddle him, impaling myself with it. He licks across my mouth, and I cling to him, just enjoying the way he fills me.

"The kids will be awake soon," I say.

"We still have time, and the movers won't be here for a while."

I start to grind on him. "Are you excited to finally move?"

"Everything excites me as long as you're involved."

I blush, getting hotter and more aroused. "I can't wait to try out every single room with you," I smirk.

"I didn't think it would be possible to get any harder inside you, but I think I just did."

I laugh and swat him playfully. This gentleness is rare. I like it rough, and so does he, but neither of us seems to mind at this moment. If anything, the sheer bliss only spurs emotions inside me, making this all the more intense.

"I don't want you to go to work tomorrow," he confesses, and I pause.

"Wh-what, why not?"

After years of staying at home, I had finally found something I liked and was ready to take on. It was at a day-care, where I would still keep an eye on our kids.

"You've gotta understand that I'll gladly tear any man to shreds who dares to look at you sexually."

I almost giggle. "You're afraid of the attention I'll get from men? Mike, I only have eyes for you."

"I know, but you're mine, and everyone should know that." He raises his hips a bit, lodging his length deeper inside me, and I gasp. I cling to him and start to slowly ride him until we shatter and give into our blissful orgasm.

I cup his face in my hands and kiss him, smiling against his mouth. "I'm all yours, baby... always."

A COUPLE OF HOURS LATER, we are placing the last of the boxes inside our new house with the kids happily running around, exploring every room and trying to decide which one is theirs.

I still can't believe we finally have our own home – no more apartments. Mike had decided that he wanted to be the one to build our home, so after he quit fighting, he made it a priority to learn all he could about construction. He had worked hard to make that possible and now we had it all; the white picket fences, the kids... the happiness. After the life I'd had in the past, I never thought any of it would be possible, but then Mike came along and made me believe everything was. He is my rock, and I am his.

"We have a surprise for you, Mommy!" I turn around at the sound of little Dylan's voice. They're all standing there – all three of them with grins on their faces. Mike has something behind him, but I can't even catch a glimpse because his big frame blocks it all. They're beaming with happiness, and it all seems to radiate on me.

"Really? What is it?"

Lylah is jumping on her toes with her two ponytails bouncing against her shoulders. She has a wide grin, showing the missing tooth at the front. I watch Mike as he moves his hands from behind him and presents a small cage. My mouth falls open when I realize a puppy is inside – a Border Collie, to be exact.

I slap my hands over my mouth and scream into it, causing the kids to bounce around even more. I rush toward them and take the cage in hand, picking up the puppy and smiling from ear to ear as I take in his big, bright eyes.

Mike stands with pride as he watches the interaction, and I feel like crying as my love for him bubbles over. He didn't forget. He didn't forget when I told him I wanted the kids, the house, and the dog. He told me then that he would make sure I had it all. And I do. I am surrounded by happiness all because of Mike, my savior, my protector, my reason for life.

I bound toward him and kissed him hard and kept

letting him know just how much I appreciate him and all he has done for me. "Thank you."

"Anything for you, my queen."

Daddy's Bully-Heir

Izzie Vee

Erotic & Forbidden[1]

IZZIE VEE[2]

1. https://www.amazon.com/s?k=izzie+vee&i=digital-text&crid=31LQJTEQYT2EE&sprefix=izzie+vee%2Cdigital-text%2C121&ref=nb_sb_noss
2. https://www.amazon.com/s?k=izzie+vee&i=digital-text&crid=31LQJTEQYT2EE&sprefix=izzie+vee%2Cdigital-text%2C121&ref=nb_sb_noss

Cover Design by Izzie Vee
Cover Photo by Vishstudio on Depositphotos.com

Table of Content

Chapter 1

Anna

I could feel my eyes watering as I listened to what the person was saying on the other end. I couldn't believe this was happening, but it was, and every detail thrummed through my head like a nasty headache.

"Mr. Nash has left his cabin and requested in his will that you are to scatter his ashes at his favorite place – I'm assuming you know where that is?"

My foggy eyes traced the room for a second as my brain raced to understand what he was saying. "Y-yeah."

"Again, I'm very sorry for your loss, Miss Cambridge; we'll be in touch." The line went dead, and I stood frozen on the sofa, feeling a warm trail of wetness slide down my face.

My best friend Maria came up to me, immediately lacing her hands around my shoulders as she pulled me in to give me comfort. She didn't know what it was; she was just there, collecting all my tears on her shoulders as I sobbed against her. Memories that seemed distant came crashing back, making this even more overwhelming. Those memories had been buried – dormant – for a very long time, but one phone call erupted it all.

"Anna, what's happening?" Maria asked, her tone soft, the expression on her face pained as she pulled back to look at me.

"Everything is just falling apart," I choked, attempting to wipe my face with the back of my hand, but only more tears came.

"Hey, Hey... you can talk to me, y'know." Her hand moved to my face as she used her thumb to caress my cheeks and wipe at the fallen tears.

I sniffed, trying to find the courage to do just that, but my heart felt like it was about to burst in my chest with the sorrow that currently took claim of me.

"Remember I always told you about Patrick Nash when I came here and how he was basically the closest thing to a family I had growing up?"

Maria nodded immediately. "He's gone," I choked out.

Maria's blue eyes glistened. "Oh, Anna, I'm so sorry."

I nodded, fighting back the tears. "Nobody bothered to call me and tell me until now. There was no funeral – nothing – just his cremated body in an urn."

Maria had her hand over her mouth, the tears just a blink away from falling. "Jesus, Anna, I'm so very sorry."

I sniffed and nodded. "That was his lawyer explaining everything. He wants me to come to Northern California and sort things out with Patrick's house and ashes. He left it all to me." My lips trembled, but I bit down on them and willed myself not to cry.

"Fuck... how did he even die?" she asked.

"An aneurysm...it was unexpected. He must have been all alone when it happened." The mere thought made me want to bawl my eyes out.

Maria shook her head and sighed. "So when are you planning on leaving."

My eyes snapped to hers. "I don't think I can – not yet."

"Why not?"

"It's still winter, and I have work. It's just too much," I shook my head as if to clear it of the idea.

"Although the circumstances are not ideal, this may be exactly what you need, Anna."

I gawked at her. "How so? This isn't even a train stop away, Mar; it's thousands of miles away. I-"

"Listen, you still haven't given yourself the time to fully get over what Hector did."

Another lump formed in my throat that I forced myself to swallow. "This isn't about Hector."

"All I'm saying is, the time away might be good."

I pondered on it for a second. "Greenvale just has so many bad memories for me," I whispered under my breath, staring at my folded hands.

"And you're going there to celebrate the only good one you've ever had there," she smiled. "Think about it for a while. I'm gonna order us some pizza and ice cream, and then we can watch Outlander again for the hundredth time," she laughed.

I smiled, watching as Maria got up to do just that. Shuffling down on the sofa, pulling the blankets over my shoulders, I allowed my thoughts to overwhelm me. Patrick's face came to mind, and all I wanted to do was cry. The fact that I had called him last week amazed me. He was chirpy as always, with a voice that always seemed to be filled with joy, even when he was serious. Back in Greenvale, it was one of the many things about him that held me together. My family had been falling apart, I was being bullied at school, but Patrick had been there, helping me get through all of it. He was my anchor when everything was sinking around me. The fact that he was gone was like a huge boulder that came crashing into me over and over again, nailing me a little harder with each thought of him. Going back to it all would be too much; I would be swamped with even more memories, but I had to, didn't I? Patrick meant so much to me – the least I could do was honor his wishes.

"Okay, the order is in. What do you wanna do in the meantime?"

"I'm gonna take a few days off and go to Greenvale, and then I'm gonna come back and get my life in order."

"What- Anna, your life is fine." Maria seemed confused.

"As much as I love living with you, I need to find myself a new place again. It's been almost two months since Hector and I ended things. You were right... maybe this little trip will help me regardless of the circumstances," I smiled.

Maria's mouth fell open. "Anna, you can still live here when you get back. We can still be roommates."

"I know, but we aren't in college anymore, and I can't spend the rest of my life pining over a man who didn't want me," I exclaimed. Maria seemed to recoil as she looked at me, the tension easing from her face, which told me she understood where I was coming from."

"I just need to do this," I continued. "For myself."

She sighed and nodded. "I know," she said, pulling me in for another hug.

A DAY LATER, I HAD put in for some personal time off at the office and was packing a bag to leave the state the following day. Each piece of clothing seemed heavy, but thanks to Maria, I was well on my way to getting it all done.

"Do you even know anyone else back in Greenvale? I mean, all your family moved back here, right? The place is kinda underpopulated if you ask me."

I laughed. "There are a few people – none that I was close to, but I bet I'd still recognize them if it ever came to that."

"What about your friends in high school? Where are they?"

"Um, I only had two friends, and we went our separate ways after we graduated. We stayed in touch for a while, and then we didn't," I shrugged.

Maria nodded, and I bit my lips as I contemplated telling her a part about my childhood that I had never told her about before. This seemed like a convenient time anyway, seeing that I would be heading back to the very place it all started.

"I was bullied in high school, so I only stuck to the people I knew initially and stayed away from everyone else. Patrick was mostly my go-to. I liked that he was secluded from everyone else and had a big lake near his house. It was everything – it was peaceful."

"Anna, you never told me you were bullied," Maria exclaimed, her eyes wide as she stared at me.

"It was just a part of me I couldn't bring myself to tell anyone because I was so ashamed."

Maria's brows furrowed. "Ashamed? How?"

"This guy made my life a living hell on a daily basis with his verbal abuse, but I still found myself attracted to him somehow, even though I hated him so much," I scoffed and zipped up my suitcase.

"Wow, so where is he now?" Maria asked.

I shrugged. "I don't know. Patrick mentioned once that he was still there, and I'm not surprised. He's not the type to venture out and explore. People like him would rather suffocate in that stagnant town than go out and see actual life. I just hope I don't bump into him when I get there."

"And what if you do?"

"Maybe I'll develop enough courage to tell him a piece of my mind."

Maria grinned. "Oh, I would pay money to see that."

I smiled. "I probably won't anyway. He lived on the other side of town. There's a slim chance I'll see him."

Maria choked up a laugh. "The same town with a population of about three thousand?"

I rolled my eyes. "My point is, Carter Strande can go to hell for all I care. I'm not going there to reacquaint myself with anyone or catch up on the past. As soon as I scatter Patrick's ashes, I will be home."

"Speaking of, what do you plan on doing with his house?"

"I don't know yet. I still find it hard to grasp the fact that he's dead. I haven't thought so far ahead."

Maria nodded, pinning her golden tresses behind her ear. "Well, I haven't seen the place, but I think it would be a great vacation home," she smiled.

I raised a brow. "Vacation in Greenvale? Yeah, I don't see that happening," I laughed.

"Well, I don't care for the people there, but the spot seems nice. A cabin in the woods with a lakefront. I'd say that's a catch. Sometimes, the city can be overwhelming – I'm sure you know that."

I shrugged. "I guess."

Later that night, I sat in bed, checking Hector's Instagram for the millionth time since we broke up. I assumed he already had a woman, seeing he couldn't find a solid reason to end things. I figured that maybe he got bored of me – bored of the relationship. '*This isn't working*,' was all he said – all he left me to base the breakup on, and I had to accept it as hard as it was for me to do. No amount of begging him to explain himself changed his mind. He was done with me, and I could see it in his eyes, a coldness that was as plain as day – one that I hadn't expected. But Hector was always unpredictable; I just never thought that the unexpected gifts or roses... the random dates he would bring me out of nowhere. I just never knew that the unpredictability would be something that ruined what we had.

My eyes stung, and I hugged myself, but I paused as my fingers touched the scar on my arm. I traced my hand over it, wincing, feeling the need to cry even more as an old memory filled me.

Ok, Emmie... I'll see you tomorrow." I waved at my best friend as I made my way out of the school gates and on the path home. I had a smile on my face because, for the first time in a long time, I had not bumped into my bully. Today was a good day, and I was thankful for small mercies such as this. As I neared home, I decided to make a detour and visit Patrick. It was a Friday evening, and he was probably by his lake fishing. I got excited at the thought, knowing that he'd make the best dinner out of it after fishing. I preferred that to pizza and the loud arguments I'd get home to.

But as I started to tread the road to Patrick's cabin, I paused in my tracks, my heart immediately picking up pace – my palms gone sweaty. My stomach felt tight because Carter Strande was on the same path as me... walking towards me with a smile on his conniving face. I wanted to run, but I was seemingly frozen in that spot as he approached me with his swagger and the dangerous glint in his whiskey-colored eyes.

"Well, well, well... if it isn't the little shrimp."

I swallowed hard. He stopped in front of me, his gaze roving over my body as he gritted his teeth. "Missed me today?"

I remained rigid, casting my gaze to the ground – anything to avoid eye contact. What are you even doing in these parts? Rich little princess like you."

I licked my lips. "This is a free country, Carter," I developed the courage to say, not too pleased with the sound of my voice.

"And yet it doesn't really feel like it. Not with your pops running around acting like he owns the place."

My eyes shot up to his. "My father was the one who gave yours a job so you could live the measly life you live now. It's not our fault this town is too drunk and lazy most of the time to actually do something about their pitiful situations. You were lucky when my family moved here; otherwise, you'd all be just a bunch of nobodies, taking up space where actual good people belong!"

I didn't know where the words came from; I just knew I regretted them as soon as they left my mouth. I was breathing hard – fuming even. I wasn't really a fan of my dad, but he was the only one who gave this place hope. Ungrateful people like Carter couldn't see that – they refused to.

But I knew I had ventured on dangerous grounds. Carter's eyes were piercing, his teeth were clenched, and I could see that with his visibly hardened jaw. He looked deadly, and at that second, I feared for my life. This was my first time standing up to him, but unlike the movies or the novels, he didn't seem like the type of bully to stand down. He was lethal.

"I swear to God, shrimp... if you don't fucking run, I'll do something I won't likely regret." Each word was a threat. I could feel it sizzle against my skin... down my spine. I could feel the rage filtering off him, making me fearful.

I swallowed, took a step back and almost gasped from the crunch of my footstep. Carter's hands were balled into fists as he towered over me like a giant. Heck, his height alone should've been enough of a red flag before I decided to be sassy.

I feared what he would do at that moment, and so I took off running, my pants echoing in my ear as I tried my best to get away from him. It occurred to me that Carter wasn't the type that was all bark. He could have snapped my neck if he wanted to. My eyes got blurry; the tickle on my face made me realize I was crying as I burrowed through the bushes for safety, but I must not have looked where I was going because I came to a sudden halt when pain ripped through my body. I screamed and squinted at the tears as I assessed the damage. My sweater was soaked red and so was the tip of a broken branch hanging into the road.

I looked back to see if Carter was behind me and thankfully, he wasn't.

I sighed in bed and brushed away the last of the memory. No matter where I went and how many times I tried to forget my high school bully, this scar would always remind me of him no matter how much I willed myself to forget.

Chapter 2

Anna

Maria followed me to the airport the following day, wanting to be by my side until she no longer could.

"I'll miss you...even if it's for like four days," she said with a nonchalant shrug.

"Maybe less," I reassured. "I'll miss you too, bestie."

"Ok, go before I start sobbing again!" she exclaimed, laughing.

I grinned and reached for my suitcase. Maria jumped into my arms and hugged me one last time. "Don't forget to call me as soon as you get there."

"I will."

We parted ways, and half an hour later, I was inside an airplane. All I could do was think about how the time spent would be. All the memories... I didn't know if I was prepared for any of it, but I knew it was something that had to be done.

When I arrived in Greenvale, I was thankful I had decided to get dressed in winter gear because even though it wasn't snowing, it was very cold. My car arrived, and I took a breath of the crisp, fresh air, looking at the small town, which had come a long way since I was in high school. I had thought the town would go back to square one after my dad left for the big city, but apparently, they were inspired and decided to make something of themselves. The homes were lovely now, and there were a few structures that hadn't been there when we were around. Memories flooded through me when I passed the refinery my dad had owned. It was abandoned now and not as sophisticated as it once was.

Many people earned a living from it, and to this day, I was still puzzled as to why he decided to shut it down in the first place. Whenever I asked, he always said it wasn't what he hoped it would be in the long run and that it cost him more to keep it going than the profit he was making. I never really questioned his decision to pick up and leave a town we had spent ten years in anyway; I was so happy to leave that I gladly welcomed anything.

That desperation was because of Carter, who filled me with fear each passing day. I couldn't fathom living in Greenvale forever after being bullied by him constantly. So when my dad told me we were leaving, I welcomed the news, even though I knew I would be leaving behind Patrick and my friends. Saying goodbye to Patrick was the hardest, though. He was more family than my dad, who thought he could buy my love with lovely things, and my mom, who was an alcoholic for as long as I knew her. Neither was reliable and didn't care much about my opinion, but I didn't really mind that when I left Greenvale and knew I'd be off to college and away from them for a long time.

The ride to Patrick's cabin seemed longer than before and was overcrowded with bushes I knew would become problematic. The car suddenly came to a stop, and the driver turned to look at me.

"This is as far as I'll go, missy. Can't risk getting stuck up there."

My eyes widened as I stared at him, waiting for him to say something. But the look in his eyes told me to get out, so he could go about his day. I huffed as I paid him and struggled as I pulled out my small suitcase and carry-on. He drove off as soon as my things were out, and I was left fuming at the lack of chivalry—typical Greenvale.

Sighing, I made my way up the narrow path, struggling to roll the suitcase's wheels along the bumpy, pudgy path. But I was happy with the distraction of the dewy forest scents, the green trees – nature. I couldn't help my smile, and in no time, I was staring at the cabin, which brought back so many memories at one glance.

If one thing remained the same in Greenvale, it was this. It was just as I remembered; it was a small, cozy wooden cabin with a big, beautiful lake view that I couldn't get tired of seeing.

"Ms Cambridge, you're here." A tall, dark man stepped from inside the house with a jacket over his tailored suit. I recognized his voice as the one I had spoken to on the phone and knew it was Patrick's lawyer, Mr. Hendricks.

"I hope your flight was good; it's nice to meet you, although I wish it were under better circumstances," he smiled.

"Likewise," I offered. "My flight was great, thanks. I'm surprised you're actually here. I know you said you'd meet me here when I arrived, but I didn't actually think you'd make the trip."

"Oh, I'm a man of my word, and I figured I'd officially welcome you back to Greenvale."

I managed a tight smile.

"Plus, there was something I wanted to discuss with you in person before you settle in."

I quirked a brow as I stared at him, curious more than ever. "What's that?"

Mr. Hendricks' eyes dropped to my suitcase. "Let me help you with that. I made a fresh pot of coffee before you got here."

"Oh, I'm not really a fan of coffee," I informed, watching as he pulled my luggage to the house.

Hendricks flung his head back and gave me a sceptical glance before he chuckled deeply. "American?"

I laughed. "Yeah, most people can't believe it either. What else did you want to discuss?" I was getting impatient.

Hendricks flung the door open, and I paused in my tracks as memories filled me and tears threatened to spill. I could smell Patrick all over. The cigarettes were faint, his brand of old spice fragrances and the pungent smell of cedarwood. It was so masculine – so Patrick. A painful lump formed in my throat, and I could feel it rising ...

"Miss Cambridge?" Mr. Hendricks's voice brought me back to reality.

I shook my head. "Yeah, I er- call me Anna, please."

He smiled and gave me curt nod. "Well, in that case, call me Randall."

I smiled. "So, what did you want to talk to me about?" I asked.

"Hey, Randall, I'm sorry I'm late. I kinda got held up at the bar." A voice suddenly came from the front door. My heart instantly began to thrum in my chest, and it felt like my throat was closing up as the slightly familiar sound resonated in my head. I felt sweaty; I felt confused and angry as emotions threatened to overwhelm me.

"No problem, man. Carter, I'd like you to meet Anna Cambridge, although I know you two are already familiar with each other," an oblivious Hendricks said, confirming my suspicions - making this all the more difficult.

The silence that filled the room could be cut with a knife. I turned around to face my fears and was shocked at the findings. It was Carter alright, but he was somehow even more handsome than the last time I saw him, though his eyes were the fucking same – dangerous and cold, causing a shiver down my spine. He seemed shocked to see me, too, but for the first time in forever, the look in his eyes didn't resemble pure hatred as he stared at me, which confused me. But the longer I stared at him, his good looks seemed to fade and all I could remember was my bully who made my life a living hell...

"What the hell are you doing here?" I blared, my voice sounding a lot harsher than I had expected.

His Adam's apple bobbed as he shifted in his spot and ducked under the door, staring at me as if it were the first time. "Nice to see you, too, Anna." The corner of his mouth quirked in a smirk as he crossed his arms and leaned against the doorway he filled out completely.

When was it not *Shrimp*? The name that I hated so much – the word that made me feel some odd resentment towards the seafood. When did that change?

I huffed and turned to Hendricks, shooting a brow up at him. "What's going on here? And why is he here?"

Hendricks held out his hand as if a signal of surrender. "Listen, how about we sit and have a civilized, adult conversation?" he said as he shuffled towards the sofa in the living room.

I snapped my head back to Carter, who I found staring at me. I swallowed hard and watched as he shrugged and moved past me to sit alongside Hendricks. The last thing I wanted to do was sit and talk with Carter around. I wanted to run for the hills, but being so curious about the issue at hand, I forcefully walked and flopped down on a single-seated sofa facing them.

"What is this about?" I asked.

Hendricks took a deep sigh. "Patrick made everything profoundly clear in his will, including that he didn't want a funeral and asked that his body be cremated and his ashes scattered by both of you."

I swallowed as I shook my head. "I don't understand how he's involved in any of this," I said, darting a glare at Carter.

"When you moved away to your little city, I was the one who stuck beside Patrick," he said with a voice that seemed to vibrate through my whole body.

"When since? In high school, all you did was cause the old man trouble with your group of delinquent assholes!" I shot at him.

He scoffed and shook his head. "Here we go again. You never really came off that high horse, did you?" he spat. "How could I expect better anyway when you moved to be surrounded by people just like you."

I opened my mouth to talk, completely enraged, but Hendricks beat me to it. "Guys, guys! Let's calm down, shall we? Mr. Nash adored both of you equally – he had nothing but good things to say about you."

I shook my head. "I refuse to believe that," I mumbled under my breath. Carter shook his head.

"Miss Cambridge, on the phone, I told you that Patrick left the property to you, but truth is, it was left for the two of you."

I eased back in my chair, my mouth slightly hanging open as I processed what he was saying. I could tell that Carter was surprised, too, but he didn't wear his emotions on his sleeve unlike me.

"What?"

"You two were the closest thing Patrick had to a family. He wanted you to have this," Hendricks was saying. I was still utterly confused about Carter's role in all of this. Patrick rarely talked about him when I left Greenvale and after the trouble he was in high school...there had to be a mistake.

I darted my eyes towards Carter. "Did you blackmail Patrick into this?" I hissed at him.

Carter stared at me as if I'd lost my mind and scoffed as he got up and moved towards the door. "I don't have to take this bullshit."

"Carter, wait!" Hendricks called, shooting up to his feet as he moved towards him. He huffed out a breath and stood between us. "Can you guys please stop for a second, please? This is what Patrick wanted – forget about yourselves for a second and consider his dying wish. He wanted you both here for a reason."

You could hear a pin drop on cotton after that statement as I pondered Hendricks' words. I was still confused and knew it would be hard to fathom any of this, but the truth was there, and there was no reason for Hendricks to lie. I was just completely baffled.

"Sure, I can be civilized," Carter said as he jabbed a cryptic glare at me. I bit my tongue and allowed silence to take course.

Hendricks sighed and managed a smile. "Good, well I don't think there's much left to say. There will be a few paperwork left for you guys, and then the rest is all for you to figure out amongst yourselves."

"Why didn't you just tell me this over the phone?" I asked.

"Because I feared you wouldn't make the trip if you knew, and I knew that Patrick wanted you here more than anything."

I hung my head and swallowed, ashamed of myself because I didn't know how I would have reacted over the phone and if I would even be here if I'd known that Carter would be here too.

"Patrick didn't have any family except for you guys. And he wanted to thank you both by giving you all he had."

I glanced at Carter and somehow, I still felt some sort of resentment for the remorseful, sad look on his face. This was my moment – my moment to bask in the memories and mourn Patrick the way I wanted to, but here he was, taking that away from me, and I hated it. I hated that he seemed like a far cry from the bully he was in high school. I had pictured seeing the man again, but nothing prepared me for this. I wish I was confronted by stained teeth instead of pearly whites and the ghastly look I had expected from him being a bum who had nothing to contribute to society. But he was the complete fucking opposite, and it irked me somehow. So fucking much, to be honest.

"Well, I'll leave you guys to it. If you need anything, you know where to reach me," Hendricks said, breaking the small silence.

My heart skipped a beat. "Wait, you're leaving?"

He chuckled. "Well, yes. I have work to get back to, and I'm sure all this has nothing to do with me, dear," he smiled.

I glanced at Carter who pushed his sleeves further up his elbow as he crossed his arms – accentuating his bulky muscles. He must have figured out what I was thinking because as soon as his gaze met mine, he scoffed and shook his head.

"Don't worry, I'm not going to hurt you or anything remotely close to it," he said, but I didn't want to believe any of that was true. But what choice did I have anyway?

"I'm sure you guys will get along in no time. I'd better be on my way," Hendricks said as she moved past Carter and went outside.

"Don't count on it," Carter mumbled under his breath, and I rolled my eyes.

Soon, it was just the two of us in the cabin, and quite frankly, I didn't know what to expect from a man I had not seen in years – a man who'd done nothing but make my life a living hell in the past. Could I trust him? I most certainly could not.

I wandered around the house, reacquainting myself with some old things I had last seen when I left for the big city. Some things were new, but they all reminded me of Patrick regardless. I moved to a small wall table he had made all my himself for photos. Each one was framed and in neat order. The black and white one of him and his mom was in the back. It was the only one he said he had left of her after she died when he was just a teen. The front ones were bursting with color, and I recognized myself in a few. Most were taken in summer when the sun was mostly out, and we had made a habit of going fishing. My first catch was photographed and if it weren't for the photo, all of it would have been a distant memory. But looking back, every detail of that day came rushing back, and my eyes started to sting.

I had the biggest smile on my face and the smallest fish in hand, but I was still so proud, and so was Patrick. For a man who barely smiled, he had a huge one in place with his hand slung around me as we smiled for the camera. I became even sadder when I looked at the other photos of us over the grill or eating dinner – we made the most out of every situation and photographed every bit.

I was smiling – close to tears – when everything crashed into the anger that suddenly bubbled up inside me. Carter was there in some of the frames as well. Drinking beer with Patrick, laughing... it was all so strange to me. So infuriatingly strange, but there was no denying that they adored each other based on the pictures.

"That one was last summer." I almost jumped, quickly reminding myself that I wasn't alone. Carter was behind me, and I could feel him as much as I could smell the sweet musk of his perfume. A shiver ran down my spine despite the warmth his presence brought, but I didn't want any of this. I didn't want this effect he had on me – the way my heart skipped a beat but not in fear this time around.

I had to remind myself I hated this man – it was the only way I could get through all this with him being here.

"You just had to, didn't you?" I snapped, grinding my teeth as I looked at the photos.

"What?"

"You just had to figure out a way to agonize me even when I wasn't here?" I seethed as I spun around to face him, almost gasping when I realized he was so close – so handsome. I had to look up, but it was worth any neck strain I would have in the future. Carter was a beautiful man – even more now than in high school.

His thick eyebrows narrowed and that lethal gaze retook residence – making me doubt this entire conversation. "Patrick was my friend, and he was the only part of Greenvale that I cherished with my whole heart, then you of all people just had to come and make this entire experience bitter for me!" I exclaimed as my chest rose and fell.

"Well, maybe you should do a better job of treating the people you 'cherish' better!" he threw back at me with air quotes that made me even angrier.

"Patrick was like a father to me, so don't you dare come in here and act like you know my life better than I do!"

"You left here eight years ago and never looked back even for Patrick's sake and then you claim he was like a father to you," he scoffed. "I might have done some fucked up things in the past, but I made up for the wrongs I did and was there for Patrick every step of the way. So don't come marching back now that he's dead, pretending to be a fucking saint!"

My vision became blurry, but I was fuming so much I could almost feel the steam through my ears. "Fuck you, Carter!" I snapped, pushing past him and running from the house.

My feet were set in the direction of the lake, so that's where I went as tears streamed down my face. I'd die if I let Carter see me like this. As angry as I was and as much as it hurt to hear the words, I knew I wasn't exactly innocent in his claims. He was right. I never visited Patrick in the eight years since I left Greenvale and had thought that calls and video calls would suffice, but I could have done more – I should have. I was just too hell-bent on staying away from a place as wretched as this, but here I was again, facing my demons. And this one was a fucking sight for sore eyes.

Chapter 3

Carter

Shit!

The last thing I wanted was problems, but I knew I couldn't avoid them from the moment I saw Anna Cambridge. Patrick talked about her countless times, so I somewhat expected to see her here when he died, although I wasn't holding my breath. When I walked through that door earlier, she was the last person I expected to see, yet the image of her face at that moment was one I wished to see many times after. Anna was a beautiful girl in school, but the transition to womanhood most certainly suited her more. Every feature was accentuated over time, and I knew she had to be the most beautiful woman I'd ever laid eyes on.

If it were anyone else, I'd be looking for a way to charm the socks off her, but in a split second, I was reminded that this was Anna – the person I had loathed back in high school. A part of me still wished that I still carried that resentment, but over the years, with Patrick's help, I had learned to let go of my hatred and constant anger toward the girl. Ironic since she still obviously felt the same way about me.

Not that I could blame her, but Anna needed a constant knock off her high horse and years of being away only seemed to make that worse. Still, I felt a tad guilty for causing her to flee the cabin. I had caught the glistening in her eyes and knew that maybe I'd gone a bit too far. I blew out a breath and raked my hands through my hair as I left the house searching for Anna. She couldn't have gone far considering there wasn't a car, and her bags were still here. As soon as I went outside, my eyes traveled to the lake, and I saw her sitting there on the little bench I made for Patrick. She was overlooking the lake as she hugged herself – her glossy brunette hair being tousled by the wind.

I was hesitant, but I made my way there and paused just an arm's length away from her.

"I didn't ask for any company," she bit out without even having to look around at me.

"I shouldn't have said all that; I'm sorry," I said, sheathing my hands with the warmth of my pockets.

She scoffed. "I didn't know you were capable of such things," she quipped drily.

"There's a lot you don't know about me, Anna."

"I know enough," she put in almost immediately. A part of me wanted to challenge her on what she meant by that, but the last thing I wanted was another argument, and I knew that would be the only outcome if I did.

I moved toward her and sat beside her on the bench. She glanced at me through the corner of her eyes and shuffled a little. I started to regret my decision as soon as a bout of wind came and filled my nostrils with her scent. It was refreshing and expensive – I could tell – but it made me warm all over.

"Listen, we don't have to like or even pretend to like each other while you're here. We just have to tolerate each other enough to get through all the arrangements."

She didn't say anything – just kept ignoring me as she stared ahead at anything but me.

"We need to decide what we're going to do with the house, especially."

She finally looked at me with fiery green eyes, flattered by long, spiky lashes. "Name a price."

I scowled at her. "What?"

"I want the cabin. Tell me your price, and I will buy back your portion," she firmly said.

My mouth must have been hanging because of my shock. "What makes you think I'd want to do that?" I asked her. This would be a lot easier if she weren't so fucking beautiful.

"Don't act as if you'd have any use for this house, Carter," she said as she rolled her eyes and trapped a lock of loose hair behind her studded ear.

"Oh, and you do? As soon as you move back to your fancy little city you'll sell it to the highest bidder! I'll be damned if I let that happen!" I exclaimed.

"I'm not-"

"You're just like your old man, aren't you? You both have this God complex and think you can flash your money around and it will fix anything," I scoffed, watching how her eyes blazed at me.

"You don't know anything about me or my father!"

"More than you know!" I snapped.

She got up again, ready to flee, and I almost laughed to myself. "Great, do what you do best, Anna, run," I said as I stood.

She paused in her tracks and spun around, shooting daggers at me with piercing eyes. Her face had gotten a little pink, and her ears were red. "I wouldn't have to run so much if it weren't for you!" she jabbed, pointing at me – so fucking close I could feel her breath against me. "You made my life a living hell here every second of every fricking day!"

I took a step back as if she had struck me. It wasn't like I could forget that I had bullied her throughout high school. The memories were still ripe and vivid, but I had my reasons and managed to get past them. Why couldn't she do the same?

I sighed. "Look, I was stupid and was looking for someone to be angry with; I'm sorry about the past."

She stared at me for a long minute before she shook her head and started her trek to the house. I followed behind her and paused at the door when I saw her picking up her things.

"What are you doing?"

"None of your business, Carter."

"I thought you'd be staying here."

"You thought wrong."

"Well, it's either this or some run-down motel in town. You don't look like a fan of cockroaches or drug dealers."

She paused in her tracks, her face going pale as she stared at me. "This house is ours now; you can stay here. I have my own place, so you don't have to worry about me."

"I wasn't," she quipped.

"Figured. Anyway, how about you get settled in, and I'll leave you to it. In the morning, I will stop by, and we can try again at a level-headed conversation. You must be jet-lagged anyway."

I was happy when I was welcomed with zero sass. She was still looking at me, but I could see she was just trying to process all this in her pretty little head. She had the cutest pout, I doubt she was even aware of, and I couldn't help my smirk.

"Fine, you know anywhere around here other than Lassie's where I can get a good meal?"

I chuckled. "I know just the place. Lassie's has been out of business for quite a while now anyway. Not much you could get there." I glanced out front and remembered mine was the only vehicle present. "Want a ride?"

She shifted and adjusted the bag on her shoulder before looking to the floor. "I guess." I held back my smile and nodded as I walked outside with Anna following behind.

When we hopped in the van, we were silent for a while until she said. "How did you even get up here? The cab I took from the airport said he couldn't get so far," she mumbled.

"I know my way around," I shrugged.

And just like that, we were met with silence again, but I didn't want to say anything for this to turn into world war three, so I kept quiet and observed the way she looked out the window to ignore me. I smiled at the seatbelt strapped around her and knew I shouldn't have expected any less. That was Anna Cambridge, alright. We rode into the small town area and arrived at the bar. She finally glanced at me with her brows furrowed.

"This is new. When did it go up?" she asked as she unbuckled herself.

"A year ago. Guaranteed to have the best food in town," I smiled as I stepped out and moved to Anna's side. She came out after with her eyes trailing all over the place. I waited for the moment and when it arrived, the reaction didn't fail.

"This is yours?" she asked with widened eyes and an open mouth.

She looked back to the sign *'Carter's Bar & Grill'* and then to me. I couldn't help my smile. "Yep!"

The expression I would pay to see again faded and that cold, cryptic Anna took over once again. "Not bad, Strande. Nice to know that the cycle of laziness in this town didn't hit you." She managed a tight smile and walked towards the entrance while I had to bite my tongue from saying something I'd likely regret.

I blew out a breath and followed behind, happy to see the people that littered the inside. However, this time, all the eyes weren't on me. Instead, they were on Anna, who paused a little to take in the curious eyes before she headed for the counter. The boisterous conversations and the country music died down to collective whispers.

I rounded the counter and stood before her after I slipped on an apron. "what can I get you?" I asked.

Anna reached for a menu and scanned it before she looked up to me with her mouth in a twist. "I guess I'll have the Greenvale Classic chicken sandwich?"

I smiled. "Good choice."

"Of course it is," she mumbled.

She reached for her phone as she waited, obviously not interested in a conversation with me or anyone for that matter. She was seemingly unfazed by the whispers or the fact that she had gotten the attention of everyone in the bar. It was like no one existed but her.

The burger came under fifteen minutes, and she finally looked up to assess it. I was busy serving someone else, but I watched her reaction as I did so. When she took a bite, her eyes fluttered, and I could have sworn I heard a moan despite the noisy bar.

"So Cambridge is back," my best bud, Andrew said as he chugged his beer and glanced at Anna who was busy mauling her food.

"Yep, not for long, though. She's just here to sort things out regarding Patrick."

"I didn't know they were still in touch."

"Yeah, they never lost the connection."

Andrew chuckled. "She must still hate your guts."

I grinned. "Of course, she still does."

"But I bet you wish you were in hers," he said as he slyly looked at me over the rim of his glass. "She's a fucking beauty, that's for sure. Has a nice ass too, from what I saw when she came in."

I rolled my eyes. "She's alright."

"All you need to do is say sorry and explain why you hated her, and you'll be on her good side."

I gave it a second's thought. "Yeah, I don't see that happening. I'm not going to try and butter up to her, and the last thing I want to do is rehash all that from the past," I shook my head and refilled Andrew's glass.

"Well, you know what they say; secrets always find a way of coming out."

"That wasn't exactly a secret. I don't care if she knows or not."

A thick brow rose. "So you wouldn't mind if I walked over and spilled my guts to her?"

I flashed him a hard stare that anchored him to the chair. "That doesn't matter anyway. I shouldn't have bullied her in high school. It wasn't exactly her fault."

Andrew scoffed. "So where's she staying?"

"Up at the cabin," I didn't hesitate to say.

"All by herself?"

I nodded and watched as the expression changed on Andrew's face. "You know the low-lives in this town won't hesitate when they hear a beautiful woman is up there all by herself."

"She'll be fine, and I doubt she'll be here long anyway."

Andrew rose a brow, not at all convinced about the 'fine' part, and I wasn't sure I was either. I hadn't given it much thought, but this town was in fact filled with the type of people Anna thought I'd become. She would be all alone in the woods, perfect for people who wanted to take advantage.

I glanced her way and realized she had a bite of the burger left, which would be trash food from the looks of it, but I was somewhat happy that she enjoyed it. Which was weird considering I shouldn't give a rat's ass about what she thought of me and my business. She wiped at her small, naturally pink mouth and took a sip of her coke before reaching for her phone which started to ring.

She immediately slid from her bar stool, glanced at me with the phone to her ear and then left the bar. I sighed as I watched her go. Andrew was right; she had a nice ass.

Chapter 4

Anna

I looked around to see if anyone was nearby and was happy when I realized no one was.

"Yes Mar, I'm sorry I didn't call earlier to tell you I arrived safely but things just kinda went superfast," I explained to an upset Maria on the other end.

"What do you mean? What happened?"

I rubbed my temple as I leaned against a rail at the front. "So, remember I told you I was bullied in high school?"

"Yeah... wait! Did you bump into him?" she almost shrieked. "Did he cause you trouble?" she fumbled.

"Er... well, yes I did bump into him and it turns out that Patrick left the property for the two of us."

There was a slight pause before, "What? How is that even possible? I thought the lawyer said it was all yours..."

"He left out the other part because he thought I wouldn't make the trip if I knew."

"Damn, so they were friends all this time?"

"Apparently. There are pictures of them at the cabin and..." I trailed off and sighed. "I just can't believe Patrick didn't tell me about it."

"Yeah, he maybe didn't want all that contention in your relationship. But how is this bully guy? Is he the bum you expected?"

I bit my lips for a sec. "Far from that. He's so good-looking Mar and even owns a bar that seems to be doing pretty well, too," I said as I glanced back at the wooden structure with the huge windows and colorful signs.

"Damn, but you still hate his guts, right?"

I swallowed. "Of course I do. He gave a half-assed apology about the past, and that was it. After all he put me through, I don't think that will suffice."

"So, what will?"

I shrugged. "I don't know. I don't know about anything at this point. I just can't wait to get this over with so I can come home."

"That makes two of us. I'm starting to miss my best friend."

I could see Carter making his way over through the corner of my eye. "I miss you too, Mar. Listen, I've gotta go; I'll talk to you soon."

"Ok, be safe."

"Will do, bye."

I ended the call just in time to find Carter standing behind me. He had this worried look as he stared at me with his honey blonde hair blowing in the wind. I tore my gaze away and turned my back to him, staring into the parking lot.

"Can't a girl get some privacy around here?" I hissed.

"Well, that's actually what I'm here about," he said.

I turned to look at him. "Why? What happened?"

"I might have some concerns about you staying at the cabin."

I could feel my eyebrows coming together in a scowl. "Really, and what might those be?" I asked dryly.

"Staying at the cabin all by yourself might not be a wise choice. You of all people know this town isn't crawling with upstanding citizens."

I could feel the blood drain from my face and an acidic taste on my tongue as I realized what he meant by that. "Right, I forgot this place is the ultimate paradise for low lives," I scoffed, shaking my head.

Carter had a scowl on his face. "You do know you don't have to be this judgemental all the time, right?"

I balked at him. "So you just said that I can't stay at the cabin because there's a possibility they might break in and do God knows what, and then you're blaming me for being judgemental?" I raised a brow, and he sighed.

"Anyway, I just thought I'd let you know. Anya still does her bed and breakfast. There might be available rooms if you're interested. That's the other option apart from the crappy motel."

"What choice do I have at this point, right? Do you have the number to a cab I can call?" I asked, feeling a little too desperate for my pride at this moment. It would be dark soon anyway, so I had to figure this out soon.

"Not if you want to wait for two hours-plus for one. Come on, I will drop you."

I crossed my arms with a huff. "I can take care of myself y'know."

"No one said you couldn't. I'm only making this easier on ya." He was already headed in the direction of his pick-up. I blew out a breath and followed behind, wishing I had stayed in contact with someone else apart from Patrick, so I wouldn't feel like my bully was the only option in this wretched place.

AS SOON AS WE ARRIVED at Anya's bed and breakfast, I knew I'd have issues getting a room. There was a big truck with pest control written on it and men in suits gearing up to enter. Anya was there talking to one of them, but as soon as she spotted Carter's truck, she waved him off and approached the truck with a huge smile on her face.

"I don't think we need her to explain the obvious," I murmured to Carter, who still had his hands glued to the steering wheel.

Anya came and stopped by his window, smiling broadly with her red lipstick a little smudged and her grey-streaked, mousy brown hair blowing in the wind. "Hey, Cart, what brings you here today?" she asked, her eyes shifting to me. Her brows furrowed a bit, and then recognition dawned after a second of staring at me.

"Well, I'll be damned! Anna? Anna Cambridge?"

I managed a smile. "In the flesh."

"Girl, you're looking prettier than ever. Isn't that right, Cart?" she asked as she glanced at Carter with a mischievous glint in her eyes.

I found myself holding my breath for an answer from Carter, but he cleared his throat instead and said, "Er, we just came to see if you had any available rooms here, but from the looks of it, I don't think you do."

"Ahh, yes, we had a little termite issue that I want gone before it starts to snow again. We will be good in a day or two, but I have a few other things that need tending to before I open back up," she smiled, licking her lips before her eyes darted to me again. "Oh, Anna, are you planning on staying for long?"

"Er no... I'll be leaving soon."

"Oh, well, I'm sorry I couldn't be of more help, dear."

"Thank you," I said.

Anya glanced back to one of the guys who was signaling to her. "Well, I better get back to it. It was nice seeing you two."

I released a heavy sigh and plopped back into the seat, closing my eyes. "Great."

"There's another option. Although I'm not sure you'll like it," Carter said. My eyes popped open to meet his.

"Well, what is it?"

"There's a spare room at the cabin. I can crash there until you're ready to leave," he shrugged as he started back up the van.

I scoffed. "And what makes you think I'll feel safe with you, of all people? You're still a bully."

"Was a bully... and I've been driving you around all day. If I wanted to do anything to you, I could have already."

I rolled my eyes. "Well, that's reassuring."

He chuckled. "Trust me; you have more to be afraid of than me. I won't get in your way, so don't worry."

I chewed on my bottom lip as I pondered his words. Carter seemed like a changed man, and I assumed he had to be if he was friends with Patrick. But I couldn't completely trust someone who put me through hell in the past and had not managed to apologize to me like a real man. Maybe it was easy for him to forget and pass it off as nothing, but I had to live with real trauma that still plagued me to this day. What if this were a front that he was putting up? What if it were all an act?

I certainly believed him when he said being alone in the cabin wouldn't be safe. I'd lived in this town long enough to know that anything was possible with the addicts and bums that resided here, and I wasn't willing to take that chance. An available hotel was miles away, and I didn't have the time to be going back and forth and depend on cabs that were almost non-existent in this place.

"Ok, fine. I swear, if you try anything, my best friend knows my every move."

He snorted. "Don't flatter yourself."

I rolled my eyes and crossed my arms as we drove back up to the cabin.

CARTER DROVE BACK TO the bar and later grabbed a few things and dinner for the both of us. After that, we were on our way back, and in no time, we were there again. It was already getting dark, and the sunset had cast a purple-ish hue in the sky. The air was crisp, and I knew if there was anything to love about Greenvale, it was probably this. The fresh air, the filling scent of nature – pinewood, cedar, moist earth. I could never get tired of it. I was outside, just taking it all in and admiring the scenic mountains, when Carter came out of the house and stood behind me. His scent added another drooling combination to what I was already experiencing, and I almost moaned.

"Beautiful, isn't it?" he said.

"Very."

He smiled and peeled off his shirt, which he threw on the wooden steps. My heart started to thrum, and despite the wind, I suddenly felt hot all over. I couldn't help it; I was staring at the man like his image was the only thing my sight could allow. I took my time to drink in the view of each hardened contour of his upper half – his defined pecs, which were dusted with a bit of hair that looked undoubtedly soft. My fingers inched to touch it and his stone-hard abs. Was there a gym in Greenvale? There wasn't one last time I checked, and yet, this man would shock a gym-goer.

"What are you doing?" I couldn't help but ask after realizing that I was probably staring for longer than necessary.

Carter must have caught on, too, because he had a goofy grin that highlighted a dimple I didn't even know he had.

"This is the best time to take a swim, sweetheart," he said as he grinned while unbuckling his belt.

I swallowed. "It's freezing cold!"

"This is as warm as it gets for a while. I'm taking advantage of every second." The pants were gone as he kicked them beside his shirt, only now sporting underpants that clung to every delicious inch of him. I didn't want to look, but how could I not when he was right in front of me? I only caught a glimpse of his bulge before he dashed down the lake and towards the deck.

I was breathless for no reason as I watched him before he dived into the cold lake. I couldn't believe it! I was freezing by just standing here and there he was taking an ice bath. I didn't dare move further down to look – I didn't want to make it seem like I was interested or anything like that, but I would die to see his strong body moving around in the water.

Fuck, but what was I doing fantasizing about this man of all people. I should hate him as much as I did in high school, but the feeling wasn't as strong for some strange reason. I wanted to hate his guts, but it was hard when he was this hot and...nice? I was pitiful! He was only acting. I'm sure he hated me as much, but my body didn't want to believe that. I could feel the heat in my core, begging for attention. I could feel the moistness between my legs and knew that I couldn't control my thoughts or my body's reaction to this God of a man.

A few minutes later, he came out soaking wet and dripping all over. Well, at least two of us were soaking. I watched unabashedly as he made his way toward me and knew that I must have been as red as a tomato with the heat that suddenly rushed to my face.

His shoulder-length hair was clamped down on his head but managed to make his angular face more defined. The underwear had traveled slightly lower, exposing his strong V-cut and his obviously big manhood. There was no denying that he was a well-endowed man, and I almost salivated at the thought of having it all.

"You should have joined me," he said with a smile. "I'm gonna dry off, and then we can have dinner." He moved past me and went inside, leaving me there to collect my thoughts from the pit of hell.

He was unfazed, as if he made a habit of swinging his goods around and exposing his body to anyone. But should I expect any different? Carter probably had women at his beck and call – a different one every night. He wasn't the man to stick to one person. He was a heartbreaker, and I hated that more than anything.

But why should I care? It wasn't like I was planning on hooking up with him. That was never going to happen. I would be back home in a few days and forget any of this ever happened.

The problem was getting through the days. It was going to be harder than I thought.

When I went back in, he had on another flannel shirt that he rolled up to his elbows and jeans that were cut off at the knees. He placed the plates on the table and the takeout boxes in the center. I watched him keenly, somehow finding the whole thing sexy. What was with me? Was I this sexually deprived? It had only been two months since I last had sex, and that was just before Hector and I ended things. I'd gone for far longer in the past and was fine.

"I only bought beer from the bar; I hope that's fine," Carter said, causing my head to snap up when I realized I was lost in thought again.

"Er, yeah, that's fine, I guess."

"Well, dinner is ready."

I took a seat around the small circular table on the opposite side of Carter, who had already started to dig in and serve himself. I did the same, eager to take a bit of the chicken linguine. I hadn't had it in a while and was excited to try Carter's take on it.

He watched as I took the first bite, and I could tell he was looking for some type of approval just like he was at the bar when he thought I didn't notice him staring at me when I ate the burger. But how could I, despite my grudge against him, not tell him that this was the best linguine I had ever tasted. The flavors were bursting in my mouth, and the spice was potent. My face must have been a dead giveaway because he smiled.

"It's good," I managed with a full mouth.

"Thanks."

We continued to eat in silence. There were so many things I wanted to say but didn't want to at the same time. I should hate him; his very presence should irk me, but the fact that it didn't puzzled me.

"I think this was Patrick's favorite meal other than fish," Carter said.

I smiled. "He loved his fish."

"All types... cooked, uncooked. It didn't matter to him."

"He was so happy when I caught my first one. The pic is back there," I said as I gestured towards the table.

He nodded as he ate. "I saw it, and he told me the story too. Said you were a natural."

I chuckled. "Well, I don't know about that, but I always liked doing it with him."

Carter paused to look up at me. "You were really important to him. He said he was really proud of you."

I blinked a few times to stop the stinging in my eyes. I didn't want to cry now. "He was very important to me too."

There was a small silence before I said, "When are you planning to scatter his ashes?"

"It's really up to you. You're the one who has to get back to your life," he said as he took a drink.

"I guess we could do it tomorrow."

He nodded and stood, bringing the plates to the sink.

I headed to the bathroom and took a shower. There was no sign of Carter when I came out, so I went to the porch and started scrolling through my phone because there wasn't really anything else to do. I went on Instagram to stalk Hector's profile but was surprised when I saw that there was a text message from him. I held my breath as I tapped on the message. My chest rose as I read what he had to say:

Hey beautiful, can we talk?

Why would he want to talk months after a failed engagement? I was tempted to close the chat and ignore it, but more than anything, I was curious as to what he wanted to say.

What is it? I replied.

I'd prefer if we discussed this in person. Are you free tomorrow?

I'm not in the city. Why was I even telling him this? It was none of his business.

Where are you? Another message came.

"Hey, care for some company?" Carter's voice came. He was already sitting before I could give an answer, sporting a smug smile on his face, which told me his actions were intentional. This wasn't exactly the best time, but maybe it was better than Hector and his confusion. Maybe I needed some time before I replied to him anyway.

I glanced at the small antique-looking box in his hand and then at him. "What's up?"

"These are some things that Patrick left behind," he said as he opened the box. "He always said he wanted to give you these whenever he got the chance."

I looked in the box and took note of the jewelry: the rings, the clips and the necklaces.

"This was his mother's," Carter said as he took up the blue-gemmed hair clip. "He always talked about giving it to you on your wedding day. Something blue." My eyes started to sting again, but I wasn't sure if I could stop the tears this time.

"Last time I heard, you were engaged. You could bring it back with you."

I blinked, but instead of keeping the tears at bay, they came streaming down my face, and there was nothing I could do to stop them. My heart felt so bare at that moment.

"Me and my fiancé broke things off about two months ago. I couldn't bring myself to tell Patrick because I didn't want him to be disappointed in me," I sobbed.

Carter stared at me in shock. "I'm sorry," he said. "He would have understood. He wouldn't have judged."

"I know," I snapped unintentionally. "Things were always just so perfect whenever we talked. I didn't want to ruin that."

"I understand."

I sniffed, biting into my trembling lips. "I should have visited. I should have been there for him in his last moments. I just assumed that everything was fine. He was old, but it didn't occur to me that, at any given time, he could die. I got used to the calls and assumed that was enough," I sniffed, wiping at my tears as they fell.

"There was no way of knowing. Patrick was healthy otherwise. No one could have predicted this. Things like this happen," Carter was saying. I tried my best to cling to his words and find comfort in them, but I just couldn't help but hate myself in this moment.

"You were right. This isn't how you treated someone who was like a father to you. He was more of a father to me than my own. I cherished every single moment I spent with him, but it wasn't enough. I should have done more."

"Hey, Anna, look at me," Carter said. More tears streamed down my face, but I managed to turn to look at him. His brown eyes were soft and kind. "You were the most important thing in Patrick's life. He had nothing but good things to say about you. He could have felt your love despite the distance, trust me. You did enough."

I nodded slowly, thankful for his words and the look in his eyes, which spoke a lot more than words. The familiar heat consumed my body once again, and I was almost lost in Carter's eyes. I found myself leaning in like he was a magnet pulling me in. Maybe that was true because we were complete opposites, and I couldn't pull myself away. His eyes lowered to my mouth, and I could feel his breath against me. A part of my brain wanted me to see logic, but I was too far gone. I wanted to taste his mouth. I wanted to savor the flavor and the feel of his skin on mine. My body was begging for the caress, and I was sure my panties were sodden again. How could I stop myself? I couldn't. My fate was inevitable, and all the stars were aligned for this moment.

When my lips touched his, I held my breath and reveled in the feathery softness before his mouth parted and took mine in. I moaned because the pleasure that coursed through me was like no other. Our lips only brushed against each other – as if testing the waters before the big dive, but I was so hot – so eager and impatient for more. My hands circled his neck and pulled him closer, going deeper until I could taste the flavor of mint on his breath and the sweet warmth that rushed through my veins like a bolt of lightning. Carter's hands found my waist as he pulled me closer to him to further bask in the kiss. My hard nipples pressed against his chest, and I had to keep myself from moaning once again. My fingers raked through his still-damp hair as I urged him deeper into my mouth. His stubble tickled my skin, but his tongue was doing wonders in my mouth. I was burning at a fever pitch that wouldn't die down anytime soon.

My core tightened at the thought of him between my legs or my own straddled over his. I was craving more – more than this could possibly offer.

But then my phone vibrated again, which brought me back to reality. I pulled away, breathing heavily, staring into Carter's darkened, lust-filled eyes. I was tempted to damn it all to hell once again, but then logic won over, and I shifted a little on the chair to create some distance between us.

"I er... I shouldn't have done that; I'm sorry."

"N-no... it's my fault I shouldn't..." Carter trailed off and raked his hand through his hair, scratching the spot.

"I should head in. It's getting late anyway. Good night."

I got up and dashed to the bedroom, flopping down on the bed as I tried to process what happened out there and how quickly it did. However, my brain didn't allow me much but memories of it. It was as if I could still feel his mouth on mine; how his teeth grazed over my lips and gently tugged them before he entwined my tongue with his in a passionate caress. My heart was still beating fast, and I knew that if I stayed a minute longer, it would probably burst in my chest. I had never experienced something so intense in my entire life – not even with Hector.

I still craved more. The taste of his lips, his calloused hands around my waist, the crisp scent of his clothes and the freshness of his skin. I had always found Carter attractive, but never in my life had I ever expected to feel this way because of him. Could I go back to living life as usual, knowing this man had the potential to make me feel so much more?

My phone vibrated again. Frustrated, I reached for it and almost rolled my eyes when I saw that it was Hector again.

'??' was the first text, followed by;

Well?

I huffed out a breath and threw the phone to the side. For the first time in a long time, another man occupied my mind for the night.

Chapter 5

Carter

Never in my life had a woman plagued my thoughts as much as Anna did now. Maybe it was that I never had to wait or do much to get them. I usually got whomever I wanted, but here Anna was different in so many ways. As attractive as she was, I hadn't expected the kiss to be that good. Damn, more than good even. There was no way of describing how incredible her lips had felt against mine – how sweet her mouth was. How warm.

As I lay in my bed, desperate for some other thought, Anna kept coming back. The memory would stick; I knew. But that wasn't the hard part. The hard part was waking up tomorrow, knowing I couldn't have her. Knowing that even though she allowed this, she wouldn't allow it to happen a second time. The days would be torturous... I already knew that as much as I knew that I wouldn't likely get any sleep tonight with her just in the other room. I was fucked, and yet I was far from it.

I was hard as a rock, and all I wanted was her to quell the hunger than raged like wildfire inside me. Fuck my life and the universe for being so spiteful. This was the karma I got for bullying her in high school. I was now the one in agony, and there was nothing I could do about it.

The following day I got up, feeling like a walking dead. I didn't get an ounce of sleep because my thoughts were reckless, and so was the constant boner that came and went like my past lovers.

I entered the kitchen hoping to get some coffee and found Anna there, making something that didn't smell like coffee. I paused in my tracks, unsure of how to react now that it was a new day and things had become clearer.

As if sensing my presence, she turned to face me. Her eyes swept over my frame, and she managed a brief smile before she spun around to do what she was doing before I entered. "Good morning. I made enough tea just in case you wanted some," she said.

My eyes roamed over her from behind. I took the chance, knowing I probably wouldn't be as bold if her eyes were on me. She still had a robe on but had managed to grip it so tight that I could still see the delicious flare of her hips and her round ass. Her hair dangled in her back, a bit tousled, almost brushing her ass. My manhood stirred in my pants, and I resisted the urge to mutter a curse. Her body on mine was what I'd want for breakfast...to explore every inch of smooth, supple flesh. Oh, what I'd give.

"Tea is great, thanks," I said, putting my thoughts to a halt before I could stir up an embarrassing boner.

I watched as she poured me a cup, and I approached her. She handed me the cup, and our gazes met for a brief second before she tore hers away and took a sip of her tea.

"I was thinking maybe we could scatter the ashes before I head to the bar. I might not have time after."

She slowly nodded, her green eyes on me once again. "Sure, I guess we could do that."

About twenty minutes later, we both got dressed. I picked up the urn, and we both went out front. Anna paused and stared at the water body ahead, seemingly nostalgic as she did so.

"He said he wanted it scattered in his favorite place," she said just above a whisper.

I nodded. "I guess it's the lake, right?"

"It is, but there was a part that he liked the most. He always said that it was beautiful and peaceful and that he just couldn't get enough. If I remember correctly, it's up a little hill, and then we walk down to a graveled path."

"I think I know where you're talking. Let's go."

We started our trek, and it wasn't long before I realized Anna was admiring the vegetation as we walked. She even stopped at times to listen to the birds, and I smiled to myself when her face lifted with a genuine smile that I found myself longing to see more of. There was this undeniable innocence in her – almost like the weight of the world had been lifted off her shoulders as she breathed in the fresh air and ran her hand along any available branch in her path.

"Ever thought about living in a place like this?" I asked.

She glanced at me, her forehead wrinkled. "I had for ten years."

"But not quite this part."

"I guess I could, but I also like the city, which is just a burst of possibilities. What job would I have in Greenvale?" she scoffed.

"Greenvale has potential too. It just needs the right people to see that."

"Last time someone saw that, people didn't take it well. These people are just not fans of growth."

"And by someone, you mean your dad?" I countered, and she paused, turning to me.

"Right. I might not be a fan of him, but it isn't because he was a bad person, it was because he was a lousy dad. All he ever did was try to better this town."

I scoffed and shook my head. "Oh, that's definitely what he wanted everybody to think."

She raised her chin and crossed her arms. "You disagree?"

There were so many things I wanted to say – could have said that would break the wall of defense Anna was building up as we spoke, but I decided not to. I could feel the anger blooming inside me at the memories and knew this wasn't an ideal time to let it all out.

I sighed. "I don't want to get into it. I don't want to start an argument now, so can we please just... not."

Her mouth opened to talk, but she quickly clamped it back shut and managed a curt nod before she spun around again and continued to walk. We were silent until we got to the spot Patrick wanted us to be.

"Wow... it's even more beautiful than I remembered," she said as she looked at the vast expanse of lake water. It was similar to the view at Patrick's with the mountainous ranges in the background, but the water was clearer here – so clear that you could see the bedrock beneath the water at the shoreline. But that wasn't even the best part. It was the variety of winter flowers that bloomed around us, all in different colors, huddled together to create a beautiful bed.

"I see why it's Patrick's favorite spot."

She nodded with a smile and glanced at the urn in my hand, her eyes softening. "So this is it?"

"This is it."

I opened the container and walked closer to the edge, observing the direction of the wind. "You will be missed, old man. I will always be grateful to you for being there for me at my worst and my best. You made me believe all hope wasn't lost in the world, and that I could do anything I wanted if I were passionate enough. I'll miss you, but I'll hold onto the memories," I said as I glanced at an empathetic Anna and spilled the ashes. Some landed in the water before us, and the wind carried some before it disappeared. I cleared my throat in an attempt to rid myself of the lump that had begun to form.

I glanced at Anna and handed her the remains. She was already crying as she took it. "You were my anchor, the light I had to lead me in the darkness. My fondest memories were spent with you, and I can't thank you enough for them. I love and miss you, but I know you're in a better place and if I'm lucky, I might see you again," she croaked before she sniffed and emptied the rest of the ashes into the lake. We both watched as the particles flew high before they were no more. For me, it indicated a finality that I had not allowed myself to grasp until now.

Anna started to sob, and I did the only thing I could have done in that moment. I reached for her and allowed her to cry against me while I tried to hold back my own tears. She felt so small and vulnerable in my hands – something new to me – and it prompted me to hold her even closer. She felt right in my arms as if here was where she belonged – with me. As she was being racked with sobs, I knew in my heart that she was my person. The burst of emotions that constricted my chest was mostly because she was sad more than anything else.

I didn't know what it was that led me to have this sudden train of thoughts, but I wanted to be there for Anna in moments like these. Be her shoulder to cry on – the person she went to when she was sad. Nothing else mattered more than holding her, and I didn't want to let go.

ONCE WE ARRIVED BACK at the cabin, I already knew that it would start snowing soon, by the looks of it, and I had some things to take care of before it started.

"I'm gonna head to the bar for a bit. You could come for breakfast."

"Nah, I'm good. There were some leftovers, anyway. I think I'll have that."

I nodded, and our gazes met. "Ok, I'll be back soon. You'll be safe here. The bad guys only come out at night," I smiled, and she nodded.

I was about to turn in my tracks when I paused, hearing her call my name, and feeling her small hands wrapped around my wrist. I honestly wished she hadn't done that because it was like she had triggered something in me. Something primal and needy – craving to finish what we had started the other night. I swallowed and looked from my hand to her soft blue eyes.

"I'm glad you were there with me today. I don't know what I would have done if it were me alone."

I smiled. "I'm glad you were there too."

I couldn't take my eyes off her. Not when she looked so beautiful with her hair down, framing her small, oval face. Her cheeks flushed from the cold. The woman was stunning, and I wanted her as much as I wanted the air I breathed.

Like a moth drawn to a flame, I gave into the attraction once again, stepping a little closer, watching as her small mouth parted in anticipation. Her scent filled me with longing, and I stood directly in front of her, taking in it all. I lowered my head to her, and she tipped a little to meet me as our mouths crashed against each other. My body instantly remembered the taste and feel of her cotton-soft lips – the sweetness. The memory ran hot through my veins, and I was in paradise for the second time when my tongue caressed hers and melted the chills in my body. I pulled her against me, scouring the contents of her sweet mouth while my hand traced up her slender back, resting at her neck where I held her firmly in place. She moaned against me, and the vibrations rang through my body like an electric force.

My pants started to tighten as my length expanded and sought release. I was right at her stomach and knew she could feel me against her the longer we kissed. To my surprise, it seemed she even tried to wiggle closer to get a better experience of my erection against her. She started to tug at my buckle while I kissed her like her mouth had endless treasures.

I could feel how much she wanted me, and I hoped she could feel the same energy radiating from me. I peeled off her coat and threw it to the side, exposing the tight blouse underneath that clung to her skin and imprinted her hardened nipples.

Gosh, Anna was everything, something I couldn't get enough of, no matter how I tried. My hands traveled up her own, but I paused when my fingers hit a small bump that interrupted the flawlessness of her supple skin. She gasped, and I pulled back to look at her and her arm.

It was a small scar that went wide across her arm. "What happened here?" I was curious to know, especially seeing the expression that took over her face and how she tried to pull the sleeve down to cover it.

"It's nothing," she said as she reached for her coat, but I recognized the sudden edge to her voice and knew that it was definitely something.

"Seemed like the injury was pretty bad."

She raised a brow. "I guess you could say that," she said as she adjusted the coat and looked at everything except me.

I sighed, feeling a little frustrated. "Anna, I'm trying here. The least you could do is meet me halfway."

She stared at me for a long second before she scoffed and shook her head. "We don't have to do anything, Carter. In a day or two, I will be gone. Maybe our heads are a little fuzzy with emotions, but we both hate each other at the end of the day!" she snapped.

I was taken aback by her harsh words but knew there was some truth in them. "I don't hate you."

She seemed taken off guard by my response but quickly shook her head as if to clear it. "Well, you might have evolved from the person you were in high school, but I definitely can't forget what you put me through."

I scoffed. Here we go again! "I told you I was sorry for all that. I was stupid and was looking for someone to blame for my problems. I didn't think it was that big of a deal. It was high school!" I exclaimed.

Her little nostrils flared, her mouth set in a pout, and the softness in her eyes from earlier was long gone. "Part of the reason I hated this place so much was because of you. I lived in fear for most of my time because I didn't know what you would say or do to me!"

I swallowed. "I never laid a finger on you, and neither did I plan to. I never would."

"You never did, but when I stood up to you for the first time, I was scared out of my mind especially after you threatened me. I ran from you because I believed you when you said you wouldn't regret what you would do if I didn't run. This scar on my arm was from running from you!" she spat, tears now streaming down her flushed face. I didn't dare say a word because I was too shocked.

"So you might think it was nothing but the usual bullying, but I hated you for most of my life because of it."

I couldn't meet her gaze. I was too ashamed to do anything but hang my head. I remembered the day as clear as day. How she had shamed my family and the town. At the time, I was shocked that she was standing up to me, but nothing beat the anger that had coursed through me. I threatened her because I couldn't bear to look at her, but I knew I would never lay a finger on her, no matter how angry I was.

"I'm sorry – I didn't know. I'm sorry I put you through all that, Anna," I said, finally managing to look at her.

"Why, though? Why me? I didn't do anything to you. I don't even remember having a conversation with you before the bullying," she said. "It was like you got up and decided that you would make my life hell."

I swallowed as I contemplated telling her my truth. It was something I hoped would stay buried forever because I never wanted to relive the moment, but how long could I at this point?

"I hated you because I hated your dad," I blurted.

She scoffed. "What did my dad ever do to you people? I don't get it. All he tried to do was help and make something of this dump!" she snapped.

That familiar anger started to slowly grow inside me again. "You're so blind to everything, aren't you? It's high time you take your family off that pedestal you have them on because they are far from saints!" I exclaimed.

"Oh, fuck you, Carter!" she said as she turned to leave.

"Why do you think he picked up and left Greenvale?" I called, and she paused in her tracks before confidently turning around to confront me.

"The refinery wasn't profiting!"

I scoffed. "And you believed that? There was a Benzene exposure because your dad was busy running shortcuts. My dad was exposed and found out a year later that he had cancer. Your dear old dad did nothing to help, even when he still continued to work with the diagnosis. He couldn't stop because he wanted to care for me and pay his medical bills. Your dad said it wasn't the factory's fault that he got cancer, but then two more persons became ill with the same cancer."

Anna's eyes were wide, her face pale as she listened to me.

"They wanted to lawyer up, fight the matter in court, but none of the lawyers they could afford wanted to go up against Sylas Cambridge. Then he picked up and left because he was a coward who didn't want to face up to his responsibilities. And my dad died because of it."

She still didn't say anything, but I imagined she was processing all that I was telling her, which was warranted because this was a lot.

"I was angry for a very long time, and because I couldn't get to your father, I let it out on you."

Her lips trembled as she stared at me. "My dad would never-"

“If you don’t believe him, ask him yourself. He knows the truth,” I said before sidestepping her and leaving the house. Whatever conclusions she wanted to draw from what I told her was up to her.

Chapter 6

Anna

Carter left me with a pill that I had difficulty swallowing even an hour later. He had left for the bar, and I was still here with tears streaming down my face because I couldn't begin to fathom his words being true. But surely, this was something he couldn't make up. I wanted to put my mind at ease, and so I fished out my phone and dialed my dad's number because I couldn't wait until I got back to the city to confront him.

"Anna?" he answered, probably shocked that I called, seeing I hadn't done so in a while.

"I'm going to ask you something, and I want you to give me the honest truth, nothing less," I said and was happy with the firmness in my voice, although I was slowly crumbling on the inside.

"Of course. What is the matter, sweetheart."

"Why did we leave Greenvale?"

There was a bit of hesitance on his end before he said, "Honey, I told you, it wasn't working out. It cost too much..."

My lips quivered. "People's lives?"

"What?'

"Was the refinery giving people cancer because you were too cheap to follow proper protocols?" I asked.

"Anna, where did you –"

"I asked for the truth, Dad!" I snapped as tears flowed down my face.

The line went silent. "There was an exposure, yes." His voice was low, and I knew right away that he was guilty.

"You could have easily footed their medical bills and made it better. What kind of person are you?" I sobbed, feeling myself shake.

"Anna, I-"

"You are a horrible dad, but I still defended you against these people who were right all along!" I shouted. "This is the last time you'll be hearing from me! You're dead to me as of today." Without waiting to hear a reply from him, I hung up the phone and pulled my knees to my chest and started sobbing.

I couldn't believe it. I couldn't believe that my dad was guilty and that I had foolishly defended him. I had spent the better part of my life hating Carter because I thought he was being the typical high school antagonist with no real reason behind his bullying. But he was in pain, battling with things far greater than I had to deal with. As hard as it was to do, I understood his reasons – why he did it and why he was so angry at me.

I was innocent in the matter, but I understood. I understood it now, but I hated the unintentional hurt and not knowing. I wanted to cry my eyes out... I felt so stupid and hurt all at once. For years, I had just accepted my father's lie and went along with it because it never crossed my mind that the issue would be so severe.

For the rest of the day, I felt like crap and quite frankly, I didn't know what I'd say to Carter when he came back. I should apologize because it was the right thing to do, although I doubt anything I did would fix the damage. His father was dead because of mine, for Christ's sake! How could I even look him in the eyes after this?

It started to snow later that day, so I went inside and huddled in bed after making myself some tea and snacking on some chips that had been left in the pantry.

I heard the door open later that evening and knew Carter had arrived. This feeling of anxiety took over as I dreaded the impending conversation. A few minutes passed while I listened to him shuffling around the house.

I almost gasped when a knock came at the door, accompanied by his bassy voice. "I brought dinner if you're hungry," he said and then there was silence again.

I felt that familiar burning in my throat, which was usually accompanied by tears. Despite what had happened, he was still managing to be kind. I didn't know whether to cry my eyes out at the chivalry or feel more guilty for what had happened. All this time, I'd been hating someone I thought was a monster when really, he had just been hurting.

I pulled in a breath, peeled myself off the bed and went to the small living room where Carter sat with the take-out bags in front of him while he scrolled on his phone. His hair was in a high ponytail that was a bit messy, and for the first time since I'd been here, he wasn't wearing flannel. Instead, he wore a white t-shirt that showed his strong arms even more.

He didn't look up even when I moved closer and took a seat beside him.

"You were right, and I'm sorry, Carter. I had no idea," I began. "Nothing I say will make it better, but I'm deeply sorry for all you went through because of my father."

He finally looked up at me. His features were soft, and so were his eyes, which seemed to glisten under the lights. "You called him."

"I did; he tried to defend himself, but I knew he was lying. I just wished I'd known earlier."

He shook his head. "I guess I should have told you back then. I just thought you were just like your father and you wouldn't care for the truth. Either way, it's no excuse for what I did to you all those years. I shouldn't have bullied you, and I'm deeply sorry."

I smiled. "Apology accepted. I guess we can stop hating each other now."

He chuckled. "I stopped hating you a long time ago."

I smiled and tucked a lock of loose hair behind my ear. We ate the food he brought and settled into light chatter until we both realized it was starting to snow harder.

"I'm gonna crank up the heat a bit more. It's gonna be a cold night here."

I cleaned up and opted for an extra blanket when Carter returned.

"Well, I'd better head to bed. It's going to be a long night. Good night, Anna."

"Good night, Carter."

We went our separate ways; I flopped down in the bed with a sigh, staring at the blank ceiling as I listened to the howling wind outside. I was never a fan of the cold weather, so I had hoped that coming here would be sunny long enough until I got back home.

I pulled up the covers and shuffled around in the bed, knowing the night ahead would be reckless. All I could think about was Carter and that he was in the other room. It was harder now that I had no reason to hate him again. The kisses we shared started to plague me, and I grew even more reckless by the passing second. All I wanted to temper my chills was a warm body pressed against mine. Carter was more than capable of making that happen with his large, taut body.

I closed my eyes and huffed a sigh, but all I could see was the sexy, rugged beast who had managed to stir more emotions in me in one day than I had managed in years. I couldn't believe it, but here I was, fantasizing about my former bully – wanting him more than I did anything else.

I even contemplated walking over to his room and offering myself to him because I felt that needy. But I feared rejection more than anything, and there was a high possibility that Carter would if I made such a bold move. Or would he? I had felt how he kissed me and knew he wanted me as much as I wanted him. I could feel it in the way he kissed me – the way he held me against him – and, of course, how could I forget the way his boner had pressed against my stomach. Big and hard, ready to take me whichever way he could.

I twisted and turned in the small bed for hours until I decided to damn it all to hell. I swung my legs over and licked my lips as I stood, ready to do the boldest thing I had ever done in my life. I was in pajamas – the least sexy thing – but I knew I had to make it work.

I timidly walked from my room and went to where Carter was. My heart was beating a mile a second, but I couldn't dare turn back now. Not when I was so close. I swallowed the nervous lump in my throat and was happy to find that his door wasn't fully locked. I licked my lips and pushed the door open, feeling as if my heart was about to burst out of my chest any second now.

"Carter?" I said in the darkness, holding my breath.

The bedside lights were immediately flicked, on and there he was, shirtless in bed with his hair loose and brushing against his strong shoulders. He eased up and stared at me with a look of curiosity in his eyes – maybe wondering what the fuck I was doing in his room so late in the night.

"Anna, is everything okay?" he asked, voice slightly groggy.

I swallowed. "Er... I couldn't sleep." That was the truth after all, but the bigger question was, why?

There was a bit of realization in his eyes as they swept my form before settling on my face. Wordlessly, I moved towards him, and he scooted off the bed a little, so he was sitting at the edge in boxers. I didn't know what the hell I was doing. I was never this bold or spontaneous, but here Carter was, bringing all of it out.

I stood before him and met his darkened gaze, licking across my lips. I wanted to kiss him so badly, but what if all this blew up in my face? What would I do then?

He swallowed, and his Adam's apple bobbed. "Are you sure this is what you want?" his voice was low and incredibly sexy, with a bit of huskiness that sent chills down my spine.

I nodded and folded my lips. We were both silent after, but then he reached out with his big muscular hands, wrapping them around my waist as he pulled me close. I almost gasped, but I took his reaction as a sign to do what I had been craving for hours. I kissed him, and I kissed him hard, not holding back for even a second. Unlike the others, which had started sweet and soft, this was the complete opposite. This was pure need between two people, and I was burning with each stroke, each lick into my mouth, each possessive tug and nip that made up this kiss.

Carter's lips briefly left my mouth as he went to suckle on my sensitive neck. An erogenous zone that I had not even spoken about. Yet here he was, causing a river to flow within my panties the longer he kissed me there. I almost squealed when he started to suck on the flesh with his hot tongue. I didn't care if he left a mark – I was just living for every second of this amazing moment.

"Oh, yes," I whispered, arching my neck higher to grant him more access. He took the opportunity to suckle the spot needily while his hands traveled beneath my top and explored my heated flesh. I shivered against him as his hands traveled up both my sides, his thumb brushing against my tits.

"Fuck, your skin is like velvet," he stated huskily, moving further down my chest. I gasped, my knees almost giving out when he caught one nipple in his mouth through my clothes and tugged at it. The heat that seared through me was blinding, and I knew I was probably so wet that my juices would soon begin to slither down my legs. When he pulled away, a wet spot remained on the thin fabric. He smiled down at it, and I almost lost my mind at the whole thing.

"Hands up, sweetheart. I want my mouth against your flesh." The way he said it was like a demand that had my heart doing flips.

I held up my hands and allowed him to peel off my top, exposing my naked chest. He didn't go at it right away. He just took his time to admire each round swell of flesh with the lust building in his gaze. Somehow, despite his thorough inspection of me, I didn't feel self-conscious. I felt even more confident in myself because this man was looking at me like I was a prize he had just won.

When he finally reached out and took my breast in his mouth, I arched my neck and closed my eyes. Each breast fit perfectly in his mouth, and he smoothed his tongue along its perimeter until he sucked at the nipples, releasing them with a 'pop' when his mouth left them. He stroked each with his tongue with skillful accuracy, giving both just the right amount of licks before he suckled and wrapped them around his tongue. My hands were busy making streaks in his hair as he spent his time heightening my arousal.

When he was done with them, he knelt before me and peeled my pants off. I was in lacy blue underwear that he didn't waste any time in shoving down my legs. He knelt in front of me on two knees like I was some God he was cherishing. My chest rose and fell as I anticipated his next move, but what he did next was something I had not seen coming.

He wrapped his arms around my hips and pulled me closer to him before he stuck out his tongue and licked across my vagina. I gasped when he picked me up in that same position and flopped me on the bed. My ass was barely at the edge of the bed, and he was still kneeling in front of me. I had closed my legs, but one look from him prompted me to open them.

I held my breath and watched the darkness that loomed in his eyes as he observed my heated flesh, which was probably glistening with wetness.

"You're so beautiful, Anna." Just the way he said my name caused my flesh to clench up in front of him, and heat immediately rose to my cheeks.

He held up my legs – pried them apart with his strong arms, and then he lowered his head to my most intimate flesh. I moaned and fell back on the bed when his warm mouth made contact with my skin. He moaned against me as he sucked on my sensitive flesh, lapping up my juices but creating more with his own. I started to writhe in the bed when he started to lick me with his strong tongue from top to bottom, flicking lightly at the hole before he went back up and repeated his actions. I was burning up... so, so hot as Carter did wonders to my flesh.

He found my tiny gape and decided that he would give it some attention. When he probed deep and began to flick it, I damn near lost my mind. I couldn't stop my moans or the movements of my body as I thrashed from side to side. Carter held my legs in place and didn't let up for even a second until I was screaming and shaking on the bed, my orgasm hitting me like a boulder.

"Oh, my gosh! Oh!" my voice even sounded hoarse – my body feeling drained. Yet, he still continued to bathe my flesh with his tongue, causing me to quiver over and over again. He finally got to his feet and licked his lips, looking like a God with his hair flowing and his muscular chest left to my hungry gaze.

Despite my mind-boggling orgasm, I felt myself wanting more. My eyes lowered to Carter's lower half, and I could see his manhood visibly straining against the fabric, creating a tent that pointed in my direction. I licked my lips, and he must have followed the direction of my gaze because he immediately hooked his fingers in the waistband and pulled off his boxers. His dick sprung free and bounced a little before it settled, pulsing at me. I almost salivated for a taste.

"I want to taste you like you did me," I said and was happy my voice didn't break.

He ran his hand through his hair and climbed on the bed, leaning against the headboard. I crept up to him and settled between his spread legs, capturing his cock in my hand, which perfectly fitted my palms. It was huge and beautiful, and I had to briefly ponder whether or not he would fit.

However, I gave it little thought – more eager for a taste at this moment than anything else. I licked my palm and started to stroke him with it, slowly going up and down his length. He moaned throatily, and I continued, amping up my pace a little until I saw clear precum oozing from the tip. I used my thumb and spread it across the head before lowering my mouth over him and taking him inside. The tangy, slightly salty taste exploded in my mouth, but I enjoyed the feel of my tongue on his sensitive skin. My saliva pooled on him as I went back and forth in the sloppy blow-job. Carter moaned and reached for my head, massaging my scalp as I went down on him. It motivated me to move faster until he started to grunt and thrust his hips up, sending his length further into my throat. More saliva pooled on him, his moans becoming louder as I relentlessly blew him off.

"Fuck, Anna, I can't hold back," he warned. I upped my pace a little, pausing as he bucked and muttered a curse, his hot semen shooting at the back of my throat. My mouth remained over his head, collecting every drop until he was empty. I sucked him a little despite my full mouth and went all the way up the head before I finally emptied his semen back on his length.

"Oh, fuck!" Carter exclaimed as his cream coated his entire length.

I licked my lips and swallowed what I had left in my mouth, smiling shyly at him. He was still hard as a rock, his manhood still upright as it slightly throbbed.

"Damn, you're perfect. Come here," he said as he reached for me and clamped my mouth to his yet again. I kissed him hard, tasting myself on him just as he tasted himself on me.

The dusting of hair on his chest caressed my nipples as we kissed, almost tickling yet arousing me beyond measure. Carter's hands moved down my back until he reached my ass, squeezing each globe. I rolled my hips against him, his cock resting just below me. I wanted him so much; I couldn't wait a second more. I raised my ass and reached between us to capture his length. I met his gaze as I impaled myself on him, watching as his lips slowly parted as my flesh slowly sheathed his.

I gasped as I lowered myself on his slick member, feeling incredibly full the farther he went. It almost became overwhelming as I took in his entire length, but I managed to do so without cumming at once. All the while Carter's hands were busy exploring my body, igniting little fires all over.

He kissed my open mouth, and I quivered at the shift in movement. He held me as I began to roll my hips on him, feeling him all the way inside me; it felt so good that I had to close my eyes for a second and bask in the amazing feeling.

"You feel so amazing," he said as he found my neck again and peppered it with hot kisses and licks. I moved against him, feeling the heat radiate from both our bodies as we made love. Carter held my hips and started to control my movements, pushing me back and forth on his steely length. I slid against him effortlessly, pleasure rippling through me with every stroke. I clung to him, wrapping my hands around his neck as I moved on him – the sounds of our body's connection creating rhythmic music inside the room.

I started to move faster as the pleasure started to build more and more within me. I didn't want the feeling to stop and sought more of it with each thrust, each tug on my skin. It was everything, and I was close – so incredibly close as I rode on my high. A scream bubbled up from inside me, which I tried to suppress, but the feeling was too intense.

My mouth fell open, and I could feel my flesh clamping down on him even as he continued to move within me. I screamed his name and threw my head back as a whirlwind of emotions crashed into me. I was quivering – my brain had gone completely putty...

But Carter wasn't done with me yet.

Carter

I'd never experienced pleasure so intense. Each stroke inside Anna was like bliss. I was on cloud nine as I slid back and forth into her. Her skin was soft and supple, and I could smell her sweet perfume that was almost an intoxicating smell mixed with the scent of sex in the room. When she came around me, I felt everything... there was nothing between us as she offered me all she had.

Her orgasm almost triggered my own, but I was hell-bent on holding out as long as I could because I didn't want this to end. Her silky flesh hugged mine, clenching and unclenching as more of her juices sheathed my shaft. I held onto her and collected all her tremors, kissing along her open mouth, tracing my tongue along her sweaty nape.

Grabbing her hips, I held her and flipped her over on her back while I towered above her. Her hair was sprawled out behind her head, and her face was flushed – lips incredibly pink from my incessant kisses.

Her chest rose and fell, drawing my eyes to her erect nipples, which were like cherries resting on her small mounds. There was this eagerness in her eyes that told me that though she had orgasmed, she wanted more. That's my girl. She was possibly exhausted, but she wanted more of me inside her. Who was I to resist? I began my kisses again, starting at her collarbone and moving down her breasts. I saw the scar on her arm, and my stomach churned as I recollected the story she told me. It was all because of me, and I hated myself for it. It should have been enough of a buzzkill to soften my erection, but then Anna reached for me as if reading my thoughts and kissed me soulfully. I sucked and licked at her lips before I lowered myself and gave her neck the same treatment.

After the first kiss to her neck, I realized it was a soft spot. I enjoyed the moans that almost seemed automatic whenever I kissed her there and would live a lifetime doing just that to hear them over and over again. My kisses traveled to her arm, and I kissed the scar before I strayed to her tits. I would spend a lifetime kissing it and telling her how sorry I was for putting her through all that agony in high school.

"I want you again, Carter, please," an eager Anna whispered as she raised her hips to meet my body. I didn't hesitate for a second longer. I found her heat for the second time and muttered a curse when I slid all the way inside her.

There was an involuntary clench that made me move faster inside her. She was hot and soft and was like velvet as I moved. She started to mewl, grabbing onto my neck as she pulled me down on her body. Our slick bodies moved together, and as slow as I wanted to take it for Anna's sake, I couldn't hold back. I started ramming into her with sharp and hard thrusts that made the bed beneath us creak. Her moans got louder, she held me tighter, and I swore I would pass out whenever I orgasmed.

"Oh, yes! Oh my God, Carter! Yes!" she repeatedly exclaimed as her flesh started to clench again.

"You're so fucking perfect," I managed before I bucked into her and paused, releasing my seed into her. It seemed endless; the pleasure soaring through me was almost crippling as I pumped loads inside her. She collected every drop with a quiver until I collapsed beside her, totally spent and unbelievably satisfied.

Chapter 7

Anna

I woke up to a sweet ache between my legs and Carter's big arms wrapped around my waist. He was still fast asleep, and I could tell by the gentle snores and the heaviness in his hands. I shuffled away a bit and took his hands up before gently placing them on the bed. He slept so peacefully – features completely at ease with his hair tousled, but it was probably the sexiest thing. I contemplated staying just to be in his arms a little longer, but the stickiness between my thighs reminded me that I needed to shower.

I got off the bed and went in search of my scattered clothes before I quickly padded to the bathroom. Each sweet ache from the result of every movement made me smile. I could definitely get used to this – to the idea of waking up with Carter every day. No man had ever made me feel like this. No man had ever given such a stellar performance in bed. He definitely had the whole package.

I took a quick shower and went to my room, where my phone immediately started to ring. I knew it was Maria without even giving it a second thought, and it actually was.

I smiled. "Heeyyy!"

"Well, someone is in a chipper mood. Care to tell your best friend what happened?" she prodded.

I bit my lips and nibbled on a nail for a second. "I'm not."

"Anna, you sound like a morning person right now, and you're definitely not one. It's not even eight," she acknowledged with a little bit of chirpiness in her voice.

Of course, Maria could tell. I sighed as I sat on the bed. "I slept with Carter," I blurted.

There was a small pause before she said, "Carter, as in the guy who bullied you throughout high school?!"

"Yeah," I almost squeaked out.

"OMG, what the hell? How did that even happen?"

"It just kinda did. We kinda figured things out," I said as I rubbed at my jaw and smiled.

"Oh, my gosh, so how was it?"

I immediately felt the heat rising to my cheeks. "Amazing! Out of this world," I said, lowering my voice a bit as I looked to the door.

"Damn, I need all the details when you get back!"

"Of course."

"But I guess what I'm about to tell you is gonna put a damper on this, and I'm so sorry!"

The smile dropped from my face. "Mar, what is it?"

"Hector came by the apartment and was going on about you not replying to his texts and that he needed to talk to you. He said he really wanted to talk to you, and, of course, I didn't tell him where you were, but then he kinda got insanely nagging, and I feared it could be serious, so I told him you were in Greenvale," she sighed.

I rolled my eyes. "Oh, my gosh," I said as I shook my head. "Don't worry about it, though; it's not like Hector will hop on a plane to come see me," I snorted.

"Thing is, that's exactly what I think he's going to do. He seems desperate and seems to have this big apology lined up."

I rolled my eyes. "Doesn't matter. I might be back by tomorrow, anyway. I'll text him and tell him not to."

"Ok, good, but if he tries to worm his way back into your life, don't let him. You deserve better," she warned.

"I won't."

"You always had a soft spot for him, Anna."

I rubbed the nape of my neck. "True, but I've had time to think these past few months, and I was really doing myself a disservice by being with Hector, anyway."

Maria giggled on the other end. "The last two months or last night when you realized he was crap in bed all this time."

I blurted out a laugh, instantly slapping my hand over my mouth. "Shut up; Hector was good in bed too."

"But didn't hold a candle to Carter, right?" she prodded.

I bit my lips. "I'm not talking about this with you right now."

"Right, you have to get back in bed for some delicious morning sex," she exclaimed dramatically.

"Oh, my gosh, you're the worst. Goodbye, I'll talk to you later."

Maria laughed. "Ok, goodbye, my little nymph."

I was grinning as I rolled my eyes and disconnected the call, sighing heavily. I immediately texted Hector on Instagram and told him that flying out to Greenvale wouldn't be necessary. As a man who was a social media presence and was always online, he wasn't now.

What was he thinking anyway? Did he think he could just dump me and get me back whenever he pleased? I'd cried non-stop for over a week after our breakup, but after, I had actually gotten time to clear my head of him. Yes, I still stalked his Instagram to see what he was up to, but now more than ever, I was clear that I didn't want him back.

"Hey, you weren't trying to run from me, were you?" I looked up to find Carter at the door with a towel draped around his waist while he leaned against the doorpost.

I smiled as my eyes consumed the length of his sexy body, and I could feel the heat rising in my body again. "Nah, I just had to take a call." He approached me and pulled me against him, my small body pressed against him.

"Is everything alright?" he asked, his forehead wrinkled.

"Yeah, everything is fine."

"Great, I'm gonna take a shower, and then I'm going to make us some breakfast."

I smiled. "Sounds perfect," I said, and he kissed me softly before he pulled away and left the room.

I bit my lips and watched as he left before I plopped back down on the bed with a sigh. Leaving would be hard; I could see that now that I knew that Carter was becoming addicting. Just his mere presence had caused my heart to flutter and my stomach to churn. I also knew I had been blushing with the heat that warmed my cheeks as soon as he touched me. How could I leave this all behind when he had managed to make me feel like a new person in one night?

I went back to his room and made the bed, my memories becoming more vivid with every piece of linen I touched.

Fifteen minutes later, Carter was out of the shower with his hair in a wet bun at the top of his head. His stubble had grown out a little more, making him a little rugged, along with a red flannel that he threw on. He had a few more buttons loose this time, showing off a little of the hair on his taut chest. He went to the kitchen and started to prepare eggs and pancakes, which were ready in no time.

I dug in first because I was famished, especially after going rounds last night. "Where did you learn to cook like this?" I asked as I cut into the pancake.

"YouTube, and then I just kind of experimented with a few things after," he said.

"These are literally the best pancakes I've ever had."

"Thanks."

"The linguine was great too. I mean, you could make good money in the big cities, and there would be more opportunities, too," I said as I ate.

"Sounds like someone's going to miss me when they're gone," he grinned, raising a brow.

I rolled my eyes. "Don't flatter yourself. But I'm serious; have you ever thought about leaving Greenvale?"

"Not really; Greenvale has always been my home. I wouldn't want to change that."

I nodded slowly, knowing that even if I wanted Carter for a little longer, he wouldn't move to be with me. His heart was set here, which further confirmed this would be a fling and nothing else. There was no future for us when our hearts were in different places.

"How about you? What kind of work do you do?"

"I'm an HR manager for a cosmetics company."

"Wow, that's impressive."

"Says the guy who owns his own bar."

He gave a nonchalant shrug. "Yours take a lot of brainpower."

I smiled and bit my lips. "I just realized I didn't even ask you if you had a girlfriend," I geeked.

"Do you think last night would have happened if I did?"

I shrugged. "I don't know. You don't seem like the committed type."

His mouth fell open as he laughed. "Oh, wow, well, sorry to break the news to you, sweetheart, but I am."

"You're full of surprises, aren't you?"

"Way to keep the excitement going," he winked, and I felt it all the way to my stomach.

"My ex-fiancé was somewhat of the same. Unpredictable in every sense until he dumped me out of the blue," I said with a dry laugh.

"His loss." Our eyes locked, and I bit my lips as I stared at him.

"How long do you think it'll keep snowing?" I cleared my throat and asked.

"Maybe for the rest of the day."

"What do you plan on doing?"

He looked at me with a familiar glint in his eyes. "You."

I RAISED MY HIPS A little and moaned into the bedsheets as Carter kissed a trail up my back, spending a little time at my neck before he kissed my cheeks. His hand slipped under me to grab one of my tits at the same time he slid into me. I gasped at the delicious intrusion and gripped the sheets as he started to move slowly against my ass. His breath was hot against my neck, and so was his body against mine as he rocked in and out of me. He moved at a controlled pace for a few minutes until I started to clench against him and heard the way his groans became more guttural.

His pace increased as he eased up off me, placing his hands on my hips where he held them in place and started to thrust inside me at a wilder pace. I shimmied a little on the bed, wanting to spread my legs a little because he felt too big, and I was on the threshold of pain and pleasure in this position. But Carter had me pinned beneath him, moving more erratic to the point where I almost became overwhelmed.

"Oh, my ...ahh!" my words were muffled in the bedsheets, my head spinning as I tried to make sense of the emotions overriding me.

He started to spread my cheeks with his hands, and I'm guessing the sight must have been something because he immediately muttered a curse and went even faster. At this point, my moans were loud and pleading as my body neared a release. But each time I moved closer to cloud nine, I came back down when he slowed his pace.

"Please." Frustration began to take a toll on me, and I feared I would pass out from the sheer pleasure and agony of it all. "Please, I need to cum..."

He upped his pace again at the simple demand, and I squealed when I got to the point of no return. I quivered, my flesh clenching around him as he stroked me with powerful thrusts. I screamed into the sheets and clamped my eyes shut as I rode the waves of my orgasm and came back down to find that Carter was still not there.

Two more thrusts from him, and I was quivering again, hit by another orgasm. But this time, he bucked and dug deeper into my skin before he quickly pulled out and slathered his seed all over my ass.

"I swear you're fucking perfect, Anna. So beautiful," he said between breaths as he rolled me over and kissed me like his life depended on it. I kissed him back in my state of bliss, knowing there was no way I could leave Greenvale and not have Carter with me.

Chapter 8

Carter

I was over the moon, and I didn't know if it were the sex or I was falling for Anna every second of the day. Every inch of her body was mine – every inch explored for hours on end. I couldn't get enough. She was a drug, and I was an addict who sought more constantly. Just when I thought I'd had enough, she would smile or do something that set me ablaze again.

How was this even possible? Compared to the start we had, this was a miracle. We had warmed up to each other and had spent the last day getting more familiar with each other's body while the snow fell, giving us more reasons to stay trapped inside.

But today, there was no snow and a hint of sun in the sky. I was somewhat disappointed because I knew this would come to an end very soon. Anna had to return to work, and her flight was already booked. It was all finalized while I was there, dreading every moment. The thought of having her gone was painful – the idea of never seeing her again was something I never thought would make me so sad. All of a sudden, it was like I couldn't live without Anna Cambridge.

She came out of the shower with a robe wrapped around her while she mussed up her wet hair. She smiled at me, and her glow was just so beautiful. She was like a ray of sunshine in this gloomy place.

"Wanna drive me to the airport later on?" she asked as she came over and straddled my lap. I moaned as I pulled her in and gave her a small kiss on the lips.

"I wish you didn't have to leave," I groaned, nuzzling her neck.

"Then come with me," she said.

I chuckled at the offer. "To your big city? Are you saying that you like me?" I teased, and her cheeks ripened with a blush.

"Maybe just a little bit."

I grinned. "Not too loud. You might cause a blizzard after that statement."

She swatted me playfully. "I'm serious, though; you can come to New York. You're great at what you do and will be on your way to success in no time."

I licked across my lips, knowing that Anna wasn't the type of person to come right out and say she wanted to be with me, but the feeling was bittersweet.

"I can't just pick up and leave my life behind, Anna," I said. She got up off me, and damn, I knew it was only good while it lasted.

"I don't get why you're so obsessed with this place!" she exclaimed with a dry laugh. "You'd rather stay here and be in your comfort zone than go out there and experience life for a change!"

"Or maybe I'm just happy with my life as it is!" I bit back.

"What life?" she scoffed. "You may have turned out better than most people here, but living like this gets old fast."

I shook my head. "I'm not having this conversation with you," I said as I got up and attempted to go anywhere but here, but then I paused and turned to her, feeling there was something I needed to get off my chest first. "You know, for as long as you've lived here, you never once complimented this place. You always saw everyone as less than you and never thought this place was anything other than a piece of dump!"

"I never looked down on anyone here!" she defended fiercely, her green eyes wide as she stared at me.

"Really? Have you ever stopped to listen to yourself? You have no faith in this place or the people!"

"One of the most important persons in my life was from here."

"And he might have been the only one you truly saw!"

"Because you made most of it hell for me!" she spat.

I clenched my teeth. "I've spent the last day apologizing and telling you how sorry I am for putting you through that. Whether or not you want to believe me is up to you at this point. I'm done." I moved past her, seeing the tears glisten in her eyes and feeling guiltier than ever, but I was too angry to stop – to apologize again or make this better. Maybe there was no happily ever after with Anna and me.

I was packing my overnight bag, ready to leave as soon as I got the chance, when I heard her name being called from the outside. Curious more than ever because I didn't recognize the voice, I got up and moved towards the door, almost bumping into Anna, who had a mostly shocked expression on her face. Without a word, she moved toward the door and opened it. A tall, slender man was on the other side, wearing a beanie and a coat while he shivered in the wind. For a brief second, he looked at Anna, and I could see his hazel eyes soften with relief, but then he spotted me and the expression on his face became as cold as the snow outside.

"Hector, what are you doing here?" Anna exclaimed, her face gone pale at the sight of him.

"I came to see you, of course. You weren't answering any of my texts."

"I told you not to bother because I was leaving soon. What are you doing?" she asked with an obvious edge to her voice, which told me she was annoyed, but it didn't take long for me to figure out that Hector was the ex-fiancé.

Hector's eyes lifted to my face, Anna's, and then to mine again. Obviously, this guy wanted an introduction that none of us was willing to give.

"Can we talk, please?"

She folded her arms and glanced at me through the corners of her eyes. "Come in."

I stepped aside, feeling a little angry and jealous that this guy just barged in, ready to stake his claim. I was about to head to the bedroom, thinking it was none of my business, when I paused at the sound of Hector's voice.

"Anna, mind introducing me?"

I stepped forward and extended my hand. I managed a smile that seemed to creak at the edges as I stared at Hector. "Hi, I'm Carter, Anna's...friend." Hector took my hand and nodded slowly as his gaze trailed across my face. He then looked to Anna, a visible clench to his teeth as he managed a smile similar to mine.

"Oh, I didn't know Anna had friends here," he said, looking between us.

I turned to Anna and raised a brow. She shot me a glare that could have killed me on the spot if looks could kill, but I decided to play with fire for a bit longer. "We go way back."

Hector's brows shot up. "Oh, Anna never mentioned you," he said, his eyes twitching a little.

"I could say the same," I smirked.

Anna stepped between us, turning to me with a warning in her mesmerizing green eyes. "Could you give us a minute, please?"

There was the little pout in place that I didn't even know she was cognisant of. It almost made me smile, but the feelings storming through me at the moment couldn't warrant such an action. I gritted my teeth and looked behind her at Hector, who had his brows furrowed as he tried to make sense of the situation.

I gave a curt nod and excused myself as I continued to pack. There was little I could hear, but some things I could make out from where I was.

"I heard about Patrick; I'm sorry."

"Thanks, but you need to tell me what you're doing here."

"I realized I made a big mistake letting go of you, and trust me, Anna, I would do anything for another chance," he said, and I gritted my teeth.

"It's been two months. While you were busy realizing the mistake you made by ending things, I was busy getting over you."

I almost smiled.

"I know deep down you still love me, and with just another try, we can be what we used to..."

"Hector-"

His voice lowered to a hushed whisper, and there was nothing else I could hear but faint mumblings, but the conversation was lengthy, and that probably wasn't a good sign for me. The idea of her warming back up with her ex caused me more inner turmoil than I could have anticipated. I was on edge, my palms went sweaty at the possibility of Anna reigniting an old flame. But what chance did I have against this bum, anyway? He knew her better than me – they had history, which wasn't a nightmare like the one we had.

But I couldn't picture her with someone else. I couldn't stand the thought of her wrapped in another man's arms, giving her smile to someone else – her body. The feeling was like a dagger to the heart.

I've never been so conflicted in my life – all for a woman who came into my life a few days ago and flipped it around in the best possible way.

A few minutes later, the door was pushed in, and Anna's face came into view. She couldn't meet my gaze for one second, and I guess that was enough of an answer for me.

"I'm leaving with Hector."

I clenched my teeth as the world crashed into me – as the thing I had feared the most became a reality. Anna had made her choice, and it wasn't me. Of course, it wasn't. I wasn't good enough for her, and she knew that as much as I did.

"Okay," I managed, my voice a little hoarse.

She stood there for a couple more seconds before she finally said, "You can have the house. There's obviously nothing left for me here." And then she was gone before I could even react.

I wanted to run after her, tell her that I wanted her with everything I had within me. I wanted to tell her that we could make this work and figure something out, but I knew it was a reach. We were just two people who were good in bed... that's all.

But somehow, my heart had something else to say.

TWO DAYS AFTER ANNA left, nothing seemed the same. It was as if I had found the missing piece in my life, and it was gone again now that she was. My nights were restless because all I wanted was her body on mine, snuggled up against me while I took in lung fills of her sweet scent. I was back home, and my bed was cold while she continued to plague my mind with her sweet memories.

But she made her choice, and I had to accept that and get her out of my head no matter how hard. I couldn't fit into Anna's idea of life, and I probably couldn't be with someone who hated the place I loved with all my heart. But could I even blame her for hating the place when her experience here was mostly hell because of me? Her throwing it in my face when I thought we had gotten past it was even worse.

"You look like shit," Andrew scoffed as he pulled up a chair around the counter.

"Thanks," I replied dryly.

"I heard Cambridge went back to the big city."

"She did."

"I thought you'd look happier."

"Well, I'm not exactly in a mood," I said as I filled his cup with his much-loved beer.

"Don't tell me you fell in love with the minx," he laughed.

"Don't be silly."

"I saw the way you looked at her."

"It doesn't even matter at this point. She is back home, and I'm where I need to be. Simple."

"Something tells me you want to be with her," he said as he raised a brow and drank his beer.

"We don't always get what we want in life, do we, Andrew?"

"It doesn't hurt to try."

"I can't just pick up and leave my life behind-"

"Why the hell not?!" he exclaimed. "This place has nothing to offer but fresh air!"

I rolled my eyes. "What's wrong with you people thinking Greenvale is trash?" I snapped.

"It's not exactly Dubai, bro. I'd choose a pretty woman and good pussy anytime over this place," he said, choking up a laugh.

I shook my head and continued to wipe the washed glasses.

"The only time Greenvale ever had some hope was when the Cambridge's came, and then that turned out to be the biggest shit show ever. All I'm saying is, the town needs a little work, and until someone is willing to come along with big pockets to change that, it isn't worth it," he shrugged. "You find a girl like Anna Cambridge in your lifetime, man, you fucking chase her until she stops. Life is too fucking short not to take the risk."

I stared at Andrew as he drank his beer. By morning, he would probably forget ever saying any of this to me, but I knew it would stick with me for a lifetime because it was definitely food for thought.

Chapter 9

Anna

"ARE YOU SURE YOU'RE okay?" Maria asked, a look of concern and pity on her face.

"Come on, Mar, you've asked me the same question a dozen times."

"And each time you've provided me with answers that are far from the truth," she defended as she shot up a brow.

"How do you know they're not the truth?"

"Because I know you!"

I huffed out a breath. "Fine, I am not okay, but it's pointless to miss a man who probably doesn't even feel the same way about me."

'You don't know that."

"Well, he isn't here, is he? Carter will never leave Greenvale," I said as I shook my head and reached for the tub of ice cream on the coffee table.

"You've got to give him more credit than that. People can surprise you."

I rolled my eyes. "I'm a little tired of surprises at this point. I just want to move on with my life, like he's obviously doing right now."

"It doesn't help that you left the cabin hand in hand with Hector. I mean, what's the guy supposed to think?"

"I didn't-" I sighed. "Hector and I aren't together. I was just angry with Carter and wanted to leave. He didn't put up a fight when he saw me leaving."

"Okay, so maybe you both should swallow your pride for a sec, but there's no point in being here moping all the time when you could get his number, call him and tell him how you feel," she said before she walked off, leaving me there with nothing but my thoughts.

I shook my head and jammed the spoon in the tub of ice cream as if it were the cause of my frustrations. It was stupid to expect Carter to come chasing after me, anyway. After all, we had never discussed feelings or a future and the closest we came to that it started a fight. I should never have asked him to come to New York; I should have just accepted that what we had was just a short fling and nothing else. There was no future for us. Carter was in one place, and I was in another, plain and simple, but why was I missing him so much? Sure, the sex had been great, but something else made my heart flutter whenever I thought of him, and surely it was insane, seeing we had just been together for less than a week, but there was no doubt there was something else there... something that now made me feel incomplete.

A MONTH HAD PASSED since my visit to Greenvale. I was in a new apartment, and was finally moving on with my life. Even though I still couldn't stop thinking about Carter, I would get over him eventually. Just as I did Hector, who was still fighting for a chance in my life. There was just no getting back together with him. Hector's chapter in my life was over. I still wished I could swallow my pride and get in touch with Carter, but I couldn't force a man to do something he didn't want to do. He was obviously happy in Greenvale, and there was nothing I could do to change that. It was just not meant to be.

I shuffled out of bed, but I could feel bile rise to my throat as soon as I did. Slapping my hands over my mouth, I ran to the bathroom to spill the contents of my stomach into the toilet bowl. I suddenly felt weak and nauseous as I sat on the floor, trying to regain my strength. As soon as I tried to get up, the feeling came again, and I found myself heaving even more.

Ten minutes later, I finally got hold of myself when the feeling started to fade. I groaned as I made my way to the bedroom and lay in the bed, trying to figure out where this feeling came from. Yesterday, I was fine, and today, it felt like I was going to die. I hadn't even eaten anything out of the norm, so I was a bit puzzled as to why I was feeling like this. There was one explanation at the back of my mind, but the very thought made me feel like throwing up all over again.

It couldn't be possible! My stomach churned at the possibility of pregnancy. It had to be something else. No matter how many times I tried to convince myself it was something else, it returned to this. I could feel it in the pit of my stomach but was scared to think of such a thing. I had been on birth control.

Wanting to ease my mind, I got up and searched through a small box with random things from my last apartment. I had bought two pregnancy tests once when I had a scare with Hector and had only used one when it turned out negative.

My hands started to shake as I took the stick and headed for the bathroom. It felt like I had run a marathon with the way my heart was beating fast. I was breathless as I waited for the results, sweat beading on my forehead as I waited for the time to pass.

After five minutes, my palms were sweaty, and I was scared more than ever to look down on the stick. Somehow, I knew before I even looked that it would be positive. It was just a feeling I had, and when I finally looked, it was confirmed.

I gasped as I stared at the two bright lines and felt my lips tremble as tears flowed from my eyes. The feeling was bittersweet because I'd always wanted a child, but on the other hand, it was with a man who I wasn't even sure I'd see again. There was no way I could tell him this when I didn't even know if he wanted kids. Would he even believe me? I could feel myself spiraling the longer I thought about it. There were so many questions, and yet not enough answers.

My eyes were puffy when I stopped crying, but I managed to take a shower and get myself something to eat before I dragged myself to bed again. As soon as I was about to lie down, a knock came at the door.

I was in no mood for company but figured it was Maria, which was probably a good thing, seeing I needed some support right now.

I pulled on a robe and dragged myself to the door, but the person standing there was not my best friend.

I could feel the blood drain from my face when I laid eyes on Carter.

He was here, and he looked more handsome than ever. His stubble had grown out to a medium beard, and his hair was even taller as it hung past his shoulders.

"Ca-Carter, what are you doing here?" I said in what sounded like a whisper.

He took a hand from behind him and presented a bouquet with a smile on his face. "I er – I wasn't sure which one you liked, so I got a little of everything," he said.

I bit the inside of my lips to stop them from shaking as I acknowledged the beautiful flowers in front of me. I felt as if I were going to swoon, and I didn't know whether it was because I was still exhausted from spilling my guts or seeing him again.

I took the flowers. "Thank you, but why are you here?" I swallowed.

He looked over my shoulder. "May I come in? This doesn't seem like the right place to talk."

It took me a second to process before I stepped to the side to allow him entry. He ducked under the doorpost and walked to the living area.

"Have a seat. How did you even find me?" I asked as I put the flowers down and took a seat.

"I er... I found your address in one of Patrick's journals."

"I always told him that whenever he wanted to visit the Big City, he'd know where to find me."

Carter nodded and placed his elbows on his knees as he looked at me. "I've had some time to think these past weeks, Anna – to really think about what I wanted for myself and my life, and certain things have become clear."

I swallowed as I listened to him, my heart galloping in my chest.

"I know you and your ex are probably back together, but I didn't want to let more time pass without telling you how I feel. I've never felt more alive than I did when I had you by my side.

You made everything seem better, and I only realized how big of a mistake I'd made by not telling you sooner..."

My eyes became foggy, a single tear hanging on my lash as it awaited a blink to fall. "Carter..."

"You don't have to feel the same, but I don't want to live life knowing I never tried. I love you, Anna."

The tears finally fell at his words, and my heart did a double flip in my chest as I looked at him and saw that he meant every word. I wanted to tell him I loved him, too, but so many other things needed to be sorted out. We weren't on the same page with a lot of things.

I sniffed. "Hector and I aren't together. I told him no before I left the cabin," I confessed and his face visibly lit up, his whiskey-colored eyes wide. "But we have different views, Carter; your heart is in Greenvale, and mine is here. There's no way it would work."

He briskly moved to sit beside me, holding my hands as he stared into my eyes. "I'd gladly move to the end of the earth as long as you're by my side. I realize that now. I can have someone manage the bar there while I find something else here. I have it all figured out, Anna. Just tell me you'll have me."

More tears streamed down my face as I listened to him. My heart was bursting with joy, and all I wanted to do was throw my hands around him and kiss him, but it wasn't fair to expect him to do all this for me, was it?

"I can't ask you to do that. It was unfair of me to expect you to pick up and leave everything behind," I cried.

His hands tightened in mine as he held my gaze. "All I want is right here, right now."

I managed a smile and was about to do what I was desperately craving to do for weeks – kiss him, but then the breakfast rose to my throat, and I had to rush to the bathroom to empty it. I prayed that Carter wouldn't follow me, but as soon as I flushed, he was at the door, looking down at me with wide eyes and an open mouth as his face changed into one of pure concern.

"Are you okay?" he asked as he came in and peeled me off the floor and into his arms. I realized the test was still sitting on the counter from earlier, and as soon as I spotted it, so did he.

He stiffened against me, and I paused as I watched the series of emotions play across his face. He looked to the stick and then at me repeatedly before his gaze finally settled on mine for answers.

"Is...Is this real?" he asked, searching my eyes.

I nodded.

"Whose... Is it mine?" his voice cracked, his eyes glistening.

I sniffed and nodded. "Yes."

He didn't react right away. It was as if he hadn't processed the information right away, but when he did, he choked up a laugh and placed one hand over his mouth as he looked to the stick again. I couldn't help but smile at the evident joy on his face. The way he pulled me tighter against him and hugged me.

"I just found out this morning," I told him while inhaling his scent, feeling at home.

He held my face in his palms. "Were you planning on telling me if I hadn't shown up here?" he asked.

"Of course, I just didn't know how, but I would."

He smiled from ear to ear, each pearly white in perfect view. "You have no idea how happy you've made me," he said, kissing me. I kissed him back, feeling so much lighter than I had felt hours ago. There were so many things that we had to talk about now, but all that mattered was that Carter was by my side.

"I love you, too," I said, and his hold tightened on me.

I brushed my teeth and went back to the bedroom to find him seated at the end of the bed, smiling when he saw me.

My stomach churned as I looked at him, but it wasn't from nausea. It was that I felt everything just by looking at him. I slowly moved across the room, and he stood – our eyes never leaving each other. I stood before him while my heart beat like drums in my chest. My eyes trailed across the wide expanse of his chest – drinking in every muscle that was imprinted, the small bits of hair exposed beneath the opened buttons. I swallowed as I raised my hand and slid it along his neck, using my thumb to caress his skin.

He didn't say anything; he just kept looking at me with undeniable lust in his darkened eyes. The atmosphere became thick as we stood there, breathing in each other. I wanted him so badly that it took everything within me to go slow, but I wanted to take note of every single part of Carter. Plant him in my memory.

I started to unbutton his shirt, dropping it to the floor as I came in contact with his beautifully sculpted body. I then reached for his buckle and pulled down his pants, giving it the same treatment.

He stood naked in front of me, just watching me watch him. I licked my lips, almost salivating at the sight of him. Every single inch of his body was hard, including his cock, which throbbed between us. My body was on fire – the room felt congested as I refrained from jumping Carter.

I placed a hand on his chest and dragged my hand across his bulky pecs and his hard six-pack. I circled him as my hand continued to slide across his skin while he just stood there, allowing me to admire him. My fingers explored his firm buttocks, taking in every detail before I was in front of him again.

He had a smirk on his face but said nothing at first. Carter was truly a God in his own right, and truthfully, I had never seen a more beautiful man.

"I think it's only right that I give the same treatment." His voice was husky and raw as he said the words, and my breath hitched as I awaited his touch.

His hands found the straps of my silk nightgown. I held his gaze as he peeled them from my shoulders and watched as the fabric shimmied to my ankles. I swallowed hard as Carter's eyes went along with it, his eyes taking in my hardened nipples. His gaze traveled lower to my belly, lingering there before a faint smile crossed his lips. I couldn't help my own smile but almost caved when his fingers finally touched me. A single finger circled my nipples before he slid it across the other. Shivers ran down my spine as his hand began to bathe my flesh as if binding it to memory.

"Your skin is so soft," he said. "So perfect." He caressed the flare of my hips, moving straight around my ass before he pulled me into him. I gasped as my skin met his, his cock crushed against my stomach with his precum seeping into my skin. Carter's hands trailed up my back before he paused at the nape of my neck, forcing me to pry my neck up to him.

My open mouth was an opportunity for him to claim it because, in the next second, I was tasting his hungry mouth, sucking on his sweet tongue as fire consumed my body. I moaned as I kissed him, my nipples becoming harder at his touch.

Carter's hands found my ass as he pulled me into his arms. I wrapped my legs around his narrow waist, latching my hands around his neck as I tried to show him all I felt within one kiss. He then turned, and I fell to the bed with him hovering over me. We broke from our kiss for a brief second but found our way back within a second. I sucked on his tongue and could feel myself pooling between my legs. Carter was right there with his cock brushing my sex in a tease that almost drove me mad. My mind was reeling, I was on fire, and all I needed was him inside me. It was that simple.

"Carter, please... I want you so much," I whispered against his mouth. He stared down at me, his hair framing his face while the sun coming through the window highlighted every strand.

I felt his cock at my entrance and held my breath as the hard head teased me, causing me to spread my legs even further apart. My mouth slowly parted as he entered me, inch by inch. I closed my eyes to bask in the bliss.

"Look at me," he demanded brusquely.

My heart was about to jump out of my chest as I opened my eyes to his. A single vein was popping in his forehead as he took his time entering me. "Oh, oh God," I mewled, reaching for his face to caress it as he caressed my pussy with his cock.

I could feel my sensitive flesh parting to accommodate him, every single nerve in my body on high alert as pleasure flowed through my body. I knew I was soaking because, despite his size, he was sliding effortlessly inside me. The feeling was almost overwhelming as I stared into his eyes while he made love to me – it was something I had never considered would be so intense.

Carter lowered his lips to mine as he kissed me while he slowly started to move inside me. I moaned against his mouth as he released every inch inside me before pulling back to go again. My flesh hugged his, and I started lifting my hips to experience the feeling of having him deep inside me. He sucked on my lips and nipped my flesh with his teeth as he filled me with slow, agonizing thrusts that made me feel like losing my mind.

"Oh, Carter... please fuck me harder. I'm about to lose my mind," I whimpered as he paused and looked down at me.

"Won't it...I don't want to hurt you or the baby," his forehead wrinkled in confusion.

I caressed his cheeks and smiled. "I promise you won't," I said to him.

He kissed me yet again and eased up on his knees, and pulled me up a little by my ass. He entered me with a single stroke that had my mouth falling open. He then started to move inside me with long and hard strokes that had my tits jiggling in my chest. I gasped and bit my lips, stretching to reach his chest, which was out of reach. But then he leaned into me, his cock sinking keeper as he kissed me yet again and began to slam into me. I gasped against his mouth and tied my hands around his neck, keeping him in place.

My pussy tightened, a small quiver racking my body as he moved from my mouth to suckle on my neck, still moving inside me. I arched my neck, closed my eyes and hung to Carter, my nails scraping his flesh as I floated in pleasure. My hands slid from his sweaty back to his ass, pressing him deeper into me as shockwaves started to flow through my body.

I opened my mouth to speak, but a scream came out instead. My pussy started to clench around him, every stroke becoming better – more intense. Too good. I couldn't hold back. I started to quiver, all my nerves on end as I orgasmed.

Carter's body slid against mine as he looked down at me and licked across my mouth. "I love you so much," he said between breaths before he bucked inside me, and the warmth of his seed filled me.

I lay there in complete bliss as my body reached new horizons and came back down. Every touch after my orgasm made me sensitive, and I couldn't help my shiver every now and then. But even after Carter pulled out, he slid down my body and kissed my stomach, which rose and fell from my heavy breaths. He kissed my skin, and I could feel it all the way in my stomach.

Epilogue

"ARE YOU SURE YOU WANT to do this, Mar?" I asked as I paused my packing to get her reaction.

"I'm positive, Anna; you don't have to worry about me regretting my decision further down the line," she smiled. "And plus, you know I never really liked the city, to begin with."

I smiled as I resumed the task at hand. "Well, I'm happy I'm going to have my best friend with me every step of the way."

She grinned. "Me too. Jason is beyond excited too. He has so many ideas for Greenvale," she said, referring to her fiancé.

"I'm happy."

Maria moved toward me and hugged me. "I'm really proud of you, you know."

"Aww, thank you."

"You and Carter have come really far. He's basically famous for his recipes, and now that you'll be moving back to Greenvale, I'm sure it'll attract many tourists, which will be good for Jason's resort," she geeked, rubbing her hands together in excitement as she suppressed a squeal.

"Exactly. It'll be perfect."

"Where are they, anyway? Our flight is in two hours."

"Carter went to get some diaper cream for Joshua. They should be back any minute now."

We continued to chat for a few more minutes until the door flew open when Carter bustled through with baby Joshua on his side. As soon as she saw me, he gave me a toothy smile, and I couldn't help the joy that bubbled up inside me at the precious sight. I moved toward them and kissed Carter before I took the baby and ruffled his silky blonde hair.

"I hope we didn't keep you guys waiting too long," Carter said as he looked between me and Maria.

"You're just in time. We should get going soon," Maria said as she pulled up a bag and fished out her phone from her pockets. "I'm gonna call Jason and see where he's at. He should be there before us."

"Ok, I'm gonna get Joshua into some fresh clothes and then we're all set," I said as I moved to the bedroom to do just that. Carter followed behind me and claimed my mouth as soon as I placed the baby on the bed.

I moaned against him, feeling the sliver of desire that coursed through me when his lips touched mine. Nothing had changed; Carter could still manage to get me all aroused with one kiss, and I had the same effect on him. His hands crept down my ass and held it in a gentle squeeze as he deepened the kiss. I moaned and tore my lips away from his, laughing lightly.

"Remember, we have company."

He groaned and pulled me in to nuzzle my neck. "I missed you so much," he said, and I almost shivered from his hot breath on my skin.

"I missed you too, but we've gotta go, or else we'll miss our flight," I warned.

"Yeah, I can't believe we're moving back to Greenvale," he said.

"Are you happy?" I asked.

"I am. As much as I loved the city, it's nice to be back. It's been a year and a half," he said as he smiled at me. "The big question is, are you happy?"

"I am. I love that I can go back and do what my father couldn't, which is to make it a better place."

Carter smiled at me and pulled me in for another kiss. "That's my girl. I love you; have I told you that lately?" he asked as he smiled down at me.

I made a face. "Um, maybe not as often. A few hours is a long time," I grinned.

He chuckled. "Well, I love you."

"I love you too, babe. Now let's go; we have a plane to catch."

BEING BACK AT GREENVALE always brought back memories, but it was safe to say this time was different. There was no bitterness – just an abundance of love I could feel around me. I had my family and friends who had grown to become just as close – here to make a difference with me.

It wasn't like this was the first time I'd been back since I left Carter here. We came back five months after getting married when Maria came to us with the idea of transforming Greenvale. Of course, Carter hopped on to the idea, and the more we spoke of our plans, the more we were willing to make them a reality.

Carter still had his bar and was planning to expand in the near future while he worked the first year at Jason's resort, which had spiked up the employment rate in the area. It was the talk of the town, and everyone was eager for the official grand opening, which was to take place in a few days.

Carter had made a name for himself in the city and created a reputation that wasn't limited to New York, and everyone was excited about his next move.

There were new developments in Greenvale and that was clear as day when we landed and began to drive to the cabin after dropping off Maria and Jason at the resort.

"Can you believe that one year has made such a vast difference?" I said in amazement as I looked out the window.

"Yeah, that's a lot of time. I fell in love with you in less than a week, and look how much difference that made," Carter said, and I turned to him with a smile.

"That's a very good point." I kissed him lightly on the lips while Joshua shuffled around in the middle.

I sighed when we arrived at the cabin and couldn't help my smile as I feasted my eyes on the beauty. We had expanded a bit and incorporated the rustic cabin look with a bit of a modern vibe. The windows had been replaced with large, floor-to-ceiling ones that added a lot of natural light to the house. Superb for the content creation I would do at home while still keeping in touch with nature. It had been a lot as we didn't want to change the whole thing. We wanted what Patrick had to remain but still wanted it bigger for our family.

It was perfect, and now that it was summer, everything seemed lush and bright with the glow of the sun, which just made everything better. Carter came up behind me as I gazed at the beauty ahead of us and wrapped his hands around my shoulder.

"Well, When Hendricks told us that Patrick had left the house to us, I never imagined this would be the outcome," he said as he smiled at me.

I grinned. "Nothing we have now ever crossed my mind a year and a half ago," I admitted.

"But I'm glad we crossed paths again. I can't imagine my life without you in it, Anna."

His words were soft as he looked deep within my soul and said the words to me. I felt it deep inside my heart and felt a burst of emotions overwhelm me. My eyes got foggy as tears began to pool in them. Carter reached for me and kissed me hard, wanting to seal it all with a toe-curling kiss.

This was home.

Off-Limits Coach Daddy

Izzie Vee

Erotic & Forbidden[1]

IZZIE VEE[2]

1. https://www.amazon.com/s?k=izzie+vee&i=digital-text&crid=31LQJTEQYT2EE&sprefix=izzie+vee%2Cdigital-text%2C121&ref=nb_sb_noss
2. https://www.amazon.com/s?k=izzie+vee&i=digital-text&crid=31LQJTEQYT2EE&sprefix=izzie+vee%2Cdigital-text%2C121&ref=nb_sb_noss

Cover Design by Izzie Vee
Cover Photo by VitalikRadko on Depositphotos.com

Table of Contents

Chapter 1

Bella

"Oh my gosh, Bella, I can't believe it's almost the end of summer, and you haven't allowed yourself to have some fun," Dian rolled her eyes and threw her phone to the chair in a huff.

I looked up from my notebook and placed it to the side to study her from across the room. "I've had fun," I simply said before deciding to elaborate. "We went rock climbing and went to the movies a couple of times," I defended.

Dian scoffed as she approached me, sitting at the edge of my bed. "I'm not talking about that sort of fun, silly," she said as her green eyes met mine. "I'm talking about some skin-to-skin, sexy time, kind of fun," she grinned, looking at me wickedly.

I bit the inside of my lips, feeling the heat that assailed my cheeks. I looked away, but Dian reached for my hand, demanding my attention. I licked my lips, trying to meet her gaze. "Dian, you already know I'm not that kind of person," I almost whispered.

She huffed and slumped her shoulders with her gaze now lazy. "Are you really planning on leaving college a virgin?" she asked, raising a brow.

I swallowed. "I'm in no rush to hook up with random people I'll maybe regret later on in life."

Dian rubbed her forehead and shook her head. "You aren't even open to having a real relationship, anyway. It's like you've completely written off men!" she exclaimed with a bit of mirth to her voice before glancing at me with wide eyes. "OMG, I didn't even think about it, but are you... are you into girls?"

It was my time to roll my eyes. "No, I'm not but..." I trailed off with a sigh. "I don't know. I just want to get through college without the drama."

Dian sighed heavily. "Ok, but can I ask two things of you before we head back to campus this term?"

I stared into her soft green eyes. Dian had grown to become my best friend, but I didn't know whether I could agree to a promise, especially after the conversation we'd had. Surely it would be something related to me finding a boyfriend or having sex.

"What is it?" I asked, clearing my throat.

She shuffled a bit closer with a smile on her face. "Can I take you shopping for clothes that aren't gowns and skirts?" she laughed.

I bit back mine. "I actually like my clothes," I said.

"I know, but we don't have much time left in college. Can you be a bit more spontaneous for me ...please?" she said with a cheesy grin.

I straightened. "Dian, are you ashamed of me?"

Her eyes immediately widened. "What? No, never! Why would you think that?" she said, clearly taken aback, and I immediately felt bad for assuming such a thing. "You could wear garbage bags for all I care. I just know you're missing out, and I don't want you to leave college, regretting that you never did certain things. I want you to see that you can have your As and your fun at the same time."

I bit my lips in thought. "What was the second thing?"

Her eyes lit up again. "There's a new club opening on the weekend, and I want us to go together. You're my best friend, and I want to share the experience with you."

I would have said no right away, but the last bit really warmed my heart in some strange way. I appreciated that Dian was my best friend, and she could see that as much as I could. We were complete opposites, but here we were by some source of nature. Dian was a socialite, and I wasn't. She had over fifty thousand followers on all social media and was the 'it girl' at school, but she didn't mind that I didn't act crazy or swoon in her presence. She said it was refreshing that I wasn't fake, and I was happy that she wasn't either, despite being a popular face. She always kept it real, and I loved her for it.

"Ok, sure. I will revamp my wardrobe, and I'll go to the club with you," I said.

She squealed and clapped her hands as she stared at me with adoration.

"OMG, I can't wait to go shopping!" she exclaimed as she got up and went for her discarded phone. "There are a few online stores we could try too. I'm an ambassador for one downtown that's doing really good since I did that haul on my YouTube. We could try that and then maybe head to the mall. Are you planning on doing something about your hair too? Pink highlights like me, maybe?" she clasped her hands and smiled at me.

I was barely processing all she was saying with how fast she spoke, but the last question caught me off guard when I did. "Er no... I never really gave it much thought. I think I'll let it stay as it, plus, I don't think I could rock pink hair," I laughed timidly as I reached to fiddle with strands of my long brown hair.

"You could rock anything, trust me. You don't even have any idea how gorgeous you are," she said as she typed away on her phone. "Sometimes, I wish I had your big brown eyes and your long legs," she groaned.

I smiled. "You are beautiful, and I'm sure you know that, Dian."

She looked up from her phone at me. "I know, but still..." she sighed. "I can't wait to get you all dolled up! Omg, this will be epic, just watch and guess what – you don't even have to worry about the cash. I will cover everything!" she said, flashing a smile at me.

My mouth fell open. "Dian, I can't ask you to do that."

"Good thing you don't have to ask," she said as she jumped on the bed and shoved her phone in front me. "Anyway, I don't want to hear any arguments about it. I can, and I will... look through their page and tell me if you see anything you'd like. It's better to secure it if you're sure, y'know."

There was so much going on. I almost felt overwhelmed but was distracted by Dian's constant prodding and the clothes that immediately caught my eye as I started to inspect them. "I think I have the red to this, but the black would definitely suit you," she said as she tapped on a bodycon dress that was just simple and sleek. "I'm gonna grab a coke in your fridge and be right back – want anything?" she said as she placed her phone in my hand and stood.

"No thanks."

I sighed as she left the room and scrolled through the options. I tried to imagine myself in each piece of clothing and found it a tad bit difficult to do so. There wasn't anything as modest as the type I wore. There were tiny dresses, skin-tight leather pants and shorts and other stuff that looked like they weren't even finished. I wanted to throw the phone to the side and go to bed, but I wanted to do this for Dian, and if I were completely honest, part of me was excited to see myself in such a light.

I got up from the bed and walked to the standing mirror at the end of my room. I was wearing this nude-colored dress that fell down my body like it was twice my size. I bit my lips and gathered a bit of fabric behind me, pulling it back so the dress latched onto my skin. I scraped my hair to the side and tilted my neck as I stared at myself. I never imagined myself in such a position – so sexually appealing – but I definitely saw where those dresses on Dian's phone would hug my body as this did with manual adjustments.

My heart thrummed in my chest, and for the first time in forever, I decided to open up myself to the idea of a complete makeover.

For as long as I can remember, I've always been the shy girl so focused on her studies and making her parents proud that seemingly nothing else mattered to her. I had one friend in high school who was more of a study partner than anything else, but it worked for the time being until we graduated and went our separate ways. That gave me more reasons to believe that maybe I wouldn't be a socialite in life, but I was brilliant, and that was all that mattered to me for a while.

I never imagined that once I got to college, my roommate would be a firecracker who implored me to take life by the balls, literally. The very moment Dian Maynard found out I was a college virgin, she made it a priority to convince me to make a change. '*This is college,*' she would say. *'We should be studying dicks more than subjects.'* The very idea grossed me out, but I always enjoyed her rather graphic take on sex and college life.

The truth was, I didn't even think I was capable of attracting members of the opposite sex. After being embarrassed in elementary school for almost kissing a boy I thought liked me back, I had made it a priority to steer clear of them. I chose to wear long skirts and sundresses with sweaters, knowing they wouldn't show even an inch of skin. Though I got teased about it in high school, the goal was achieved, and I was happy about that, at least.

But now, with Dian, the pressure was on, and I frequently contemplated ditching my whole wardrobe just to give her kind of lifestyle a try. I was tempted, especially when she bragged about the men she'd been with and how great the sex was. I guess part of me wanted to explore such intimacies. The closest I ever came to sex was watching romance movies, and I felt some sort of tingling between my legs. It was strange, but I knew what it was, though I'd never given myself the satisfaction of even trying to please myself. I didn't know what it was, but part of me was scared to make such a huge step.

DIAN STAYED THAT NIGHT, getting up at the peak of dawn just because she was so excited for the day ahead. I hauled myself out of bed and brushed my teeth before going down for breakfast. My mom was already in her scrubs and looked between us and smiled as she plated scrambled eggs while my dad sat there drinking coffee and reading the morning paper.

"You guys seem to be in a chipper mood," Mom said as she approached the counter with two plates she placed in front of us.

Dian perked up and smiled brightly – definitely the morning person I wasn't. "We are going shopping today. I'm pretty excited about it."

My mom's gaze immediately landed on me. "Oh, that sounds fun." I scratched my head and reached for the toast, allowing Dian to take the lead.

"Yeah, I can't wait. We have so many places in mind."

My dad finally looked up. "Honey, do you need cash?"

I opened my mouth to answer, but, of course, Dian beat me to it. "Oh, don't worry about that. It's all on me," she smiled.

Mom's smile fell as she glanced at me and then at my best friend. "We couldn't ask you to do that. You are a student yourself," she said with a half-laugh.

Dian playfully fanned her off. "Oh stop, it's not a problem really," she said, her gaze moving towards her phone, which started to ring. "That's my mom... excuse me," she said as she got up and walked to the other room.

Mom walked towards me and sighed, holding my hands. "Honey, are you okay with all this?" she asked, blue eyes boring into mine.

"I am, Mom; Dian means well," I smiled, but she didn't look at all convinced.

"Judging from Dian's excitement, something tells me you aren't going to be shopping for your style of clothing," she gave a tight smile and squeezed my hands. "Just know you don't have to feel pressured to-"

I pulled in a breath. "Mom, I'm not being pressured. This is something I really want to do," I said as I looked over my shoulders. "I'm just allowing my fashionista best friend to lead the way."

"Well, let us give you some cash at least," Dad intervened. "I heard what Dian said, but you should always practice independence. Who knows what can happen?" he said as he reached for his wallet and handed me a few bills.

I sighed and took it. "Thanks, Dad."

Mom reached for my cheeks and caressed them with a smile before she returned to the stove. I filled my mouth with eggs as I went into deep thought. I glanced at my parents and suddenly realized that I was probably the way I was now because of how my parents treated me. I was their only child – a miracle really – since my mom had gotten pregnant with me when they had both thought it was impossible. They met in college, and my dad was my mom's first-ever boyfriend. I guess she was a lot like me in that sense, but I'd have found a boyfriend already if that were the case.

My mom had always made it her duty to tell me to stay focussed on what was important, and she didn't allow me to guess what that was either. She always said my studies came first – being successful – as no one could take that away from me.

That had become a mantra, and maybe without realizing it, I had taken those words to heart... but it was now time to make a change. Well, not really, but I was always good at multitasking.

WE WERE AT THE SPOT Dian had basically reserved for us two hours later. As soon as I entered the store, I felt out of place. The remarkable fits on the models and even the ones the employees wore were so stark in difference and quality than what I wore. I immediately hugged myself and glanced down at my dress that brushed my ankles and the all-stars on my feet.

Dian reached for my arm and tugged me towards the clerk at the front, who had a smile on her face until she saw me. "So, this was my friend I was telling you about – Bella."

I managed a smile, and she did her best to do the same, although I could tell it literally pained her to do so. "I see why you were in such a rush." Her smile came easy after that statement because she thought her 'joke' was funny.

"Could we see the ones I had asked you to pick out, please?" Dian asked while I tried to do anything but stare in the face of the blue-eyed bleach blonde.

"Of course, this way," she said as she moved from around the counter to a rack with a few pieces.

We started sorting through them, Dian just beaming as she examined each fit placed against my body. The clerk watched with folded arms as she scrutinized each fit with a twisted mouth. I assessed myself in the mirror and found myself smiling when a few fits were to my liking. I tried a few while Dian sat as a judge outside the changing room. Luckily for me, someone with seemingly more wealth and fashion sense had come in and caught the clerk's attention. Somehow, I felt more confident not having her here – seeing the joy on Dian's face when I stepped out time after time. She was literally jumping on her feet and clapping, and I couldn't help my grin and the happiness that bubbled up inside me at the sight.

"Oh, my gosh! I could literally cry right now," she squealed and wiped fake tears from her eyes when I came out in a dress that reached mid-thigh. It was a soft lilac with fine straps and dipping cleavage. The material had that kind of scrunched look with adjustable strings at the side, which, to my amazement, could make the dress tighter and even shorter. I turned to the mirror, and Dian came up behind me, squeezing my shoulders as she grinned.

"Well, it's pretty obvious which one you'll be wearing to the club."

I giggled. "We haven't even checked the other stores yet."

"Doesn't matter. This is the one. I swear, it's perfect – except for the bra – you'll have to ditch that." My eyes went to the black straps that were peeking out along with the cups at the cleavage.

"Yeah, you're right."

"So, what do you think?"

My eyes roamed over my body, and I could feel the heat in my cheeks as I admired myself. "I love it."

"Well then, there's still hope in this world after all," she teased, and I grinned, swatting at her hands.

We checked a couple more stores and decided to have lunch at the mall – close to the last store we went to. We were sitting under an umbrella and eating burgers. I was pretty exhausted from all the walking and was happy to be at one spot away from the crowd.

"Well, today wasn't so bad, was it?" she asked as she bit into her food.

"Not bad at all. It was fun actually," I smiled.

"Great. I think we have a fair amount, too," she said.

I glanced at the clutter of bags at our feet and raised a brow. "Well, that's one way of putting it."

We ate in silence until I almost choked on my fries when I heard a voice behind me.

"Dian?"

Dian looked up, her eyes widening. The person moved from behind me while Dian stood to accept the hug he offered. "Oh, my gosh, Jace, what are you doing here?" she asked as she pulled apart from him to examine his face with wide eyes.

He chuckled. I still couldn't see anything, but his ashy blonde hair as his back was turned to me.

"We decided to move here since it was a bit closer to school. My dad also got a new job offer, so that's that."

"That's awesome man; welcome to L.A."

"Thanks."

"Jace, I want you to meet my best friend, Bella. You might have seen us on campus a couple of times. Bella, this is Jace... football prodigy and soon-to-be captain of our team come this semester."

He chuckled and turned to me with his smile still in place. His clear blue eyes were the first thing I was drawn to – they seemed hypnotic, and I hadn't even realized they were as such until now when I was this close to him. I knew of him on campus – he was the popular kid – and would always see him with his friends or the girls who would frequently swarm him.

I extended my hand and offered a smile. "Nice to meet you."

His grip was firm, but there was a softness in his hands I wasn't expecting, considering the sport he played. "The pleasure is all mine."

He had a smile that I wasn't too innocent to understand, and I knew was partly the reason why the females loved him so much. I didn't know if it were natural or just a tactic he used to charm females, but I knew better than to think of the latter with a guy like Jace. There was no way he would find me attractive – especially in this get-up.

The handshake lingered for longer than necessary until I pulled my hand away and cleared my throat.

Dian flashed me a look, a smile on her face that told me she was up to no good. "So, Jace, how's LA treating you so far?"

"Great, I just need someone to show me around the place. The good spots, that is," he smiled, looking between us.

Dian's eyes lit up. "Oh, there's this club-"

I instantly stepped on her feet beneath the table and watched as she cut herself off and bit her lips, flashing me a dangerous look, but I figured she got the gist. Jace looked confused.

"What club?" he asked.

Dian shrugged. "Um... this new one that's opening up on the weekend, but um... we won't be able to go until next week," she lied.

"Oh, maybe we can all go together and hang out?" he said, looking at me.

I swallowed and looked to my burger.

"Yeah, sure; we can exchange numbers." Through the corner of my eye, I could see Dian handing him her phone and vice versa.

"Awesome, well, I'm looking forward to seeing you guys," I looked back up and found his eyes were still trained on me. "It was nice meeting you, Bella."

I managed a smile. "You too."

He smiled, "See you guys," and then he was gone.

I sighed and reached for my drink, taking a huge gulp.

"I can't believe you were gonna invite a complete stranger with us on Saturday," I argued.

"Jace is not a complete stranger. He's a great guy who, by the looks of it, was really into you," she wiggled her brows.

I scoffed. "Oh, please. Have you seen him?"

"Have you seen you? You've got to give yourself more credit y'know," she said with a warning look.

"Hmm, he's not really my type, anyway," I mumbled as I drank.

Dian's eyes widened. "You have a type? Since when?" she choked up a laugh.

I shrugged. "Well, I guess I just prefer dark brunettes like myself."

"Ouuu, but Jace is definitely handsome," she argued.

"He is, but I dunno, there's no spark or anything like that."

Dian laughed. "This isn't the movies or the romance novels, Bella. Electricity isn't going to run through your veins when you find 'the one'. It's all bull, and you're smart enough to know that."

"My parents said they knew they were each other's soulmates when they met. I believe it exists, and I don't think Jace is mine."

Dian rolled her eyes. "Well, no one is looking for soulmates in college. We're all just looking for a good time, and I'm confident Jace is someone who can show you that."

I sighed. "Ok, you already convinced me to change my wardrobe and go with you to this club. Maybe just go easy on the Jace argument, please. That's a definite no."

Dian sighed. "Ok, fine, I'll stop all the Jace talk," she said as she drank and eyed me over the rim of her cup.

I knew Dianne enough to know it would just be for a while before she started again.

Chapter 2

Bella

The weekend came faster than I was anticipating. I didn't know how exactly to explain the knot in my stomach, but it was there. I was by my vanity applying a little makeup to my face, happy that I had picked up on the skill in high school and intrigued by the technique. I was no pro, but I knew enough not to make me look like a plain Jane.

Dian was in the back, straightening her hair after deciding to add some more pink highlights a day prior. We were already dressed – me in my lilac dress and Dian deciding to go for leather leggings and a lacy crop top.

"I promise you, Bella – this is gonna be epic!" Dian said as she tried to suppress a scream.

I smiled, not knowing how true that would be, seeing I'd never been to a club in my life to gauge the experience. I didn't know what to expect, except for a ton load of people and loud music. Right now, I wasn't too keen on that either. I didn't anticipate the wandering gazes of men or their non-consensual touches. I didn't want any part of it but figured I would give Dian the pleasure by agreeing. Plus, a voice in my head constantly told me to get out of my shell. I didn't know how tonight would aid in that cause, but I guess there was only one way of finding out.

"Ok, ready?" she asked as she stood behind me with a smile on her blood-red lips. She brought her clasped hands to her mouth and stared down at me. "You look so fucking amazing, bestie."

I couldn't help my smile. "Thank you. Of course, you don't need me to tell you that you look stunning."

Dian grinned. "Ok, let's go... it's almost ten and it's ladies free before."

We got up and grabbed our purses before leaving the house. I was happy it was my parents' date night, and they had gone out. I don't think I could live down the look on their faces if they ever saw me in such a scandalous outfit. They were quite content with my conservative fits and had no qualms in accepting otherwise.

"So when we get there, stay by my side, okay. It's gonna get pretty hectic, and I just know the place is already packed," Dian said as she drove, eyes trained on the road.

I smiled at her motherly tone. "Doesn't sound like there will be room to even have fun."

"Don't worry, once we get a few drinks in, we'll be living for it," she glanced and me and winked.

I swallowed. "I er- I don't think I'll be having anything to drink," I admitted softly.

Dian darted her gaze toward me. "What? You can't be serious."

"Someone has to be the designated driver, and I know you'll be pretty out of it, so... I'm choosing not to."

"Listen, Bella. I don't need you to sacrifice your fun for me. If both of us get wasted, I know a lot of people I could call to get us. Don't worry."

I managed a smile and remained silent until we arrived at the club named *'Enigma.'* Dian parked, and we got out, facing the entrance. My eyes roved over the huge black building with the pop of neon lights that emphasized the name at the top. The bassy music could be heard from a mile away, and a few people were being searched at the front, where a huge man stood in all black.

I sighed when Dian came and stood beside me, her eyes set in the same direction as mine. "Well, this is it. Let's go," she said as she reached for my hand and tugged me along with her. I almost tumbled in the four-inch heels I had on but quickly regained my balance and followed behind an eager Dian, who was basically hopping as we approached the entrance. As we got closer, the music got louder, and I could make out a few people inside. I craned my neck and looked up at the man in front, who stood with a somber expression on his face, a metal detector in his hand as we stood before him.

Without saying a word, he swiped it across our bodies and nodded towards the opened door. Dian grabbed my hands and pulled me along, and before long, we were swallowed up inside. The beams of colorful lights flashed across my eyes, and I had to blink a few times to adjust it. All I could smell was perfume – a mix that made my stomach churn. Dian turned to me and smiled, pulling my hands as we bore through people and made our way to the counter at the front. I had thought it would have been less crowded, considering it wasn't even ten yet, but the place was already booming, and I was sure I'd have a headache in the morning.

"Ok, what are you drinking?" Dian exclaimed.

"A club soda to start," I said, watching as her brows furrowed while she paused as if contemplating whether or not to argue with me. She turned to the counter and yelled the order to one of the four bartenders who moved at the speed of light to get their jobs done.

I rubbed my arm and looked around at the vibe that was inside. There were couples, singles, and groups of people who came together to celebrate. Champagnes were being popped, shots were being served, and a chorus of shouts and celebratory noises contested with the sound of the hip hop music blasting in speakers while the DJ stood on the second floor at a small section reserved just for him. He caught the attention of a few persons on the ground floor, staring up at him and boosting him as they danced to the song he was playing. He paused to shout out a few people, scratched his equipment and then went to another song with a similar rhythm. I nodded my head and smiled without realizing it until Dian came and shoved my drink in front of me.

"Not so bad, is it?" she smiled, flashing me that I-told-you-so look.

I shrugged and took a drink, glancing at Dian's. "What're you having."

"My favorite; Henny and coke. Come, let's go mingle with the crowd a bit." Without waiting for a response from me, she was already leading the way, one hand in the air, her hips swaying as she vibed to a song. We went deep into the dancing bodies, and I held my drink tight, afraid that it would spill on people, but ironic enough, a few drinks were spilled on me as soon as I settled at a spot on the dance floor. I was squirming, but as I looked at Dian, I realized she was having the time of her life while she spilled her drink on people in the process. It didn't seem to faze them, though – everyone was just busy having a good time, and part of me envied them for that.

Dian laughed as she stumbled in front of me. "Loosen up, girl. What's wrong with you!" she exclaimed, turning her drink to her head and gulping it down in one go. "Ok, now that that's out of the way, let's have some fun," she said, tipping my glass further towards my mouth.

I decided to damn it all and drank down all of it. Dian grinned and took my glass, passing it on to a nearby waitress. She then grabbed my arm and tossed it in the air, trying to match the energy around us.

I was starting to get hot with the people that surrounded me – bouncing against me while I inhaled their sweat and the alcohol on their breath. But no one seemed to mind all that, and I wondered if I could do the same thing if I allowed myself to loosen up. So I started to sway my hips rather awkwardly, but heck, nobody was judging or even seemed to care, giving me a little confidence boost.

Soon after, it was as if I were moving along the waves of the music around me. The DJ switched to a more upbeat tune, and the crowd seemingly went off in a frenzy. Dian grabbed my hands and twirled me around, and I giggled, not finding this bad after all. I was starting to enjoy myself, and it was as if people could see that. They came to snuggle up to us, dancing against us but not too daring to touch us out of the ordinary. I started to hop on my feet because, apparently, that was what I knew how to do best. My hands flailed in the air, and I closed my eyes while I soaked up all that was being offered.

I didn't know how long it continued, I just knew that I was having the time of my life with my best friend beside me, who was just like an energizer bunny. It was like I was feeding off that, and it felt damn good. Soon, I could feel sweat trickling down my back and knew it was probably time for me to catch my breath.

I leaned into Dian. "I'm gonna get us some more drinks, okay?" I yelled, and she immediately grabbed onto my shoulders.

"I can go if you want!"

"No, no. I need to catch my breath, anyway," I admitted.

"Okay, I'll be right here when you get back!" she said, and I nodded, shoving off into the sea of people who wouldn't even hear my excuses if I said it.

Once I got to the bar, I realized it was even more crowded than before, and people overran the spot I had stood earlier. But nevertheless, I made my way through to the front and yelled until I got served. As fun as all this was, it was pretty exhausting, and I knew without a doubt that I would be sleeping for hours come tomorrow.

I was making my way back to Dian when I bumped into something rock hard, causing the drinks to spill over. The first thing my brain registered was the musky perfume that made me feel light-headed in the best possible way, but when it dawned on me that I had bumped into an actual person, my eyes widened, and my mouth fell open.

My heart started pounding in my chest as my eyes met his and traveled all the way up to his face. This man could probably step on me in any given situation. Fuck my luck.

"Oh, my gosh, I'm so sorry," I said as my eyes moved back to his drenched black shirt, which stuck to his skin like a glove, emphasizing the hard ridges of his stomach.

I didn't know why my heart was beating so fast. Either I was blaming myself for being such a klutz, or this man was the most beautiful I had ever seen. Once I took in every detail of his face, I found myself staring while he was maybe thinking of ways to knock me out.

His blue eyes were intense – probably the most intense I have ever seen – causing an unexplainable shiver to sliver down my spine. But despite the intensity in his eyes, a smile was still on his full lips.

"Don't worry about it," he said. That should have been enough to slow down my heart, but instead, it started galloping at the sound of his voice, which seemingly contested the bass in the room.

I lowered my gaze to hide the blush that crept to my cheeks. "At least allow me to buy you a drink to make up for it," I heard myself saying.

"After making you spill yours, I don't think so," he chuckled. "Allow me to buy back yours."

My gaze found its way to his beautiful face again, and just like that, I was captivated for the second time. How could one man be so beautiful, and added to that, he was looking at me in a way that made me feel like swooning right there on him. My mouth opened to produce a reply while he watched every single wordless movement. I clamped it shut and bit my lips, my brain seemingly gone to mush in the presence of this man.

"O-Ok," was the only word my lips could allow me.

He smiled, and we moved off towards the bar once again. I almost gasped when I felt his hand on the small of my back, ushering me through the crowd. I could feel the warmth radiating from his hands through my body, which caused a tingling between my legs.

I knew I was treading on dangerous grounds with this man, but it was as if I were blind to everything else but him. He stood at the counter, towering over everyone else as he commanded the waiters' attention. His scent was still in my nose, and it seemed all I could smell at this point–a sweet musk that was kind of citrusy and animalistic, yet with a sweet undertone that made me feel high from just one whiff.

He turned to me, and I paused, knowing I must have been red as a beet at the realization of getting caught staring at him. "What were you having, sweetheart?"

"Er... club soda and a henny and coke for my friend."

He nodded and relayed the order to the waitress, and waited a few seconds before it was served to him. He offered me the two cups, and I took it with a smile. "Thank you, although you didn't have to."

"I kinda felt like I did. I got you wet, too," he said as his gaze went down my dress. I froze. There was one kind of wet I could think about: the feeling between my legs. I was hot all over–too shocked to say anything, until I finally realized he meant the spillage, and I almost kicked myself.

I immediately looked down at my own body and noticed the wetness across my chest, knowing my nipples were poking through my dress like pistols. His eyes were glued there. He clenched his teeth before he tore them away and settled them back to my face. Somehow, his inspection of me didn't make me feel self-conscious. I felt sexier than ever for some reason.

"I'm Logan, by the way," he said with an extended hand.

I stared at his big palm before placing mine into it and instantly felt my nipples tightening as well as my core. "Bella," I managed to say.

He held my hand, and I didn't want him to let go. It was like the world had stopped, and all that mattered was how this complete stranger roiled up everything inside me. How his touch made me feel and how it was something I was suddenly craving more of.

"Pleasure to meet you, Bella. What do you say we show these bums a few moves on the dancefloor?" he said with a teasing smile.

I giggled. "I can't dance to save my life."

"Well, good thing you're not dying. Let's go," he said, arching an arrow-straight brow.

I bit my lips and nodded at him, moving past him to lead the way. I still had no control over my heart and the way it was beating fast in my chest. I looked into the crowd and met Dian's gaze. Her eyes shifted to Logan behind me, and she flashed a smile at me, looking prouder than anything else.

I handed her the drink while she still continued to sway her hips, looking at Logan over my shoulder. "Who's the hottie?" she asked, and my cheeks flamed.

"Er – Logan. I met him at the bar when I spilled my drinks on him," I said, trying to get as close as possible to her so only she could hear what I had to say.

"Well, that's one way of getting someone's attention," she laughed. "He's totally into you and definitely your 'type,'" she winked, and I folded my lips to hide my grin. Dian got back to partying, mingling with a male and female who were seemingly amused by her energy.

I smiled and turned to Logan, bobbing his head to the music while people danced around him. As soon as he saw he had my attention again, he smiled, and I felt it all the way to my knees.

"I take it you're not much of a dancer yourself!" I exclaimed.

He ran his fingers through his tapered cut as he assessed the dance floor. "Not really, but maybe we can be better together."

I licked my lips and took a sip of my drink as I watched him while contemplating his words. I knew I probably shouldn't engage, but there was just something about him, like a magnet pulling me closer. The way he looked at me made matters worse. It was like he was devouring every inch of me with his intense gaze, and I enjoyed it. There was this dangerous aura to him, but it made him all the more attractive. He couldn't take his eyes off me, and I couldn't take mine off him, even though I was probably as red as a beet.

The music switched to something more sensual, completely transforming the couples around us, who immediately started to move against each other in a hypnotizing fashion that took me by surprise. I glanced at Dian and realized she was already caught up with a man with his hands around her waist while she swayed her ass against him. She reached up and trailed her hand along his face, allowing him to move closer to nuzzle her neck.

I turned to Logan, who watched me like a hawk, just waiting for me to make a move. This was what I wanted after all, wasn't it? To let loose – have some fun. I inched closer to him and started to sway my hips as well, turning my back to him before our bodies touched. My breath hitched, and I stiffened for a bit, but then his hand was at my waist, rolling it from side to side. I was sure someone could see my heart beating out my chest when his hands found my body – my back pressed against his hard chest. He was warm, he smelled good, and I felt safe, despite knowing I was probably losing my mind thinking such a thing.

But I wanted this experience. I wanted to revel in the feeling that being so close to Logan brought me, so I started to gyrate against him faster, matching the rhythm blasting from the speakers. He rolled his hips against me as I rolled mine to meet his soft thrusts. My body was on fire, and this time, it wasn't from the heat. It was because this man had managed to awaken every single nerve inside my body.

"See, it's not so bad," he said against my neck, his heated breath almost causing me to shiver. I didn't know what was happening. My body had never had such a reaction toward a man. I was flustered and confused, and quite frankly, I didn't want the night to end.

I became more comfortable in his arms, bracing into him with each passing second while my body grew needier. His hands started to slide up and down my side slowly, teasing my flesh – sending jolts through my body. I pressed my ass further into him and could feel as he briefly stopped, his hands coming to a halt on me. I ground on him and could have sworn I heard him growl as his fingers pressed into my skin.

Logan's body became tenser the longer we danced until I could feel something hard pressing against me. My eyes widened, and I stiffened as I turned to face him. His eyes were dark, and I could tell he was enjoying this just as much as I was. My gaze dropped to his pants, and from there, I could see the evident bulge in his pants that he didn't seem ashamed of. My heart started to gallop at the realization that such a stellar man as Logan was attracted to me – was so attracted that I could arouse him.

Surprisingly, the idea didn't frighten me, which should be frightening in itself, but here I was, wanting all this man had to offer for tonight and the rest of my lifetime. I licked my lips and pressed myself into him, my hardened nipples flattening into his hard chest. I could feel his boner in my stomach, and I knew I was completely sodden by now. I could feel it as I moved – how wet I was for this man. The feel of his length made me putty; I knew I needed him and had never felt so clear about anything in my life.

As if our gazes were a language of their own, my eyes met his, and I watched with bated breath as his head lowered to mine. When our lips touched, the feeling was heaven on earth. His lips were soft as they brushed against mine in a teasing manner. I smiled against his and swallowed the lump in my throat before I leaned further into him and experienced my very first real kiss.

This wasn't the kindergarten-type peck on the cheeks that was purely innocent. This was something else on a whole other level. As soon as my mouth opened up for his, I knew one thing was certain – this was the man I was supposed to spend my life with. Don't ask me how I knew; I just knew I had never felt so alive in my life. As his tongue probed in to mingle with mine, I was lost – in a world of my own that this man provided. Nothing else existed but what was happening around me. Tremors vibrated through my whole body, more rigorous at certain spots that had me wanting more and more of him. His hands were on me, I was pressed against his taut body, and my mouth was experiencing a level of passion not known to man.

I moaned against him and could feel the bulge in his pants grow against me. I was on fire – burning at a fever pitch – as I became intoxicated with him. His medium stubble against my skin was bittersweet, but nothing compared to the feeling of his mouth against mine.

I've never kissed someone like this – I had no idea what I was doing. But Logan's tongue guided mine, he sucked against mine, and I did the same to him, reciprocating every action the best I knew how.

I hadn't even realized my eyes were closed until they popped open when he broke the kiss. I stared at him with an open mouth, trying to find some answers there.

"I don't think I'll be able to stop myself if we continue," he exclaimed huskily against my ear.

I swallowed, breathing heavily. "I- I don't want you to."

He smiled, one large hand coming up to cup my face, his thumb caressing my cheek. "May I take you somewhere more private?" he asked as his gaze searched mine.

My mind and heart were on a racecourse, and I felt breathless at how fast they were going. I was buzzing from the invite, but at the same time, I wanted to be logical. Yes, Logan was nice, but could I trust a beast in a nightclub? My heart already knew what it wanted, and my brain was not far behind. Truth was, I wanted this more than anything I had ever desired in my life. If I were lucky like my parents, then Logan would be my forever man. I could feel it in his touch, and I knew it deep down in my heart. It was that simple.

"I'll respect whatever choice you make, Bella." Even my name on his lips was like a gentle caress that made my decision more certain.

"Okay." I turned to Dian, still dancing away, her pinkish blonde hair damp with sweat and her makeup now glowing. I bit my lips as I approached her, somehow dreading her reaction to me telling her that I was willing to leave with a man.

"Hey!"

She glanced at Logan and then at me. "Is everything okay?"

I quickly nodded, fiddling with my fingers. "I er...I'm leaving with Logan," I said.

Dian paused, her mouth falling open while her eyes widened. "What?"

"I will be careful... I – I want this."

Her big green eyes softened, and her mouth transformed into an open-mouthed smile. "Look at you being a baddie and not afraid to express what you want," she exclaimed proudly.

I rubbed my arm. "I will text you, okay."

She grinned with a nod. "Sure. Have fun and use protection," she said, flashing me a warning look.

I blushed. "See ya."

I left Dian's side and went with Logan who held my hand and walked us out of the club. The cold night air whipped my skin as soon as I stepped out, and I shivered. But Logan was there with a hand around my shoulder as he walked us to the parking lot. He stopped at a Prius and opened the passenger's seat door before he turned to look at me.

"After you."

I smiled and stepped in, hoping to have the ride of my life.

Chapter 3

Bella

We parked in front of a small two-story house with a small porch and a huge front yard. When he said he was bringing me to his place, I wasn't thinking the whole thing. I was thinking of an apartment, but Logan looked mature enough to have things like this. I knew he was way older, and yet he was fitter than most of the men I had seen on our campus back in college. It suddenly dawned on me that this was an experienced man, and I didn't need to know his age to come to that conclusion. Logan had looks to kill, and I was certain that just as I was hypnotized by his mere beauty, a lot of other females had been too.

My stomach sank at the thought. In the back of my mind, he only had eyes for me just as I had for him, but I knew not to be foolish by thinking such a thing. Regardless, I was sure I wanted him, I was sure that my gut feeling was right, and I had found my prince charming.

Logan shuffled out of his seat and came around my side to do the same for me. I tried to hide my smile, but I couldn't stop myself. The chivalry was swoon-worthy.

"This is me, Bella," he said as he stared ahead at his house and then at me.

"It's really nice."

"Thank you."

He led the way and opened the door, allowing me to enter first. As soon as I stepped in, I noticed his scent was all over the place. Well, at least I was now certain it was his. We were in the living room, with hardwood, and huge brown sofas that sat on a huge red and cream Persian rug. A section of the cream walls was reserved for photos of all types and frames. I was suddenly tempted to look – see the people that were part of his life.

"Can I get you something to drink?" he asked as he came to stand in front me. I saw something I hadn't seen in the poorly lit bar. There was a tattoo of an eagle at the side of his neck – so intricately designed that it seemed like the bird was about to fly off his skin. My hands reached up to touch it, and I was glad he allowed me to, though I didn't want to seem too inquisitive. My fingers trailed along the thick column of his neck, lingering on the smooth skin where the bird was drawn. I looked at Logan again and realized his eyes had darkened again as he stared at me. My heart skipped a beat as he held my hand in place and pulled me against him with the other. I almost gasped as my body came in contact with his again, and just like that, I was burning up.

I looked into his eyes, awaiting the moment when my lips would meet his. But he just stared at me as if trying to see into my soul.

"I need you to tell me that this is what you want, Bella," he said. "I need to know that you are completely on board with what's going to happen. I don't need you to regret anything in the morning. All I want you to think about is me and how great this will be for you," he said.

I swallowed and nodded.

"Say it."

"I want you, Logan – without a doubt."

He smiled and gave me what I'd be longing for. A kiss that weakened my knees and had me latching my hands around his neck as I marveled in it. There was no delaying this – we both knew what we wanted and were in the process of taking it.

He swept me into his arms, and I gasped, holding onto him tighter. He climbed the stairs and carried me to a bedroom with the neatly spread bed and dark furniture that matched his overall aura. He placed me on my feet, and I licked my lips as it dawned on me what was really about to happen.

"I- I've never done this before," I said in what sounded like a whisper.

"What, sleeping with someone you just met?"

"A one night stand-"

"I know I'll want you for more than just one night, beautiful. This isn't what this is," he said, his words making me dizzy.

It made what I was about to say next a lot easier. "I- I'm a virgin," I said.

His eyes widened, and his brows rose. "You've never had sex before?" he asked.

My cheeks heated as I shook my head.

"How old are you, Bella?"

"Twenty-three. You?"

"Thirty-three."

I was expecting thirty, but that wasn't far off. It didn't make me want him any less. He reached for my face again with that reassuring touch that had me quaking in my boots.

"I'm gonna make certain you don't forget tonight," he said.

"I wouldn't want to."

He smiled and kissed me again, his hands trailing across the small of my back as he deepened the kiss to a mind-numbing degree. I latched onto him like life itself depended on it and kissed him back the best I knew how. His lips were so soft, so alluring; his mouth sweet as stroke after stroke set me ablaze.

Like a hungry little kitten, I started to claw at him, wanting to touch his skin and feel it against me. My fingers crept up under his shirt, grazing bulks of hard flesh that made me moan against his mouth. Logan broke the kiss and stared at me, his eyes a story of passion. He pulled his shirt over his head, and my eyes dropped to his slightly hairy chest with his taut muscles glowering at me. He was a beautiful specimen of a man, and my body couldn't wait to have him. Looking at him, I could feel myself pooling with liquid heat.

He reached for me again and kissed me hard, one hand at the strap of my dress, which he gently pried down my shoulders. My exposed breasts were pressed against his muscular body, my nipples even tighter from the contact. I found his buckle and started fumbling with it, simultaneously wondering where I got the courage to be acting like this. But it was as if I had known Logan for a while, and knew that my body was explicitly meant for him. He broke the kiss yet again and caught my gaze as he pulled my dress down my body. He knelt in front of me, and I swallowed as he drank in the sight of my naked breasts and my lacy royal blue panties, visibly wet from where he stood.

His hands slid down the curves of my hips, leaving a fiery trail in its wake. "You are so perfect, Bella. Your skin is like silk; flawless, supple," he said, his breath hot on my legs as he spoke.

I swallowed hard. "Th-thanks."

He looked up at me and smiled before he pulled me into his arms and lifted me, placing me on the bed. I propped up on my shoulders and watched as he loomed over me, his muscles flexing as he walked. He pulled me to the edge of the bed and pried my legs apart before he hooked his fingers in the waistband of my panties and pulled them off. His eyes were fixed on me, fixed on the area between my legs that was absolutely dripping for him. There was the darkness in his eyes that I began to know too much. My eyes shifted down his body, and it seemed the dent in his pants got even bigger.

I was almost out of breath when I realized what this man was about to do. I had expected to feel his penis inside me by the look on his face, but when he positioned himself between my legs, I damn near lost my mind.

"Wh-What are you doing?" my voice came out shakily.

He looked up from between my thighs, and I swallowed as I awaited his response. "I'm gonna taste you. I want every drop of juice on my lips before I have it on my dick," he said matter-of-factly. What could I say to that? Nothing.

I was speechless as I watched him with my heart hammering in my chest. When his mouth found my flesh, I flinched, taken off guard by the tonne load of sensations that assaulted my body with one single touch. Logan's eyes were on me as he stuck out his tongue and swiped it across my needy flesh. I moaned, my whole body tingling as he reigned pleasure on me with lick after lick.

"You taste better than I expected," he said, and I quivered when his hot breath caressed my skin. "But now it's time for me to eat," he said, and I held my breath as I awaited his next move.

I gasped when his whole mouth went down on me, his lips flat against my sensitive clit while his tongue stroked my hole. Unable to hold my body up, I flopped back into the bed and stared at the ceiling, which seemed to be spinning around me. My chest rose and fell as Logan's hot mouth lapped up my juices. I could hear the sounds of my wetness and felt my cheeks flame. I gripped the sheets, trying to make sense of the pleasure with an open mouth. I couldn't believe it felt this good – I couldn't believe that someone was pleasuring my body like he had known it for ages. I moaned, I snapped my eyes shut, and I writhed as it got more and more intense. Logan's tongue was doing wonders, and I couldn't make sense of the feelings that inhabited my body. But then, just when I thought it couldn't get any better, he started moving faster, sucking my flesh, which resulted in a series of whimpers from me. I eased up to look at what he was doing but crashed back into the bed just as fast when a bolt of pleasure rippled through me.

"Oh- oh my gosh," I exclaimed, feeling like I was losing my mind. He didn't let up for even one second – he just stayed there as if my vagina was his home. I pushed my hips against him because, as great as he was doing, a sensation was building inside me, which made me want more. I moaned and whimpered, reaching for his head, mussing up his hair, wordlessly begging him for more until I received my full share.

I squealed, crashing back into the bed as a glorious feeling built inside me, getting higher and higher the longer he stayed there.

"Logan!" I screamed and froze in the bed, staring at the ceiling as a wave of unexplainable bliss took over my body, settling at my core. It was like an explosion that paralyzed me before I started to tremble in the aftershocks. A gush of liquid rushed to my core, and Logan collected it with his resilient tongue, which had me quaking over and over again. My mouth was wide open but couldn't produce any words, my eyes wide open, but all I could see were stars. My body seemed weightless as it went to cloud nine and back.

Logan finally eased up, licking his lips as he loomed over me. I could see traces of wetness around his mouth that somehow caused me to be aroused all over again.

"How was it?" he asked me, a small smile on his face.

I swallowed. "T-That was the most amazing feeling in the world," I whispered, still in a state of stasis.

He chuckled. "One of..." he said, propping on an elbow beside me.

I turned to him, trying to catch my breath. "You are really good at that."

He smiled, his hands sliding over my overly sensitive nipple, down my stomach before lingering between my legs. I swallowed, staring into his clear blue eyes. "Could I taste you too?"

Something flashed across his gaze. "Maybe later. Tonight is all about you, Bella. We're gonna have a lot of time after tonight to try everything," he smiled, and my heart skipped a beat when his finger slipped between my folds.

I tried to get hold of my composure. "You want more than tonight?" I said breathlessly.

"Don't you?"

"Yes," I said in what sounded like a gasp as his fingers repeatedly slid over my sensitive clit.

"It'd be a sin not to have you again after this." His voice was husky as he spoke, trapping my gaze as he fingered me. "Your body is mine tonight and will be for a long time." He slipped a finger inside me, and my mouth fell open as I started to breathe heavily again.

"Tell me everything that you want, Bella. Let me know how to please you," he said, his words like a promise.

My brain spun. "I- I want you to kiss me," I said as I reached for his face, running my thumb along his stubble.

Without another word, he lowered his mouth to mine and sucked my lips in a gentle caress. I could taste myself on him, and my heart soared, remembering what he had done minutes earlier. As he kissed me, he used his finger to stroke my flesh, going back and forth with his middle fingers before he added another. It slipped inside me easily, seeing I was still so wet for him – even wetter now that his saliva had lubricated my flesh. His fingers glided inside me, massaging my walls, causing me to pry my legs further apart as he stroked me. The kiss added another degree to the pleasure I was already feeling. This was different from what he had done earlier. His fingers were hard and more dominant as they moved within my flesh. The sensations grew quicker – I was close to another orgasm within seconds of him adding another finger.

I moaned and kissed him harder, feeling like I was about to cum. I started to roll my hips to reach the pleasure I knew was near, but I didn't get the chance because Logan pulled out and left me empty. He broke the kiss at the same time and stared down at me.

"Do you think you're ready for me, Bella?"

"Yes," I said. "I want you so much." I didn't know where such bold words came from, but I knew I meant that more than anything I'd ever said in my life.

Logan rolled off the bed and stood, staring at me before he peeled his jeans down his waist, leaving him in only boxers. I watched with bated breath, acknowledging the huge lump between his thighs that seemed to strain for release. Logan was a beast – I could see that now in every single muscle he possessed. He was a God of a man – the most beautiful I had ever seen, and quite frankly, to have such an experience with such a man felt like a dream.

He pulled his boxers down, and his manhood strained against it before it sprang free, dangling for a second before it pointed at me, throbbing. I nearly lost my wits at the sight, now feeling a trickle of panic overcome me. As wet as I knew myself to be, I doubted he could fit inside me.

Logan must have seen the look on my face because he was quick to assure me. "Don't worry... I'll ensure you know nothing but pleasure," he said as he approached me.

I couldn't take my eyes off him; off the bulbous shiny head and the veins that lined his length like roots. There was an anticipation growing inside me despite the anxiety I was currently feeling. This was about to happen. I wasn't going to be a virgin anymore, and the thought excited me. I was confident this was the man I wanted for the job. I could feel it in my soul.

Logan came onto the bed and hovered over me, blocking the light in the room as his beautiful face and broad shoulders came into view. He kissed me, kissed along my neck, and I whimpered at the pleasure that sizzled through me. He took his time to knead each breast in hand before he covered each with his mouth, sucking gently as ripples ran through my body. He kissed a line to my belly button before he came back up and did it all over again.

My hands were all over him – sailing across his back, through his soft hair. I wanted everything. His length grazed my leg, my core pooling with need at the simple touch. My body was begging for him, burning at a fever pitch.

Logan came back up to my face and paused. "It's going to hurt for a second when I'm inside you, but then it's gonna get better. If it gets too much for you, just tell me. Tell me what you want and what you don't want," he said, positioning between my legs.

I nodded as he guided the shiny tip of his manhood to my entrance and rubbed it up and down my slit. I moaned, my heart pounding in my chest as I waited for him to enter me. I was aware that he wasn't using any protection, but I wanted to feel every inch of Logan with nothing between us. My flesh against his flesh, fully joined because I was convinced that he was going to be my man after tonight. He slid his length down my clit and propped the head inside my hole. I stiffened and awaited the pain as he slowly slipped inside me. My body was already railing with pleasure, my flesh parting to grant him access. I was so wet and could feel it with every movement of his dick.

He pushed a little deeper, and I bit down into my lips as my flesh tore, and he gained access inside me. He was right; there was pain, but not as much as I had expected. Just a slight sting and a bit of tenderness that slowly began to fade as Logan pushed inside me a little further. But then he paused, and I could feel my insides familiarizing itself with the sweet intrusion.

"Are you okay?" he asked me, his forehead slightly wrinkled with worry.

"Yes, I'm great," I said as I reached for him and kissed his addicting lips. His manhood slipped deeper, and I moaned, feeling so stretched with his length inside me. I made an effort to spread my legs a little further while he went deeper and deeper.

I was on the verge of tears with how glorious he felt inside me. This surpassed the oral sex and the fingering. It was like he was filling me with a missing piece I had not known existed until now. The further he went, the more it felt like I was going to pass out from the sheer bliss.

"Do you like what I'm doing to you, beautiful?" he asked me as he slowly began to push back and forth inside me with half his length yet to feel the insides of my vagina.

My walls hugged him, and I could feel myself seep with more juices, making Logan's movements even more fluid. He was hard and huge, but I was getting used to it with each stroke – used to the bigness that stretched me to the limit. His stroking my flesh echoed in the room – my wetness against his hardness. It was a sound I knew would stick with me for a lifetime – the sound of our bodies becoming one. I couldn't get enough of it; I couldn't get enough of Logan and how the room carried his scent, branding it to memory.

He sunk deeper, deeper than he had ever been, and I gasped as my walls clamped down on him. He increased his pace, and each stroke made me spiral more and more out of control.

"More," I found myself saying, curling my legs around his hips as I urged him further. Logan obliged and sunk his whole length inside me. I immediately started to shudder, clamping down on him when he stroked something inside me. It immediately set me off, and I found myself experiencing my first orgasm via penetration.

Logan didn't let up; he continued to thrust into me, his movements getting faster and faster as he slammed into me.

"You feel like heaven...fuck!" he exclaimed as he moved inside me, giving me orgasm after orgasm. Just when I thought I was recovering from one, there I was in another. My heart was full; there were no words to describe what was happening to my body as Logan went deep inside me, his girth stretching me further open as his steely cock raged inside me.

Chapter 4

Bella

"Oh, oh God. I-" He thrust into me sharply, cutting off my words, and I screamed as I latched onto him, feeling my eyes roll back into my head as he buried himself completely inside me.

"Is this what you want, Bella?"

"Oh, yes! Keep going... don't stop, please," I begged him. His muscles flexed as he went to town inside me, a single vein popping up at his neck, right through the tattoo. Sweat started to bead on his forehead, our skin already slippery from all the action. I was so wet that I could feel it trickling down my ass as Logan pumped into me. I knew I would be sore the following morning with how fast Logan was going, but I had no plans to tell him to stop. The pleasure with the slight pain was maddening. I didn't know what to focus on- I just knew I was on cloud nine, my body begging for release yet again. His hand found my breast, and he pinched a nipple, setting me off as I screamed and clamped around him.

Logan released a guttural moan and bucked, thrusting deep within me a few more times before pulling out his cock and spraying his cum across my stomach and pussy. I was writhing beneath him as I collected every warm drop while basking in my own orgasm. My pussy clenched, but it gripped onto nothing, and I suddenly missed the feeling of him inside me.

I looked up at him as he juiced the last bits from his penis and smiled down at me. "You're mine now Bella, as much as I am yours."

My heart fluttered in my chest with the happiness that seemed to overwhelm me. "Yes." Despite having the most amazing orgasm of my life, I found myself wanting more and more of Logan – I couldn't get enough. He laid on his back, his cock still hard and throbbing as he tried to catch his breath.

My gaze drank in every glorious inch of him, and I couldn't help but wish this moment lasted forever. My exhaustion ran deep, but I still needed this man inside me for a moment longer.

I eased up from the bed, reached for his still-hard cock and straddled him. Logan looked surprised, but he didn't say anything. Instead, he just lay there and accepted his fate. I impaled myself with his length and flinched when his manhood rubbed against the tenderness caused by my broken hymen. I didn't stop; I continued to slide down on him until I had all of him inside me as hard as it was to do. In this position, he felt even bigger, and I felt fuller. There was a slight bit of discomfort, but then I started to roll my hips against him. He felt like he was in my stomach, and I felt like I was going to cum as his manhood rubbed against my g-spots. His cum rolled down my insides and settled at the base on his cock as I rode him. Logan held my hips and eased up, crashing his mouth against mine.

"Fuck, you're incredible," he said as he wrapped one hand around me and used the other to squeeze one of my tits. I started to thrust into him while he did the same. The heat grew between our bodies, his hands slick against my sweaty one as he fucked me. I latched my hand around his neck and gave my all while Logan did the same. We were both burning up – I could feel the heat radiating off Logan as we made love. His eyes were on my lips, and as if he was unable to help himself, he kissed me hard while we continued with our thrusting. At that point, I was done for. Logan's mouth and length were a combination I wasn't strong enough to hold back on. I shattered on him, squeezing him hard as my orgasm took its course. He quickly pulled back, slipped from inside me and showered my stomach with another load of cum.

I collapsed on the bed, exhausted and completely satisfied, finding it hard to believe that I was lucky enough to find the man of my dreams in one night. When he wrapped me in his arms and held me close, I had no reason to believe Logan wasn't my forever man. I cuddled up to him, so close to saying, 'I love you.' I knew it wouldn't probably freak him out as much as it did me, and so I decided not to. Maybe I was still fuzzy from the sex, anyway – I didn't want to jump the gun, but I couldn't ignore what was so clear to my heart.

MY EYES FLUTTERED OPEN, a smile immediately blooming on my face as images of last night flashed through my head. The soft light coming from the closed curtains told me it was morning, and I had spent the night with Logan, having sex every chance we got.

Without even moving, I could feel the soreness between my legs – a sweet dull ache that made me want a repeat of the night before. I turned to Logan and realized he was still sleeping – one heavy hand thrown over my waist as he held me in place. I smiled as I stared down at his face – now completely relaxed and seemingly taking years off him. He seemed even more beautiful in sleep – hair all ruffled, his stubble a bit longer, giving him a rugged look and lashes any girl would envy.

I wanted to stay by his side, but I badly wanted to pee, so I gently pried his hands off me and shuffled from the bed. The ache grew more intense as I moved, and I almost moaned aloud. I glanced at the bedside table where both our phones were and picked up mine – wanting to assure Dian that I was fine – great actually.

Multiple texts were on the phone, and I started to blush as I read them.

It's just dawning on me ...

I can't believe you are no longer a virgin.

OMG, text me back Asap, I need to know the details, and I need to know that you are fine!

Damn, girl, it's almost nine. Sleeping in? Was it that good?

Call meee!

I covered my mouth to hide a giggle and was about to head to the bathroom when Logan's phone buzzed. I knew I had no business looking, but I couldn't help it. My brows furrowed as I read the name on the screen; Jenny. My brain began to race as I tried to figure out who Jenny was. It was probably a friend, his sister? His mom? The possibilities were endless, right? And yet I couldn't help the wrenching feeling in my gut. I hadn't even bothered to ask Logan if he had a wife or a girlfriend. What if that was who was calling? But that couldn't be possible; he had said he wanted more than just one night. If he had a girlfriend, then –

A text came in, and I paused in my tracks as the phone lit up and I viewed what was written on the notification bar.

Babe, pick up the phone. I really need to talk to you.

I miss you, came another.

I paused, feeling the blood drain from my face as I read what was on screen. My head started to spin, and I had to steady myself to keep myself from falling. My throat began to burn, and soon my eyes did the same as I glanced back at Logan on the bed and reflected on last night.

Had he been lying to me to get me in bed? To make me feel good before he fucked me? Tears trailed down my face as I tried to fathom the idea as reality. He said I was his, and he was mine, but clearly, he hadn't meant a word of it. I was just the virgin he wanted to fuck to add to the notch on his bedpost. He meant none of it – clearly.

The phone buzzed again, and I almost jumped out of my skin. Another text popped up, which sealed the deal for me.

I love you.

More tears tumbled down my face. How could I be so fricking stupid to believe a guy like Logan was single or wanted just one woman? He was a cheater, and a liar, and that feeling of regret started to build inside me like a tsunami threatening to flood me. I was so stupid – so fricking stupid. He was a player who would have said anything to get me in bed. I should have known that. I should have.

I stumbled across the room and blindly searched for my clothes as tears fogged my eyes. As much as I was in a hurry to leave, I knew I had to be quiet. I didn't want to confront him about it; I didn't want to see his face – I just wanted to go home. I hastily pulled on my clothes, not caring if I looked like I just walked out of an alley, and ran for the door. When I reached the outside, I choked a sob and tried to hail down a cab – feeling totally destroyed.

Just my luck. Just when I decided take on life by the balls, as Dian would put it, it turned out to be a complete shit show.

The man of my dreams had turned out to be a fricking nightmare.

Chapter 5

Logan

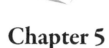

It had been over a month, yet I had not been fortunate enough to find Bella. I returned to the club where we had met, hoping to see her there again, but there was no trace of her or her friend. I regret not asking her surname on the very first night, but I had been so confident in seeing her again that it had never crossed my mind to find out then. I thought we had a lifetime, but apparently, it was just a couple of hours.

She left without a word, fleeing my bed like Goldilocks. For weeks I had tried to figure out the reason and came up blank each time. I hadn't seen it coming – our chemistry was off the charts, and I genuinely thought it'd be for more than just a night. But maybe I was the one kidding myself. Maybe she lied about all that we had that night. The thought of it made my blood boil – the not knowing. She was mine, and I didn't need a lifetime to know that. I knew it as soon as I saw her, as soon as we touched, as soon as we talked.

The trouble now was finding where the hell she was. I had never met a woman like her – never met a woman capable of making me feel so much. It was otherworldly. She was rare, and she belonged to me. I believed we'd meet again in due time, but until then, every passing day was agony.

I wanted her plain and simple. Not just for her innocent touches or her good pussy. I wanted her for the rest of my life. Maybe I was pussy whipped, but nothing had ever been clear as much as this was. Bella was my woman and my woman only.

As hard as her leaving was for me to accept, I had to admit the days leading up to today weren't so bad. I was finally getting a shot at my dream job after succumbing to an injury in the past that had prevented me from going pro.

Two days ago, the administration at Westgate University called and asked if I was willing to coach the football team because their head coach had an accident and was in a pretty bad condition. I applied years ago but to no avail. I thought it was a no-go, so imagine my surprise when I received the phone call that was about to change my life. It wasn't permanent – I knew as much, but this could potentially open doors for me, and that was what I wanted. If I could lead the team to victory this season, people would be knocking at my door, wanting me to be part of their team.

The idea excited me. It was great to have that sense of passion back into my life, and I knew that I couldn't blow it. I only wished I had a woman like Bella at my side through all of this – someone I could come home to, tell about how my day went, someone that I could spoil and give the world while all she had to offer was herself. Even the thought of her was enough to get me hard. Her beautiful face, and her big brown eyes that had gone through a series of emotions as I made love to her. Fuck, no other could compare. I've had my fair share of women throughout my life and none held a candle to the petite little virgin who had rocked my world harder than one could imagine.

I couldn't get her out of my thoughts, my nights were plagued with images of her, leaving me needy, but I had no other woman to turn to. I couldn't dare touch someone else after her, even if I was dying to do so. I wanted her and her alone, so on countless nights, I had gripped my cock, wishing it was her until I had the release that would give me temporary relief.

I smoothed the lapels on my jacket and grabbed my keys from the table before I stepped out and into my Prius. I only hoped today would be a good one.

I STEPPED OUT AND INHALED the crisp air as I stared at the plain brown building with its huge lawn littered with students. I couldn't help the smile that tipped at my lips. It was good to be back at my alma mater – the place which developed my love for football. It was just a pity how it ended. Nevertheless, it was great to return to the place that had groomed me to become the person I am today.

I adjusted my jacket and headed to the Principal's office, where I had a short discussion regarding my position and what was required of me. Typical employee/employer stuff. I knocked and entered to find Principal Cole seated around his huge desk while another man sat before him in one of the chairs at the front.

"Mr. Taylor, right on time. Great," Cole said as he stood with an outstretched hand.

I approached him and shook his hand. "This is assistant coach Steve Barkley," he said as he gestured to the other man that stood with a smile on his aging face. "Steve here will get you acquainted with the team and tell you all you need to know to get you comfortable."

I turned to Steve, who had a proud smile on his face.

"Hey man, nice to meet you," I said as I shook his hand as well.

"The pleasure is all mine. I was a big fan of yours back in the day. You were a beast," he said as he slowly shook his head and took in my form. "Pity what happened, y'know."

I shrugged. "Yeah, it is what it is. Shit happens," I said as I turned to Cole, who watched the interaction. "Speaking of, I'm very sorry to hear about what happened to Coach Peters."

Cole nodded, a remorseful expression on his face. "Yeah, very unfortunate. He's doing pretty well, though – should be fully recovered in a few months," he said as he sat. "Until that time, I want you to make Westgate proud. Lead our team to victory, as you have seen many times. I'm confident that you will, Taylor."

I nodded firmly. "Yes, sir."

Barkley sat back in his chair and rested his ankle on his knee. "We have a great team this year. And we are blessed by the likes of our star player and captain, Jace Bradford. Kid's a real-life prodigy," Barkley said with enthusiasm evident in his voice.

"Yeah, the kid is great, but his academics aren't the best," Principal Cole put in.

"Yeah, well, you can't have it all, can you?" he chuckled. "You're gonna have to keep an eye out for that one. He has real talent but can get pretty wrapped up in all the attention he's been getting lately. The guy is a chick magnet," he snickered.

Principal Cole raised a brow and turned his attention back to me. "Well, it's definitely great to have you back, Logan. I expect nothing but great things from you."

I smiled. "Thank you, sir, for the opportunity. I'll definitely put my best foot forward."

"I expect nothing less."

HALF AN HOUR LATER, I made myself comfortable in the small office assigned to me. The stacks of paper on the table were all Peters' stuff. The framed photos on the walls of him and the players – it was all him, and from the looks of it, he had a good relationship with the guys that would seem impossible to top. But I wasn't here to make friends, was I? I was here to do the job to the best of my abilities, so by the end of it, I got a sparkling recommendation or a permanent spot. It was game time, and I had to develop an excellent game plan to guarantee my success.

As I skimmed through the documents, I realized Peters must have been great at it. His tactics were awesome, but I had to have my own play – something more solid. I skimmed through the student files, trying to know everyone on paper before I actually met them face-to-face later this evening. My attention lingered on the talk of the town for a second – the supposed prodigy in all of this. Jace Bradford. Apparently, he was the key to most of the wins last season, and quite frankly, I was a bit eager to meet him.

I eased back into the chair with my hands propped at the back of my head. I couldn't get the woman of my dreams, but I had my dream job right in front of me, and I couldn't allow anything to get in the way of that.

Chapter 6

Bella

The only thing that could get my mind off what happened this summer was my books. I had been knee-deep in my studies, desperate to think about something else apart from Logan and that entire night. But no matter how hard I tried and how hard I worked, he was still there. Every waking morning, every night – the memories were constant. There was nothing else to do but go back to my comfort zone. I wasn't as lucky as the others who had taken risks and had left unscathed.

The one time I decided to be a bit rebellious, it backfired in my face. So I was back to square one, except I had kept the new clothes. It had hurt like hell – even now, more than a month later. The hurt was still ripe, the deceit, the lies. Even now as I reflected on it, my stomach churned, and tears threatened to spill from my eyes. I didn't know when I would get over it. I had truly thought that Logan was the man for me. He was a fricking stranger whom I knew nothing about, but in the moment, it didn't matter because, as he said, it would be more than one night with us. All lies. And I had been foolish enough to believe.

I was a straight-A student who knew my way around anything, and yet I had not seen through the façade this man presented. I had truly felt like I was in love with the man, even more so when he made love to me. It was bliss, but sometimes I wished it hadn't been that great. Maybe it would be easier to get over him then, but it was hard to get over someone as beautiful as Logan, someone so skilled in bed, someone who made me believe that anything was possible at the time.

The hardest part was, now that I was no longer a virgin, I craved him more than anything. Some nights were reckless when all I could think about was someone I couldn't have. I wanted him inside me and all over me. It was that bad. It was a craving that ate at me and made me feel like I was losing my mind at times.

But I blamed myself. I shouldn't have hooked up with someone at a damned club. He was fire and desire, and that alone should have been a big red flag for me.

I was possibly the hot topic among his friends – the virgin he had picked up and made a fool of. I had begged him to have me; I had called his name endlessly as he made love to me. That had probably boosted his ego – a decoration to add to his rather large bedpost he shared with his girlfriend at night. Damn cheater!

"Christ!" I snapped, slamming the book shut and covering my eyes as tears streamed down my face.

My roomie and best friend, Dian, immediately perched up on her bed and stared at me. "Hey, is everything okay?" she asked from the other end of the room.

I sniffed and used the back of my hand to wipe my eyes. "Yeah," I croaked, but she wasn't too convinced. She immediately got up and walked towards me, sitting at the edge of the bed.

"Hey, talk to me."

"It's Logan. I just can't fricking get him out of my damn head!" I exclaimed, raking my hand through my hair.

She nodded understandably. After finding out Logan had a whole other woman, I ran to my best friend for comfort, telling her everything that happened, although it had been embarrassing even to say out loud. Dian had been there to collect every single tear and assure me that everything would be fine.

She rubbed my leg and stared at me. "The first is usually the hardest to get over with anyone. What you're going through is normal, Bells; it will hurt for a while, but I promise it gets better."

I cleared my throat and swallowed. "I was just so... entranced, y'know. He was perfect, he made me feel perfect, and I swear it was that love at first sight type of thing – I'm not even kidding," I said as I dropped my gaze to the bed, embarrassed.

"Good sex will make you feel like that –"

"You don't understand," I said, cutting her off. "I felt the sparks; my whole body was alert with a single touch. I couldn't explain it, but it was different, and I knew there was something there. I –" I trailed off and shook my head.

"Arousal will make you feel like that, and I understand because Logan is actually really pretty hot."

I rolled my eyes. "You don't understand what I'm saying. It was like I had found my soulmate."

Dian sighed. "I'm trying to understand you, but at the same time, I'm letting you know that attraction can do that sort of stuff. This asshole isn't your soulmate, Bells. You only felt that way because you wanted him, and he wanted you. It might have been perfect in the moment, but I bet even if things didn't turn out the way it did, and you actually gave a relationship a shot, it probably wouldn't work," she shrugged.

I sighed. "You're probably right. I just felt so lucky, y'know. It was almost like a dream."

Dian patted me on the legs. "Come on, no more moping around and allowing that asshole to fuck with your headspace. It's time to get over him and under another dick."

My mouth fell open as I gawked at her. "What?"

"Trust me; you will meet someone way better than Logan. You just have to give it a chance..."

I sighed. "Dian, I don't want someone better – I don't want anyone. Not now, anyway."

"I know, but do you remember Jace, whom we met summer?" she asked, and without waiting for a reply, she continued. "He's been asking about you ever since, and because of the whole Logan thing, I figured I would give you some time, but it's been over a month now, Bells; you need to get back out there," she said.

"What's the rush?" I snapped. "I did most of what you asked, and it turned out to be a fricking shit show, so stop. Maybe your advice isn't the best, Dian," I exclaimed before I flopped back down on the bed and turned my back to her.

She didn't say a word after, which was unlike her, and I immediately felt guilty. I knew she only wanted to see me happy, but it all felt too overwhelming. I just wanted to wallow in my self-pity and continue to miss the man I couldn't have. Logan was still a constant on my mind, and I didn't want to get involved with anyone else until this feeling passed. But maybe Dian was right; maybe all I needed was to distract myself with someone else in order to heal. But was that even fair to the new person? I sighed as I curled up into the bed and gave it more thought.

It was obvious that Logan wasn't the man for me, no matter what I had felt at the time. Maybe all this pining and sadness was blocking my path to who was actually right for me. I knew it wasn't Jace – I had felt nothing for him despite his good looks and charm, and could I even see myself with someone so popular and... outgoing? I was the complete opposite who didn't want the attention. I couldn't be the quarterback's girlfriend. The mere thought was ridiculous. People would think so less of me, as I'd seen a million times over. I didn't have groupie energy or any energy at all for that kind of lifestyle. What did Jace even see in me, anyway? A part of me wanted to know that because it was possibly the biggest mystery in history.

He could be with anyone he wanted on campus – girls way hotter than me, and here he was, gunning for the nerd. Or was it that he wanted someone else on the side? My brain couldn't stop working with questions I didn't have the slightest idea of the answers.

There was this five percent inside me that wanted to damn it all to hell and be as spontaneous as I had been at the club with Logan, but then the majority didn't want me taking such risks again, only to lick my wounds and cry in the end. Dian often bragged that this was what the twenties were about. Dating, having fun, finding out what you wanted, having your heart broken... the list was endless. I didn't know if I wanted all that; I wanted to be like my parents, who found each other with one shot and have been in love ever since. Was that too much to ask for?

An idea suddenly came to me, and I rolled off the bed with my phone in hand as I headed toward the door. Dian was curled up in bed on her phone, watching me through the corners of her eyes, but she didn't say a word. I made my way out and began to walk down the narrow passage as I dialed my mom's number.

"Hey, sweetheart," her voice came, immediately putting a smile on my face.

"Hey, Mom, are you busy?" I asked as I made my way outside.

"No, we just had dinner. Your father is taking a shower, and I'm chilling on the porch," she chuckled. "Is everything okay?"

"I er – I actually need your advice with something..." I said, biting my lips.

"Of course, hon; what is it?"

I cleared my throat and hugged myself as I continued to walk. "So, I've been giving the dating thing a shot, and I thought I found the right guy, but it turns out he wasn't, so now I'm scared to put myself out there again," I confessed.

"Oh, honey, you never told me you were dating," she said softly, a little disappointment in her voice.

"I- It was nothing serious, I guess."

There was a brief pause. "Okay, well, I'm happy regardless. Not everyone finds Mr. Right right away honey-"

"I guess I just wanted to have what you and Dad have," I murmured.

"Listen, I kissed a lot of frogs before I found my prince charming," she laughed.

"I thought Dad was your first," I said, a bit confused.

"He was my first love and my first lover, but I dated people before him; I just didn't have sex with them," she clarified, and I immediately prayed the ground would swallow me up right at that very moment. I went and had sex with a guy I thought was the one, so there was no way I could have what my mom had. I'd already made the biggest mistake of my life in that regard.

"Bella?" my mom's voice came, pulling me from my thoughts.

I cleared my throat. "Yes, Mom, I'm here."

"Yes, so all I'm saying is you will find your person. It doesn't necessarily have to be on your first attempt or even second, but you will find someone who will love and cherish you for the person you are. There's no race; there's no timeline on it. You just have to be open to the idea."

I finally stopped outside our dorms, the chill night air reminding me I should have brought a sweater with me. "Thanks, Mom, I appreciate it."

"Don't mention it, and honey, if you need to talk more about these kinds of things, I'm here," she said, and I just knew she was smiling. That was the kind of person my mom was. Always proud of every step I took in life.

"I'll keep that in mind, Mom," I said as I leaned against the exposed brick building. "I'll talk to you later. Tell Dad hello for me."

"Will do, sweetheart. Goodnight. I love you."

"I love you too, Mom," I said before I hung up and mustered a sigh. Talking to my mom always did the trick, but after this conversation, I was still left a little confused. Should I put myself out there again now or later, was the big question. Maybe I should sleep on it, I thought as

I turned to make my way back up, but then I almost froze when I spotted Jace moving toward me with a smile on his face. I wished he hadn't seen me, then maybe I could escape before he actually did, but he was staring right at me, his intentions clear.

I managed a smile and glanced down at my sweats and the large T-shirt I had stolen from my dad last summer. From laying down for almost the entire day, I knew my hair was tousled, my face bare, and I probably looked like Friday the 13th. Jace approached; his hair had grown a little bit more since I'd last seen him in summer. It was faded at the sides and neatly combed back at the top, a single lock of hair falling to his forehead. He wore the University's jacket and jeans that were impressively not clinging to him like a second skin. I never liked that.

The closer he came, the more I realized why girls made such a fuss about him. He was very attractive and confident enough to know it was a quality people were amazed by. But he didn't make my heart skip a beat – I felt nothing like I had felt for Logan from a single glance. Though he was good-looking, Logan was more attractive in a more masculine, rugged type of way. They were probably the same height, but the muscles on Logan were what I knew guys like Jace prayed to have on a daily.

"Bella, hey," he said as he stopped before me, pearly whites on full display, and honestly, I was expecting the dramatic sparkle that toothpaste commercials often included.

"Hey, Jace."

"How are you?" he asked.

"I'm great, you?" I asked, clearing my throat and hugging my shoulders.

"Yeah, I'm good. I was expecting to see more of you in the summer, but you guys were nowhere in sight."

"Yeah, we were pretty busy."

He nodded slowly, his eyes slowly taking note of me, making me a little self-conscious. "You look great, by the way."

"Thanks."

He licked his lips and raked his fingers through his hair, slightly spiking it up. "So I don't know if Dian mentioned anything to you, but I'd really like to get together sometime. Go on a date, maybe?" He shrugged, "Anything really; I'd just like a chance with you."

My heart started thudding in my chest, and it wasn't because Jace had that effect on me; it was because I couldn't believe this was actually happening now. It would have been easy to tell Dian no when she had asked, but here Jace was, looking like an eager puppy with a vulnerability I didn't even know existed until now. Was this player tactic, or did he really want a chance with me?

My mouth opened up, but I couldn't find the right words to say. That five percent of rebellion was fighting hard.

"One date, and if you don't like it, I'll accept and leave you alone," he said as he raised a challenging brow, waiting for me to reply.

I licked across my lips. "Okay, one date."

A broad smile immediately bloomed on his face. "Great, how about this weekend.? I could pick you up at around five?"

"Yeah, sounds great."

He was grinning. "Perfect; do you mind if we exchange numbers?" he said while fishing out his phone from his pocket.

"Sure," I said as I unlocked mine and handed it to him while he did the same. "Well, I'd better get back up; I'll see you then, Jace," I smiled as I handed him back his phone.

He smiled with a nod. "Can't wait."

I made my way back up to my room, feeling some trepidation for actually agreeing to a date with Jace. In the moment, it would have been hard to say no to his face, so I was allowing this date to happen because, as he had said, if I didn't like it, it didn't have to go further. I was sure that I wouldn't. I could already see myself seated in a pizza shack while Jace spoke solely about himself and his career. That was the type of thing guys like him did – egotistical and wrapped up in their own selves.

Once I returned to the room, I contemplated telling Dian about what transpired, feeling even more guilty for snapping at her earlier, especially now that I had done the same thing she was drilling me about. She was still on her phone but looked up at me as I entered. I could tell she wanted to know where I had been, but she didn't dare ask. I paused in front of her bed and fiddled with my fingers.

"I bumped into Jace," I said, and she immediately perked up, putting her phone down. "He asked me on a date."

Her eyes brightened enough to light a dark room. "What did you say?" she asked.

"I said yes, but we agreed that if I didn't enjoy it, it wouldn't go any further," I shrugged.

Dian was grinning. "And you think you'll get off the hook on date one? I don't know, Bells; Jace is a pretty nice guy. He might surprise you," she said as she perked up a brow.

I sighed and flopped beside her on the bed. "I don't want him to. I still can't stop thinking about Logan," I sighed.

She shuffled closer to me. "And I get that, but it's not like Logan is gonna magically appear and redeem himself. He was good for a night – you can still be grateful for the experience."

I stared at the blank ceiling as thoughts rushed through my head. I didn't want to be grateful for an experience that didn't amount to anything. I always said, if I didn't see a future with someone, what sense did it make to lose my body to them? Still, I had to admit, the feeling was bittersweet where Logan was concerned. On the one hand, I hated how it ended, but on the other, I loved how it started.

I couldn't believe my life had gotten so messy in a matter of weeks.

Chapter 7

Logan

With each passing day, the excruciating need to be with Bella became more torturous. The meek virgin had managed to occupy every second of my thoughts to the point where I considered having a private investigator look for her. But what did I even have to go off on either; all I knew was her first name and nothing else. I didn't know anything else about her apart from her body, and that couldn't exactly go into someone's search engine.

I didn't want her just to be some girl I met at a bar; I wanted her to be my woman in every way possible. I wanted it all with her, but at the same time, I had to question her reasons for fleeing. In my head, it didn't make any sense. That night, we had shared so much – were so mutual in our feelings – and the next day, she was gone. Maybe she had decided she couldn't be my woman – that she couldn't commit to anyone. I'd understand that better if she wasn't a virgin – but she was. That had been as clear as day. I had been inside her, felt as I breached her hymen and as she gripped me in the moment of pain. I had seen the evidence, seen it in her eyes and spent hours stretching her inexperienced flesh. There was no denying that part, but her leaving without a word was a mystery that boggled my mind with each passing day. Truth was, I wasn't going to accept it. There had to be a reason, and I wouldn't stop until I found out what it was.

My phone shrilled, bringing me from my thoughts. I looked at the caller ID and almost rolled my eyes when I saw who it was. I had half a mind to answer it – in fact, I should have blocked the caller a long time ago, but it never occurred to me until now.

"What do you want?" I asked, reaching into the refrigerator to grab a beer.

"No need to be like that; can we talk?"

"We have nothing to talk about, Jenny. Enjoy the rest of your night," I said, hanging up out of spite and pure despise for the woman.

No sooner than I did that, I heard a knock on the door. Sighing, I moved toward the front door. All I wanted was an evening to unwind, prepare myself for tomorrow and stroke myself to thoughts of Bella until I was satisfied and exhausted enough to fall asleep. I opened the door and muttered a curse, standing face to face with the woman who had just been on the phone with me.

"You've got to be fucking kidding," I hissed as I stared at her.

"I knew you wouldn't want to talk on the phone, but I really need to talk to you, Logan," she said as she pushed past me and entered the house without another word.

I huffed a breath, closed the door and followed behind her to the living room, where she dropped her bag and sat.

"You've got a minute, and then I'm kicking you out," I said as I stood before her, arms crossed.

She tucked her brown hair behind her ears and pursed her lips. "I made a mistake," she blurted.

I scoffed. "With what?"

She swallowed and met my eyes. "Leaving you."

I couldn't help my chuckle. "You've been saying that for two months now, and I've been telling you, no matter what you fucking say, nothing will change. I'm done with you, Jenny. Get that through your head," I exclaimed, feeling the anger rise within me.

She bounded from her chair, now standing. "Why? I've been begging you for the past two months, and it's like it has meant nothing to you," she said, her voice cracking a little.

"It doesn't. You made your choice when you left this relationship searching for greener pastures. You can't come running back just because it didn't suit you."

Her green eyes glistened. "Logan, please, I'm so very sorry. I wasn't thinking straight, I-"

"You fucked someone else for months during our relationship and left me for him. Don't give me crap about not thinking straight," I hissed, and she paled as she hung her head.

I knew this move too well – knew Jenny too well to know exactly what this was. She sniffled and played with her fingers, and in the next instant, her tears were falling to the floor. As expected.

"What do you want?" I asked, irritated by the overplayed antics.

She lifted her glossy eyes to me, and any man who didn't know the type of woman she was would fall for it in a heartbeat. But not me – not again. The big, bright puppy dog eyes wouldn't work on me again.

"I want another chance," she said. "I want you back, Logan."

"Why?" I asked her, and she hesitated with a reply. I knew that whatever sob story she came up with would be a lie. Truth was, after living the lavish lifestyle with someone else, she either revealed her true colors or had become boring. Jenny wasn't spontaneous, but she was greedy and had the looks to appease any man for a while.

I had been so caught up in her good looks and her sex appeal that I was blinded to what was really in front of me. Luckily for me, I hadn't married her before finding out all this.

"I missed you," she finally said, and I wondered how deep she actually had to dig for that one. "I missed us, Logie." Here with the ridiculous nickname that I had found cute a long time ago. She approached me and trailed her fingers down my chest. I expected to feel something because as much as I disliked the woman, she had always managed to make my cock stand for her. But surprisingly, that wasn't the effect she had on me now. My skin crawled at her touch – I couldn't bear the thought of another woman touching me apart from Bella. It felt wrong. Jenny paled so much in comparison in many ways to Bella that I hadn't realized until now.

I reached for her hands and dropped them at her sides. Her eyes widened, and I could see a bit of confusion there, which was expected, seeing that I could never resist her when she was this near, this daring.

"Why are you being like this?" she asked, "Is there someone else?" there was this dramatic look of horror in her eyes which was almost laughable.

I hesitated with her question. There was someone else who plagued my mind like a drug, but physically, there wasn't. How could I voice that aloud without sounding like a complete idiot?

"Yes," I said as she took a step back as if she had been slapped.

"Who? Where is she?"

"That's none of your business, Jenny. None of what I do anymore is your business," I said. "I gave you more than a minute, and now it's time for you to leave," I said, leaning my head towards the exit.

More tears started to stream down her face. "I won't stop until you're mine again, Logan. I won't give up so easily on us," she sniffed before she walked away and left the room. When the front door slammed, I scoffed and shook my head. It was obvious Jenny was delusional – in some fairy-tale land that I wanted no part of. If I hadn't met Bella, I didn't know how this conversation would have gone. I wondered if I would have conceded – forgiven everything and given her another shot. That was the type of person Jenny knew me to be, and I knew this rejection was probably strange to her, but there was no going back to her toxicity. I didn't even realize how alive I could feel in one night. How alive I continued to feel even after.

That was the Bella effect. Jenny was history.

Chapter 8

Bella

I skimmed through my closet, searching for something to wear while Dian hovered over me, her excitement almost tangible.

"Where exactly is he taking you again?" she asked as she assessed the clothes I had thrown on the floor.

"He wouldn't say, but he did say to keep it simple," I shrugged, pulling up a few bottoms. "Maybe I wasn't so wrong in the pizza shack theory after all," I murmured.

"Let's be a bit more positive, shall we?" Dian countered as she pulled out denim shorts. "How about this? Your legs are really nice and tempting."

I rolled my eyes. "The last thing I want to do is tempt him."

Dian laughed. "It wouldn't hurt. Or you could keep it girly?" she said as she wiggled her brows and held up a yellow dress with daisy prints. My mouth twisted as I gave it some thought.

"Hmm, maybe. But anyway, what do you plan on doing while I'm gone?" I asked, continuing with the task at hand.

Dian shrugged. "I might upload a new makeup tutorial to my YouTube or go chill with Matthew," she said, referring to her new boy toy.

"How's it been? You've been dating for a few weeks now," I said.

"He's okay, I guess. Good in bed, but that's about it."

I laughed. "So why are you still seeing him?" I asked.

"Didn't you hear the good in bed part? It's hard to find someone who can make your toes curl like that. I'm not ready to let him go just yet."

My stomach fluttered at Dian's words, and I couldn't help but think about Logan. He had been able to do that – more than that. The thing was, it wasn't just the sex with him; I'd wanted to know more about him, and the way we connected was more than just on a sexual level. But why was I thinking about him again when I should be getting ready to go on a date with another man? I should be thinking about Jace, but it all felt so wrong. For some crazy reason, my heart was only set on Logan, and anyone else felt like a threat. It was crazy – maybe this was the virgin attachment I'd heard about plenty of times. Maybe this was me finding it hard to get over the man I had lost my virginity to. I had no clue, but maybe I would bring myself closer to finding the answers after this date with Jace.

We had texted, and I had found that he was a pretty decent guy with some humor up his sleeve, but I couldn't exactly use that to judge his character until I was face to face with him, observing every response and reaction.

Fifteen minutes later, I finally settled on the flowy daisy-printed dress and a jacket. It was fast approaching six in the afternoon, and I knew it would be a chilly night. I let my hair down, happy that I had decided to brighten the blonde highlights a few days ago. I put on minimal makeup, applied a few finishing touches and then I was ready to leave.

Dian was grinning from ear to ear, her hands clasped at her mouth as she stared at me with admiration. "I'm so proud. I can't believe you're going on a date with the most popular guy on campus," she shrieked.

I managed a tight smile. "Me neither."

She clapped her hands and hopped towards me, grabbing my shoulders. "It's gonna be great, I promise!"

"I hope so," I smiled.

"Have a good time, and I'll be here waiting for you to tell me all the juicy details when you get back!"

I snorted. "There won't be any 'juicy' details," I retorted as I grabbed my purse.

"Whatever; I'll be happy with any details. Have fun!" she exclaimed, kissing me on the cheeks and jumping in excitement.

"Thanks, Dian; I'll see you later," I said as I stepped out of the room and down the hall. Jace had texted about five minutes ago, saying he was out front. There was this feeling of nervousness inside me because although I had been with a man before, I'd never really been on a real date. This was my first in that regard, and quite frankly, I didn't know what to expect. I already dreaded the conversation – knowing I'd be too awkward to keep the conversation flowing. The idea that this would all turn out to be a complete shit show crossed my mind, filling me with trepidation.

I wanted to run back to my room and bury myself under the covers, but I had to remind myself I wasn't getting any younger and couldn't allow life to pass me by. I had to explore the playing field – find out what I liked and what I didn't like.

I spotted Jace in a red pickup, his hand resting on the open window while he smiled at me with his glistening white teeth. I managed a smile as I moved closer to him. He pushed open the door and hopped out, moving to the passenger's side to open my door. But he paused in front of me, and my heart almost leaped out of my chest for some reason.

"You look beautiful," he said, that look of pride on his face.

"Thanks," I said, skimming over his pale jeans and navy blue sweater. "You don't look bad yourself."

He smiled and cranked the door further open. "After you," he said, and I stepped inside his pickup, which was fairly clean, but smelled a bit like worn socks barely masked by air freshener. Jace smelled nice, though – despite not hugging or anything remotely physical, I had smelled his cologne from a mile away. He was seemingly drenched in it, and it tickled my nose a bit.

He hopped back into the driver's side and turned to me. "So I was thinking maybe we could watch the sunset for a bit and then a picnic?" he said, blue eyes intense as he awaited an answer.

The whole pizza shack theory was still stuck in my head, and so I hadn't been expecting anything remotely close to what he was suggesting. "That sounds like a great idea."

He beamed at me before he started the engine, turned on the latest rap music and drove off.

"I'm really glad you decided to come, Bella. You have no idea how long I wanted to ask you out," he said, looking from the road to me.

"Really?"

"Yeah, I just didn't know how. I kinda hinted at it to Dian, but she never really picked up on it, I guess. When I saw you this summer, I knew I couldn't hold off any longer," he said, a smile curving his lips.

I bit my lips. "You don't seem like the type to be hesitant about such things."

He chuckled. "People constantly misjudge me, so I get it, but I'm not a stereotype. I'm not a loser, I'm not a dick, and I'm not a manwhore. That's where a lot of people go wrong."

"Well, I can't exactly take your word for it; I guess I'll just have to find out," I said, and Jace glanced at me and laughed.

"True. I guess so, Bella," he nodded, still smiling. "So how comes I've never seen you with anyone on campus?" he asked.

"Were you paying that much attention to me to realize?" I asked, brows raised.

"I have when I get the chance," he admitted.

I fidgeted my fingers. "I'm not really an open book, Jace. I value my privacy," I said, though there had been nothing to be private about. He was right. I was never seen with any guy on campus because there weren't any. If I hadn't been to that club and met Logan, Jace would have been the only guy I'd ever had a solid conversation with, except for my group partners in the past.

"I appreciate that. So if this date goes well, and we decide to give this dating thing a shot, would you mind the attention you would get when people see that we're dating?" he asked, glancing at me.

I opened my mouth to answer but clamped it shut when I realized that answering would be harder than I had expected. Initially, this had been one of the first thoughts that had crossed my mind, but somewhere along the way, I had forgotten that part of putting myself out there with the school's quarterback was allowing a thousand eyes to scrutinize, judge and draw a whole lot of conclusions. Was I ready for that? Shy me, who had tried to avoid male attention for almost all of my life? I didn't have to answer that. I was still working it out in my head.

"Let's just see where today takes us, and then I might be able to give you an answer," I said, and Jace nodded.

"Fair enough."

We continued the rest of the journey with light chatter until Jace parked on top of a hill that overlooked the city. I was in awe, but before I could fully appreciate it, he was jumping out and running around the other side to open my door. I wondered if this was even genuine chivalry, but I still appreciated the effort.

I stepped out and watched as he pulled down the tailgate of his pickup and hopped up in it. I hadn't realized before, but there were a few things wrapped up in the back. Blankets, cushions, a basket. Jace pulled everything apart, laying out the blanket in the back before he picked out things from the basket and did the same. There was a variety of food – sandwiches, cookies, pies, fruits and candies that really had me just staring.

Once done, he smiled at me and reached for my hand. I took it, and he helped me up into the back of the van, facing the view of the city.

"Wow, Jace, this is amazing," I said as I settled on a cushion beside him.

"I'm glad you like it. I don't mean to brag, but I prepared everything myself," he grinned, reaching for a bottle of wine.

"You're kidding!"

"Serious as a judge. My dad is a chef, so he has shown me the ropes ever since I was a kid.

I smiled. "I don't even know what to choose!"

He laughed. "You can try the chicken salad sandwich; it's one of my faves. Always puts me in a good mood."

"Ok, here goes," I said as I unwrapped it from the clear foil and took a bite. I closed my eyes as the flavors burst in my mouth and opened them to find Jace grinning at me, eyes trained on my lips.

"Mmm, this is really good," I said, my mouth full.

He licked his lips. "Thanks; I always said that if football doesn't work out, I have this to bounce back on," he laughed. "My dad would prefer that any day as well."

My brows shot up as I swallowed. "Really?"

"Yeah, he has this plan for us to start our own little restaurant once I graduate. It was really my uncle who got me into the whole football thing."

I nodded as I looked at him, trying to read him. "So which do you prefer?"

"I like both equally. Football is like an outlet, but cooking really brings me peace, so I might just do football for a couple of years and then be a chef for the rest of my life," he shrugged.

I nodded as I took another bite. "You could."

He started to eat too. "So what about you? What are you studying?"

"Finances."

"Wow, you must really like math."

I laughed. "I do."

We continued to chat while the sunset became more beautiful – a vibrant mix of orange, pink and yellow that was possibly the most beautiful thing I had ever seen.

"Sunsets in LA are really the most beautiful," I said, glancing at Jace.

"So true. I can't decide which is more beautiful, you or it," he said, and I turned to him, trapped by the look in his eyes. They had darkened, and his eyes were on my lips as a barrage of thoughts seemingly rushed through his mind. I knew he wanted to kiss me, and I weighed the idea in my mind for a brief second, wondering if his lips would be as soft and welcoming as Logan's - as sweet. A part of me wanted to test the waters, to explore something new in an attempt to rid my memory of Logan. That feeling of need roamed through me like a wild animal as I thought back to the seemingly endless nights of missing Logan and wanting him by my side again. I craved the feeling – wanted to have it again, but this was Jace, and there was no fire between us, no matter how smoothly the conversations went or how easily he had managed to make me laugh. With Logan, it had been instant – one look, and I knew I wanted him more than anything. It had me considering if that was a once in a lifetime occurrence for me or if I would live to experience that feeling again.

But Jace was leaning in, ready to take the next step with me while my heart beat a mile a second, trying to decide if this was actually what I wanted. But his mouth was on mine in the next instant. His lips were soft and welcoming as he probed within my mouth with his hand and latched on to my waist to pull me closer. I decided to give in to whatever this was without any restraint. I didn't hold back and instead allowed whatever to happen, happen. I kissed him back, desperate to feel something – anything, not knowing that while I was doing that, I was urging on Jace even more. He moaned against my mouth and pulled me even closer to him – placing me in an uncomfortable position that he didn't seem aware of.

His warm tongue explored the contours of my mouth, sliding against my teeth in an almost sloppy manner while his hands ran up my back. I was still desperately wanting to feel that passion – that need that seemed to make me go all mushy, but all I could ever feel was pleasant. Just a pleasant kiss that did nothing but exercise my tongue.

But the longer he kissed me, I realized there was this need within me, but it wasn't for Jace. It was for the man I couldn't have. Here I was, wishing it was Logan kissing me, that it was his body pressed against me – that this was us. My core tightened at the idea; I could feel the liquid heat boiling inside my body at the prospect of Logan. I wanted him so badly and was desperate enough to use Jace to have my way.

I found myself kissing him back hard, clinging onto him while I envisioned Logan in his position. I was burning up – wanting something that would clear my mind even for a second. I reached for Jace's buckle, and he tore apart to look at me with wide eyes.

"Are you sure?" he asked me between breaths.

"Yes, Jace, I'm sure," I said as I fumbled with his pants.

His mouth crashed into mine again while he clumsily tried to get his pants off in the same breath. At this point, I was burning up despite the wind that passed between us. We broke apart for another second, Jace taking off his pants while I slipped off my panties. For a brief second, he slipped around into the truck and came back with a condom which he easily slipped on his length. I couldn't think straight. I just wanted a repeat of what happened with Logan.

Jace was naked from the bottom half down, his sweater still on, his manhood dangling between us as he hovered over me. It wasn't as astounding as Logan's had been. It was long and slender. I spread my legs, and he kissed me again, harder this time as he lowered himself on me. Jace guided his penis to my flesh, and I moaned when the hard tip touched my sensitive skin. There was no foreplay, thereafter, no teasing. He just drove his length inside me, and I stiffened, realizing I had not been completely aroused. There was a bit of discomfort, but I didn't voice my thoughts, and Jace didn't ask.

"Fuck, you're so tight!" he said between clenched teeth, his face at my neck, and he shoved himself further. Half his weight was on me as he thrust back and forth quickly. As much as I tried to envision this was Logan, this experience couldn't create such an illusion. As I stared into the darkening sky, I only prayed this experience would be over, but it ended way quicker than expected. A couple of seconds later, Jace started to fuck me a little faster, and I knew I would be sore when it ended. He didn't stop as he sunk me deeper and deeper into the hard van. He then grunted like he was in pain, stiffened and filled the condom with his seed.

I sighed, swallowed back the tears and waited for him to get off me. When he finally did, he had a smile on his face while sweat beaded his forehead.

"I swear, you're amazing, Bella," he said as he reached for his discarded clothes. I managed a tight smile and pushed my dress down over my private area, wishing it had stayed private.

That should have been enough to cancel any ideas of a second date, but I had been foolish enough to have sex on the first date. I had to see it through, hoping things would get better. I couldn't have two bodies that meant nothing in less than two months. So later that night when we drove back to campus, Jace asked me how it went.

I smiled. "Great, I was really impressed by all you did, Jace." *Except for the sex*, I was tempted to say but held my tongue.

He grinned. "Good, because I didn't want just one date from you, Bella. In fact, today went better than I had planned. Us making love was just the icing on the top."

I wanted to cringe; I wanted to cry, I wanted to bury myself to rid myself of this embarrassment, but there was nowhere to run.

"Now that you've seen my culinary skills, I'd really like it if you stopped by at practice one of these evenings – see how I dominate the field," he winked.

"Sure, I'd like that," I heard myself saying. Jace reached across and quickly kissed me on the cheeks before he turned his attention back to the road.

When he dropped me off and I began my walk up to my room, I could feel the evidence of the disaster between my thighs. Unlike Logan, it was not from the result of something incredibly mind-blowing; it was just plain disaster. As I opened the door to my room, I dreaded the conversation with Dian. The last thing I wanted to discuss was what happened - explain how I acted like a slut and had slept with the quarterback on the first night. It made me feel sick to my stomach, but when I entered, I was pleasantly shocked to find she wasn't there. Probably decided to 'chill' with Matthew. Hopefully, it was going better than mine had gone.

I immediately headed to the bathroom and took a quick shower before I came back into the room and flopped down on the bed, replaying everything in my head. I had hoped that although the sparks had not flown when Jace and I were together, the sex would at least be good. But it wasn't, and maybe my standards were a bit high after Logan, but I didn't expect the need to still be there, and I didn't think Jace would come that quick.

I groaned and shuffled beneath the sheets, wanting the release that Jace couldn't give. My fingers trailed along my open leg and to my vagina, where I teased my flesh through the fabric. There was still that bit of sensitivity – that ache I wished would go away. I found my hardened bud and began to massage it while I allowed my thoughts to go back to that night of pure pleasure. Logan's mouth on me, his fingers trailing all over. I wanted my body on full alert, the feeling that had swam through me when he pinned me with his intense blue eyes and then his hands. I wanted it all. I wanted his rock-hard member parting my slit, massaging my clit before he sunk deep within my flesh and proceeded to give me an unending amount of pleasure.

I'd simply die if I didn't experience that feeling again in this lifetime – I was already on the verge of doing so. So sex-starved that I think I'd lose my mind at any given moment. I wanted Logan. I wanted the man who had made me feel so sexy and alive, who had opened a world of pleasure I didn't even know existed until him. I wanted that. I wanted every second of it and tried to do the best I could to have that now that he couldn't. A simple thought of Logan could get me wet... just thinking about him in such a manner had me soaked. My fingers trickled under the waistband of my panties and found my dripping core – a single touch causing a shockwave of sensations to plummet through my body.

My middle finger slid over my saturated flesh, the feeling like a touch of silk as pleasure erupted through me. I moaned and closed my eyes as images of Logan flashed across my thoughts. His mouth against my slit, his manhood in it. It was all too much. My fingers began to circle my clitoris, causing my core to pool with more wetness as I further aroused myself. My body clenched, and I could feel the juices oozing from me and down my ass. I was so ready to be stuffed by something that it almost became unbearable. Without a second thought, I slipped my fingers from my hard clit and inside my hole. One finger slipped in with ease, caressing the bruised walls that Jace had caused, but I needed more. I needed to feel something close to what Logan had made me feel. Another finger joined, and I could feel the juices sluicing down my fingers as I pleasured myself. With each stroke, the desperation for release increased, and I found myself moaning and writhing as I basked in the sensations I'd created for myself.

I closed my eyes and sunk my fingers as deep as my snatch could allow, whimpering when I touched a spot that had me clamping my legs together. But I wasn't done yet, regardless of the orgasm beating at my gates. I moved my fingers faster and faster until all I could feel was an insurmountable pleasure. But I wanted this feeling rippling through me for longer, so I pulled them out, circled my drenched clit and went back in again, feeling as I opened up in welcome. The feeling of discomfort faded, and my fingers began to thrust even deeper and faster before my mouth opened up, and a surge of blinding pleasure wrenched me. I bit down on my lips in an attempt to suppress my cries as my body quivered and convulsed in the wake of my orgasm. My fingers were still inside, my walls clamping down on them as my orgasm riddled my body.

I felt so weightless afterward – similar to how I had felt with Logan but nothing compared. My eyes started to flutter open and close as sleep threatened my form. I allowed the bliss to float through me as I fell asleep, the most contented I had ever felt in weeks.

Chapter 9

Bella

Dian scoffed, mouth opened in shock as I relayed the events of the past evening to her. I'd prefer if I had kept it a secret, but Dian was always my go-to, even though she didn't always give the best advice, and I knew she would ask as soon as she had the chance to, anyway. So when she came back this morning, it was the first thing she inquired about after taking a shower.

"So you're telling me Jace Bradford is a three-minute man?" she exclaimed, green eyes wide.

I nodded. "And the three minutes weren't even good?" she asked.

I shook my head. "It wasn't."

"OMG, this is headline-worthy stuff; I can't believe it?" she said as her eyes searched the room, her brain obviously spinning. Her gaze snapped back to me. "So why are you even making plans to go out with him again?"

I sighed. "I don't want to end things after one date, especially since I had been stupid enough to have sex with him," I scowled.

Dian nodded understandingly. "But the date went great, right? – Apart from the whole sex thing."

"Yeah, he wasn't so bad in that department after all," I said, and Dian giggled.

"Maybe it was just because it was the first time. Some guys can't hold out for long, but it might get better," she shrugged.

I picked at my nails. "I'm not holding my breath."

Dian blew out a sigh and reached for my shoulders, giving them a gentle squeeze. "Not every love story has sparks flying right away or incredible sex. Some take time. I'm pretty sure Jace will eventually get there."

I shrugged my shoulders and rolled off the bed. "We'll see. Anyway, he's been blowing up my phone since last night and has invited me to see his practice this afternoon."

"Aww, seems like poor Jace is in deeper than we thought," Dian grinned.

I rolled my eyes. "I hope not because I'm not looking to rush anything."

"I heard they got a new coach anyway. Word is the guy is hotter than the players. I'm dying to see who it is," Dian geeked.

An idea immediately popped up. "Oh, you could come with me then; that way, you would know as well as keep me company!" I said as I beamed at her.

Dian made a sad face. "Sorry, Bells. Around that time, I'm gonna be collecting clothes from a sponsorship and ohh – I want you to please take some photos of me in them. My tripod is broken, and having the new one delivered will take a day or so."

"Ok, sure, when?"

"Around five or so."

"Yeah, sure, I'm sure practice will be done by then, and if it isn't, it's still a pretty good excuse to leave. I'm not a fan of the sport."

Bella laughed. "Join the club. Do you think I need to brighten the pink for the photos?" she asked, weaving her fingers through her hair.

"No, the blonde is barely even showing at this point."

"True," she said as she flashed me a sly smile. "I can't believe that you are slowly becoming the girlfriend of a star player! Watch out for the other girls, Bells; they are gonna be watching you like a hawk and maybe want to pick your eyes out too."

I groaned and did a face palm. "Don't remind me!"

Dian laughed. "Don't worry, I'm sure it won't be so bad."

"I hope not."

I MADE MY WAY THROUGH an economics test, and a few other classes, and before I knew it, it was almost time to see Jace play. I realized something that had never been evident before. People were staring at me, and while some always did because I was the best friend of the biggest influencer on campus, this time, it was different. Not only were they looking, but some were also whispering as I passed – eyeing me from top to bottom. I wanted to curl up in my shell and go back to when I was almost invisible to people. This wasn't the type of attention I wanted to attract. Not because of Jace, of all people. I could just imagine what they all had to say about me – what assumptions they were drawing based on the fact that Jace and I had gone on one date! Did he tell people that we had sex? As the thought came to me, I wanted to sink through the ground. Guys had a way of bragging to their friends, and while Jace would have liked to convince everyone that he wasn't the typical guy, he was a guy nonetheless. A guy who obviously sought validation from people's opinions.

I felt sick to my stomach and considered heading home but realized the walk to my dorm room would be longer than the walk to the stadium, and I couldn't go through all that again. I quickly made my way there, happy I was wearing skinny black jeans and a black crop top. That wasn't exactly plain.

The stands were almost empty except for a few groupies and people who came to support. The guys were dressed in gear, doing warm-ups, and I made it a mission to sit the furthest away from everyone but still close enough to see what was happening. I didn't know the first thing about the sport and wanted to laugh at how ridiculous this whole thing was. Who was I kidding?! There was no way I could fit into this lifestyle – there was no way I wanted to, which became clearer with each passing second. I should never have said yes to a date with Jace – I should have stayed moping over Logan, who I was still fricking moping over regardless of being with Jace. Being with someone else should have made things better, but all I could do was compare; see all the things that Jace lacked that Logan had possessed. It was fricking torture!

"Bella, right?" I heard a voice behind me say. My head snapped around to see two girls standing behind me, long legs exposed beneath their little mini-skirts and crop tops showing their blinding navel rings.

I cleared my throat and managed a smile. "Yeah."

They both plastered a smile on their petite little faces and came to sit on opposite sides of me. The brunette flipped her hair and stretched out a hand to me. "I'm Lilly, and that is Carmen. My man is the wide receiver, and hers is the center," she smiled, and I shook her hand.

"Nice to meet you, guys," I said, glancing at the dark skin who had not said a word. Only smiled.

"Word is, you're Jace's girl," Lilly said.

I could feel the blood draining from my face. "I er – we're not really official or anything like that," I said.

Carmen laughed. "Tell that to Jace. All he does is brag about you, but he was right, though, you are a real beauty, I must admit," she said as her gaze roamed over me in the most seductive manner. Who was she here for again?

I swallowed. "Thanks."

"I like your hair. Where did you get it done?" Lilly asked, weaving a few strands through her fingers.

"Er, I don't quite remember. My friend Dian actually brought me there, I-"

"OMG, I love her so much. I live for her videos!"

"And her Instagram. The girl is a straight up baddie," Carmen gushed. "And have you seen her body? – To die for!"

"How did you guys become friends?" Lilly asked as she ran her gaze over my fit.

"She's been my roomie since first year," I said as my brows furrowed.

"We should all hang out sometimes. Us and the guys and Dian, of course!" Carmen exclaimed.

"Totes!"

My mind was racing. It was hard to keep up with these two. Dian was enough of a chatterbox for me; I didn't need these two joining the club with their high-pitched voice and personalities I'd have to take my time figuring out. It was overwhelming.

"Oh, they've started!" Lilly shrieked, and I almost jumped as my gaze snapped to the field to see the guys had formed into two teams and were competing against each other. I squinted my eyes and could spot Jace, who immediately waved at me despite the tussling.

"Awww!" the girls chirped in unison.

A blush warmed my cheeks, and I waved at him before he dashed across the field, chasing one of the players. I winced when they began to crash into each other, the sound of their helmets and gears crunching as they made contact. I couldn't help but squirm at every contact, and I knew I would never get to the point of liking this sport. I realized the goal was to get the ball at a certain point while wrestling for it. All the protective gear made sense, and with Lilly and Carmen at both ears, it was hard not to pick up on what was happening. Still, it wasn't the most entertaining or interesting sport I had ever seen, and I would choose a book over it any day. As a matter of fact, if the girls hadn't decided to come and keep my company, I might have pulled out a book to distract myself and pass the time, but I didn't want to seem like that girl in front of anyone. And heck, I didn't want to hurt Jace's feelings either.

Minutes seemed like hours, and an actual hour later felt like a lifetime, but things quickly began to wind down, and I was aware of that thanks to the girls who bragged it was a good practice overall.

"This new coach seems to really be putting in the work," Carmen said.

"And OMG, have you seen him?!" Lilly exclaimed. "I swear he is like a God. I'll drop my man any day if I get a chance to climb that stallion," she said and giggled, Carmen joining in as they gushed about the coach.

Heck, at this point, I was now pretty curious to see what he looked like – see what the fuss was all about.

"Oh, come on, Bella. Let's go congratulate the guys on a good practice match!" Carmen said as they both got up and waited for me to do the same. I held back a sigh and did as was asked, following the chirpy girls to the field to meet their partners. I didn't know why my heart was beating so fast – it wasn't as if I hadn't seen Jace before. Or maybe it was because I was certain I would draw even more attention, being Jace's new girl and all. All his friends were on the team – the people he bragged about me with.

Jace spotted me from afar, a smile lighting up his face as he saw me. He began to walk faster toward me, jogging a little as he pulled his helmet off – still padded in football gear.

I smiled because it was like his joy was radiating off him on me. I could see that my being here was important to him for some reason, and although he was dripping with sweat and stained with dirt, I didn't exactly cringe when he came and hugged me, lifting me off the ground as he spun me into a little circle. I laughed – I actually laughed and clung to him. He smelled like sweat and cologne, which wasn't the most pleasant, but I still allowed myself to bask in the moment. People were looking at us, his friends nudging each other as they watched, but I didn't mind – not now.

"I'm glad you came," he said when he put me down.

I smiled. "I'm glad I did too. It was great seeing you out there. You were a beast," I said, repeating the word the girls had used to describe him.

He smiled broadly and ran his fingers through his damp hair, spiking it up a bit. "Yeah? So what do you say, this football thing could actually work for me?"

"Definitely." He lowered his head and kissed my lips lightly, smiling hard when he pulled away. Jace seemed like such a great guy so far – I just wished I shared the same feelings. And it kinda made me sad because I knew that if I weren't so hung up on Logan, I would be more open to giving this a fighting chance, but sadly, Jace didn't hold a candle to Logan.

"Come, I want you to meet some of the guys," he said as he held my hands.

I remained grounded. "Jace, we agreed we would take it slow," I whispered, looking at the guys who were obviously eager to meet me. They couldn't stop staring.

His smile faltered a little. "I know, but everyone knows we're dating already..."

I stepped closer toward him. "By any chance, did you mention that we slept together?" I whispered, feeling my cheeks warming.

His brows furrowed, a look of confusion crossing his face. "To the guys – no. That's our business," he said, and I immediately felt a sense of relief overcome me, but I wasn't a hundred percent reassured.

"Hey, Bradford – a word, please," a voice said from behind. My body stiffened as familiarity dawned, and my brain raced to put a face to it. But that didn't take long. I knew who it was, and when Jace turned to acknowledge him, and he came into view, my world crashed before me. I couldn't believe it; I couldn't believe that what I was seeing was true. He was right there. The man I had pined over for weeks – the man who had occupied my thoughts for weeks on end was standing right in front of me. My knees weakened, and it was like I had lost my grip on reality with how my head was spinning. Logan was right there, his eyes widening a bit when he saw me, that pure lust and wonder taking over his blue eyes. Our gazes met, and everyone else became non-existent.

Suddenly, I was reminded of everything – every touch, every caress. That entire night came swimming back into my head so vividly, it felt real. A series of emotions came crashing within me, and I was there, thinking about the wonderful night we had and what I had awakened to in the morning. It spilled out of me, and I could feel my eyes sting as the wound I had been working so hard to repair ripped wide open.

He was staring at me with those intense blue eyes, looking sexier than the day we met in his t-shirt that clung to every muscle and shorts that showed off his toned legs. His beard was still low cut, his hair had grown out a little, and the tattoo was still so visible on his neck. I remembered kissing along it, tracing every line with the curve of my tongue. The tears fell from my eyes, and before Jace could see it, I dashed from the field, not caring how ridiculous I looked. I couldn't be there for another second – I couldn't stand to look into his face and feel the happiness that bubbled up inside me, along with the despise I also felt for him and what he had done. It was all too much. Too overwhelming.

Chapter 10

Logan

I had been optimistic about the day from the very moment I got out of bed this morning, but nothing could have prepared me for what I was now witnessing. Bella was right in front of me. After looking for her for all these weeks, hoping I would see her again, being obsessive about it with each passing day, she was actually here. At the most unlikely spot with the most unlikely set of people I had expected to see her with. I was so caught up in finding her and seeing her again that I had not fathomed the idea of her being a college student. How could I not have guessed? How could it not have crossed my mind even after getting this position?

None of it mattered now, anyway. She was here now, and I couldn't let her slip through my fingers yet again. I couldn't believe it. She was beautiful, small, with that look of innocence she still possessed even after I had taken her over and over again. This time, though, there wasn't any makeup on her face, and fuck, if she wasn't even more beautiful with her beautiful ivory skin, her lush lips, her expressive brown eyes that were bigger now in her state of shock. Bella was delectable, and my body was on full alert as my cock stirred, and my fingers itched to touch her.

As I stared at her, completely dumbfounded, her eyes began to glisten, and before I could give it any thought, she was dashing away with tears streaming down her face. My first thought was to run after her, and I was about to, but then Jace – who I had completely forgotten was before us – spoke, and reality kicked it.

"Er – could you give me a sec, coach? I'm gonna go see what's wrong with my girl," he said, and before I got the chance to respond, he was running off behind Bella. His words resonated in my head, and I came to the startling realization that Bella was someone else's girlfriend. Jace Bradford.

I could feel the fire rushing through my veins as the thought of another man with my woman dawned on me. Bella was mine, and I had made it clear that night. She was mine to touch and mine to keep. But here she was with another man with me just a memory in the back of her mind. But I refused to accept that.

I stormed from the field and into my office, wanting to punch something. When I saw nothing was available, I resorted to the wall, slamming my fist onto it, knowing I would regret it later.

"Fuck!" I exclaimed between clenched teeth, pacing the small room as my brain raced.

There were so many things I needed the answers to. The first, why she had stormed out of my house the following morning after the amazing night we had. I needed her to look me in the eyes and tell me where I had gone wrong and why she had moved on so quickly. Did it really mean nothing to her? Had she forgotten what we shared so quickly? I couldn't see myself with another woman but Bella, and yet she had moved on with her life as if nothing had happened. I didn't know why I was so angry – things like this happened all the time. At one point in my life, I had been the one fleeing in the mornings. Was this Karma? It also gnawed me to see her with someone younger, someone more handsome – more fitting for her – more in her age range. She was a college student for Christ's sake! What was I even thinking to be acting like this? If the board found out I had been involved with a student, they would kick me out faster than I had entered. Staff and students were an absolute no-no.

For a brief instant, it made me wonder if this was just how things were supposed to go – if Bella and I had only been good for one night and one night alone. But I was quick to debunk the thought as soon as it came. I knew that she was mine with every fiber of my being, and though this career was everything I had ever dreamt of, I was willing to risk it all for a chance with Bella. It was that simple. I couldn't lose her again, and I didn't give a fuck about who stood in my way of having her. No one else mattered.

I made my way out of the office, intent on finding her and almost bumping into Jace in the process. I instantly felt territorial as I sized up the young man with greater scrutiny. It amazed me a bit to find that Bella was with someone like Jace. From what I had observed, she didn't seem like the type for the limelight.

"Sorry, coach," he quickly said.

"Is everything alright?"

"Yeah, Bella is fine. I'm just gonna change, so we can leave. Could we have that talk tomorrow?" he asked, that hopefulness in his eyes – the eagerness to quickly hurry back to his girl. My girl. I gritted my teeth.

"Yeah, sure," I said, eager to have him leave. He smiled, patted me on the shoulder and ran toward the locker room. I began to walk as fast as I could as my eyes scanned the area in search of Bella. I found her along the sides of the bleachers, hugging her shoulders and sniffing while she used her shoulders to wipe at her wet cheeks. The very sight tore at my heart. Seeing her cry tore at me completely, and feeling that it was because of me left me undone.

When she saw me, she paled, but I was already right up on her for her to run away. I stood before her, drinking in her beautiful facial features.

"What do you want?" she croaked, sniffing.

I was taken aback by her words but curious more than ever to find out what the problem was. "I thought that was obvious from the very first night, Bella. I want you."

Colour returned to her cheeks, but her scoff had her contradicting what was so evident on her face. "Don't mess with me, Logan; I'm no fool," she snapped.

"Where is all of this coming from?" I asked, confused more than ever.

"Don't stand there and pretend that you're innocent and I'm the bad guy!"

I shook my head as if to clear it and took one step closer to her. I could smell her perfume – the same one she had worn the night at the club, and fuck, it was doing things to me. I narrowed in on her neck like a vampire, desperate for a taste. She was perfect, but I had to remind myself about the matter at hand.

"Talk to me, Bella."

She swallowed, pressing her back against the cold iron behind her. "I saw the texts," she whispered between tightly clenched teeth. "I would have appreciated you telling me the truth from the get-go, but you're just a fricking asshole like I should have known you to be!" she hissed, and although my head should be reeling with confusion, I was more captivated by her fiery tongue.

From the corners of my eyes, I spotted a shadow and knew it had to be Jace. Grabbing Bella by the arm, I pulled her around to the other side and pinned her between the rails and my body. She gasped as I lowered my mouth to her ear and whispered, "We need to talk. Meet me at my apartment tonight." Touching her brought my cock to life, but I had no time to act on my desires when I could be caught at any moment. While the idea didn't scare me as much as it should, I knew I had to think this through more with a clear head.

I stood at the corner and watched as Jace approached and placed a small kiss on Bella's forehead before he placed his hand on the small of her back and led her away. I wanted to rip his hands off her and steal Bella away for safekeeping, but I knew I couldn't.

As they disappeared around the corner, I relayed Bella's words through my head and realized what she had said. *I saw the texts*; it was a statement that left me utterly confused, and I hadn't even had the chance to ask her what she was talking about. I almost gave myself an aneurysm trying to figure out what she meant but decided to check my messages to see what had come in the following morning. As sad as it sounded, only two people were in my text message box was: an old friend from coaching high school football and Jenny. As soon as the name came to me, my heart began to beat fast, knowing there was a hundred percent chance that she was the one.

I skimmed through a series of unanswered texts and went back to the date of the morning Bella had left. I muttered a curse as I read the three text messages that had come in that morning. I had been so hellbent on finding Bella and trying to figure out why she had left that I hadn't noticed that the answers were right in front of me. She had obviously seen the texts from Jenny, assumed she was my partner and fled without a second thought.

"Fuck!" I hissed, kicking at nothing in particular.

A simple misunderstanding was all it was, and I had suffered for weeks because of it. If only I could go back in time and block the woman from the very start, I wouldn't have this problem to deal with. Then my fucking student wouldn't be sporting around my woman in his arms. I raked my fingers through my hair and hoped that Bella would accept my invitation. I had to tell her the reason; I had to let her know that I made her mine from the very moment I saw her and wouldn't dare go against my word. I had to regain her trust.

THAT EVENING, I WENT home a bit earlier than usual, deciding to skip a drink at the bar and instead head home to prepare dinner. If Bella came, then she would have something to eat. I'd make this all romantic, apologize to her and explain what had happened. I was no chef or anything remotely close to it. I debated ordering take-outs or taking her somewhere, but I wanted her to see the effort and being out with her was maybe not the wisest idea now.

I was wiping sweat from my brow as I prepared a piece of steak and some greens. With trying to look at the recipe I had seen online and preparing the actual meal, I was pretty much exhausted. If Bella decided to come, I had no idea of the time, but I wanted all this to be done by eight at the latest.

I set the table, took a shower, and when I came back, everything was ready. I glanced at the time and realised that it was some minutes past eight, hoping that she would have felt something that night that convinced her to come. But minutes turned into an hour, and by then disappointment was running deep. She didn't come and that cut deep, but I knew tomorrow was another day for trying. And I wouldn't stop until I had her again.

Chapter 11

Bella

I still couldn't believe that I had seen Logan and had actually spoken to him – felt his touch that had awakened everything inside me. It felt surreal and bittersweet. There was still the anger I had harboured for what I had discovered that morning. And yet when I had confronted him, he had seemed really confused. It made me wonder if he was that good at pretending or if he truly had no idea of what I was talking about.

Part of me wanted to accept his invitation and head over to his house – I had memorized the address, so it wouldn't be hard, but I was scared of what I felt with Logan and what could happen if I actually went. It would bring back too many memories – rehash too many feelings. Part of me wondered if that would be a bad thing, but I knew it would be, seeing that I had moved on with Jace, who had been so clueless about the whole thing. I hated to lie, but I had to tell him that school was taking a toll, and I had randomly broken down in tears. It was a stupid lie, but he had bought it, not for a moment thinking that it was because I had slept with his coach.

The whole thing was a mess, and I could see how things would turn out if I gave in to Logan's temptations. He could lose his job if he was caught, and the rumors would simply kill me. The very thought caused my stomach to churn. I couldn't do it – I had to stay far. No matter how many times I tried to convince myself of that, my body was in turmoil. It was like it had found the missing piece again and was desperate for completion.

I didn't know what I was going to do. How could I still be with Jace, knowing there was no way I could love him, especially with Logan around? I had to end things with him, and I had to avoid Logan, but thinking it was much easier than giving in to the actions.

Even now, I itched to damn it all to hell and head over to Logan's place, but I was trying to be logical at the same time. Damn, adulthood was hard.

Dian entered through the door, and I almost jumped out of my skin. She furrowed her brows when she saw me and flung her bag to her bed. "You look like you've just seen a ghost," she scoffed.

"Not exactly a ghost," I said. "Logan."

Dian continued to peel her jacket off but paused when she processed what I said, her head snapping to me. "What?"

"He's the new coach," I said, not holding back.

Dian hastened towards me and sat on the edge of the bed. "You've got to be kidding!" she exclaimed, eyes searching my face. "What happened? What did you do when you saw him?"

"I ran away crying in front of him and Jace. It was a disaster," I said as I shook my head.

"Fuck."

"Yeah, and then I confronted him privately, and he acted like he had no idea about what I was talking about."

"What a loser."

"And then he asked me to come by his place to talk."

Dian's eyes widened. "Well, what did you do?"

"I'm here, aren't I? I couldn't go."

"Damn, Bells, I don't even know what to say. The fucking coach, and your boyfriend is the quarterback."

"He's not my boyfriend, Dian."

"Well, do you want him to be?"

I licked my lips and pondered on it for a second. "I don't know what I want anymore. This whole thing is a mess," I sighed.

"True, but what does your gut say?"

"That I should be at Logan's listening to what he has to say."

"Then why aren't you?"

"Because I'm with Jace, and I'm afraid I might be passing up a good guy for someone who's just interested in playing games. I'm also afraid of the overall outcome this may lead to. There's no fricking way Logan and I can be together either, Dian. He's a member of faculty!" I sniffed.

Dian scratched her head, and for the first time, I realized she was speechless on matters regarding this. She always had a lot to say and some advice to give, but even she was confused this time around, which was understandable.

She reached for my hand and smiled. "At the end of the day, things will work themselves out, but Bells, if you aren't feeling Jace and don't think you ever will, there's no point in leading him on in hopes that your feelings will change... because what if it doesn't, and he ends up being in love with you while you don't share the same feelings?" She raised a quizzical brow at me and sighed. "Maybe Logan isn't the guy for you, and maybe he actually is – who knows? But he's back in your life, and maybe that's a sign that more is supposed to happen between you two."

I nodded and reached for her, pulling her in for a hug. "Thanks Dian; I don't know what I would do without you."

"I wonder the same thing every day," she giggled, and I joined in.

I SLEPT ON IT AND WAS willing to make a decision the following morning. I asked Jace to meet me at the Starbucks in town and sat there drinking my favorite – strawberry cheesecake – when he entered through the door, a wide smile on his face. I immediately felt guilty but managed to smile back and kissed him lightly on the lips when he was near enough before he sat.

"Is everything okay?" he asked.

My eyes scanned the scanty café, happy with myself for choosing a seat at the far back and away from inquisitive ears.

"I um- I don't think we should continue this," I said, licking my lips and staring at the wooden table.

When he didn't say anything, I looked up and saw the utter confusion on his face, as well as the disappointment that was so clear in his blue eyes.

"Why? I thought we both enjoyed our date and –"

"I did," I was quick to say. "I just – there's no chemistry, Jace, and I don't want to lead you on," I said, lowering my voice a tad.

His Adam's apple bobbed, and he started to fidget his fingers. "But I do feel something with you, Bella... you're different from all the other girls I've dated," he said, scratching the back of his neck. "Couldn't you give this more time to see if that'll change?" he asked, eyes searching my face.

I licked across my lips. "I'm sorry," I softly said.

He scoffed. "So this is it?" he exclaimed, and my gaze snapped beside us to see if anyone was near. "We fucked on the first day, and less than a week later, you want to call it quits? Maybe you're worse than the other sluts I've been with!"

Heat engulfed my cheeks, and a painful lump rose to my throat. I wanted to die in that very spot, especially when I realized a few people had started looking.

"Jace, please –"

"No, fuck you, Bella!" he said, pushing back in his chair and causing it to scrape loudly against the wooden floor. I blinked a few times to keep myself from crying, but I just couldn't help it. Grabbing my bag, I hurried from the café and away from the curious gazes of onlookers.

As soon as I was far enough, I stopped to catch my breath and breathed in a lungful, choking sobs as I rested my palms against my knees and leaned against a nearby building. The tears flowed, but they weren't solely because of Jace. It was because of all that had happened and the mess that was turning out to be. How did I allow myself to be in such a position?

But I still had to do one thing, even though it already felt like the hardest thing I would do in my entire life. Nevertheless, I collected myself as best as I could and made my way through a few finance classes. I was still gaining attention from being Jace's new conquest, but I wondered how that would change after the news hit that we were no longer dating. I couldn't wait for whatever it was to come and eventually die down. I couldn't wait for my life to return to normal, and heck, I might even revisit my old closet – be the girl that nobody saw again.

When the clock struck six that afternoon, I knew what needed to be done. My heart was already beating so fast in my chest, I feared I would collapse before doing what I was supposed to. I made my way over to Logan's, taking a cab and instructing him where to go. When he dropped me off in front of his house, I knew I hadn't been mistaken. His Prius was parked out front, which also confirmed that he was home. Every footstep toward the door felt like it carried a tonne. I was at his house, uninvited, not knowing if he had someone over – a woman perhaps. My gut sunk at the thought, and my armpits felt sweaty, my lungs out of breath. It would appear as if I had run a marathon prior to this, but this was the slowest I had ever walked, yet it was the most exhausted I had ever felt.

When I arrived at the small porch, right in front of his door, I took a deep breath and scraped a few tendrils of hair behind my ear. I rubbed my now sweaty palm, rolled it into a fist and rapped on his door, the sound like thunder in my ears.

Waiting for him to open felt like eons had passed, but when the door was finally pulled open, Logan stood there with a look of shock on his face, but I could barely look at his face when he was shirtless, with grey sweatpants drawn over his narrow hips. Who even opened the door like this? I questioned myself, swallowing the saliva that had pooled inside my mouth.

"Bella, come in," he said, stepping to the side.

I licked my lips, still a bit hesitant and stepped inside the familiar, not-so-familiar house. As expected, the night we met came to mind when I had admired the cozy feel of his house before he had carried me upstairs to make love to me.

"I'm glad you came. I was expecting you yesterday, but I'm still happy you came. Can I get you anything to drink?"

"No thanks, I just came to clear the air," I said, clearing my throat. "What we had that night was fun and all, but that was it. It's over, and nothing else can happen between us," I said, the words feeling heavy on my tongue.

Logan's jaw visibly clenched. "What we had was more than just 'fun,' Bella. I think we both know that," he said, his voice a little gruff.

Something inside me ticked. "Actually, I don't, Logan. I thought so for a while, and then I saw for myself that all I was to you was a side piece – someone to pass the time. Have a little fun with – to add another notch to your bedpost!" I exclaimed.

"I figured out what you were talking about. Those texts you saw were from my ex, who I haven't been with in over two months," he said.

"Yeah, right. An ex who calls you babe and tells you she loves you," I scoffed, feeling the anger rise within me.

"She wanted to be back in my life, and I have turned her down many a times, but believe me, nothing was going on between us when I met you."

"And now? Have you rekindled the relationship?"

He took a step toward me, and I could feel the mint on him – the freshness that swirled down my nostrils and through my body. "Don't you understand that after being with you, there's no other woman I could have touched or laid eyes on. You were mine from that very night, and you still continue to be mine even after you left."

A chill ran down my spine, and a fire started to trickle through my body. His eyes were intense, and they were glued on mine as if letting me know that he couldn't lie to me. My heart began to beat faster; part of me wanted to dive into his arms, while another part told me I needed to do what I came here to do.

I swallowed the lump in my throat and dropped my gaze to his chest. "I can't do this Logan. Not now... not again."

"Tell me why – look me in the eyes, Bella."

With every step this man took closer toward me, I began to lose my train of thought. "You are a member of staff, Goddammit, and I'm a fricking student. So even if I wanted to, I can't," I said, my eyes now foggy with the tears that threatened to spill.

"I'll gladly quit that fucking job and go back to what I had before if it means having you for the rest of my life. Everything I said to you that night, I meant with every fucking piece of me."

The tears finally spilled. "I can't ask you to do that," I croaked. "I can't ask you to jeopardize your career and your future for me."

"You don't have to ask when I would willingly give it all up in the blink of an eye. You don't have any idea how it was for me not waking up to you after having the most amazing night of my life. Every inch of my body ached to have you; my soul yearned for you. Not many people are lucky enough to experience what we have, Bella, and I know you fucking feel it too. Don't try to fight it."

He lifted my chin, forcing me to look into his eyes, which said so much that words couldn't. My mind knew what I should be doing, but my heart couldn't allow it. I gave into the temptation that was this beautiful hunk of a man, went on tippy toes and met his lips, which had lowered to meet mine. Who was I kidding? There was no resisting Logan, no matter how hard I tried. I believed him when he said there was no one else, and I believed him when he said he would drop it all for me, although I didn't want him to. There must be some way we could figure it all out.

When his lips touched mine, it seemed like anything was possible at that moment. I latched onto his lips, allowing myself to bask in the pleasures I had been deprived of for so long. It felt like the first time; the feeling was the same, the instant arousal was the same. His hands trailed up to the back of my head, anchoring me in place as he kissed me with so much need it left my knees weak. I was already burning up, a sweet fire consuming every part of me. Logan's hands were magical, his touch was magical – I had missed him so much.

The need grew the longer we kissed – the intense need to have his skin on mine, to have him inside me. I scoured the sweetness of his mouth as he did mine, my hands hastily reaching down beneath his slacks, feeling the swelling lump between his legs. Fire instantly sparked through my skin, my body yearning for him to a mind-numbing degree.

"God, I missed you so much," he said against my mouth, which trailed from my mouth and to my neck, licking against the sensitive area. He hoisted me in his arms, and I wrapped my legs around his waist as he pressed me against a wall. There, he bathed the length of my neck with licks and hungry kisses, hastily moving to my mouth again to kiss me. My aimless hands trailed along the expanse of his broad back, gripping his skin when he explored a few spots, which had me pooling with wetness. I wanted him so much that I didn't care for the foreplay this time around. I wanted him inside me, I wanted my body to rejoice from his presence again.

"Please, Logan, I can't wait any longer," I said breathlessly, leaning my neck to the side as he showered it with kisses. "I want you inside me, please," I said, just in case he hadn't heard my earlier words.

My core hummed with need, the knowledge that his cock was just mere inches away made it worse. He paused, looking at me with his intense blue eyes while his lush lips hung open, warming my skin. I slid to the floor and used it as an opportunity to pull my panties off and pull my small dress over my head. Logan watched with hunger lurking in his eyes, kicking off his sweats in the same breath. In seconds, we were naked, standing in front of each other – drinking in the beauty we saw in each other. His eyes lowered to my tits, causing them to tighten instantly. His cock was rigid and thrumming, measuring the distance between us.

"I'm gonna fuck you in every room of this house, Bella. Mark my words," he said, his fingers trailing a lazy line down my side. I shivered and swallowed, my chest rising and falling.

"You're killing me here, Logan. Please," I begged, knowing he was the only man I could ever beg for pleasure.

Both his hands found my ass as he lifted me in his arms for a second time. He kissed me again, and I could feel the juices rushing to my core. My hands tightened around his neck as I felt his length graze my flesh. I prepared myself and wasn't disappointed when he entered me with one hard stroke that almost took my breath away. It came out like a strained gasp, my walls clinging to his massive size. But there wasn't any trouble accommodating Logan when I was practically dripping with arousal for him. The pleasure that seared through me with each stroke that he issued sent me closer and closer to cloud nine. My body rubbed against his, my clit grating on his skin as he buried his entire length inside me.

"Oh Logan, oh God," I purred in the midst of my pleasure, throwing my head forward as I kissed his strong neck and clung tighter to him.

"How could I want anyone else but you, princess?" he announced gruffly as he increased his pace, filling me with harder strokes.

I whimpered at his words, almost on the verge of tears again because I couldn't help the flicker of guilt that rushed through me. Though we weren't together at the time, I regretted being with Jace and not having him as the one and only man for me. This feeling I was experiencing right now should have sold me on the very first night. I had been a fool to think anything would have worked with anyone else.

His thrusts became more frantic, his name sliding off my lips as pleasure swirled through me. Our bodies were hot against each other, the pungent smell of sex, the sound of his cock in my wetness. I couldn't hold back anymore. I shattered around him, my walls squeezing his unyielding member. My screams echoed in the room, stars floating across my eyes as my orgasm plummeted through me. Logan was still thrusting inside me, rubbing against my sensitive walls that clenched around him with each thrust he administered. Ripples of pleasure still continued to consume me until he twitched inside me and grunted loudly. He pulled out, allowing his cum to splatter against the walls and my legs instead of my insides. Somehow I wanted that to happen. I wanted it all.

We were both breathing heavily, but Logan picked up my exhausted form and carried me to his bedroom, placing me on the bed and lying beside me. I smiled, not wanting the day to end – wanting to live like this forever.

"Are you hungry?" he asked. "We could order something to eat."

"I'd like that," I said, realizing I hadn't really eaten anything except for the drink when I met up with Jace.

Logan kissed me quickly on the lips and rolled off the bed. "Give me a sec; I'm gonna go get my phone," he said, smiling before he dashed through the door. I smiled dreamily and snuggled up to the pillows, basking in the bliss of the moment. And that was exactly what this was; a moment. When reality hit, we had a lot to consider, but for now, I didn't want to burden my mind with it. I just wanted to be here with Logan for as long as I could.

He returned with a phone in hand, completely naked, as he made his way over to me. Every inch of him was ripped and so insanely tempting; I just couldn't believe how lucky I was.

"Your pick. What would you like to have?" he asked as he came to sit beside me again.

I twisted my mouth in indecision. "How about pizza?"

He smiled. "Pizza it is."

After placing the order, he came to lay beside me, holding my gaze. "Can I ask you something?"

"Yeah, sure."

"Why Jace?"

I momentarily stiffened. "I er – he was the one who asked me out, and I guess I thought I needed someone to get my mind off you," I said, dropping my gaze to the bedsheets.

"And did it work?"

"Obviously not," I said, choking out a laugh.

A smile appeared on his lips that quickly vanished as soon as it came. I knew there was something else, and I had a feeling what it was.

"Did you guys..." he trailed off, the muscles working up in his jaw.

My heart fluttered. "Only once," I whispered, watching as his jaw clenched as his eyes darkened. "I didn't think I would see you again, Logan. I thought you were only playing me at the club-"

The muscles in his jaw bunched as he pinned me to the bed with his eyes. "I told you that you were mine from day one..."

"And I believed it in the moment, but after seeing those texts, I had to rethink," I quickly put in.

His Adam's apple bobbed. "Do you know how much it tears at me knowing that someone else was touching you, kissing you... making love to you?" he said between clenched teeth, his eyes wild.

My eyes stung. "Does that make you think less of me?" I croaked. "Don't you want me anymore?" I asked, confused.

His eyes slightly widened. "What? Of course, I do. Don't you understand that nothing you do would ever make me think less of you? I need you as much as the very air I breathe," he said as he reached for my face and tilted my chin closer to him, caressing my skin with his thumb.

"You broke things off with him, right?"

"Yes," I said, holding my breath as his hands trailed down my neck, between my breasts and between my legs.

"None of that matters now," he said, his fingers parting my wet slit, finger pressing against my clit. "All that matters is that you're here – mine again, and no man will dare to look at you after. This pussy is mine, and my cock is yours, princess." I pulled in a breath and parted my legs, allowing Logan's finger to slip into the spot his cock had been just minutes ago.

My chest started to rise and fall as my arousal heightened, the craving intensifying. I was looking at Logan, and his gaze seemingly bore through my soul as he continued to pleasure me with his eyes never leaving mine.

It all felt too intense – too overwhelming. When he slipped another finger in, I gasped as his digits slowly caressed the inside of my flesh. "Promise me that if you ever have any doubts about us, you will come to me first before running away," he said, voice thick with lust.

I licked my lips and nodded my head the best I could in this position. "I promise," I said almost breathlessly.

He pushed his fingers deeper, pushing me one step closer to losing my mind. "Believe me when I say I want you more than anything in this world, Bella. Don't ever question it. Just know I'd gladly lose everything if it meant having you."

I believed him now, and I believed everything else he could say to me in the future. It felt all so insane what I was feeling for this man. It was raw and pure, not only driven by sex but a desperation to have him in my life forever, learning everything about him – getting through life together.

His fingers began to move back and forth within me, my pussy walls like silk along his long fingers. I could feel the juices flowing from me that were not from the result of an orgasm but the arousal that stormed through my body because of Logan's presence.

"I want you inside me," I said, reaching for his face to kiss his lips.

He smiled and shook his head. "I enjoy watching you like this – seeing everything."

I slammed my head against the pillows and moaned as the pleasure built inside me. My legs opened up further to grant him more access – to have him probe deeper within me. He went knuckle deep, flickering his fingers inside me, hitting a few spots that had me writhing on the bed and oozing more juices. Pulling out for a brief second, he used his saturated fingers to rub my clit into circles before he slipped back inside me again, moving even faster. I wanted to touch him so badly, I wanted to feel his body on mine. This almost felt like agony.

My mouth opened up, and a strained cry left my lips, my body convulsing as I gripped the sheets and onto Logan's arm. My body trembled as another orgasm took hold of me.

I closed my eyes, allowing my heart and body to settle. When they fluttered open, Logan was smiling as he slipped his fingers from inside me and held them up to our gazes. My cheeks flamed as I took in the sight of his creamy fingers.

"Taste yourself. Experience what I taste when my head is between your legs, princess."

I caught his fingers between my lips, sucking off my own essence and moaning at the taste. Logan watched every second, and once he pulled his fingers out, his mouth was on mine as we shared the taste of my pussy.

Chapter 12

Logan

The pizza came, and we stayed in bed and ate. Bella was telling me about her plans for the future, and I realized I simply could not get enough of this woman. Not only was she ambitious, but she was also bright and full of life and unfiltered beauty. Any man would be lucky to have her, but I was delighted to be the lucky bastard. I could spend forever with her, reminding her of why I was the better choice than Jace or any other man for that matter.

Even now, as I was reminded that she had been with someone else, it left a sour taste in my mouth. I'd wanted to be the only man for Bella, and learning that someone else had explored her glorious body had been like a sucker punch to the gut. But I blamed myself; I blamed myself for not blocking Jenny as soon as the relationship ended. If I had done so, then none of that would have happened.

However, I tried not to think of it and instead tried to focus on the present, reminding myself of how Bella's face had contorted with pleasure when I touched her – knowing no other man could make her feel what I made her feel. I knew that to be a fact. I was that confident in my skills and Bella's body, which I was learning more about as time went by.

"So after college, my dad said he would line up an internship for me at the bank where he works. I'm hoping that will put a head start on my career," she said as she picked at the last slice of pizza, the smile falling from her face. "Logan, I know you said you would gladly drop everything for us, but what then? What will you do?"

I smiled and circled her nipples with my fingers because I couldn't be so close and not touch Bella. "I got myself an agent as soon as I accepted the position at Westgate. He has already started looking at potential opportunities if things don't work at Westgate."

"But how long does stuff like that take?" she asked.

"I'm not sure. It all depends on available opportunities and if I'm what they're looking for."

"But you said you have experience teaching high school football, too, right? If you lead Westgate to victory this season, won't it better your chances?" I could see the excitement shining in her eyes. The hope caused my heart to surge. No one had ever been so hopeful or excited about anything in my life, and that simple fact gave me more reasons to believe that this was the woman for me.

"It would."

"We have to keep things on the low for a while then until Westgate wins a couple of matches."

"Bella..." I started to protest.

"Please, Logan. I wouldn't be able to live with myself if I caused a dent in your future," she argued.

"You won't –" she placed a finger on my lips to keep me quiet.

"Please, just this one thing," she said softly as she snuggled closer to me. She then removed her finger and replaced it with her lips, kissing me softly and tenderly, hardening my cock more than it had been. I pulled her against me – we were both on our sides – kissing and running our hands along each other's skin. Bella's skin was like velvet, pure and soft – without a single blemish. I pulled her against me, my erection now pressed against her lean stomach. Wordlessly, she lifted her leg and placed it over my hips while I shuffled down on the bed a little, still kissing her.

I grabbed one of her ass cheeks and pulled her down on me, my cock fumbling a bit at her small entrance before it parted her lips, and the head pushed its way inside with a small pop as it passed a tight resistance in her opening. Bella sighed against my mouth and deepened the kiss, her soft, lithe body pressing against mine as I pushed my cock further into her.

The silkiness of her flesh, the warmth, the tightness was something I knew I could never get used to. Each time I entered her, it felt new all over again. She was gushing with wetness, allowing me to slide effortlessly back and forth in her sweet little cavern that hugged me upon each thrust. Her sweet smell was intoxicating, the scent of her sex filling my nostrils. It was heaven on earth.

I thrust deeper and harder into her, holding onto her plump little ass cheeks as I pulled her back and forth on my cock. She started to gasp, latching onto me tighter as she moved her hips of her own free will, trying to meet my thrusts.

I knew my length was creamy with her wetness by now. I could feel it pooling at the base of my cock after every single stroke and knew it would be trailing down my legs soon. The imagery I created inside my head caused my cock to swell and my arousal to heighten.

"Fuck!" I exclaimed, capturing her lips again, gripping her in the small of her back as she continued to rock back and forth on my member. She whimpered, which would have been enough to undo me, but Bella shifted positions, causing me to roll on my back while she straddled me and sat on my cock.

She arched her neck and gave herself a moment to get used to the new position, her palms on my chest, my cock buried entirely inside her tight passage. I propped my head up on a pillow, wanting to see each movement. Her lips were spread over my length, her creaminess latched onto both our sexes, and I swore it was the most erotic thing I had ever witnessed in my life.

"How does it feel, princess?" I managed.

She swallowed and looked down at me. "So great, Logan – so fricking incredible," she said as she started to roll her hips, closing her eyes and arching her back, which caused her beautiful brown hair to tumble down her spine and her breasts to jut out further in her chest. I reached for them, fitting each into my palm as she continued to ride me. Her breathing came out in small pants, a whimper leaving her lips when I caught both nipples between my fingers and twisted them into circles.

Her hands were now behind her, resting on my legs. My own hands faltered from her boobs and went to her creamy slender legs, which were sprawled out on both sides, to take me. She started to bounce on my cock, and from this angle, I could clearly see my creamy cock come into view before it disappeared inside her again. I muttered a curse and gripped her legs, watching the beautiful sight in front of me. Her tightness started to squeeze me like a vice grip, and I knew her time was near. Her movements became more frantic, and her actions became a mixture of bouncing and grinding as she used my dick to pleasure herself.

I held her hips and guided her, raising her up and down on my length, loving the sounds of her cries and the sweat that beaded on her forehead as we fucked. My cock swelled, and I released a guttural grunt as I lifted Bella off, so I wouldn't come in her. But she held my hands, looked straight in my eyes and said something that had me busting inside her right away...

"I want to feel all of you, Logan. I want to feel your cum inside me." My cock continued to expand and shoot loads in her, which triggered her own orgasm. She cried and whimpered, her tightness squeezing every drop of semen from me.

"Oh, Fuck!" I exclaimed as I rubbed along her leg, almost dizzy from the feeling that bolted through me.

Bella continued to tremble for almost a minute before she slowly eased off my length, both of us watching as it slipped out and flopped to my stomach. She sighed, her insides clenching and unclenching as a dollop of cum fell from her hole and to my spent cock.

"My gosh, you are perfect," I said between breaths, kissing her when she collapsed beside me.

BELLA HAD DECIDED TO stay the night, and we had spent it talking, making love and just being in our own world – somehow afraid of what reality would bring. It didn't matter to me as long as I had her. The feeling was strange and unlike anything I had ever felt before, but I embraced it. It was quick; it was intense; it was like a whole box of goodies that I couldn't get enough of.

She slept, looking so peaceful it would be a sin to ruin it. Her mouth was slightly opened, her long lashes flattering on her face while her shiny hair flowed behind her like a river. The way she used both hands as a pillow was adorable, causing her tits to squeeze together, her nipples pointy and hard. My cock twitched, that unending need sweeping through me again. Gosh, when could

I ever get enough? It was impossible with her. I watched as she slept and couldn't help but run my hands along her arms, teasing the pads of my fingers with the softness of her pristine skin. A smile curved her lips, her eyes still closed, and I fucking knew right then and there that I loved this woman. It didn't matter how much time we spent together; my heart had never felt so full, and I had never experienced so much joy just by someone's mere presence. It was a feeling I was willing to risk it all for.

My cell phone vibrated on the bedside table, and I had half a mind to leave it alone, but I didn't want the sound to wake Bella. I reached for it, and my stomach churned when I saw it was Jenny. With a scowl, I hung it up and went straight to blocking her – something I should have done a long time ago.

Bella twisted in the bed and groaned, a smile still on her face, her eyes still closed while she stretched and snuggled up to me. Her eyes fluttered open, welcoming her beautiful brown eyes as she smiled at me.

"Hey," she said, voice a little husky from sleep.

"Hello, beautiful. How did you sleep."

Her cheeks reddened. "Better than I ever slept in my whole life."

I smiled and kissed her on the lips. She didn't hesitate in kissing me back, snuggling up even closer as heat sizzled between us.

"Logan!" a voice exclaimed, and I knew it wasn't Bella's. Just as my brain registered, the door burst open, and Jenny stepped in, her eyes going wide and her mouth hanging open.

"What the fuck!" I exclaimed, pulling up the covers to sheathe Bella, who gasped and jerked up on the bed. "What the fuck are you doing here?"

"You've got to be fucking kidding me! Who the fuck is that?" she asked, shooting daggers at Bella.

"None of your fucking business," I snapped as I pulled on a pair of shorts and grabbed her by the arm, ushering her out of the room. "How the fuck did you get in here?" I asked, once in the hallway.

"I know where your fucking spare is!" she snapped, crossing her arms. "I've been asking you for a second chance, and already you have someone in your bed? How old is she, by the way? She doesn't even look old enough to drink?"

My jaw ticked. "I have nothing to explain to you; get the fuck out!" I said, pointing down the stairs.

She stood grounded, staring at me before her eyes lit up for some reason. Her mouth opened in incredulity. "Don't tell me she's a college student!"

When I didn't answer, she scoffed, green eyes twinkling with mischief. "She fucking is, isn't she?" she laughed dryly.

I grabbed her arm again and led her downstairs. She shrugged out of my hand when we arrived at the base of the stairs. "Do you know how much trouble you could get in for fucking a student, Logan? I wouldn't want you to ruin that pretty little new job of yours now, would I?" she smiled slyly.

I was at boiling point. "What the fuck do you want?"

She licked her lips and crossed her arms, lifting her chin. "I want a second chance."

"Not a fucking chance in hell!" I almost laughed in her face but was too angry to.

"I said I was sorry for cheating!" she exclaimed in frustration.

"And I'm telling you to fuck yourself with your apology!" I shot back.

Her eyes glistened, her mouth drawn in a thin line, and I realized Jenny wasn't even all that. What the fuck had I seen in her?

She blinked a couple of times, and the artificial tears fell. "I need your help, okay," she sniffed, folding her arms and hanging her head. "I'm short on rent for this month, and my landlord is threatening to evict me. I don't have anywhere else to go," she admitted, refusing to meet my gaze.

Of course, there was something else. "So you're telling me fucking all those rich men behind my back had been in vain?" I raised a mocking brow.

Her lips twisted. "Please, you're the only one I can turn to."

"Get a fucking job, Jenny," I hissed as I walked toward the door and opened it up, waiting for her to get the gist.

She cleared her throat. "I don't wanna have to report your little secret to the board, Logan, don't push me," she threatened.

By this time, I was seeing red. "I don't give a fuck what you do. Go!"

She took a step closer to me. "Do you really want your little girlfriend to spend the rest of her college life being the center of attention for the wrong reasons? People will fucking alienate her, laugh at her. You'll just be fired, but she has to live with it on a daily basis. Don't you give a fuck about that, Logan, or does she mean so little to you?" The soft, remorseful tone she had carried earlier was gone, replaced with pure spite and dread. As hard as it was to accept, her words had me thinking. I had been so wrapped up in having Bella that I had not thought so much about the long-term effects.

"Two grand in my account, and I will leave you alone, but my lips will start moving if I don't see it by this afternoon."

I took a step toward her, looking down at her, seeing the way her throat bobbed with fear. "Fine," I said between tightly clenched teeth. "But after that, if you dare to threaten me or my woman again, I will wring your fucking neck on the spot. Don't push me," I warned, my eyes not leaving her.

Finally, she conceded, swallowing hard as she sidestepped me and left the house. I clenched my teeth, slammed the door shut and was about to head back upstairs when I saw Bella coming down the stairs. She was fully dressed, had her hair wrapped in a ponytail, and her eyes were glistening with tears.

I immediately rushed to her. "What's wrong?" I asked, searching her face for answers.

"I can't do this," she said as she pushed past me.

My mouth hung open as I ran after her. "Bella, I'm sorry about Jenny. She's fucking crazy, but I promise that was the last we'll see of her," I said, stopping in front of her.

She sniffed. "It's not about your ex, Logan. What she said was right, and no matter how many times you tell me you'll risk it, I can't." her lips trembled. "In our heads, this would have worked a million times, but in reality, it's complicated," she said as she attempted to move past me.

I held her wrist, putting her to a halt. "Don't do this; we can work it out. We discussed this – we can keep things under wrap until this first season, and then I could quit."

"And what if we're caught like we were just now? What then?" she asked me, wide-eyed. "I'm sorry, but I can't."

I clenched my jaw. "What I feel for you – what we feel for each other should be enough to want to get through this together," I argued, watching as the tears spilled from her eyes.

"I'm sorry, but it's not," she sniffed, using the back of her hand to wipe her tears before she tugged out of my hand and left me there, speechless.

The only way I could stop Bella was if I tied her to a bed, and while the idea of that might seem amusing, I knew I couldn't. I could only hope that she would come around – no amount of me begging was going to change her mind now. Not when she was so emotional. It cut deep – seeing her leave, knowing I could lose her for a second time. I wasn't ready for that; I wasn't ready to let her leave my life.

But it was all a waiting game from here on. I could wait an eternity for Bella, and if that was how long it took for her to realize she already had my whole heart, then that is what I would do.

Chapter 13

Bella

Two weeks had passed since I walked out of Logan's house and every day since, I had cried about it, knowing deep down it was a stupid decision, but I also knew I was doing the right thing. I dreaded the implication, I dreaded what people would think of me, and I hated the idea of me willing to risk it all only to have it fail in the end. Those prospects gnawed at me, roaming relentlessly around my head with each passing day.

There was not a single thought I could muster without it involving Logan. I often thought back to what we shared at his house. Our dreams and aspirations together, plans. It all seemed so surreal then – like everything could be made possible with the snap of a finger.

But then Jenny had come in like a wrecking ball, reminding me that our reality was shitty. It was better this way for both of us, I frequently told myself. Over time, I would get over Logan and move on. That was hard to think as much as it was going to be hard to do because there was one problem: I loved him. I had foolishly worn my heart on the sleeve, and Logan had stolen it – his to keep forever.

The tickling sensation on my face made me realize I was crying, and before I could brush the tears away, a knock came at the door. I stiffened, quickly wiping my face before I rolled out of bed and went to the door. I didn't know who to expect, but when I saw Jace standing there, I realized he was the last person I would have thought of. He had a huge smile plastered on his face and a bouquet of roses in hand.

My brows furrowed. "What's this; what are you doing?" I asked, genuinely confused.

"I come bearing gifts and an apology. I'm sorry for how I reacted at the café, Bella. I didn't mean to come across so disrespectful and harsh," he said.

"It's fine," I shrugged, taking the roses he jutted out for me to take."

"No, it wasn't. Let me make it up to you. A home-cooked dinner with no strings attached," he said, wiggling his brows. That would have sounded good to any other girl but me.

"I'm sorry, I can't accept."

A scowl appeared on his face. "Why the hell not?" he exclaimed, and I suddenly wanted to roll my eyes. He sighed. "Come on, Bella, I'm trying here," he said as he slumped his shoulders.

"I'm in love with someone else, Jace. That's the honest truth!" I blurted, a bit frustrated.

"That doesn't make any sense; we were together just two weeks ago," he said, grimacing.

"I know, but I fooled myself into thinking I could get over him by being with you, and it didn't work," I said.

He raked his fingers through his hair and scanned the room floor before his eyes met mine again. "So I was a rebound?" he asked, brows furrowing.

My gaze drifted away from him, unable to look into his eyes. "I'm sorry," I whispered, and he scoffed.

"So you fucked me to get over someone else," he stated rather than asked. "In what world does that happen?" he laughed drily. "I'm Jace Bradford... it should be the other way around, dammit."

"We were a mistake, I'm sorry," I said as I reached for the door to close it.

He clenched his jaw. "You really are just a bitch like the others," he scoffed. "I wasn't wrong in that assumption." He shook his head and turned to leave. I closed the door and sighed, too drained to feel guilty about what had just happened with Jace. But I didn't even get a chance to collect my thoughts when Dian came through the door.

"I just saw Jace; what's going on?" she asked. I hadn't even bothered to look at her. I went to my bed and wrapped myself in my blanket.

"Nothing. Literally," I sighed. "I'm not really in the mood, Dian."

"Bells, you've been like this for weeks, and it's worse than the first time," she said, moving toward my bed.

"Can't I just do what I want without you having something to say all the time?" I snapped, rolling my eyes.

"No, because you don't know what the fuck you want sometimes, Bells," she exclaimed.

"Just leave me alone."

"You're wound up about Logan, who would be willing to drop it all for you, but you're here moping because you can't see a good thing even if it kicked you in the ass!"

I bounded from the bed. "I already told you why Logan and I can't work! Why are you acting like this?" I argued, glaring at her.

"Bells, you're afraid of what people might think. People who don't even give a fuck about you, to begin with. You're willing to let the love of your life pass you because you are a fucking chicken!"

"You wouldn't understand how hard this has been for me?" I exclaimed.

"Why, because you think all I want to do is fuck with no intentions of finding love?" she said with a raised brow.

"I never said that!"

"You are a fucking coward who always has to analyze every single thing, Bella. Don't let life pass you by because you're trying to figure out how to live it. Nothing is ever going to be perfect; there are things you're gonna fight for, and there are things that will make you uncomfortable, but you have to figure out whether or not it's worth it. I say Logan is fucking worth it because I can see that you love him, and it pisses me off to see you can't even admit that to him or yourself."

I stood there trembling because it was the first time seeing Dian so angry – on the verge of tears because my well-being mattered to her so much. I flopped down in the bed and started to sob because I knew she was speaking the truth. I always looked at life from a logical perspective, which was a good thing but disallowed me from seeing the beauty within the risks. Yes, I was afraid of failure, I was afraid of judgment and realizing that was a hard pill to swallow.

Dian sighed and came to sit beside me on the bed. She draped a hand around my shoulder and rested her head against my shoulder. "You can move on and move past Logan, but I don't want you to look back on life and say you regretted not giving this a chance. Life is too short not to accept love when you find it, Bells."

I sniffed. "What if I'm too late? What if my biggest mistake was leaving his house?"

"There's only one way to find out." She smiled, and I turned to hug her.

Chapter 14

Logan

Somehow, though I had made it my life's mission to love and enjoy the sport I had dedicated most of my life to, it seemed lacking all of a sudden. There was no motivation, no real interest, just a task I wished would be over as soon as possible. Each day, I was tempted to explore the dorms searching for Bella but caught myself when I realized it was not what she would have wanted.

It had been almost three weeks, and admittedly, I'd been patient – the most patient I'd been in my entire life, but each day started to feel like a losing battle.

One evening at practice, I went searching for Jace since his footwork had started to get sloppy on the field. I entered their locker room and nodded my greeting to a few players, who immediately went into their shells as they saw me, clearing the way as if my mere presence was a ball of destruction.

"Have you seen Jace?" I asked as I made my way through and was directed to the back.

The closer I got, I recognized his voice and realized he and another teammate were having a conversation. I didn't mean to eavesdrop, but the closer I got, the clearer their words became.

"Yeah, dude, Sally is not really my type," I heard Jace say.

"Hmm, so what happened to that brunette, by the way? The one that hangs with that Instagram chick, Dian."

My brain raced to make a connection as I remembered the talks we had several weeks back when we had just laid in bed talking. Bella had mentioned her friend – she said that's who she was with at the bar when we met. And Bella was a brunette who had been with Jace.

Jace scoffed. "I'm telling you it's the quiet ones man. The ones you least expect shit from; they're the ones with the most fucking drama."

The friend chuckled. "What the fuck happened?"

"We went on one date, fucked, and a couple of days later, she tells me she's not into me." My teeth gritted at how he was talking and bragging that he had been with my woman.

"Sheesh!"

"Yeah, and even then, I tried to make things right because heck – I wouldn't mind some more of that pussy – tight as fuck, dawg!" he laughed, and the friend joined in.

At this point, I thought I'd heard enough as anger raged through me. I was about to make an appearance, but he just kept talking. "Then the fucking slut tells me she's in love with someone else," he scoffed.

I marched to the other side, too angry to see anything but red but also picking up on one small thing as I did so. As I turned the corner, Jace and the other guy's eyes widened, and I figured it was more because I was storming toward them like I intended to kill more than anything else. I couldn't hold myself back. I couldn't control the anger that stormed through me. I approached Jace and punched him squarely across the jaw, sending him jolting back toward the lockers as they made a resounding crashing sound. He immediately grabbed onto his presumably busted lips as he stared at me with shock and confusion.

"What the fuck, coach?!"

"Don't you dare talk about Bella like that!" I barked but quickly caught myself. "Any other female, for that matter." I quickly added, and he seemed even more confused. I had half a mind to pounce on him again, just to let out my frustrations, but then I saw that the friend was still there with his mouth hanging, and footsteps started to approach.

Assistant coach Barkley was the first to enter and see Jace slumped on the ground, looking up at me with his eyes wide.

"What the fuck happened?" he demanded, looking to Jace and then at me. My fists were still folded, and I was still shooting daggers at Jace while he sat there like a scared cat. It was easy to see what happened here.

"Tell Principal Cole he'll have my resignation in the morning," I said to Barkley before walking through the small crowd and out of the building.

As soon as I was on the outside, I raked my hands through my hair and muttered a curse, deciding to head home. Of course, that wasn't my wisest choice, but heck, maybe Westgate wasn't for me at all.

I headed home and had to blink a few times when I parked and realized someone was on my porch, but not just someone – Bella. My heart soared in my chest as I quickly got out and made my way toward her. Since the walk seemed endless, I began to jog a little until I was near enough to see and smell the beauty that had captured my heart.

"Bella," I said, searching her face, eager to know what this would lead to.

She fidgeted with her fingers and managed a small smile. "Can we talk?" she asked.

I nodded, "Sure," gesturing towards the long wooden chair.

We both sat, and I was just there staring into her face, admiring her beauty, reflecting on the days when she was mine.

"I'm sorry, Logan, I shouldn't have left the way I did... I shouldn't have left at all," she said, biting her lips before her gaze dropped to her hands. "These past weeks, I've had some time to think and realized that I would never be happy if I didn't have you by my side. I was scared of all the complications reality would bring, not realizing that losing you meant more to me than what people would say. I'm sorry I took so long to realize it," she said, looking at me with her pleading eyes.

I smiled. "I would have waited for you no matter how much time it took because I love you, Bella," I confessed, and her lips started to tremble, her eyes glistening.

"I love you, too," she choked as she leaped into my arms and kissed me. "So very much."

I hugged her tight, not wanting to let her go – afraid she would slip through my fingers if I did. "Promise me that you won't run again. Promise me that whatever shots life fires at us, we will armor up and face it together."

She broke apart and looked me straight in the eyes as she nodded. "I promise. And I don't care if the whole school knows about us. I'll be happy with anything as long as I have you at the end of the day."

My heart warmed, but then I reminded myself what I had done earlier. "I quit my job, so you don't have to worry about that," I confessed.

"What? Why?"

"I overheard Jace making some snarky comments about you, and I punched him. They would have probably fired me anyway," I scoffed, smiling, but Bella didn't seem too amused.

"Logan, you didn't have to do that!"

"I did. You are mine, Bella, and that means protecting and loving you, and being able to go to the end of the earth for you. I would do that in a heartbeat – know that."

She smiled. "So what will you do now?"

"My agent is still putting in the work, but if football doesn't work out, I have a few things to fall back on and enough money to guarantee our security for a while."

She hugged me. "I love you, Logan."

"I love you more, princess."

Epilogue

Bella

I watched the game ahead from the VIP section that had been reserved for us. There were a couple of minutes left in the game, and everyone was on high alert to see who would win. My phone shrilled beside me, and I almost jumped out of my seat as I picked it up and recognized who the caller was. I smiled and answered.

"Hey, Mom," I asked, looking ahead at the players.

"Hey, baby, how's the game going?" she asked, and I smiled.

"Great so far; we're in the lead. It should be finished any minute now," I informed.

"Awesome. Let me know the results as soon as it's over," she said.

"Will do, Mom."

"When will you guys be back? We miss you guys."

My heart swelled in my chest. "In a couple of days. Logan has a few things to finish up, and then we're on our way," I said.

"Ok, can't wait. Anyway... my shift at the hospital has just ended, so I'm on my way home to make dinner for your father."

"Ok, tell him hi for me," I said.

"Will do, baby; I love you."

"I love you too, Mom."

I ended the call with a smile on my face, a bigger one spreading my cheeks when Dian came up behind me with Emmet in hand. She grinned at me, her excitement geared at the game ahead.

She handed me Emmet – the toddler who seemed to understand what was happening around him. Dian pulled out her phone and turned the camera to the playing field while she spoke to her followers on the other end. I smiled as I reflected on how far she had come. What had just started out as being a social media personality ended with her having millions of supporters, who enabled her to live the life she was living now. This was her job; traveling and exploring new things, which she showed to the world.

I smiled down at Emmet, who started to play with the buttons on my shirt but paused to assess his surroundings when the stadium erupted in celebratory noises. I bounded from my chair with him in hand, jumping on my feet as excitement consumed me. I watched as the players sprinted toward each other, bumping chests before they hugged. I couldn't believe that a sport I had hated so much three years ago was now one of my favorites. It was now something I looked forward to and followed up on as often as possible, and that couldn't have been possible without Logan. My life changed completely when I met him.

From where I was, I could see him there congratulating the team while reporters rushed to speak with them. I couldn't wait for all that to be over, so I could have him all to myself. While it sounded selfish, one of the things I hated about Logan being out there was the attention and the groupies that swooned for him, even when they knew he was a married man.

"See, that's Daddy," I said to Emmet, whose eyes were in the same position as mine.

He smiled, a single dimple popping up as he watched more intensely. I held him tight and smothered his cheeks with kisses as we waited for Logan to come up.

Almost half an hour later, he entered the VIP box with a huge smile on his face when he saw us. Seeing him was like falling in love all over again. It was like that every time, and the effect he had on me hadn't waned in the time we had known each other. If anything, it got stronger.

"Hi, coach," I grinned, and he did too at the title.

"Well, if it isn't my two favorite people in the world," he said as he kissed me and took Emmet, who started to laugh when he hoisted him in the air a couple of times.

"Great match."

"Thanks, babe. I don't know about you, but I'm ready to go home."

"Well not home, home," I said, raising a brow. Home for me was LA, and we were miles away from it. Logan leaned in and kissed me gently, and I could feel it all the way through my body, settling between my legs as need consumed me.

"Home for me is wherever you guys are," he said once we broke apart, and I smiled, knowing that that was the only true answer.

Daddy's Little Birthday Girl

Izzie Vee

Erotic & Forbidden [1]

IZZIE VEE[2]

1. https://www.amazon.com/s?k=izzie+vee&i=digital-text&crid=31LQJTEQYT2EE&sprefix=izzie+vee%2Cdigital-text%2C121&ref=nb_sb_noss
2. https://www.amazon.com/s?k=izzie+vee&i=digital-text&crid=31LQJTEQYT2EE&sprefix=izzie+vee%2Cdigital-text%2C121&ref=nb_sb_noss

Cover Design by Izzie Vee
Cover Photo by VitalikRadko on Depositphotos.com

Table of Content

Chapter 1

Collin

It was funny how Mark and I had been in business for years, and I had never met his family. His wife was always on business trips, and his daughter was mostly off to college. But it was summer, and he had told me his daughter would be home for a while, and his wife was on leave from work. He thought it was the perfect time to meet everyone, seeing that I might not catch everyone together again anytime soon.

I looked up to Mark; he was ten years my senior but had good values and work ethic. He was also a family man, and although I was currently single, I looked forward to having my own someday soon. One bad divorce should have changed my mind, but I was still hopeful that good women were out there. It had been two years. It had been two years since I'd had a woman in my bed because I told myself I was giving myself time and believed that rushing into things never really paid off. Whenever I actually found a woman, I would get to know her as much as I could before anything else.

I parked my car in front of Mark's house and stepped out with a sigh as I looked around at the beautiful neighborhood. There wasn't a shabby house in sight. Everyone had modern architecture with the latest cars parked out front. It was nothing like my small Condo. I adjusted the lapels to my jacket and cleared my throat as I made my way to the front door.

I rang the doorbell and waited for it to open. Mark popped up on the other side with a bright smile, and I couldn't help my own.

"Collin, so glad you could make it," he said as he opened his arms. I smiled and patted his shoulder.

"Of course. This has been long overdue," I said, and he chuckled.

"Come in, come in," he said as he stepped to the side and allowed me entry. Mark led the way to the living room while I admired the glistening marble tiles, the accented walls filled with family portraits I was too far off to see, and the white leather couches with the compartmentalized coffee table, an art piece of its own.

"Lovely home you've got here, Mark," I said as he gestured for me to sit in one of the single sofas.

"Thank you, my wife Amy really put her foot into it." His wife immediately entered the room with a tight smile on her face, wearing a sundress that brushed her ankles, showing off her slender form. Her brunette hair was scraped back into a neat bun – not a single strand out of place. She was an aging beauty with piercing blue eyes and wide lips smothered with red lipstick.

I stood as she approached me. Mark smiled proudly and stood beside his wife, his hand going to the small of her back. "Collin, this is my wife Amy," he said, chin up as he did the introductions.

I smiled at the woman who held out her hand for a shake. "Nice to finally meet you, Collin. Mark has told me great things about you," she said as she smiled up at her husband.

"Likewise," I said as I took her soft hands and offered a handshake.

"Lauren should be down any minute now; she was on a call with her aunt," Amy informed. "Could I get you something to drink? Lemonade perhaps? I just made a pitcher not too long," she said.

"That would be great; thanks."

"Let's go around to the back," Mark said as he led the way through the large white-themed kitchen and out the back where a pool was and a small patio gazebo with wooden furniture. We sat down, and within a minute, Amy came with a pitcher of lemonade on a tray. She served it and took a seat. I took a sip of the refreshing drink and overlooked the beautiful backyard when my eyes caught a figure coming from the kitchen.

For some reason, my heart started to pound in my chest as the petite beauty came into view. She was small but had slender legs beneath a yellow pleated mini-skirt. My eyes traveled further up, taking note of her buttoned-down crop top that showed just a hint of her stomach. As my eyes went further up, my breath almost stopped at that moment when I saw her face. She was moving closer toward us, and the clearer her appearance became, the more she seemed to take my breath away. Her small face was surrounded by long, flowing blonde hair that seemed to sparkle in the sun, bouncing down her shoulders in waves as she walked. When she came up to us, I could smell her sweet perfume that would be lodged in my nostrils forever – a reminder of the first time I ever laid eyes on her.

"Finally. Collin, this is our daughter, Lauren. Lauren, this is Collin, who your father has talked so much about," Amy informed, but I could barely hear what she was saying, being so captivated by her offspring. Fuck.

A smile curved Lauren's glossy pink lips, and she stretched out a hand to me, her clear blue eyes trained on me. I got up from my seat and took hers in mine, my big one swallowing her small, delicate digits. But as soon as I touched her, I immediately knew what the movies and the books had meant when they said they felt sparks flying. This woman's touch sent a sensation bolting through my body, going straight to my heart, which started to pound a bit faster. She continued staring at me while I stared at her, watching her throat bob with a swallow. She folded her lips, looked away and pulled her hands from mine, but her cheeks were red after – something that I alone seemed to notice.

I couldn't believe it. I couldn't believe that a simple touch from a stranger would arouse so many emotions in me. Not only had she set my heart ablaze, but she had awakened my resting cock – reminding it that it had not felt a woman in a long time. I fucking knew – as crazy as it sounded – that this was the woman for me. She was mine, and it was that simple.

She sat beside her mom and crossed her slender legs at the ankles, and I immediately itched to touch them – to run my hands and my tongue along the slender column.

"Lauren here is about to complete her final in dentistry and will be celebrating her twenty-second birthday this weekend," Amy proudly informed as she glanced at me. "She skipped a couple of years. You must be so excited, honey," she said as she looked at her.

Lauren cleared her throat and glanced at me before she looked away. "Yeah, I guess so. I don't really have any plans, though," she shrugged.

"What about your friends, sweetheart?" Mark said a bit sadly.

She laughed dryly. "Dad, you know I've never had any real friends. Plus, everyone I know is already off doing their own thing this summer. No one wants to hang with me," she murmured under her breath, and I could see the momentary sadness that took residence on her face. There was an urge inside me to fix that – fix the sadness that was so obvious in her eyes.

"Aww honey, I wish I could be here to take you out, but I have to take a trip out to New York," Amy explained.

"Collin and I have this tech seminar to attend. I'm sorry, sweetheart; we thought you already had plans," Mark said with a somber expression on his face.

"It's fine, guys. It's not like I've ever done anything extravagant for my birthday," Lauren muttered, hanging her head as she fidgeted with her fingers.

"Yes, but still, you've been doing so well. You need to celebrate," Amy said.

Lauren shrugged and reached for a glass of lemonade. I couldn't take my eyes off her even if I tried – even though I knew that Amy and Mark were right in front of me and could see me devouring their daughter. This was my woman – I could feel it in every fiber of my being and knew that it wouldn't just go away anytime soon. This wasn't just lust; this was a need for me to have this woman in many ways than one. I wanted her for a lifetime.

Despite my attraction and the intense chemistry that collided between us, I tried to bear this sense of logic in mind. Many factors could prevent what I already knew to be real, but I wasn't too focussed on that. I just knew that I had to have this woman, and nothing would stop me.

I gulped down my lemonade in an attempt to temper the fire that was blazing wild throughout my body. Each second without touching her felt like something I had been craving for and could not have. But how was this feeling even possible when I had only known the girl for just ten minutes?

"How long will you guys be gone for?" Lauren asked. "Mom, you literally just came back. I thought you'd be here for longer this time."

"It'll just be for a couple of days, and then I hope to be home for a long time afterward," she smiled.

"The seminar is just for the weekend. We leave Friday and come back on Monday. After that, I'm sure we can celebrate, honey," Mark reassured with a smile.

Lauren heaved a sigh and nodded as she picked at her nails. Amy was about to say something, but her phone rang as soon as her mouth opened to talk. She quickly reached for it, glanced at the caller ID and excused herself as she walked back to the kitchen.

"Busy bee, that one," Mark smiled as he watched Amy disappear into the kitchen.

"Must be hard being the number one event planner in the city," I said, and he chuckled. I glanced at Lauren and realized she was sipping at her lemonade while she watched me over the rim of her glass.

"Amy handles the pressure well," he said before his phone started to ring as well. "Oh, look at that; it must be a busy day for all of us," Mark said as he fished his phone from his pocket and stood. "Guys, if you'll excuse me," he said and went in the direction Amy had gone.

Before long, it was just the two of us seated there in silence, Lauren looking towards the house like she wanted to come up with an excuse to flee as well. I took a drink of my lemonade and leaned back in my chair as I watched her.

"So, is there any place you would have liked to go for your birthday?" I asked, trying to build a conversation as well as get to know her better.

Her head snapped towards me, her eyes widening a bit before she shifted in her seat and cleared her throat. "Er...not really," she said.

I wasn't buying it, though. I had seen a sparkle in her eyes that quickly faded as soon as it came. "Come on; there must be somewhere," I challenged, and she swallowed.

"I... I guess I always wanted to go to Las Vegas," she shrugged, crossing her hands beneath her breasts, causing them to push up and hint at her creamy cleavage. She wasn't even aware of it, which made it even more alluring.

My brow shot up at her reply. I had been expecting many things, but this certainly wasn't it. "Oh, wow... well, that's definitely a good pick. Vegas is great."

She perked up. "You've been there?"

"Nah," I chuckled. "It has been on my bucket list for a long time, though," I admitted.

"Hmm, well, that makes two of us," she said, the joy deflating to disappointment yet again. "I probably won't get to go until I'm around your age or so," there was a little smirk on her face.

My mouth fell open. "Are you calling me old?" I asked dramatically.

She giggled. "You said it, not me."

Lauren was just so beautiful; it was like her presence was a ray of sunshine that I couldn't get enough of. Her smile made my heart smile, and her sadness made me feel like I was in a losing battle. I should be running for the hills for having such an insane attraction toward someone so young – my friend's daughter – but instead, I wanted to draw closer.

"I think you should give it a shot for your birthday," I said.

She scoffed. "I'm not going to Las Vegas alone on my birthday."

A thought occurred to me and paralyzed me in that spot because it was probably the most ridiculous thing I had ever thought of in my life. Maybe I was about to jump the gun – maybe I was about to make the biggest mistake in my life by proposing such a thing, but the words were leaving my lips before I could catch them.

"Who said you had to go alone? I could be your wingman," I said, and her mouth opened up and clamped back shut – certainly speechless, which was the logical response. What the fuck was I thinking? Before any of us could reply, Amy and Mark came smiling in our direction. Lauren managed a tight smile geared toward them and glanced at me from the corner of her eyes.

"Sorry guys, that was an important work call that I had to take," Amy said as she occupied an empty seat beside Mark.

A conversation ensued that I couldn't even pay attention to. All that was on my mind was Lauren and how she hadn't looked at me since her parents got back. I wanted to kick myself for obviously scaring away the girl before I even had a chance with her.

An hour later, when I was ready to leave, she quickly said her goodbyes and dashed toward the house before I even had a chance to say a word to her. I'd definitely overstepped my place and was now suffering the consequences. What was I thinking to have suggested such a thing? As much as it sounded appealing in my head, I had to bear in mind that I was no more than a stranger to Lauren, and to be proposing such a thing might have seemed weird for her.

That evening when I went home, I couldn't stop thinking about it and hoping that it was somehow real in the back of my head. What I wouldn't give to be frolicking around in the sin city with the most beautiful woman I had ever laid eyes on.

A woman who was also your friend's kid, a voice in the back of my head reminded, and I had to hold back a groan. Throughout all this, I had ignored the fact that Mark was my friend and business partner, and Lauren was his kid. If the circumstances were different, then I would definitely find a way to seduce the petite beauty, but there was no way I could have her without blowing up what I had worked so hard to build with Mark in the past year. Mark trusted me like a brother, as I trusted him. Could I risk all that for someone who might not even return the same feelings?

In my heart, I knew the answer was simple.

Chapter 2

Lauren

I laid in bed, staring at the blank ceiling as if it had the answers I was looking for. I thought back to the day and how I initially thought that the man my dad had always spoken so fondly of was someone around his age. There was no way I was expecting a man who looked like he was a fitness instructor instead of an I.T nerd. I hadn't seen it coming; neither did I expect to be so blown away by his good looks and the way my heart instantly started to flutter as soon as I saw him. Maybe it was the intensity in his dark grey eyes or how he seemed to dominate the whole room, but I had never reacted that way in front of a man. As a matter of fact, no man had ever made me feel that way. When he looked at me, I felt shivers all over my body and felt an intense throbbing between my legs–one I knew that my fingers wouldn't satiate this time around. It was like I had found 'the one,' and my heart and soul were letting me in on that fact.

I had given up on relationships for a long time because I was always looking for that spark that every married couple I knew spoke about. I hadn't felt it with any man who had approached me in the past and began to think it was a hoax. Yet, today, I had felt everything and so much more for my father's business friend. I couldn't explain my body's reaction to him, and I couldn't explain how I wanted to damn it all and run to him.

I was always the good girl, but I wanted to be bad this once. I wanted to take this man up on his offer to a Vegas trip. And while he might have only said it jokingly to cheer me up, I so wished it was true. It would soon be my birthday, and I had maintained a straight-A profile. Couldn't this be my reward? I would want nothing more.

I was so tempted to ask if he was serious, but I didn't get the chance. I was too chicken – too scared of the rejection. I started to chew on my nails as I gave it more thought. Collin was basically a stranger who I hadn't met before today, but my father knew him well and often bragged that he was a good guy. He had to be.

That night, I slept on the idea and decided to confront him the following evening about it, but I quickly realized I had no idea where he lived. I went to my father's in-house office, trying to search through his old journals and books but found nothing but a number etched in the back of one of his books. I bit my lips as I stared at the digits and contemplated my actions–actions that seemed ludicrous and desperate – which were so not me. But Collin had made me feel something that made me want to abandon all sense of decency and take the leap forward. It was that intense.

I quickly dialed the number and saved it to my phone, waiting for when I knew he would leave work – assuming I was brave enough to make the call. At six, I sat with my phone in hand and decided to make the call after much contemplation.

I licked my lips and sat on my bed, my heart beating fast, my armpits suddenly feeling sweaty. I dialed the number and awaited his answer, my heart almost beating out my chest when the velvety timbre of his voice resonated through the speaker.

"Hello." I could hear in his voice that he was a little skeptical, having no idea who was calling him.

I swallowed hard. "Hey, Collin it's me, Lauren," I said.

There was a small pause. "Oh hey, to what do I owe the pleasure?"

"I er- I was just wondering if we could meet up somewhere to talk?"

"Er- sure. Is everything okay?"

I rubbed the nape of my neck. "Yeah, do you know *Carmen's Café*? It's not far from where you and my dad work."

"Yeah, one of my favorite spots," he said. "When would you like this to happen?"

"I bit my lips. "Um... this evening. In the next twenty minutes, perhaps?"

"Okay, perfect. I'll see you there, Lauren."

"Ok, see you," I said as I ended the call and fell back on the bed in a huff. I couldn't believe that had just happened and that I had been brave enough to go through with it. Still, I couldn't help the smile I felt curving my lips at the idea of seeing and talking to Collin again.

I dashed to the bathroom and took a quick shower, happy that my parents weren't home to pummel me with questions about where I was going. When it came down to what I would wear, I was puzzled, not having the slightest idea about what to wear when impressing a crush. I decided on leggings and a crop top before grabbing my purse and driving to the café in the car my parents had gifted me for my eighteenth birthday.

As soon as I arrived at the entrance to the café, I spotted Collin seated at one of the window seats, glancing on the outside while he simultaneously checked his phone. That nervousness I had felt when I first met him came back, and I swallowed hard as I walked toward him.

I just couldn't get over how good-looking he was. This time he was in a full suit with a few buttons of his undershirt loose, exposing the light dusting of hair on his chest.

The nearer I got, his head shot up, and a smile immediately flourished on his face when he saw me. I couldn't help my own smile, watching as he stood to greet me.

"Hey, thanks for coming," I said when I arrived at the small table, not knowing whether I should hug him or just take a seat. I didn't want to seem too presumptuous with a man I just met, but in hindsight, what was even more presumptuous than this meeting and what I was about to ask.

"No problem; is everything alright?" he said as he took a seat while I did the same in the one opposite him.

"Yeah, I um-" The waitress came, and I paused while she took our orders and went on her way. "I – that thing you suggested at the house; were you actually serious?"

His grey eyes were planted solidly on me, and my heart was still raging out of control. He managed a slight smile. "I was."

I licked my lips and shifted in my seat, feeling as heat rose to my cheeks. "I um- I thought you and my dad had this seminar thing to attend," I said, watching his every movement, knowing that the little smile on his face and his intense grey eyes would make a woman swoon any day.

"You don't have to worry about that, Lauren. The big question is, do you want this or not?"

I managed a sigh. "Why would you do this for me?" I asked, almost whispering.

"Because I don't think there's anything I wouldn't do for you after meeting you yesterday," he said.

My heart fluttered. "What?"

"I'm just gonna be blunt, Lauren," he said as he leaned in closer to me. "I felt a connection with you yesterday, and I'm still kinda trying to figure out what it means, but I just know I want to do this for you. Tell me I'm crazy; tell me you didn't feel it as well, and I'll forget all of this and go."

I knew my face was probably as red as beets, but there was no way to stop it. Not when Collin was right in front of me, admitting to something I alone thought I felt. Joy erupted inside me, but at the same time, I knew this would all get complicated.

I bit my lips. "I did, too, but Collin... my dad."

He nodded curtly. "I know, and that's why I don't want to jump the gun, but I can and want to give you that Las Vegas birthday trip, Lauren, if nothing else."

I opened my mouth to speak, but the waitress returned with our orders, placing the cup of black coffee in front of Collin and the cheese Danish in front of me. "Thank you," we said in unison before she smiled and left.

I cleared my throat. "I know we just met, and this whole thing is kinda strange and unlike anything I had ever felt in my life, but... I'd like a trip with you, Collin."

Our gazes met. "Great, but you still have a few days to sleep on it. I don't want you to feel pressured into anything."

"I don't feel pressured. I just don't want my parents to know about this."

"Understood."

"We go, we have our fun and then we return to our normal lives," I said, knowing deep down that that might have been the furthest thing from the truth.

Chapter 3

Collin

I couldn't believe that Lauren had actually agreed to go to Vegas with me, and it was all I could think about ever since our meeting yesterday. I still couldn't get her image out of my head and how she managed to be even more beautiful than the first time – which was almost impossible, seeing that Lauren was the most beautiful woman I had ever laid eyes on.

I knew this trip was something she might have wanted to be platonic, but I wasn't sure how I could keep myself from touching her soft skin. Blood rushed to my cock every time I thought of her; I could only imagine the sweet torture I'd feel when I was by her side almost all the time. The anticipation was sweet, but I knew better than to think this would be all fun and games.

We had exchanged numbers, and she hadn't texted me since, but I was willing to give her the time she needed to think this through. Maybe I was nothing more than a companion for her on this trip, but I still believed that she wasn't lying when she had said she felt a connection with me too. That one declaration put me on cloud nine, and for as long as I had Lauren, I would stay there.

I tapped my pen to my laptop and gazed through the glass doors at the working personnel on the outside. Mark was on the other side, and I couldn't help but bring him into play. The man had believed in me when nobody else did – saw my idea and decided that he wanted me to join his team. I owed him everything – this sudden splurge of success was all because of him.

I felt awful for what felt like an impending betrayal. To be talking and making plans with his daughter behind his back felt wrong, and yet the need I felt to do this with Lauren seemed to drown out everything. I was waiting for that logic to kick in – to tell me that the only reason I felt that way toward Lauren was because she was beautiful and sexy and all that good stuff. But I had been in the playing field long enough to know the difference between sexual attraction and emotional connection. With her, it was both. I wanted to fuck her senseless, and yet I wanted her to be by my side in everything I did. I had spent hours, wanting this to be a fluke, waiting for the attraction to wane, but the need intensified every single day.

The big question was; what did Lauren see in me anyway? She could have any man she wanted, yet she had admitted to feeling an attraction toward me. It was insane, and right now, I was counting her as part of my continuous blessings.

"What's got you up in here daydreaming like that?" I snapped myself from my thoughts to find Mark leaning against my door with a smile on his face. I immediately felt guilty because he would have my head on a stake if he only knew what or, rather, who it was.

I quickly cleared my throat as my eyes searched my desk. "Er- just work," I lied.

He sighed. "You push yourself too hard," he chuckled. "I'm heading out to lunch... wanna join?"

"Er – no, you can go ahead. I have a few things to finish up first."

He made a face as he looked behind him. "I really wish you would join. Ben just asked, and I told him I was heading out with you."

I almost rolled my eyes. "What's with that guy anyway? He's such a fucking push-up."

"Don't I know it. He'll be on vacation for a while anyway, so at least you won't see him around here for a bit."

I scoffed. "Looking forward to that."

"Sooo... coming or not?"

I sighed. "How about you indulge Ben this time around; I'm sure he'll give you a break after this," I smiled.

Mark rolled his eyes comically. "Okay, suit yourself, but can I get you anything?"

I rubbed the nape of my neck. "No thanks, man, I'm good."

"Okay then, well, I'll be back," he said as he turned to leave.

A thought occurred to me. "Mark!" I called.

He turned to me. "Yeah?"

"About the seminar this weekend..." I began, not even sure about the excuse I would give.

He huffed. "What? You don't wanna come?"

"Er-"

"It's fine Collin. I know you don't like the boring stuff or the formal interactions," he chuckled. "I'll spare you this time around," he smiled.

I blew out a sigh. "Thanks."

"It's all right. As long as one of us attends, it's good. Plus, unlike you, I'm looking forward to it. You make really good connections at places like these."

"I bet. I'll definitely be there the next time."

"We'll see," he chuckled before he left.

I sighed and flopped back into the chair, happy that that part of it went well. Mark was a kind and understanding man, and all this would have been a lot easier if he wasn't.

LATER THAT DAY, I WENT home, took a shower and warmed up some food before I went to bed. Lauren was the only thought that occupied my mind lately, so one could imagine my joy when a text message came in on my phone with her name in the notification bar. I almost broke my thumb with how quickly I tapped on it, eager to know what she said.

Hey, may I call you?

I didn't know why that made me smile, but I was geeking ear to ear in my empty apartment like a schoolboy just discovering the opposite gender.

I didn't bother to reply. Instead, I sent out the call to her instead and was even happier when her voice came over the line.

"Hello."

"Lauren, how are you?"

"I'm great. I hope I wasn't disturbing you or anything."

"Not at all. In fact, this is quite a pleasant surprise," I admitted.

There was a brief silence, and I knew she was probably smiling. "Good. Well, I just wanted to let you know that I slept on it like you said, and nothing's changed.

I smiled. "It has only been a day."

"A lot can happen in a day, Collin. If I didn't know any better, I'd say you're trying to convince me not to go with you," she said, her voice falling a bit.

My heart skipped a beat. "Of course not. I just want you to be comfortable with the idea. No regrets."

"I am. Aren't you?"

"Trust me, I want nothing more."

The line went silent again. "Thanks for doing this with me, Collin. I know we've just met, but my dad used to talk about you a lot whenever I was in school, and he would call. This feels right to me."

"You have no idea how amazing it is to hear that."

She giggled. "Well, we should start making arrangements then."

I fluffed the pillows behind my head. "Yeah, I'll book the flights as soon as I can. We can leave on Friday."

"Preferably Friday evening. Dad's leaving in the afternoon, and Mom is leaving in the morning."

"OK, sure."

She sighed. "Well, we'll talk. I don't want to keep you any longer; I know you need your beauty sleep."

I laughed. "You flatter me. You're the real beauty here."

Silence, so I knew she was smiling again. "Good night, Collin."

"Goodnight, Lauren."

The call ended with a smile on my face. The joy I felt when it came to this woman was like no other I had ever felt in a lifetime. I had been a married man at one point in my life, yet the union had never made me feel as happy as I was now. All for a woman I had just known a few days ago. Lauren made me feel alive again – made me look forward to each day with bated breath. What I wouldn't do to continue hearing her soft-spoken voice or be lost in her clear blue eyes. There was this burst of energy that consumed me, and I knew it was all because of her.

As I stared ahead at the blank wall, thoughts raging, I couldn't help but reflect on my lonely night and wish Lauren was here with me. Just a whiff of her perfume would do me in – that warm, dewy scent that would stain my sheets as she laid beside me, her tiny body curled up on mine.

My cock started to harden in my pants, and for the first time in a long time, I didn't need porn to get me off. I'd found something better. Pushing my hand beneath my boxers, I grabbed my hardening cock and gripped it tightly, imagining that it was Lauren's walls that gripped me. Soon after, I reached over into my bedside table and retrieved the small bottle of lotion that had been stacked there for this particular purpose. Soon my hands were gliding effortlessly down my steely length, my arousal building as I thought about Lauren.

Just to have her perched above me, lowering herself on my length, I would give the world to have such an experience. Her warmth encasing me, her juices flowing down my length. Fuck. I started to pump my flesh faster, moaning and muttering curses when it all seemed too intense. I could imagine her tiny tits that she loved to cover beneath crop tops, all perky and perfect as she bounced on me. Her small mouth open, her sun-like hair bouncing down her naked flesh...

I couldn't hold back myself any longer. I grunted and stiffened, muttering a curse as my seed spurted from my cock and coated the bedsheets. I laid heaving in bed, unable to believe what had just happened. If masturbating to Lauren was so powerful and otherworldly, I could only imagine what the real thing felt like. Fuck, it made me want her even more – which was pretty impossible at this point.

Chapter 4

Lauren

"Oh, honey, I'm so sorry we're not going to be here for your birthday," my mom said that following Friday morning as she pulled along her small carry-on suitcase into the living room.

"Don't worry about it, Mom. I understand," I reassured.

She smiled and approached me, clasping my face with both her hands. "I promise we will do something together when we return."

"I'd like that very much," I smiled, and she kissed me before running back to her luggage.

"Safe travel, sweetheart," Dad said as he entered the room with a smile.

Mom smiled. "Thanks, honey; you too."

They kissed, and we waved mom goodbye as she piled her things into the uber she had called. In the next minute, she was gone, and I was left with Dad, who stared at the vehicle until it disappeared around a corner. I patted him on the shoulder.

"I can tell you miss her already," I said.

"I always do, but I'm looking to get some time this winter. I'll be giving most of the power to Collin for some time."

"What do you mean?" I asked.

"You'll start working in less than a year. Maybe have your own practice someday; Collin is the only person I trust capable of taking over when I retire. I have to start getting him in the frame of mind soon," he said, and I swallowed the lump in my throat as I gave it thought. Guilt ate at me because the last thing I wanted to do was jeopardize the relationship between him and my father. But at the same time, it was like something within me called for Collin. This was my dad, who I've known all my life, and then there was a man I had met less than a week ago.

"I should start preparing to leave," he said, breaking through my thoughts. He smiled at me and left; I flopped down on the sofa beside me and reached for my phone that was on the coffee table. I bit my lips and stared down at the device, knowing that the right thing to do would be to call Collin and tell him that I couldn't make the trip.

How could I spend a weekend in the most sinful city on earth with someone my father depended on in so many ways? But this trip was innocent, right? Although Collin and I shared a connection, we had no plans to sleep with each other, right? But who was I kidding? How could

I resist the first man I had ever felt sexually and emotionally attracted to? For the first time in forever, I had naughty dreams that involved this man and only him.

"Lauren?" a voice came, and my heart almost jumped out of my chest when I realized I had sent out the call to Collin.

"Er...Collin hey..."

"Ready for later?" he asked, and I could hear the excitement in his voice. I bit my lips as my mouth opened up to tell him that I couldn't go with him, but the words weighed on my tongue.

"Lauren, is everything okay?" he asked and I closed my eyes.

"Yeah, sorry. I was just slightly distracted, but yeah, everything is fine. I was just calling to see if you're all set," I said as I bit my lips and cringed at myself.

"Yeah, I'm packing my bag as we speak."

"Last minute packer, I see."

"Nah, I still wanted to give you some time to think about this. I almost thought this call was you calling it quits on it."

I swallowed. "I had a bit of cold feet earlier, but I really want this, Collin."

"Me too. I'll pick you up at six, then."

"See you then."

I shouldn't be smiling after knowing what my father had plans for a man who I was lusting over, but I couldn't help the joy that filled me whenever I talked to Collin or even thought about him. Maybe it was a crush that would fade after Las Vegas; I didn't know. I wanted this weekend more than anything, yet I knew I couldn't do anything but be platonic with Collin if I wanted to keep the peace.

With a sigh, I ran up to my bedroom and packed the remainder of the things I wanted to carry with me.

SIX HOURS LATER, WE boarded the plane, and my heart started to gallop in my chest. I felt sweaty, and my heart seemed as if it would lurch out of my chest any second.

"Hey, wanna take the window?" Collin asked.

I shook my head and took a seat beside him, wiping at my forehead and clearing my throat. I gripped the armrest when it started on the runway and stiffened when it took off into the air. I was heaving, and it seemed I would pass out; no one seemed to exist in the room except me and my fear.

But then I felt a large hand enclose mine, the warmth spreading through my body. I popped my eyes open to find Collin staring at me, concern etched on his face.

"It's alright. Everything is gonna be fine," he said.

I shook my head and resisted the urge to cry. "It's stupid, I know, but I just can't get over this part," I exclaimed shakily.

"Hey, look at me," Collin said as he peeled my hand from the furniture and took it into his. I stared into his grey eyes and blinked away the fogginess in my own. "Take a deep breath and just imagine the fun we're about to have soon," he smiled. I looked at him because he said so and because it was hard not to look when he was this good-looking. His strong jawline, arrow-straight nose and the small dusting of freckles, which you could only see if you were close enough. His gaze held mine, and it was like a magnetic field was between us. His hand on mine didn't make matters easier – the warmth spreading through my body, the need that throbbed between my legs.

Suddenly, the flight wasn't the reason for my speeding heart, but my nerves had calmed, and I no longer felt like my world was going to end. If anything, I felt safer, knowing that Collin was here beside me.

When I calmed, his hold on my hand had not faltered. "Why didn't you tell me you were scared of flights?"

I shrugged. "I didn't want it to ruin anything, and I hadn't been on a plane in such a long time; I just thought I'd gotten over it."

He nodded. "Well, you don't need to be scared of anything once I'm beside you," he said with a smile of pearly whites.

I smiled. "I know that now."

Collin held my hand for the rest of the journey, even when I was absolutely calm. Regardless, it gave me some comfort and deep down, I knew this was probably the closest I'd come to having him this close to me – to be touching me.

WE TOOK A CAB TO OUR hotel room, and though I had not given it an ounce of thought, I felt sad to know that we had separate rooms. It was silly thinking, but a girl could dream, right?

"Well, we're officially in sin city," Collin said. "What do you plan to do on your first night?"

I blew out a breath as my eyes scanned the busy hotel lobby. "I have no idea. Could we maybe stay in tonight? I don't think I have enough energy to roam the streets of Las Vegas tonight."

He laughed. "Sure thing. We can order room service. Your room or mine?"

Somehow, that had me pausing for a bit as if the question meant something completely different. My cheeks flamed, and by the look in Collin's eyes, I knew he saw it.

"Er mine... Could you just give me about twenty minutes to take a shower and get settled?"

"Yeah, sure."

We took an elevator up to our room. Collin went to the room that was opposite mine. I sighed as soon as I got in, wanting to temper the heat that blazed throughout my body in his presence. The lavish interior was much of an attention grabber with its pure white walls and the huge bed that rested on light grey hardwood flooring. As I paced the room, I realized the center of attention was the glass doors that led to the balcony, reflecting the colorful lights of the city. I opened the door and was greeted by the cold wind and the noisy hustle and bustle of the city. Collin had picked a hotel in the center of it all, and my mouth fell open as I soaked up the jubilant display of life around me.

I was smiling from ear to ear, already knowing in my heart that this would be a great weekend. This was already a great start. I dashed to the bathroom and took a quick shower before I pulled on a cotton shorts set that I had ordered for this particular purpose. I bound my hair in a ponytail, checked the time, and then texted Collin as soon as it hit the twenty-minute mark. When he knocked on the door, it was back to square one with him and how he made me feel.

I opened the door to find him on the other side, dressed in grey shorts and a black T-shirt that highlighted his beefy pecs and his muscular arms. After I realized I had been staring for too long, I had to catch myself and clear my throat.

"Come in." He dipped under the doorway and came inside. I could smell the soap on him – the same one stacked inside my bathroom. But he had on his signature perfume, too – the mixture creating the most swoon-worthy scent in history. Collin took a seat in one of the lounge chairs while I hopped on the bed.

"So, what will we be ordering?" I asked.

"I wouldn't mind a juicy double cheeseburger right now with large fries," he said as he perked up a brow at me.

"I think I'll get the hot wings."

"Ok, well, then it's settled. I'm starving," he exclaimed, and I giggled.

"Hold your horses, big guy; you're not dying on my watch."

He chuckled heartily while I reached for the phone and made the order. Collin didn't take his eyes off me as I did so.

"So I did my research before we got here and checked out some of the places we could visit. We're definitely going on the high roller," he said.

"What's that?" I asked.

"A giant rotating wheel that gives you a pretty good view of the city," he said, clearly amused.

"That sounds great, but this right here is the second best thing," I said as I looked toward the balcony and then at him. "Collin, you didn't have to do this – this place is clearly expensive...but I'll definitely give you back my share of expenses," I said.

"Are you kidding me?" he chuckled. "What kind of man would I be if I allowed that to happen? Lauren, don't worry about it."

I sighed, and he shuffled in his chair. "Come on, tell me about college life," he said as he relaxed, ready for a story he was sure I would tell.

I licked my lips. "Well, college is pretty much blah for me. But I know what I have to do, and I haven't let anything get in the way of that."

"Well, that doesn't sound like much fun," he said as he raised a brow at me.

"Is school ever fun?" I asked as I made a face.

He laughed. "It can be if you make it."

"Well, I can just imagine you being the cool guy in school; everybody wants to be your friend," I said, and he laughed and rubbed the nape of his neck, guilty. "Tell me, how does a guy like you get into tech?"

"A guy like me?" he asked, mirth in his voice. "Should I be offended?"

I grinned. "No, but I mean... I know there's a stereotype, and I might be guilty of it... but aren't tech guys usually puny and nerdy?"

"I mean, you have your dad as an example, who could blame you," he said, and I burst out laughing while he sat with a smile on his face, watching the whole thing.

I blushed and cleared my throat. "So... how did you get into the tech business?"

He shrugged. "I don't know. I guess I was always fascinated by it, so I watched a couple of videos and did some research. It kinda came naturally. I didn't always use my powers for good, though," he smiled. "In high school, I was hacking into the school's computer system for tests – and in college, I just got better at it. The coding stuff, I mean, not the cheating."

I grinned. "How did you meet my dad?"

"Well, I was working for this small company a couple of years back, and your dad came in; I pitched an idea to him, and he took me on his team. It was a huge deal for me, so I didn't stop until he saw that I was actually good at what I do. Last year, he decided to make me a partner, and my life hasn't been the same since. I owe everything to him," he said.

I hung my head and started to pick at my fingers in my lap. "I like you, Collin," I said in what sounded like a whisper. "More than I've ever liked any guy in my life, but I think we both understand that nothing can happen between us," I looked back up at him, and our gazes met. "Even if we want it to."

"Lauren-"

"If my dad finds out, who knows what he'll do. I don't want to ruin multiple relationships by risking it all for one."

"Lauren –"

A knock suddenly came at the door. "Room service!"

"We'd better get that," I said as I slid off the bed. I could hear Collin's deep sigh behind me.

Chapter 5

Collin

I knew Lauren had a point, yet it was hard to concentrate on anything apart from her slender, creamy legs housed in shorts that barely covered her ass. How could I think logically when she had sat there on the bed, leaving me with no choice but to think about the things I could be doing to her on it. Logic was lost with me – and call me stupid, but nothing mattered more than having Lauren in every aspect of my life.

We were already less than five hours in the sin city, and temptation was running wild. We were inside her hotel room, with no one to watch or judge, and my cock knew that. I knew that with a little seduction, I could have her beneath me, moaning and writhing. But Lauren deserved the best, and I wouldn't make a move unless she asked me to. Right now, she was still skeptical about what she wanted, and I was willing to give her the time to decide. But fuck, it was torture.

We ate in relative silence because we were both hungry and took our time to eat before he got another conversation going. As I watched as she tore at the meat like a scavenger, I smiled. Somehow, I had expected her to be shy in that aspect- heck, I was expecting a salad instead of chicken wings, but here the petite beauty was again surprising me. I could watch and admire her all day, even when her cheeks were filled with food, her small lips were greasy, and her fingers were filled with sauce.

I never imagined I would enjoy such a thing, but I didn't know what about Lauren I wouldn't like. What would seem like imperfections to others were simply beautiful to me.

She wiped her hands in a napkin and swallowed what she had left in her mouth before gulping down her drinks and finally looking at me. She must have realized I'd been staring because her cheeks immediately flushed red, and she looked away.

"You know, all of a sudden, I'm not feeling tired anymore. Wanna go for a walk?" she asked.

I glanced at my watch. "Are you sure? It's almost ten."

"And it's Las Vegas. Come on," she said as she got up and headed for her suitcase, where she pulled out a coat.

"Okay, just give me a minute to grab my wallet. I'll meet you in the lobby."

"Okay."

THE LAS VEGAS STRIP was just full of life, and who better to explore it with than Lauren? There was this permanent smile on her face as she walked and looked around – feasting her eyes on everything and being amused by anything. There was a sparkle in her eyes that told me I had made the right decision by bringing her here. What I wouldn't do to see this look on her face for a lifetime.

"Come on, I have something to show you," I said as I grabbed her small hands and wielded her along a different path. She giggled and hopped along beside me, bursting with joy and energy.

"Where are we going?" she asked as she ran beside me, her ponytail bouncing down her back.

"You'll see," I said, and before long, we paused in front of a fountain, where people had started to gather, phones out to capture the moment.

Lauren looked at me with a look of puzzlement on her face. "What's going on?" she asked, her eyes roaming over the small crowd.

I chuckled as I glanced at my watch. "You really don't know anything about Las Vegas, do you?"

She grinned. "Nah, just what I saw in movies. I just know it's fun."

"Ok, so all you know is getting hitched and gambling because that's all the movies show."

"True."

Our attention strayed when the fountain in front of us erupted with beautiful, colorful spurts of water. Lauren's mouth fell open as she looked at it and then glanced at me. I smiled as I watched the waterworks and how captivated she and everyone were by it. Classical music came on, and it was like the water was dancing to every beat, the spurts swaying from side to side as the colors changed, as well as the formation of the fountain. A series of 'ohh's and ahhhs' filled the air as the amazed spectators captured the moment with their phones.

Lauren glanced at me. "Oh, my gosh, this is amazing!" she exclaimed, eyes fastened to the attraction yet again.

We watched the masterpiece for about four minutes until it stopped, to be active again soon. After that, people started to leave, but some stayed, and more came on for the other one, which would be on again soon.

"That's legit the coolest thing I've ever seen!" she said in awe as we left the spot and started walking down the strip again.

"Yeah, it's pretty cool," I said.

We passed a chapel with people lined up, waiting to get hitched. Some were in casual clothes, while others had taken the time to dress the part in wedding attire. Lauren paused to look before she glanced at me.

"People are this eager to get married?" she asked as she stared at the small gathering.

"You'd be surprised. A couple of years back, I was the same."

Her head flashed to me. "You were married."

"Yeah, didn't last a year. I quickly realized I had made a mistake," I explained.

"Why?" she asked.

"She didn't know what it meant to be loyal. The whole thing was a joke really."

"Did you love her?"

"I thought I did but quickly realized that I didn't. That was just one crazy part of my life that I'm happy is over."

She nodded. "Well, it's late. We'd better head back to the hotel."

We walked back as we engaged in small chit-chat. When we got back, Lauren paused at the front of her door and turned to me with a smile on her face.

"I really enjoyed tonight, Collin. Thank you."

I smiled. "Don't mention it."

Before I saw it coming, she crashed into my arms and hugged me. I froze at the unexpectedness but quickly welcomed the feel of her soft body pressing against mine. She felt so incredibly small like I could wrap her away and keep her all to myself. Being so close, I could smell the shampoo in her hair and took a hearty whiff of her sweet scent. She was warm, and her body fit into mine perfectly.

My cock started to stir as my hands slid around her small waist, which was probably small enough to measure with one hand. When she broke apart, my heart sank, but she didn't step away.

Instead, she remained there, staring up at me. She licked her lips, and I could tell she was nervous. My eyes were suddenly drawn to the spot, forced to admire the lush pink and the juicy fullness.

She went on tippy toes as her lips drew closer to mine. I knew what was about to happen, and I knew the right thing would be to step away. But I couldn't resist. Not when she was so sweet – not when my body was responding to every single inch of her.

I lowered my lips to meet hers, and when her soft, feathery lips touched mine, I knew I was a goner. I wrapped my hands around her and pulled her closer to me, allowing her body to be pressed against mine again while I scored the sweetness from her mouth. I found her tongue and quickly guided mine over hers before I sucked on her lips and went back in again. My body was burning at a fever pitch, each second getting even hotter. My cock started to expand in my pants, and I knew she could feel it. She moaned, and I kissed her deeper, almost lost in the taste of her sweetness. I pressed her against me, letting her feel my hardness against her, so she knew how much I wanted her.

She gasped against my mouth and lightly sucked on my lips before she pulled apart and folded her lips.

"We shouldn't; I'm sorry," she said. I took a moment to process because it took everything within me not to pull her against me and kiss her hard and deep again before pushing her into the bedroom to fuck her the same.

I shook my head as if to clear it and then cleared my throat. "Yeah, you're right. I..." I trailed off, not knowing what the fuck to say.

"Goodnight, Collin."

"Goodnight, Lauren." She smiled, and then she disappeared into the room. I muttered a curse as I raked my hands through my hair and kicked at nothing in particular.

Chapter 6

Lauren

It was almost noon, and the plan was to go to a museum in the day and then the popular high roller later tonight. Yet I couldn't seem to get myself out of bed. I'd been stuck daydreaming about Collin and the kiss we'd shared the previous night. It was like a scratched record in my head – one that I couldn't get tired of no matter how many times I played it over. I still felt warm and fuzzy on the inside, as I had felt last night when it happened. Everything was still vivid in my head. How soft his lips had been, how warm and fresh he had felt when I was so close to him.

But something had stood out to me – literally. It was his manhood that had been pressed against me while I kissed him. I had no doubt that it was big; I just knew it. A flutter had been in my stomach ever since, and it was hard to shake – not that I wanted to. An intense need was building inside me now–a craving I had never felt before. Part of me wanted to explore it in its entirety, but then I was brought back to my dad and the plans he had in store for Collin. The attraction I felt toward him was one thing, but sex would take this to a whole other level that would complicate things more than it already was.

I moaned, dragged myself out of bed, took a shower, and pulled on a little sundress and decided to sport it without wearing any bra. Then, blowing out a sigh, I left my room and proceeded to meet Collin in the lobby where we had agreed.

As soon as I saw him, I could feel the blush warming my cheeks at the reminder of last night. He was wearing fitted denim and his usual T-shirt with sunglasses on that made him look like a movie star. He just had it all, didn't he?

"Hey," I said as I approached him.

"You look great," he smiled, adjusting his shades.

"Thanks. So, what's on the agenda today?" I asked.

"I guess we could walk around, get some lunch. I really wanted to visit the museum, though..."

"Then the museum it is," I said.

We visited the mob museum, where we were given a guide on the most renowned criminals in history. Collin was soaking up every bit of information while I, on the other hand, was just fascinated by the artifacts that were inside. An hour later, we had lunch, visited a few shops, and before we knew it, it was nighttime.

"Are you having fun?" Collin asked me after we began our walk to another of Las Vegas's attractions.

"Are you kidding me? This is the most fun I've had in my entire life."

He grinned. "Good. Now for what I think will be your favorite part."

"Ouu, let's see!" I almost squealed in excitement.

When we got there, we paid and joined a line that flowed into a huge pod housing more than thirty people. Collin and I stepped inside the glass structure, and I was amazed to find that there was also a bar inside.

"Can I get you anything to drink?" he asked, glancing toward the bar area.

"Er, a margarita...but not too strong," I said.

Collin smiled, "Noted," and moved towards the bar.

I walked toward the windows, astounded by the whole thing. Soon, the gears started to get in place, and the pod was lifted off the ground. Collin returned with the drinks and handed one to me. I thanked him as I glanced at what seemed to be whiskey in his hand and took a sip.

"Perfect; thank you."

Before long, the giant Ferris wheel started to rotate, slowly welcoming the view of the beautiful Las Vegas City. Everyone was in awe – including myself as the skyrises with the colorful lights came into view. We could even see the fountain we had visited the previous night and the waterworks it had going on for it.

"This is just so beautiful," I said in awe, my words so low that I doubted Collin even heard me.

"Indeed," he simply said. I glanced up at him to see his gaze transfixed on the beautiful view ahead. A small smile was on his face, and my heart felt whole just looking at this man. I knew I was in too deep, but maybe that wasn't such a bad thing,

WE WALKED BACK TO THE hotel room, laughing over some joke Collin had shared. I was just so filled with happiness that it was hard to put it into words. This whole experience had been the best thing that ever happened in my life, and that was all thanks to Collin.

He walked me to my door as usual and watched as I opened the door before he tucked his hands into his pockets and smiled.

"Well, today has been great; I'll see you tomorrow, Lauren," he said as he turned to leave.

My heart started to plummet in my chest, and I knew if I let this opportunity pass, I might never get the chance again. There was a lot to lose by doing this, but I was optimistic that there was a lot to be gained as well.

I reached for his hand and grabbed onto his wrist. Collin turned around with a puzzled look on his face as he searched my eyes.

"Is everything okay?" He asked.

I swallowed and slowly nodded. "Don't leave.... Stay, please," I said just above a whisper.

He was silent as he tried to find meaning in my words. "Lauren...?"

I didn't wait for a possible rejection. Instead, I flung myself at him, crashing my lips to his as I hoped for a repeat of the other night. He kissed me back with just as much neediness, his hands wrapping around me as he kissed me so passionately, my toes curled in my sandals. That familiar heat sluiced through my body in powerful waves, settling between my legs.

He broke apart for a brief moment to look at me, his lush pink lips apart as he tried to speak. "I swear you're fucking killing me right now, Lauren."

I licked my lips and met his gaze, wanting him to see that I was serious about what I wanted.

"I know things can get complicated, but can we just live in this moment?" She asked. "I want you to make love to me, Collin."

His eyes darkened, and his sharp jawline clenched as he stared down at me. I didn't know much about desire, but it was clear in his grey eyes, and I knew he wanted me just as much as I wanted him.

"Are you sure?" He asked, his voice suddenly husky.

"I'm sure," I said softly.

He stepped toward me, held my face with both his hands and kissed me hard. We were still in the hallway, where anyone passing could see us, but I didn't care. Collin seemed to wield a power that made me forget anyone existed in the moment but him. I didn't see anything else; all I could feel was his soft lips against mine, his low stubble that slightly tickled my skin while his hard body pressed against mine. The longer we kissed, the more I could feel his blooming erection – the evidence of his desire for me.

I moaned against him as we stumbled inside, Collin using his foot to kick the door shut. I started to fumble with his belt while he pried down the straps of my dress from my shoulders. My perky breasts jumped out at him because I had decided earlier that I wouldn't wear any bra. He stepped back, tearing his mouth from mine as he stared down at them with a dangerous glint in his eyes. My chest rose and fell as I stared back at him, feeling my body flush with the heat from his inspection. There was no self-consciousness; in fact, with how he looked at me, I felt like the sexiest woman in the world.

"Fuck, you're gorgeous," he exclaimed before he swiftly pulled off his shirt and tossed it into a corner of the room. My eyes wandered over the hard ridges of his chest, taking in every muscle that was carved over his body. He seemed more giant as he looked over me in his purest form, his hair a little rugged from the intense kiss we'd just shared.

As he watched me, I decided to peel my dress further down my body until it pooled in a pile at my ankles. His eyes traveled the length of me, settling on the red lace panties I had on.

"You're so beautiful, Lauren; you know that?" He said raspily while pulling down his pants at the same time. I watched with bated breath as he did so, my mouth falling open at the tent in his boxers. I didn't have time to process how long it was because, in the next instant, Collin was pulling it down just to show me how much. I gasped as his manhood sprung free, dangling a bit before it steadied upward. I couldn't take my eyes off it even if I tried. Suddenly, I began to wonder if I was jumping the gun by doing this. Collin was a well-endowed man, and I didn't have the experience to match up to it, though I already knew how wet I was. I could feel the arousal that pumped through me and the wetness pooling in my vagina.

"I– you're big," I stuttered.

He chuckled as he approached me. There were no words to deny it because he knew it was true.

"I'll be gentle, I promise," he said.

I licked my lips and opened my mouth to the kiss he offered, his bare length pressing against my stomach. It was hard and beefy, and if I paid close enough attention, I could feel it throbbing against me. But it was hard to keep up with what I was feeling because I was feeling everything. It was like my body had entered another universe, and I was experiencing the newness that came with it.

We moved towards the bed with our lips joined. He guided me until my back pressed against the mattress while he hovered over me.

My heart was beating fast, and the AC in the room did nothing to temper the heat that assaulted my body.

Collin captured one of my small breasts in his mouth, and I gasped as he sucked on it, his warm mouth intensifying the pleasure that sucking on them was already giving. My back arched, and I moaned as he went from one to the other, giving each the same treatment as he lapped on them with skillful accuracy. As he did this, his hands slid down my hips and across my stomach before he finally settled them between my legs.

I was becoming breathless, the anticipation killing me.

"Oh, Collin," I whispered as I thrashed around on the bed.

His fingers found my slit, dancing along the sensitive flesh with feather-like strokes before a single digit parted my lips. I moaned and reached for his head, raking my fingers through his hair. I didn't know what to do, but Collin seemed to have it all figured out.

I parted my legs a little, wanting to give him more access as his finger rubbed the bud of my clit.

I swung my head from side to side as his fingers dipped inside me while he sucked hard on my tits. I gasped and stiffened when his fingers went a bit too deep and felt my face redden when he paused to look at me.

"Lauren...."

I swallowed the lump in my throat because I wanted to cry for not telling Collin about this sooner. The last thing I wanted him to do was to stop, and he was on the verge of doing so as he looked to me for answers.

"I've never had sex before," I admitted, watching as his eyes widened.

"Wha– how's that even possible?" He asked, clearly confused.

"I just never thought anyone was good enough – until now."

He stared at me wordlessly. "Lauren, you realize that nothing can go back to normal after this, right?"

I bit my lips. "Can we worry about that after, please? Right now, the only thing I can think about is you making love to me," I admitted truthfully.

He smiled. "Yes, ma'am."

He was back to the kissing. Kissing me all over my face and then to my breasts, which I realized would probably be a future favorite – assuming there was one to be had after this. His fingers found my flesh again as he dipped it inside my snatch.

"You're so wet for me, baby," he said as he went up to kiss my mouth. His finger continued to drive back and forth inside me until he added another that made my head start to spin. I gripped onto the sheets and closed my eyes to bask in the bliss as his strong digits pleasured me. I had thought that one finger would be big enough for my virgin hole but apparently, two fit easily, and it made me less nervous about taking his length.

Collin filled me with gentle strokes before he pulled his fingers out and rubbed the wet digits along my sensitive clit. I shivered at the wave of pleasure that passed through me and reached for his hand to put it to a stop.

"I want you now... please," I begged because it was the only thing I could ever beg for. Pleasure that was inevitable with a man that my heart was just bursting with joy for.

Collin eased up a bit and ran his wet fingers over the bulbous tip of his stellar manhood. I grew even wetter as I watched the sight before me, anticipating the moment when it would be buried inside me.

I pulled his mouth down to mine and kissed him while he adjusted himself between my legs. His cock grazed my thighs, and I moaned. Soon after, it was grazing my glistening lips as Collin guided it to my entrance. I parted my legs as wide as I could because I knew I'd need as much room as possible.

"It'll hurt only for a moment, but I promise to make you feel good afterward."

I nodded and held my breath as his hardness breached my flesh and gained access inside. He only had the tip in, but I already felt so stretched and filled. He kissed me again, his lips never leaving mine as he drove his cock deeper, thrusting a bit harder as he broke my hymen. I clamped my eyes shut and groaned against his lips as brief pain shot through my body.

Collin paused, brushed back a few tendrils of hair from my forehead and looked deep into my eyes.

"It's okay; the worst part is over," he said softly, placing a brief kiss on my nose before he started to move inside me.

My mouth fell open as his dick stroked my tender walls. He was so big that I doubted there would be any pleasure after all, but he didn't stop moving until all the discomfort started to fade.

His eyes were still pinned to mine, taking in every emotion that passed across my face.

He was so gentle that I felt like crying. What better man to lose my virginity to than him? My nipples brushed against his chest as he fucked me, his pace increasing as pleasure took over my body. Collin started to slide inside me with a bit more ease as he tried to get more of his cock inside me each time.

"Oh!" I exclaimed when he hit a spot that almost had me coming on the spot.

"Do you like this baby? Do you like what my cock is doing to you right now?" He asked, his voice thick with desire.

"Oh, yes, Collin, everything feels so good, yes," I purred as I clung to him.

"Do you want more?" He asked, and I nodded because I was too speechless for words.

He drove the rest of his cock inside me, and I screamed at the pleasure and pain that erupted through me. He paused again to help me adjust, kissing along my neck and my face.

"Fuck me, please."

He obliged, moving even faster now, the sounds of our sexes creating music in the room. I was so wet, which was evident in the 'schlopping' sounds my pussy made when he moved back and forth inside me.

My flesh clamped around him, hugging his cock for the amazing job it was doing. I felt overwhelmed; I felt like I was about to lose my mind in the best possible way. I wanted more; I wanted everything.

"Harder, please," I begged as sweat glistened on my body.

Collin held my leg up, pinched my nipples between his teeth and started to fuck me relentlessly.

I started to scream out, but it wasn't in pain. It was the complete opposite.

"Ohhh, oh yes!" I exclaimed.

"I want you to understand that after tonight, you're mine, Lauren. No other man will ever say they've had this glorious pussy. You're mine." He hissed as he continued to fill me with hard, deep thrusts.

"Yes, Collin! Yes!" I shouted back as my walls clamped around him.

His cock slipped out for a brief moment, and I gasped at the dismissal. I felt so empty, but soon I was filled again in one hard stroke that had me coming and screaming my orgasm.

I thrashed around on the bed and muttered words I knew wouldn't make any sense later. Everything was all too intense. My heart was pounding out of my chest, and the state my body was currently in was something I couldn't use mere words to describe. I clung to Collin in the midst of my orgasm, but he still continued to fuck me, feeding off the tightness in my milking pussy.

"Oh, fuck! Yes, baby... come for daddy!" He said.

His words might have triggered another orgasm from me. Collin as my daddy Dom was too much to fathom.

I quivered as he continued to rail me until he grunted and finally pulled his cock out. He used his hands to pump it twice, and then his cum was shooting all over my stomach – all the way up to my breasts.

He moaned aloud until every last drop was emptied onto me. I laid there as I came down from my own high, too fulfilled to do anything but lay there.

Collin propped himself up on his elbow beside me and smiled down at my exhausted form.

"How do you feel?" He asked.

"Better than I've ever felt in my entire life," I said as I tried to catch my breath.

"Good," he said as he kissed me.

I licked my lips, and my cheeks warmed at my impending question. I bit my lips. "Can we do it again?"

Collin's eyes popped out. "Well, aren't you the insatiable minx."

I giggled.

"You don't ever have to ask, baby. My cock is yours to take whenever you want it."

Chapter 7

Collin

I went to the bathroom and prepared a warm cloth before reentering the bedroom to find Lauren lying there with a smile. Her whole body was flushed, her nipples still tight and pointy with arousal. Even now, I still salivated over tasting them. They were like little pebbles that tasted like a lollipop. Her whole body was sweet – a kind of drug that you couldn't get out of your system.

My cock still throbbed to have her. Heck, I'd have her a thousand times over in the same night. My boner hadn't died; it was still raging, and after the request Lauren had made earlier, there was no calming it anytime soon.

I felt like the luckiest man in the world as I stared at her on the bed, ready to have me again. Her hair was tousled, and she was glowing in the aftermath of our lovemaking.

I approached her and used the cloth to wipe at her entrance before I wiped away the cum I had dispensed on her. She moaned still, her small hands sliding down my arm as I did so. As I stared at her naked pussy, I wanted to have her right then and then. It was so small that it was a wonder she had managed to take my cock. It was like I could still feel her tightness wrapped around my length, incredibly warm and soft, as she worked to juice the cum from my cock. I've had a lot of women in my bed, but nothing compared to Lauren's virgin cunt.

Unable to stop myself, I placed the cloth to the side and kissed Lauren hard and deep, exploring her warm, sweet mouth that caressed me just as needily.

"I want you on all fours, baby. Do you think you can handle that?" I whispered in her ear. She ran her hot little fingers down my body, and my cock hardened to steel.

"I think so," she said almost breathlessly as she rolled over, arched her back and looked over her shoulder at me.

I muttered a curse as my eyes latched onto her ass, which was perched in the air, her pretty pink pussy on full display and her cute little rosebud above.

I slid my hands down her pristine body and went under to squeeze her full breasts, which fitted into my palms perfectly. Lauren moaned and spread her legs wider, eagerly waiting to have my cock again.

Her round little ass cheeks were soft to the touch – unblemished like the rest of her body. I squeezed each and parted them with my hands, watching as her pussy lips stretched open from the action.

"Gosh, I don't know when I'll ever get over how beautiful you are," I said as rubbed her velvet-like pussy between my fingers.

She moaned and shuffled a little on the bed, pushing her ass out to me.

I smiled to myself and obliged her as I guided my throbbing cock to her entrance. I watched the whole time as the head of my length popped inside her warm cavern, her flesh parting to the side as it granted me access. I licked my lips and resisted the urge to curse again as I sunk inch after inch inside her, watching as it disappeared into her warmth.

"Oh, Collin!" Lauren mewled as she gripped the bedsheets, probably as tight as her pussy was gripping me right now.

"Nice and easy, baby," I whispered as I got three-quarters of my cock inside her. I pulled back and watched as her pussy creamed my length before I went back in again.

"So tight," I said between clenched teeth as I grabbed her ass cheeks and started to up my pace.

Her moans were constant as she went back and forth on my length. Her pussy was so juicy that it started to sluice out from her lips as I impaled her repeatedly. Yet, she was still as tight as a vice grip, persuading an orgasm from me maybe sooner than I had anticipated.

My cock swelled inside her as I fucked her, and while I didn't want to hurt her, I also couldn't hold back the feeling that washed through me.

I started to pound her hard, driving my cock inside her to the hilt before I pulled back and went again. Lauren's cries echoed through the room as her pussy tightened around me.

She wailed and flung her hand back to stop my thrusting.

"Oh, my God, Collin. I don't think I can handle anymore. It's too much this way," she said breathlessly.

Guilt tore at me. I pulled my cock out of her and settled behind her as she went on her side on the bed. I kissed her shoulders.

"I'm so sorry, baby. I didn't mean to hurt you," I whispered.

"You didn't. It just felt like I was going to pass out," she said, and her cheeks flushed a bright red. "Maybe we could try that one again another time?"

I kissed her ear. "Of course."

She turned to me with a smile on her face, her sweet musky scent making me heady with arousal.

"We could try like this," she said as she kissed me, her small fingers running along my jawline.

My hands slid down her body, down the slight flare at her hips. I held her ass cheeks and pulled her closer to me, so close I could feel her nipples pressed against mine.

She lifted her legs and draped them over my hip while I adjusted myself and used one hand to guide my cock to her entrance. I filled her with one stroke, and she gasped, her heated breath adding to the heat already raging between us.

I held her ass and pushed myself up into her, her wetness lubricating my way. She already started to clench down on me while I tried to hold onto every bit of control not to bust into her. We collected each other's breath as the pleasure soared between us. Lauren was whimpering like a baby as I drilled her, her cute little mouth opened.

"Cum for me, baby. Come for daddy," I exclaimed as I grappled on to her slippery body, giving her everything I had.

Her fingers dug into my skin as she cried out and started to move her hips to meet my thrusts. I rolled her over on her back without dislodging and fucked her in missionary until she was calling my name like I was the God she prayed to. The sweet rush of her orgasm bathed my cock as she quivered and writhed beneath me.

I grunted as I pulled out. A second slower and I would have been coming inside her. My seed plastered her pussy lips, some landing on her stomach in a small puddle.

I collapsed beside Lauren, who was breathing hard as she stared at the ceiling fan, her mouth slightly opened as she tried her best to catch her breath.

I glanced at my phone on the side table and smiled as I turned to her.

"Happy birthday, baby."

Chapter 8

Lauren

If someone had told me a week ago that I would be spending my birthday with the man of my dreams, I would have laughed in their face. This had already been the best birthday I'd had in my whole life, and all thanks were due to the man who laid across me in the bed. He was still asleep with one hand propped across his chest and the sheets barely draped across his midsection.

I bit my lips and watched him, reflecting on the night we'd shared. It was hard to keep track of how many times we had made love, but after what seemed like the millionth round, we finally collapsed in exhaustion and fell asleep.

I could feel the soreness between my legs – evidence of all that had happened and what Collin had done to me. I blushed at the reminder and snuggled up to him. Although this man had fulfilled me on degrees, I didn't even think anyone was capable of; I still wanted him over and over again.

It only proved that this Las Vegas trip couldn't be a one-time thing. I couldn't just go home and forget everything that had happened between us and return to normal. I didn't see it being possible. Not now, not ever.

My hands crept below the sheets, and I caught his length in my hand, which was still surprisingly semi-erect. He shuffled a bit as I started to glide my hand back and forth on him, feeling as he hardened in my hand. It was still so fascinating, and I wondered if it were something I'd ever get tired of. I didn't think I'd tire of seeing Collin's length, touching it – feeling it inside me. The only thing left to do was taste it, and even now, as I thought about it, I could feel the saliva pooling in my mouth.

Deciding to be spontaneous, I shuffled down on the bed and settled myself between his toned legs. I held his cock, massaged it for a little while and then opened my mouth to take in the tip. The slightly salty taste and the tanginess caught me off guard, but its smoothness had me wanting to taste more.

Collin finally opened his eyes, which widened when he saw me perched there.

"Lauren, what—"

"Shhh, I want to do this," I said as I slid my tongue over the pinkish head. He moaned and propped himself up to look at me. I felt motivated to do my best, even though this was something I had never done before.

The tip of my tongue dangled in the tiny hole in the head, creating wet circles around it until I covered it completely with my mouth. I opened my mouth as wide as possible to accommodate him, trying to get more than just the tip in my mouth. The corners of my mouth stretched, and my saliva started to drain down his length. But with one quick swipe, I lapped it all up and went down on him again.

"You're fucking incredible, Lauren!" Collin exclaimed as he started to breathe hard. I started to suck on him, bobbing my head back and forth on what I could manage to take in. More saliva ran from my lips, but I didn't let up on pleasuring the cock that had done wonders to my pussy.

I started twisting it around the base with one hand while I sucked on the top, plucking it from my mouth in a pop occasionally.

Collin's hand found my hair as his strong fingers massaged my scalp.

"Just like that, baby," he said huskily, and I increased my pace. Emboldened by the desire in me and Collin's encouraging words, I tried to take all of him in my throat but failed drastically. As soon as the tip touched my throat, I gagged, saliva pooling in my mouth.

Collin was still massaging my head as I bobbed my head on his cock. He held my head in place and thrust his hip upwards, sending his length deeper into my mouth but not deep enough for me to gag.

I tightened my lips around him and continued to suck him until his enthusiasm could be felt throughout the room.

"Fuck, Lauren, I'm gonna come!" He said, but I still didn't let up. If I couldn't have his cum in my vagina, then I would have it somewhere else.

His cock twitched inside my mouth, his hips thrusting for a brief moment before I felt a huge spurt hit the back of my throat. I eased up slightly as he dispensed a mouthful in my mouth. I knew I had to get used to the salty tanginess, but I swallowed what I could and allowed the rest to seep from the corners of my mouth and down on his cock.

Collin laughed in disbelief and looked at me with that lust in his eyes.

"Come here," he said.

I used the back of my hand to wipe my mouth and went to lay beside him with a smile on my face.

He turned and kissed me even though I'd just had his cock in my mouth. "I'm never letting you go," he whispered.

AN HOUR LATER, WE SHOWERED and went down for breakfast. I couldn't stop smiling, and Collin couldn't stop staring at me. Unlike the day we met, what I felt for him now was not just attraction. It was something deeper, and I knew it was partly because of the sex but not entirely. He had more to offer, and he had offered it all. There was nothing more that I wanted than to just be by his side. I feared the reality that we would have to go back to because I knew it wouldn't be as blissful as being here with him was. I didn't want the moment to end, but I knew it would end in a few hours when we would catch our flight back home.

"So what do you want to do for the rest of the day, baby? We only have a few hours left," Collin said as he sipped on his coffee.

I shrugged and sighed dreamily. "I don't know. Being here with you is enough."

He smiled. "I have something for you," he said as he pulled a box from the pocket of his jean jacket.

I held my breath and took it as he handed it to me. "Collin, you didn't have to. This trip was already more than enough; last night."

"Nothing I can ever offer you will ever be enough in my eyes. You deserve the world, Lauren."

My eyes started to sting, but before the tears came, I opened the box to see what was inside. I gasped as soon as my eyes made contact with the exquisite piece of silver jewelry lined with little diamonds around the infinity sign.

I choked up a sob. "Collin, it's beautiful. You didn't have to," I sniffed, my hands shaking as I took it in hand and held it up to admire the beauty more closely.

Collin got up and came around to my side, where he took it and helped me go put it on. It was beautiful, and the gesture was just as amazing; I couldn't stop my tears.

"Thank you," I said. "I love it."

"I'm happy to hear that," he said as he kissed me on the neck.

"Collin?" A voice said. We both looked up to see a middle-aged man standing before us with a quizzical expression on his wrinkling face. He looked between us, and I could see recognition dawn on his face while the blood drained from mine.

Fuck, fuck, fuck! This wasn't happening!

"Lauren... you – Collin, I thought you went to that seminar with Mark," he said as he looked between us, trying to connect the dots.

Collin cleared his throat. "Not really my crowd," he shrugged.

The man's brows furrowed. "I see — are you guys dating?" He asked as he pointed at us, eyes moving from me to Collin.

Collin's eyes met mine. "Er... no," I was quick to say. "We just er..."

"You guys seemed pretty close to me. Does Mark know?" He asked as he raised a brow.

"Listen, Ben, I'll see you at the office. Now, will you excuse us?" Collin exclaimed with an evident edge to his voice.

Ben seemed taken aback. Without saying another word, he left, but the look in his eyes told me there would be trouble ahead.

I started to breathe hard, as if someone was stepping on my lungs. I couldn't breathe and found it hard to catch my breath. A hand reached out to mine and gave it a gentle squeeze. My eyes met with Collin, and I found some reassurance in it.

"Baby, everything is going to be fine," he said with a curt nod.

I shook my head. "No, Collin. He's going to tell Dad that he saw us, and the whole thing will blow up in our faces!"

"And would that be such a bad thing?" He asked.

I gawked at him as if he had lost his mind. "Are you kidding me? The last thing I want is my parents to find out from some guy at the office. He probably has Dad on call as we speak," I hissed, rubbing my forehead.

"I knew this was a bad idea from the start. We shouldn't have done this, Collin," I said and immediately regretted the words as soon as I saw the sadness and disappointment on his face.

"Lauren, come on, don't say that."

I shook my head. "We knew the complications being together would cause, and we both knew this probably wouldn't work outside Las Vegas. That's become even clearer now," I sniffed.

"I'll talk to your dad and let him know how I feel about you. It probably won't go over well, but at least he'll know the truth."

My thoughts were all over the place, and it took me a moment to realize the words Collin had spoken. My gaze flashed to him, and I blinked back the fogginess from my eyes.

"Dad has plans for you, Collin. He's going to give it all to you once he's retired. If he finds out about us, I don't think he will." Shock took over his face as my words resonated through to him. He didn't say anything as he stood there looking clueless as if trying to work the pieces together in his head.

I used the opportunity to get up and flee to my hotel room, but I could hear Collin's footsteps behind me as he called my name. I finally stopped at my door with tears flowing down his face. The look on his face was pained as he stared back at me.

"Lauren, these past days have been the best I've ever had in my life, and no, it wasn't because I am in one of the most vibrant cities in the world, it's because I had you by my side," he said. "I don't care about the plans your father has for me, I don't care if this ruins the relationship I have with him ... I just want you."

His words gave me some sort of reassurance, and I couldn't stop the tears that flowed from my eyes. But it was still bittersweet. Collin was willing to make that choice, but I couldn't allow him to. I couldn't ruin what he'd obviously worked so hard for, and though he might have been saying this now, I didn't want him to resent me months or even years down the line. Maybe we were just in the honeymoon phase of a would-be relationship, and all this spark and excitement would die down soon. So although I knew in my heart that what I felt for Collin wouldn't ever go away, I still had to make a choice between his happiness and mine, and I chose his, which was what he had worked so hard for over the years.

"I'm sorry, but this won't work, Collin. Let's just appreciate the fact that we had a good time, and now it's over. We're done," I said as I went inside and closed the door behind me. I leaned against the hardwood as soon as I entered, and my body slid to the floor as I broke into sobs.

Chapter 9

Collin

The door closing in my face signified a finality that I couldn't bring myself to accept but that I couldn't force. Maybe Lauren needed some time to process, or maybe she meant every word. Whatever the case was, I was willing to give her time to make a choice with a clear head.

I dragged myself back to my room with a heavy heart and emotions I had never felt in my life. I reflected on her words, especially the last bit she had said about Mark having plans for me after his retirement. A week ago, the news would have made me feel like the luckiest man in the world, but the excitement that should have come from such an announcement wasn't there. If it meant not having Lauren, then I didn't care for it.

I almost felt stupid. I had worked my ass off to get where I was, and then a beautiful woman walked into my life and gave my life new meaning.

This was more than the attraction I initially thought this was. Lauren was my soulmate, and I found that out even before we had sex. To lose that once-in-a-lifetime opportunity was like losing life itself.

Even now, knowing that tomorrow I wouldn't wake up to her in my bed gnawed at me. I needed her every waking morning and for her to be the last thing I saw before I closed my eyes at night.

I was reckless throughout the rest of the day, hoping she would send me a text or even knock at my door, but nothing came for hours straight until it was time to leave, and she asked me if I was ready.

I had so many things to say to her during our ride to the airport and as we settled on the plane. But I also didn't want to force anything. I was giving Lauren the time she needed to think and clear her head, and I would respect any decision she made, even if it wasn't to my liking.

Her anxiety returned as soon as the plane was about to take off. She didn't say a word, but I still held her hands and felt the nerves slowly leave her body. She glanced at me with so much emotion in her eyes that her lips failed to convey.

I didn't let go of her in fear that it would be the last time that I held her and simply because touching her gave me some sort of peace. When we got back to LA, waiting for our Uber at the airport, she turned to me.

“Thanks again for everything, Collin. This weekend was really amazing,” she said with a small smile on her face.

I nodded. “I wish it was more than the weekend.”

She hung her head and tucked a few tendrils of hair behind her hair.

“We both knew what we were getting ourselves into.”

“Yes, and I thought we could get past the complications. I still think we can,” I said.

She shook her head. “It’s just wrong timing. I’m sorry,” she sniffed.

I stepped closer toward her and kissed her hard, feeling as the desire for her rushed through me tenfold. She kissed me back for a brief second with as much eagerness as I had offered but quickly tore herself away and swallowed.

“We can’t... I’m sorry,” she said as she glanced at the car parked a few feet away. “That’s my ride. Goodbye, Collin.” With that, she left and stepped inside the car. She didn’t look at me once, but I watched as the car disappeared around a corner, and just like that, a familiar emptiness filled me once again.

WHEN I MET MARK AT the office for the next few days, I knew something was up. He wouldn’t meet my gaze, and all he said was the usual formalities which was pretty much unlike Mark. It was strange that he hadn’t filled me in on the seminar that he went to. Nothing. I knew he knew, and it was just a matter of when the confrontation would be.

The right thing to do would have been to approach him and set the record straight, but I didn’t want Lauren upset at me for doing it alone.

Regardless, the tension could be cut with a knife, and I hated working in an environment like that. If Mark decided he no longer wanted me as part of his company, I would respect that, but I’d sleep better knowing my conscience was clear. Knowing Mark, he already knew what happened between Lauren and me and was just waiting for me to be ‘man enough’ and come to him about it.

I smoothed the lapels of my jacket and got up from my chair as I headed toward his office. I was as nervous as hell because even though I knew I would drop it all for Lauren, I still hated that I could potentially lose my relationship with Mark.

I swallowed hard as I rapped on his door, and he gave me the go-ahead to enter.

He didn’t look up from his laptop, and there was a grim expression on his face. He knew for sure.

“Could we talk?” I asked as I approached the chair in front of his desk.

He finally looked up at me with a danger in his eyes that I didn't think was possible with a guy like Mark. His silence for me was consent, and I took that as a sign to say my piece.

I cleared my throat. "I'm in love with your daughter." Those were definitely not the words I had planned, but apparently, they were the ones that needed an out. I hadn't admitted it to myself, even though I knew from the start that what I felt for Lauren couldn't be anything but love.

Mark's jaw ticked. "You son of a bitch!" He hissed through tightly clenched teeth.

"I didn't mean for any of it to happen, Mark, but it did. I'm in love with her.

He slammed the laptop screen shut and threw daggers at me with his gaze. "I fucking trusted you, and you went behind my back and fucked it all up. You lied to my fucking face!"

I hung my head and managed a sigh. "I'm sorry..."

"And then you have the nerve to come in here and say you love her?" He scoffed. "I know the reputation you have with women, Collin. You don't have any good intentions toward my daughter, and you've only known her for a fucking week. Have you lost your mind?!" He asked as he stared at me wide-eyed.

"Maybe, but I'm telling you that what I feel for her is unlike anything I've ever felt for a woman. I love her, and you can hate me for it or whatever, but that's not gonna change the fact!" I exclaimed.

He laughed sardonically and shook his head. "You're a piece of work, you know that? I gave you the opportunity of a lifetime, and this is the fucking thanks I get. I brought you into my house, and the first thing you thought to do was prey on my daughter!"

It was my time to laugh. "I didn't fucking prey on anyone. Lauren is twenty-two years old. She can make her own decisions!"

Mark's eyes blazed fire. "Get the hell out of here!"

I stood to do just that, feeling angry at myself, at Mark – at this whole fucking situation.

"I swear to God, Collin. If you don't fucking end it with her, I'll ruin you."

"You don't have to worry about that, Mark. You got your wish before you even knew you wanted it! You'll have my resignation in the morning!" I hissed as I moved toward the door and slammed it shut behind me.

I muttered a curse as soon as I got back to the office. Leave it to fucking me to poke the bear and add gasoline to the fire.

Chapter 10

Lauren

"Honey, you need to eat something," Mom said as she entered my room with a distressed look on her face.

"I'm not hungry, om," I croaked out.

"You haven't had a sensible meal in days. You're not doing any good to your body by treating it like this," she argued as she came to sit beside me at the edge of the bed.

"I'll be fine," I sniffed.

She sighed heavily. "Honey, you will get over this and realize in due time. This has been your first attempt at love; your feelings are justified, but you'll find the right man one day, trust me," she smiled.

I shook my head and eased up on the bed. "You don't understand, do you? I love him with all my heart, Mom."

"Honey–"

"I know what you're gonna say, but it's not some stupid crush that I'll get over anytime soon. I feel happiest when I'm around Collin. Just the thought of him makes me happy. Why can't you understand that?" I exclaimed, my voice almost breaking as I spoke.

"I'm trying to – believe me, but you've only known him for little over a week. I'm just worried that it's a bit too soon for you to have such strong feelings or to think you have. I don't want you regretting this further down the line, sweetheart."

I shook my head and curled back up in the covers, trying to avoid my mom as best as possible, but she was still there minutes later in the silence that took over the room.

"He resigned from the company," she said some minutes later.

I shot up from the bed, my eyes widening. "What?"

"He and your father got into an argument yesterday. I spoke to your father earlier, and he said he hadn't too long brought in his resignation."

"That idiot," I muttered under my breath.

"Excuse me?"

"We're not together because I didn't want him choosing me over the job."

"Wha–"

"I've gotta go see him," I said as I threw the sheets from over me and rolled off the bed.

"Honey, are you sure this is what you want?" Mom pressed.

"I've never been more certain about anything in my life, Mom."

She sighed. "Ok, well, in that case, go for it," she said as she reached in to kiss me. "I've gotta head out shortly. Let me know how it goes."

I smiled. "Will do, Mom."

After she left, I took a quick shower and pulled on a pair of shorts and a T-shirt. I couldn't believe Collin had made such a stupid decision. I had spent days crying because I thought I'd lose the love of my life, but at the same time, I was happy he had the job of his dreams.

Dad said he had no plans to fire him, although he wouldn't look at him the same again. I was content with that, but Collin resigning didn't make any sense.

Tying my hair in a ponytail, I grabbed my purse and ran downstairs, hellbent on finding Collin's apartment one way or another.

To my surprise, as I swung the door open, ready to leave, I almost bumped into Collin, who was on the other side, his hand mid-air, ready to knock.

My eyes widened, and so did his. We both remained silent and stared at each other as if we had both discovered the most beautiful thing in the world. I drank in every inch of him, realizing that his hair had grown a bit and so had his beard. There was this rugged look to him that added layers to the already strapping man that he was. The heat that suddenly filled me told me I was attracted to him despite the changes.

"I was just coming to see you," I finally said.

He smiled. "Beat you to it."

I bit my lips. "Come in."

He moved past me, barely inside, before he turned to me. "You know I said I'd give you some time to think us through, but I got impatient," he said. "Do you know what that necklace means for me, Lauren?"

I subconsciously touched the piece of jewelry that I hadn't taken off since Collin gave it to me. I shook my head.

"It means I'll love you till the end of time. Infinity."

My heart was just bursting in my chest. My lips started to quiver. "Collin..."

"We might not be what other people want, but I know what I want more than anything in this world, Lauren, and that's you. Nothing will change my mind."

I smiled amid my tears. "I love you too, you big teddy bear," I laughed as I bounded toward him and clamped my mouth to his. It was like a breath of fresh air to be touching him again, to be in his presence. I latched onto him like my life depended on it, and he held me tight, his hard body pressed against mine. Collin broke free to look at me while he cupped my face into his strong hands.

"I missed you so much."

"I missed you."

A DAY LATER, I WAS in Collin's bed, though the truth was, I hadn't left it since we made up. I didn't want to leave it, either. I wanted this moment to last as long as it could, even though I knew there wouldn't be any uncertainty about our future this time around.

I snuggled up to him and slid my naked legs over his narrow hips. He smiled up at me, a dangerous glint in his eyes as he trailed his hands down my hips and up to my breasts. Heat sizzled through me; the constant craving raged wild throughout my body. I was sticky with cum, drenched in sweat and only a few minutes away from bone-deep exhaustion, but as long as Collin was here, I was always ready for another round.

I climbed atop of him and reached for his manhood, setting it into place before I impaled myself on it. A wholesome sigh left my lips as his length filled me, the girth stretching me to the max. I was able to take all of him in, allowing myself a second before I started to roll my hips, feeling as his cock moved within me, creating spasms throughout my body.

Collin held my hips and helped to guide my movements. I ran my fingers down his hands and later leaned into him for a kiss as I lifted my hips and slammed them down on him. He filled me with sharp thrusts that had me moaning against his mouth, but I didn't let up. Collin reached for my ass and eased me down on his stealthy cock until my pussy started to convulse, and my orgasm started to beat at my gates.

His hand slid over my ass, his fingers tracing the rim of my rosebud. I continued to bounce on him as the pleasure soared within me. He slipped the tip of his finger inside, and I screamed aloud as my orgasm crashed into me.

Collin grunted at the same time, pressing me down on him, so all of him was buried inside me. I started to tremble as his cum filled me for the first time, warm spurts filling my insides that had me coming again.

I collapsed on his chest, breathing heavily with his length inside me. He held me close, his hands rubbing down my back as we came down from our orgasms. A minute later, his cock slipped out, a dollop of cum following in its wake.

I couldn't even find it within me to move from off him. My body was humming with pleasure, and I was exhausted to the bone. Just as my eyes started to droop, he rolled me over on the bed and headed to the bathroom. A few minutes later, I was picked up from the bed and carried to the bathroom, where I was placed in a warm tub of water doused with essential oils and bath bombs.

Collin joined me, sliding behind me while he held me and used a sponge to bathe me. I sighed against him and closed my eyes, too satiated to do anything but enjoy the moment.

WE WERE HAVING TAKE-out sometime later and enjoying each other's company when a knock sounded at the door. I glanced at Collin, who also had a curious expression on his face.

He shrugged and got up, brushing off his hands before he walked toward the door.

I wiped my mouth and prepared myself for whoever it was, happy that I was wearing clothes this time around.

"Mark...what a pleasant surprise," I heard Collin say and immediately stiffened.

What was my dad doing here?

"Can we talk?" Dad said his tone firm.

"Yeah, come in."

I watched the entrance with bated breath, feeling as if my heart was going to hop out of my chest. My dad made an appearance seconds later, pausing for a bit when he saw me.

"I figured you'd be here."

I bit my lips. "Is everything okay?" Collin asked.

Dad sighed and loosened the button to his jacket before he took a seat beside me.

"Truth be told, I still feel betrayed and disappointed," he began, and I hung my head, embarrassed.

"I'm sorry, Dad."

"I felt like shit hearing about it from someone outside of this family," he turned to Collin. "I don't know if I can look at you the same again – I'm gonna need some time."

"Dad..."

"I still can't quite wrap my head around it, but I guess it isn't for me to understand. It's just crazy how after one day of knowing each other, you both decided to go to another state together for a whole weekend."

Collin moved closer toward me. "I guess you could say it was love at first sight for me," he said, and I blushed.

Dad scoffed. "I don't want to see my daughter hurt, Collin, and if that happens, we're going to have problems," he said firmly.

"I wouldn't dare-"

"See, you say that now, but this whole thing is still fresh, and, of course, it all seems perfect now, but time has a way of revealing things."

"Mark, if you're afraid my feelings will change for your daughter, that won't happen. I love Lauren," Collin defended just as firmly.

"Didn't you love your ex-wife as well, and we all saw how that turned out," he jabbed dryly.

Collin scoffed and shook his head. I felt like this was taking a turn. "Dad, please, if you're just here to put us down, please don't. If we make mistakes, that's on us; we're both adults here. You don't have to worry about anything," I intervened.

He sighed. "I just want what's best for you, sweetheart."

I stepped toward him and held his hands. "I know that, but I'll be fine. Collin makes me happy," I smiled.

He nodded. "That's all I want," he said as he hugged me, looking over my shoulder at Collin. He cleared his throat as we pulled apart, straightened his posture and looked to Collin. "You do great work and have made such a huge impact to the company... I er - I'd hate to lose you."

Collin nodded. "Thank you."

"Please come back."

"Will do."

I flung myself into Dad's arms yet again. "You have no idea how I appreciate this."

He kissed me on the cheek. "Anything for you, sweetheart." He sighed as we broke apart. "I'd better get going; your mother is expecting me for dinner."

We said our goodbyes, and I turned to Collin with a grin on my face. The excitement was radiating off me in waves, and I couldn't control it. I leapt into Collin's arms, and he caught me with a chuckle.

"See, everything has a way of working itself out."

Epilogue

Lauren

The multibillion-dollar company has created another video game that has the world in a frenzy, accumulating more than a billion users worldwide.

I smiled as I read the article, turning my head to the bathroom where Collin was.

"Babe, you're in the papers again!" I exclaimed.

He came out with a towel draped around his waist and a smile on his face. I bit my lips at the beauty that he was, still managing to be as fit as a fiddle despite the six years that had passed. Nothing changed about Collin except for the few strands of grey that lined his temple. He still looked as good as the first day I saw him – even better.

He came beside me and glanced at the paper in my hand.

"I look good in that shot, don't I?" He smirked.

I took a moment to glance at the photo of him in his royal blue suit. The color made his skin pop, and every inch of it was seamless and tailored to perfection.

"You always look good, baby," I said.

"Not as good as you," he teased, his eyes dropping to the cleavage of my camisole.

I grinned and kissed him, feeling the sudden burst of arousal that ran through me. Every day felt as new as the first. Nothing had changed between us, even for a second, and each day I was thankful that a love that had formed so quickly didn't end just as fast. As Collin kissed me, his hands started to trail up my leg, and I parted them to allow him access, but we didn't get far because my phone started to ring, and I forced myself apart from him.

"Don't answer that," Collin groaned, still kissing me all over the face.

I was tempted not to, but when I glanced across at the screen, I saw that it was my mom and couldn't resist.

"It's Mom," I said, which seemed to have done the trick because he eased up and watched as I took the phone and answered.

It was a video call. Collin shuffled up beside me and plastered a smile on his face similar to mine as soon as my mom came on screen.

"Hey, sweetheart!" She yelled over the breeze in the background.

"Hey Mom, how are you guys enjoying your time?" I asked.

She squinted her eyes as if finding it hard to hear me and gestured further down the beach where the others were. The wind was whipping her hair all over, and her skin was sunburnt, but the smile on her face was priceless, as well as the view in the background.

"We're leaving the beach now to go have some lunch. Cameron wanted to talk to you guys."

The four-year-old suddenly appeared on screen with a smile on his face, his blonde hair ruffled, a tooth gone from his smile.

"Hi Mama, hi Dad," he said, and my heart melted.

Dad held him in his hand while he, too, smiled proudly at the interaction.

"Hi, my sweet boy. Are you having fun with grandma and grandpa?"

He nodded. "We went on a boat and saw some fish!" He was quick to say, the enthusiasm rich in his voice.

"Aww, that's amazing, bud. I hope you are being a good boy for your grandparents..."

He nodded vigorously, his hair bouncing in the process. I smiled, on the verge of tears by the simple act.

Collin chuckled. "Ok, bud, we miss you. Can't wait for you to get back!"

"I miss you too!"

"We love you honey! Enjoy and be a good boy, okay."

"Okay, Mommy."

He bounced on his grandpa's lap and went to play with a beach ball beside them. A little girl about his age ran up to him, and they started to play together.

"We went on a glass-bottom boat ride earlier," Mom said. "He was so excited. I'll send you the pictures after this call."

I smiled. "I still can't believe you guys decided to bring him with you. He can be such a handful at times, and you're on vacation."

Mom fanned me off. "He keeps us on our feet, but he truly makes us happier," she said as she glanced at dad, who shared a smile as well.

"Speaking of, how's our soon-to-be granddaughter?"

I glanced down at my swollen stomach. "Looks like she's being a good girl today. She isn't trying to kick out my stomach today," I giggled.

They all burst into laughter. "Well, it's still early," Mom teased. "Are you planning on going to work today?" She asked.

"Not today. Collin and I saw this house on the market that we wanted to check out. We're hoping to have a bigger space for when the baby gets here."

"That's amazing, but you should get some rest too, honey. This is one of the pros of being your own boss; you don't have to push yourself too much in times like these."

I sighed. "I know, Mom, but I'm just fine, trust me."

"Ok, sweetheart; Cameron must be hungry so we're gonna head to the restaurant to get some food. I love you guys."

"We love you too, Mom. Kiss Cameron for me."

"Will do, sweetheart. Bye."

I ended the call and smiled at Collin, who was already leaning in to kiss me.

"Come on, we don't have much time. We'll have to leave soon," he said and I giggled as I wrapped my hands around him and kissed him. I fell back on the bed with him atop of me because clearly, we couldn't get enough of each other.

My Roommate's Sexy Daddy

Izzie Vee

Erotic & Forbidden[1]

IZZIE VEE[2]

1. https://www.amazon.com/s?k=izzie+vee&i=digital-text&crid=31LQJTEQYT2EE&sprefix=izzie+vee%2Cdigital-text%2C121&ref=nb_sb_noss
2. https://www.amazon.com/s?k=izzie+vee&i=digital-text&crid=31LQJTEQYT2EE&sprefix=izzie+vee%2Cdigital-text%2C121&ref=nb_sb_noss

Cover Design by Izzie Vee
Cover Photo by VitalikRadko on Depositphotos.com

Table of Content

Chapter 1

Jane

"Hey, nerd girl, my dad's coming over for a bit. You can stay, or you can leave. It's up to you," my roommate Courtney exclaimed as she typed away at her phone before casually fanning me off with a flicker to her wrist.

I resisted the urge to roll my eyes as I glanced at her. "It's fine. Just pretend I'm not here," I said as I flipped through the pages of my notebook.

"Well, that won't be hard," she murmured loud enough for me to hear.

I sighed and shuffled further into the bed, praying for the day to be over as I had done every day since this semester. It was an unending cycle and every day seemed worse. I missed my old roommate and wished she hadn't moved across the continent. But just my luck. Having someone I actually clicked with was a once-in-a-lifetime occurrence in my life, so when it actually happened, I was over the moon. Now I was back to earth and back to a dreadful reality, where my new roommate was like the spawn of satan and everything I feared and hated growing up. A mean girl. I had been foolish to think I'd get someone like my friend, Bailey, who was incredibly caring and sweet. Even though we still stayed in touch, I still felt like crying whenever I thought about her. But I was encouraged by the fact that I just had a couple of months left before this was all over; college life.

I sat there reviewing some notes for my economics class when a knock sounded at the door. Courtney immediately bounded from her bed, a huge grin on her face as she dashed toward the door, her bob bouncing around her neck as she did so. I shuffled further into my bed, now wishing I had taken the opportunity to head out instead of enduring Courtney and the person who helped bring her into this world. Surely, they were just the same; Courtney had to get her meanness from somebody.

I bit my lips and buried my head into my notebook, pretending to study because I knew there was no way I could do the real thing with a parent in the room. I already felt nervous for some reason. Maybe it was the fear I felt for the impending snarky remarks. I could just imagine it now. How she would whisper in her dad's ear as she glanced at me. Then they would laugh together while I stayed perched in my little corner.

My cheeks grew heated at the thought.

Courtney squealed. "Daddy, I'm so happy you came!" I didn't even look in fear that one glance from Courtney would force my head back in my books.

"Of course. I missed my baby girl," he said with a voice just as smooth as velvet and as deep as the ocean. I wasn't expecting that voice on a man who was probably nearing fifty, but what did I know about men anyway?

Courtney giggled, which was so unlike her; it was almost scary.

"I bought everything you said you needed," he said, and I could hear a few bags shuffle.

"Thanks, Dad, you're the best!"

"Anything for you, sweetheart," he said. There was a silent pause that I dreaded. "Who's your friend?"

I sat on the bed, hoping someone else had entered the room and he wasn't referring to me.

"Er ... we're just roommates, Dad," Courtney said as she cleared her throat. "That's Jane."

I finally turned out of respect, preparing to offer a fake smile before burying myself in my books again. But I wasn't nearly prepared for what or rather who confronted me as I did so. My eyes widened, and my mouth must have been on the floor while my heart began to race in my chest. Courtney's dad was unlike anything I would have expected. He had the face and body of an action movie star with his sharp jawline and athletic body. I was dumbstruck, too amazed to utter even a word. And what made it worse was that he was staring right back at me with a small smile on his handsome face.

A flutter appeared in my stomach, and my palms suddenly felt wet. There was just something about how he looked at me with seemingly pitch-black eyes that seemed to bore through my soul.

"Hi, Jane," he said as he moved toward me. I was certain I would pass out any minute with the way my heart was beating. Suddenly feeling self-conscious, I looked down at the pair of pajamas I hadn't bothered to change out of this morning. It was pink and blue and had hello kitty all over it. I could feel my cheeks burn, and I felt like sinking through the floor with embarrassment.

But I couldn't prove to be the complete loser that Courtney thought me to be, even though I looked like I had just come out of somebody's nightmare with my tousled brown hair and bare face.

I cleared my throat and straightened up on the bed. "Hi, nice to meet you, sir," I croaked and immediately wanted to kick myself.

He chuckled and extended his hand. "Please, call me Elliot."

I swallowed with a nod and reached for his big arm with a complete sleeve of tattoos that disappeared beneath the sleeve of his snug T-shirt.

When my sweaty palm finally touched his, I had to hold back the gasp that threatened to spill from my lips. He was warm, and his big hands were firm. I didn't know how to explain the feeling

I had, but my entire body grew heated from the single touch, and I could feel my nipples growing hard beneath my shirt.

I quickly drew back my hand as if I'd been burnt and cleared my throat, glancing at Courtney, who had no care for the interaction that completely uprooted me.

"Nice to meet you, Elliot," I said, my voice barely above a whisper.

His eyes lingered on me for a second, the smile not waning from his angular face as his eyes roamed over me.

"So, Dad, do you wanna go get dinner or something? I know you hardly cook, so you must be hungry," Courtney said, and I almost jumped.

Elliot looked away, his attention on his daughter once more. "Er– sure. Sounds good."

"Great, let's go. I'll unpack these later," she said as she briefly glanced at the grocery bags before pulling a jacket from the portable closet.

Elliot turned to me again, and just like that, my heart was in a marathon. "Would you like to join us, Jane?" He asked.

My mouth fell open, but Courtney was already beating me to it before I could reply.

"Er ... Jane is busy studying, Dad," she said as she looked at me. "I'm sure that's more productive than ruining our family time," she said as she raised a brow at me.

My cheeks flamed as I glanced at Elliot. "Yeah, sorry. I really have to study."

There was a small silence as he looked at me like he was trying to see the real truth within me.

"Okay, well, it was a pleasure meeting you, Jane. I'll see you around," he smiled.

I nodded and returned his smile. Courtney rolled her eyes, grabbed her purse and waited as her dad moved toward her and ducked beneath the door before she followed suit. The door closed with a soft click, and I sighed heavily as I plopped back down onto the bed.

It was hard to believe that Elliot was Courtney's dad when he didn't look a day over thirty. There wasn't even a grey hair in sight, and his body was a far cry from the famous dad bods. The complete opposite, actually. Elliot looked like he spent his days crushing weights and eating spinach.

I could still feel the firm grip on my hand and how he dominated the room with his presence. His scent still lingered – a musky, citrusy scent that was probably more intoxicating than any drug on the market. I brought the hand he had held to my nose and took in a whiff of it, the scent still ripe on my skin. I closed my eyes, and for the first time, I was daydreaming about a man — a man who was probably twice my age.

Catching myself, I opened my eyes and bounded upright, shaking my head. "What are you doing, Jane? Get a hold of yourself," I scolded myself.

How could I be attracted to someone's father? And yes, he was handsome and sexy and charming and consisted of all the good stuff that made girls like me swoon, but he was a dad, and worse ... the dad of the girl I dreaded.

A few guys had approached me on campus, but I hadn't given them the time of day because none of them appealed to me. Yet, an older man came along, smiled at me and said a few words, and I was ready to risk it all.

Risk what exactly, Jane? A voice in the back of my head exclaimed, and I almost laughed at myself. Surely, I was getting ahead of myself. Yes, Elliot had spurred up unfamiliar feelings in me, but this was nothing but a new crush and nothing else. I could only watch and admire from afar, too afraid to make a move because that was definitely not the person I was... and because I was pretty sure Elliot saw me as nothing more than a little girl like his daughter. Not to mention the fact that Courtney would have my head on a stake if I were to try anything.

I sighed, knowing it was pointless to think of would-bes when the chances were zero.

My phone started to ring, and I was happy for the distraction. The last thing I should be doing was thinking about a man I couldn't have – one that would probably laugh at the idea of being with me.

A smile bloomed on my face when I saw the caller, and I knew it was just the right person I needed to take my mind off things.

"Hi, my favorite brother in the whole world!" I exclaimed chirpily.

Troy chuckled. "I'm your only brother in the whole world."

I grinned. "That makes you a lucky bastard."

He laughed. "Definitely that. How have you been? I've been a bit swamped the past couple of days. I'm sorry I couldn't call as usual."

I hugged my pillow and smiled. "I understand; don't worry about it. I know by now that when I don't get a reply, you're busy with work," I said a bit sadly, though that wasn't the intention.

"I don't want you to feel like your second priority, sis. You know you always come first," he said.

"I know, and I don't feel like that. We aren't kids anymore; I know you won't always have the time."

"Well, you'll always be my baby sister no matter how old we get," he said.

I smiled, and my lips trembled. "Stop, you're gonna make me cry," I sniffed.

He chuckled. "Okay, so on a brighter note, guess who's heading out to L.A. next weekend?" He said as his voice raised a pitch.

I could already feel the happiness bubbling up inside me as soon as I heard the words. I couldn't resist a squeal as joy exploded within me.

"OMG, OMG!"

Troy laughed on the other end. "I already booked my flight. I'll be there by Friday!"

My eyes stung with tears of happiness, and I hugged the pillows tight, wishing it was Troy instead. "Oh, my gosh! I can't wait!" I exclaimed. "Eek, you've truly made my day, big bro."

He was laughing on the other end. "Happy to hear it. Clear your schedule, sis. You're in for the most amazing weekend of your life!"

I squealed. "Can't wait!"

"I have to get back to work, but if you need anything, don't hesitate to call."

"Noted. I love you."

"I love you too, sis, bye."

I ended the call with a huge smile because that was the effect Troy always made when he called. With a single word, he could make my day ten times better. Suddenly, I was waiting for this weekend to pass, so I could welcome the other and see my brother. It had been well over two months since I last saw him, and I had missed him every day since. It sucked being a state apart, but I had school, and he had work, and we had to find a way to make it work.

A few hours later, I took a shower, made some ramen and decided to watch a movie when the door opened, and Courtney made an appearance. She was humming to a song as she got inside and immediately went to her side of the room. I was automatically reminded of her father, Elliot, and how he had made me feel earlier. There were a lot of things I considered ever since we met, and one of those things was if I actually preferred older men.

But the more I thought about it, the more I realized I had never taken a liking to any man in particular until Elliot. There was this one guy in high school whom I had a huge crush on, but he was a jock, and I wasn't even close to being in his league. I guess the situations were a bit similar now, seeing Elliot was a complete eye candy who maybe had a string of models lining up to be with him. I was nowhere close to that.

"Hey, nerd girl!" A voice exclaimed, and I dragged myself from my thoughts to find Courtney there, looking at me annoyed, her stained lips set in a scowl.

"Yeah...?"

"'My man is coming over tomorrow evening. You can stay to watch us fuck, or you can give us the time," she shrugged nonchalantly. "It's up to you."

My cheeks flamed at her bluntness, and I could swear I felt a little bile in the back of my throat at the very thought. "Yeah, I'll be out your hair, don't worry."

"Hmm," she replied as she crossed her legs on her bed and typed away on her phone.

I rolled my eyes and decided to scrap the movie, thinking that the faster I fell asleep, the less likely I'd need to tolerate Courtney.

THE FOLLOWING DAY, Courtney had made it clear that she would be indisposed in the evening. I had no friend to hang out with, so I decided to head to the café I worked last summer. It was always my go-to to clear my head and study, and I figured it wouldn't be any different this time around.

I pulled on a pair of leggings and a cotton shirt, grabbing my laptop before I headed out. As soon as I got there, I ordered my favorite – French vanilla and took one of the window seats that overlooked the busy street. I sighed with a smile already on my face as I got comfortable. It would be a while because I knew I couldn't risk possibly going back to the dorm to find Courtney wrapped up with her boyfriend. The idea was repulsive, and I wanted no part of it.

"Hey, are you free?" A text came in from Bailey.

I smiled and quickly replied. "Of course."

The next second, my phone started to ring with a picture of her on the screen.

"Hiiii!" I chirped, smiling into the phone.

Bailey was in bed, looking like she just woke up with her curly hair splayed across her pillows, her eyes a bit droopy.

She grinned at my voice. "Well, someone's in a good mood. How are you? I missed you so much!" She said, making a sad face.

"I miss you too! Life hasn't been the same since you left."

"Ugh, same... I thought South Africa would be cool, and it has been, but at this point, I've seen it all already. I just want to come back home!" She moaned.

I smiled. "Well we only have less than one year of college left. You can come back after?" I said, hopefulness in my voice.

"Definitely. So how's your new roomie?"

I rolled my eyes. "An absolute nightmare. She insists on calling me nerd girl, even though I literally struggle with some of my subjects!"

Bailey laughed. "Struggle and still get straight A's?" She asked as she raised a brow comically. "You need to stand up to her and talk back, Jane."

"Yeah, if I wasn't afraid that she'd maul me in my sleep."

Bailey giggled. "Don't be dramatic. I'm sure she's just all bark and no bite."

"I wouldn't be too sure. You should see her dad. He's like a handsome version of hulk."

"Oh, you've met her dad? See, you two are becoming friends already," she teased.

"He came by to drop off groceries for her, and then he left."

"So he's an asshole too, like his kid?"

"The complete opposite from the looks of it. He was really nice to me."

Bailey's mouth dropped open. "Why are you blushing? OMG, you like him!"

I quickly caught myself but ended up blushing even harder. "What, no! He's someone's father, Bailes! My enemy's father at that," I defended.

"Oh, please, as if that has anything to do with it. Tell me the truth!"

I groaned and slapped one hand over my face. "Okay, fine. He's really sexy, and I got that tingly feeling when he was around!"

Bailey's brown eyes widened to saucers. "You want to fuck him!"

At this point, I was as red as a beetroot as I looked around the café to see if anyone had heard Bailey's outburst. Luckily, no one was in earshot of hearing us.

"OMG, stop. I don't!"

Bailey laughed. "Oh, please. I know you, and you've never gotten this flustered over boy talk – only he's not a boy, he's a man. A man who can give you the time of your life!" She grinned.

I shook my head. "Just kill me right now. Bailey!"

"Come on, Jane. Your coochie probably thinks you've died. It needs some action!"

I glanced at the air vents because I was burning up from all this lewd talk. "Nothing is going to happen between us. Heck, he was just nice in a fatherly way. Nothing to get my panties in a bunch about."

She scoffed. "Have you seen you? You're fucking hot, and he's a man. They can't resist, Jane."

I couldn't help my smile but quickly remembered. "I was in pajamas when he saw me."

Bailey choked out a laugh. "Well, hey, you're beautiful too."

I smiled. "You really know how to boost people, don't you?"

She smirked. "All I'm saying is, the best way to get back at your hater is to fuck her father."

"That's never going to happen, and I'm not trying to 'get back' at anyone," I almost whispered as I glanced around the café. "Anyway, isn't it like midnight there? How are you up?"

She sighed. "I slept early, woke up and thought about you. I know we don't talk as often with the different time zones, so I took the chance, and here we are," she smiled.

I smiled. "Aww, I'm so happy you called, though. God knows I needed it," I sighed.

"Hey, just a couple more months, and you'll be done with college and forget your bitchy roommate ever existed – Courtney, that is."

I grinned. "I can't wait," I said as I raked my fingers through my hair, my eyes moving toward the cashier, where a short line was with people waiting to order. I did a double-take when I recognized someone. But not just anyone; the person who had been plaguing my mind since yesterday. Elliot was there with a knapsack on his back, and although I could only see his side profile, I had taken enough of him in to know it was him.

"What is it?" Bailey asked on the other end. "You look like you've just seen a ghost," she said.

I momentarily glanced back to the screen. "Not exactly. It's him," I whispered.

"Who?" She asked eagerly.

"Courtney's dad – Elliot!" I whisper-yelled.

"OMG, lemme see, lemme see!"

My palms felt sweaty again, even more so when I flipped the camera and tried my very best to slyly aim it at him. "Oh damn, he's hot from what I see. You sure he's her actual dad?"

I scoffed. "I thought the same thing. He is, though!"

Just then, Elliot turned, and our eyes locked. Bailey squealed on the other end, and I seemed to have lost all thinking. I shifted my phone abruptly, causing what was left of my coffee to spill over and my phone to land right in it. I muttered a curse as my eyes searched the table for a napkin. Luckily, I had gotten one with my coffee and quickly dabbed up the spillage and wiped it from my phone.

"He's so fucking hot. What!" Bailey was saying, despite my tragedy.

I already felt flustered, and to top it off, when I glanced back to the register, Elliot was making his way over to me with a worried look on his face. I wanted to take my purse and run toward the door, but he was already so close there was no escaping.

"Bailes, he's coming over; I've gotta go, bye!" I quickly whispered into the phone before I ended the call and slapped the phone to the table, plastering a smile on my face.

Elliot appeared right in front of me, one bulky hand clutching his backpack, causing the muscles to pop up more in his hand. He wore a snug black T-shirt and clad denim that showcased his toned legs.

"Jane, hi, is everything alright?" He asked, still looking worried with his thick, narrow brows drawn together. My eyes roamed over his face unabashedly, and though I knew it was impolite and weird, I couldn't stop myself. The man was a looker. Though this time, I realized he looked a bit scruffy with a small bruise on his cheek and a small cut on his brow bone.

I cleared my throat. "I'm fine... just clumsy me," I said, wanting to kick myself. "How are you? I er – you should put something on that," I said, my hand moving to my own cheek.

An emotion crossed his face, and he quickly cleared his throat. "Ah, that's nothing. I'll be fine," he said, those dark eyes boring into me again.

There was a short silence. "Would you mind if I joined you?"

My heart started to thud faster. "Er, not at all..."

Just then, the barista called his name, and we both looked to the cashier. "Just a sec," he said as he went to get his order. I swallowed hard and adjusted my shirt, trapping a few tendrils of my loose hair behind my ear. Elliot returned with a cup and what looked to be a sandwich. He smiled as he took a seat on the opposite end of me. My eyes lowered to his hand that gripped his cup. I took note of his red, bruised knuckles and had to wonder what type of a man he was. Yes, he had the tattoos and was huge, but I didn't want to automatically assume he was a bad guy. Maybe he got into a bar fight, I surmised. Everything still looked so fresh; it made me wonder. What if he were a bad guy who was just putting up a nice front, so I couldn't see through the façade.

"I hope I wasn't disturbing your studying," he said as he took a drink and glanced at my laptop.

"Er, no. I haven't even started. I just usually come here to clear my head."

He nodded. "I'd expect you to be out with friends partying. But you don't strike me as the average college kid, Jane."

He called me a kid, great. "Yeah, I'm not really into that stuff. I'm very much an introvert," I said, managing a tight smile, trying to do anything but look into his eyes.

He chuckled. "I see. So are you from around here? L.A., I mean."

"No, originally from Arizona. I'm just here for college. How about you?"

"Yeah, I live about twenty minutes from here. Court wanted the whole college experience, so she decided to do the whole dorm thing. But I just think it's an excuse to go out whenever she wants."

I smiled, not knowing what to say. I looked to my cup for a distraction but remembered it was empty.

"You should join us for dinner sometime," he said as he eased back in his chair.

"I'm not your daughter's biggest fan – I hardly think she'd like that," I said, managing a tight smile.

"She can be a bit snarky at times, but I promise once you get to know her, she's the sweetest," he said.

I wouldn't hold my breath for that to happen, as I would probably end up dead.

"Yeah, we'll see."

He cleared his throat and glanced at his watch. "Well, I'd better get going, Jane. It was a pleasure seeing you again," he said as he stood.

I stood, too, my knees hitting the table and almost causing me to knock it over. "It was nice seeing you too, Elliot."

"Give that dinner invite some thought?"

I smiled tightly. "Will do." I knew I wouldn't. Not with Courtney there, anyway. He nodded, smiled, and I watched as he left the café with his broad back flexing, a single tattoo peeking over the neck of his shirt. How many tattoos did this man have? I was somehow curious to know, but not only to see the tattoos – something else completely. His scent lingered behind and filled my nostrils, and I almost shivered. That flutter had returned to my stomach, but this time, it was more intense. It was bittersweet because, on the one hand, I wanted to bask in the feeling, but at the same time, I knew I couldn't because things would get complicated way too fast, and

Courtney would maul me for sure. Then there was the fact that he was probably twice my age, and society would look down on us — it just couldn't happen. *Best to take your mind off it,* my subconscious spoke.

But that was easier said than done because all I could think about for the rest of the day was the charming older man.

Chapter 2

Jane

Although Courtney was being her usual self throughout the rest of the week, I didn't mind because the anticipation of seeing my brother was greater than anything else. All the snarky remarks she passed at me were like dust that quickly floated away as soon as they came. I was free that Friday morning, so I took the time to wash and press my hair and pluck my brows before Troy came. I didn't want him to see how bad I was taking the whole college thing, so I had scoured every inch of me, and I was practically glistening by the end of it. For the first time in what seemed like forever, I let my hair out, happy with the luscious bounce that fell to my back. I waited, seeing Troy had not given me a specific time when he'd be here.

Courtney entered that afternoon, glancing at me through the corners of her eyes but quickly doing a double-take when she saw me sitting on my bed.

"Wow, look who finally managed to crawl out of their little dusty shell," she scoffed.

I resisted the urge to roll my eyes, instead managing a tight smile and bearing in mind that Troy would be here anytime.

"Finally realized that college doesn't have to be a snooze fest, huh?" She continued with a dry laugh.

I huffed. "Why do you always have to be such a bitch?" I snapped, feeling the blood drain from my face as soon as I said the words.

Her head snapped toward me, her eyes wide, brows raised with a look of disbelief on her face. "What did you just call me?"

I swallowed, deciding to speak my mind before anything happened. Things were already going south, anyway. "I've been nothing but tolerant of you since you got here. I've stayed out of your way, and I've allowed you to take countless jabs at me. Give it a rest, Courtney!" I exclaimed, my chest heaving as I spoke, now too afraid to even move. She shot daggers at me with her intense green eyes, and I started to regret everything I had said as she approached me. But before she got any closer, a knock came at the door, and she paused in her tracks, gritting her teeth before turning to the door.

I sighed in relief, watching as she opened the door and Elliot made an appearance. My heart started to beat fast — the usual effect when he was around, and my palms got sweaty. I watched as Courtney flung her arms around him, squealing in the embrace.

"Dad!" She exclaimed in a voice that had gone higher – the complete opposite of how she'd spoken to me earlier.

Elliot chuckled as he embraced her, squeezing her tight before kissing her on the cheek. "Hey, pumpkin," he greeted, smiling down at Courtney.

His eyes met mine, and I swallowed, trapped in the heat of his gaze. His eyes darkened as they roamed over my entire body in mere seconds.

"Jane... hi," he said as they broke apart.

Courtney rolled her eyes and walked toward her desk to pick up something. I licked my lips and managed a smile. "Hi."

"You look lovely," he said, unabashedly giving me a once-over that had my knees going weak.

"Thank you."

"Come on, Dad. We have to get going before the store closes," Courtney mumbled as she pushed the shopping bags Elliot had brought to the side.

"Still haven't taken me up on my invite, Jane?" He asked.

I cleared my throat. "Maybe some other time."

Just then, Troy appeared at the door that Elliot hadn't bothered to close. He had a huge smile on his face as he dropped his bags to the floor and opened his arms to me. I screamed as I bounded from the bed and flung my body into his. He laughed as he picked me up and spun me around twice while I latched onto him and soaked up everything he offered.

"Oh, my gosh, you're here!" I grinned, almost on the verge of tears with happiness.

"I told you, didn't I?" He grinned as he put me down and looked me over. "You look so beautiful."

I blushed as I slapped him on his bulky arm. "You don't look too bad yourself."

Troy gave his charming smile and pinched my cheeks before his eyes moved past my shoulder to Courtney and Elliot, who stood there curious. Courtney, however, looked more intrigued than anything else. I glanced at Elliot to see that his face had hardened, and he didn't look as welcoming as he had earlier. Instead, he looked ready to kill someone, and I found that to be the most confusing thing ever.

"Er... this is my roommate Courtney and her dad, Elliot," I informed Troy. Courtney hopped up in front of Troy, a huge smile on her face. My brows furrowed.

"This is my big brother, Troy," I said, watching as Courtney's brow raised.

"Nice to meet you," Troy said with a smile, reaching out to shake Courtney's hand. She took it eagerly, a sly expression on her face.

"Pleasure is all mine."

The grim expression had gone from Elliot's face, and he now had on the smile he had when he had just entered. He greeted Troy with a handshake, and I watched as I mentally compared them.

They were around the same height, but surprisingly, despite being the gym enthusiast that Troy was, Elliot stood out more – more strapped in every aspect. Maybe it was the tank top he had on today, but every hardened ridge of his body seemed magnified – taut and riddled with tattoos.

"Love the ink, man. Who's your guy?" Troy asked.

Elliot glanced at his arm. "Er, I had these done years ago, so that part of my memory is a bit foggy," he chuckled. "But there's a guy on eight that's pretty good too."

Troy nodded. "Cool. Luckily, I have my baby sis here to show me where that is," he smiled as he looked down at me. Elliot did the same, and my cheeks flamed a bright red.

"Well, it's nice meeting you, Troy. We'd better get going," Elliot said as he glanced at Courtney, then at me. "Jane..."

"Bye," I said before dropping my gaze to the floor.

I bit my lips and watched as they left, Courtney doing a cute little finger wave as she left.

I turned my smile back to Troy, who started to examine my room. "It's a wonder you fit in this thing." He said as he took his bags.

"I'm not nearly as big as you. It works," I laughed.

He grinned a straight line of pearly whites. "True."

I sat on the bed. "So, where are you staying?"

"I booked the weekend at a motel in town. Nothing fancy; just somewhere to lay my head," he winked. "I'm starving. Let's go get something to eat and catch up."

"Now you're talking my language," I grinned as I grabbed my purse.

Half an hour later, we were at Troy's favorite fast-food joint whenever he visited. We ordered and sat there eating – Troy having decided on a double cheeseburger. He closed his eyes as he chewed, the corners of his mouth packed with food.

"So, how's the roommate?" He asked between swallows.

I rolled my eyes. "The worst."

His thick bushy brows furrowed. "Really? She didn't seem so bad to me."

"That's what she wants you to think. I can't wait to be done with her," I sighed as I sipped on my soda.

"You must miss Bailey, huh?"

"More than you know. We talk as often as we can, though."

"Well, that's great, at least. How's she doing?"

"I think she's done with the place and wants to return home."

Troy chuckled. "Well, once school is over, you two can reunite again."

"Yeah, I can't wait. Seriously."

He smiled and reached across to pat my hand. "So, who's the lucky guy?"

I almost choked on my drink. "What?"

"You're glowing. Has to be someone."

My cheeks flushed. "I'm not. I'll let you know I made an effort to look extra pretty just to see you."

Troy grinned. "You don't have to make an effort, sis. You're beautiful, anyway."

I couldn't hide my smile. "But that still doesn't answer my question," he insisted.

"There's no one, I swear. These college guys are all idiots."

He laughed as he wiped his mouth. "No argument there."

"How about you? I know you must have a girlfriend by now."

He scratched the nape of his neck. "I don't know. She wants to be exclusive, and I don't know if I want that yet..."

"Why not?"

He shrugged. "It'll become more real, I guess. I kinda like my freedom in a sense."

"So... are you seeing other people?"

"No, I..." he trailed off and raked his fingers through his sandy blonde hair. "I just have a feeling things will move too fast afterward, and she'll want to move in and then she'll wanna get married..."

I laughed. "You're definitely thinking too far ahead. Do you love her?"

He looked up at me from under his eyes, a sly smile on his face. "I'm not having this conversation with my baby sister," he laughed.

"What?!" I gawked. "I'm not so much a baby anymore, you know."

He shrugged. "You'll always be to me. You're the only person I've got left in this world, Janey."

I hung my head to the table and fiddled with my fries. "I wish Mom and Dad were here," I said, feeling a lump in my throat as sadness took me over.

Troy reached across to take my hand, giving it a gentle squeeze. "Me too. But we've got each other, and as long as we have that, we'll be okay," he smiled. I smiled back and nodded. "Now come on, we didn't come here to rehash the past and get all sad about it. We're gonna have some fun," he said as he pushed back into the rickety iron chair, causing it to scrape loudly against the checkered tiles. Troy then pulled a few notes out of his pocket and laid them on the counter before reaching for my hand with a smile on his face.

I grinned as I took his hand and hopped behind him as we left the café.

WE WENT TO AN AMUSEMENT park, rode the Ferris wheel, played some games and took advantage of every fun thing in sight. I had a smile on my face the entire time because this was the happiest I had ever been in months. Later that night, I followed Troy back to his hotel room and crashed on one of the beds. I would have gone back to the dorm, but I was afraid of what might happen after the way I left things with Courtney earlier. I was too tired for a confrontation and too happy to let anything spoil my day.

That Saturday morning, I got up and washed my face, preparing to head back to the dorm to freshen up before I met with Troy again.

"I'm gonna go take a shower and change, and then we can meet up somewhere."

He nodded. "I think I'm gonna head to that place your roommate's dad suggested. I've been planning on getting a fresh tat."

"Do you even know where that is?" I asked.

"I was hoping you'd come, but I'll just ask around."

"I can follow you."

"Nah, I'll be fine. While you're getting yourself together, I'll be doing that. It'll save us some time."

"You sure?"

"Yeah, don't worry about it," he said, kissing my forehead.

I smiled. "Ok, well, I'll see you in a few."

"Hey," he said, and I paused in my tracks, turning back to look at him. "There's this boxing thing I wanna go to tonight. Heard about it online. You don't mind coming, do you?"

Although the idea of cracking bones and blood didn't appeal to me in the slightest, this was Troy, and I would do anything to see him happy. He loved this sort of stuff. "Of course."

A hundred-watt smile appeared on his face. "Sweet!"

Chapter 3

Jane

I didn't know if I had suddenly attracted a spurt of luck, but I found myself counting my blessings when I arrived at the apartment, and Courtney wasn't there. I smiled to myself as I quickly took a shower and changed into something for the coming evening. Troy had offered to take me shopping before his boxing game. At least I had one thing to look forward to. I'd been starved for a closet upgrade anyway.

Two hours later, I met him there, and we explored a couple of malls, got a few things and went back to my dorm to put them down. After that, we had something to eat, and at seven, I could see the excitement on Troy's face.

"We should get going," he said. "I don't wanna miss even a minute."

"Where is this place anyway?" I asked as I hopped into the rental he had gotten for the weekend.

"Um, a basketball court. A friend of mine said he'd tag me the location."

"Are these things even legal?" I asked, furrowing my brow.

He grinned. "It's fun; that's all you need to know," he winked.

I rolled my eyes and groaned, knowing that was enough of an answer to my question. I didn't recognize the street we were on, but the further I went, the more cars I found were parked ahead. Troy filled in one of the empty slots that surrounded an old basketball court and glanced at me with excitement evident on his face.

A loud ruckus could be heard further up, which sounded like shouts and boos all mixed together. My stomach churned at the idea of what I was walking into, but Troy was just buzzing with excitement as he bounded from the car, waiting for me to do the same. I hugged my shoulders as soon as I got out, regretting that I hadn't taken a jacket with me.

"Come on, sounds like it's already started," he said as he closed the doors and walked ahead to where a huge crowd had gathered around the court. I skipped a little to catch up with Troy, and he held my hands as we moved through the thick crowd that glanced at us with scowls on their faces as we bore through. I was scared of any sort of confrontation but knew no one would dare approach Troy with his giant-like build. Heck, they probably thought he was there to put on a show as well.

We settled at the front, having a clear view of what was happening before us. There was only a small circle left for those who were fighting, people lining the edge with fists in the air as they cheered their favorites on. I shuffled as close as I could to Troy, who had his eyes glued on the two men in the ring. One was tall and slender, while the other one looked like he belonged on the front page of a fitness ad. Though the other had the height advantage, I imagine one punch from baby hulk would floor him.

That became fact in a matter of seconds as the bulky one took a swing right in the face of the slender one. I cringed as the loud crack resonated through the crowd, blood spewing from his nose, which he quickly grabbed onto and staggered back into the crowd. The people pushed him back as they cheered for him to get back out there, but before anything else could happen, he slouched to his knees, one hand in the air as a sign of surrender while he continued to hold his nose with the other.

The people burst into a chorus of noises, some clearly disappointed but the majority cheering on the winner. My stomach churned as I watched the victor slap his chest and meet the crowd's enthusiasm while two men came and peeled the loser off the floor, helping him out of the ring. I glanced at Troy, who was literally buzzing with excitement, his eyes wide, a smile on his face as he watched.

"I'm fucking ready to floor someone else... right now!" The bulky man shouted, gaining a number of whistles and howls from the reckless crowd.

"Oh, shit, I'm putting my money on that guy," Troy exclaimed as he dug into his pockets and took out his wallet, almost fumbling with the task as excitement ran through him.

"You don't even know who the other guy is yet," I put in.

He scoffed. "Do you see the muscles on that guy? No one here stands a chance!" He laughed.

I found myself glancing around the crowd to see if I saw anyone who fit the bill. But, unfortunately, nobody from where I stood did, and I had to admit, he had a point.

"So, who's ready?!" The guy shouted, "cause I fucking sure am!"

For a few seconds, no one entered, but then a man walked up to him and peeled off his shirt, throwing it to the side. I couldn't make out who it was as his back was turned, but I realized they were both the same in muscle size, but the new guy was a bit taller.

"Holy fuck!" Troy exclaimed. "Now there's some competition."

A series of murmurs erupted in the crowd, and I stood looking to see who it was. When he turned around, my breath caught in my throat, and my lips hung apart. It was Elliot. I didn't know how I hadn't noticed the entire sleeve of tattoos on his arm, but he was the last person I expected to see here. Or was he? He looked like just the type to be at places like these. Yet I was too mesmerized to think of the hows and whys. I was too intrigued by his bare upper body and how every inch of him looked as hard as a stone. There were tattoos along his side, and as he turned around to acknowledge the crowd, I couldn't take my eyes off the wings on his back. This time, he wore shorts that showed off his toned legs and his firm ass, which made me suddenly feel hot on the chilly night.

"Wait, what the hell. Isn't he – is that the guy who was in your dorm. Your roomie's dad?" Troy asked as he glanced at me, his brows furrowed with curiosity.

I nodded. "Yeah."

"Holy shit, this is intense. Wait, did you know he did this sort of thing?" He asked.

My head snapped to his. "No. I don't know anything about the guy other than the obvious."

"Shit, well now I don't know who the fuck to bet on. They're both huge," he said as he looked around. "Stay here, and don't move. I'm gonna walk around to see what the people think, and then I'm gonna place my bets. Don't move, okay?"

I sighed at the baby treatment. "Okay."

I couldn't take my eyes off Elliot, and for some reason, there was a nervous knot in my stomach for him. As I watched him, things started to become clearer. The bruises on his hands and face. It all made sense. This was the sort of thing he did, but for a living? Did Courtney know all this? Was this the reason she was always so mean? Because she knew her dad could break someone's neck if they dared tried her? I had too many questions and nowhere near the answers. The man I had been crushing on for the past week did street fights and was probably a bad guy. I didn't know what to think, but did any of it change how I felt about Elliot? No.

Ten minutes later, Troy returned with a sigh. "Okay, so from what I've heard, it's fifty-fifty. These guys never lose and have been doing this sort of thing for a long time. There's a shitload of money on the two of them, but since your guy there put me on to that tattoo artist, I put my money on him. Fingers crossed, sis."

"He's not my guy," I murmured under my breath, though hoping that it would somehow be true.

I sighed, and a few minutes later, the fight commenced. I hugged myself and tried to calm my beating heart but knew there wouldn't be any relief until this was all over. There was no way of knowing who would win just by looking at them. They both had the same muscle mass and looked just as deadly as they squared each other up as if trying to predict their next move. The crowd was louder than ever, and I realized a few more people had gathered around us, some sitting on the tops of fences as they cheered on their favorite.

The first guy tried to issue the first blow, which Elliot skillfully dodged and took the opportunity to swiftly jab him in the face. The guy staggered back, shook his head a little and hopped on his feet, preparing himself to go again. As he launched forward, he kicked at Elliot, and I gasped, but Elliot grabbed his leg and flung him to the floor. The crowd erupted as the two beasts fell to the ground in a rustle, Elliot on top as he dropped punch after punch in his face. My heart rejoiced a little, but the excitement quickly dimmed when the other guy wrung his leg around him and gained the upper hand, bringing Elliot on his back while he assumed the position Elliot had been in earlier. Two punches had Elliot's head flashing to the side, and I covered my mouth as terror made its way through me.

My eyes filled with tears for some reason I couldn't comprehend, my heart feeling as if it were about to gallop out of my chest. As he laid there collecting punches, his head snapped in my direction, and our gazes locked. I gasped, and his eyes widened as he stared at me in shock. The tears finally fell from my eyes, and Elliot's darkened. In one swift movement, he punched the guy and got him off him. They scrambled to their feet, but the other guy didn't have time to collect himself because Elliot's legs were in his chest as he brought him to the floor again and trapped in a chokehold. The other guy scraped at his hands aimlessly as his face reddened, and the veins began to pop out in his face. He bared his teeth and held onto Elliot's bulky muscles, but it did nothing to alleviate the pressure.

I couldn't believe my eyes. Tears were streaming down my face, and there was no way to stop them as I continued to watch the scene in front of me. Finally, the big buy slapped the floor and the crowd went into a frenzy before Elliot finally let him go, leaving him there as he coughed and tried to catch his breath.

"Yesss!! That's what I'm fucking talking about. I knew there was something I liked about that guy!" Troy said with a grin. One that quickly faded when he saw the look on my face.

"Janey, what's wrong?" He asked, worrylines etched across his forehead.

I sniffed. "Just take me home, please."

I took one last glance at the ring and realized Elliot's eyes were glued to mine. Wiping at the tears, I briskly turned on my heels and pushed through the swarm of people.

Troy ran behind me. "Janey, I don't understand. What's the issue here?" He asked as he ran behind me.

"Nothing," I snapped. "This just isn't my crowd."

He sighed as he looked back to the ring and raked his fingers through his hair. "You can stay if you want. I'll just stay in the car or find some way to get back to the dorm," I said.

He bit his lips as he weighed the options. "Just stay in the car, please. I swear, one more fight, and then I'm done," he said as he clasped his hands at me.

There was no way of denying Troy this one thing when he had sacrificed so much for me over the years. He always tried to make me happy and though we had different views on things and liked different stuff, I didn't mind coming to a compromise just to make him happy.

"Ok, I'll stay in the car until you get back."

He grinned and kissed me quickly on the cheeks, my small face nestled between his big palms. “Thank you. I love you, and I’ll be back before you know it!” He said before he bounded off toward the crowd.

I sighed and went to sit in the passenger’s side of the car. Elliot was the only thing on my mind and how lethal he had looked as he stood in that ring. I was confused about whether he was a good guy or a bad one. I didn’t want to judge, but that’s all I had to base things on.

A knock suddenly came at the window and I jumped with fright as I looked to see who it was. The revelation didn’t make me any calmer. If anything, it made me a lot more flustered. Elliot stood there with a shirt now draped over his top and a towel slung around his neck. I swallowed hard as I wound the windows down and met his toe-curling gaze.

“Hey, Jane. Could I have a minute?” He asked me.

I bit the inside of my lips as I glanced around the car. I cleared my throat. “Do you wanna sit?” I asked as I gestured toward the empty driver’s seat.

He thought about it for a second before he nodded, “sure,” and went around to the other side.

I shifted in my seat and glanced down at the little dress I wore that had most of my legs exposed. I tugged at the hem and tried to cover up as much as possible before Elliot entered. When he did, he completely filled out the car, more than Troy did, who was also very big in the small car.

He smiled at me, and I smiled at him, the tension already so thick that Elliot could punch through it.

His Adam’s apple bobbed. “I didn’t peg you as the type to like street fighting,” he said.

“I don’t,” I blurted. “I only tagged along with Troy because he does,” I said, staring at the bruises on his face, the tiniest one on the corner of his lips. Compared to what had been happening inside the ring, he didn’t look too bad. I had expected worse.

He nodded slowly as he cleared his throat and shifted in the seat to look directly at me. “I er – I’m sorry if I made the whole thing uncomfortable for you.”

I managed a tight smile. “It’s fine. I’ve seen worse.”

That made him smile for a brief moment. “I know you and Court aren’t the best of friends, but I’d really like it if you kept this between us, Jane.”

I swallowed. “We don’t even talk. You don’t have to worry about that,” I said.

He nodded, and a small silence passed between us. “Why don’t you want her to know?” I couldn’t resist asking.

“College is enough for her to worry about for now.”

I nodded. “Fair enough.” Our eyes met. “You should put something on those bruises.”

He touched the small one on his forehead. “I have a first aid kit at home. I’ll be fine,” he smiled, and I licked my lips as I watched his. I was burning alive inside the car despite the air conditioning I had turned on. Without having to touch me, Elliot was able to evoke emotions inside me that I didn't think myself capable of having. I couldn't take my eyes off him no matter how hard I tried. There was a voice in the back of my head telling me to end the conversation so he could leave, but he was staring at me, and I was staring right back at him. Our heads moved closer, and I held my breath as I sweetly awaited what would happen next, even though my heart was hammering out of my chest.

His crispy, sweet breath fanned against me, his musky cologne seeping out and filling my nostrils. When his lips touched mine, I couldn't do anything but close my eyes as the soft feather-like feeling caressed mine and sent tingles through my body. I opened my mouth and welcomed his hot tongue inside as he gently kissed me. I almost moaned against his mouth but stopped myself as I basked in the euphoria of the caress. His hand came around the small of my back, his heated touch penetrating through my skin. The sensitive area between my legs began to throb with need, and I found myself deepening the kiss, wanting more than what I was getting, while my body burned at a fever pitch. I had only kissed a boy once and only remembered it simply because it was my first. I felt like I was in another dimension with Elliot, and my body was on cloud nine as pleasure erupted through my body. I soaked up his smell, his firm touch, his soft lips. Everything played a part in making this one of the best experiences of my life. I didn't want it to end, but the voices outside forced me to pull myself apart and collect myself. I was still breathing heavily, my lips still apart as I looked at Elliot, who had an animalistic look in his eyes. My face flushed.

I licked my lips, tasting him on it. "I've wanted to do that from the very first time I saw you," he said a bit huskily.

My heart fluttered at his confession. "You have?"

He nodded. "I don't know what it is about you, Jane, but I haven't been able to get my mind off you since that first time."

Heat sparked through me. My heart felt full. "I've been thinking about you a lot, too," I almost whispered.

He smiled. "I was afraid of confronting you earlier, but I've seen the look in your eyes, and if I'm not mistaken, I think you want this as much as I do."

I swallowed. "What exactly."

His eyes moved down the length of my body. "Tell me you are wet for me just as my cock is hard for you," he said, and I gasped at his bluntness, my cheeks flamed.

"I– I am," I shyly admitted.

He smiled, and just as his mouth opened to speak, Troy came into view, stopping to talk to someone. I glanced at Elliot who had straightened in his seat.

"You should go," I said.

He nodded. "I guess I'll see you around, Jane."

Before I could reply, he was gone, and the cold air from outside welcomed me, reminding me of the gap he had left and how he had filled it and me with warmth earlier. I couldn't believe that had happened. My brain was still in shambles, trying to make sense of it. I kissed Elliot, and it was the most amazing thing in the world. Elliot, who was my awful roommate's father. I began to spiral, trying to make sense of all that had happened. Maybe he had gotten a concussion in the fight and could not think clearly. That was the only logical explanation for all this. There was no way I actually managed to arouse him, and there was no way he had liked me from the start.

"See, I didn't take long, did I?" Troy's voice came, and I almost bounded from the car in fright.

He laughed. "Hey, it's only me. Sheesh, sis. You should lighten up sometime."

I sighed and flopped back into the chair. "Sorry, I just... I'm a little angst."

"Don't worry, the horror of it is all over and look what I won," he said as he pulled a couple of hundred-dollar notes.

My eyes popped open. "What the heck!"

"Cool, right," he grinned, handing me a sum. "That's for you."

I took it confused. "What, I didn't even do anything."

"I only met Elliot because of you, and if I hadn't, I probably would have bet on the wrong guy. Buy yourself something nice."

I smiled. "Thank you. But you've already done so much by coming here, Troy. You don't need to spoil me."

"But oh I do. Who else do I have to live for?"

"Yourself, of course!"

He rolled his eyes and started the car. "Please, I love you way more," he winked, and I blushed, smiling.

....

When Troy dropped me off, I knew I had to confront reality. Courtney was probably there, although she was maybe out seeing it was a Saturday night. I made my way to our room and opened the door, hoping that I would just take a shower and go to bed thinking of her father, but as soon as the door opened, she was the first person I saw. My heart wrenched in my chest as our gazes locked. There was no escaping her. I made my way in and closed the door, second-guessing that choice in case I needed a quick escape.

"Good night," I said as I made my way to my area.

"Hey, can we talk?"

My mouth fell open at the question and the soft tone in her voice. "I er... yeah, I guess."

I took a seat on my bed, and she came to stand in front of me, already in her pajamas with her blue-streaked black hair caught in a little ponytail. "I'm sorry for being an ass," she said. It took me a while to process what she said because this was the last thing I expected she would say. "You didn't deserve it," she said.

My eyes widened. "Thanks...?"

She sighed. "You know you're pretty perfect, Wiley. I guess I kinda envied that. I didn't even realize I was being such an asshole until you pointed it out earlier," she scoffed.

My brows furrowed. "I'm far from perfect, Courtney."

She scoffed. "Not far. I mean, you're pretty, you're smart, and you have a family that loves you. I only have my dad."

I swallowed. "I only have my brother. Both my parents died a couple of years ago," I said and my voice cracked.

Her brows raised. "Oh fuck, and here I was thinking you had that all-American family with the white picket fence and shit," she said as she shook her head. "I'm sorry about that."

"No need to be. We often misjudge each other."

She nodded. "Yeah, well it's stupid and unproductive," she smiled.

"Sure is."

Scratching the nape of her neck, she said. "Well, from now on, Wiley, you don't have to worry about me being an ass to you," she said before she moved over to her side.

I bit my lips and wordlessly went to get myself prepared for bed. I hadn't anticipated feeling guilty, but that was the feeling that overcame me as I went to bed. Lusting after Elliot would have been a lot easier if Courtney had remained an asshole. Now that she was trying to make amends, I suddenly felt horrible for kissing Elliot. I wanted to pass it off in my head as just a harmless kiss, but it hadn't been. I had felt too many things to just pass it off as that. Although conflicted, there were no regrets regarding what Elliot and I shared. I couldn't forget that moment, and I didn't want to. Courtney and I didn't have to be friends, but what exactly were Elliot and I?

Chapter 4

Elliot

My finger lingered over the caller ID of a woman I had hooked up with a couple of times in the past. I enjoyed her because she knew what to do and knew that this wouldn't go beyond a couple of fucks. It was a no strings attached type of arrangement, and since that was so hard to find nowadays, I didn't want to risk losing it.

Normally, I would have sent out the call already and waited about fifteen minutes until she was at my front door, but this time, the task seemed harder than usual. I couldn't bring myself to do it, and it was fucking stupid because I knew the reason, and it didn't make any sense to me.

I couldn't stop thinking about the petite brunette who had sparked something inside me from the very first day I met her. She occupied my thoughts like a parasite, and I didn't know why. Yes, she was beautiful and sexy in that timid way, but I've seen beautiful, and I've seen sexy. I've fucked both, so what made her any different? I didn't know the answers; I just knew that she made me feel things I had never felt with a woman before. As soon as my eyes had caught wind of her, I knew in my heart that I was damned for the rest of eternity. She hadn't touched me, she hadn't said a word, and yet I wanted to have her in my house to fuck and to be by my side forever.

The most insane part about feeling something like that for someone was that she was just as old as my daughter, and never in my life had I felt such an attraction towards someone so young. I was still trying to figure out what made her so different, but I came up with nothing each time. I just knew I had to have her.

Tonight only heightened that fact more than before. They had only been thoughts earlier – me trying to figure out the attraction and trying to run around it, but tonight I had seen her so vulnerable and sweet with a need I hadn't mistaken in her eyes. I knew lust, and whether or not she knew it herself, it was all over her. She reeked of it. I couldn't resist. I knew then and there that I had to give myself a taste of what I didn't have before but what I craved more than anything in this world.

And the kiss didn't disappoint. In fact, it was more than I had imagined over the past days. I had drawn up scenarios in my mind of what she would taste like and had played the scene repeatedly in my head. Yet, she surpassed my expectations, delivering on mind-numbing degrees. I had wanted so much more – I wanted to bury my cock inside her then and there but had to quickly remind myself of where we were and who she was. She had put me in a trance and had occupied every single cell in my body, that even now, as my body buzzed with need, I couldn't bring myself to call another woman.

I muttered a curse and flung my phone to one side of the bed, finding it hard to believe that I was rejecting a woman I often depended on for my pleasures for someone I had only kissed. How was I even sure there was more to be had after that? I knew that Jane wanted me as much as I wanted her, but there were factors to consider.

I sighed as I flopped back in bed and tried to rid myself of the small little minx, but all I could see were images of her as I thought back to the kiss and how sweet and soft her lips had been. My cock had hardened to steel in an instant, even before her lips grazed mine. No one had ever had that effect on me before, and I was curious to know why that was the case with Jane. Even now, as I thought about her, I could feel a stirring in my groin and regretted not calling up my no strings attached woman. I couldn't bring myself to do it – not when I felt guilty to think about any other woman but her. I went to bed with my cock in my hand, trying to give myself some relief but found myself wanting more each time.

The following morning, after a restless night, I was tempted to head over to Courtney's dorm just so I could see Jane, but I knew that Courtney would find it strange that I was there on a weekday, and two, she was probably not even there. I went to work, and the look of distress on my face must have been evident because my good friend Isaac came into the office with a look of puzzlement on his face.

"You look like your dog just died," he said as he flopped into one of the chairs in front of my desk.

"I don't have a dog," I said dryly.

"I know, but if you had one, and it died, that's what you'd look like."

I raised my brows and sighed. "What do you want, Isaac?"

"I can't come to say hi to my boss and my best friend?" He asked a bit dramatically.

"I'm not in the best mood," I mumbled as I scribbled on a piece of paper.

"I can see that. Who's the girl?"

My eyes snapped to his. "What?"

"Well, I know this face. Only two things can have you like this: a woman or the business. Business is going great, so who's the girl?" He asked. I scoffed as I stared at him. I guess we knew each other long enough to know our triggers.

I decided to indulge him. "So yes, there's a girl, but she isn't the type I'd usually go for," I explained, leaning back in my chair.

Isaac's brows furrowed. "So she's ugly and isn't a bimbo?"

I rolled my eyes. "That's not what I mean. Of course, she's beautiful, but...she's around Courtney's age."

Isaac's eyes widened. "What the hell. How did that happen?"

"That's the thing... nothing happened. All we did was kiss."

"Oh, but that's something. Where did you even meet this girl?"

I scratched the nape of my neck. "Courtney's dorm. She's her roommate."

Isaac's mouth fell open, his hazel eyes going wide. "No fucking way!" He said before he started to laugh. "So, is she like those pushy college girls that swoon over guys like you?" He asked as he rocked back in his chair with a smirk.

I shook my head. "I doubt she's even had sex before. She has innocence written all over her," I said.

"I'm telling you, man; those are the type you need to watch out for. They'll just seep their way in like a drug, and before you know it, you're on an alter saying I-do."

I scoffed. "Don't get ahead of yourself now."

Isaac leaned into me. "Listen to me. Run. Beg Courtney to get another roomie if you have to, but this will only end with you being pussy whipped."

I laughed. "You know I'm starting to regret telling you this."

Isaac shook his head. "You've been a player for the longest while. Do you really want to risk that?"

"Would it be such a bad thing?" I said as I choked out a laugh. "I'll be forty years old soon."

"And you really think this supposed virgin, who is closer to twenty than thirty, is gonna settle down with you and give you the time of day? Elliot, once she gets her first cock, you'll be just a memory. She'll roam the continent and live her best life. Sorry to break it to you, dude, but you'll be old news. Literally. Emphasis on the old," he blinked.

I shook my head. "You're overthinking this."

"And you're only thinking with your cock, as always. Find a woman around your age and settle down if that's what you want, but steer clear from this girl."

I didn't say anything.

"Don't take this as a challenge, man. I'm warning you; this will end badly, and plus, there's Court to consider. She's had enough disappointments in her life to deal with this as well."

I sighed as that last sentence hit home. "You're right, you're right. This can't go any further."

Isaac sighed and finally relaxed in his chair. "Good."

I managed a smile at him and thought about it, knowing I would do anything to keep Courtney from hurting, even if it meant not having a woman I felt such an attraction to. And, plus, Isaac was right. Jane was young and hadn't even experienced life yet. There was so much to explore, and I didn't want to stand in the way of that. As hard as it was for me to do, I had to stay away. For everyone's sake.

THAT WEEKEND, I DID the usual and went by Courtney's dorm, so we could spend some time together. For the past couple of days, all I had tried to do was get my mind off Jane, but to no avail. Trying not to think about her did more damage than actually thinking of her. All I kept replaying was the kiss, her beautiful face with her long, dark hair and her big brown eyes. But I had promised myself to steer clear, as Isaac suggested.

I knocked on the door and hoped Courtney would answer and we would be out in the next second. As much as I wanted to see Jane, I knew I shouldn't. I knew that one look from those innocent doe eyes would break my control and my promise. I waited impatiently, but in a few seconds, the door handle rattled, and the door burst open. But it wasn't Courtney who was on the other side. It was Jane. When she saw me, her eyes widened a little, her lush pink lips slightly parted as she stared up at me. Her hair was down and tumbled down her shoulders in soft waves, and her shoulders were bare because all she had was a towel draped around her. I could bet she was naked underneath, and my cock began to stir at how close I was to tugging it away and seeing it all. I swallowed and folded my fists as I tried to cling to every bit of restraint I had.

I tore my gaze away from her and looked around the room.

"Hey, is Court here?"

She shook her head. "Er... no, she said she had to run out for a sec, but she'll be back. I didn't think you'd be here this quick," she said as she gripped onto the top of the towel.

I cleared my throat and glanced at my watch. "I'm right on time, Jane." I smiled. "You look beautiful."

Her cheeks reddened instantly. "Thank you."

"How have you been?" I said as I stepped inside. She backed up a little.

"Great. You?"

My cock was getting harder by the second. Her scent filled my nostrils, and I couldn't take my eyes off her dewy skin that still had a few beads of water in certain areas. She smelled so fresh; all I wanted to do was run my tongue along every inch of her perfect body.

"All I've been able to think about these past days is you, Jane. You've ruined me with one single kiss," I said.

She swallowed. "I'm sorry."

I chuckled. "No need to be. I just need to know that you feel the same way."

"I do... but Courtney," she said.

"I know, and that's why I'm still standing here and not inside you instead."

The smallest of gasps left her lips. Our gazes met, and I tried my best to control myself because I'd become too familiar with the look in Jane's eyes. She wanted this; she wanted me. Before I saw it coming, she sprung towards me and captured my lips with her. I collected her against me, wrapping my hands around her as I scoured her mouth like it was something I had been deprived of for eternity. Her breath was minty, her lips even softer than I remembered, and her body was the perfect fit against mine. I pulled her tighter against me, so she could feel the evidence of my arousal pressing into her stomach. She moaned against my mouth and sucked desperately on my tongue. Her small hands raked through my hair, the pads of her finger distributing heat all over my body. My hand went down to her ass as I caressed the firm little gloves through the fabric of the towel.

One movement, and I could have her bare skin on my hands if I wanted to. The longer we kissed, the more I craved for that to become a reality. I wanted her all over me; I wanted to feel every inch of her. I kissed her hard, my hand sliding up under her towel as I squeezed her firm little ass cheeks. She moaned and pressed herself further into me as if trying to feel more of my hardness on her. I almost smiled against her mouth as I massaged her flesh into my palm and slid my fingers through her cheeks and further down, where my finger grazed the sodden entrance of her pussy. She gasped and bit down on my lips. Fire erupted through me as I moved with her toward the small bed that I probably couldn't even fit on. But who said we needed it anyway. I was burning up, fire running through every single vein in my body.

But as soon as Jane touched the bed, she paused and tore her lips from mine, breathing heavily, her entire face flushed.

She shook her head and adjusted her towel. "I'm sorry, we can't, Elliot," she said

I sighed because I knew that as much as I wanted to fuck her, she was right. This was definitely not the time and place.

"Courtney is finally being nice to me, and I don't want to ruin that," she explained a bit shakily as she raked her fingers through her hair.

I rubbed my forehead and licked my lips, nodding because I understood where she was coming from. I knew the right thing to do was leave her alone, but I just fucking couldn't. I didn't have that level of control within me. This need I felt for her was insane, and if I didn't have her soon, I would probably lose my mind. My gaze shifted toward her small work desk that was toward the window. I moved over to it, my boner like a third leg as I walked. Jane watched me closely as I drew for a piece of paper and a pencil and scribbled my address and my number on it. I walked back to her and handed it to her. She looked clueless.

"That's my address. If you ever change your mind, Jane, you know where to find me."

She swallowed as she examined the contents before looking up at me. She nodded and that small sense of reassurance was all I needed to get through my days.

Chapter 5

Jane

THAT NIGHT, WHILE COURTNEY was out, I decided to call Bailey because she was always good at giving advice. I gave her a ring and hoped she would answer, although it was probably too early in the morning for her. The phone rang a few times, and just as I was about to hang up, she answered.

"Hey you," she said groggily.

"I woke you, didn't I? I'm so sorry." I said as I bit my lips.

"Don't be, my alarm was just about to go off anyway. I have a busy day ahead," she said as she cleared her throat.

"Is everything alright?"

"Yeah, my mom and I are just gonna visit a few places, is all. What's up with you?"

"Nothing much. Remember I told you the other day that Troy was in town?" I said.

"Yesss, my dream man!"

I rolled my eyes. "I left out some very important details," I said softly.

"What?" She prodded.

I paused a bit. "Well, we went to this street fighting thing and guess who I saw there?"

"Who?!"

I gave her a run-down of everything that had happened that night, including the fact that I had seen Elliot fight, and afterward, we had kissed.

"No fucking way! What?"

"I know, right. It just happened so fast, but it was great, Bailes," I explained almost dreamily.

"You're a whole lot braver than I thought, bestie," she giggled. "So what happened after that?"

"He left, but earlier today, he came to meet Courtney. She wasn't here, and we kissed again, but things went a little further this time."

"Wh– you had sex with him?"

"No, but there was a little groping — anyway, I broke things off, but then he gave me his address, and I don't know what to do!" I squealed into the pillows.

"Well, what do you wanna do?! You have to know!"

"Bailes, he's Courtney's dad!"

"Yeah, the same Courtney who doesn't give a shit about you and treats you like crap."

"She has been a lot nicer these past couple a days. I just don't want any drama, you know."

Bailey sighed. "So you're willing to miss out on this once-in-a-lifetime opportunity because you're afraid of what will happen?"

"Yes!" I exclaimed. "And this might be exactly that. A one-time thing, and I don't wanna lose my virginity to someone who'll forget me the next day!"

"You don't know that!"

"Bailes, I'm not blind. I've read about guys like Elliot, and I've seen him in movies and real life. They have girls on speed dial. They don't stick to one woman. I know that much!"

"You might be wrong, but either way, if this is something you want, go for it."

"And then what?"

"Let tomorrow worry about itself. You're almost twenty-three years old. Any longer and your cooch will be out of service indefinitely."

I laughed and rolled my eyes. "Quit being dramatic."

"You've never been this way over a boy ... ever. Who knows what's on the other side of fear? You might like it."

I sighed. "I don't know."

"Tell me something; do you go to bed with him on your mind and wake up with him still there?"

I bit my lips. "Yeah."

"Well, there you have it. I'd say it's worth it. Life's too short to be holding back on what could make us happy. Go to his house and have the time of your life. Zero chance that he will disappoint."

I groaned. "Ugh, I wish things weren't so hard!"

"They aren't. You're just trying to make it so."

After a few minutes, I ended the call with a heavy sigh, somewhat clear on what I wanted to do but still a bit conflicted. I knew I wanted Elliot, but I didn't know if I wanted the baggage that came with having him. I didn't want this to be a one-time thing. I knew I'd want more and never even liked the concept of one-night stands, to begin with. But what if that was what Elliot wanted.? A quick fling with his newest conquest before he moved on to the other. I didn't want that, but I wanted every second with Elliot, which was stronger than anything else.

On Sunday, I had made up my mind and decided that I would head over to his place in the evening. Courtney was there, but I couldn't look her in the eyes because even though we weren't friends, she was being nice to me, and it felt wrong to go behind her back. I was already guilty over something I hadn't even done yet. What was going to happen when it actually did?

I watched a movie that afternoon while she was wrapped up in bed, not having left all morning. I was tempted to ask if she was okay but wanted to mind my business in case the old Courtney snapped at me. I decided to stay out of it, but then her sniffs alerted me that she was crying. I glanced over and watched as her body trembled, and her crying became louder. I sat there, not knowing what to do or how to approach her. Yes, she had been nice, but there was still a lot that I didn't know about Courtney and her triggers. I knew nothing.

I swallowed hard and walked over to her side of the room, standing before her as I stared down at her small body, covered from head to toe in her blanket.

"Courtney, is everything okay?" I asked

She sniffed once and shuffled in the bed. "I'm fine," she croaked.

I wasn't sure what to say. "Do you want me to get you anything?"

She pulled the covers from her face and shook her head, her eyes and nose red and wet. "No thanks."

I rubbed the nape of my neck. "Do you wanna talk about it?" I asked.

She eased up on the bed and crossed her legs, her head now out, the rest of her body still wrapped in the blanket.

"My mom wants to see me."

My lips moved wordlessly because I couldn't understand what she meant by that and why it had her crying. "I– is that such a bad thing?"

She wiped her nose. "She's in rehab."

I froze. "Oh. I–"

"For a while, it was going so good. y'know. I was living with her and going to school, and she had her job. Then it all started going downhill when she started seeing some asshole..." she croaked. "It was like she became a completely different person altogether. She started doing drugs and just transformed into this person I didn't even recognize."

I swallowed the lump in my throat. "Courtney, I'm so sorry."

Tears flowed from her eyes. "That's why I moved here with my dad. I lived with him for a while until I decided to stay on campus. I'm just afraid that he'll change, too, and I'll be disappointed again," she sniffed.

My heart broke. "Courtney, your dad is a good guy. He wouldn't..."

"I'm just afraid to lose him, too, y'know. Maybe I'm the problem."

"You aren't."

"You don't know that. Look how awful I was to you, and you didn't even do anything wrong," she sniffed.

“All is forgiven. I understand.”

She hung her head. “I don’t know if I want to see her ... not yet.”

I rubbed her shoulder. “It’s okay to give yourself time to heal. You don’t have to if you don’t want to.”

She nodded as she looked up at me with so much emotions in her eyes. Before I saw it coming, she flung herself into my arms and hugged me. I was taken aback but didn’t do anything to fight it. I allowed it to happen as she continued crying on my shoulders, knowing that whatever I had planned with Elliot was off the table as of now.

Chapter 6

Jane

Days had passed, and I still had Elliot's number and refused to use it – refused to head over to his place because I knew it'd be the wrong thing to do. I couldn't get involved; Courtney had opened up to me, and breaking that small ounce of trust would be unforgivable. I thought I would eventually forget Elliot if I gave myself time – that over time, the feelings I had for him would fade, and things would be back to normal.

But every day proved that no such thing was going to happen. I was growing to miss a man I had never been with for more than fifteen minutes, which was confusing as well as torturous. I didn't know what to do. Another weekend was rolling by, and I didn't know how I would look him in the eyes when he came to see Courtney. So I started making plans to be out of the house whether he came by the Friday or the Saturday.

When Friday rolled by, he didn't come, and I was conflicted with feeling relieved as well as disappointed. It was stupid, but I couldn't help myself or the emotions I felt when it came to Elliot.

Saturday morning, Courtney got dressed, and I figured Elliot would be there any minute, so I quickly escaped to the door.

"Hey, we're going to this new restaurant in town. You might have heard of it; *Pablo's*... wanna come?" She asked.

Well, that was something you didn't see every day. "Er... nah. I'm about to head out now anyway."

She smiled. "Ouuu, have a hot date?"

I laughed. "Nah, just gonna pick up some things."

"Ok, well some other time then," she smiled.

"Yeah, sure. See you later."

I WENT OUT AND EYE-shopped for a while before settling at the café to have a light snack. It was dinner time, but I didn't feel like much except a french vanilla and a ham sandwich. I scrolled through my dormant social media, researched a few topics for my class on Monday and just sat there as I overlooked the street ahead. I thought back to when Elliot had seen me here and how he came to sit right at this very table. It was amazing what had happened since then.

My phone rang, and I glanced down at the caller to find that it was Troy. I smiled and swiped the screen to answer.

"Tell me you're out having fun and not cooped up in your room," he said, and I grinned.

"I'm not in my room, but I'm not out having fun either."

"You're at that little café, I bet."

"Correct."

"Your roomie's dad is fighting again tonight," he said.

I stiffened. "How do you know that?"

"This guy I met at the court when I was there. He filled me in."

I swallowed. "I bet you wished you were here."

"Yeah, not only for that. I miss you too."

I smiled. "I miss you."

"Want me to cashapp you some money so you can bet on him."

My mouth fell open. "Are you kidding? Troy, I'm not doing that!" I exclaimed.

He laughed. "I know, I know, but it wouldn't hurt to go see what he's up to and maybe fill me in," he said casually.

I rolled my eyes. "You know it isn't my scene, and what happened to your guy? Isn't he gonna be there?" I asked.

"Unfortunately, no, that's why he asked me. He's gonna be out of town, I guess."

I sighed. "I guess I could drop by to see how he's doing," I said but knew it wouldn't be so much for Troy, but more so myself. I guess I wanted that peace of mind knowing he was okay, although the whole thing was such a tear-jerker.

"Great. I heard it starts at 7:30 PM, but it's best to be a bit earlier in case."

I removed the phone from my ear to glance at the time. I had thirty minutes to an hour. "Okay."

"I'll text you the address. Be careful, though. Stay where others can see you."

I laughed. "Troy, I'm not five years old."

"I know, but still."

"I love you; I'll talk to you later," I said. We said our goodbyes, and I hung up with a sigh, dreading the whole thing. But half an hour later, I was taking an Uber to the location he had texted, which was not the same one as last time. This place was an old junkyard with old cars stacked on top of each other. The good cars were parked outside the fence where I was dropped off, and a few people were going inside where the excitement was. I pulled at the hem of my dress and rubbed my arm as I followed the thin line of people. The closer we got, the more boisterous the noise was, and before long, there was a small ring like the last time with people forming the circle. Two men were already inside fighting while people boosted them on, some standing on the tops of cars so they could get a better view of what was going on. I looked around and regretted my decision to come. There were only a few females around, and some of the men looked like they belonged in biker gangs. The place was dark for the most part, except for the small light posts that went through the premises. I was probably the shortest person there and the smallest too.

I went in front of a car where a vacant spot was and rested my back against an old car. A few people were in front, but I had a clear view of what was happening inside the ring. The fight ended shortly, and the other was ready to begin. I hoped it was Elliot because the quicker I saw what was happening, the quicker I would leave. Elliot entered the ring shirtless, in jeans alone, his body looking as hard and muscular as ever. I licked my lips and crossed my arms, looking around to see if anyone was seeing how I blatantly drooled for him. Luckily, everyone was too focused on the fight ahead to even care what I was doing.

The referee gave the go-ahead to start, and both men started to hop around the ring before making their first move. Elliot was the first to tumble back when he received a punch in the jaw. I gasped, but he quickly collected himself and kicked the guy in the stomach. He fell to the ground but quickly got back up before Elliot could charge at him again.

With another kick from Elliot, he fell flat on his back with a thud that echoed through the noisy crowd. Elliot didn't give him any time to recover this time. He charged on top of him and straddled his legs over his chest before he started packing punches to the guy's face. I cringed, feeling bile rise to my throat at the blood that oozed from the guy's face. The referee ran up to them and pulled Elliot off before he flung his hand in the air, sending the crowd into a frenzy.

I quickly made my way out, regretting I hadn't called an Uber earlier. I walked out to the front for some quiet and made the call. A few minutes later, I stood there waiting and looking around to see if I was safe enough.

My heart started to plummet in my chest when I saw two men talking and smiling at me. I tried to swallow the fear in my throat but to no avail. I was close to shitting my pants.

"Hey, beautiful," one with grills on his teeth said as he walked up to me. "We can take you home if you want," he said as he nudged the other in his side and snickered at him. He joined in on the joke as they both moved toward me, smiling.

I took a step back. "Please, I don't want any trouble," I said, hating that my voice didn't come out the way I wanted it to.

"Oh, we don't want any trouble at all, love. We just wanna get to know you," the same one shrugged.

I swallowed. "I'm not interested, sorry."

The grimy smile fell from his lips. "I don't remember asking your opinion," he said with a firmer tone. I was close to having a heart attack with the way my heart was beating and a second away from screaming.

"Jane?" A voice came, and my head flashed to the right to find Elliot standing there with a scowl as he sized up the two men. "Everything alright here?" He asked as he approached.

"Hey, man, why don't you just mind your business," the instigator exclaimed. The other looked at Elliot and then at his friend as if he had lost his mind.

"This is my business," he said between clenched teeth. He was still shirtless, his body glistening as he unwrapped the gauze from his hands.

"Come on, man; we should just go."

He scoffed at the friend. "Don't tell me you're afraid of this asshole!" He said with a sly grin.

"He just knocked down a guy in less than five minutes. What the fuck. This chick's not even worth it," he said as he gestured to me, eyeing me up and down scornfully.

"Oh, I think she is," he said, and I gasped as he pulled me into him. Before I could process what was happening, Elliot was right in front of us, and a loud crack sounded, followed by an even louder howl. The guy's grip on me loosened, and he staggered back, clutching his bloody nose and crying tears. The other friend's eyes widened as he looked at his friend. Elliot gave him one hard stare, and he went running off, leaving his friend behind who tumbled behind with his hands red with blood.

I looked at Elliot, and a shiver ran down my spine at the look he had on his face. The devil himself would be scared.

"Are you okay?" He asked, eyes roaming across my face.

I nodded, pinning a lock of hair behind my ear. "Yeah, I'm fine."

His face eased. "What are you doing here all by yourself? I thought this wasn't your scene," he smiled.

I cleared my throat. "My brother is your biggest fan now."

He smiled. "And here I thought you were here to see me. Where is he?"

I blushed. "He went back home. I'm here alone."

"You shouldn't be. A lot of assholes come to places like this."

"I'm starting to see that."

He smiled. "Come on; I'll take you home."

I shook my head. "That's okay, my Uber is on its way."

"Let me," he said with a tone that could make any woman drop to their knees.

"Okay," I said as I walked with him toward his car. My body was already on fire, and there was no stopping the flames. I hopped in his new RAV4 and waited for him to enter.

"Give me a minute; I'll just go grab my stuff," he said; I nodded, and then he was gone.

I eased back into the cool leather seats and managed a sigh. I knew the logical thing to do was to go home. I couldn't trust myself around Elliot, but at the same time, my panties were already soaked for him. All he needed was to look at me, and I would get wet. It was that simple. These past weeks had been the hardest, and now that I was seeing him again, it became even more surreal – more intense. A small percentage of me wanted him to just drop me home, but I wanted more than anything for him to bring me to his house instead.

When he returned, I squeezed my legs together and stared at the road ahead, knowing my wandering eyes would probably get me in trouble.

"Ok, let's go," he said as he started the car.

"I er - I'm sorry I didn't actually take you up on the invite – I ..."

"Jane, you don't need to explain. I understand."

"You don't. I was actually ready to do it, but then Courtney opened up to me, and I just couldn't."

He glanced at me. "Well, I'm happy to hear that, at least."

I stared at him. "Are you? She's afraid to lose you, Elliot. She's afraid you'll disappoint her as soon as she moves in with you. That's the real reason why she doesn't want to live with you."

His brows furrowed. "What?"

"She thinks she's the problem. It's like she thinks everything will turn to shit once she touches it."

He cast his eyes back to the road, and his Adam's apple bobbed. "Courtney knows I love her more than anything in this world."

"I'm sure she knows. She just wants a little reassurance, I guess."

He nodded. "Thanks for letting me know, Jane."

I nodded in return. "I don't want us getting together to break her. I know she'll hate me and resent you..."

"Courtney is a big girl, Jane. We're all adults here."

I raked my hands through my hair. "It still doesn't excuse the fact."

He immediately pulled over to the side of the road. He turned to look at me, and my heart plummeted. "For the past weeks, I haven't been able to think about anything but you. That has never happened before, and I'm finding it hard to just pass it off as a simple crush."

My cheeks warmed, and heat began to pool between my legs. "We might be making a mistake," I softly said.

"And what if we aren't?" He challenged.

I swallowed, speechless. "I know you feel it, too, Jane. Don't try to deny it. It's written all over your face."

I must have been as red as tomatoes at that moment and hotter than the Sahara desert. What was the point in controlling something so inevitable? Something so pure and intense. I had never felt like this in all my life, and the truth was, I didn't want to ignore it.

I bit on my lower lips for a quick second. "Take me to your place."

Chapter 7

Jane

As soon as I stepped into Elliot's two-story home, he moved toward me and cupped my face with his hand. He smiled down at me and kissed me on the forehead. "You'll wait until I take a shower?" He asked.

I nodded. "Yeah."

He smiled. "Would you like me to get you anything to drink? To eat, perhaps?"

I smiled. "I'm fine, I promise."

He nodded, kissed me quickly, and then moved to the bathroom. I bit my lips as silence welcomed me. I was in Elliot's home, which was just as masculine as him, with the black leather sofas, and the grey and white walls. Everything was dark except for the few artificial green plants he had that gave it some color. However, everything was crisp and clean and in perfect order, and that caught me by a bit of surprise.

I bit my lips because the closer I inched upstairs, the more I could hear the shower running. I had a thought that I couldn't believe even crossed my mind. I entered his bedroom and glanced at the neatly spread bed and the soft grey carpet. I kicked my shoes off, pulled my dress over my head and tore my undies off – left completely naked. I walked softly to the adjoining bathroom with my heart in my mouth. This was the most spontaneous thing I would ever do in my life.

As I stepped inside, I could see his frame through the fogged shower mirrors. I swallowed hard as I watched his silhouette, my eyes moving down the length of him, stopping at his midsection where his erect penis was long and hard. I bit back my gasp as I feasted my eyes on him and wondered if I could even fit him. There was this nervous knot in my stomach, and yet I could feel the wetness between my thighs that told me I needed every inch of him.

I slid the glass door across, and his head snapped toward me, a look of surprise on his face.

"Jane," he said as his eyes moved from my face and down the length of my body. His Adam's apple bobbed, and his eyes darkened lustfully. I couldn't get enough of his body or how the water trickled down every taut inch of him, caressing every crevice. I longed to have my body against his in such a way.

I stepped inside and almost gasped when the water hit my body and flattened the hair on my head. I could feel my nipples hardening under the warm spray, my core begging for pleasure.

"I couldn't wait," I said as I raised my palm to place it on one large pectoral muscle.

He reached for my hand and clasped it in his before placing a gentle kiss on the back of my hand. My lips parted for him, and he obliged me with a kiss that weakened my knees. Nothing stood between us now. It was just skin against skin, and my body acknowledged every inch of his. My nipples were like hard pebbles against his slightly hairy chest, his length resting like a pipe against my stomach. Heat radiated between us, and my body buzzed from the sheer bliss of the moment. I kissed him like I was starved, reacquainting my lips with the feel of him. It felt like forever since I kissed him and wanted to cherish every single second. My hands roamed the plane of his broad back while he squeezed my ass – one glove seemingly fitting in the palm of his hand. He spread my cheeks, and I could feel as my core puckered almost audibly for action.

"Ohh," I sighed against his mouth, leaning my neck to the side as he left my mouth to suck on the slender column. My eyes rolled over as a bolt of pleasure shot through me. My hands moved against him, going to his hard buttocks before I slid it between us and captured his hardened length in my hand. He held me tighter, sucked on my skin deeper, and I moaned as I wrapped my fingers around him, sliding my palm over the smooth head that drew a moan from him.

He was so hard, so strong. I could feel the power in that single muscle and was too eager to have it inside me.

"Oh, Jane. You have no idea what you're doing to me," he whispered huskily against my ear, nipping the lobe for a brief moment before he captured my mouth again. In the next instant, I was in his arms, wrapping my legs around him while my lady-bits rested on his upright cock like a chair. With a single movement, he could have it inside me, and I was hoping that would be the case, but he turned the shower off and stepped out with me in his arms, pressed against his firm body.

We were dripping all over the place, and I was pretty sure mine wasn't just water. He laid me on the bed and hovered over me, taking in every inch of my body.

"My gosh, you're beautiful," he said as he knelt before me. "Tell me this is what you want, Jane, and I promise to give you the best experience of your life," he said, lips pinker than usual.

"I want you, Elliot. More than anything," I said, finding it hard to believe that I was actually saying those words to a man. This was actually happening, but it suddenly occurred to me that I had left out one very important fact in all this.

"But there's something I've gotta tell you," I said softly as I eased up on the bed. He looked at me with a puzzled look on his face.

"What is it?" He asked.

I looked away from his gaze. "I– I'm a virgin," I said in what sounded like a whisper.

My heart thudded as I awaited a response. I half expected him to cancel everything, but then he smiled, and I was the one who was left confused. "I know. It doesn't change how much I want you."

My lips moved wordlessly. "How did you know?" I asked.

He smiled. "I just did," he said, but I boiled it down to experience. He'd probably been with so many women, he could spot the different types from afar. But how could I expect less when Elliot was a man who had it all?

He moved in to kiss me passionately on my lips, and I could feel the juices pooling between my legs. I moaned as I clung to him, his mouth moving from mine to my neck, where he took his time to caress every erogenous zone with his tongue. I arched my neck and rested my palms behind me on the bed as his tongue sparked flames on my skin. One hand moved to my breast as he kneaded it into his hand, his mouth covering the other as he sucked on it gently. His hot mouth covering one of the most sensitive parts of my body drove me nuts. I was already writhing on the bed, rolling my hips as I tried to make sense of what was happening to my body.

"Ohhh," I whispered, my fingers raking through Elliot's silky soft hair as he pleasured me. He moved from one breast to the other, giving the other the same treatment as the previous one. I began to moan, because with each passing second, the pleasure got more intense, the arousal almost explosive inside my body. If Elliot continued like this, I would definitely cum over and over again without using his cock.

He finally eased up, smiled and kissed me briefly on the lips before placing his hand on my chest and gently pushing me back to lie on the bed with my feet hanging off the edge. He was still kneeling before me and I gasped when he pulled me by the hips, allowing my ass to rest at the edge while he parted my legs.

My heart thrummed in my chest as it occurred to me what he was about to do. I propped myself on my elbows and looked at him perched there, looking at my vagina while his hand caressed my thighs.

"Elliot," I said, swallowing hard.

He looked up at me with lust-clouded eyes. "I swear I'm salivating to taste you," he said. "Every inch of you is breathtaking, Jane."

I couldn't say a single word after that. Just watched as his eyes returned to my flesh, as he used a single finger to rub on my hardened clitoris. I whimpered and trembled at the sudden pleasure and how sensitive I was to the smallest touch. His finger went up and down my slit, and I reddened as our gazes locked.

"You're so wet for me, baby," he said huskily before he dipped his head and lathered his tongue across my flesh.

"Ahhh!" I voiced, falling back on the bed.

Elliot was right between my legs with his tongue on my cunt, and the longer he stayed there, the more surreal this became. This was actually happening, and I couldn't formulate thoughts that went beyond him. He occupied every cell in my brain.

I moaned as his strong tongue parted my slit and went up and down my clitoris and then my tiny hole. I knew I was wet, and his tongue added another layer as his warm saliva oozed against my skin. He licked me and sucked each of my lips in his mouth before he went to tongue-fucking me again.

My back arched on the bed, my legs twitching, but Elliot still held them up, so he had as much room as possible. "Oh, my God!" I exclaimed.

Without even easing his mouth off me, Elliot added a single finger inside me and worked it in while his tongue flickered on my clit. My body jolted as I gripped the sheets, hoping to regain some of the control I had lost on myself. His other hand moved up my damp body, clutching onto a single breast while he continued to work my cunt. His ability to multitask was mind-blowing.

"Oh, Elliot, please," I found myself saying, not knowing exactly what I was asking for; I just felt like I was about to lose my mind.

He squeezed my tits and added another finger. My mouth formed an 'O' at the sweet intrusion that stretched my flesh and magnified the pleasure within me. He gently worked that finger in as it slid effortlessly inside me due to my wetness.

"Fucking hell, Jane," he rasped. "Do you think you're ready for me?" He asked as he moved faster.

"Y- yesss," I managed, my head thrashing from side to side, my body curling.

He met my gaze and continued to thrust them inside me until the pleasure built and overflowed inside me. I stiffened, words failing to leave my lips as my heart pounded and pleasure erupted inside me. It was the most glorious feeling–one I had no control over as my walls clamped down on Elliot's firm finger, and a sudden rush of juices flooded my vagina.

Elliot moaned and pulled his fingers out, rubbing the wetness over my slit and my clit. I flinched, feeling too sensitive to the touch. My chest rose and fell rapidly as I rose and descended on my high.

Elliot came beside me on the bed and kissed me softly on lips that were still gaped open and a body that was still trembling. He had a proud look on his face, which was warranted after what he just did.

"How do you feel?" He asked as he shuffled behind me and pulled me up against him, his head right at my ear, one hand propped beneath me, the other over me.

"So amazing," I whispered, rubbing up against his hard body, feeling his cock right beneath my pussy. I wanted him so much it ached.

"Do you think you'll come just as hard for my cock?" He asked, his warm breath fanning against my skin, his hand trailing up and down.

I didn't think it was possible to get wet with mere words, but I gushed a little at the question. "Harder."

He chuckled and kissed me on the ear. "That's my girl."

I jutted out my ass, and he adjusted a little and placed my leg over his. The arm under my head held one breast while he used the other to rub his smooth hardness at my entrance. I gasped, closing my eyes as I awaited the pleasure. He pushed himself inside me, and I stretched with acceptance of his length and girth. He only had the tip in, but my head was already swirling with pleasure.

"It'll hurt for a bit," he said as he rubbed my clit a little, forcing my walls to clamp around the head. I reached around for his ass, pressing my palm against it as I urged him to continue. With one single thrust, he inserted himself deep inside me and broke my hymen. I screamed, clamping my eyes shut as brief pain assaulted my body. Elliot paused and kissed my face as his hands slid against me.

I acquainted myself with his size, the tears at the brim of my eyes. But it wasn't so much because of the pain; I was so overwhelmed, finding it hard to believe that I was finally with my dream guy. My pussy burned while Elliot throbbed inside me, but after a second, he started thrusting slowly, ridding me of the ache with his huge cock that provided me with the sweetest invasion. My moans were constant as every thrust made me feel better each time. I was soaked for him – so incredibly wet that I could clearly hear each thrust.

"You're so tight, baby – fuck," he said against my ear as he held my hips and squeezed my tits with his other hand.

I realized he got deeper each time, but he was still moving incredibly slowly, as if afraid to hurt me. Admittedly, there was still a dull ache there, but the pleasures I was getting from his manhood made it feel almost non-existent. This was better than his fingers, and although his mouth had done a fantastic job, I just couldn't get enough of him in me. I felt the connection to my heart and knew this certainly couldn't be a one-time thing for me. I suddenly feared the idea of it being just that for Elliot. What if he didn't feel the same? However, I wasn't going to allow it to ruin the moment. I was on cloud nine, and I wasn't planning on coming down anytime soon.

"Faster, please," I whispered.

Elliot paused for a second as if unable to believe his ears. "I don't want to hurt you," he said, the concern evident in his voice.

"You won't. I want to feel all of you, Elliot," I said, emboldened by pleasure.

Without another word, he pushed himself deeper inside me, and my breath hitched as pleasure erupted through me and an ache when he pushed too far. I gasped repeatedly after each thrust that went to unknown territories. I was so full, so stretched, and I was still oozing juices for him. Elliot started to move inside me relentlessly, not holding back, and for a second, I second-guessed my earlier request.

I was tender, but the more he fucked me, the pleasure overcame every bit of discomfort that I felt. His hands slid around my hips and found my clit, which he slowly rubbed as his cock disappeared inside me. My mouth hung open before I bit back down on my lips to prevent a scream.

It was so intense. Elliot was right behind me with his body moving against me, him inside me, one hand planted on my breast and the other on my clit. The distribution of pleasure was making me heady, the heat in the room.... Our slippery bodies. He started to move even faster inside me, and my whimpers and moans were endless. The mattress creaked, the headboard was loud against the wall as Elliot fucked me like the stallion he was.

"Oh, my God, Oh Elliot!" I purred.

"I won't ever get enough, Jane," he rasped as he filled me over and over with his cock. "This pussy is mine and only mine; tell me you understand that."

His thick voice sent shivers down my spine, and my pussy clenched at his words.

"Yes! Oh, yes, Elliot! Ahh!" I said as I clamped my eyes shut, trying to hold out while my orgasm beat at my gates.

"Are you on the pill?" He asked, and I froze up for a bit.

My heart was bursting in my chest. "N- no, but I want you to cum inside me."

"Jane–"

"Please," I said, and just then, the dam broke inside me, and I screamed as my orgasm took its course. My body convulsed, and my walls clamped around Elliot while his cock continued to rage rampage inside me.

I trembled, my body shaking violently as my orgasm racked my body. Then, just when I thought I'd pass out from Elliot's length still inside me, he filled me all the way and bucked, grunting as he released his seed deep inside me. A tear fell from my eyes as my body went into a deep state of relaxation – almost like I was floating and the weight of the world had been lifted off my shoulders.

Elliot moaned and sighed as he ran his hands along the flare of my hips, his cock still throbbing inside me as he emptied every single warm drop of cum. My pussy continued to clench around him until he withdrew and then clenched at the emptiness.

Elliot turned me around, and as my legs closed, I knew the pleasure might have numbed the aches, but I would surely be sore the following day.

We were face to face, and he smiled at me. "How do you feel?" He asked, pushing my hair back away from my face.

"Like I'm in a dream or something."

He smiled. "I'll take that as a good thing."

"I never imagined my first time to be this good, but it was truly more than I expected," I smiled, my eyes fluttering.

He kissed me on the forehead. "I'm happy to hear that, baby."

I felt warm all over, and the bed suddenly felt like cotton. I snuggled up to him with a smile, and he leaned back on his back, allowing me to rest my head on his chest.

I smiled as my hands trailed down his taut body, documenting every inch of him to memory. He did the same to my back; everything felt right in the world. But then my fingers passed over something at his side – just below his ribs, and I eased up to see what it was.

It was a huge, long scar, and I gasped as I inspected it and how it had marred his skin. My eyes instantly filled with tears as I glanced up at him.

"What happened?"

He got up with his back against the headboard and pulled me to him, kissing me gently on the lips. "I was in the army for almost ten years. Enlisted two years after Courtney was born. Things were going great before I er – I got shot and almost lost my life," he said with a tight, unhumorous smile that went as quickly as it came. "I had to have a kidney removed because of the damage from the gunshot. It was one hell of a time, princess," he genuinely smiled this time.

I glanced back to the scar. It wasn't obvious to the naked eye, and I might have missed it if I hadn't felt it. He had tattooed a feather in and around it, making it almost spotless.

"I'm so sorry that you had to go through that," I said, my voice a bit shaky.

He kissed me on the forehead. "Don't worry about it. I'm alright now."

I clenched my jaw tight as a thought occurred to me. "But why are you even doing the street fighting? Elliot, one hard blow down there, and you can be seriously injured." My voice got higher as the seriousness of the situation resonated with me.

"Jane, I'll be fine."

"But you don't know that!" I said to him, knowing I had no right to. I didn't want to turn Elliot off by passing my place.

He sighed lightly. "After I recovered, it felt like I was losing control over my life. I loved being out there, but in one single moment, it was all taken away. I was angry for the better part of my life, battling PTSD. And then a friend brought me to this other junkyard on the other side of town. That was when I started the whole street fighting thing. I felt so alive, Jane, you wouldn't even understand. I felt in control again, and things started falling into place. I started my manufacturing business, and things have been great since. I don't know what I would do if I lost that."

I bit my lips, totally understanding where he was coming from. "But what about Courtney? You haven't even told her about it. What if she finds out?"

"She won't. Now stop worrying your pretty little head about it and come here," he said, pulling me in for a kiss.

I caved despite the serious conversation that was just had. All it took was his lips on me and his hands making trails over my body for me to forget everything else but what was happening in the moment.

Chapter 8

Elliot

I clenched my teeth and muttered a curse as I feasted my eyes on the way my cock was disappearing in and out of Jane's creamy pussy. The way her small tits bounced up and down in her chest, and her mouth hung open while tiny gasps escaped her luscious lips. I couldn't have enough of the silky softness of her cavern and the warmth that radiated through my cock and my body. She was tight and wet, her juices glistening on my length as I thrust back and forth inside her. Her lips were stretched to the max from my size, battered pink from the relentless fucking.

I grabbed onto her hips and pulled her into me, allowing her to meet my thrusts as I went hard and deep inside her. She whimpered, and the sound was like music to my ears that gave me some sort of encouragement. If I had no control, I would have filled her cunt with my seed again, but I wanted every second to last as long as possible. Jane had already had her orgasm, her tightness trying to milk the cum out of me, but I had held on like my life depended on it and held back, wanting to give her two orgasms before I had mine.

Her sweet pussy contested that as she met each thrust with a clench. I bared my teeth and dug my fingers into her skin, burying my entire length inside her before I fell atop of her and met her heated body. Her gasps filled my ears as I continued to fill her with sharp stabs. Her fingers trailed down my back, skewering my flesh with her sharp nails.

Our slippery bodies moved against each other, her hardened nipples rolling against my chest and increasing the pleasure. She collided again, screaming loudly as her inner walls hugged my cock, and her fingers went deeper into my skin. I muttered a curse, and my legs buckled as the pressure built and I released my load inside her. She was whimpering like a baby, and I was grunting as her tightness drained every drop from me. Once again, I had filled her with my seed, and I would do it over and over again as I was already addicted to the sight.

Breathing heavily, I kissed her softly and eased up as I slipped from inside her warmth. She moaned and closed her eyes in her state of bliss while I watched as her pussy lips closed after my cock's retreat. Her flesh moved in and out, her wetness smeared all over her cunt. I clenched my jaw as a dollop of cum rolled from inside her and down her tight rosebud.

The sight was enough to get me hard again, but Jane was clearly exhausted as we had fucked throughout half of the night. It was now morning.

I collapsed beside her and watched as her eyes fluttered, a smile on her face as I caressed her dewy cheeks. Truth was, if Jane had asked me to stop fighting, I would have in a heartbeat. It was crazy how I was willing to let go of something I had held on to for so long for a woman I had only known for a couple of weeks. As her eyes closed and sleep took over her form, I came to the conclusion that losing Jane would be worse than losing my chance to fight. And then there was Courtney, on the other hand. She had been so devastated throughout my recovery that it would be almost ruthless to break her heart in such a manner again. The last thing I wanted her to think was that I was in danger. Fighting would be an absolute no for her, and after all, she was going through with her mom, it would simply be too much.

I smiled as I looked down at Jane. Never in my life did I anticipate for this to happen. She was young and just about ready to take on the world. I didn't want to stand in her way, but, at the same time, I didn't want to lose her. I didn't know what to do or how to ask her if she wanted to be my woman. I had been so versed with women, but none had made me feel the way Jane had, especially in such a short time. It was frightening, and maybe I should be running, but running meant not being able to have her by my side, and I couldn't have that.

I fell asleep beside her, and we both woke up some hours later to make love again before ordering some food. She told me about how she had lost her parents and that her brother was the only one she had left. I wanted to reassure her and let her know that she had me as long as she wanted me, but I didn't want to scare her away. We weren't a hundred percent transparent with our feelings, and there was still the elephant in the room. There was so much to be discussed, but I was afraid that reality would knock us back on course, and I wasn't quite ready for that.

She sighed as she pulled on her discarded clothes and smiled at me. "I wish I could stay longer, but I have to finish up a few assignments for class tomorrow."

I walked up toward her and hugged her. "You'll come back here tomorrow?"

She kissed me. "I will."

I walked her to the front door and watched as she climbed into the Uber and left. I sighed, the sudden emptiness taking its course within me. Prior to this, I was always contented with being alone, but after a night with Jane, I was pretty sure I wanted her in my bed and by my side day after day.

That following evening, I came in early to prepare dinner, wanting it to be a surprise for her. I prepared steak, greens and a side of mashed potatoes and was happy with the outcome. I waited for Jane and smiled when I heard a car being parked out front. I immediately wiped my hands and moved toward the front door to welcome her. Much to my surprise, the doorknob rustled before I even got there, and before I could open it myself, it popped open, but it wasn't Jane who was on the other side.

"Court!" I said, my body gone stiff.

She smiled and looked at me with a hint of confusion. "Is everything okay, Dad?" She asked.

I cleared my throat. "Of course, I just wasn't expecting you is all," I said as I managed a smile and hugged her.

We broke apart, and her eyes scanned the living room. "Is that food I smell?" She beamed. "Are you expecting someone?"

I glanced at my watch, following behind her as she moved toward the kitchen. "Er – kinda. Is everything okay?"

She turned to me with a huge grin after seeing the meal and the glass of wine I had put out. "OMG, why didn't you tell me you were seeing someone?"

I rubbed the nape of my neck. "I was er- I was waiting first. I didn't want to speak too soon."

She approached me with a warm smile. "Well, I'm happy for you, Dad. I can't wait to meet her!" She grinned.

I paled. "Is everything okay, Court. You don't usually visit on weekdays."

She huffed out a sigh and propped herself on one of the kitchen stools. "I'm in a bit of a dilemma. I want to get your opinion on something, and it's been really gnawing at me lately."

Curious and concerned, I took a seat beside her as well. "What is it, sweetheart?"

She licked her lips and cracked her knuckles. "Mom has been asking to see me."

My brows rose. "What?"

"She's saying she's getting better and wants to see me. I'm confused, Dad. I don't know –

"Hey," I reached for her hand. "If you aren't ready, you don't have to. You went through a lot with her, and she knows that. Part of her healing is allowing you to heal as well."

She nodded. "But what if she doesn't see me come and relapses again? I don't want that to happen." Her eyes filled with tears.

"Court, your mom is in a very good place and has professionals taking care of her. She'll be fine, and she'll also understand if you're not ready," I said.

She sniffed and nodded. "Ok, but maybe I can visit her in the summer. Would you come with me?"

"Anything for you, baby girl," I said as I pulled her into my arms and hugged her. She tightened her hold on me, and my heart warmed.

"Thanks, Dad, you're the best."

Just then, the doorbell rang, and I froze. Fuck! Courtney pulled apart with a beaming smile and hopped off the chair.

"Oh, that must be her!" She squealed as she ran into the living room toward the door.

"Courtney, wait!" I called, trying to keep up with her.

But I was too late. She opened the door, and Jane stood on the other side, her face instantly going pale when she saw Courtney standing there. She looked like she was about to pass out as she stood there in her little pink dress, her hair flowing down her shoulders. Shit!

"Jane, what are you doing here?" Courtney asked, her brows furrowed with confusion as she turned to glance at me with her gaze full of questions. Courtney was a smart girl. No sooner had that question come, I could see her fitting the puzzle together in her head. She looked from me to Jane.

"What's going on here?" She demanded firmly.

"Court, lemme just explain..." I intervened.

Realization dawned on her face suddenly, and her eyes widened, already glistening with tears. "You've got to be fucking kidding me!" She exclaimed. "You two?" She asked as she pointed at both Jane and me. "She's the date, Dad?" She asked me, her eyes wide with terror as she looked to me for answers. I could see the disappointment in her eyes, and it broke my heart.

"Sweetheart, let me explain..."

"What's there to explain?!" She snapped. "You've been going behind my back and fucking my roommate!" She turned her anger toward a frozen Jane. "And you have been acting like a goody two-shoes all this time when you're really just a fucking slut. I opened up to you, I started to like you!" She exclaimed.

"Courtney!" I scolded.

"I'm so sorry, Courtney. The last thing I wanted to do was hurt you," Jane cried.

Courtney scoffed. "And yet, in the space of a fucking month, it became the last thing. If this were your idea of getting back at me for all the smack talk I hurled at you, con-fuckin-gratulations, job well done!" She exclaimed as she shoved past her, almost knocking Jane to the ground.

"Courtney!" She called as she ran to her car. I pulled her out of the way as Courtney sped off, just inches away from running over Jane.

I pulled her against me as she sobbed. "Hey, everything will be fine. She just needs some time to process and cool off."

Jane peeled herself from me as she sniffed. "This was a mistake," she sobbed. "I knew the shit would hit the fan, and I still allowed myself to be caught up in you. I knew nothing good would come from it, and I was only fooling myself!"

I clenched my teeth. I've felt pain in my lifetime – understood it to a 'T,' yet her words pierced me harder than any weapon ever could. I swallowed. "Come on, Jane, don't say that."

She forced a dry laugh through her tears. "Just admit it, Elliot. I was only good enough for you for a few fucks, but I knew you would soon get tired of me and move on to the next best thing. I was just going to satisfy you for a while, and as great as it was for me, I knew I would be the one to get the shitty end of the stick."

"That's not true," I defended.

"Isn't it? You're going to move on, and I'm gonna have to move on because this won't work."

I clenched my teeth at the idea of someone else touching her – someone else being inside her. "You're mine, damnit. Only mine. No other man will call you theirs as long as I live."

Her jaw worked up, and her small mouth drew thin. "I'm not your property, Elliot. I'm not something you could have whenever you feel like it!" She said between clenched teeth.

Fire was pumping through my veins, and my thoughts were still a mess from what had just happened, but I couldn't ignore the fire in Jane's eyes and how I was itching to touch her – to taste her despite the magnitude of the situation. I clamped my mouth to hers and kissed her hungrily and passionately, more than I'd ever done before. There was a slight hesitance from her, but she opened up to kiss me and reciprocated the passion that I offered. However, it was short-lived as she tore her lips apart and slapped me, the sting coursing through my body.

I flinched as I stared at her wordlessly while she did the same, her chest heaving. That should have been enough to make me take a step back, but I didn't, and neither did Jane. Much to my surprise, she collided into me and kissed me again, hard and deep. Joy erupted through me, and I kissed her back, kneading her soft lips into my mouth, which was a bit salty from her tears.

My cock swelled in my pants; I pushed her back against the wall and kicked the door shut as my hands roamed over her body. She reached for my belt and fumbled with the buckle, eager for my cock. When she opened it, I pulled it down and stepped out of it. Jane gasped when she felt my girth that throbbed to enter her. I reached between her and hoisted her dress, bringing her panties to the side before I lifted her in my hands. She wrapped her legs around me, and I kissed her again, both of us seemingly out of breath as we raced for the pleasure that was so near but which seemed so far. I reached for my length and guided it to her entrance, filling her with one single thrust that had her mouth opening against mine.

I moaned at how wet she had gotten in the short space of time. No foreplay was needed because Jane was already soaked for me, and that simple fact brought me great joy.

I buried my face in her neck and pushed myself inside her, wanting the walls of her hot pussy to sheath the entire length of my cock. Her heat encased me, the headiness of her perfume made my head swirl as I fucked her hard and deep. Her whimpers filled the air again, and I continued to fuck her hard and deep, so I wouldn't stop hearing them.

Feeling like I was going to bust, I pulled out and flipped her around, so her ass was against me. I reached for her breast and pushed my fingers through the low-cut cleavage, filling my palm with the firm mound and pointy nipples.

I entered her from behind, and she gasped as I buried myself inside her. She oozed more juices as my cock effortlessly slid back and forth within her, her round ass cushioning every thrust I made. I parted her ass cheeks, wanting to get as much of my cock inside her as possible. She cried out and briefly rested her forehead against the wall as her pussy started to clamp down on me. I slowed my pace a bit, pulling her up against me and forcing her back to arch as I held her throat and kissed her exposed neck.

"You're mine, Jane. Fucking mine," I rasped against her ear as I emptied my seed inside her. She moaned as her knees buckled, too satiated to utter a word.

Chapter 9

Jane

I woke up in Elliot's bed, my mind too fogged to remember how I ended up here. He was fast asleep beside me, and little by little, the night before became clear, and guilt started to poke at me. I couldn't believe I had succumbed to Elliot's lustful ways - couldn't believe that I lacked so much self-control that I had caved in the most intense situation. I should have spent the entire night apologizing to Courtney, yet I had been wrapped up with her father all night.

I felt sick to my stomach, and my eyes stung as tears threatened to spill. Leaving Elliot's side was the hardest thing to do, but I knew it had to be done. I couldn't stay and allow his daughter to resent him. Hating me was fine, but I just couldn't sit back and watch as their relationship fell apart. We weren't friends, but I would have done anything to have my father for another day. She had hers, and I couldn't ruin that.

Sniffing, I slowly eased up from the bed, the sweet aches in my body telling me that I should stay. Elliot was a fantastic lover, and it was easy to get caught up in his charms and great sexual abilities, but it was just the worst timing. We couldn't happen.

With shaking hands, I pulled on my dress and bound my hair in a ponytail. My heart ached as I watched him; I gently placed a kiss on his cheeks before I gathered my things and went downstairs to call an Uber. Tears were already streaming down my face, and I didn't do anything to stop it. My heart ached too much. Before I left, I went in search of a piece of paper to leave a note. I found a notepad on the coffee table in the living room and quickly scribbled a message: *Please don't come after me. This won't work. I'm sorry.*

I used the back of my hand to wipe my eyes, I slowly walked to the kitchen, my vision cloudy from the tears. As I stopped in front of the fridge, I wiped my tears again and the long streaks on my cheeks. I sniffled, and tensed my jaw to do what I had to. I looked at the note, then at the fridge. I tried hard to stop the tears, but they only kept flowing.

As I stood there, trying to fight my tears and toughen up, I saw the pots and the wine that were left out, and my heart tugged. Elliot would have been the perfect man if things hadn't been so complicated. I would gladly call him my forever man, but we were two different people living in different worlds.

I stuck the note to the refrigerator and left the house, waiting down by the gate for my ride and hoping that he wouldn't wake up before then.

I cried all the way to the café because I didn't know how I could face Courtney. And plus, if she saw that I'd come back in the same clothes, she'd know I'd stayed at Elliot's house. She would hate me even more, and I just couldn't deal with the guilt that would bring me.

I ordered a strong coffee and dialed Bailey's number.

As soon as she answered, my sob broke free. "Jane, is everything okay?" She asked.

I sniffed and attempted to wipe my eyes before I attracted any attention. "I slept with Elliot," I choked.

"Wh- Jane that's great, but why are you crying? What happened?" She asked.

"Courtney found out, and now she hates the two of us."

"Wait a sec— how did she find out?"

"I went over to Elliot's place, and she was there. Things just got so out of control. I made a mistake, Bailes."

"What mistake?" She asked. "You loved being with Elliot, didn't you?"

I sniffed. "I did."

"So how is it a mistake when you were only making yourself happy?" She asked, sounding genuinely curious.

"Don't you get it? She feels betrayed. Just when we were starting to get along, this happened. And plus, she's all sad about her mom being in rehab and — it's just too much, Bailey."

She sighed. "Listen, Courtney is an adult, you're an adult, and Elliot is an adult. You're all adults in this situation. If she wants to bitch about who her dad dates, then maybe she needs a couple more years to mature. Don't ever beat yourself up for putting yourself first," she exclaimed.

"But it's selfish..."

"No, what's selfish is her acting like you belonged on the cross next to Jesus. Now, as short as the time was, I've never seen you this excited about anything as you were about Elliot. I know you care for him, Jane. You may regret this opportunity if you walk away."

I rubbed my forehead. "I just wished things weren't so complicated, y'know."

"Life is never easy. Sometimes, we just have to make some tough decisions. Talk to Courtney and apologize for not telling her earlier, but at the same time, also tell her about what you feel for her dad."

I smiled. "I don't know what I would do without you."

She giggled. "You've got this.

After an hour, I returned to my room and took a shower. Just as I was done getting dressed, Courtney stepped in. She paused when she saw me, her gaze deadly, and her mouth formed in a scowl.

My heart lurched in my chest. "Courtney, I'm sorry."

"I don't need to hear it, Jane. I'm already in the process of requesting another roomie," she said as she moved toward her bed and picked up the stuff she had laid out there. She snapped her head toward me. "The fact that you stayed there even after all that happened just shows how fucking uncaring you are, so don't come here and act all innocent," she said as she rolled her eyes.

I swallowed the lump in my throat. "I really care about your dad," I blurted.

She scoffed. "You haven't known him for a month! And just to break it to you, Jane. My dad doesn't settle with one woman, so all this back-stabbing was all for nothing."

"Listen, you can be mad at me all you want but don't be mad at your dad.

"Aww, isn't that sweet?" She exclaimed dryly. "You could have had any man you wanted, but you just had to choose my dad, of all people."

"Courtney, this wasn't intentional. I didn't set out to hurt you. If it's any consolation whatsoever, we broke things off."

She scoffed as she got her things and left the room. I plopped down on the bed with a sigh. There was just no way things would get better.

AFTER TWO WEEKS, COURTNEY had moved out, and I was left alone in my dorm for a while. That would have been the dream a few months ago after Bailey left, but now it just didn't feel right. I still felt horrible for the way things ended, and no amount of apology would get me Courtney's forgiveness.

Plus, I had not seen or heard from Elliot ever since I left that morning. Regardless of the note, a part of me had hoped that he would try to reach out. But I supposed it was just a clean escape for him. Courtney had said it, and I knew that Elliot wasn't a one-woman man. Yet, I had inserted myself into his life as if begging to get myself hurt. He'd probably moved on to the next woman already, and I was forgotten.

A tear rolled down my cheeks at the thought, and I shuffled up to the pillows that I had used as a placeholder during my lonely nights. They collected my tears again as I huddled there, thinking about the one man I probably shouldn't have. My heart was breaking in two, and my throat burned from the endless sobs that threatened to spill from me.

I didn't understand the emotions I was feeling. I didn't understand why my eyes stung each time I thought about Elliot. Being away from him was probably a good thing, but my body rebelled against the idea, and my heart was sore from losing a piece every single day.

It was simple. Elliot had ruined me for anyone else, and I was certain I would die with him being the only man I ever touched.

Chapter 10

Elliot

Two weeks felt like forever; that was when I last saw Jane. I had woken up with a smile that morning, content with the fact that she was beside me, but oh, how I quickly realized that she wasn't. I didn't need to search the house for her because I knew in my heart that she was gone for good. I found the small note later on the refrigerator that made me feel worse about everything. All I wanted to do was hop in my car, head over to the campus and convince Jane to stay, but then I remembered Isaac's words.

Jane had her whole life ahead of her, and I didn't want to imprison her. She didn't have to deal with my mess and had already gotten a share during our short time together.

She deserved better, and though it was hard to convince myself of that fact, I knew it to be true. She deserved better than a messed-up army man with family issues.

Every day, I reminded myself of that – that she was better off- it was the motto I used to get through each day. I had gotten Courtney's forgiveness, and we were on good terms again after she had bragged about Jane telling her that we were over. That small bit of info really allowed me to face reality, however harsh.

It was a Saturday evening, and I was having dinner with Courtney, trying to concentrate on everything she was saying but unable to stick anything to memory.

I twirled my fork around the linguine and watched as it fell off before I repeated the process again.

"Dad, are you even listening to me?" She asked, irritated. My head snapped up to meet her gaze

"Sorry, sweetheart, what were you saying?" I asked as I put my fork down and eased back in my chair

She rolled her eyes. "You're thinking about her, aren't you?" She asked. My lips moved to deny it, but what was the point?

She scoffed. "What is it about her? I've seen you date better women."

I shook my head. "I've never met anyone like Jane, Courtney. No one compares," I was quick to say.

Her mouth fell open as she looked at me. "Oh, my gosh, you love her," she exclaimed matter-of-factly.

There was no denying that either. I realized that a week ago.

"My gosh, I can't believe this is happening! Why her?!"

"You don't choose who you love, Courtney. I was just drawn to Jane. It was like my heart knew before I even realized that she was my person."

"Dad, I can't have a stepmom who's my age!" She exclaimed in frustration, sighing heavily.

I couldn't hold back my chuckle. "Court, you don't have to call anyone anything."

"But that's what she'll be, and that's what people will see her as," she whined before rolling her eyes. "Anyway, I think I've lost my appetite," she murmured as she stood. "Good night."

I opened my mouth to talk but clamped it back shut, deciding not to. It was obvious Courtney was still not happy with the idea of Jane and me, and I couldn't force it. What point did it make now, anyway? Jane had made it clear she wanted no part of a relationship between us. I had gotten Courtney's forgiveness, and that should have been enough. Yet, it didn't feel like it. I eased back into my chair and glanced at the untouched food in front of me that I had no appetite for. With a sigh, I signaled for a waiter, instructing him to pour me a glass of scotch.

I WAS HOPING TO HEAR something from Jane for the next few days, but nothing. I burned with a need to see her and be with her. Each day was like torture when I realized I couldn't have any of those things.

I sat in the café, nursing a cup of coffee I had no care for while occasionally looking over my shoulders. I tapped my fingers against the wooden table, my eyes focused on the entrance. People probably thought I was weird for looking around so much, but if they knew my intentions, they would probably pity me.

A petite brunette stepped through the door, and my heart lurched. I craned my neck as I tried to see her face, but as soon as she turned to face me, my heart quickly fell, realizing that it wasn't who I wanted it to be.

With a defeated huff, I left for the office, thinking this was maybe the karma I got for ghosting females and playing with their hearts in the past.

That weekend, Courtney and I went to have our usual dinner at a fast-food joint in town. I picked at my fries and sipped at my coke while she devoured a two-layer cheeseburger, a contented look on her face. I smiled because regardless of all that was happening, Courtney was happy, and that was all that mattered in the end, wasn't it?

"I'm so glad they gave me a single room. I promise, if I had gotten someone I didn't like, I would have moved back home," she said as she shook her head and used her tongue to clean the corners of her mouth.

I smiled. "You know, that wouldn't be such a bad thing," I said.

She shrugged. "In a few months, I'll be done with college and have my own place. I don't want to be moving back and forth."

I nodded and lowered my gaze to the fries as a small silence passed between us. I glanced at Courtney and realized she was staring at me.

"Is everything okay, sweetheart?"

She cleared her throat and reached for a fry, which she circled around in the pool of ketchup. "You know, I've thought about what happened to you and Jane a lot..."

I straightened in my chair. "Court, I'm sorry –

"No, Dad, you don't have to apologize," she said as she met my gaze. "You've been alone for so long, Dad and have been through so much; I want to see you happy."

A small smile appeared on my lips. "I've realized that hasn't been the case since the whole incident."

I reached for her hand to give it a reassuring squeeze. "I'm fine, sweetheart."

She shook her head. "I was being childish and selfish..."

"You were hurt, and I will always regret putting you through that," I said.

"If Jane is the person that makes you happy, then I guess I owe her an apology and a thank you."

I smiled. "Thank you, sweetheart, but it really doesn't matter now. She doesn't want anything to do with me."

"We'll see about that. Jane has a big heart. She'll take you back. Come on," she said as she got up from her chair and reached for my hand.

"Court, are you sure about this?"

She smiled. "I don't wanna be the reason you miss out on the love of your life, even if it's my ex-roommate, who's the same age as me."

I grinned as I got up and ran alongside her.

We came upon Jane's dorm half an hour later. Courtney was smiling as she knocked and waited for the door to open while I was there, nervous as hell with my palms gone sweaty. But I believed I would feel better if she rejected me rather than living my life, regretting I never went for the opportunity.

The door opened, and Jane stood on the other side in oversized pajamas with her hair caught in a messy bun at the top of her head. Her puffy eyes widened when she saw us, looking at us from one to the other, her face pale with shock.

"Wh-what are you guys doing here?" She stuttered.

Courtney was the first to talk. I just couldn't stop staring at Jane and missing her even more, even though I was curious to know why she had been crying.

"I'm sorry for bitching about you guys being together. I know I said some mean things, and I'm sorry.

She scratched her neck and nodded. "It's fine," she said as she briefly glanced at me.

"It's not. I was being selfish, and that wasn't fair to you or my dad."

She cleared her throat. "I'm sorry, too, for not telling you."

Courtney fanned her off. "Ahh, it's fine. Anyway, I should get going. You two have my blessing," she said before she reached up to kiss me on the cheeks before running off.

I looked back to Jane, and our gazes locked. "Are you okay?"

She immediately wiped at her eyes. "Yeah, I'm fine. What are you doing here, Elliot?"

I felt nervous for the first time in my life. "I came to tell you I love you, Jane."

She froze. "What?"

"I love you, and I wish it hadn't taken me this long to realize, but I believe I fell in love with you from the very first day..."

"Elliot..."

"I know you might not feel the same, and I know that you have your whole life ahead of you, but please make me a part of it," I said, watching as her eyes filled with tears. "I'm not perfect, but if there's one thing in this world I'll do right, it'll be loving you."

The tears tumbled down her face, but she managed to smile through them. "God, I love you too. I love you so much!" She said as she bounded into my arms and hugged me. I chuckled as I held her against me and basked in the bliss surrounding us.

"I was afraid that I'd lost you," she sobbed.

I pulled away to look at her face. "I'm all yours, Jane. Just as you are mine." I lowered my mouth to hers and kissed her hard, wanting to make up for all the lost time in a single moment. But I had a lifetime to show her just how much she meant to me.

Epilogue

Jane

I sighed heavily, my chest heaving, as I dropped the last box to the floor and glanced around at the lot that littered the living room. Elliot came up behind me with two in hand, seemingly unaffected by their weight. He carefully placed them on the floor and turned toward me with a smile.

"That's the last of them," he said as he placed his hands akimbo and glanced at the clutter.

I bit my lips as I moved toward him. "Babe, are you sure you're okay with me moving in?"

His brows shot up. "Am I sure? I've never been more certain about anything in my life," he said, wrapping his hands around my waist. "Do you know one of the many perks of you moving in?" he asked and I could see by the sly look in his eyes where he was heading.

I played dumb, shaking my head as I wrapped my hands around his strong neck. "I get to fuck you every second of the day."

My cheeks flamed and I grinned. "Well, not every second; you have a company to run."

"*We* have a company to run. If I don't fuck you here, I'll do it at the office – doesn't matter," he shrugged.

I was already on fire for him, and he knew just how much. "You just can't get enough, can you?" I teased.

"Can you?" he shot back, pressing me against his body so that I felt the lump in his pants. My heart fluttered, and my core pooled with arousal.

Elliot dipped his head to mine and kissed me tenderly, each soft caress increasing my need. His hands trailed down my back and to my ass, where he squeezed the firm flesh and molded it into his hands. I moaned against his mouth, my nipples now tight against his chest.

I pulled apart, my lips just mere inches away from him. "I have to go take a shower and then meet Bailey, babe," I said through ragged breath.

Elliot's head dipped to my neck, sucking on my flesh. I arched my neck and closed my eyes, clinging onto him.

"Cancel," he muttered against me, continuing with his deed.

I laughed. "I can't. This is the only time she'll have off, and I haven't seen her in more than a week."

He finally eased up, his eyes dark with lust as he looked down on me. "Babe, you can't leave me like this. I'll go mad," he said huskily.

I bit my lips as I contemplated on his words. Truth was, I didn't think I could leave myself like this. I could already feel the evidence of my arousal between my legs and with Elliot right in front of me, how could I even resist?

"Ok, but we'll make it quick?"

He raised his brow with a grin that told me this would go otherwise, but I wanted this as much as him. No matter how long it would take.

I LAID ON THE BED, breathing heavily on my back while Elliot came and hovered over me, pushing my legs back to my chest. He glanced at my nakedness, and I could see him visibly clench his teeth as he drank in the imagery of my gaping wetness. Holding my legs in place, he inserted his cock, and I closed my eyes, sighing as he filled me. My flesh gave a resounding squelch as he entered me and started to thrust into my heat.

He muttered a curse as he went back and forth inside me, his cock popping out occasionally before he filled me harder and deeper again. I moaned and held my legs up, panting hard as he took me. He went fast and then slow, the mixture driving me insane.

"Elliot, please," I managed, moaning hard.

He bared his teeth and fucked me hard, glancing at my face. "Tell me where you want daddy's cum, baby," he said.

"I wanna taste you," I whispered, sounding breathless.

He smiled and buried himself inside me to the hilt, repeatedly hitting that button that had me quaking and shaking in the bed. My walls clenched around him as he triggered my orgasm, my juices flooding his cock.

"Oh, yes!" I whimpered, squeezing his length until he grunted and quickly pulled out from inside me.

Elliot quickly shuffled up to my head, straddling his legs around my chest before he fed me his creamy cock that was lathered with my juices. I opened wide and took him into my mouth, sucking off my own sweet flavor all the way down my throat.

"Fuck!" he muttered as he eased up and braced his cock down my mouth. He thrust a few times, battering my throat before he grunted and paused, his cum shooting down my throat. I moaned and slid my hands over his firm buttocks while he filled me up with every drop.

Once done, he pulled out, and I swallowed, watching as a dollop of saliva mixed with cum slid down the tip. His manhood throbbed and slowly deflated as he shuffled up beside me, one bulky hand thrown across my chest.

"I don't want you to leave," he said, trailing his fingers across my nipples.

I laughed. "Babe, you promised."

"It's the weekend and the only time I can fuck you 24/7. Plus, you just moved in," he argued.

"We'll have all of tomorrow," I said.

He sighed. "Alright, but maybe when you're done with Bailey, we could go out for dinner or something?"

I smiled. "I'd love that," I said as I leaned over and kissed him.

Elliot reached for his phone on the nightstand and glanced at the time. "I think I should call Courtney and check up to see how she's doing," he said.

"I texted her earlier. She said the band was performing in Toronto tonight."

He smiled. "That's great. I'm so lucky to have both of you in my life, Jane."

I blushed and snuggled up to him. "I'm the lucky one. I found the love of my life in one go."

"I truly hope you know how much I love you, Jane."

"I do." I said as I kissed him.

Huge Mountain Daddy

Izzie Vee

Erotic & Forbidden [1]

IZZIE VEE[2]

1. https://www.amazon.com/s?k=izzie+vee&i=digital-text&crid=31LQJTEQYT2EE&sprefix=izzie+vee%2Cdigital-text%2C121&ref=nb_sb_noss
2. https://www.amazon.com/s?k=izzie+vee&i=digital-text&crid=31LQJTEQYT2EE&sprefix=izzie+vee%2Cdigital-text%2C121&ref=nb_sb_noss

Cover Design by Izzie Vee
Cover Photo by Vishstudio on Depositphotos.com

Table of Content

Chapter 1

Jenna

"I can't believe you're really doing this?" I heard my mom say as I stuffed clothes into my little suitcase. I then pressed my knees into it and forced the zipper around the perimeter before I bolted upright with a sigh and scraped away the hair that had fallen to my face.

"Yeah, me neither, but this is a good thing, Mom, I promise," I said with a grin.

She still didn't look all too convinced, but I knew she wouldn't press the issue for long.

"Yes, but I still think it's a bit reckless that you're traveling across the country for this. You could have bought a cabin from anywhere."

I sighed. "Yes, but I fell in love with this particular one."

She shook her head and rubbed her temple. "Well, I guess the only thing left for me to say is good luck and wish you a safe travel," she smiled.

"Thank you. Don't worry, Mom; I'm just going to see how the area is and then I'll be back before you know it," I smiled.

She raised her brow and said nothing after, but I knew there was judgment there. As she hurried off to the living area, I finished getting my things together before I took a bath and got dressed. Mom was still waiting to bring me to the airport as I pulled my suitcase and carry-on into the living room.

The drive to the airport was fairly silent except for when my mom would talk about the trip and that I should call as soon as I got there. I had too much on my mind to talk, and so much my mom had no idea about. This trip was more than just buying a cabin in the middle of nowhere – it was a getaway trip.

"Ok, baby, I love you. Be safe," she said as she dropped me off and helped me to get my things out of the car.

"I love you too, Mom," I said as she hugged me tightly. The tears threatened to spill, but I swallowed the lump in my throat and tried to compose myself as best as I could.

I waved and blew kisses at her until I couldn't see her anymore. Finally, the tears fell and didn't stop falling even as I boarded the airplane and took my seat at the window. I knew it was stupid, but I couldn't help myself. I hadn't allowed myself to cry ever since it happened but now, in the most unlikely circumstances, I was pouring my eyes out on a fucking plane. The lady seated beside me looked at me strangely but didn't bother to ask if I was okay and I was happy for that. I just needed to bask in my own self-pity and use this trip as an opportunity to unwind.

Clearing my throat, I mustered the courage to check my Instagram. His particularly. I heard through the grapevine that things were becoming serious, and if I knew Emma well, I knew she would have something on her social media.

I was right. As I scrolled through her profile, I clicked on her recent story and saw them cuddled up together in bed with the caption, 'The best part of my day.' My heart sank as I stared at the images of laughing faces and bodies snuggled up under sheets. The happiness was evident on their faces while mine was withering and trembling with tears that fell harder with each passing second.

It had been two weeks, but I was still not over it. How could I be when I had thought he was the love of my life and she was my best friend.

I choked out a sob and the lady's head snapped to mine, her blue eyes moving up and down my face, her forehead wrinkled with curiosity.

"Are you alright, dear?" She asked.

I cleared my throat and aimlessly wiped at my face. "Yeah, I'm fine. I'm sorry," I said before she gave me one last glance before turning her head back to the front.

I heaved a sigh and adjusted my neck pillow, trying to clear my head as I prepared myself for the long ride.

I TOOK IN A WHIFF OF fresh air as soon as I stepped out of the airport and zipped up my fleece jacket. There was a subtle glow of sun that tried to bore through thick white clouds and the wind was still a bit chilly, but that was expected for Alaska.

The taxi service I had called was out in the parking lot. I hopped in and searched up the directions I'd been given from the seller and gave it to the driver, who looked too old to be working.

As we drove, my eyes remained focused outside. The melting snow, the vast amount of greenery with the houses neatly tucked between. This town was a small one, and I could see that now. See how everyone looked at me, a mere stranger, as I looked at them through the untinted glass.

"You have folks around here, ma'am?" The driver asked, bringing my attention to the front.

I cleared my throat. "Er, no. Just interested in property."

"I see," he mumbled.

I fiddled for the keys that had been sent through the mail as soon as the car dribbled to a stop. I was anxious and excited, my fingers barely able to grasp anything. I grabbed it and smiled, my head popping up to finally see where we had parked. My brows furrowed, and I looked at the driver, who met my gaze in the rear view.

I swallowed and shook my head, looking at the structure before us and then at him. "Are you sure this is the right place?" I asked, slowly feeling the blood drain from my face.

"I've been in this town all my life ma'am. I know it like the back of my hand. Unless the directions you gave weren't correct."

I shuffled for my phone and searched for the directions again before reciting it to him.

"Yep, this the one."

"That can't be possible!" I snapped, looking at the building which was nothing like I saw in photos and videos.

"Well, we can stay here and chat about it all you want, but it's gonna cost you extra," he said as he began to chew on something, resting his hand against the door.

I scoffed and pulled out some money before I handed it to him. He shoved the door open with a squeak and went around the back to pull my suitcase out. I stood at the door, flabbergasted, unable to believe what I was really looking at. The driver came and placed my belongings at my feet, standing beside me as we both gazed at the property.

"So I'm figuring this is the property you were talking about?" He said as he dug into his pocket and brought out a cigarette and a light. I didn't answer him; I was too shocked to produce words as a series of emotions passed through me.

The old driver popped the cigarette in his mouth, lit it and chuckled. "This old junk has been sitting like this for years. I bet Rosco wanted a quick penny and figured he'd make a scam out of it." A cloud of smoke passed across my nostrils, tickling them.

"Good luck, missy. You'll need it for that neighbor of yours, too," he laughed before he moved around to the driver's seat and started the engine.

Tears pricked my eyes as he drove off and left me standing there by myself. The emotions overflowed me. I felt hot despite the cool weather, and my hands were shaking.

With a sniff, I pulled my suitcase along the dirt road to the cabin which looked like it hadn't had life in it since it was built. I climbed the short steps of the porch and was welcomed with creaky floorboards, which had a few missing pieces. The log structure was weathered, and plants had begun to grow on the walls.

Hoping that inside would be better, I pushed the keys through the dingy lock and pushed it open. I stepped inside and a cloud of cobwebs had me stepping back and clawing at my face. Though the inside was better than the outside, it vastly smelled like mildew, and there was a hole in the roof with a rotting patch of floorboard right beneath.

I muttered a curse and stepped further inside, using my hands to clear the path in front of me. The furniture was alright but needed some polishing and maybe some renovations. The house needed some deep cleaning, and some changes needed to be made.

With a huff, I fished out my phone and dialed the number to the seller, but it went straight to voicemail.

"Fuck," I exclaimed, slamming the device onto the small, circular table.

I got up and decided to walk around the outside, looking at the amount of work that needed to be done on a property I thought was spotless. But the longer I stood there, gazing out, the more I could hear a sound in the distance. My ears perked up, and my head snapped around as I tried to see where it was coming from in the vastly vegetated area.

I began to walk and found that the noise was becoming louder the closer I went. It became obvious what it was – it was chopping wood, and I paused in my tracks as the revelations came. I thought back to what the taxi driver said and suddenly remembered I had a neighbor. One who wasn't so friendly by the sound of it.

I wondered if I should even approach. I was a stranger who didn't know my way around the place and was basically in the middle of nowhere.

But it was too late to turn back because he was just a few meters away, and he would see me if I made the slightest movement. But it wasn't like I could move anyway. Not when I was so entranced by this being. He was placing logs on a stump and splitting them with an axe, his muscles swelling with each hit he took. His arms were probably the size of my legs, bulging each time he swung.

I'd never seen a man like that in my entire life; my mouth was probably on the dewy ground, and my heart had already started to pick up pace. I swallowed hard and was just about to turn back when he looked up, and our gazes locked.

My cheeks flamed as I watched him stare at me under bushy brows.

He straightened up, his gaze questioning.

I swallowed hard and approached him, ignoring the weakness in my legs.

"Hi," I said upon reaching his cabin, which was what I'd expected mine to be. He was in full view now, his narrow hips covered in a pair of denim pants that clung to his toned legs. It was a wonder how he was out in the chill, shirtless.

"Not interested in anything you have to sell," he said, his voice thick and bassy – almost like thunder.

I bit the inside of my lips and allowed myself to take in his bare back that he now turned to me. His dark hair grew past his shoulders in soft waves, a few streaks of silver interspersed.

"Ugh, I'm not selling anything. I er – I brought the house across from here."

"Hmm," he said, splitting a log that had me flinching.

I cleared my throat. "Do you know the previous owner?" I asked.

He sighed, his shoulders dropping slightly as he paused and turned around to look at me. His eyes were grey, I could see that now, and a scar ran right through his right brow, separating the hair to make it easily mimic a slit. A long beard covered half his face, but his lush pink lips couldn't be mistaken. I could see that he was handsome – just rugged and intimidating.

There was something about the way he looked at me that made a shiver run up my spine. His gaze ran along the length of me, and I could swear I saw something flash across his eyes before he quickly turned back around to continue the task at hand.

"I know you're probably dumb or desperate to buy that dump."

My skin burned with embarrassment as I stared up at him. I was taken aback by his words but knew I couldn't contest them, knowing I was exactly what he described.

"It just needs a few repairs. I brought it at a good price."

"I bet," he said dryly as he put his axe down, turned around and moved past me.

On instinct, without even giving it a thought, I reached out and grabbed his hand, fearing he would head inside and close the door in my face.

My heart slammed in my chest when he paused in his tracks, my slender fingers not even fully wrapped around his wrist. My body grew heated, and liquid heat pooled between my legs, taking me off guard. I'd not expected such a reaction towards a man – him at least.

He slowly turned to me, his piercing grey eyes holding mine before they traveled to the area where our bodies touched. My heart thrummed even faster as I was face to face with him now, my neck craned so high I feared it would ache later.

I swallowed hard and slipped my hand from around his. I still couldn't find the words right away – I was seemingly paralyzed by his presence and the effect he had on me.

"D– do you know someone I could call for repairs?" I asked, hating the way my voice sounded.

"No," he said and my gaze fell to the patchy ground.

Without another word, the beast left for his cabin, his footsteps like thunder against the pleading hardwood floor.

Pulling in a breath, I tried to calm my raging nerves. I didn't understand what was happening to my body, and I didn't understand why it was the case with a man who was as cuddly as a cactus. I've never ached for a man before – not even my ex. Yet, one touch from a mere stranger, and I was already feeling the urge to satisfy myself. But I had bigger problems at hand – one this man couldn't help me with. It reminded me why I should still be angry for the mess I was welcomed with.

Pulling my phone from my pocket, I marched back to the cabin, scrolling through my contacts while simultaneously hopping over fallen trees in my path. I paused as soon as I reached the cabin door and sent out the call to Rosco Miller – the man I'd been foolish enough to buy from. It rang three times before I heard a beep, which ended the call.

"Shit!" I spat, raking my fingers through my hair. "Fucking perfect!" I exclaimed as my lips trembled for what I knew to be impending tears.

My phone shrilled and my heart swelled with hope, but quickly deflated as soon as I saw that it wasn't who I wanted it to be. It was my mom instead.

I took a seat and rested my elbow against my knee as I brought the phone to my ear. "Hey, Mom..."

"Sweetheart, you said you'd call.." she said with some disappointment to her voice.

"I know, Mom and I'm sorry. I just literally settled in."

"Oh... how is it?" She asked, her voice raising a bit.

My eyes scanned the confines of the room, and I faked a smile as if she were right in front of me. "It's just as I imagined. It's really great, Mom." I cringed at myself for the lie.

"That's great, sweetheart. Send pictures!"

I bit my lips. "Er, maybe tomorrow when I've sorted out the internet here."

"Okay, honey. Well, I won't keep you. I know you must be tired and pretty excited. Stay safe, okay."

"Will do, Mom. Love you."

"I love you too."

The phone call ended, and the tears that had threatened to spill earlier came tumbling down. My body trembled as I bawled my eyes out, unable to believe this was the bad luck my life had turned into. I had expected this would be a getaway for a new beginning, but it was as tragic as my life was at the current moment.

I stayed crying and sniffing, hiccupping for what seemed like hours before the tears stopped, and I forced myself to get up from my stupor and face my problems head-on.

It would be dark soon, and I didn't have any blankets and hadn't even bothered to check myself in at a motel.

Muttering a curse, I pulled my suitcase to the bedroom, which was surprisingly not as bad as the living room. The furniture was still in good quality, and it was quite cozy. I pulled a few things from my suitcase, stuffed them in the large tote and closed the door behind me.

The town was visible from where I was and maybe about ten minutes' walk. With a sigh, I slung the bag over my shoulders and began my walk. The crisp fresh air really motivated me – a stark contrast from the air-polluted city. I saw a few trees and fallen branches before stepping on asphalt, which really felt like civilization.

I couldn't help my smile as I walked toward a bar with a few people outside. I figured someone would know a hotel around here and someone who could fix the busted roof, and hey, I was pretty hungry too.

As soon as I stepped inside, the place quieted to whispers, and I must have sprouted a second head with how everyone looked at me. I swallowed hard and managed a tight smile at the enquiring eyes before I walked to the front, my footsteps piercing through the silence like a two-edged sword.

The whispers got louder before it was back to the usual ruckus with some jazz music playing in the background. I pulled out a stool and took a seat at the counter, happy to be looking at a variety of drinks instead of faces.

But I must've spoken too soon because soon after, a blonde slid in front of me with a smile on her wide lips, curiosity in her pale blue eyes.

"Visiting for the summer?" She asked as she wiped a glass behind the counter.

"Er– I guess you could say that," I smiled back.

"Welcome to Nevis. What can I get you?"

She shoved a laminated menu before me, allowing me a few seconds to scan the contents.

"A double cheeseburger and fries would be good, thanks." I said.

"Any drink to go with that?"

"Actually, could I have some coffee."

"Of course," she said before moving through the back double doors.

I fiddled with the straps of my bag while I waited, my eyes scanning the fairly packed bar. I met eye contact with a few men who nodded and winked at me, holding their beers high before they chuckled and went to whisper amongst their peers. A shiver snaked up my back, and it suddenly dawned on me that I was in a strange place with strange people. I didn't know anyone, and if anyone of them wanted to do anything to me, there wasn't much I could do to stop it.

"Here ya go." I gasped when a voice spoke to me, but as my head snapped around, I realized it was the waitress with my coffee.

"Sorry I startled you."

"Don't worry; thanks," I smiled.

She nodded. "Your food will be out shortly."

I nodded. "Er, can I ask you something..?"

"Of course."

"Do you know any motels around here. I did a silly thing of not booking one before I came here."

She grinned. "Of course. There's one about a mile up the road. I could ask one of the boys to take ya," she said as her gaze traveled over my shoulders to the men behind.

She must've seen the look on my face because she was quick to continue. "There's no need to worry about them, honey. Everyone is like family here. They might tease or look like beasts, but I swear, they're all harmless," she winked.

I managed a smile, but just then, the room quieted, and the whispers started to float around. I figured another tourist had stepped in, but as I spun around to see who it was, I realized it was the giant from earlier – my neighbor. He filled out the door, little natural light being able to pass through. His gaze scanned the room and the persons inside snapped their heads around as if they hadn't even seen him to begin with. This time he wore a black T-shirt with a black jacket strapped over his broad shoulders.

"Well, I can't say the same for this one," the waitress whispered.

My brows furrowed and fear crept up my spine. "He's dangerous?"

"Just as he looks, sweetheart. I'd steer clear of that one. He's done a few years in prison for murdering someone."

I felt as if the blood drained from my face. "What?"

"He got out after a retrial but, come on, the guy is as guilty as he looks," she scoffed.

I swallowed hard and glowered at my steaming cup of coffee that I suddenly had no appetite for.

"Wh– what's his name?"

She leaned into me and whispered, "Cullen," which sent a small tremor through my body.

I cleared my throat. "Can you make my order to go, please? And I'd really appreciate that ride you mentioned earlier."

She nodded. "Of course."

I turned my head to the side and saw Cullen seated in a corner, his chair seeming as if it were made for a toddler and not a man. He already had a beer in hand, drinking it occasionally while his gaze scanned the place. Then suddenly, he turned, and our gazes locked. My first thought was to look away, but I found that hard to do. It was like a magnetic field that pulled me closer to him. His eyes squinted, and there was some question in his eyes as they darkened. Heat evaded my body again; if it weren't for the waitress I would probably be burning myself alive.

"That'll be five ninety-nine."

My head snapped to the counter where the waitress had my order wrapped in a brown paper bag.

"Oh, thank you," I said as I dug through my bag and paid the bill.

"I'm Lilly, by the way."

"Jenna."

"Nice to meet you, Jenna and enjoy your stay," she said, waving over a guy who was there in seconds. "Pete here will get you to the motel safe and sound."

I smiled. "Thank you."

"Don't mention it."

As I collected my things, I couldn't help but give one more glance to Cullen who was staring back at me as I looked at him. His jaw visibly hardened, but I tore my gaze away before he could do anything else.

Chapter 2

Jenna

I twisted and turned in the queen-sized bed. Though it was comfortable with thick, soft blankets, I just couldn't sleep. How could I when there was so much to consider? Suddenly the repairs at the house had seemingly gone on the back burner and all I could think about was the ex-convict living beside me. How could I even go back knowing that we were the only persons around that area in about half a mile? Who's to say I didn't already piss off this man who maybe had it out for me?

Muttering a curse, I flashed off the sheets and flung my legs over the side of the bed. I reached for my phone on the bedside table and walked to the adjoining balcony at the side. I'd expected less when I initially thought of a motel, but this was more like a bed and breakfast vibe without the breakfast. It was like a mansion that someone had decided to profit off. I rubbed my shoulders as soon as I went outside and was met with the cold morning air. I had half a mind to go back in and get a jacket, but I wouldn't be long anyway, and I really couldn't get over the fresh air.

I searched for Rosco's number again while I gazed at the beautiful lawn ahead. People were walking their dogs, and though it was early, the town ahead seemed to be in full swing. I almost breathed a sigh when I heard a hello on the other end of the line, but my frustrations came back and so did my anger as soon as I heard his voice.

"I really can't believe you!" I spat.

"What's the matter Ms. Hendricks?"

"What's the matter? You scammed me and made me believe that the house I was coming to was what I saw in the pictures–"

"It is!" He cut in.

"Bullshit! There's a freaking busted roof and floor. Grass has taken over the whole place, and some things have started to mildew!" I ranted.

He was silent, and that aggravated me even more. I could feel my ears burning as anger fueled through me. "I need you to fix it, or I'm calling my lawyer!" I threatened.

"Okay, okay, I'm sorry, okay? I knew the place wanted some TLC, but I never knew it was that bad. I haven't been to Nevis in years! I didn't–"

"That's no excuse!" I cut in.

He sighed. "Okay, true. Listen, I'll send someone over today to do the repairs and get you whatever else you need, okay?"

I bit my lips, not hating the way that sounded. I guess that could work, seeing I didn't completely hate the place. "Fine."

"Great!"

Another thought came to me. "And why didn't you tell me I was living next to an ex-convict!"

"Who? Cullen? He was found not guilty. The guy's innocent!"

"Well, you seem to be the only one around here who believes that," I said as I rolled my eyes.

"Listen, Cullen isn't going to hurt you. You have nothing to worry about."

"You said the same thing about the cabin!" I snapped back.

His heavy sigh came. "Trust me on this one. He's a good guy. Just not the friendliest."

"Hmm. Anyway, you better not be shitting me about someone coming for the repairs. You don't want to piss me off further, Mr. Miller."

"Someone will be there before you know it. My apologies again, Ms. Hendricks."

"Okay," I said before I hung up the phone and breathed a sigh of resignation. There was some relief, but I still felt some trepidation over the whole Cullen thing. I'd like to take Rosco's word for it, but that did little for me in the past.

I flopped back down on the bed, staring at the ceiling and the fan in the center that looked like it hadn't been used in decades. I felt the urge to check my ex's social media, but I had to quickly remind myself that this trip was so I wouldn't think about them and the betrayal that they had done to me. I didn't want to think about them, but each time I was alone for too long with my thoughts, with nothing to do, it was all I could do.

With a huff, I peeled myself off the bed, deciding on an early morning. Half an hour later, I was at the bar slash diner, getting some coffee.

Lilly came from around the back, sporting a smile on her face as soon as she saw me.

"Well, hey there. You look well rested," she said as she settled in front of me on the other end of the counter.

"I am, thanks to you."

"Don't mention it. I'm glad I could help."

I smiled.

She lingered there as she looked around and scratched her head. I could tell there was something else she wanted to say, and she didn't hold back.

"So word around here is you bought Rosco's cabin," she said, raising a brow.

My mouth fell open. "Wow, news travels fast around here," I laughed drily.

She laughed. "Yeah, one of the woes of a small town."

"I see, but yeah, I did."

"Was that why you kinda freaked out yesterday and left when I told you about Cullen? Him being your neighbor and all."

I trapped a lock of hair behind my ear and cleared my throat. "Kinda, yeah," I said as I smiled stiffly.

"I didn't mean to freak you out–"

"No, no, I'm glad you told me," I quickly said.

She bit her lips and sighed. "Hey, he was found not guilty after all. Maybe he didn't do it," she shrugged, but she wasn't convinced, and neither was I.

I finished my coffee while Lilly and I engaged in a little chit-chat. Once done, we said our goodbyes, and I started walking around the town, eye shopping and actually shopping for a few blankets and food for the rest of the week, assuming Rosco was true to his word and would have someone come by today. Nevertheless, I held onto the hope that someone would.

A taxi brought me back to the cabin a couple of hours later. As I climbed out and went towards the cabin, I paused when I heard a noise. I placed the shopping bags on the busted floor and moved around the side, a scream piercing through my lips and my heart almost galloping through my chest when I saw a half-naked Cullen around the side.

His eyes fell on me as he paused in his tracks, a long shiny machete in hand.

I swallowed hard, my heart beating too fast. "W– what are you doing here?" I asked, unable to help myself from looking at his toned chest or bulky arms — the huge bulge in his tight jeans. Get a hold of yourself, Jenna!

"What does it look like?" He quipped with an edge to his voice.

My eyes widened as a thought came to me. "Did Roscoe send you?" I asked in disbelief and wonder.

"Hmm," he grunted before he twisted the machete in his hand and chopped off a vine from the house.

That asshole!

I swallowed and crossed my arms. "I thought you didn't know anyone who did this sorta thing," I challenged.

He shot me a glance before he was back to doing his task. I almost rolled my eyes as I stomped inside the house and grabbed a broom that was perched in a corner. I cleaned the bedroom, changed the dirty ruffled sheets and replaced them with some new ones I bought. I'd expected to feel some fear and discomfort knowing that a potential criminal was right outside, but I didn't. It was weird that I didn't feel fear when it came to Cullen – only desire.

Around midday, he was on the roof, repairing the hole. There was not much I could think about with the constant banging, but I figured I would make some sandwiches.

As I was preparing to bring them out, he appeared at the door, still shirtless, his body glistening with sweat and from the warm glow of the sun reflecting off his skin. That familiar weakness appeared in my knees again as I stared at him. Things were happening to my body that I couldn't understand. It was strange, and even stranger was that he was a stranger.

"I'm done with the roof, but I'll have to get some more supplies for the floor," he said. "I'll come back in a day or two to fix it," he said.

I nodded, clearing my throat. "Y–yeah. I er – I made some sandwiches if you'd like," I said, shoving the platter towards him, a smile on my face.

His eyes moved to the tray in hand before returning to my face. "I'm good."

"Please. It'll go to waste if you don't help me eat it," I said.

He was silent as he looked at me as if contemplating what to do. It felt like forever before he grunted and moved toward me, taking off a triangular piece.

I smiled as I moved to the small table in the corner and placed the tray on it, gesturing towards the empty chair.

"I have beer, too, if you'd like."

A glint appeared in his eyes. "Thanks."

Feeling accomplished, I dashed toward the fridge and pulled one from it before I returned to him. "They're not too cold as yet, seeing I just bought them."

"It's fine," he said as he popped the cap open and took a gulp.

"My name is Jenna, by the way."

"Cullen," he said.

"I know."

His gaze flickered to mine. "Did your research or did the town's people volunteer the info?"

My cheeks flamed. "Er–"

"I take it it's the latter," he said as he eased back in his chair and looked at me.

"Yeah, what can I say? Small town, fast gossip."

He nodded. "You catch on fast, but you really shouldn't believe everything you hear."

"I know that."

"What do you think... Jenna?" He asked, the sound of my name on his lips causing heat to course through me. I folded my legs.

"I er... I don't know. I don't know you," I stuttered.

He seemed to think on it for a few seconds before he stood with his beer in hand and picked up another slice of sandwich. "I should get going; have a nice day."

I stood, too, almost falling over the chair from the haste I moved. Cullen reached out and grabbed my arm, steadying me before I was face-first with the ground.

"Easy there, tiger," he said, hands planted on my waist.

My brain was all fuzzy from his touch. Somehow, the fear of a possible injury didn't shake me as much as his grip on me. His hands were warm and big, and I could feel the heat from them move past my clothes and radiate on my skin–a warmth that spread through my body, hardened my nipples and caused the area between my legs to pool with need. He looked down at me, and I could see the intensity there – how his eyes darkened and his gaze spoke to me. I was compelled by them, wanting to seek out more from this strange situation. My body was humming with need, and I knew that the only person capable of ridding me of it was the man standing right in front of me.

I moved closer toward him, acting off his touch that still sizzled through my body. Not a single logical thought could be formed in my head at the moment; all I wanted to do was act on the desire lunging through me.

My lips were inches from his as I went on tiptoes, almost desperate to feel his lips on mine. The closer I drew to him, the more I could feel the woodsy scent of his body, a whiff of cologne that had faded during the hard labor.

I was just an inch away from having my fantasy turn into reality when he shifted a little and whispered, "I'll see you around, Jenna."

I swallowed the lump in my throat as my skin flustered, my body seemingly drenched with a bucket of cold water. His hand fell from my body as he stepped away, giving me one last glance and then he was gone.

"Shit, shit!" I exclaimed, smacking myself in the head as I scolded myself. I couldn't believe what had just happened. I couldn't believe I threw myself on a man like that. A man who was obviously not interested in me. A man who had served time!

What the hell was wrong with me? I asked myself. Maybe my brain was still messed up from the Kyle and Emma affair, but it still didn't explain my feelings toward Cullen. I had never felt this way before – I'd never ached so much for a man in my entire life. Though the feeling was alien, there was nothing I wanted more than to explore these feelings. I wanted him in every way possible; it was that simple.

THAT NIGHT, I WAS RECKLESS, but Cullen was the only thing I had on my mind. Not the fact that he was an ex-con; I just wanted him more than I had ever wanted anything in my life.

A part of me told me to forget whatever desire I had looming inside of me, but I knew it wouldn't be that easy. The rejection had been harsh, but it didn't make me want him any less. I was still hot and bothered, desperate to have his hands on me again. But the likelihood of that happening was slim.

Even now, as I lay in bed, his robust body was all I could think about and what it would feel like to have it against me. I felt a tingling between my thighs that filled me with an instant need to satiate. My heart started beating fast as I snuck my hand beneath the sheets and under the waistband of my panties.

The breath hitched in my throat as my middle finger ran along my wet slit, which oozed with liquid heat. There was no denying what my body wanted, and though I couldn't have the real thing yet, I still had to seek release somehow.

My fingers started to move back and forth, gently parting the folds of flesh to explore deeper. When it slid over my hardened clit, I almost gasped with the pleasure that suddenly coursed through me.

I adjusted myself in the bed and bit my lips as I rubbed the most sensitive spot into circles. I moaned as I thought back to Cullen and what it would be like to have him do this. Of course, his fingers would be much bigger as they left my clit and went to my drenched hole.

As I drove my finger inside my warmth, my back arched on the bed, and I gripped the sheets with another hand. I drove that finger back and forth, listening to the sound of my aroused sex. It made me even wetter, filling me with the urge to go deeper.

I closed my eyes as I did just that, an array of pleasure filling me. But the longer I pleasured myself, the more the need increased. I decided to add another finger, my lips parting as a sigh left my lips. I was soaked and knew that the evidence would probably be visible on the sheets when I was finished.

Still, I didn't stop. Two fingers felt like I was stretched to the limit – like the way I'd want Cullen to stretch me with his manhood. I went deeper, envisioning him in my mind.

He filled me with deep strokes while he towered over me, his hips rolling back and forth as my insides convulsed around him. My body moved on the bed by the force of his thrusts, his full length buried to the hilt. Just then, I shoved my fingers to the limit until I felt a barrier and stiffened as a bolt of pleasure riddled my body.

I wanted this to go on as long as possible but knew I didn't have much time with Cullen's face in mind. I let my fingers stay buried, flickering them on my flesh and moaning as the pleasure increased inside me. It grew gradually while my heart raced frantically. I lifted my ass off the bed and whimpered as my orgasm crashed into me.

Pulling my fingers out, I went to thrash my clit, my body quivering as I climbed the high of my release.

I was breathing heavily in the aftermath; sweat beaded on my forehead while the temperature in the room rose a few degrees. I clamped my legs shut, still basking in the small aftershocks that riddled my form.

I felt so light afterward, like I'd been carrying a load that had been lifted off my shoulders. It was great, but as amazing as it was, I knew I'd never truly be satisfied until I got the real thing.

Chapter 3

Cullen

Just when I thought I'd secluded myself enough from people, she had to come along. One of the reasons for living away from people was the peace it brought. Plus, I knew that a few people probably felt better with me some distance away from them.

When I had bought the old log cabin, I'd been aware of the other one behind me. I just never thought someone would really buy the place.

I never expected that it would be someone so pretty, either. The very first day, I'd thought I'd been seeing things when the petite woman walked up to me in leggings that showed every curve of her shapely legs. I'd seen beautiful women in Nevis, but none compared to this one with her beautiful tanned skin that seemed to glow under the sun, which we'd been lucky to have. Her hair seemed like it had been caught ablaze with long orange tresses that fell over her tiny tits and down her small waist.

My cock had acknowledged her right away, a stirring that I knew wouldn't go away anytime soon. There was so much I wanted to know about her in that moment. Heck, I wanted to grab her and fuck her against my cabin walls, but I had to keep my guard up. I wasn't the luckiest bastard when it came to women and had sworn myself off them. All of them were tempting vixens with the heart of the devil, and I knew I'd be better off without them.

Still, this one had affected me in ways I'd felt with no other. It was more than about fucking her senseless. It was just a need to have her in every way possible.

But I knew the cold shoulder would be better for the two of us. The town's people would corrupt her mind soon enough, and she'd be just like the others. I knew that would be the case and didn't want to waste my time regretting anything.

When Rosco had called to help with the repairs, my first instinct was to say no, but although my mind wanted to stay as far away from her as possible, my body wanted to draw closer. I had given in to the latter, thinking I'd just do the job and be on my way.

I never expected the tease, and I never expected to be so affected by it. In the past, I wouldn't pass up on the opportunity to have her pale pink lips on mine, but my experiences had taught me control. As hard as it was to do, I had to leave her there. I've been through enough to know not to concede to the wiles of a woman.

Something told me this one was different, but I didn't have any real reason to testify to that thought. Yet, I found myself in the wee hours of the night, watching her cabin like a guard dog, watching to see if anyone would want to hurt her.

It was silly; the woman was nothing more than a stranger to me, yet I still felt this sense of obligation as if she were mine to keep.

The idea of her being mine crossed my thoughts and filled me with something I hadn't felt in years. I'd give anything to rut inside her tightness, squeeze her small tits in my hand and suck on her soft lips, but I had to get her out of my head. I had to; it wasn't healthy, and she was no doubt a temptress. I've had my share of those, and it didn't end well in the past.

I reached for a cigarette and lit it, taking a few draws before I pressed it in the table and decided to head to bed, but sleep didn't come that easily.

The following morning, I had enough time on my hands to complete the job, but I figured I'd give myself some time away from Jenna. Maybe a day would clear my head – allow me to see reason and not just a desirable woman. From where I stood in the yard, I could see her walking about and knew it couldn't be something I could get tired of seeing. Her redhead was the first thing you saw in the sun, moving about in the greenery surrounding her. I was tempted to walk over and change my mind about the repairs, but I knew I wouldn't be doing myself any favors.

So, instead, I went on my usual job as a lumberjack, rounding up some fallen trees from the day before and transporting them to the sawmill. When I got back, it was getting dark, but I picked up some food at the diner in town and headed home in my pickup.

I spotted Jenna walking home, a shopping bag in hand, as she tried to walk over the small hill. I almost smiled at her misery but drove up towards her and stopped at her feet.

"Get in," I said, watching as her cheeks flamed while she stood there, giving it some thought.

She glanced at the bags in her hands and the path ahead as if working out the distance and her capabilities in her head.

"You're just a ray of sunshine, aren't you?" She quipped, and I resisted the urge to smile.

"You shouldn't stay out this late in a strange place."

"Yeah, and here I am, taking a ride from a stranger. Guess I didn't do well in stranger danger education," she laughed humorlessly as she climbed in.

"Guess not," I mumbled.

A pregnant silence fell between us. I could tell she wanted to say more, but I didn't ask about it. It was better this way, anyway. But the silence alerted me to a few things, such as her fruity perfume that lingered in my nostrils. I knew that I wouldn't forget the scent anytime soon and quite frankly, I didn't want to. Having her so close was doing things to me, things that I'd tried so hard to fight against. There was a stirring in my cock, and I knew that if I allowed myself to think about her, I'd be sporting a boner that I couldn't hide.

When her cabin came into view, I almost blew a sigh of relief. She opened the door and hopped out, pausing as she glanced at me.

"Er– would you like to come over for dinner?" She asked, and my brows furrowed in wonderment. That was the last thing I expected.

"I got dinner in town," I said, glancing at the paper bag sitting on the dashboard.

She bit her lips before her eyes lit up again. "We could eat together; I have a bottle of wine to spare," she smiled.

I should say no, but I was intrigued by her. Everything about her. Whether she would damn me to hell, I didn't know, but I was willing to take the risk for tonight.

"Fine, I'll head over and freshen up. Be there in ten," I said, and she smiled. A smile that made me feel warm and fuzzy – like all my problems turned to dust right away.

I watched as she entered her cabin before I drove over to mine and sighed once I was inside. I shouldn't be allowing Jenna to crawl under my skin like this. She was a temptress, and it was obvious what she wanted.

It puzzled me. Despite knowing what she probably did about me, she still wanted to be close to me, and there was no fear. I've gone close to a lot of people in town, and everyone always seemed to cower in my presence, except Rosco and now Jenna.

She was either stupid or truly believed me to be innocent of the crime I'd been accused of. There was hope for the latter, but I knew better than to hope.

Maybe if I fucked her hard enough, she would get her fill and be on her way. The idea was tempting, but I'd sworn never to get attached to another woman ever again. Although I wanted to claim Jenna, there was something else that drew me to her that I couldn't quite place my finger on.

I moved toward the bathroom and took a quick shower before getting dressed in a pair of sweats and a jacket. I took my takeout and headed over to her place, contemplating my actions with each step I took.

I paused at her porch and mustered a sigh before I lifted my hand and knocked on the wooden door.

"It's open!" She called, and I shook my head. She still had a few things to learn, apparently.

I made my way in and closed it behind me, my nostrils immediately filled with her scent. A sweet scent that alerted every single nerve in my body. My cock stirred without even seeing her, but I couldn't help but think of her small little body and her lush pink lips – how I'd wrap her in my arms as I thrust my cock back and forth inside her.

"I'm in here! Could you help me out with something?" She asked. I didn't give it a second thought as I made my way inside what I realized to be the bedroom. As soon as I entered, I saw Jenna standing beside the bed in an olive-colored negligee that brushed her slender thighs. Her long hair was out and more lustrous than I had ever seen before, falling over her shoulders. Most of it was scraped to the back, giving me the perfect view of her tiny, tight nipples pressed against the fabric of her clothing.

I swallowed hard and brought my gaze to her face, seeing the soft blush on her cheeks as she bit her lips and waited on a response from me.

"What's going on?" My voice was husky and firm.

She fidgeted with her fingers in front of her, somehow shy despite her bold move. "I– I want you to make love to me, Cullen."

I began to harden in my pants, but I tried as hard as possible to find some logic in this. "I don't make love," I said, and she paused for a bit before she moved toward me.

She was now right in front of me, with her scent taking my senses by storm. I was fully hard now – I could feel my cock straining against my sweats. Her tiny fingers brushed against mine, and that's where I lost all sense of thinking.

"I don't care," she said as she leaned into me. "I just want you inside me.... Please." She was on tiptoes, her minty breath fanning against me. I lowered my head, drawing closer to her open mouth. I couldn't stop myself. I needed this woman as much as I needed oxygen.

Her lips finally brushed mine, and just as I'd imagined, they were soft, making me crave them even more. I pulled her toward me, her petite body smashed against mine while I suckled on her sweetness. She whimpered, and I could tell she felt the bulge in my pants pressing against her stomach. *I have a huge cock. I shouldn't do this,* I contemplate with myself. *I will split her small body in two. I am not only big, I am rough. But I want nothing more than to make her mine. I'm throbbing for her. I should warn her.*

"You should be afraid of me, sweetheart," I said, pulling away my lips briefly and clasping her face in my hands.

She looked up at me with those big, blue doe eyes, her skin flushed pink. "I'm not. I'm trusting my gut, and my gut tells me you're a good guy," she said. She had no idea what those words meant to me and how much they sent heat rushing through my body.

"I wouldn't be begging you to have me if I didn't think you were," she continued, moving in closer to kiss me again.

My hands slid over her soft curves to her ass which was firm yet soft to the touch. I molded each cheek with my hands, pressing her closer into me until I was certain my cock would leave a print on her. She moaned as she kissed me, her hands moving to the waistband of my slacks, her warm little finger going under, blindly searching for my manhood.

I had no idea this would happen, but I was happy when I decided not to wear any boxers. She found my length and moaned again, her slender fingers sliding over and under as if estimating the length.

She pulled apart from me, her eyes widen as if caught off guard by a horror movie and her cheeks as pink as peonies.

"You're *hugeee.* No. *Hung!*" her mouth hanging open in shock. Or fright. Or both. She didn't move, her expression was as if she sensed some danger but yet remained still as if she was calculating something. I know she was small and I am hoping I'll fit. I don't want to hurt her but I know my size is way beyond average. Long and Thick. A little monster. And when I get lost in the moment, I can get too rough.

"I'm a big guy, sweetheart," I said, I searched her eyes, waiting for her to back out.

"Makes me want you even more," she smiled confidently before putting a naughty smirk on her face.

"Are you sure?" I searched her eyes.

"Never been surer about anything in my life." I didn't make a move and she observed my hesitation.

"Come on. I'm a big girl. I want you. Please." Her voice was soft, raspy and laced with need. She wanted me, needed me, regardless of my size. "Please, Cullen." Her small hand grabbed on to mine. Her arousing voice makes my cock so hard, I can't resist her a second longer. I reached for the hem of her dress and peeled it over her head, giving me a full view of her perfect, naked body, which looked like a piece of art. Lithe. Limber. Her limbs slender, her skin looking creamy-soft, unblemished, her radiant skin almost a pale, angelic glow, her body looking so tender and supple. She stood still and allowed me to drink in every inch of her, from her round little breasts, her tiny waist and her delicious curves. My eyes lingered at the area between her thighs, which was completely bald, smooth and so small. My pulse thrummed as need overcame me, my blood as hot as a raging furnace.

"Perfect," was the only word I could utter – the only one that came to mind.

She smiled and moved towards me, hauling my jacket off my shoulders and staring at my bare chest when she was done with the task. I pulled my pants down, freeing my cock, which sprang from the confines with a gentle bob. Her eyes were strained there, wonderment in her clear irises.

As I stared at her, and she stared at me, I wondered how such a fragile being could handle my pleasures. Jenna looked as if she could be broken in two, and I was a beast who acted just like it. Still, her temperament to have me drove me insane – it drove me wild with lust.

"Are you sure I am what you want. I can walk through that door right now if you change your mind, but fair warning, sweetheart, I don't do gentle."

She swallowed and licked her lips, nodding after a second. "Okay."

Chapter 4

Jenna

After seeing Cullen's size, the logical thing to do was run and never look back, but I was too enticed for that. Somehow, his size didn't scare me as much; I was just too excited to have him inside me.

Tonight was the boldest thing I had ever done in my life. I had to wonder where this sudden burst of courage came from, but it was already a done deal when I had climbed into his pickup earlier. Nothing had been clearer. I wanted him and knew that nothing could stop me from having him. Of course, there was the matter of his past, but I knew in my heart that he wasn't a bad guy – that he was innocent.

The dinner had been a genuine request, but as I had taken my shower, my hands all over my body, I imagined that it was Cullen's running all over me. I wanted him, and the need was aching as time passed.

The feeling was one I had never felt before, but I was willing to hold on to it for as long as it lasted. I wanted this for myself – I wanted this because it was what my body craved.

Both of us were naked. He towered over me, looking at me as though he wanted to devour me. I was already wet – so wet that I felt it dribbling down my thighs. The need was intense, and it grew more consuming with each second.

My fingers traced the hard ridges of his body, moving from his taut stomach to the place which made me pool with more need. I couldn't get over how big he was – how well endowed with girth and length.

My fingers slipped along the tip, and I was taken off guard by the slipperiness before I quickly realized it was Precum. My heart thudded in my chest as he held me by the waist and led me to the bed.

I fell on my back, adjusting to a comfortable position before spreading my legs apart. His eyes moved between my thighs, and I could see them darken as he grunted.

Cullen climbed up on the bed, looking gigantic above me before he dipped his head and kissed me hungrily. I could feel the dire need in his kiss and I gasped as his teeth scraped against my lips before biting into it and tugging at it.

I felt the tip of his erection at my entrance and became wetter from mere anticipation. He rubbed it up and down my slit, lubing his monstrous length with my juices. My mouth hung open as I stared into his eyes, trembling each time the firm tip grazed over my sensitive clit.

"I haven't had a woman in so long, I don't know how fucking long I'll last, but I'll make it worth your while, sweetheart," he said. A second later I was squealing as he slowly pierced between my flesh and entered me for the first time. *Oh my God he's huge!* My lady-parts has never been stretched open so wide apart before. God his cock is really, really thick. Even though I'm so wet it still stings, it burns as he pushes deeper into me, feels like he's just too big for entry. Tears sprung to my eyes as his hard member breached past my hymen and evaded my tightness.

He paused, his eyes going wide as he looked down at me with question. I reached for his hairy face, clasping it in my hands and opened my mouth to produce words that seemed hard to formulate.

"Don't stop," I begged, the pain evident on my face.

His eyes were still searching while my lady-parts was slowly getting accustomed to the feel of him inside me and the pain fading away.

"You're a virgin." It was more of a statement than a question.

I bit my lips, my eyes blurry with tears as I tried to nod. "Yes. But please don't stop," I begged again as I raised my hips to feel him move inside me, but the ache wasn't quite gone as yet, and I ended up gasping instead.

He swallowed, his face filled with worry and his Adam's apple visibly bobbed as he carefully moved within me. *Oh shit!* The pain is on the rise again when he moves. I grabbed his arms and spread my legs further apart as he slowly increased his pace, my insides getting wetter and slicker around him with every stroke. But still, I felt like I'd been broken in two with the pain that echoed through my body. Despite being so wet for him, he still felt so big.

I gripped his arm and gasped as I writhed on the bed. He was definitely too big, and he could see that as much as I did.

He withdrew from me, and I could feel the cool air of disappointment wash over my heated body. The tears tipped from the rim of my eyes, and all I wanted to do was curl myself into a ball and weep, but Cullen didn't leave my side.

He slipped from the bed and pulled me in, my ass resting at the edge of the bed while he knelt between my legs.

I eased up on my elbows, my heart thrumming as I wondered what he was about to do.

"Wh–"

"Just relax," he said gruffly, using his hands to spread my legs. I feared I would have a heart attack with how my heart was beating, but I laid back on the bed and trusted what would happen next.

My body quivered when I felt his breath fanning against my most sensitive area, and before I could fathom what would happen next, his warm mouth was against my aching flesh. A moan instantly erupted from my lips, my eyes closing as I basked in the pleasure that now filled me. He sucked softly, licking my slit delicately as his hand snuck up to my tits.

I whimpered, trailing my hand across my body as I focused on what Cullen was doing. His tongue then started to stroke me, massaging the spot where his manhood had been just minutes ago. The ache started to fade, and I could feel the pleasure consuming my body yet again. His strong tongue bathed my crevice, stroking back and forth as it lapped up my juices and circled inside my tiny hole.

I was losing my mind because while all this was happening, Cullen had my nipple between his thumb and index finger, rolling it gently and sending sparks all over my body.

My head thrashed from side to side as his warm mouth explored my most intimate spot, his beard tickling my skin but adding a sensation that made this all the more mind-blowing. My hand found his head as the need increased within me, my fingers raking through the wavy mass as I urged him further inside me. He looked up at me with those intense eyes of his, and I moaned, writhing on the mattress.

"Oh please.... Yes!"

"Patience, sweets, I need you soaked enough to take my cock after this," he said.

His tongue started to flicker on my clit, and I could feel myself rising, the pleasure intensifying as my body grew heated. Goosebumps riddled my skin as I rose to my peak, and just as I came, Cullen inserted a finger inside me. I squealed, my flesh clamping down on him as my orgasm overrode me. He thrust into me slowly, massaging my walls with a single finger and making me quiver like a leaf in the wind.

My whole body was in a state of bliss, incredibly sensitive to the touch, but Cullen still didn't let up. He added another finger, knowing he had to stretch me good to fit, and I was sure I would lose my mind from the oversensitivity at the spot inside me he fingered.

"Please!" I begged him, reaching for his hand. He filled me with a few more strokes before he pulled them out.

I made an attempt to close my legs, but he was quick to pry them further apart as he got to his feet.

I shuffled back so he would have some space to enter. I glanced at his manhood, and to my surprise, it was dripping precum and seemingly harder than before. Despite the failure some minutes ago, I was anxious to have him inside me.

Cullen towered over me yet again and lowered his face to mine. My cheeks grew heated when I saw the evidence of my juices on areas of his beard. He didn't make an effort to wipe it off;

instead, he lowered his mouth to mine and allowed me to taste myself on him. I moaned as I kissed him, not knowing it was possible to get even wetter at this moment.

He slipped a finger inside me again, and I gasped. I had just recovered from my orgasm, but my body was ready again for another. He finger-fucked me, not so gently this time, as the squelching sound of my wetness echoed in the room. It slid back and forth with each stroke, making me hopeful that it would fit this time around.

"I need you... please," I begged, reaching between us to massage his hardened flesh. He grunted and lowered himself, allowing me to direct his manhood to my entrance.

I did so with bated breath, my lips falling further apart as I impaled myself with his length. He moved inside me slowly, inch after inch disappearing inside me until he paused halfway. I already felt so full, and only half of him was inside me. I couldn't even imagine what it would be like to take all of him.

My lady-parts still burned, but it was certainly better than the first attempt. Cullen was inside me, feeling out every single corner of my cunt.

I looked up at him and saw how flushed he was from the neck up, a single vein protruding from his forehead. I could see that he was trying to hold back, and I admired that. My heart was swelling as I lay there.

When he started to move within me, my moans couldn't be contained. With each thrust, it seemed like he had ventured into new territory that provided a different level of pleasure. I clung to him, staring deep into his grey eyes as he gave me more pleasure than I'd felt in a lifetime.

Cullen started to move faster, moving further into me while my flesh stretched to accommodate him. He bared his teeth and muttered a curse, clamping his hand around my breast as he slammed into me.

"Oh!" I exclaimed, feeling the full length of him inside me. He dipped and licked across the swell of my breast, grazing his teeth across my nipples as he moved relentlessly inside me. The dull ache was still there, but the pleasure was too intense to give it any attention.

Before I could fathom what was happening, Cullen slipped his hand under my back and peeled me from the bed. I wrapped my hands around his neck, my legs around his hips as he moved and stood with me in hand, his palms on my ass as he held me. I was so tiny against him and felt even more so when he started to thrust within me in that standing position. I was his toy to do whatever he pleased, and I was just as manageable as a rag doll.

He pulled me back and then slammed me onto his full length, and continued for minutes until he pressed me against the wall and started rolling his hips into me. Our bodies became slippery, and I could feel myself moving toward my high once again.

"Fuck!" Cullen exclaimed loudly as he slammed into me, filling me over and over with his cock. My body grew weak, almost weightless as my orgasm started to beat at my gates.

"Yesss, ohhh!"

"Do you want my cum, sweetheart?" He asked, his voice thick and bassy against my ear.

I licked my parched lips and nodded. "Yes, give me all of it... please," I said, knowing I'd probably regret it later, but there was nothing I wanted more at that moment.

He slammed into me again, burying his manhood to the hilt before he sprayed his seed inside me. My orgasm hit simultaneously as I cried out, my inner-walls clamping around him as we both came.

He growled in my ear, and my body quivered as he pressed his sweaty body against mine, still pumping his cum inside me. Breathing heavily, I kissed his neck and raked my shaking hands through his hair.

Cullen moaned as he moved with me toward the bed. His member slipped out of me as he put me down, and my insides clenched at its dismissal, not liking the feel of emptiness.

I lay there spent, feeling his essence seep from my cunt and onto the bedsheets. Cullen came and lay beside me, reaching for a blanket, which he pulled over our bodies.

A smile smeared my face as my body buzzed with happiness. I snuggled up to him and rested my head on his chest while he gently rubbed my hips from under the sheets.

"Thank you for that," I said in what sounded like a whisper. I was utterly exhausted.

He grunted. "You shouldn't be thanking me just yet. Now that you've given me a taste, I'll be forever starved for it. I'll fuck you every chance I get," he said, and my heart skipped a beat at his words.

I smiled as I made circles on his broad chest. "Would that be such a bad thing?"

"I guess not," he said.

My cheeks heated as I lay there beside this naked beast. I could tell he was still hard from the way he was making a tent in the sheets, and it made me needy all over again.

"Is it weird that I want to do it again?" I whispered.

He chuckled. "If that's the case, then we're both weirdos."

I grinned as I eased up to look into his eyes. He was serious, but I didn't need his words to testify to that. It was visible. I flung the sheets from around him, exposing his bottom half where his member was hard and mighty.

I knew I'd be sore tomorrow, but I was still riding on my high and ready to make the best of the night.

I straddled him and positioned myself just above his penis, holding it up with one hand before I lowered myself onto it. A deep sigh escaped my lips as he slid inside me with so much ease, making my heart soar. My pussy puckered, and as I slid further down on him, his cum began to ooze around his shaft.

Cullen muttered a curse as he held my hips and pulled me down until my naked lips were rubbing against his slightly bushy front. His hands moved to my breasts, gently squeezing them as I started to roll my hips against him. A couple of seconds later, he reached for my hips and tried to raise me up, but I held his hand and anchored myself to him. My neck arched, my hair tumbling down my back as I used Cullen to pleasure myself. I didn't want to move; the pleasure was so incredible like this, and I couldn't risk letting it go anytime soon.

I glanced at Cullen, and he had a contented look on his face as he watched me. I didn't stop until I was screaming his name while my orgasm shot through every inch of my body. He came with me like before, filling me with his seed again.

When I lifted myself off him, a dollop of his cum fell to his cock, coating the already creamed length. I collapsed beside him with a smile on my face while the exhaustion ran deep within my bones.

We lay there silently for what seemed like forever until I bit my lips and decided to head to unchartered territory.

"What happened?" I asked. Cullen was silent, and by it, I knew he understood what I meant.

"I'd rather not talk about it," he said gruffly.

"Ok," I said, hoping I didn't scare him away with the question. But he stayed, and we remained silent for a few more minutes until he cleared his throat.

"Six years ago, I was working at a lumberyard in the city. This girl came along, and we kicked things off. It was going good until she got herself caught up in some bad company – some so-called friends from her past..." he scoffed, and the softness that had been in his eyes earlier was now gone, replaced by the looming darkness that had been there before.

"They did some shady shit, got into a confrontation, and she shot one of them. I panicked and picked up the gun when it happened and tried to get her out. The cops came, she ran, and I was left with a sentence," he said with a scoff.

A lump formed in my throat at the revelations. "That's messed up; Cullen, I'm so sorry."

"You have nothing to be sorry about."

"What happened to her?

"She was on the run for a few years until the law caught up to her. I got myself a good lawyer after years in that hellhole and here I am."

"You loved her," I said.

"I thought I did for a very long time," he said with a sigh.

"I understand what betrayal feels like, especially from someone you loved."

"Do you?" He said, sounding surprised.

I shifted my gaze from his face. "A few weeks ago, I found out my boyfriend cheated on me with my best friend."

"Boyfriend?" He said, his gaze moving over my body.

I grinned. "We were together for about three months–"

"And you never had sex?" He asked, his forehead wrinkling.

"It just never felt like the right time. I guess he couldn't wait, so he moved on to the closest thing."

Cullen was silent for a second. "So this is what, a rebound?"

I eased up as I stared at him, taken aback by the question. "What?"

"Are you using me to get over your ex, Jenna?"

I was beginning to get confused. "Wh– what, no?"

He stared at me as if trying to see through me. My heart thudded in my chest as I awaited what he would say next. He looked deadly, but most of all, disappointed. "This was a mistake. In a couple of days, you'll probably be back to your city while you rent out the cabin to some woman like yourself who wants to live out a fantasy."

My eyes pricked with tears. "Cullen, I don't understand where all this is coming from," I exclaimed.

He shuffled off the bed and reached for his pants on the floor. He paused to look at me after pulling them on.

"I don't appreciate being used," he said firmly, causing me to flinch.

"I wasn't—"

"I'll see you around, Jenna," he said as he grabbed his jacket off the floor and moved towards the door.

I blinked a few times, unable to fully comprehend what happened and how everything moved from zero to a hundred in seconds. The door slammed on the outside, and I was welcomed with a silence that brought tears to my eyes. I sniffed and snuggled up in my blanket, crying my eyes out for a man I'd only known for a couple of days.

This wasn't how I expected my first sexual experience to be. Yes, Cullen ticked all the boxes when it came to the sex, but I hadn't expected the fight that had escalated out of nowhere.

I tried to understand his take on the situation, and I felt even worse. Maybe I did sleep with Cullen because part of me wanted to see if I could get over what Kyle had done. But it was deeper than that. I didn't have Kyle in mind as I had stripped myself naked and given myself up to Cullen. He certainly wasn't on my mind when he was inside me, his body pressed against mine.

As a matter of fact, whenever Cullen was around, it was like everything else seemed non-existent. His presence consumed any other thought I could possibly formulate.

I'd thought that the fact that I was a virgin would make him see that, but sadly, he hadn't. I brushed the tears from my face and moved to the bathroom before I went back to bed. I didn't take a shower because I wanted to bask in the aftermath of our lovemaking for a bit longer. This might be the only time Cullen and I ever touched each other, but I still had no regrets. The only regret I could think of was allowing Kyle to enter my life in the first place.

Chapter 5

Jenna

I woke the following day to the sound of someone calling my name outside. I quickly bounded from the bed and glanced at the time, realizing it was almost ten in the morning.

"Shit!" I muttered, quickly reaching for my robe on the end bench. My hair was tousled, and I probably looked a mess, but I scurried to the living area and pulled the door open. A tall, bearded man presented himself on the other end, but it was definitely not Cullen. He had a bag slung over his shoulder, and his pick-up was parked right in front of the porch.

"Good morning, ma'am," he said as his gaze ran over my body before he quickly brushed his nose and cleared his throat.

On instinct, I tightened the robe and hugged my shoulders. "Good morning; can I help you?"

"Yeah, I came to do the floor repairs."

My brain was still working overtime to try and process what he was saying until it became clear. I glanced over to Cullen's cabin and felt a pang in my heart as I did so.

I cleared my throat. "Cullen sent you?"

He nodded curtly. "That's right, ma'am."

I nodded slowly, trying to understand why I felt hurt by his actions. I thought maybe the argument last night was something he'd sleep on and forget the next day, but apparently, he was still upset.

I had half a mind to confront him and clear the air between us, but Cullen was right about one thing. I'd be gone in a few days and back to the life I had before coming here. What was the point in immersing myself deeper into a relationship that would end in a few days? I asked myself the question over and over in my head and realized it brought no clarification, only a sense of sadness.

The thought of leaving and never seeing Cullen again made me sad, and I couldn't quite understand why.

I TRIED MY BEST TO stay occupied for the rest of the day but found that to be almost impossible with the noise being made by the repair man. A call came in on my phone around midday; I glanced at the caller and realized it was my mom.

Muttering a curse, I quickly grabbed the device and stepped outside, almost running as I tried my best to escape the noise.

When I answered, I almost sounded breathless. "Hey, Mom."

"Hi honey, how's it going? You sound tired."

I pulled in a breath and rubbed my forehead, glancing around at the trees and the view of the town ahead.

"Yeah, I'm doing great. I was just er, taking some firewood from around the back to inside for later," I lied.

She chuckled softly. "So, how's the place? You still haven't sent me those pictures I asked for."

I smacked myself. "Completely slipped my mind, Mom. I'm sorry."

"No worries; how are the people there?"

Cullen was the first person who came to mind, and my cheeks grew heated. "They're okay; I met this girl who was really nice. She worked at this bar in the town."

"That's nice. I bet Kyle must be missing you a lot."

I froze, the smile dropping heavily from my face. It reminded me that I still had not told my mom about our failed relationship or the complications surrounding it.

"Yeah, I er– how's Dad doing?"

"Busy with work as usual. Says he misses you."

I smiled. "I miss him too – both of you."

"Well, hurry and get back, so we can stop missing each other."

"Ok, Mom, talk to you later," I said.

After saying our goodbyes, we ended the call. I sighed, thinking about how I'd break the news to my mom. This was the first secret I'd ever kept from her; worse, she liked Kyle. A week didn't go by where she didn't discuss the babies we'd have, or the wedding she hoped would be early down the line. Everyone liked Kyle, which simply made this whole situation a big mess.

As I walked back to the cabin, I spotted Cullen's pickup leaving his cabin, and my heart fluttered that he was still giving me the cold shoulder while I was busy feeling butterflies and repeating the night we'd shared in my head. As much as I wanted to reassure him that he wasn't a rebound for Kyle, I didn't know how to explain what he actually was.

That afternoon, I decided to head into the town to get some dinner. Lilly welcomed me with a smile as soon as I entered the pub, and I was quite surprised that this time around, people didn't stop what they were doing to stare.

"Hey you. For a sec there, I thought you went back to the city."

I smiled as I took a seat in front of the counter. "Nah, I have a few days to spare before that happens."

She nodded. "What can I get you today?"

"What do you recommend?" I asked.

She glanced away in thought for a second before looking back at me with a smile.

"Our cook makes a mean Alfredo."

I moaned. "Oh, I haven't had that in a while. Sounds great."

She grinned. "It is. Should I run the order around the back?"

"Of course."

"Give me a sec," she said as she moved toward the double doors behind her.

I sighed as I sat there, fidgeting with my phone and glancing around the room, which wasn't as busy today. My eyes locked with a man at the far end, and I froze, realizing he must have been staring at me first for that to happen. He wore a beanie, but his black curls still sprouted at the edges, making him look almost boyish. Unlike the rest of the people in this town, he was clean-shaven with small thin lips and small, beady eyes. A smile curled his lips as he gave a tiny wave that made me smile back.

"So when do you plan on going back, Jenna?"

My head snapped around to see that Lilly had returned, her elbows planted on the counter as she gazed at me.

"Maybe on the weekend. I don't know; I haven't even bought my ticket back as yet."

"Place is growing on ya, huh?" She smirked.

I laughed. "I guess you could say that. I like waking up and just stepping outside to inhale the glorious fresh air, and I like how quiet it is."

She nodded, smiling. "I feel you on that. I came here from Arizona one summer after college to visit my grandma, and I never looked back," she stated, raising a brow.

My eyes widened. "Really? That's insane."

She chuckled. "That's what everybody says, but there's just something I love about small towns and cold weather."

I laughed.

"How long have you been working here?"

"Since day one. Worked as a waitress for a couple of years until George decided to make me partner."

"That's amazing."

"Yeah, how about you? What kind of work do you do?"

"I teach at a preschool."

Her perfectly arched brows shot up. "Oh wow, you look kinda young to be a teacher."

I laughed. "I'm gonna be twenty-five in a few months."

She nodded slowly as if processing the information. "You know, funny thing is, they're actually looking for a teacher here. The last one had a baby a few weeks back, and word is, she's resigned to be a stay-at-home mom. I bet you could fill the gap if you ever decide to stay in Nevis," she winked.

"Oh, I don't think I will. Maybe just to visit when I can, but my family and my life is in L.A.," I said.

Lilly's brows raised as she smirked and scurried around the back. I scratched the nape of my neck, my brows furrowing as I allowed the thought to settle in my mind. But before I could ponder on it, Lilly was coming back with a plate of steaming Alfredo in hand and a smile on her ever-pleasant face.

"Enjoy," she said as she placed the plate before me, a pleased look on her face.

"Thank you," I said as I rubbed my hands together and stared down at the beautiful plate of food. "This looks delicious."

"Be sure to tell me how it is once you're done."

I nodded. "Will do. Could I have a glass of Merlot, too, please."

"Coming right up, beautiful."

I smiled as I reached for my fork and dug in, my brows shooting up as soon as the flavor hit my tastebuds. I harped it down in what felt like seconds, licking my lips and gazing at the empty plate. Taking the last sip of my wine, I gave a thumbs up to Lilly who was at the far end, serving another customer. She smiled before she continued with her task.

"I'm sorry if I came off as creepy earlier. I didn't mean to stare." I turned to find the man who had been at the far end right beside me.

I offered a shaky smile, shifting in my chair. "No worries."

He smiled at that, his gaze roaming over my face. "I just have never seen someone as beautiful as you before."

"Thank you," I said politely.

"Can I get you something to drink," he glanced at my empty glass. "Another glass of wine, perhaps?"

"No, that's fine, thanks."

I wasn't in the mood for a conversation but watched as this stranger called over for a beer for himself and got himself comfortable on the bar stool beside me. I cleared my throat and tucked a lock of hair behind my ear.

"I'm Tim, by the way," he said as he extended a hand.

I was a bit hesitant in taking it, but I decided to for the sake of being polite. "Jenna."

Just then, the bar quieted, and I figured someone new had stepped in. But as I turned to see who it was, I made eye contact with Cullen, who gritted his teeth and glanced over at Tim. He paused for a second as his eyes darkened, his brows drawing a bit closer together. Without a word, he moved to one corner of the room, taking a seat around the same table I'd seen him at when he was last here.

"You know that guy?" Tim asked. For a moment, I'd forgotten he was beside me.

"Er... not really."

He nodded as he took a swig of his beer. "Probably a good thing. The guy's a criminal."

I frowned. "Well, he was found innocent in court."

He scoffed. "We both know the justice system is fucked up. Anyway, enough of that big pile of muscle; tell me about yourself, Jenna."

I glanced at Cullen through the corner of my eyes. Lilly had just served him a beer, which he brought to his head right away. His head slightly shifted in my direction, his eyes on me. But then, just as my heart fluttered with hope, he turned around and proceeded to act like I didn't even exist.

Anger coursed through me at his nonchalant behavior. Cullen couldn't see reason if it walked up to him and slapped him in the face. If he wanted to act like what happened between us didn't happen, that was fine, but I wasn't going to beat myself up over it. Not anymore.

I glanced at Tim as he sat there awaiting a response from me. Cullen obviously didn't care, but Tim was being nice, and he was available to chat. I turned to him and smiled as I continued the conversation.

Chapter 6

Cullen

It was like fire coursed through my veins as I sat there watching Jenna. The beer felt bitter in the back of my throat, and despite the steady chillness in the evening air, I felt like I was burning up.

I was still angry about what had happened the other night. Though I'd wanted to relax in the aftermath of wonderful sex, the idea that Jenna had been using me to get over someone else didn't sit right with me. I'd spilled out my guts – something I'd never done before. That too with a woman I hadn't even known for a week, and she couldn't even deny that what I had implied was true.

Although I'd taken her virginity, which should have felt like a prize I'd won, I couldn't get over the matter of being a rebound.

The emotions that overcame me at that moment were almost crippling because some I couldn't quite figure out. After I'd left, I'd given myself some time to clear my head of her, but that was futile as the only thing that I could fucking think of was her. Her beautiful face, her slender body, her dazzling eyes – everything. Each memory of her was like a plague that ate at me, gnawing at every single cell in my body.

Not a minute went by that I didn't think of my cock entering her and how her sweet mouth had opened as she collected each stroke with a peaceful gasp. The imagery of her naked body was a permanent memory in my head, and I knew the only thing that would rid me of it was death.

I missed her, I missed her sweet perfume and her smile. I just fucking missed how I felt when I was around her. Seeing her with someone else made me feel murderous.

My hands tightened around the beer bottle, and I knew that with a little bit more force, it would shatter in my hands. My jaw clenched when I heard her giggle, my head flashing around so fast that I feared my neck would ache later. She still continued to laugh with this Tim guy – this asshole who used women just as much as he used the fucking toilet. He wanted to get into Jenna's pants; I knew that. And she was just sitting there, laughing at what I presumed to be horrible jokes because Tim didn't have a sense of humor.

I could see the faint blush on her cheeks, the way she looked at him as if he were the only living man on earth, and it fucking drove me insane.

I was probably blood red and breathing smoke through my nose, but I didn't stop looking even when people looked at me. When Tim shifted toward Jenna, I nearly lost it. His hands snuck around the small of her waist, and he held her there before whispering something in her ear.

She was fucking mine, and there was no way I could sit here and watch another man make a move on my woman. Touch her.

I got up, pushing the wooden chair back and causing it to scrape gnawingly on the hardwood floor. A few persons turned to look as I made my way toward Jenna and Tim, my footsteps echoing as I walked.

They both turned to see what was happening when I was inches away from standing next to them. Tim's face paled, and Jenna's eyes widened as I stomped toward them.

The only thing that prevented me from pushing Tim over was my already bad reputation in this town. My hands curled into fists as I stood before them.

"Let's go," I said, my voice thick and heavy.

Tim's brows rose as he looked to Jenna as if trying to figure out what I had to do with all that was happening between them.

"What? No," she said, her small lips set in a pout, her brows furrowed.

My chest rose and fell with deep breaths. Our gazes locked, and I could see the fire blazing through hers. I was waiting to see if she would heed my request, but she didn't budge. I scoffed after a few seconds. "So this is your new little boy toy, huh?"

Her jaw tightened, and her blue eyes glistened. "Cullen, please leave," she muttered between tightly clenched teeth.

Tim jumped off his stool and stood before me, looking at my face with his lips set in a thin line. I knew this bravado was just to impress Jenna, but Tim couldn't win a fight with me even if he brought an army.

"You heard the lady, big guy," he said, crossing his arms.

"This is none of your business, Baker. Step away before I fucking step on you," I hissed.

He choked out a laugh and scanned the room to see if anyone would join in on the laughter, but no one did.

"You think because you went to jail and you have some muscle, you own this town, huh?" He spat, twisting his mouth. "Well, let me tell you something, I'm not afraid of you," he said as he jabbed me in the chest with a finger.

My teeth clenched, and all I could see was red. This guy just couldn't fucking keep his hand to himself, could he? With a grunt, I picked him up by the collar and pushed him into a line of chairs by the counter. They collapsed on top and around him, causing a series of gasps to ring out in the diner.

I turned to Jenna, but her eyes were teary, and she had this look of disbelief on her face, making me regret what had just happened. But I wasn't going to admit that, and neither was I going to leave her here when it was about to get dark. She went to help up Tim but as soon as he was on his feet, his face red with embarrassment, I held onto Jenna's hands and started walking with her outside the bar.

As soon as we were on the outside, she pulled her hands away and stood her ground, now seething.

"What the hell is wrong with you?" She snapped, her small chest rising and falling.

"Do you think I'd just sit there and watch as another man runs his hands all over you?" I hissed back with the same fire in my tone.

She scoffed. "Don't be fucking ridiculous!" She spat, and I was shocked and taken aback by the filthy word that came from her pure little mouth. "You don't own me! We are nothing!" She said as she stomped away, moving in the direction of our cabins.

I stood as I watched her walk away, processing what she'd just said. I breathed heavily, but I couldn't accept it. There's no way I could, even though her words pierced me to the core.

I caught up with her as she moved between trees and bushy paths, each step purposeful as she made an effort to out-walk me.

I grabbed onto her hand, and she spun around to meet my gaze, a frown on her face as her face reddened.

"You became mine the moment you opened your sweet little thighs for me. You are mine, Jenna," I said, focusing on her pout and expressive blue eyes.

She attempted to tug herself free, but I held her firm. "I'm not your property, and if you ever fucking pull a stunt like that again, you'll regret it," she threatened. As angry as I was, I couldn't ignore her touch or how her vile words set me ablaze. I was hard for her because no woman had ever spoken to me with such a fiery tongue and so much passion that matched the vixen she was in bed.

"You give me the cold shoulder for a fucking day, and the minute I decided to forget you, there's a problem. Fuck you, Cullen!"

My grip tightened on her. "What man would be pleased to hear they're a rebound?" I hissed.

"I didn't say that. That's just what you chose to believe in your big freaking head!" She snapped.

"Then what am I to you, Jenna?" I barked back. "I can't fucking think straight when you're around, and all I can think about when you're not around is still you. You're like a fucking drug to me, but to you, I'm just a piece of meat to pass the time and mend the heartache!"

Her lips quivered. "You took my fricking virginity. If that says nothing to you, I don't know what will," she exclaimed as she pulled herself free and stomped away.

I held onto her again and pulled her against me. My eyes snapped shut, and heat engulfed my cheeks as she pressed a firing slap to my face. My heart slammed in my chest at the unexpectedness of it, but before I could look at her, her lips were on mine. She kissed me deeply, and I felt it all the way to my toes. But then she pulled away, and a tear slipped from her eyes.

"You're so stupid," she exclaimed, her eyes now gone sad, and it ripped away at my heart.

Unable to resist the fire pulsing through my veins, I reached for her and kissed her again. There was no resistance in the caress, just pure passion, which made me even harder. Overcome by the need consuming me, I groped her ass and pressed her small body into my erection, allowing her to feel how much I wanted her. Jenna wrapped her hands around my neck and kissed me, her lips roaming over mine in a sinful caress. I suckled on her lips like my life depended on it, enjoying the sweetness and wishing I'd never strayed from them, to begin with.

Jenna started to fumble with my belt, which caught me by surprise. It was getting dark, but if someone walked by us, they would definitely see what was happening. She didn't seem to care about that, and neither did I as I helped her to loosen the straps.

I staggered with her with my pants falling down my waist and pressed her against a nearby tree. She gasped against my mouth as her fingers moved to free my cock. Meanwhile, I was fumbling with her skirt as I gathered it in my hands and tried to pull everything above her waist.

The cold pinched my skin as my boxers went next, exposing my skin, but nothing could temper the heat that burned within me. I felt starved, and the only person who could satiate me was Jenna.

She wrapped her legs around me, and I parted her panties, my cock fumbling at her entrance before I finally shoved it inside her and sheathed it with her moist warmth.

She moaned against my mouth as I sunk inch after inch inside her. Jenna grunted as I held her up and repeatedly went back and forth into her warm cavern with my pants pooled around my ankles.

"You're mine, Jenna. Every inch of you." She sighed against me, burying her face into my neck as she clung to me. She was just perfect, perfect as her tightness clothed my cock and her small body pressed against mine.

"Say it," I ordered, slamming into her and causing her to whimper.

"I– I'm yours, Cullen," she softly said, her warm breath heating my burning skin.

I held her against me and fucked her hard and deep, making sure I filled out every inch of her hot pussy. Her soft whimpers were like gasoline on the fire that burned within me, and I couldn't get enough.

She was wet, still tight as the first time I'd fucked her and every bit of mine. The dewy scent of nature filled my nostrils, mixed with the sweet scent of her perfume. She gripped tightly around me, and I grunted as I began to fuck her faster. Her quim held me tight until I could feel the pressure building in my balls.

Jenna's sweet cries echoed in my ears as she came, her insides squeezing and releasing as I continued to plummet into her. But there wasn't much further I could go with my release just seconds away.

I plunged into her two more times before I stiffened, my ass clenching as I spilled my seed into Jenna. I released every single drop inside her until I became semi-erect. Jenna was breathing heavily as I placed her on her feet and watched as she fixed her panties and pulled her skirt down. Her hair was a mess, and her face was flushed, making the view of her the most beautiful I'd ever seen.

She licked her lips and adjusted her clothes while I stuffed my cock back into my pants and buttoned it. I raked my fingers through my hair and mustered a sigh, staring at her. But she refused to meet my gaze.

"Jenna, I'm sorry about what happened earlier," I told her because admitting I was wrong was better than watching the resentment cloud her eyes.

"It's fine," she said as she turned on her heels and headed for the cabin without another word said. I sighed as I watched her go before looking back into the town. My van was still parked at the bar, so I had to go get it, but afterward, I had to make things right with Jenna.

I watched as she climbed the small slope before arriving at her cabin. She reached into her pockets and took out her keys, and she was inside the next second.

Chapter 7

Jenna

I brushed the tears from my face and sniffed as I slammed the door behind me. I couldn't have allowed Cullen to see my tears, but they were all because of him. I didn't understand what I was feeling or how despite how angry I had been, I just couldn't resist him. While I was busy screaming at him earlier, my body was screaming for him. And like the pathetic person I was, I'd given in to him, only to be discarded like old cloth at the end of it.

After getting what he wanted, he hadn't even bothered to walk me home. That was the type of man he was, and like an idiot, blinded by desire, I'd told him that I was his.

I felt like I belonged to no other man but him, but confessing it to him was just an ego boost I'd fallen for. He'd ruined me for any other man. I knew that now. I could feel it and knew that no other man could touch me but him for as long as I lived.

I felt ridiculous, but throughout the heated conversation we had, followed by the rough sex, something had become clear to me. I'd foolishly fallen for the beast.

The tears still continued pouring from my eyes as I made my way to the bathroom and started to strip my clothes. My body was still flushed, and it was almost as if I could still feel his touches – the way he'd been inside me just moments ago.

I stripped my panties, and my lips quivered as I saw the evidence of our lovemaking on the lacy cloth and against my thighs. Somewhere through my haze, it occurred to me that Cullen and I never once used protection. It wasn't even a thought whenever we did it because everything just seemed so natural, but now the thought of pregnancy left me anxious. I wasn't on any birth control. But the idea didn't seem all too frightening. I couldn't picture myself having a kid with anyone else but Cullen.

After my shower, I figured I'd watch a movie and call it a night, but as soon as I pulled on a pair of my pajamas, a knock came at the door.

My brows furrowed as I wondered who it could be. When I opened the door, I was shocked to find Cullen on the other side with some firewood in hand and a bottle of wine.

"What's going on?" I asked, genuinely curious.

"Weather report says it might snow late tonight. I figured you'd need this and some company," he said.

"It's July."

"It's Alaska," he retorted with a raised brow.

I bit my lips and stood my ground. "Why are you really here, Cullen?" I asked as I rested my shoulder against the door post.

"I told you already," he said. My heart dropped, but I quickly cleared my throat before my emotions overwhelmed me.

"I'm fine," I said as I attempted to close the door in his face.

He reached out and stopped it with one hand, stepping an inch further. Sighing, he met my gaze and swallowed.

"I– I'm sorry, Jenna. For how I acted earlier, I shouldn't have done what I did," he said before clearing his throat.

I crossed my arms and looked at him. "You'll apologize to Tim?"

His face hardened, his jaw clenching.

"I don't regret what I did; I only regret making you upset," he clarified.

"I'm still upset," I said.

He looked over his shoulder and sighed once again. "Well, can we at least talk about it inside. It's freezing out here."

I bit my lips and, after a second, pushed the door open and moved aside so he could enter.

We moved towards the living room, and I took a seat, watching as Cullen placed the logs beside the fireplace. He then took a seat around the table, staring at me.

"I don't know what you're doing to me, Jenna," he started off by saying. "It has only been a couple of days, but I can't seem to stop thinking about you. I want you all the time, and if I don't have you, it feels like I'm losing my mind,"

I licked my lips, feeling my heart begin to race in my chest.

"For the first time in my life, it feels like I have something to live for," he said.

My lips quivered, and a burst of emotions erupted inside of me. It was hard to believe that it was Cullen saying these words, but I was witnessing everything as he sat before me with his eyes gone soft – the big bad wolf seemingly hidden.

"We must be losing our minds," I said, choking up a laugh.

He smiled, a straight line of teeth on full display.

"I'm falling for you, Cullen," I said.

"I think I'm in love with you, Jenna," he said.

I laughed, tears resting at the brink of my eyes as I moved over to him and sat on his lap. I clasped his face with my hands as I looked into his eyes. He leaned into me, circling his big hands around my waist before our lips met.

I moaned as desire shot through me. I knew I'd already been wet because from the very moment Cullen arrived at my doorstep, my body had been quick to respond to him. Now that my body was against his, my desire grew tenfold. There was no resisting him even if I tried.

I straddled my legs over his and kissed him hard while his hands roamed over and under my shirt, his touch sizzling against my skin.

His erect manhood was just beneath me, growing more solid with each passing second. I could feel my wetness pool between my thighs and wanted so much to feel Cullen inside me again.

I started to grind on him through our clothes, our kiss becoming sloppier as our sexes ached to be reunited. His erection poked at my lady-parts, and I knew that if it weren't for our clothes, he'd be inside me.

Desperate for that to happen, I got up, breathing heavily, as I shoved off my pajama bottom and watched as Cullen did the same to his pants.

He sat back down on the chair and stroked his pulsating flesh for a few seconds before I went back over and straddled him, impaling myself on his hard length. I sighed, closing my eyes in pleasure as inch after inch escaped into my tiny hole. My flesh stretched to its limit accepting him, but I was happy that there was no resistance as he effortlessly made his way in.

Cullen grunted, hands planted on my hips as he gently eased me down on his full length. When he was buried to the hilt, he drew his mouth across mine, hungrily licking down my neck as I slowly moved on him.

A loud tear and the tapping of buttons on the hardwood floor were what alerted me to the fact that he had ripped my blouse open. My hard nipples stood out at him, pert and pink and pointing directly at him. Cullen's hungry gaze inspected them, his mouth slightly agape before he dipped his head and took one soft swell into his mouth. I moaned, a gasp following suit as his teeth grazed across my sensitive nipple, a shiver running down my spine, causing me to clench on him.

"Oh, you feel so good," I whispered, throwing my head back as I rolled myself onto him.

"Not as good as you, baby," he said as he took a fist full of my hair and pried my head back. I gasped, a bit taken off guard by the roughness but even more aroused. "Your pussy is so fucking hot and wet for me. How can I not lose my mind if another man even dares come close to you," he muttered, slathering his mouth over my tits again and sucking on them.

"Ahhh!"

"Tell me if I'm too rough for you, sweetheart."

"Yes, Daddy," I mewled.

His eyes darkened.

"Say it again."

"Yes, Daddy!"

He grunted before he picked me up and placed me on my feet. He flipped me around and made me lean over on the table, my face pressed against the furniture and my ass propped up in the air.

My breathing became more frantic as I anticipated what Cullen would do as he stood before me. My insides clenched, and I could feel my juices trailing down my legs.

"Do you want Daddy again, sweet girl?" He asked as he reached for my hands and placed them behind me.

"Yes," I said, my mouth gaping open as he held both my wrists in one of his hands.

"Beg for it."

I licked my lips, trying to catch a glimpse of him over my shoulder.

"Please, please. I want you so muc–" my words stopped short as soon as he rammed himself into me, my body shifting on the table that would maybe cause a bruise later. My yelp echoed through the house as Cullen plunged into me repeatedly, his pelvis smacking against my asscheeks. He still held my hand but released them after a few minutes. He was big and filling every crevice inside me with hard strokes that had me clasping around his length.

"You're mine, Jenna. Every inch of you. I'll fucking commit murder this time around if someone dare touches you or even looks at you too much!" He said between clenched teeth, still moving like a rocket inside me.

I couldn't find the words to say, but I knew he meant every word of it. I could feel it with each stroke and the passion in his already bassy voice.

I quivered as my orgasm took its course, my body completely abandoned to the pleasure that assailed every single inch of my form. Cullen continued to fuck me, giving me orgasms over and over again until I feared I'd pass out from all the pleasure.

Then I felt something happening inside me. An even more powerful wave of pleasure building up from deep within my core. This feeling was different, it felt urgent and was coming fast, ripping through me violently. But just as it was about to peak, I felt an urge, like I wanted to pee.

"I want to pee!" I shouted, but Cullen didn't stop he kept on fucking me even after all my orgasms.

"You're about to squirt... Oh yes, squirt for me baby ... fucking squirt for me," he ordered through gritted teeth, pummeling even harder and more determined as if the idea of me squirting all over his cock while he was still fucking me turned him on immensely.

"Come on ... don't tense," he instructed.

Then I felt a firm spank on my ass. *Splat!*

"Bad girl ... bad, baaad girl ..."

Splat! Splat!

Two more quick, firm spanks across my asscheeks. The sound echoing through the room.

"I can feel you tensing ... Just relax ... Be a good girl. Just let it flow ... let it come, Baby." His voice throaty, low and insistent. A man on a mission.

"Squirt for me.... Arrrh ... Squirt for me, my Sweet-Little-Thing... Arrhh ... Arrhhh ... Squirt ... Squirt for Daddy."

Fuck, I'd never squirted before and I didn't want to. I didn't want to make a wet mess all over his table and floor, but it seemed as if he was too aroused by the kink of having me squirt for him to worry about the mess I would make.

I tried my best to hold it back, but he was determined to get the squirt out of me, he kept on pounding, bringing me closer and closer to my peak. The pleasure was doubling over in me quickly. It was too much for me to bear, I just couldn't hold back my squirt a second longer. Then I felt the most powerful, body-wracking pleasure I had ever felt as the squirt erupted through me, a warm thick stream spraying on and on with such great force it caused me to shake uncontrollably as it wreaked havoc on my entire soul.

"Oh shit! Oh fuck, I'm squirting, I'm fucking squirtinggg!" My warm liquid dousing his cock, the table and the floor without prejudice, and even after ten-seconds passed I was still squirting as he continued his wicked onslaught.

"Yes baby, you're doing good ...Arrhhh ... You're doing fucking great!" He encouraged, as my knees buckled underneath me. I couldn't stand anymore. I was slipping off the table, and he grabbed me tight by either side of my waist, held me still and continued to fuck ever last ounce of squirt out of my body, grunting like a wild animal as he rammed into me, giving me non-stop pleasure.

"Fuck!" He exclaimed before he pulled out, leaving me empty and quivering. The warm blast of his cum hit my buttocks, slipping betwixt my crack and trailing down my pussy and my legs. When he was done, a cloudy puddle was mixed with my squirt on the floor, right between my legs. My body still sporadically shaking from just the mere aftermath of such a huge orgasm.

I was totally spent, I was too exhausted to even blink – too satisfied to do anything but bask in the aftermath of such wonderful sex.

Cullen leaned over and kissed me on the shoulder before he picked me up and carried me to the shower. He washed every inch of me with such delicacy that was far from how he'd been just minutes ago. I clung to his huge form as he bathed me, making me feel the safest I'd ever felt in my life.

When he was done, he wrapped me in a towel and carried me to the bed. I snuggled up to the sheets with a smile on my face, feeling like I was in a dreamlike state. After lighting the fire pit, Cullen returned, moving beneath the covers behind me.

He spooned me, wrapping me into his warm embrace, his warmth spreading throughout my body.

"You could never be a rebound, Cullen. You're the only man I've ever felt this way with," I whispered and felt his hold on me slightly tighten.

He kissed me on the neck. "I don't want you to leave," he said, and my heart lurched. I turned around to him to see his gaze as he talked. His grey eyes were soft, and somehow, he seemed so much younger.

"You want me to stay?" I asked, feeling a stinging in my eyes.

"I meant what I said earlier. It's only been a couple of days, but I feel like a new man with you, Jenna. I don't want to lose that."

I blinked a couple of times. "I – my whole life is back in LA. I have to get back to my job once the summer is over –"

"Then spend the rest of the summer with me then," he said. "Let's just enjoy the time we have," he said, kissing me softly.

I conceded to that idea but knew that when the summer ended, we would be right back to this conversation, and I knew it would be harder because by then, I would be fully head over heels in love with this beast.

THE NEXT DAY WHEN CULLEN went into the town, I dragged my sweetly aching body out of bed and picked up my phone, deciding to give my mom a call.

"Hey, sweetheart, how are you?"

"I'm great, Mom. Never better."

"Mmm, someone sounds like they're enjoying their little break," she teased.

I smiled and bit my lips. "I am. Mom, there's something I've gotta tell you," I said as I took a seat and adjusted my robe.

"What is it, honey? Is everything okay?"

I swallowed hard. "Er, I'm in love with someone," I said.

She laughed softly. "Of course, I know that, honey. You and Kyle are perfect together," she chirped.

"We're actually not, Mom. We broke up three weeks ago," I said, listening to the momentary silence on the other end. "I found out he was cheating on me with Emma."

"What?" She gasped, horror filling her voice.

"I came here because I thought it would be good for me to get over him, and I have. I feel so happy, Mom."

"Wh– Jenna why didn't you tell me?" She exclaimed.

I sniffed. "You guys loved Kyle so much I didn't know how to break the news to you."

"Of course we did, but we love you so much more. Your happiness is all that matters to me."

I brushed at my tears. "I'm sorry for not letting you know earlier. I was so embarrassed."

"Oh, honey! I can't believe they did that to you — I always told you that Emma was no friend of yours. You didn't believe me."

I managed a smile through my tears, remembering that to be true.

"But I don't understand; who are you in love with if not Kyle?" She asked.

Anxiety rose to my chest again. "I met someone here," I said, wondering if she even heard what was said.

"What, honey, you haven't been there a week," she reasoned.

"I know, Mom, but he's everything that Kyle isn't. I have never felt this way before–"

"Listen to me, you're just fresh out of a heartbreak; this isn't love, sweetheart. This is just you trying to heal your heart."

"Mom, I know what I feel, and I've decided to stay here for the rest of the summer."

"Jenna!"

"Trust me on this, Mom, please."

After a moment of brief silence, she released a deep sigh.

"Okay, but try not to be heartbroken again once summer's over."

That left me with something to think about.

For the rest of the holiday, Cullen and I lived like the world would end anytime soon. He took me hiking, and bear sighting, and for the rest of the time, I was in his bed, or he was in mine. We talked about everything and did all that a small town allowed, but as it drew closer to the end, the elephant in the room grew bigger. It was a topic we avoided until the very last minute.

The night before I left, Cullen and I stayed curled together in bed. I figured he was fast asleep, but I couldn't seem to close my eyes, busy thinking about what would become of us come the following day.

"I can hear you thinking, you know," Cullen said, and I almost gasped in fright hearing his voice in the dead silence.

I turned around to face him, seeing the question in his eyes. "Just thinking about tomorrow," I confessed. "I wish I could stay, but I have so many things that need taking care of in the city."

"I know," he said as he trapped a lock of hair behind my ear. "But I've been thinking... what if I come with you?"

My eyes widened, a smile teasing the corners of my lips. "You'd do that?"

"I love you, Jenna and I don't want to lose you – not even for a minute."

My lips quivered. "But what about your job – your life here?" I asked, my voice shaky.

"I can find something else, and my life will be perfect as long as you're with me," he smiled. "Plus, I think I need a new start; the people don't even like me here."

"I love you," I said, smiling at him with my heart soaring with happiness. "You have no idea how happy you've made me. I've been stressing these past few weeks, not knowing what would happen to us," I exclaimed with a short laugh.

"Well, you don't have to worry your pretty little head about anything for as long as I live."

A grin plastered my face as I reached for him and kissed him, enjoying how his beard tickled my skin. A few more minutes, and we were lost in the throes of passion. My heart felt like it would burst open with joy because I would never have imagined that a trip aimed at healing my broken heart would actually lead me to the love of my life.

Epilogue

Cullen

I entered our bedroom to find Jenna standing on the balcony through the double doors. She had on a sheer nightgown that brushed her ankles and was almost translucent as the warm glow of the sunset shone on her. Her hair was out and even longer than it had been when we met. It brushed her ass, bringing my attention to the pert little mound being caressed by the soft fabric.

As if sensing my presence, she turned around and smiled, my heart galloping at the sight of her beautiful face. She was radiant, and every inch of her carried a glow I could never get tired of seeing. But now, she seemed to take my breath away more than any other day. She was beautiful – skin like ivory and her hair like fire.

As she turned to face me, my eyes lowered to her small breasts with nipples straining against her gown. I could see the faint tinge of their pinkness and could feel my manhood stir in my boxers. Jenna's eyes lowered to my midsection, and she visibly swallowed, a little color warming her cheeks.

I moved toward her, unable to help myself as I reached for the flare of her hips and rested my hands there. She smiled as she wrapped her hands around my neck and kissed me softly against the lips. Fire coursed through every inch of my body as I trailed my hands along her body and inhaled a heavy whiff of her heady cologne.

I wanted her all over again despite having had her earlier in the morning. But I'd been away for the entire day and had missed her- I couldn't stop thinking about coming home to her. I wondered when this obsession would end, when I could actually look at my wife and not want to be deep inside her. Not that I was complaining, but I simply found it amazing that I couldn't have enough of her over the three years we'd been together. I was the luckiest bastard alive – I knew that now and knew that for as long as I lived, my cock would still stand for this woman.

She moaned against my lips and ran her fingers through my mass of loose hair. Each second with her was making me harder, and as she deepened the kiss, I knew there was no turning back.

"How did I become so lucky?" I asked as I kissed along her cheeks and then to her neck.

"I could ask the same thing about myself," she said as she reached for my cock. The breath hitched in my throat as her slender fingers wrapped around the length of it.

Pulling her up into my arms, I carried her inside the bedroom and dropped her on the bed. Her gown shifted, leaving one of her ripe nipples exposed to my hungry gaze.

"Fuck!"

Feeling like time was against me, I pulled off my shorts and moved between Jenna's legs. She gathered her gown over her hips and left me in perfect view of her pretty, pink, bald pussy. Her small hands reached for me, bringing my face to hers as she kissed me passionately. My cock twitched, and unable to resist for a moment longer, I plunged into her, grunting as her warmth consumed the entire length of me.

She sighed against my lips and pushed her hips down to meet my thrusts. My body grated against her; I could feel her hard nipples rubbing against my chest as I fucked her with my face now buried at her neck. I sank deep into her, enjoying her whimpers each time it hit home. Her tightness squeezed around me, and I felt myself spasm as I plunged deeper.

This was home. Moments like this with Jenna made me feel complete. Her touch was like a pacifier, and I couldn't get enough. As sweat beaded on our bodies, the pressure increased as well as an animalistic need to fuck Jenna as hard as I could. I propped myself on one hand, staring down at her while the other hand went to caress her breast.

"Yes, just like that, Daddy!" she whimpered. I gritted my teeth as I fucked her, sliding against the creamy walls of her tight pussy. Her mouth formed an 'O' as I swelled inside her, pounding her harder.

I grunted as Jenna's tightness hugged me even tighter, but I couldn't go much further. With a growl, I buried myself deep and collapsed on top of her, dispensing my cum deep within her.

When I was finished, I rolled off her and laid on my back as I tried to catch my breath. We remained silent for a few seconds as Jenna tried to do the same.

"I think that one did the trick. I'm confident there'll be a baby this time," I said as I rolled over on my side and pulled her close.

She smiled shyly and bit her lips as she stared at me. "I don't think so."

My heart dropped, the smile immediately fading from my face. Swallowing the lump in my throat, I sought some answers. "You don't think we'll be successful this time around either?"

She smiled as she shook her head, and quite frankly, I was confused.

"Babe, why are you smiling."

"Because I'm already pregnant, you big teddy bear," she grinned.

The confusion still hadn't left my face but after processing what she'd said, my eyes widened, and my mouth fell open as joy erupted in me.

"What?" I asked as I bounded upright.

Jenna laughed, her eyes glossy with tears as she nodded. "We're gonna be parents, Cullen!"

I blinked a few times and raked my hands over my face, somehow still finding it hard to believe but feeling like the happiest man alive at the same time. My eyes grew foggy as I reached for Jenna and pulled her in for a tight hug. I couldn't remember the last time I cried, but Jenna's shoulders were soaked at the moment. She was crying too but was laughing as well, and I couldn't get a grip on myself.

"We'd been trying for two years, and it's finally happened," I croaked, briefly pulling apart to look at her. "How long have you known?"

She sniffed. "This morning. I was waiting for you to get back from work."

I nodded and raked my hands through my hair as my gaze searched her still-flat tummy. I touched the spot where the little human would grow and felt a flutter in my heart.

"You're going to be the best dad ever, Cullen."

I managed a smile. "You truly think so?"

"With every bit of my heart."

I pulled her in for a hug again and kissed her softly before whispering against her ear. "You complete me."

Grumpy Christmas Mountain Man

Izzie Vee

Erotic & Forbidden[1]

IZZIE VEE[2]

1. https://www.amazon.com/s?k=izzie+vee&i=digital-text&crid=31LQJTEQYT2EE&sprefix=izzie+vee%2Cdigital-text%2C121&ref=nb_sb_noss
2. https://www.amazon.com/s?k=izzie+vee&i=digital-text&crid=31LQJTEQYT2EE&sprefix=izzie+vee%2Cdigital-text%2C121&ref=nb_sb_noss

Cover Design by Izzie Vee
Cover Photo by Vishstudio on Depositphotos.com

GRUMPY CHRISTMAS MOUNTAIN Man

Chapter 1

Victoria

I dodged a few people in my office corridor, trying to not to fall while rushing to my boss' office. It's a hard feat. Not only am I late; I'm juggling two cups of coffee, a paper bag containing breakfast, my laptop bag and a folder I just picked up from the lobby security. My hands are so full, there's no space for even a strand of my hair.

"Hey, watch out!"

I gasped, braking to a stop. Still, it wasn't enough to stop me from bumping into Oliver, the office heartthrob. His strong arms held me in place, preventing me from toppling over. By some miracle, the cups of coffee remained intact. The universe probably realized how much I needed this pick-me-upper.

"Sorry, Oliver," I mumbled. "It's one of those crazy mornings."

"Don't worry about it." He gave me the signature flirty wink that made the other journalists swoon, but it only amused me. Oliver was the perfect guy—physically at least—perfect height, hair, body—even his teeth were white and straight, always glistening when he smiled. For some reason, he didn't make my pulse trip whenever he came around. There was no man alive who ever did. "Just be careful, okay?" he continued. "I wouldn't want you to get hurt."

"Thanks for your concern, but I'll be fine."

He smiled again, his head jerking to the coffee in my hand. "Things are that bad, huh?"

"What do you mean?" I asked.

"I've never seen you with two cups of coffee. You must be extra stressed."

"Oh." I shook my head, holding up a cup. "This one's for Mr. Pearson."

"Okay, then it's really bad. You *never* buy Mr. Pearson coffee. What's up?"

I shrugged. "I don't know. He called me last night for an emergency meeting this morning. He didn't even tell me what it's about."

Oliver winced. "It doesn't sound too good, Vic."

I blew out a sigh. "You too? And here I was, hoping I'd been worrying too much. You think he's about to fire me?"

"Nah." Oliver squeezed my shoulder reassuringly. "Mr. Pearson is a hard-ass, but I doubt he's heartless. You'll be fine."

"I hope so." My watch beeped with the hourly notification. It's nine o'clock. "Gotta go, Oliver. Talk to you later."

My armpits were already sweaty despite me just getting to work. The uneasiness in my gut told me this was not going to be a fun meeting. With a huff, I paused for a brief second at the large mahogany door and used my shoulder to push it open, almost tumbling over my feet when it flew forward much quicker than I expected. I straightened, meeting the hard gaze of the tall, handsome man standing behind the large mahogany desk.

"Good morning sir, I'm sorry I'm late," I explained, trying to catch my breath as I moved toward his desk and placed a cup of coffee before him. The folder that I had stuck under my arm slipped a little, and I quickly caught it with my free hand.

Mr. Pearson didn't reply, his hard stare remaining in place, which made me more nervous than before.

"Uh... the line at the café was a real bummer and my colleague—she usually works the morning shift—well, she called in sick today. It took me double the time—" I stopped, clearing my throat when I realized he couldn't care less why I was late. "You wanted to see me?" I asked, pulling at my top, that was probably smeared with my sweat.

With a sigh, Mr. Pearson eased back in his chair, his eyes still locked on me.

"Take a seat, Miss Danvers," he said, his tone firm, giving me a clue of his agenda for this meeting.

I took a seat and eyed my cup of coffee, desperately wanting to take a sip. After waking late that morning, I had no time to grab breakfast and just enough time – or lack thereof – to grab coffee. My stomach churned with queasiness, and I didn't know whether it came from my hunger or those pair of intense green eyes staring back at me.

With a great eye for fashion, I always dressed impeccably for work. People came to me for styling tips. Makeovers were my forte. But from the way Mr. Pearson stared me down, it made me double-check the snug pencil skirt and flattering chiffon top that presented the aura of professionalism. I didn't need a mirror to confirm how great I looked, so why did this meeting give me flashbacks of being called to the principal's office back in high school? I remembered it like yesterday, when I'd skipped school to sleep with Brian Matthews – who turned out to be an absolute douchebag by the way. He took my virginity and gave me a heartbreak in return. It took me years to get over that dickhead.

However, this situation was more serious – my career could possibly be at stake. Correction: it was at stake. I could feel it in my gut.

"It's the middle of the month, Miss Danvers, and I'm yet to receive a draft of your story for the next issue. Care to explain why?" he asked, rocking side to side in his chair with his fingers entwined.

I reached for my folder right away, pretending that my expense report was the draft of a story in the works. The truth was, I had nothing the memory of a headline I saw online this morning. "Er, I was thinking about the Ponzi scheme involving our former mayor. The cops refuse to indict him for it, but all know he's the mastermind. I'd like to get to the bottom of it—"

I cut myself off when his mouth tightened, his eyes going dull. "That's something I'd expect Pete to write. An okay story, but nothing to get people to pick it up at first glance. There's no proof the mayor's involved, and even if he was, the story has been beaten more than a stubborn mule at this point."

"I understand what you're saying, Mr. Pearson, I can put a spin on it—"

Miss Danvers, you've been working here for a little over a year now and you came in like a thunderstorm, especially with that head-turning fracking story—the one we broke exclusively. Not to mention the piece you wrote on those kids who tried to cover up their friend's murder. Remember how that issue of your interview with that cult leader flew off the shelves? Have you forgotten the awards we'd gotten for your hard work? I'd expected to see the same drive, but you've been off your game for months now. Makes me wonder if you have nothing left to give," he said, and my stomach dropped. Glancing at my hands, I saw how white they were. I imagined my face was just as pale.

"Mr. Pearson, please. I've been trying my best to find a decent story. I er –"

"You need to try harder, Victoria. Your career depends on it. It's bad business for the company to keep paying your hefty salary with nothing in return. I'm giving you one last shot, and if the story isn't doesn't blow people out the park, I'm afraid I'll have to let you go," he said with a shrug and a derisive twist of his thin lips.

I sat transfixed in my chair, his words freezing me in place. I suspected what this meeting would be about, but hearing Mr. Pearson say the words was too surreal and heart wrenching. Working at Grapevine Buzz was everything I'd ever dreamt of, and when I got hired right out of college, I felt like the luckiest person alive. But as I sat there wondering what his next words would be, it felt like a nightmare.

"You have a day to present your story. You may leave, Victoria," he said dismissively, reaching for his cup of coffee and taking a sip.

Having not a clue of what to do next, but knowing time was my enemy, I hurriedly closed the folder and grabbed my coffee before I exited the room. My heart rate was still on a high when I plopped in the chair in my cubicle with a view of the busy city. It was always inspiring seeing all the activities below; people going about their business, knowing each of them had a story the world needed to hear about.

I pulled down the blinds, covering the window, shutting out the distraction below. *I should focus. People-gazing won't save my job.*

Turning my laptop on, I scanned the internet, searching for something to trigger my next ground-breaking piece. After two hours, and with my brain falling asleep, I convinced myself this was my last day working for Grapevine Buzz.

When the clock struck five, I went home more defeated than I'd ever felt my entire life. It was a wasted day doing research and finding nothing inspiring enough to secure my job.

I drew for a bottle of wine after taking a shower, curling up on the couch to binge-watch my favorite reality series and unwind. I was halfway through the first episode when my roommate and best friend, Ashley, entered the front door.

She groaned when she saw me, her bag falling to the floor as she released it. I made way for her on the couch as she kicked off her comfortable, closed-toed shoes and flopped down beside me.

"What is it this time?" I asked, knowing she came home every night with a similar expression.

She turned to look at me, her hazel eyes a little droopy. "Tell me why I decided to become a nurse again?" she asked, genuinely curious for a response.

"Well, it's everything you've ever dreamt of since we were in high school," I replied, and she rolled her eyes. I grinned. Ashley loved to complain, even about the things she enjoyed. I often wondered if she got a kick out of it or something.

"Well, it's not anymore. I regret using Grey's Anatomy as inspiration," she said with a scoff.

I pull her close, running my fingers through her thick, blonde hair. I remember her obsession with the hospital drama series back in high school. The cast made hospital procedures seem effortless, but Ashley discovered during her internship how far from the truth they were. Back then, it was too late to turn back.

"Things will get better, babe," I said.

"You think?" she asked.

"I know." I didn't feel as confident, but I hoped the words were enough to trigger positive energy in the room.

Ashley blew out a sigh and turned to the television, her brows furrowing when she saw what was on. "Seems like I'm not the only one who's stressed." This time she eased up and turned toward me, her eyes scanning my face as if trying to figure out the problem before I fessed up.

"Why do you think I'm stressed?" I challenged.

"Come on, you only watch this thrashy series when you're stressed out. What is it? Come, on tell me."

I raked my fingers through my hair, releasing a resigned sigh. "I'm about to lose my job, Ash."

Ashley's brows shot up. "The hell? What do you mean?"

"I haven't submitted a decent story in ages. Pearson is giving me one chance time to produce another hit or I'm out. His words. I don't know what I'm going to do because I can't think of anything!" I moaned, smashing a small cushion in my face.

"Wh– are you sure he said that?"

"Yes. I have a day to present a draft and a week for a full story. I feel like I'm stuck, Ash."

Ashley removed the cushion from my face and shook my shoulders. "It's not the end, Vicky. You just need to dig deep for something spectacular. You always do; maybe you're overthinking it."

I shook my head. "I'm not, Ash. I've been stuck for a while, struggling to find the spark I had when I just started my job."

"Your brain is probably overworked. It's been a year since your last break, remember? You need some time off, Vicky," Ashley suggested.

"Nah, I can't afford a break. I'll have to come up with a story, regardless of how tired I am." I sighed. "I don't want to lose my job, Ash."

She immediately reached for my hand and gave it a gentle squeeze. "That's not going to happen. You're good at what you do. Sleep on it. I'm certain something will come."

I didn't feel Ashley's confidence, but I smiled anyway.

"I'm going to take a shower, then maybe we can go over some topics for your story. Do some research, maybe?" she suggested.

"Ash, you must be tired. Don't worry about it; I'll figure this out," I said, not knowing how true it was, but wanting to reassure my best friend.

She shot me down with a wave of her hand. "I'm not that tired. Plus, I'll be working the night shift tomorrow, which gives me plenty time to sleep in," she said before patting my legs and bounding from the couch. "I'll be right back," she said before dashing to her bedroom.

I smiled, more thankful than ever for a friend like Ashley who'd been there for me through thick and thin. It was a mutual dependency from the day she moved across the street from me and knocked on the door with her mom who introduced them as our new neighbors. We remained close throughout high school and college. Now, we were almost joined at the hip.

With a sigh, I reached for the remote and shut the TV off, deciding to reach for my laptop instead, since I really had to research my next story if I planned on keeping my job.

Half an hour later, Ashley raced from her room with an expression like she'd just won a million bucks. Her hazel eyes were wide with pleasure and her smile competed with the lighting in the room as she approached me with her phone in hand.

"I don't know how I didn't think of this sooner!" she exclaimed, throwing the phone at me.

I quickly caught it and gazed on the screen. It was a video of a woman discussing a book she'd read—one that totally awed her, based on her review.

I glanced up at Ashley. "What's this about?"

"Griffin Holt – the author. He's all everyone's talking about on social media." She frowned at me. "Have you been living under a rock?"

"Of course, I'm not, but–"

"Shh, so apparently, this famous blogger, Christine James, read a mystery thriller written by Griffin and it's been blowing up the place ever since. Everyone's reading it – which reminds me, I need to get a copy, but anyway, it's the new hot topic on Booktok and people have been giving reviews and all that stuff and it's just epic. I don't know why I didn't tell you sooner. It's everywhere."

I shook my head to process the information coming at me. "Ok, but I still don't understand what this has to do with my story, Ash."

She rolled her eyes and scoffed. "You can be so dense sometimes. Griffin Holt basically vanished off the face of the earth after writing this best-selling story years ago. No one has heard from him since and that's pretty suspicious, especially after creating a story like Hangman. One would think he'd kept writing, especially after how it blew up back then. But there's been nothing. No sighting of him, no new book coming out. Now, seven years later, the book's blowing up again. People are speculating this may pull him out of hiding. You need to get the story on him."

"What story?"

She stared at me like I had no brains. "The story of why he vanished. Can you please keep up?"

"Ok, but if he vanished off the face of the earth, how am I supposed to find him?"

"Well, you need to figure that out, but listen to me, social media is at its prime and he's trending now – it's a wonder how you hadn't heard about this before now – you need to find him and get the tea. Imagine how your career would skyrocket. Pearson would be begging for you to stay," she said with big, bright eyes.

I bit my lips. "How do you even know this story will take off? It might not be enough for Pearson to give me a second chance. Plus, for all we know, this man is just not digging the spotlight anymore."

"Oh. I forgot to mention. Him going viral isn't only connected to *his* disappearance, Vicky."

"Huh?"

"There are rumors going around about his personal life. He had a wife and a baby on the way when he went off the grid. No one has seen or heard from them, either. People are saying he might be holding both wife and child prisoner wherever he is."

I rolled my eyes. "Come on..."

"Or worse."

Again, I rolled my eyes.

"Believe me; no one has found his family. It's like they've also vanished. Something's fishy here, Vicky, and if you can figure out what it is, Pearson will be kissing your feet for months to come."

I scratched my head and glanced back at the paused video, which had over ten million likes. I tapped on the comments and scrolled through the list, with majority of them asking what happened to Griffin Holt. Some were even saying he'd made the book a reality, massacred his family, and was hiding out somewhere. A chill ran down my spine and I turned my gaze to Ashley who seemed edgy for my response.

"I'm telling you, Vicky. Even celebrities are on this. I say it's worth the shot. Bring the idea to Pearson and see if he approves it, then you find Mystery Man and get him to tell his story."

"And what if he doesn't want to?"

She thought on it for a second. "I doubt that. I mean, who can resist your pretty face?" she teased with a cheesy grin.

I snorted. "Ash, the man's married with a kid," I emphasized.

"Still a man, regardless." She shrugged, smirking.

"You're terrible, you know that?" I said, a little amused. Ashley had a warped moral compass, especially with men and relationships.

She grinned. "Oh, whatever. You love me anyway."

I smiled. "I do. This may be a long shot, but it's definitely more than what I have, so thank you, Ash. I honestly don't know what I'd do without you."

"I ask myself the same thing every day."

I laughed and shoved her playfully.

Jokes aside, I had an uphill battle ahead, one that made me. Desperation made me push the doubt aside. Whatever it took, I had to find Griffin Holt. Deep down, I knew this was the break I needed.

Chapter 2

Victoria

That night I stayed up late, trying to learn everything about Griffin Holt. Ashley was right; he'd gone viral. Social media, Google, even a morning show on cable mentioned him. Millions of people had seen the original video that went viral and thousands had shared, acquiring numerous views as well. His books were now bestsellers and the most popular one had blown up with sales. It made me curious to read and see what the hype was all about. Besides, if I was going to interview the man, I had to get inside his head—at least, a little. So, I ordered his most popular book, *Hang man.*

After placing the order, I scoured the internet for more information on him. There were no recent photos, of course, but I spent a few minutes more than necessary gazing on the ones I saw online. For someone who wrote murder mysteries, I didn't expect a cheery-faced man wearing glasses. He was exceptionally tall, not muscular, but athletic-looking and handsome in a boyish way despite being about thirty years old in that last photograph.

I grew more engrossed in my search, learning about his pregnant wife. She was a nurse who had just taken maternity leave around the time she disappeared. Like Griffin, no one had heard from her, which left me even more intrigued. Where was Rachel Holt? What about their baby? Were they alive?

Ashley was right. This story might be a good shot to secure my job and prove to Pearson that I still had the touch. All I had to do was find the source.

That night I stayed up late, reading between the lines of Holt's very private life and wondering if there was something that hinted at his hideout. But there was nothing apart from information that the couple lived in LA for a while and went MIA before the birth of their baby girl.

I found nothing else, but I didn't make room for discouragement. A good journalist always kept good sources. Tomorrow, I hoped they would lead me to my mystery man. For the rest of the night, I packed my brain with as much info as I could while mentally preparing myself for Pearson. I only hoped that after showing him the evidence, he would approve.

It was a solid plan, but not enough to help me sleep that night. Not when the following day held my fate.

I ROSE EARLY THE FOLLOWING morning and hurried through a shower, determined not to be late. Ashley lay sprawled out on the living room couch because she always took advantage of her mornings off by watching her favorite TV shows until two in the morning.

I tried my very best to be quiet, knowing she needed the rest, but as I dashed past her on my way to the kitchen, my shin caught the coffee table. A screech rang out. I quickly slapped my hand over my mouth, hopping around on one leg, but it was too late. Ashley was a light sleeper, and my commotion had already woken her up.

"What's going on?" she asked groggily while rubbing the sleep from her eyes.

"Shit! Sorry Ash... I didn't mean to wake you."

She fanned at me playfully as she sat up on the couch, her eyes half open as she directed her gaze at me. "Don't sweat; I was getting up anyway. I'm starving." She yawned with an elaborate stretch. "What's for breakfast?"

"No time. I don't wanna be late today. I'm meeting Pearson again," I said as I moved to the kitchen and poured a cup of coffee. A bagel had been left in the toaster from the day before. I pulled it out, giving it a sniff. Not the freshest, but it was enough.

"Oh yeah! Let me know how it goes! I'm certain I'll still be here at the time."

I reached for my bag with the bagel trapped between my teeth and the cup of coffee in hand.

"Wish me luck," I mumbled as I swung my bag over my shoulder and took a bite of the bread.

"Always! Good luck!" she called just as I closed the door.

I ran down the stairs of my apartment and hopped in the mini-cooper my mom bought for my eighteenth birthday, a few weeks before she took ill. I cruised to the office downtown, smiling when I realized I didn't have to break my neck to get there because of how early I was. I took my time, blowing out a breath, thankful my sweat glands weren't overactive this morning. This was a positive sign that day would go well.

After settling at my desk, I powered up my laptop and rehearsed my winning pitch for Pearson. Around me, my colleagues appeared busy, the sound of clicking keyboards filling the room. I couldn't suppress my envy, wishing my month had gone well, too. With a deep sigh, I shook it off. There were still two weeks left in the month. I had time to make an impact.

"Hey Vic, Pearson wants to see you in his office," Oliver said as he passed with a stack of files.

My heart suddenly did a sudden somersault. Although I expected our meeting, it didn't make Oliver's words less nerve-racking. I took a gulp of my warm coffee and cleared my throat, lifting my phone as I stood. There was no sense writing a report when I had all the information on my phone.

I tucked a few loose strands of hair behind my ear and moved towards Pearson's office. The door was left open and as I entered, Pearson's head lifted, his eyes doing a slow-motion scan of my body. My tailored pants are a little fitted and my top was made of a sheer material, but my outfit was still modest. Still, it didn't ease my discomfort and made me wish for a large sheet to cover myself. I summoned a smile, closing the door.

"Good morning, sir."

"Victoria. For once, you aren't late. Good," he quipped.

My cheeks burned a little, but I didn't reply as I sat before him with my hands in my lap.

"I assumed you have a pitch for me. Right?" he asked.

I cleared my throat and straightened my posture. "I er—yes, Griffin Holt."

"Who?" he asked, thick brows drawn together.

"Griffin Holt — author of the Hangman and a few other popular books," I informed.

"Ok... and what does Griffin Holt have to do with your story?"

I picked up my phone and selected the folder containing all the information I gathered on Holt. "He's an internet sensation right now. The world wants to know where he is and what he's been up to," I said.

Pearson took my phone, glanced at it for a few seconds, then tossed it on the desk.

"BookTok is going crazy over him," I added.

His brows furrowed. "BookTok?"

"Yes, it's the side of TikTok that focuses entirely on books."

"Danvers, this isn't reader's digest. No one wants to know about an author," he said, his tone flat.

I swallowed. "That's not true. There's a mystery surrounding his disappearance; rumors that have piqued people's curiosity even more — just take a look please."

I handed him the phone again, suppressing my relief when he skipped through the contents of my folder. He paused on a video, his forehead creasing as he listened to the commentary about the author.

"Read the comments," I prodded.

He tapped the screen and scrolled through the list of comments, his expression growing more intrigued as he read.

Optimism filled me. "I'm sure no one has contacted him –"

"And you can?" he asked, a brow raised.

"I can," I said firmly, hoping he read my smile for the confidence I didn't feel. "Wherever he is, I can find him and get a story."

He stared at me, his gaze never leaving mine as if he wanted to find the credibility in my words. My posture remained straight as he sized me up. Pearson knew he was intimidating and mostly used it to his advantage. Today, I was determined to not let him get to me.

"Okay," he finally said. "I'm giving you a few days to get your story. If this falls through, you're out, got it?" He returned my phone and I took it with a nod, surprised when he didn't let go.

"You should be lucky I like you, Danvers. Otherwise, you'd be out of here a long time ago," he said before he finally released the device.

A chill ran down my spine. His words weren't professional. I hadn't been laid in ages, but I knew when a man was coming on to me. The unmistakable lust in his eyes made my stomach clench. Pearson was an attractive guy, but his douchebag attitude was such a turnoff. I wasn't that desperate for a man in my life. I hoped he wouldn't try to make a move. The last thing I wanted was another interference with my job.

Maybe I'm overthinking it. I've been out of the game for two years, anyway.

Two years ago, broke up with a Jeremy, a guy I'd been seeing for a few months when I realized he only dated me for money and an occasional place to stay when he had issues with his roommate. Since then, I'd been celibate, focusing on work.

"Are you still here, Danvers?" Pearson asked, doing that slow-motion scan of my body again. "Is there something else you needed?"

With a quick headshake, I hurried from his office, still feeling his gaze on me as I left, relieved when I finally reached my desk and in my chair – away from his prying eyes.

I didn't waste time relaxing. Not when my ass was now on the clock. Lifting my phone, I quickly dialed a number and waited patiently for an answer. It came after the first ring.

"Heyo, my sweet Vicky," the deep, smooth voice greeted.

I couldn't help my smile. "Is that how you greet someone you haven't heard from in ages?"

James, affectionately known as Jimmy, my friend from college choked a laugh. "And whose fault is that? I'm sure if you check your inbox, there's a ton of unanswered messages from me."

I bit my lips and cringed, knowing that to be true. "Er– I've been crazy busy, Jimmy. I'm sorry."

"Yeah, yeah. That's always your excuse isn't it? I won't hold it against you, though." He chuckled. "What can I help you with, sweetheart?"

I felt horrible asking a favor after I ignored his messages, but Jimmy had gotten the gist from college after I'd made it clear countless times. We couldn't be anything more than friends.

"I er– I need you to find someone for me."

"Who's that?"

"Griffin Holt," I said softly, sliding down in my seat.

"Griffin Holt," he muttered, as if the name meant something to him. "You mean that author dude everyone's been talkin' bout?"

My eyes widened. "You've seen it too!"

"Yeah, I can barely scroll on my TikTok without seeing some mention of the guy. I see him more than my family!" He laughed and I joined in.

"Yeah well, I want to run a story on him, but I need to find him first."

"That's gonna be tough, Vic. He's been MIA, or did you miss that part?"

"Yeah, but I trust your skills." Jimmy was the best tracker I knew. He got hired for an internship by a well-known security firm before we even graduated. Within a year, he'd gotten a permanent job as a cyber security engineer. "You've always helped me out of some tight spaces."

"Imagine that, yet I still can't get you to have dinner with me," he teased.

I rubbed my neck, a flood of guilt washing over me. Jimmy had saved my ass more than often than I could count, especially after I got hired at the magazine. Yet, he asked for nothing return—at least not much. "Ok fine. If and when we find this guy, I'll have dinner with you," I replied.

"Well damn, I'll say that's a deal I can't refuse." He chuckled. "I'll find you your mystery man, boo."

I grinned at his term of endearment. "Thanks Jimmy."

"I'll have something for you before the end of the day, I promise."

"Thank you."

The clicking of a keyboard sounded in my ear, telling me the search had already begun. "Don't mention it, beauty."

I smiled as I ended the call, suppressing the urge to squeal. Things were finally looking up. I had no doubt Jimmy's skills would lead me straight to Griffin. Which meant preparing for dinner with Jimmy. It wasn't a big deal. I could handle a date with a guy who only wanted to get under my skirt.

Jimmy was an amazing tracker but a terrible boyfriend. Scratch that. He wasn't boyfriend material at all. Back in college, I lost count of how often I saw him with a new girl on his arm, or the fights that broke out over him, or the lies he told to get a one-night stand off his back. I hated how he played women like puppets, but his response was, "Everyone knows I'm a dog, Vic. Just don't put me on a leash. I hate that shit."

There were no safe women on campus. Not even me, who knew where all the bodies were buried. It didn't surprise me when he tried making a move right before we graduated. He didn't get offended when I told him no, and he didn't back off, either. Two years later and he was still shooting his shot. Bless him, but he would never get that chance.

I didn't plan on being celibate much longer, but I wanted my next lover to be my last. Someone who made my heart dance when he walked into the room. Someone who made my body tingle like the heroines in the romance novels I read. A man with eyes only for me.

Ashley swore that person didn't exist, but deep down, I knew she was wrong. Mr. Right was out there waiting for me. All I had to do was search for him.

Which I planned to. Right after I broke the biggest story of my career.

Chapter 3

Victoria

The day went by smoothly until Jimmy called me back an hour before I left work. I snatched the phone off my desk and brought it to my ear, excited for the call.

"Hey, what do you have for me?"

Jimmy sighed; a terrible sign. "Nothing, I'm afraid. The guy's a ghost, Vic."

My shoulders slumped. The smile quickly faded. "Nothing? Are you sure?"

"Not a single trace. And trust me, babe, I searched."

I bit my lip, dragging my fingers through my hair. "Fuck." If Jimmy hit a wall, it meant there was no hope. I envisioned Pearson slapping a 'you're fired' letter on my desk.

"Listen, this still ain't over. I want that date, so I'm gonna make sure I find him. Alright?" he said.

I smiled, somehow reassured by Jimmy's words and the confidence in his tone. "Thanks, Jimmy."

"Don't give up on me now, baby girl; I'm gonna come through for you."

After a brief conversation afterwards, I hung up, the doubts returning the second I put the phone down. Jimmy never once had a problem locating his target. Would this be his epic fail?

I dragged myself through the rest of the day, my eyes darting to the clock continuously. There was no story without knowing where Griffin Holt was and no story meant no job. Defeated, I left work that evening, hoping Jimmy would call with a breakthrough, but as the time passed, I realized it was wishful thinking. As I stepped into my apartment lobby, my phone rang. Hoping it was Jimmy, I quickly dug into my bag and pulled it out. My heart sank when I saw Ashley's name on the screen.

"Hey," I mumbled as I climbed the stairs.

"Is everything okay? You don't sound as excited as I'd hoped," she said.

"I'm at a dead end, Ash. No word on Holt. I don't know what I'm going to do." I sighed, shoving the key into the lock of my apartment.

"Did you call Jimmy?"

"Yes, I did. He can't find him, either."

"Oh, dang."

"Yup. My sentiments exactly."

"Listen, we're not giving up. I'm sure Jimmy will find him; he always does."

"I hope so..."

"Have a little faith, will you? I've got to head back inside but chin up. It will work out. I'll see you when I get home, okay?"

"Okay, see you then," I said before disconnecting the call.

I stepped inside, dropped my bag and made a beeline for my bed, exhausting washing over me. I stared at the blank ceiling and wondering of karma was out to get me for something terrible my ancestors did.

Despite being tired, sleep did not come. I waited up until midnight, hoping to get Jimmy's call, but nothing came except for the awareness that my job didn't exist anymore. I couldn't go back to Pearson and tell him I didn't find Griffin Holt. Not after being so confident and convincing in our meeting yesterday. He'd definitely fire me on the spot.

"Don't worry bout things that are beyond your control," my mom would always say when I got flustered. With those words in my head, I pulled the covers over me, mentally preparing for the day ahead. I did everything in my power to find Griffin. If this was the end of my tenure at Grapevine Buzz, then so be it. My resume needed a little update, but there shouldn't be much problem finding a new job. The salary won't be as attractive, considering my current employers were the best around, but it beat being unemployed.

I woke up the following morning and dragged myself to the bathroom where I took a shower and got dressed for work. My phone rang and I ignored it at first, assuming it was Ashley telling me she had picked up a double shift. That was the case sometimes.

The phone continued to ring as I dried my body with the towel. My heart lifted when I saw Jimmy's smiling face on the screen. My fingers scraped against the bedside table as I grabbed up the phone and slammed it against my ear, excitement bubbling in my chest.

"Hey!" I answered.

He chuckled. "What did I tell ya?"

I held back a squeal as I gripped the phone tighter. "You found him?"

"Well not exactly," he began and my stomach dropped.

"But I found his sister. She lives in Beverly Hills... I'll send you the address. I dunno, maybe you could get her to tell you where her bro is holed up."

I rubbed the back of my neck and mustered a sigh. "I guess that's something, but I doubt she'll tell a stranger where her brother is."

"Worth a shot, isn't it?"

"Yeah... thanks Jimmy; I'll let you know how this plays out," I said.

"Please do. Alright, we'll chat. Good luck with this one."

"Thanks," I said before I hung up the phone and mustered yet another sigh.

Although my spirits had improved a little, I wasn't a hundred percent confident I'd get the information I needed. If Griffin's sister was as secretive as him, then I was doomed, but I kept my fingers crossed.

After Jimmy sent me Kourtney Holt's address, I sent Pearson a text with my agenda for the day. Five minutes later, I gathered my things headed out. Beverly Hills was just fifteen minutes away. With the GPS in my car and the information Jimmy had given me, I parked in her driveway in no time.

I got out and walked toward the door of the two-story house, glancing down at my attire before I knocked. A few minutes later, a tall, slender woman opened up. She looked striking, her thick hair a beautiful blanket of rainbow colors, the silky length flowing to her waist. Multiple piercings decorated her eyebrows, nose and ears. Her eccentric appearance clashed with Griffin's indistinctive look, but she was no doubt his sister. The resemblance was clear as day.

Her grey eyes narrowed at me as she frowned. "May I help you?" she asked, leaning against the door and folding her arms.

"Hi, I'm Victoria Danvers. I'm a writer from Grapevine Buzz. I was hoping to talk with you, if you don't mind," I replied, stretching out my hand.

Kourtney glanced down at my outstretched hand, her expression growing more confused. "What's this about?" she asked before taking my hand for a gentle shake.

"I was hoping we could talk about your brother, Griffin Holt," I replied, bracing for her response.

She swallowed, her chest bouncing with a harsh sigh. For a moment, I expected her to slam the door in my face, but she stepped aside and allowed me to enter. My eyes scanned the high-ceilinged foyer and the beautiful artwork against the wall. At her gesture, I followed her to the living room that was designed as colorful as she was.

"Would you like something to drink?" she asked after I sat in the plush, single-seated sofa.

I shook my head, giving her a gentle smile. "No, thank you."

"Okay... so, what is this about? Why are you asking about Griffin?"

"Er– I'm sure you've seen that your brother has gone viral recently," I began.

She nodded with a scoff. "Yeah, it's not easy seeing strangers accusing him of a crime he didn't commit," she said bitterly. "I wish they would just stop already."

"Well that's why I'm here. I was hoping to set the record straight... have a talk with him, maybe?"

She shook her head. "Griffin doesn't live here."

"I know, but that's the thing. I've been searching all over for him with no luck. Is it possible that you—"

"No." Her eyebrows drew closer as she scowled. "Griffin decided to go off the grid and he wants it to remain that way."

"Ms. Holt—"

"Listen, Griffin is a very private person and I'm sure he wouldn't want to be disturbed. I haven't even heard from him in a while, anyway."

I pulled in a breath and breathed out slowly, clasping my hands and resting them on my knees. "Please... I won't visit him with a crew or anything like that. It'll just be me. I just want to ask him a few questions and that's it, I promise."

"I just told you, Ms. Danvers. He doesn't want to be disturbed. I can't tell you where he is; surely you understand that."

"I do, but my career is on the line. If I don't produce an eye catching story, I'll be fired... please," I begged, locking my gaze with hers.

She shuffled in her chair and shook her head. "Griffin has always made it explicitly clear I shouldn't disclose his whereabouts unless there's an emergency—"

"I really need this, Ms. Holt. I promise to be out of his hair in no time and if he asks, I'll tell him I found him through another source. Please..." The desperation in my voice was a thick as hard dough bread, but I had no shame. I needed this story. If it required groveling, then so be it.

Kourtney bit her lips and lowered her gaze to her lap as she twiddled her fingers. My breath paused as I awaited a reply.

After what seemed like hours, she huffed a deep sigh. "Ok, sure, but if I tell you, you can't reveal it to anyone else, please. Griffin has grown to be a tough cookie, but he still has feelings. I don't want him to get hurt any more than he's been."

I nodded while wondering what her last line meant. "I promise, I'll keep the information safe."

She sighed, moving to a cabinet on the other side of the room. "The world needs to hear his story," she said. "I hope he gives it to you." I hear a drawer open, then she returned with a small notepad and a pen. There, she scribbled his address and tore the paper from the pad before handing it to me.

"Thank you." My eyes dropped to the paper, a tiny gasp leaving my mouth when I read the address. "Alaska?" My gaze shot to hers.

She shrugged. "How bad do you want that story, Ms. Danvers?"

JUST MY FREAKING LUCK! Of all the places Griffin Holt could have been hiding, he had to choose the coldest state. It was November. Alaska was probably shitting snow by now.

Damn it! Why do I keep taking two steps backward?

Disappointment followed me back to my apartment. I slammed the door shut, glancing at the time and wishing Ashley was home. I sorely needed someone to help me hash out this dilemma. Ashley was always my go-to when I faced problems like these.

Maybe I could call when she took her break. While I waited, I considered on my options. If I took time off from the office, I could book a flight to Anchorage, then find a cheap hotel for a week's stay, at least. One week. That was all the time I needed. Ashley was right. I had the skills required to get the information that would save my job.

But what if Griffin was an anomaly? If I couldn't crack his armor, what would I do next? Based on Kourtney's response, it seemed there was an uphill climb ahead. Griffin's past interviews were lighthearted and fun, but considering he'd moved across states and disappeared from the real world, I didn't even expect a smile.

'The world needs to hear his story', Kourtney had said. There was a great story there. I had no doubt. Come hell or high water, I would get to the bottom of it.

The conviction was enough to spur me into action. Pearson had said he would give me a few days to get the story, but I didn't need to be in the office to get it done. Kourtney Holt begged me to keep her brother's whereabouts private, so I couldn't disclose it to my boss. I sent a request for time off to HR, hoping it would suffice. Next, I pulled out a small suitcase, packed enough warm clothes for two days, then rehearsed my introductory speech for the elusive Griffin Holt.

ASHLEY CAME HOME AT nine, looking as drained as she always did after completing a twenty-four-hour shift. She stopped by my bedroom, plopping down on the bed with a groan.

I smiled at her predictable behavior and reached for her shoulder, giving it a reassuring rub. She turned on her side sighed at me, then her eyes narrowed as she spotted the suitcase on the far end of the bed.

"Wh– what's happening? Where are you going?" she asked.

"I found out where Holt is, Ash. I'm going for that interview," I replied, unable to suppress my grin.

Her expression brightened. "Yes! Didn't I tell you Jimmy would come through?"

"Yeah, you did. Turned out you had more faith than I did."

"Which means you need to trust what I say when I say it." She pokes my side, then her smile slowly faded. "Wait a minute. Where exactly is he?"

"Alaska—Anchorage to be exact," I said casually, watching as her eyes widened.

"What? That's miles away!" she exclaimed, sitting up.

"I know, but I have to do this, Ash."

"Do you really? This is Alaska we're talking about, Vicky. A-las-ka," she slowly enunciated, staring like I'm a three-year-old learning the alphabet. "Have you considered this is biting off more than you can chew?"

My forehead creased. "Why do you say that?"

"He moved far away for a reason, Vic. It's obvious he truly wants privacy. What if he's a raging psychopath?" she asked, her expression tight with concern.

"I'll take that risk. My job depends on it." I shrugged nonchalantly, but the thought of Griffin hacking me to death makes me want to shit my pants.

"This just seems so wild to me. I don't know Vic... are you sure about this?"

I push up on my knees, giving her a direct stare. "Ash, you put me on to this guy. You made me invest in his story. I can't stop now, not when I'm on to something."

She pulled in a breath. "I don't want either of us to regret this."

"We won't; I promise. At the end of my trip, I'll have a story that will put my name on everyone's lips again. Mark my words." I winked at her, but Ashley didn't seem too convinced.

But that was my best friend. Always getting excited over things and then being fearful of the outcome later.

Chapter 4

Victoria

"But I don't want you to go," Ashley whined, tugging at the handle of my carryon. "I don't want to stay here by my lonesome."

I pulled the handle from her grasp, pushing the carryon in front of me. "I'll be back before you know it. Besides, you'll be too busy to miss me."

"You're right." She wiped her eyes, nodding. "Work will be a bitch."

"And Damon will be a perfect booty call," I added with a grin.

She gasped which made me laugh out loud. "Busted! I heard you on the phone last night, Ash. I know of your little plan to keep 'busy' while I'm gone."

"Oh, my God." Ashley palmed her face. "I'm so ashamed."

"That you're still sleeping with your ex?" I removed her hands from her face. "No judgement Ash. If it makes you happy, then do it. I'll feel less guilty about leaving you here, too."

"It's just sex. We're not getting back together or anything," she clarified, looking guilty. I was there when he broke her heart last year. When she vowed it was over between them.

"I said no judgement, remember?"

She smiled. "No judgement."

"Now, help me get these bags to the car."

The nerves settled in when Ashley dropped me at airport, and they grew worse during the five-hour flight to Anchorage. If this interview didn't pan out, not only would I lose my job, I would have wasted twelve hundred dollars in flight and hotel fees.

A blast of chill hit my face as I left the terminal, prompting me to double wrap the scarf around my neck. Lucky for me, I'd taken Ashley's advice and booked a taxi service. It was already waiting for me by the curb, identified by the driver holding a sign with my name. With no hesitation, I slid in as the driver opened the door, sighing when warmth welcomed me.

"Welcome to Alaska ma'am; where to?" the driver asked.

I gave him the address to the hotel and reclined on the leather seat, taking in the view outside. It's already dark, so there wasn't much to see except the white blanket of snow covering the town. Having lived in LA all my life, I fell in love with the sight.

"First time here?" The cab drive asked me, his eyes meeting mine through the rear-view mirror.

"Yeah," I croaked, clearing my throat.

"Business or pleasure?"

"Business," I was quick to say.

He smiled. "Let's hope you wrap up business in time to have a little pleasure before you go. You can't visit Anchorage this time of year without fat tire biking or downslope skiing. Oh, and don't forget to view the aurora lights."

I nodded. "I'll keep those in mind." *As if I'd have the time.*

Pity.

I wished it wasn't so late. The urge to hit the ground running was even greater than checking into the hotel. What if I found Griffin tonight? I could use the rest of my trip to enjoy the town. It was the perfect time for a well-deserved break.

Perking up, I touched the cab driver's shoulder. "How far does your service go?"

He twisted his head to glance at me. "As far as you want, as long as you have the cash," he replied.

I hastily dug through my purse, searching for the piece of paper Kourtney Holt had given me. When I finally found it, I handed it to him. "Could you get me to that address?"

He glanced at the paper then back on the road. "Tonight?" he asked.

"Um... yeah, tonight."

"Lady, this is way up in the mountains. Are you sure you want to go there?"

"Yes, I'm sure. Is there a problem?"

He shrugged. "There are a few Airbnb cabins up there, but nothing that suits a city girl like you. You'd get bored with nothing to do, trust me."

"You mentioned Airbnb cabins. Are they occupied?"

"Usually in the summer. Most visitors keep to the town this time of the year. Snowstorms can keep you snowed in for days up there." He flicked the paper. "This cabin is the only one in use all year around."

"What do you know about whoever lives there?"

"Not much, except that it's some guy. At least, that's what I heard. Never seen him. He's a mystery, they say."

My heart flipped and I resisted the urge to pump my first in the air. Kourtney didn't send me on a wild goose chase after all. "About the other Airbnb's; how do I book my stay?"

A wild thought crossed my mind; what if I canceled my hotel booking and switched to an Airbnb in the mountains instead? I'd have closer access to Griffin, thus being able to work on my story much quicker than I planned. The faster I got the information, the sooner I could take my break.

The driver shrugged. "For most of them, you'd need to book in advance. There's only one where the owner comes in for the winter. If you show up with cash, he'll take you in."

"Sounds awesome. Can you take me there?"

"Well I could, but keep in mind, with the constant snow fall these past couple of days, I don't know far I'll get," he admitted.

I bit my lips. "Could you try?"

He nodded, taking a U-turn, the city lights zipping by as he pressed gas. Soon, we turned on a narrow road and began an incline. Pitch-black on each side, an occasional beam of light that signaled some sign of life, we traveled through the city until I was seeing mostly trees with only a few houses in sight. A few snowflakes started to cloud the windows of the car and I shifted in my seat as I grew anxious. I was never a fan of the cold, but I was this far already; I couldn't turn back. For what seemed like hours later, we started to climb up a mountain with just a path to indicate that this was a road. I could see a mist forming at the very top and trepidation started to fill me as I anticipated the end of the journey.

The car suddenly slowed, the tires screeching. I grip the back of the passenger seat as the engine stuttered. My eyes flashed to the driver, blood draining from my face as fear crept up my spine.

"What just happened?" I asked.

"It's as I feared. My car isn't fit to make the journey," he said, now turning to look at me, his expression concerned. "We need to turn back."

I shook my head even before he finished. "I can't do that. I need to talk to him," I said.

"Who?"

"The mystery guy you mentioned earlier," I replied.

The driver scoffed. "Is that why you're making this crazy trip? He'll be there tomorrow. Come on. Let me take you to the hotel." He turned the key and the engine gunned to life.

It was foolish of me to not listen to reason, but I was being led by an instinct stronger than my commonsense. "No. I want to see him now."

"Jesus, lady. You're more stubborn than my goddamn wife. Well, you can trudge through three-inch snow and risk getting hyperthermia, or you can take my advice – a guy who's lived here all his life. You probably won't make it to that cabin in this weather."

"I'll take my chances." I pushed the door open, refusing to listen to another word from him, pulling out my suitcase with me. "This is very important to me. If I freeze to death, at least I tried." I handed him my fare and swung my handbag over my shoulder, pulling the luggage behind me.

"You're one persistent young lady!" he called after me. "Have it your way. Don't say I didn't warn you!"

A gust of wind swirled around me as the driver reversed down the hill, leaving with the only source of light. I got out my phone and turned the flashlight on, seeing nothing but snow-covered trees. Not ready to regret my decision, I pulled my suitcase—a challenging feat — trying my best to trudge through the snow. The longer I walked, the harder my movement.

It was as if a sky-dam had burst, dumping heavy snowfall on my shoulders. I shrieked as the icy droplets soaked my face, numbing it. What was a gentle, whistling breeze mere minutes ago, now turned into a howling, angry wind.

"Holy shit," I muttered. "What the hell was I thinking?"

I wanted to stop and rest, but if I slowed down, I could be buried in snow in no time. Plus, moving helped to ward off the cold.

Until it didn't.

Numbness traveled downwards, shutting me down. My parched throat stopped me from calling for help. Not that it would have made a difference. There was no sign of life for miles around.

Dragging myself to the side of the road. I dropped the suitcase beside a tree and sat on it, pulling my knees to my chest as I rubbed my gloved hands together. I looked to the fading road and couldn't see much. I'd expected to have seen a house by now, but there was nothing but trees. Where the hell was Griffin Holt?

I blew out a breath and a cloud of mist left my dry lips. Stupid me; I should have listened to that cab driver. As always, I figured I could do this on my own like everything I'd done in my life.

The snowstorm got heavier. My eyes drooped, and I slapped my cheeks. There was no way I could remain sitting there. If hypothermia set in, I'd be done for. I pressed my palm against the tree trunk, using it as leverage, but it wasn't enough to get me on my feet. My knees wobbled before giving way and I land on my ass again.

I throw my head against the tree trunk with a defeated groan, which soon gave way to tears. My body shivered as I cried, resigning myself to dying right there, covered in ice. Would anyone find me? Or would my story end right there in the wilderness?

My eyelids grew heavy again, and this time, I didn't fight it. A soft sigh left my lips as I succumbed to the beckoning darkness.

Chapter 5

Griffin

Apparently, there was an expected blizzard for the next few days. A bummer for some, but for me, it was welcome news. No trekkers up this side of the mountain, definitely no tourists to the Airbnb up ahead. If I had my way, there would be a blizzard every other week.

After getting enough supplies for a few months, I loaded everything in my truck, closing the back with a satisfied sigh—well, it was more of relief at my task being done. I tried my best to limit my visits to town, conscious of the curious stares, ones that made me concerned. Curiosity often led to a desire to research. I didn't want the town to know who I was. Sure, I looked nothing like the old Griffin, but the Gen Z's were smarter than my generation. I'd seen them solve mysteries far greater than mine.

I gunned the engine of my truck, ignoring the nonstop notifications on my phone. There was no need to check the screen. I already knew what they were about. For the first time in years, my books were all on bestsellers list again, an accomplishment that should've made me joyful, but it didn't. Not when it came with the attention I'd been hiding from all this time.

Lucky for me, no one knew where I was, and I'd made great efforts to ensure it stayed that way. Reporters would be pounding on my door by now, ready to snake themselves into my life for information. I didn't miss them prying into my life. In fact, I wasn't looking forward to it again. Which reminded me to call Kourtney. My sister would never reveal my whereabouts unless there was an emergency, but I still needed to check in. No doubt the vultures were circling her house, hoping for scraps of juicy info.

The shitty service in the mountains limited my access to the internet, but I saw enough. Bloggers on TikTok, most of whom had never gone to law school or trained at the police academy were busy speculating, analyzing, trying my case and sentencing me for a crime I didn't commit. A crime that didn't even exist. It would have been easier to come out of hiding and set the record straight, but I didn't want to. I kind of enjoyed the mystery, too.

With a grunt, I turned my headlights on and headed up the mountains where it was cold enough to snatch your balls off, but beyond worthy of my peace.

Light snowfall sprinkled on my windscreen as I drove, but based on my experience, it would be snowing heavily by nightfall. Thirty minutes later confirmed how right I was. The wheels on my truck groaned as it pushed through the rising snow.

Almost home, I slowed to a pause when I spotted a small bundle along the path to my cabin. At first I thought it was a deer, but immediately canceled that notion. We were too far up the mountains, especially this time of year. It was a human being, a tiny thing, nestled beside a tree, all curled up with their knees drawn to their chest.

"What the fuck," I muttered, pressing on the brakes and pulling up the handbrake.

My heart fell, assuming it was a child. Without a second thought, I swung the door open and jumped out, rushing to the bundle. I reached down and pried their head up, realizing it was a woman, whose face was as pale as the snow.

"Fuck!" I cursed, checking her pulse, breathing a relieved sigh when its steady beat bounced beneath my fingers. I slapped her cheek. "Wake up! Can you hear me?"

Her eyes fluttered open for a brief second before they closed again. I lifted her into my arms, throwing her over my shoulders. I laid her on the backseat of the truck before doubling back for her luggage. Her fucking luggage. Where the hell was she going in this weather?

Dashing back to the front, I started my truck and amped up the heat before heading to the house. Before even cutting the engine, I jumped out, taking her in my arms again. She was still asleep, although some color had returned to her cheeks. Even in this state, there was no hiding how beautiful she was, with a small, round face flattered by long lashes, a straight nose and the perfect full lips.

I laid her on the couch and wasted no time getting blankets to cover her up. Next, I moved to the fireplace, taking some freshly chopped logs and starting a fire. I glanced over to her, my eyes stationed on the rise and fall of her chest. The wise thing to do was get her out of those clothes, but she might be offended by a stranger removing them without permission.

I imagined her getting frantic, getting her lawyers involved, which meant pushing me in the spotlight. But damp, cold clothes weren't going to do her any good, so I decided to risk it, anyway. With a prayer on my lips, I stripped her coat and boots. She wore a sweater underneath which seemed fine, but her pants were soaked to her skin.

"Shit," I muttered, taking off her hat, watching the lustrous brown hair spilling from it, covering half of her petite face. Not knowing how to go about doing the rest of her clothes, I paused and stared down at her, hoping she would wake up to do this herself. But she was out cold – literally, and if I didn't help this stupid little damsel in distress, hypothermia could set in.

I laced a blanket over her bottom half and snaked my fingers beneath it before hooking the waistband of her pants and tugging at it. My fingers grazed against her soft skin and I gritted my teeth before I gave another hard tug that dragged it to her knees. I adjusted the blanket, knowing I'd feel guilty if I glimpsed even a bit of skin.

It felt wrong to undress her while she lay unconscious, but it was the sensible thing to do. When she woke up, I'd have a clean conscience, anyway. It was either save her life or leave her to pneumonia's mercy.

With one last pull, the pants slid over her feet and I quickly placed another blanket over her for extra warmth. She stayed snuggled there while I wondered if my efforts were enough. Was it ever?

With a sigh, I moved to the kitchen to make a pot of coffee. There was a long night ahead. No way could I sleep until she woke up. I filled my mug and added a spoonful of sugar while pondering over who she was. Except for Alan, my closest neighbor, the cabins remained empty this time of year because of the constant blizzards. Why was she here on this side of the mountain? There were no sign of anyone else on the road, so why did she come alone? The last thing I wanted was trouble, and a gnawing feeling in my stomach told she was exactly that.

I could only hope she recovered soon. As soon as she woke, I'd send her on her way.

Chapter 6

Victoria

My eyes fluttered open, my nose instantly picking up the scent of freshly brewed coffee. My mind registered how blissfully warm and comfortable I was, everything soft around me, fresh air filling my lungs as I took breaths. I couldn't help my smile, thinking I'd arrived in heaven, but as the seconds passed, my memories returned. The last thing I remembered was lying on the side of the road, so cold I couldn't move. I remembered the icy wind stinging my face, my entire body going numb before I lost consciousness. I didn't need to look around to know I wasn't on the side of the road anymore, which meant someone found and brought me here.

I bolted upright, my heart hammering in my chest as I took in the impressive floor-to-ceiling fireplace in the massive room. The walls and ceilings were planked with reclaimed pine, with a chandelier made of antique wagon wheel. A wood-planked coffee table stood between a pair of tufted sofas, one of which I'd been laying on. The room looked cozy, but it didn't ease my fear. Where was I? Who brought me here?

As if summoned by my thoughts, a giant stepped through the door, surprise on his face when he saw me. He stopped short; his thick arms laden with firewood. His blue eyes slowly ran over me. A chill ran down my spine despite the warmth in the room, and I wrapped my arms around my body.

"Good, you're awake," he grunted. "Finally, I can sleep."

His words made no sense to me, not when I had no clue what was going on. "W– how did I get here?" I asked, looking down and realizing I didn't have my coat on and — I flashed the blankets from around me without thinking of him being there. My bare thighs welcomed me. I gasped, seeing all I had on was my cotton panties.

My chest tightened with panic. I could feel the blood draining from my face. "What the fuck? What did you do?" I asked, heat coursing through my body.

He grunted, staring down at me with thick brows drawn together.

"You had no right to take my clothes off! I– what else did you do to me?" I snapped, pulling the blankets over my body.

His gaze lingered for a while, giving me those tingles again, but they faded when he shifted his eyes and walked to the fireplace. I glared at his broad back, struggling with the urge to throw a pillow at him. I hated being ignored.

He came back toward me after dumping fresh logs on the fireplace. I waited for him to say something, but he walked past me without a word. Pissed, I shuffled from the couch, the blanket wrapped around me. "Are you going to answer me, or do I need to call my lawyer?"

I swore I heard him growl, but maybe I imagined it. I had no time to decide if it was real, because he'd whipped around, his glare sharp enough to cut tires. My eyes locked with his, and two thoughts immediately ran through my mind. One: how incredibly beautiful his blue eyes were, and two: how familiar he looked.

Before I said a word, he moved past me, grabbed my clothes from the armrest of the sofa and shoved them at me. "Get out."

I took my clothes, still studying his face, my brain connecting the pieces of the puzzle. This was Griffin Holt – no denying it. He wasn't the slim, athletic man I'd seen in the photos online. His body was now six feet of thick, delicious muscles. Gone was the kindness in his eyes. They were now like ice.

Despite the chill surrounding him and the rudeness in his tone, I refused to believe he had no saving grace. He saved me from freezing to death, after all, which counted for something, right?

Maybe I was too harsh with my approach. There was no excuse for going off on him, despite waking up flustered in a strange place. I should have responded more gently.

Clearing my throat, I moved closer to him. "I'm sorry about the whole lawyer thing. I didn't mean to come off so ungrateful. Thank you for saving me."

"I don't give a rat's ass about your apology. Leave." He grabbed my shoulder, steering me toward the front door.

"Wait a minute, let me get my clothes on, at least!" I shrieked, shrugging him off and stepping into my pants. His behavior was a little too harsh, considering I'd just apologized. Was his wife and child home? Was he trying to protect them from strangers?

If so, why?

"Shit."

Griffin stood at the open front door, his broad back blocking the view outside. I didn't need to see, though. The roaring wind was enough to confirm there was a snowstorm outside. Which meant I couldn't leave. Which also meant I'd be holed up with Griffin Holt and the secrets between these walls.

A welcomed opportunity, but one that could backfire if I didn't play my cards right. I could tell him who I was, but I doubted he would give me a story, especially after being in such a hurry to put me out. He wouldn't take kindly to a reporter trying to dig into his past.

Which meant… oh, boy.

For the first time, I'd lie for what I wanted.

"You're lucky I'm not a heartless piece of shit," he muttered, walking past me. "You're welcome to stay until the storm blows over."

I contained my glee, watching as he moved to the window and yanking up the blinds. From where I stood, there was nothing to see except the mist that had formed on the windows, but from Griffin's point of view, there was something there.

He muttered a low curse, raking his hand through his thick, long hair, leaving me with a sudden urge to run my fingers through it, too. My eyes dropped to his back, covered in a long-sleeved sweatshirt and his firm buttocks strapped in a pair of jeans. I still couldn't believe this was the same man I saw online. Back then he seemed approachable, with his friendly smile, spectacles and polo shirts. Now, he was like a tall, muscled god; beautiful but unapproachable.

"Spare room's empty," he mumbled under his breath, barely audible.

"Thank you. As soon as the snowstorm ends, I'll be out of your hair," I reassured him. *Hopefully, it lasts long enough to get my story.*

Griffin grunted, making a slow turn to face me. "I've been trying to figure this out since I found you on the road. Why did you come here?" he asked, a frown on his face.

His question threw me off guard. The chill in his eyes triggered my nervousness. I racked my brain for a suitable explanation. If he knew who I was, he'd probably throw me out, but I was just a stupid, unsuspecting stranger, then maybe he would give me a story without me even asking for it.

"I er... booked an Airbnb close by, but the cab driver refused to go further when the snowstorm began. I thought I'd make it before the storm got worse, but I underestimated the damn thing."

Griffin stared me down, his intense gaze piercing me. I tried to squirm, knowing my actions could betray me. A long beat passed. I slowly released my breath, waiting for him to break eye contact. Heck, if someone ever got interrogated by this guy, they'd spill within seconds.

"You took the wrong route," he finally said, his voice deep and growly.

I shrugged. "I saw the road, thought it would lead me there."

"Hmm." He glanced to the window. "One would think you'd have the sense to check the weather reports before you came. Where are you from, anyway?"

"Lo—New York," I quickly replied, kicking myself for almost slipping up.

He turned again to look at me, his gaze sweeping over my body. "A city girl. Why am I not surprised?"

I cleared my throat. "I'm Victoria, by the way."

"Guest room is first door to your left," he said, turning to leave.

"Wha– what's your name?"

He paused; the hesitance clear on his face. "Griffin."

A tiny smile pulled at the corner of my lips. "Thank you, Griffin."

He left without another word, his huge body disappearing down the hall. I sighed, turning to the blazing fire pit, the crackling wood soothing my nerves a bit. I wrapped the huge blanket around me, the scent of fresh soap washing over me. I took a sniff, noticing the hint of male perfume. No doubt Griffin's huge body had been wrapped in it at some point.

I wandered around the living area, checking out the space. Somehow, I'd expected a sign that someone else lived here, but there was nothing – not a single photo in sight – not even of him. I thought of his family, the wife who was pregnant with his child. Where were they? Why weren't they with him? Did Griffin divorce his wife?

My mind ran all over, trying to figure out the mystery behind this grumpy man. It was somewhat scary being alone in his, presence, especially after the rumors of him being a murderer who had gotten away with his crime.

I expected to feel fearful, but I didn't. For some reason, Griffin made me feel safe. He was an asshole, but he would never harm me. It was a stupid to trust a man I didn't know, but my instincts were never wrong.

Gathering my luggage, I wandered down the hallway trying to find the guestroom, since the grump hadn't even bothered to make the instructions clear. I stopped at the first door that was halfway open, confirming it was empty before stepping inside. The room looked cozy, with a double bed, a single vanity in one corner and a lounge chair at the next. I carefully placed my things on the chair then dug through my carryon for a change of clothes. There was an ensuite bathroom, thank God. After a quick shower, I pulled on a pair of sweatpants and a sweater then used a hair tie to bound my hair into a ponytail.

I flopped down on the bed with a sigh, trying to figure out what my next move would be. There was no way to determine how long the snowstorm would last, but had the end, I had to leave victorious. Griffin's story would be mine.

Chapter 7

Griffin

With a grunt, I removed the glasses from my eyes and threw them to the table. I pinched the bridge of my nose and closed my eyes, unable to concentrate on a single thing but the woman on the next side of my house.

It annoyed me; this stupid fascination with a woman I just met. This was so unlike me. Why couldn't I get the feel of her small body out of my head? Why couldn't I stop wanting her legs wrapped around me? I remembered licking my lips when she threw off the blankets in panic. I tried to look away, but not quick enough. The urge to rip those panties off and bury myself in her heat almost sucked the breath out of me. I'd never responded to a woman like that.

Fuck.

I blamed it on not getting laid in years. It had nothing to do with her beauty, although, I couldn't deny how stunning she was.

But there were always more to people than their pretty faces and I had a feeling this woman was no exception. For a woman forced to hole up with a stranger, she didn't seem as frightened as I'd expected. Which made me wonder if she knew who I was. That wouldn't surprise me, considering the internet craze.

No. She wouldn't ask my name if she knew me. Which led me to believe she was more naïve than I thought. Lucky for her, I wasn't the monster the internet made me out to be.

Naïve or not, the last thing I'd wanted was to be trapped inside the house with a woman who triggered emotions that had been dead for years. After living with the numbness for so long, it became an old friend, a safe friend, one I didn't want to part with.

With a grunt, I rose from my chair, heading to the kitchen to pour another cup of coffee. To my surprise, I found her there doing the same thing, looking comfy like she'd been living there for years. With her hair in a cute ponytail, a sexy pair of leggings hugging her tiny body, she didn't seem out of place to me. In fact, I could picture her living in my space.

Crazy. I brushed the stupid, sudden longing aside.

Her head flew up as I approached, her hand with the pot pausing over the cup. "I figured I could help myself to a cup..."

A low rumble bubbled up in my throat. As attractive as Victoria was, I didn't need her in my space. I didn't need her around me. Staying in the guestroom was one thing, but to be bumping into her around the house was another. Regardless, I said nothing. There was enough coffee to spare, anyway.

When she was finished, I moved into the space and poured myself a cup. She didn't leave as I expected. I frowned at her, wondering why she was still standing there.

Victoria either misread my expression or chose to ignore it. "You live alone?" she asked, taking a sip and watching me from over the rim.

Without replying, I added sugar to my cup, my jaw tightening with displeasure. I didn't have to give her the time of day – I was already nice enough to allow her to stay. Surely, she couldn't be expecting conversation, too.

"Pretty isolated place to live in..." she continued, despite my silence.

I scoffed.

"Look, I'm sorry if I'm imposing; I want this snow to stop as much as you do."

I moved past her, but I could hear her footsteps following behind.

"You just expect us to spend our time together without talking?" she challenged.

I stopped short and turned to face her. She gasped, braking in her tracks to stop from bumping into me. Her coffee spilled onto her sweater and she groaned, fanning the wet spot.

"Damnit," she grumbled.

My instinct prompted me to grab a napkin to dab the spot, but I ignored it. I didn't want to touch her again. Not even for a minute.

"It won't leave a stain, I hope." She peered up at me, our eyes locking for a few seconds. A few seconds too long. Something passed between us. I didn't know what it was, but it left me longing to pull her body to mine and taste that coffee on her lips. Not willing to succumb to the urge, I grunted and moved off again.

"We don't need to be friends, Griffin, but we're alone here—"

"Don't fucking remind me," I muttered before I could stop myself. Knowing there was no physical power to hold me back made resisting her so much harder. My cock had awakened from its slumber, getting harder the longer I lingered.

"All I'm saying is, we can pass the time by getting to know each other. What's the harm in that?"

I scoffed as she flopped down in the sofa. "You just don't give up, do you?"

Victoria smirked, her thin lips stretched into a smile. "Where's the fun in that?"

The hint of mischief on her face made my brows lift. Was she really a naïve girl who booked a vacation on the mountain alone—a stupid decision I might add—or was there another layer under that façade? Time would probably tell. Or not. In a day or two, she'd be gone, a distant memory in a week.

Although, my intuition told me that won't be the case.

"You're trouble," I told her as I left, unwilling to stay in her presence any longer. Victoria was like a drug. There was no physical interaction, yet I was already intoxicated. Already wanting more of her. This was too crazy. Too scary. I needed a distraction right away.

"If I'm trouble as you say, maybe I should just go!" she called after me and I scoffed. She wouldn't leave. Not when she almost froze the last time. I wanted to tell her she could go, but I wouldn't enjoy digging her out the snow again. Maybe I should have left her the first time. If only I knew she would be this chatty and persistent. If only I knew how much she would affect me.

Victoria considered me an asshole, but it was a trait I mastered over the years, determined not to repeat mistakes from my past. I didn't want her getting attached to me, either. With her girl-next-door smile, and the innocence behind her eyes, I suspected Victoria was that type.

There was just something about her that made everything seem lightweight. Like the aura she carried around her was something special. But weren't they all, until you truly got to know who they really were?

Regardless, she intrigued me, which surprised the heck out of me, considering no woman had caught my eye in such a long time. There was just something about her that made me want to lose myself in her.

It's just the loneliness talking, I told myself. *There's no way I want this stranger in my life.*

Blowing a sigh, I finished the rest of my coffee and pored over the contents that placed me on the map again. News of me were everywhere. The sales on my books were insane, but it meant nothing, though it should. A part of me craved that excitement, but it remained confined in the depth of my soul.

Needing that distraction, I opened a blank sheet on Microsoft Word, my fingers hovering over the keyboard. My mind opened, releasing my pent-up thoughts and in an instant, words flew around in my head – a promise of a fictional world where I had the power to make the impossible possible.

LATER THAT NIGHT, STILL sitting in my office, I heard the shower running which momentarily caught me off guard. Caught up with my writing, I'd forgotten there was someone in this house. Now, I wish I didn't remember, because the only thing on my mind was the image of her in that stall, naked, water cascading over her curves. I stifled a groan when I imaged the rivulets running between her thighs, caressing her pussy—

Fuck.

I scrubbed my face with a sigh, willing the forbidden image away. Time to get some food and sleep. Exhaustion was doing a number on my head.

Exiting the office, I intended to head for the kitchen. Instead, I turned the other way, walking to the guest bedroom. I paused at the closed door before I knocked, telling myself this was a simple invitation to dinner, nothing else.

Victoria opened the door, her scent washing over me, filling me with unanticipated warmth. She still wore her hair up, knotted on the top of her head while a few tendrils gracefully fell around her face, caressing her cheeks. She wore a large T-shirt that skimmed past her knees, the neck hole draping down one shoulder and exposing soft, pristine skin. I cleared my throat and shifted my eyes to her face.

"It's been hours, but thank you for checking on me," she said, her voice thick with sarcasm.

I resisted the urge to roll my eyes. "You're not a child, Victoria. I didn't need to check on you."

"Then why are you here, Griffin?" Her tone had shifted, now edgy and tight.

"Just checking if you're hungry. There's food in the kitchen," I said.

She shook her head. "I'm fine."

I gritted my teeth, having no patience for her attitude. Pretty presumptuous, considering this was my house.

"Next time remind me not to ask," I grumbled.

She crossed her arms under her breasts, making them more pronounced under the shirt. "Oh, I don't think you'll need any help with that," she shot back.

I left her standing there, almost smiling at her frustrated groan. Considering she'd helped herself to coffee earlier, I figured she would've raided the fridge when she got hungry. If she didn't, too bad. I wasn't used to having guests in my house.

I made a few batches of ham sandwiches, wondering in the back of my mind if she even liked ham. Maybe I could ask her, but I didn't want to. Not after her snarky attitude. Everyone liked ham, anyway. I plated her share, then returned to the office with mine, listening for the sound of her footsteps going down the hall.

After an hour, there was still no sounds from her, leaving me wondering if she was madder than I thought. Deciding to let it go, I went back to work, but I soon heard shuffling, following by a clinking sound. Shortly after, a shatter sounded and I bolted from my seat, dashing from the room, worried she'd gotten hurt.

I found her muttering a string of curses, hopping to steady herself on the side of the counter, the plate of sandwiches right next to her and broken glass on the floor. She had a leg propped in the air, blood running from her feet. Her face reddened when she saw me. I didn't know if it was from the embarrassment of being caught or the pain from the injury.

I moved to her, but she fanned me away. "I'll be fine," she breathed, but her face tightened with unmistakable pain.

Without thinking – something I was stupid enough to not do – I reached for her, my arm curling around her slender back as I lifted her. Too late, I realized what a mistake this was, especially with her softness pressed against me. With her so close, my commonsense flew out the window.

Not wanting to surrender, I hurried with her to the living room, dropping her a little too hard on the couch. Victoria sucked air through her teeth, reaching for her injured foot. A tiny shard of glass remained stuck between, minimizing the blood flow.

"Don't move," I said, hastily moving my office and pulling out a first-aid kit from a drawer. I returned to find Victoria inspecting the wound while trying to pluck the piece of glass from it.

"No!"

But as I spoke, she picked it out, gasping at the heavy blood flow.

"What the hell were you thinking?" I asked, flipping open the first aid kid and yanking the roll of gauze.

She looked at me, her eyes slightly glistening as I pressed the gauze to the wound. "Don't worry, I'm not going to bleed out on your floor," she said, her manicured toes scrunched up to mask the pain.

After reducing the blood flow, I reached for the cotton to dress the wound. "I can do the rest by myself, thanks," she quickly said, reaching for the cotton. I backed off, wincing in unison each time she applied the disinfectant. The pain on her face and the obvious distress made me want to take over—made me want to take care of her. But I held back, suppressing my superhero complex. This damsel in distress didn't need rescuing.

"All done," she said after applying the Band-Aid. She shot me a breathtaking smile, one that triggered my own.

"You're not as helpless as I thought, are you?"

She scoffed, dumping the used cotton on top of the kit. "What gave you that impression, you rescuing me from the snowstorm?"

I shrugged. "Maybe."

Another scoff, and she fixed me with a direct stare. "I'm not helpless, Griffin. I've been taking care of myself since I was a kid. My mom was a single parent who worked two jobs, which meant I grew up fast. I can take care of myself. Don't let that little incident fool you."

"Noted." I raised my hands in mock surrender while admiring her a little more. Yes, definitely no damsel in distress. Before me was a tough woman who knew how to handle herself.

Which made me question, why would she make such a rash mistake coming here?

"I'm sorry for snapping," she muttered, blowing a breath. "I just hate people handling me with kid gloves because of my size."

Against my commonsense, I reached out and squeezed her hand. "I understand. It's fine."

Our gazes locked. She looked down to where our hands linked, then back at me, licking her lips. There was this intense need to kiss her, to find out if her lips were just as sweet as her face. Against the warning in my head, I reached up, brushing the stray lock from her face. Her eyes flickered shut and she breathed a sigh, prompting me to lean in.

We were so close; I could feel her breath on me. One move, and our lips would meet. Our bodies would become one. I remained where I was, my common-sense fighting against the magnetic force between us.

Victoria's eyes flew open, confusion resting between them. "Griffin," she whispered.

I heard the need in her tone, and I struggled with the urge to fulfil that need. The image of me spreading her wide on the carpet was so vivid. All I wanted to do was make her moan. But before I could do anything I'd regret later, I eased back, watching the blush spreading on her cheeks as her gaze dropped to her feet.

"Um... you should keep off that foot for a while." I pat the space beside her. "Relax. I'll clean up the mess."

"No," she protested. "It's my mess. Let me—"

I gripped her chin, tilting her head and lashing her with a stern glare. "Hey. This is my house, and what I say goes, got it?"

She stared up at me with unflinching eyes. "Got it."

I witnessed a ghost of a smile on her lips before I disappeared into the kitchen.

Chapter 8

Victoria

SCREW MY STUPID CLUMSINESS. If I hadn't been so off kilter, I wouldn't have suffered the embarrassment of getting caught like a thief stealing food. My face still burned when I remembered hearing Griffin's footsteps and seeing him appear in the kitchen before I could react. I was still mad at him for ignoring me all day, and my pride wouldn't admit how hungry I was when he offered me dinner. Instead, I sneaked to the kitchen, hoping to grab and go. I was in such a rush, I didn't notice the drink glass perched on the counter. It fell over when my hand bumped against it.

I still couldn't get over how Griffin ran to my aid, the concern in his eyes. My heart fluttered when he lifted me, and I didn't want him to put me down. For some reason, it touched me when he offered to dress my wound, although I opted to do it myself. Maybe Griffin wasn't the villain people made him out to be.

Something happened to him. I didn't know what it was, but it transformed him into someone barely recognizable. Maybe his gruffness was a tactic to hide the pain, but he still had a few redeemable qualities. Hopefully, he'd give me a chance to show the world how decent he was.

I closed my room door, biting my lips as I gingerly made my way to the bed. Griffin wanted to carry me, but I'd had enough of him. It was hell trying to control myself around him in the living room. I would fare worse in this intimate space where the cozy bed gave me a one-track mind. Sex, sex and more sex; I wanted nothing more.

Trying to recall the last time I got laid, I sat at the edge of the bed, examining the injury on my foot. The cut wasn't so deep, but it would take a week before it healed. Maybe my stay would be extended, after all. But could I handle being alone with Griffin without giving into my desire for him?

There was no denying how attracted to him I was. It didn't matter how dirty it made me feel; I couldn't help myself. My body was still on fire from the memory of his thick arms that carried me to the living room. When he touched my bare skin again on the couch, I craved for more. We almost kissed. So close, I could almost taste him on my lips. I hated myself for being disappointed when he pulled back. He had a wife and child for God's sake—at least, as far as I knew.

I came for a story, not to get laid.

A loud sigh escaped as I dropped back on the bed. *God, why can't I have both? Just once. Just a taste.*

For some reason, I doubted one taste would be enough. Not with a man like Griffin. He seemed like the kind of man who dominated in bed, leaving a mark no other man could remove.

I groaned, palming my face. Now I couldn't get that image out of my head, the one with Griffin fucking me into a moaning mess, my knees pressed to my shoulder, my fingers gripping the sheet—

No. I'm not going to lose my mind. Let me find something constructive to do.

I reached for my phone. The snowstorm had affected the signal in the mountains, making my phone useless since I got there. But when I checked that time around, I few bars were up, and I called Ashley.

"OMG, Vicky, I've been worried sick! Where the hell were you?" she asked when the line opened. "I was about to file a missing person's report, you know."

"It's a long story, but I'm at Griffin's cabin," I whispered, not knowing if he was nearby.

"Wait...it's almost nine o'clock, isn't it? What are you doing there so late?"

"Like I said, it's a long story. I'm stuck here for a while. There's a snowstorm going on that will last for God knows how long. Ash, Griffin lives in the middle of nowhere."

"What, does he know you're a journalist?"

I glanced towards the closed door before. "No. The guy's about as cuddly as a cactus. There's no way I could have told him that."

There was a short pause. "So, how do you plan on getting the story?"

I scratched the top of my head. "Maybe I could get him to open up–"

"Vicky, that's deceiving. Way too low for you."

"What do you want me to do?" I whispered. "My hands are basically tied, Ash. My job is on the line here."

"Is it worth losing your morals? You're better than this. Listen, maybe you could tell him who you are and he'll talk."

"I'm telling you Ash; that would be worse. He'd probably kick me out if he found out. It's snowing a shit ton out there. I won't survive."

The was a long beat on Ashley end. "Whatever you decide, just make sure it's the right thing," she finally said.

I sighed. "Okay. Hey, you may not hear from me for a while. The signal is crap up here."

She giggled. "Well, at least you're shacked up with a hot guy. He's still hot, right?"

"That's an understatement, believe me. His photos have nothing on the real thing."

"Damn..."

"Yup." I stifled a moan, remembering the heat in his eyes when he leaned into me.

"Well, being is holed up is definitely not the worst thing. You need to get laid. Perfect timing."

I rolled my eyes. "Please, I know absolutely nothing about this guy," I said, trying to get the almost-kiss out of my head.

"That stopped no one. Certainly not me. Random sex can be so good, Vicky."

I moaned. "You're a terrible influence."

"Although I doubt Griffin Holt is hardly your type. Don't you like them big and bearded and tough as nails?"

I cleared my throat, the heat rising to my cheeks. If only Ashley knew Griffin was exactly how she described— exactly my type. I tucked that secret to the back of my mind. The last thing I wanted was her fueling to the temptation that plagued me.

"Right, he's the opposite," I said.

She laughed at that. "Well, a change is probably what you need. How long as it been now since you got laid? Three years?"

I shook my head, trying to hold back my smile. "I have better things to think about than sex."

Ashley snorted. "You just haven't found the right person yet. Or maybe he's in the other room."

I sighed heavily. "I gotta go, Ashley. It's been a long day and I'm exhausted. Talk to you later, okay?"

"Okay. Be careful and remember what I said."

"Will do," I replied before disconnecting the call with a sigh.

I considered what Ashley said about my morals and it left me torn on what to do. Pearson expected a story—no, a groundbreaking piece—and I wasn't even close to getting one. After getting this far, could I really return with nothing?

Either way, there was no guarantee Griffin would open up to me, journalist or not. I was walking on a very thin line that grew more fragile with each passing second.

I WOKE UP THE FOLLOWING morning to the smell of bacon permeating my room. My stomach rumbled, which reminded me I hadn't eaten since yesterday. Because of my injury, I hadn't bothered to eat the sandwiches Griffin left for me.

After freshening up, I hobbled to the kitchen, careful to keep the pressure off my injured foot. Griffin stood in the open kitchen, wearing a sweater with the sleeves rolled up to the elbows and a pair of dark jeans. Simple, but sexy. I envied every piece of his clothing.

As if sensing my presence, Griffin turned and saw me, his gaze momentarily sweeping over my frame. Getting dressed earlier, I convinced myself that I didn't choose the one-piece jumpsuit for him. The appreciation on his face, and the responding warmth that ran from my head to toes made me realize I wanted to look good for him.

"Good morning," I greeted him.

"Good morning," he mumbled before his gaze dropped to my feet. "How's the foot?"

"I'll live."

He returned his attention to the stove and I stood there awkwardly, not knowing what to say. Talking to this man was like walking on thin ice. You press too hard and it's over. But I couldn't get anything out of him if I didn't talk.

"Want some help?" I asked.

"No," he answered curtly.

He'd clearly had a terrible night, considering he'd been in a decent mood when I saw him last. "Okay... mind if I help myself to some coffee?"

He released a heavy sigh and grumbled, but I took that as a yes and moved toward the pot. "Thanks," I said as I poured a cup. "When do you think the snowstorm will end?"

"I don't know," he mumbled, his jaw clenching.

"Why would someone want to live here all by themselves?" I continued. I didn't know why, but I had a childish urge to get a rile out of him.

"Peace!" he snapped, slamming his large hands to the counter and glaring at me. His nostrils flared; the edges of his lips pulled tight.

Maybe this wasn't a good idea, after all. "Sorry."

Our gazes met for a brief second and something flickered in his eyes before he slid a plate across the counter to me. I took it and glanced at the contents: bacon, scrambled eggs and a bagel.

"Thank you."

He didn't reply—no surprise. I moved to a barstool around the counter, digging in right away. My eyes flew shut on the first bite. I moaned, forgetting I had company. Griffin was either a good cook or I was simply too hungry to decide whether it was good.

I opened my eyes to find Griffin staring at me with an expression I couldn't quite figure out, but it made me warm all over. Without saying a word, he turned to leave but with a quick swallow, I wanted him to do the opposite. "Please stay... I could use the company."

He paused for a second, pivoting to stare at me as if trying to figure out whether he should stay. With the sharp intake of his breath, he came to me, taking the stool on the opposite end, a large stack of food on his plate.

"Thanks again for your help last night," I told him.

"It was nothing," he mumbled under his breath. "Especially since you did most of the work yourself."

"Well, you cleaned up my mess. That was major. So, thanks."

He grunted with a nod, shoveling food in his mouth.

A long silence stretched between us, during which I tried to find an opening for my questioning.

"So... Griffin. Don't you get lonely here all by yourself?" I finally asked.

"I don't."

"How come? There are no houses for miles around. No TV, hardly any service. What do you do for fun?"

Another grunt.

"What about a family? Ever considered having one?"

Griffin looked up at me, his eyes carrying a chill. "You really ask a lot of questions."

"Just trying to make conversation."

He eased up a little, placing his fork on his plate. "How about you tell me something about you?"

I shrugged. "There's hardly anything interesting in my life. I'd probably bore you to death."

His face brightened with interest as he drew for his cup of coffee. "Please, do tell."

I licked my lips and tore my gaze away from his, desperate for any other distraction. "I er–grew up in a small neighborhood with my mom. As I mentioned before, she worked two jobs, so she was hardly ever home, but it wasn't all that bad. I had my best friend Ashley to keep me company." I smiled, glancing at my plate. "She's a nurse who constantly complains about her job, but she loves it regardless; she loves to help people... which is why it's the perfect job for her."

He grunted as if understanding perfectly what I was talking about. I figured I wouldn't get a word out of him if I tried, and so I continued. "I didn't really have a dad; he left my mom a few weeks before I was born," I said, reaching for my coffee with a scoff. "Weird thing is, they were engaged before. Like, who leaves their pregnant fiancée hanging like that? How can you claim to love someone then betray them?"

Griffin stiffened in his seat. It seemed that bit had gotten his attention. Still, he said nothing.

"People change I guess. It's stupid to think they will always love you," I continued.

"Hmm."

I twisted in my seat, directing my full attention to him. "Do you believe in love, Griffin?" I asked.

He shoved his plate to the side. "No. It's just a lie people use at their own convenience."

It was the longest string of words he'd said since I entered the kitchen. Greedy for more, I tried to prompt him. "Meaning?"

"It's like sex, Victoria," he replied. "People use it as bargaining chip. A woman wants money from a man, she spreads her legs. A man wants sex from a woman, he says I love you."

"Or, it could be the other way around," I point out. "Women say 'I love you' to get what they want, too."

Griffin shrugged. "I guess."

"You don't sound convinced. Don't tell me you're gender biased, Griffin."

For the first time since being here, the ghost of a smile played at his lips, which made him even more attractive. Which led me to wonder; Griffin Holt was a good-looking guy—no scratch that, he was a freaking God, capable of making any woman fall to their knees. From the absence of a feminine touch in the house, it was pretty obvious he and his wife weren't together anymore. Why was he still living alone?

"I'm not biased. I'm just a realist. I've been alive long enough to know what I'm talking about. Thirty-eight years, in fact." His eyes ran over me, leaving goosebumps on my skin. "What are you, twenty? You have no clue about the ways of the world."

"I'm twenty-five years old, thank you very much. And I've been around the block a few times. I know enough."

Another smile tugged the corner of his lips. "That's not something I would admit in public, if I were you."

It took me a moment to catch on, and when I did, I reached over and slapped his arm, marveling at how firm it was. "Get your mind out of the gutter! I'm not talking about my body count. I've had to grow up fast so I'm not your average twenty-five-year-old."

"Still a baby," he replied, sliding off his stool.

I got up too, completely forgetting my injured my foot. A sharp ache shot up my leg, and I grabbed onto the counter with a shriek. To my surprise, Griffin flew my side, wrapping his arm around my waist.

"Hey, I got you," he whispered.

Our eyes met, the heat within his big, beautiful blue orbs making my stomach clench. My eyes dropped to his lips, the urge to kiss him so strong I could almost taste him. I twisted from his hold, tipping on my good toes. Would he back off if I kissed him? Did I dare try?

I couldn't deprive myself. Not when he was so close, not when the scent of his body was like a drug, slowly pulling me in. With a deep sigh, I leaned in, my lips touching his. I closed my eyes, welcoming the softness against mine. I nibbled his lips, prompting his response but he stiffened. I tried again. His erection pressed against my belly, telling me his hesitation had nothing to do with him not wanting me. I teased my tongue against the seam of his lips and he suddenly opened up, his tongue meeting mine. He groaned, pulling me closer, my chest pressed against his as the kiss spiraled into deep passion. He sucked on my tongue, sending sparks of pleasure running through me. His beard tickled my skin but didn't distract me from what a good kisser he was. In fact, an airplane crash couldn't steal my attention, not with how he ate my mouth like it was his last meal. I matched his hard strokes, rolling my body against him, my panties soaked with my arousal.

I'd never reacted to a man like this before, not with this wild, desperate need. It excited me, but it scared me, because I knew how vulnerable it made me. A desire like this only meant one thing; Griffin had the power to make me fall for him. It was the biggest contradiction to my plans. After getting my story, I planned to leave Anchorage without turning back. I couldn't afford to fall in love.

Still, it wasn't enough to make me stop, especially when Griffin gripped my ass, grinding his hard cock against my aching front. I moaned, rocking my hips, hungry for more than this dry humping. I wanted him inside me, so freaking badly. My hands flew to his belt, deftly unbuckling it, but he pulled back, shaking his head.

"Fuck," he muttered, breathing a harsh sigh.

"It's fine – I..." I trailed off, not knowing what to say. But the longer we stood there, the more I sensed the wall rising between us. My heart lurched in my chest as I reached for him. "Griffin—"

"No. We're not doing this."

Ouch. Not exactly what I wanted to hear after such a mind-blowing kiss, but it didn't surprise me. Griffin's hot and cold behavior had been constant since the morning I woke up in his living room. Right now, it was freezing cold. I wanted to give up on even trying with him – story or not. He was clearly impenetrable. There was nothing I could do to change that.

Plus, my mind was still filled with what if's about him – hell, I didn't know him at all. Until then, I'd keep my distance. No, I need to stay away, regardless.

Reminding myself of my agenda, I watched as Griffin lifted his unfinished plate and left the room. I sighed, kicking myself for my rash behavior earlier. What the hell was wrong with me?

Chapter 9

Victoria

I laid in bed staring at the wooden ceiling, bored out of my mind with not the slightest thing to do. There was still no signal on my devices. I couldn't wander around the house like I wanted to. Not after what took place in the kitchen earlier. I suspected Griffin was mad at me for making a move on him.

But I grew reckless, so I decided to go out, anyway. Better to have Griffin yell at me for getting into his private space than dying of boredom in this room. I walked down the hallway, coming upon another room at the far end which I presumed to be Griffin's. The door was closed, and I wondered if he was inside. My hands slid against the bare walls, still unable to believe that there wasn't even a picture frame in sight. There was not a drop of personality to his home and I found that odd.

As I continued, I came upon another room with the door slightly ajar. I paused, glancing down the hall as I contemplated going inside. There was not a sign of Griffin anywhere, which made me believe—and hope— that he was taking a nap.

I bit my lower lip, careful not to make a sound as I slowly slid through the half-opened door. My mouth slightly parted with surprise when I realized where I was. No doubt this was Griffin's office, the only room in the house with personality. I feasted my eyes on the ceiling-to-floor bookshelves filled with books.

"Wow," I whispered, going farther in, trailing my hands across the spine of the books arranged in alphabetical order. His desk stood in the center of the room with a closed laptop, a stack of his books on the left and several awards on the right. On the wall were photos of him at book signings, plus a few abstract oil paintings. Everything seemed in perfect order, every shelf well-polished, glistening under the glow of the single lighting in the center of the ceiling.

Griffin's scent filled the air – a perfect mix of cedar wood and sweet oranges. I could tell he spent quality time there. My eyes caught a picture frame in a corner of the room. It was a photo of Griffin and his sister – Kourtney, only younger, with sparkles in their eyes that were gone now. Whatever happened to Griffin affected Kourtney, too. I took down the frame and analyzed it, seeing their resemblance. A picture was worth a thousand words, but this one gave me nothing. I wished the answers were there. If only it could explain what happened to Griffin Holt.

"The fuck are you doing in here?" Griffin's voice suddenly demanded behind me.

The frame fell from my hand, shattering on the floor. I gasped at the deadly expression on Griffin's face. He came toward me, his dark brows drawn together, his lips in a thin line as his eyes shot daggers at me.

"I'm sorry–"

"Get out!" he exclaimed, his face darkening with a deep scowl.

"I was just–"

"Snooping around," he cut in. "A right I did not give you!"

I flinched, tears pricking my eyes. I swallowed, determined not to cry.

"I'm sorry, but I didn't do anything. I was just admiring your work."

He growled, his chest rising and falling with deep breaths. "I don't want you in my fucking space," he said between clenched teeth, each word punctuated.

The tears finally dribbled down my face. "You are such a fucking asshole!" I snapped. "You know what, I don't have to take this. Fuck you!" I marched past him and slammed the door shut behind me. I might have been desperate for a story, but I didn't have to put up with Griffin's bullshit. Not anymore.

I stomped to my room, briskly moving to my carryon. I shoved my clothes inside, tears pitching from my eyes – which was stupid. I felt stupid. Why was I crying over this asshole? He didn't deserve my tears.

Ignoring the dull ache in my heart, I slung my bag over my shoulder and pulled at the carryon, not caring about the noise as the wheels tumbled through the house. I opened the front door and a gust of wind had me pausing as I squinted. A shiver passed over me. I probably wouldn't make it far in this weather, but I'll be damned if I didn't try.

Chapter 10

Griffin

I raked a hand through my hair and muttered a curse under my breath, seeing the shattered pieces of glass on the floor, but that wasn't the least of my worries anymore. What had gotten to me was the look on Victoria's face when I had shouted at her. The panic in her eyes, the paleness her face and the tears that instantly filled her eyes.

Guilt tickled my conscience, my heart heavy from knowing I caused her sadness. That was the last thing I'd wanted, although I didn't enjoy seeing her in my office. This space was only for *my* comfort. Seeing her there threatened to uproot my peace. Which was no excuse, which meant I should apologize.

But as soon as I cleaned up the mess, I heard a rumbling through the house, followed by the opening of the front door. It took me a second to realize what was happening, but as soon as I did, I grabbed my coat and rushed after her.

I wanted to kick myself repeatedly for behaving like I did, but the damage was already done. As I opened the front door, the cold blast of air told me that Victoria wouldn't make it far.

Fuck. I hoped this wasn't déjà vu.

Lucky for me—well, her, the snowstorm has eased enough for me to see her tracks. With a prayer on my lips, I followed, surprised she was moving so fast in the deep snow.

"Victoria!" I called, hearing her name on my lips for the first time. The only reply that came was from the whistling air.

I tried not to panic, battling with the fear of her being hurt. If she was, I couldn't live with myself, knowing she left the house because of how I treated her. The cold soon numbed my face, making me aware of the drop in the temperature, I had to find her soon, or else...

No. Positive thoughts only. I will find her.

As I turned a bend, I spotted a figure in the distance, moving a slow pace, pulling a suitcase through the snow. Relief flooded me. I picked up the pace, catching up with her as she slumped to her knees.

"Fuck, Victoria." I pulled her up, wrapping my arms around her. "Relax. I'm here."

Her teeth chattered as she feebly pushed at my shoulders. "Leave me alone!"

Releasing a low growl, I tightened my grip, but she sank her teeth in my shoulder. Surprised at the attack, I let her go.

"Leave me the hell alone. This was what you wanted, wasn't it?" she asked shakily.

I blew out a breath. The apology was right on my lips, but her impulsive behavior pissed me off. Why would she put herself in danger by venturing into a snowstorm? Who the fuck does that?

Victoria rolled her eyes and dipped for her luggage with a shaking hand, which upset me even more.

"What the fuck are you doing?" I asked.

"Getting as far away from you," she replied.

"The hell you are," I growled, lifting her small body in my arms and throwing her over my shoulder. She squealed, her small fists beating against my back, the effect similar to being hit by a beach ball.

"Put me down right now!" she shrieked, kicking too, but it didn't affect me one bit. "Who do you think you are?"

I grabbed her bags with my free hand and made the rough trek toward home. Throughout the journey, she was like an annoying little parrot in my ear, doing her best to hit me where she assumed would hurt. Useless.

The cold numbed me all over, disregarding the thick coat I wore. I tried to move with speed, but it was a tedious task, considering the weight on my shoulders and in my hand.

Victoria wiggled from my shoulder the instant I stepped inside. I dropped her bags to the floor, bracing for her reaction. It took no time. Her small hand swept through the air with an attempt to slap my face, but I caught her wrist, tightening my grip.

"Don't."

"You're hurting me," she gritted through her teeth.

"Yeah, like you wanted to hurt me just now, right?"

"We both know you wouldn't have felt a thing." She scoffed, jerking her hand away when I released her. "Touch me again, and you'll regret it, big guy."

It was barely a threat, considering she was only five feet tall, about one hundred and twenty pounds soaking wet. I ignored her murmurings, moving to the dying fireplace, shoving a few more pieces of wood into the fire. My peripheral vision caught her moving closer. She positioned herself right at in front of the fireplace, curling herself into a ball as she rubbed her hands together to get warm. I went for a blanket, handing it to her. She hesitated, glaring at it, but her eyes softened as she took it and wrapped it around her.

"Thanks. It's freezing," she said shakily, rocking herself back and forth.

With the fireplace not yet blazing, it would take a while before the room got heated again. I sat beside her, struggling with the urge to wrap her in my arms and warm her up. I ignored it, knowing where it could lead. There was no doubt Victoria and I would have crazy sex. The chemistry was too intense for anything less.

A few minutes passed before she glanced at me. "Sorry you had to come after me. I now realize how stupid I was."

"Yes you were," I replied, shoving my hands toward the heat radiating from the fire.

"I'm also sorry for breaking your family photo. You frightened me, but—"

"Don't worry about it. I'll replace the glass when I'm in town."

"Good." She sighed, tightening the blanket around her. "Look, I'm not the easiest person to deal with, but I'm grateful. Thank you for everything. I'm sure when this is all over I can safely say, you've saved my life more than once." Her gaze lowered to her lap, her face scrunching, making me curious about her thoughts. I didn't want to open a question-and-answer forum. The less Victoria knew about my life, the better.

She slowly lifted her head, returning her gaze to me. My heart dipped in my chest from the softness in her beautiful eyes. I could get lost in them—in her, actually.

Who was I kidding?

I was already falling hard for Victoria. The panic I experienced when I realized she'd left, that wasn't only because of my worry for her safety. It was the fear I'd lost her before even having time to be with her. There was no denying how much wanted to explore every inch of her, how I wanted to make her mine in so many other ways.

It fucking scared me. I had only been in love once—which was a shitshow—but it took time. Rachel and I dated for years before I fell for her. With Victoria, it took two days. It was ridiculous. No way could it be real. But my racing heart contradicted all logic.

I inched closer to Victoria; her pretty, pink lips parting for me. She wanted this. *She wanted me*. I leaned in, pressing my lips to hers, losing myself in her sweet smell, her soft smooth lips and the passion they exuded for me. With my hand gripping a handful of her hair, I deepened the kiss, the heat from her mouth hardening my cock. She reciprocated the same energy, kissing me hard, her tongue tangling with mine, her soft lips roaming over mine. Her sexy moan magnified the arousal that blazed through me. My hands wrapped around her small body, pulling her closer to me.

There was no protest, just pure acceptance as our bodies pressed together. Her fingers gripped the hem of my shirt, my heart racing as she pulled it over my head.

We parted, both breathing hard, but before my shirt hit the floor, she was on me again, desperate for my taste as I was for hers. Her fingers were like fire on my bare skin, melting away the coldness with each caress.

I reached for her top, hauling it over her head. My fingers found the clasp of her bra and I unhooked it, pulling down the straps and exposing her flawless breasts. They stood round and firm; the pink nipples already hard, the sight watering my mouth.

"Perfect," I murmured, my eyes only leaving them to catch the blush that reddened her cheeks.

Unable to resist any longer, I palmed her breast, gently kneading, watching as her mouth parted with a groan that sent desire rushing through me. I held the other breast, mimicking the motion. They filled my big hands, as if they were made for me.

I took her mouth for another kiss, one she soon broke, her forehead pressed to mine. She swallowed, her soft breaths leaving me on edge. "Is there something wrong?" I asked.

"Before we take another step, there's something I need to know, Griffin," she replied, her eyes closed.

This wasn't where I expected our steamy little encounter to go, but what the hell. "Shoot."

"This is just a fling, but I need to know; are you seeing someone else? Because I don't—I can't sleep with you if there's another woman in your life."

I scoffed. "Look around, Victoria. Do you see signs of any woman around?"

She opened her eyes, giving me a hopeful stare. "No wife and kids?"

It was a strange question, but I answered anyway. "No wife and kids."

A weird look crossed her face before she pressed her lips against mine again. I didn't have time to consider what it meant, not with her hands at the waistband of my pants. My cock stood on high alert, waiting patiently for her to touch it. She fumbled with the button and I considered that the sweetest thing, but not wanting to stretch it out, I pulled them off.

Victoria's lips parted, her eyes widening slightly as her eyes swept my body, her gaze lingering at my front. She licked her lips and my cock twitched instantly. She sank to her knees, those innocent brown eyes staring up at me. What I would do to have them wrapped –

"Fuck."

I sucked in a breath as she gripped my cock. "God, you're huge," she said a whisper, the incredulity unmistakable in her voice.

I couldn't hide my smirk but said nothing. Her small hand moved along my length, gently pumping at first, her gaze still locked with mine. "I hope I'm doing this right," she mumbled.

"You're perfect," I huffed.

She smiled, a soft blush covering her neck and face, her moist palm stroking the shit out of me. I tried to hold back my groans, but it became impossible when she stroked my balls with her free hand. The sounds from my mouth seemed to arouse her even more, for her nipples got even harder. Gradually, her pace increased, matching my fast breathing.

"I want my cock inside that tiny mouth," I breathed, stroking her cheek.

She peered at me again, pushing a lock of hair behind her ear and closing her mouth over the tip of my cock. I swore, her hot mouth sending an electric charge through me. Her tongue swirled around my head making slow circles that left me digging my toes in the carpet, moaning her name. Fuck, she'd just begun, and I was already falling apart. Impressive, considering how innocent she seemed. I gripped her hair when she took me in her mouth, sucking halfway before coming back up again, my cock glistening with her saliva. Again, she sank down, coming up again, her lips like a suction around me.

"Fuck, that feels amazing, baby," I whispered. "Don't fucking stop."

Victoria wrapped one hand around my ass, the next gently squeezing my balls as she moved back and forth, the slick sounds of my cock in her mouth making me even harder.

"That's it," I managed through clenched teeth, moving her hair back from her face as she sucked the head once more. "Such a fucking good girl. Take all of me, Victoria."

With a deep moan, she complied, taking my entire length in her mouth. My body jerked from the insurmountable pleasure. It was so fucking hot to watch her head bouncing, taking me in, releasing me, saliva dripping to the floor as she steadily sucked me off. I remained still, holding onto her head as my cock hit the back of her throat. She took it like a fucking champion. I closed my eyes, muttering curse after curse, slowly losing myself. On the verge of my release she pulled back, gagging. Breathing hard, she pumped me with her hand.

"I won't last long if you keep this up," I breathed, as she licked along the base.

Victoria smiled, her lips glazed with saliva and precum. "We can't have that, can we?" she said mischievously, before taking me in her mouth again. I looked to the ceiling with a load moan as I rocked my hips, gently fucking her mouth, my rigid cock gliding like a hot knife through butter.

She held onto my hips, going all the way. All nine inches of my cock in her mouth. Her skin reddened, her eyes watering before she quickly pulled back with a cough, spit draining down her lips. After taking a breath, she took me in her mouth again, this time only halfway, her tiny fist pumping the other half. My balls tightened as my climax approached. Victoria flinched as the first spurts flew to the back of her throat, taking her by surprise, but like the champ she was, she swallowed every single drop, then licked her lips with a satisfied moan.

Holy shit. This woman was something else.

I wasn't in love with her. Not yet. It was way too soon. But as I reached for her, I couldn't deny how close I was.

Chapter 11

Victoria

"Fucking hell, that was... wow," Griffin breathed, reaching for me. "You're more than what meets the eye; you know that?"

"That's a compliment, right?" I reply. The saltiness of his semen still lingered in my mouth and my jaws were tense from sucking him so long. It was so worth it, especially with those sexy curses coming from his mouth. The way he gripped my hair and fucked my mouth... god, my pussy throbbed from the memory.

"Damn right, that was." He gave me a hard, brief kiss. "It's my turn to take care of you," he muttered.

I glanced down at his cock hanging between his thick thighs. He was still hard as steel, as if he hadn't shot a mouthful of cum in the back of throat moments ago. His strong arms lifted me, and he made an effortless walk to the guest room. He placed me on the bed, clasping my face as he stared into my eyes. "Buckle up, Victoria," he mumbled. "It's going to be a rough ride."

Oh, hell. My pussy clenched so tight it hurt, soaking wet with desperate need for him.

He pulled down my pants and threw them aside. I gasped when he roughly parted my legs, his Adam's apple bobbing as he caressed me. He shifted my panties, stroking the seam of my sex. I bit back a groan when he slipped two fingers inside me.

"Fuck, you're dripping wet," he murmured, his voice husky with lust.

My body ached for him. I couldn't stand the delay any longer. "Please," I whispered. "I need you inside me, Griffin."

He dipped his head towards mine, our lips just mere inches away. "How much do you want me, Victoria?"

I licked my lips, jerking my hips upward. "I'm so turned on I can barely think straight."

Griffin sighed, easing himself up and hooking his fingers into the waistband of my panties. I held my breath and watched as he pulled them down and over my ankles before he bunched it in his fist and took a hard sniff.

My mouth parted, heat covering my face. I'd never had a man sniff my panties before. It was slightly erotic watching him inhaling my scent, yet I wanted to hide under the covers.

"You scent is so fucking perfect. Just like you," he said, throwing the panties aside and reaching for me.

He took my mouth for a kiss that short-circuited my brain, erasing my shyness. I moaned, gripping the back of his neck and matching the hard strokes of his tongue. He lowered his warm body to mine, his cock grazing at my pussy, and I deepened the kiss when it brushed my rock-hard clit.

I whimpered when he broke the kiss, then let out a happy sigh as his tongue trailed along my neck. He bit a sensitive spot and my pussy throbbed, aching for him. I rocked my hips as he moved down, leaving a hot, wet trail from my neck, throat and cleavage. I gasped his name when he took my nipple in his mouth, tugging hard. My back arched off the floor as heat flooded my body. My hand raked down his spine, the other trying to move between us to hold his cock.

Griffin moved to the other nipple, nipping like he'd done with the other giving me a perfect mix of pain and pleasure that made me ache for more. My eyes flew open when he pried my thighs further apart, settling between them. His gaze locked with mine, the hunger so clear in his eyes. My body shuddered when he nudged my entrance, so desperate for all of him.

In one swift movement, he pressed deep inside me, filling me, stealing every ounce of my breath. Fuck, he was huge. Seeing his size was one thing, feeling every inch... now, that was something else.

I gripped his thick arms, opening more for him. He pulled back, thrusting again, his eyes filled with an emotion that made my heart flutter. Or maybe I imagined it. No way did he stare at me with love.

No way.

My pussy burned sweetly by the intrusion, stretching to accommodate Griffin's size. My walls hugged him like a long-lost lover each time he pressed inside me. He muttered a curse as he sank deeper and deeper until he was completely buried, and I was latching onto him like a woman starved.

"Fuck, you feel amazing around me," he whispered, stroking me hard and deep, touching my soul.

I whimpered, my eyes rolling to the back of my head as he repeatedly brushed that sensitive spot. "Oh, Griffin...yes..."

"Yes... fucking say my name," he ordered gruffly, his hips circling as he changed the rhythm.

"Griffin!" I screamed as he picked up the pace, making my vision blurry from the rough thrusts. The headboard banged against the wall, matching his fast rhythm. Sweat ran from my body, making me wonder if there really was a snowstorm outside.

Griffin grunted, pushing my legs forward, my knees pressed to my chest. He did warn me about being rough, but when he pressed inside me again, I didn't imagine it being so brutal.

Yet, so fucking amazing.

With one hand pinning down my arms, he did not let up, fucking me with a fervor, his balls slapping my thighs. I couldn't think; not that I wanted to. I was content with the blissful haze that surrounded me, thickening with each deep, delicious stroke Griffin gave me.

My body burned from the heat. So did Griffin's. He was red in the face, his forehead dripping with sweat and his abs glistening under the warm light. I glanced at the fireplace beside us, our shadows reflected on the other side. It wasn't the heat from the fireplace that made us sweat, but the passion that swirled around us. I didn't imagine lovemaking being like this.

No. Not lovemaking. This was sex; nothing more.

My pelvic wall tightened. A deep, pleasurable sensation filled my core. On the verge of letting go, my eyes flew open with surprise as Griffin pulled out. Desperate for my release, I reached for him, but he pulled me up and kissed me.

"Wrap your legs around me," he said almost breathlessly, still positioned on his knees. I did as he asked, wrapping my arms around his neck as well. We kissed, our slick bodies rubbing against each other.

Griffin reached under, and I could feel his hard cock against my pussy before he slipped it in. I sighed, easing myself into him as he filled me once again. Mouth still joined to his, I bounced on his cock, moaning from each burst of pleasure inside me. His huge hands held my waist, keeping me in place as we rode the waves of desire.

Him inside me was the best feeling I've had in a while—no, ever. Each passing second was even better than the last. My movements became more frantic as I craved more of his sweet cock and a desperation for an orgasm. My breathing became labored and just then, Griffin held my ass cheeks and began to aid in my movements as he too neared his release.

"O–oh yes! Yes!" I moaned, my nails digging into his skin, the ache growing more intense.

Griffin grunted and squeezed me while I cried out, tears pricking my eyes as the initial wave of my orgasm swept over me.

"Fuuuuuuck!" I screamed, sinking all the way down then back again in a fast motion that made me dizzy. Griffin growled, wrapping his arms around me, his hips rising to meet my thrusts. He moaned my name as a flood of warmth filled me. At the moment, I didn't mind that he'd cum inside me. I was too caught up in my own release, too blinded by pleasure to care.

My body trembled. I sucked in a breath as my eyes rolled over and the sweetest pleasure rushed through every inch of my body. His name was a constant murmur on my lips as I sank back to earth. From his heavy breathing, I realized he was on his way back, too.

When he finally released me and moved to stoke the fire, I pushed to a sitting position with my knees pressed to my chest, my chin resting on top. I stared at his broad back, wondering what his thoughts were. For some reason, I didn't want regret to be one of them. I hoped he enjoyed this as much as I did. I hoped he wanted more.

More?

This was a onetime thing, wasn't it?

I closed my eyes with a deep breath. Who was I kidding? Griffin saved my life—twice. He gave me a place to stay. He made love to my body with a passion no man had ever done. Did I really want to let this go?

THE SMILE WOULDN'T leave my face as Griffin spooned me, another blanket thrown over us while we curled against each other, still completely naked. My body still buzzed from the incredible sex and I had a feeling it would be for a long time.

"How do you feel?" he asked me, his mouth at my ear, the sensation sending a shiver down my body.

"Like I'm in heaven on earth," I said, then chuckled. "It's corny, I know, but it's the only description that makes sense."

His hold around me tightened as he placed a gentle kiss to my cheeks. "I'm glad you got lost in the snowstorm that night."

I giggled. "The near-death experience aside, I'm glad, too."

"Hungry?" he asked, his hand just under my breast.

I turned to face him, our noses almost touching. "I have something in mind, but I don't wanna seem greedy," I replied with a smile.

"In that case, we are both greedy." He reached for me, giving me a kiss that let me know exactly what he wanted. I wrap my leg around him, grinding my sex against his thigh. With a moan, Griffin pulled away.

"You need something in your stomach if we're going to keep this up," he said, sitting up. "I'll go make us something quick."

I sat up, watching as he moved around the room completely naked, his cock semi erect. I licked my lips, the blood rushing to my face when he caught me staring. He smirked, hauling on his boxers and heading to the kitchen. With a happy sigh as I got out of bed, deciding to take a shower while Griffin made breakfast. There was still an ache between my thighs. I still wanted him. If we continued like this, there was a high chance I wouldn't even be able to walk tomorrow. I chuckled, not minding one bit. For once, I didn't think about my job, or the story, or even Ashley and home. I felt free. I wanted this feeling always.

I stepped under the warm shower, closing my eyes as the water blasted against my skin. I couldn't help but smile as I thought of the last three days. Griffin finding me in the snow, being an asshole to me at first, then transforming into a soft, caring man when I got injured.

Our little fights that ended when I stormed out of his house, him coming back to save me, our sheet-gripping lovemaking... who knew I would fall for someone so soon?

The smile disappeared as I washed the soap from my body. There was no denying my feelings for Griffin. The problem was, I couldn't tell him. The minute he learned what I did for a living, the instant he would connect the dots. He was a smart man. I missed my window. Maybe if I'd been honest from the start...

With a weary sigh, I left the stall and brushed my teeth before I pulled on another jumpsuit and walked to the kitchen where Griffin was, cooking something that reminded me of dinner with my mom. I leaned against the counter watching him, not wanting to get used to the bliss that surrounded me. This was only temporary. As soon as I got my story, I'd take the next flight out. No looking back.

Which meant, I needed to get to work. After three days, I still had nothing, not even a draft.

"I hope you like pasta," Griffin said as he stirred the pot.

"I do, it smells wonderful," I replied. "Do you want me to set the table?"

He turned and smiled at me as if I just offered him a million dollars. "I'd like that. Thank you."

Twenty minutes later, we'd taken our seats around the small table in the kitchen, two plates of steaming, creamy pasta in front of us. I didn't waste anytime in digging in. Thirty minutes in Griffin's bed had reduced me to a starving animal. I took the first bite, unable to hold back my moan as a burst of flavor hit my taste buds.

"Where did you learn to cook like this?" I asked, pausing to look at him.

"YouTube."

My brows shot up. "And here I was thinking you were going to mention your mom."

He shook his head. "My mom was hardly around."

"Your parents didn't get along?"

"Not quite. Their marriage was more for convenience than love, I suppose."

"That must have sucked as a kid."

"Not really," he said as he cleared his throat and glanced at me. "You mentioned your mom being a single parent, but do you have any siblings, Victoria?"

I shook my head. "I'm an only child, although I consider Ashley my sister." I push the fork around the plate, considering my next move. "So... where did you grow up?"

"LA," he said, taking a sip of water.

"That's miles away from here. What brought you to Alaska?" I quickly asked.

Griffin looked back to his plate, placing his fork down as if he'd suddenly lost his appetite. "The need for change, I guess."

"Oh, come on. That's the vaguest response I've ever heard. What made you want a change?"

A dark cloud passed over his face. He pushed the plate away. "My wife."

My fork dropped to the plate. "You're married?"

He scoffed. "Wipe that shock off your face, Victoria. Rachel and I are divorced. We wouldn't have made love if I was still a married man."

Hearing him say the word 'love' jumbled the thoughts in my head and I forgot what I wanted to say. I gaped at him until he scoffed again. "We're divorced, Victoria."

I bit my lips. "What happened?"

There was a slight pause as if he debated whether to tell me the truth. I kept my fingers crossed, hoping he wouldn't hold back. I needed this story. Not only to save my job, but to get me out of Anchorage. Snowstorm or not, my time with Griffin had to end before I fell deeper.

Griffin sighed, turning his gaze to me. "Rachel and I were married for five years, during which we tried having a baby. Nothing worked. We spent thousands of dollars on fertility specialists who all told us we were both perfectly healthy. I didn't understand why she couldn't get pregnant after trying for so long. Three years later, I found her birth control pills. She didn't want kids—at least, not yet, but she didn't have the guts to tell me. It almost ripped me apart, but I agreed to save our marriage.

"Back then, my best friend Elliott managed my business. I didn't have time to market my books and handle my finances. I just wanted to write. Rachel got pregnant around the time I found out Elliott had made off with every dollar from my savings account. Five hundred thousand, to be exact. It almost ruined me. Our baby on the way was my only saving grace. Rachel and I tried to make our marriage work—at least, I did, but I sensed her drifting away. I put it down to her hormones from the pregnancy, although my instincts said otherwise.

"Two weeks before her due date, she confessed that the baby wasn't mine. It was Elliott's. She had been biding her time before packing up and moving to be with him."

I gasped, covering my mouth. Out of all the stories I'd expected to hear, this surpassed them all. "Oh, my, Griffin. I'm so sorry."

He cleared his throat. "I still didn't believe her, but when the baby was born, I got a DNA test done and that confirmed it."

His face crumpled with the memories of that pain, the tears filled his eyes, balancing on the rim. I wanted to hug him so much, but I didn't dare, fearing he would lose it. "As if that didn't destroy me enough, I found out she and Elliott conspired to steal my money. They'd been seeing other since the first year of our marriage."

"Christ." I palm my cheeks, staring wide-eyed at him.

"She gave a stupid excuse about me being too busy, as it that justified her deceiving and stealing from me all those years. For the baby's sake, I didn't press charges. We divorced, and as a condition to our agreement, she didn't request spousal support, and she gave up rights to half of my assets. I moved here to clear my head – to get away from all the toxicity. Last I heard, she and the baby are living in the Maldives with Elliott. There's no extradition to the US, not did I care. They were all dead to me."

I swallowed the lump in my throat. "I'm so sorry, Griffin. You didn't deserve that."

He nodded, wiping his face. "A few days ago, you would've said the opposite, though."

The glimmer of a smile and his teasing tone made me chuckle. "You're probably right. You were such an asshole to me."

His smile faded. "You're right. I wasn't as welcoming when you got here, and I'm sorry for that. I'm glad you're here, Victoria. Truly."

My heart lurched in my chest as he rose from his seat, coming around to kneel at my feet. "Let me show you how glad I am."

He captured my lips with his own, kissing me with such passion, triggering my tears. Guilt ate at me. I now had the story I came for, which meant my job was now secure. But could I ruin Griffin's life by exposing his past?

The snowstorm still raged outside, so I would sleep on it a bit. Until then, I wanted to enjoy him. It would be the last time, anyway.

With my arms looped around his neck, I returned his kiss with the same urgency, my need for him moving in waves over my body. He pulled the zipper of my jumpsuit, peeling it over my shoulder and I hurriedly pulled my arms through, raising my butt for him to slip it down my lower half. I pulled down his shorts, gripping his cock before he even stepped from it. He hissed as I stroked him, the harsh sounds fueling my arousal, making me want to skip the foreplay.

He spun me around, pressing his hard body to mine. I bit my lips as he kneaded my breasts. His coarse hands grazed my soft skin, the contrast arousing me even more than his actions. He ran his fingers down my back, following with sweet kisses that made me tingle all over, begging him to fuck me.

With a deep growl, he bent me over, his cock grazing my ass, his rough breaths letting me know how much he wanted me. My pussy tightened with anticipation, eagerly waiting for him to spear me.

Imagine my surprise when he licked me instead. I gripped the edge of the table, sucking in a breath as his tongue stroked the seam of my pussy, lapping my clit before making its way back, then repeating the motion.

"Fuck, Griffin... I love what you're doing to me right now."

He moaned in response, the vibration making me rock my hips, rubbing myself over his mouth. His beard tickled my thighs, riling me up. I rocked faster, moaning his name when his tongue slipped inside me, tasting how ready I was for him.

Before I fell apart from the onslaught of his tongue, he withdrew, spreading my legs even more, pressing inside me with a loud grunt. My walls clamped around him, my juices flowing even more. I reached out to steady myself on the counter, slightly arching my back as his hands roamed over my sensitive breasts and across my stomach. He filled me with hard stabs, each one punctuated and hitting my sweet spot.

"Oh yes! Griffin. Don't stop. You feel like heaven inside me..."

My knees buckled and I moaned when he pulled me back up, pressing me on the table as he stroked me harder from behind. His fingers moved against my sensitive clit, making me shiver. I grip the edges of the table tighter as shockwaves of pleasure ran through me. He continued to rub my clit as he fucked me, his pace increasing with each stroke. I whimpered as the urge to pee came with full force.

"Grif–" I managed, unable to get the word out.

He didn't let up and I couldn't find it within me to utter another word, not with ecstasy dancing through my body. I screamed as a warm spray of liquid shot out from me, running down my thighs.

"Fucking hell!" Griffin breathed, amazement in his voice. He still didn't let up, fucking me like a thoroughbred on steroids.

My knees buckled. Just when I thought I'd fall to the floor, Griffin held me up, his grip tightening on me as he climaxed with deep grunts.

Completely drained and trapped in bliss, I could only register Griffin picking me up and carrying me to his bedroom. I curled up in a fetal position, my body humming from the aftershocks of my pleasure. Griffin's kiss on my forehead made me smile. I hugged the pillows as his footsteps receded to the bedroom.

He returned a minute later with a washcloth, parting my legs as he cleaned me. I shuddered when he brushed my sensitive clit, but I didn't resist. The last thing I heard was the shower running before I fell asleep.

Chapter 12

Griffin

VICTORIA HAD BEEN ASLEEP for a few hours now, but I still couldn't take my eyes off her. Her face was the perfect picture of peace – beauty like I'd never seen before. Her brown hair flowed behind her, a few tendrils loose and over her shoulders, caressing her naked breasts, those nipples still erect even in sleep. Every inch of her was perfect and it made me wonder why she was still single. Why I'd been so lucky for her to fall right into my lap—well, on my roadway.

Surely, this was a co-incidence, right?

For a man short on luck, I could only hope this was a time for my well-needed break. I didn't understand how I'd fallen for a woman so fast, but I accepted it as life rewarding me for being patient all these years. For the first time since Rachel's deception, I had no resentment – it was like the weight of the world had fallen off my shoulders.

Victoria shifted her position with a gentle snore that made me smile. This felt right; her falling asleep next to me, my sheets hugging her nakedness, contentment on her face. There was an urgent need to hide her away, where only I could see her. She was like a treasure only I had the privilege to touch.

Again, Victoria turned, the action shifting the sheet and exposing her breasts. My cock stirred. Not that it needed much effort. Just looking at her made me want to bury myself inside her again. She made me insatiable. Borderline obsessed. She was so deep under my skin, I'd never get enough.

However, she needed rest, so I allowed her to sleep while I considered the future. There was no certainty about our relationship once the snowstorm ended. The bliss from sex would finally wane—at least, for her—and she could return to New York without a relationship with me.

Or, maybe she wanted the same thing I did. Maybe she wanted to see where we could take this fling, despite how scary and uncertain it was.

The maybe's left me confused. After keeping my heart secure for so long, was I willing to give it to another woman I barely knew?

I threw my head against a pillow with a sigh, loving the way Victoria made me feel, but hating it at the same time. The thought of being with her made me oppose every decision I made seven years ago.

Victoria shuffled in the bed, moaning softly as she turned to face me, a smile on her face. "Hey, you," she said, voice groggy with sleep, the sexiest thing I'd heard in a while.

"You slept well," I smirked.

"The effects of having sex with a stallion, I guess. Another round like that and you'll put me in a coma for sure."

I chuckled. "Sounds like a challenge."

She blushed. "I might be tempted."

I reached for her hand and allowed her to feel my hard cock. "Have your say."

Her mouth fell open as she jerked her hand away. "You're insatiable."

"I can't get enough of you," I muttered, taking her mouth for a kiss that showed her exactly what I meant. She moaned, shuffling closer to me, throwing her leg over my hip. My hand trailed down her back and to her ass where I held her in place before inserting my cock. She was still wet, allowing me a slick entry as I breached her.

Her tight little pussy hugged me. I bared my teeth, shoving myself all the way. She gasped, her breath fanning against my mouth as I fucked her. Unable to resist her pouty lips, I kissed her, filling her with long tender strokes, her pussy smooth as velvet and as warm as a fire pit. There was no way I could last long inside her. Not like this.

Switching position, I rolled on top of her, using my knees to part her legs then I entered her again. She moaned, her head thrashing to each side, her fingers gripping the sheets as she urged me to go faster. I complied, my hips zipping, my cock drilling her sweet heat.

"Griffin please..."

"Tell me what you want, baby, and I'll gladly oblige."

"I want– I want your cum inside me," she whispered, her mouth at my ear.

My cock swelled inside her, the words making me want to explode, but it wasn't time. I wanted to watch her fall apart when I made her come. I withdrew, sucking her nipples, my mouth moving along her stomach, down to the slick flesh between her thighs, feathering her skin with kisses as her moans vibrated through her.

"Oh God," she whimpered when I slipped two fingers inside her.

I swiveled my tongue across her flesh, lapping at her juices and enjoying the moans that left her mouth, her quivering thighs telling me her release wasn't too far away. I licked her up and down, scouring her tightness with my tongue before I sucked her clit.

"Holy, shit. I fucking love your mouth." Victoria's fingers found my hair, raking through the roots while I sucked her clit even harder, her taste fresh and sweet and incredibly addicting. Her thighs closed in on my head, squeezing tight.

She was almost there.

I pulled back, trying not to chuckle as she swore.

The curses died on her lips as I positioned myself between her legs again, slowly inching inside her, the wetness, the heat, and tightness too unbearable. My balls smacked her ass as I fucked her, juices flowing from her cunt, the sounds echoing in the room as I drove back and forth through her.

Her climax arrived, accompanied by her sharp nails digging into my skin, her pussy tightening around me, her lips screaming my name. She kissed me; hot and rough, moaning when she tasted herself on my lips.

"Fuck, Griffin," she whispered after pulling back. "What are you doing to me?"

"The same fucking thing you're doing to me," I muttered. "Driving me insane."

Victoria closed her eyes with a soft gasp when I thrusted hard, riding out my climax. Finally drained, I rolled to the side, the sounds of our harsh breathing filling the room. I couldn't remember ever sweating like this, nor could I recall ever being so content. It was the craziest thing, but she made me complete.

I turned to face her, confused by the tears pooling in her eyes. We had the most amazing sex just now, didn't we?

I brushed her hair aside, cupping her cheek. She shifted her gaze as the first streak broke free, running in a sad, slow flow.

My heart lurched as I wiped the tear away. "Are you okay?"

She nodded. "Yeah... perfect."

"Are you sure? Because those are real tears, Victoria."

Again, she nodded, surprising me by straddling me, taking my cock. "Make love to me again, Griffin."

I groaned as she stroked me, getting me rock hard within minutes. I lifted her hips, impaling her with my cock, waves of pleasure flooding me with each delicious thrust. Victoria came with me in mind-numbing climax that left me empty, yet, still craving more of her. There was no word to explain it; just the most insane thing I'd ever experienced in my life.

Victoria rolled off and turned her back to me, her heavy breaths matching my own. I heard a soft sob, then another. Alarmed, I pulled her into my warms, wiping the tears from her face.

"What's going on, Victoria?"

She opened her mouth and I gripped her shoulders. "Don't lie to me, please."

She sighed. "There's something I have to tell you, Griffin."

"Okay..." My curious mind tried to think of a reason she would cry like this, but I came up with nothing.

Her mouth opened and closed, but no words came out.

"Hey, whatever it is, you can tell me. Look, we haven't known each other for long, but I care about you."

"Oh, God," she whispered, her eyes welling with tears once more. "Griffin, I care about you too. But—"

My cell phone rang, cutting her words short. I frowned at seeing Kourtney's name on the screen. My sister never called unless there was an emergency. Raising a finger to Victoria, I swiped the screen. "Kourt?"

Her distorted voice came back at me. I moved away, trying to find a spot in the room for a decent signal. The call ended abruptly, so I tried calling back. The 'no signal' beep sounded in my ear, and I returned the phone to the side table while making a mental reminder to call her tomorrow.

"Now, what were you saying?" I asked Victoria when I returned to her. The tears were now gone; in its place was guarded smile.

She shook her head. "It's not important. Not anymore."

"Victoria, you were crying a few minutes ago. Whatever bothers you is important to me."

"I was just caught up in the post-sex emotions, that's all." She suddenly grinned. "I'm gonna go take a shower; want to join me?"

Her obvious attempt to sidestep the question didn't disturb me. I expected she would open up when it suited her.

She ran her fingers through her long hair, letting it fall in waves as she walked toward the bathroom, her hips swinging as she went. "Are you going to join me, or not?"

She giggled and squealed when I caught up to her and scooped her up in my arms, carrying her to the bathroom. We simply showered, too exhausted to do anything else. When I snuggled next to her in bed, my only thought was on figuring how to make her stay.

THE FOLLOWING MORNING, I woke up to Victoria nestled beside me, her ass cushioned right in my crotch and my cock as hard as a rock against her. She was still sound asleep. I smiled, loving the idea of waking up next to her, inhaling her scent and feeling her soft skin against mine.

But that was short lived when my phone rang and she twisted and turned, her eyes fluttering open. I kissed her softly on the lips before I reached for the phone that stopped ringing as soon as I reached for it.

"Seems like the signal is back."

She sat up, stretching. "Great, I'm going to take a shower while you return your call."

I smiled and kissed her before watching her leave. I checked my phone. It was Kourtney again, reminding me of last night's call.

She answered on the first ring. "God. Why is it always a struggle to reach you?" she exclaimed.

"You know what the service is like up here. Is everything okay?"

"Yeah, I saw the news about the terrible snowstorm. I wanted to see if you're okay."

I moved toward the window and drew the curtains, barely able to see anything but enough to know the storm had ended. "Yes, I'm fine. I told you to stop worrying about me."

"You're my little brother; that's impossible."

I scoffed. Kourtney knew I disliked that reference, especially since we're only a year apart. "How are you?"

"I'm doing great. I already met my target for this month, so I've taken a few days off."

"Good for you. Which means you need to get off the phone and enjoy your break."

Kourtney chuckled. "Listen, I forgot to mention, and it's probably too late now, but a girl came by the house a few days ago – she wanted to talk to you..."

My brows furrowed. "A girl?"

"Yeah, said she was a journalist and wanted to hear your story. You're still blowing up here by the way."

I swallowed. "What did you tell her?"

There was a small silence. "She seemed pretty desperate; said her job was on the line and she just wanted to interview you. So, I gave her your address—"

"You did what?"

"I'm sorry I overstepped, Griff, I just felt sorry for her—"

"Kourt, you promised to keep my whereabouts a secret. Do you know how embarrassing it would be if my story gets out?"

Just the thought of some journalist invading my space, wanting to dig in my past made me want to punch a hole in the wall. Why couldn't people mind their own business? What the hell was so fascinating about me?

In the shower, Victoria hit a high note, her happy tone clashing with my fury and winning, which calmed me down. I took a deep breath, unable to help my smile. It still amazed me that after three days, she affected me so much.

Wait a minute.

My smile faded as the wheels turned in my brain. What were the odds that Victoria showed up, but the journalist didn't? What if they were one and the same?

No. It couldn't be. Victoria wouldn't lie to me.

"Are you still there, Griff?"

"What was her name?" I asked, my mind running a mile a second. This couldn't be happening. *Please let me be wrong.*

"I don't remember her name but—"

"What did she look like?" I cut in.

"Brunette... er – stunning, with the most beautiful brown eyes. A tiny little thing, too. Ahh... I think her name was Viv– Victoria!"

Fuck. Fuck. Fuck.

I gripped the phone so tight, I thought it would've crumpled in my hands. I didn't want to believe Victoria had deceived me, but it all added up. I gritted my teeth as the fury resurfaced, burning a hole in my heart.

"Griff, say something, please."

"I'll call you back, Kourt." I hung up the phone and threw it on the bed, pacing the bedroom floor.

How could I have been so fucking stupid? How could I not have figured a young, beautiful city girl wouldn't have booked a vacation in the middle of nowhere. How could I not assume that with all the buzz on the internet, someone her age would definitely know who I was. Fuck, I was so captivated by her, so blinded by my lust. She was a fucking woman; why did I expect anything less? What made Victoria any different from Rachel? Nothing.

This was her endgame from the moment she arrived; to seduce me, get my story, and sell it the highest bidder. Like an idiot, I walked right into her trap. Now that she'd gotten what she came for, I suspected she'd be out of here in no time.

A crippling ache made me clutch my chest, taking deep breaths to get rid of the pain. I dropped to my knees, grabbing onto the bed as I tried to get myself under control. I considered confronting her for the truth, but a part of me wanted revenge; to hurt her as much as she hurt me. I had no issues with pretending a little longer, just to fuck with her head.

Yes, that was exactly what I would do.

Chapter 13

Victoria

"Oh, my God. You slept with Griffin Holt?" Ashley exclaimed on the other end of the phone.

Glancing at the half-opened door of my room, I quickly scampered off my bed and closed it. After breakfast—a quiet one, where Griffin's mind seemed miles away—he'd left to work in his office. I thought it strange he'd barely said a word to me. In fact, his replies were mostly grunting and a few head shakes. Maybe the novelty had worn off and he regretted sleeping with me.

But, why did he confess to caring about me?

"Vicky?"

"Yes, I slept with him, Ash," I whispered. "Don't judge me, please."

"As if." I imagined her rolling her eyes. "But how did it happen, though? I thought you wanted to keep things professional."

I groaned. "Yes, that was the plan, but I don't know... there is this chemistry that made it hard to resist. It just... happened."

"Well, coming from a girl who'd done more one-night stands than I can count, there's no judgement here, sweetie. Unless he was terrible in bed. Was he?"

"Not even in the slightest," I reply, chuckling. "Let's just say, I've lost count of how many times my eyes rolled to the back of my head."

"Oh, my God," Ashley whines. "I'm so jealous right now. Tell me more!"

"Nuh-uh. You know I don't kiss and tell."

"Boo! You're no fun."

"I thought we already established you're the fun one," I reply.

"Flattery will get you nowhere, missy. Come on, spill the juicy details."

"My lips are sealed, Ash. Ask me something else, because I'm done talking about that."

"How did Griffin react when you told him who you are?"

I closed my eyes, my heart dropping to the floor of my stomach. "I didn't tell him."

"OMG. Victoria!"

"I was going to. Trust me, but then I chickened out." A blew out a frustrated breath, sending a loose hair flying. "Don't ride my ass for this, Ash. I already feel bad enough as it is."

"Did he tell you his story?" she asked.

"Yes, he did—"

"Jesus."

"But I'm not going to break it, I promise. He's been through a lot, Ash. I can't give you details, but his wife—ex-wife is alive and well. So is the baby."

"Well, thank God for that. You need to tell him the truth, though. Something tells me what happened between you guys was more than sex."

"Why would you think that?"

"Because you don't do casual sex, Vic. You don't sleep with a guy unless you have deep feelings for him."

I groaned, dragging my palm over my face.

"Tell. Him," Ashley ordered in her no-nonsense voice.

"I will, but he's going to hate me, Ash. I just know it."

There was a small silence. "Listen, Vic. You made a mistake. If he cares about you, he'll understand. If not, you still have me. I'll be here waiting with a tub of rocky road ice cream and a bottle of red wine."

I sighed. "I appreciate you, Ash. God knows what I'd do without you."

Ashley chuckled. "I love you too. Now, hurry and get back to LA. I won't stop until you give me all the nasty, juicy details."

I bid her goodbye, sighing heavily as I fell against the pillows, mulling over Ashley's advice. I must have fallen asleep, because when I opened my eyes, it seemed a little darker outside. Getting out of bed, I got dressed in a sweater and a pair of thick leggings. As I opened the room door, I heard knocking outside. With a frown, I searched the house for Griffin, but there was no sign of him around. The knocking came loudest from the back door, so I opened it and found him chopping logs with an axe, dressed in only a pair of sweatpants and a tank top while his muscles bulged with each movement he made.

For a moment, I forgot my dilemma and took him in, totally lusting over how delicious he looked with his thick hair hanging loosely over his shoulders. I'd never been obsessed with a man, but Griffin made it easy. I could stare at him like this all day.

It had stopped snowing, but the temperature still danced around the low twenties. I couldn't wrap my head around him standing out there, inappropriately dressed—as much as I enjoyed the view.

"Are you looking to freeze to death?" I exclaimed, when he paused for a moment.

Griffin briefly glanced at me before reaching for another log, placing it on the stump and splitting it in two with one swing of the axe. Once done, he bunched the pile under his arms and with the axe on his shoulder, he came toward me. I stepped aside, realizing he didn't intend to stop, and he brushed past me.

"Are you okay?" I asked, reaching for him. He flinched as if he'd been slapped, leaving me more concerned. "Griffin? What's wrong?"

He hesitated, his mouth moving like he had something to say. A beat passed before he murmured, "Nothing. I'm fine."

But I could see in his eyes that he wasn't.

I followed him inside, waiting for him to discard the logs and axe. As soon as he released them, I reached up to him and kissed him softly, feeling some resistance before he melted into me and kissed me with as much passion as I gave. But I realized he was a bit rougher this time – rougher than usual. His grip on me was almost painful, the hard strokes of his tongue leaving my mouth numb.

This wasn't passion, this was... anger.

I pulled away, staring up at him. "Are *we* okay?" I asked.

"Why wouldn't we be?" he asked gruffly, gripping a handful of my hair and pulling my head back, nibbling my throat. "I just want to be inside you."

The husky words made my pussy throb, ready to give him what he wanted. I surrendered, allowing him to back me to the handle of the sofa, only stopping when my legs hit the furniture.

"Turn around," he ordered, and I did just that while he stood behind me.

I gasped when he yanked down my pants and panties to my ankles, my bottom half completely naked. He traced a finger along the seam of my pussy, feeling how wet I already was. I moaned when I heard him suck his finger off. My heartbeat raced, excited for what we were about to do.

Griffin pressed his palm into my back and made me bend over the arm of the couch. I looked over my shoulder and saw him pull down his pants, his hard cock springing from its restraint. I licked my lips as he stroked himself, envying his palm, aching to have him inside me. His eyes narrowed, anger flashing within them before he pressed down my back, making me facepalm the seat of the couch.

I sucked in a breath when Griffin roughly entered me. I instantly tightened around him as he buried his entire length. Before I got used to the sensation of being full, he withdrew again, then thrusted so hard I saw stars.

"Griffin—"

He whacked my ass, making me gasp with surprise. It stung like hell, but it aroused me, too. I breathed a moan when he slapped me again, and again, his cock stroking the shit out of me. My pussy pulsed around him, ecstasy filling my insides. I was already coming, and we'd barely just begun.

"Oh, Griffin, I'm coming—"

He suddenly withdrew, bursting the pleasure bubbles inside me. I twisted to peer up at him, the anger on his face confusing me. "Are you okay—"

My words got cut short when he lifted me, carrying me to the dining table where he spread my thighs, lashing me with his thick tongue. Confusion disappeared. Passion took over. I push myself up on my elbows, watching his tongue disappear inside me, feeling its sensation along my walls. He slowly circled it, then switched to a spearing motion, bringing me closer to the edge. He flicked my clit with his thumb; once, twice, repeatedly, applying more pressure each time. I gripped the roots of his hair with a whimper, bracing myself for an outstanding release.

It didn't come. Again, Griffin left me in the cold.

"What the fuck are you doing to me?" I whispered when he lifted me again.

He grunted in reply, fury still dancing in his eyes as he brought me to the carpet, positioning me on all fours, then pressing my upper half to the floor. With my ass in the air, my thighs spread, I waited for him to take me again. It wasn't long before he breached me, plunging harder than ever before.

Pleasure-pain rocked my body. I didn't care about the pain. I focused on the pleasure, my fingers digging into the carpet as I tried to stay in place. There wasn't an ounce of gentleness about him; not from the way he gripped my waist as he *fucked* me, definitely not from the deep growls that accompanied each vicious stroke. For some reason, I welcomed it. Maybe it was from knowing I would be leaving soon. I didn't want his lovemaking,; nothing that would make me too emotional. This was an impersonal fucking, something to tide me over until I craved my next fix.

Griffin pulled his cock out, my cunt squeezing at the emptiness. Harsh breaths left my mouth as he grazed it along my clit, sending ripples of pleasure through me. I felt the first wave of my climax as he slipped it in again, going all the way.

When I thought he couldn't fuck me any rougher, he proved me wrong. With one heel pressed to the carpet, he palmed my breasts, his thumbs and index fingers gripping each nipple. A loud rumble came from his throat as he drilled me with deep, deliberate strokes, blurring my vision.

"Yes, Griffin! Oh... yes!" I screamed, delirious from the pleasure coursing through me.

My shrieks were like adding gasoline to a fire. Griffin grunted, sweat running from his body onto my back as he grinded into me. I came hard, my knees buckling as I rose to my high, then sank back to earth with a crash. Still, Griffin didn't let up. He slapped my ass, delivering stinging pain after stinging pain until he growled, pulling out of me. His hot cum shot out on my ass, running in slow motion down my crack. He slapped his cock against my cheeks, emptying himself.

With my face still pressed to the carpet, I heard his pants zipper. Surprised, I pulled myself up just in time to see him heading out.

"I'll be in my office," was all he said before disappearing down the hall.

My cheeks burned with embarrassment from his sudden dismissal. Wiping the sweat from my face, I pulled up my panties, shimmied out of my pants and walked to the bathroom, unable to ignore the slickness between my legs.

After running a bath, I removed my clothes and slipped in, acknowledging how sore I already was. Griffin wasn't a gentle lover, but this surpassed how rough he usually was with me. There was something wrong with him; I just couldn't figure out what it was.

Was he back to being cold and closed off?

Did he really care about me like he claimed?

Should I let it bother me? The snowstorm had ended. By tomorrow, the roads would be clear enough for me to leave—hopefully. I could be on a flight to LA by tomorrow night, these last four days forgotten.

I blew out a loud breath, fanning the soap bubbles, misery taking over. Who was I kidding? Griffin had already left his mark on me. I would never forget him.

Done with my bath, I made myself a sandwich and considered making one for Griffin, but he was still locked in his office. The last thing I wanted to do was piss him off again– for whatever reason. I went to bed still miserable, a stark contrast to the previous night. I wasn't wrapped in Griffin's arms this time, nor was I on cloud nine. The blankets weren't warm enough to compensate the cold shower Griffin gave me.

AFTER A MISERABLE, sleep-challenged night, I woke up, bleary-eyed and grumpy, ready to confront Griffin about our issues. I found him in the kitchen pouring a cup of coffee. Except for the small tick in his jaw, he didn't acknowledge my presence.

"Good morning."

Nothing.

A frustrated sigh pushed me forward. "Griffin. Please, talk to me. Is everything okay between us?" I asked.

He shrugged, still not looking at me. "Why wouldn't it be?"

"Because you've been acting pissed off since yesterday!" I snapped, even more frustrated by his feigned nonchalance.

A sudden honking outside made me jump. I glanced at the closed window, wondering what it could be. Griffin seemed unaffected, like he already knew what it was. I moved to the window and peeked through. A snow truck pulled up behind Griffin's truck in the driveway. The driver, a middle-aged, white-bearded man with friendly eyes, leaned his head out the window while honking the horn again.

"What's going on?" I asked, turning back to Griffin.

He finally met my eyes, his gaze as cold as any blizzard. "That's my neighbor, Andy, the owner of the Airbnb you'd booked for your trip."

"Oh... okay." I hoped my face gave nothing away. "Why is he here?"

"To take you to the airport," Griffin simply replied, his icy gaze still locked on me.

Shockwaves ran over me, numbing my entire body. "What?"

"I figured you might be in a rush to get back to *LA* and publish my story. That's what journalists do, isn't it?" he asked, his tone as hard as his face.

The room swayed. I gripped the back of the chair for support, connecting the dots. He knew. He'd known all along. The rough sex last night, that was his punishment for my lies.

I stepped to him, reaching for his arm. "Griffin–"

He backed away. The disgust on his face made my stomach drop. "I don't want to hear it. Pack your fucking bags and leave right now."

The tears spilled from my eyes. "I was going to tell you—"

"When? After you wrote your story?" he roared. "I took you into my home, I save you from fucking death—twice— and all this time, you've been lying to me!"

"I didn't lie," I tried to defend, feeling weak.

He rose a brow. "Really? Airbnb up top; was that where you were really headed?"

I couldn't answer. He wouldn't believe the half-truth, anyway. My heart broke into pieces, damaged by a self-inflicted wound.

Griffin scoffed. "Thanks for further proving why I can't trust women anymore."

Tears flowed down my face, making it hard to see. "I'm sorry!" I choked. "But after hearing your story, there was no way I could write it. Believe me, Griffin. Please."

"Believe you?" He laughed dryly. "You came in here, lied and gave yourself to me because you wanted me to open up. Like a fool, I fell for it. I don't believe you wouldn't publish that story, Victoria. Not after all the trouble you went through to get it."

"I didn't tell you who I was, because I didn't want you to kick me out when you heard I was a journalist."

"But I'm sure you figured you'd get the information one way or another," he spat.

My gaze lowered to the floor, a single drop of tears falling to the hardwood. "I didn't plan on having sex with you, Griffin. And I didn't sleep with you because I was desperate for a story. I did it because I—"

"The truck's waiting. You can head to the airport or the city; doesn't matter. As long as you're anywhere but here," he said firmly, and my heart swelled painfully in my chest– more painful than I'd ever experienced in my life.

With tears still running down my face, I turned and left for the bedroom where I packed my things hastily– desperate to get away, though at the same time, it was the last thing I wanted to do. Griffin wouldn't see reason – not when he was this angry and I couldn't even blame him. I brought this on myself. This was the consequence for my stupid actions.

If only he'd believe I didn't sleep with him for a story. I did that solely because I wanted him. It hurt like hell to see the look on his face – to know I was the reason for his pain. After what Rachel had done to him—God, I never wanted him to experience that betrayal again.

I wiped my tears as I cleared the phlegm from my throat and left the room, taking one last glance at the folded blankets Griffin had lent me – the ones we were wrapped in not too long ago.

I squinted back the fresh tears and prepared myself for Griffin in the living room, but he wasn't anywhere in sight. Realizing his intention, and with my heart breaking even more, I left, knowing this fight was the last conversation we would ever share.

Chapter 14

Victoria

"Hey, sweetie. Are you awake?"

I groaned, pulling the sheet over my head. "No," I reply to Ashley.

The bed dipped as she joined me, and fresh air hit my face when she pulled the sheet off my head. "It's been three days, Vicky. It's time to leave this goddamn bed."

"But I don't want to," I whined, rubbing my burning eyes. After three days of crying, I doubted there were any tears left in me. My dry mouth was a sign of how dehydrated I was.

After a miserable journey from Griffin's cabin, during which I prayed he would come after me and beg me to stay, I booked a flight to LA, crying all the way home, falling into Ashley's arms with more tears as I sobbed out what happened between us. She tried to comfort me but couldn't, so she went for reinforcements. But rocky road ice cream and red wine weren't enough to mend my broken heart. Three days later and here I was, still dying inside.

"I'm done with watching you wallow, Vicky. Get out of bed, take a shower and get ready to move on. It's not the end of the world," Ashley said.

"Then why does it feel like it is?" I asked, my eyes welling up with fresh tears. Guess I wasn't as dehydrated as I thought.

Ashley sighed, staring at me with pity. "Shit, you love this man, don't you?"

I shook my head. "Don't be ridiculous."

"Vicky, you've never been in love before; I don't think you have the slightest idea what it feels like, but I'm telling you, your actions tell a different story."

"I'm just ashamed of how things went down. Griffin deserved better," I replied, sniffing.

"And you need to stop beating yourself over it. You apologized to him and you told your truth. If he can't forgive you, then I guess that's his problem."

I bit my lips, not wanting to think about Griffin anymore, not when it made me cry so much. "What am I going to tell Pearson?" I whispered. I still had four more vacation days left. He assumed I was still chasing that lead.

Ashley shrugged. "Tell him there's no story; simple."

"But I'll lose my job," I reminded her.

"Nah. I think Pearson was just bluffing. He'd be a fool to let you go."

I disagreed, shaking my head. "I don't know, Ash. He seemed pretty serious."

"Well, even if he does, you'll find another job. There are plenty of openings in the city."

"But journalism is my dream job," I pointed out.

"Yes, your dream job; but Grapevine Buzz wasn't your dream workplace.

"It kinda was –"

Ashley threw her hands up, visibly frustrated. "Okay stop! And stop feeling sorry for yourself. Things will be fine." I pouted, and she took my shoulders, shaking me a little. "You will be fine, Victoria Danvers."

Ashley only used my full name when she wanted to get a point across. I pursed my lips, breathing a sigh through my nose.

"It's hard to believe that right now but trust me, if Pearson fires you, you'll find a new job. And don't worry about Griffin. It's his loss. Mr. Right is still out there waiting for you."

I sighed. "I still wish I'd done things differently."

"Shit has already hit the fan, Vicky. The only thing you can do is move on."

I cleared my throat, Ashley's positiveness slowly seeping under my skin. "You're right. Tomorrow I'll head to the office and tell Pearson the truth."

Ashley pulled me in for a hug. "Good. Whatever happens, happens. Everything will be fine, trust me."

EVEN AFTER ASHLEY'S pep talk, I couldn't get Griffin off my mind. I desperately wanted to talk to him again – to see him, but that was impossible. Griffin wanted nothing to do with me and I couldn't even blame him.

From his perspective, I understood his anger, his reaction to what I'd done and gosh, I hated myself for lying to him. Yet, I was a little ticked off that he didn't hear me out, at least. I made a mistake. Didn't all humans, at some point? I considered what Ashley said about me being in love with Griffin and while I hoped that wasn't the case, the rapid beating of my heart told me it was.

With a scoff, I piled up my pillows and dropped onto them. "Fuck love, and screw Griffin. I'm going to focus on myself; nothing else."

Griffin wasn't the only one with trust issues. I'd never seen love work out for anybody in my life. My mom was in love with my dad and he left before I was even born. Ashley fell head over heels for Damon and he cheated on her with his roommate's girl. Love was a lie. If love was what I felt for Griffin, I could do without it. It was probably the best thing for us, anyway.

I got dressed the following morning, blowing out a sigh as I stared at my reflection in the mirror. I wore a pair of dress pants that made me feel powerful, a cute buttoned top tucked in at the waist. I donned my hair in a ponytail to highlight my face, put on minimal makeup so I don't hide my natural beauty. My four-inch heels soon followed, then my short strap handbag completed the look. After doing a final twirl in the mirror I headed out, hoping for the best, but knowing it was probably wishful thinking.

"Hey, how did it go?" Colin asked as soon as I stepped from the elevator.

Confused, I frowned at him. "How did what go?"

"Your little adventure. Heard you were off chasing Griffin Holt."

I shook my head. No doubt Pearson had told the team about my pending story, which meant he planned to fire me if I didn't deliver. "Er– dead lead," I replied with a shrug.

"Oh, bummer." He tsked. "Pearson won't be pleased; you know that, right?"

I shrugged again, then headed to my cubicle to put my things down, mentally clearing my desk. Ashley was right. As much as I loved working at Grapevine Buzz, there were many other options to consider. With my record, I could find a new job in no time.

After confirming Pearson had arrived, I walked to his office, feeling lighter than I'd been in a long time.

His face lit up as soon as I entered. "Ah, Danvers. You're back. Please have a seat," he said with the most enthusiasm I'd ever heard from him.

I managed a tight smile as I took a seat in front of him. He ran his gaze over me before clearing his throat. "So, how did it go with Griffin Holt?" he asked.

"Er– it was a dead end. He didn't want to be interviewed and he made that clear."

Pearson's face fell. "What– so you got nothing?"

I nodded. "I'm sorry, sir."

He scoffed. "Danvers, you ensured I'd get a story by the end of your time off."

I licked my lips. "I thought so too, but I – he just wouldn't budge."

He raked his hand through his hair and clasped his hands at his mouth. "You begged for a chance, I gave you one and you blew it," he gritted out.

"Mr. Pearson—"

"You know what this means, right?"

Although I'd been mentally prepared to leave, I didn't want to do so without a fight. "Please, Mr. Pearson. This job means everything to me."

"If it did, you would have made sure you got Holt's story," he replied. "Where is he? Maybe I can send a more skillful journalist to talk to him."

I swallowed the lump in my throat. "I can't tell you that."

His eyes widened. "You can't–" he choked out a dry laugh. "You've got to be kidding me."

I remained silent, watching the emotions crossing Pearson's face. He finally sighed before leaning back in his chair, his gaze trailing over me. "You can keep your job on one condition, Danvers."

I perked up in my chair. "What's that?"

He gestures between us. "A date, the two of us – my treat."

I scoffed. "Are you serious?"

"Why wouldn't I be?" he said, looking genuinely confused.

I stared at him, unable to believe what he just said. I never appreciated the way Pearson checked me out, but I never thought he would make a move on me. Asking me on a date as my boss was one thing, but using it to manipulate me into keeping my job, now that was downright disgusting.

"The answer is no, Mr. Pearson," I replied. "I don't want to date you."

His face curled with a sneer. "Stop playing hard to get, Danvers. I've seen the way you look at me."

"Maybe you need to get those eyes checked, Sir," I returned stiffly, and his expression darkened.

"You're a little too feisty for someone whose job is hanging on the line. I could fire you right now, you know."

"You know what, don't even bother. I quit anyway," I said, shooting up from my chair, the force causing it to tip backward, almost falling over.

Without waiting for his response, I stormed to my cubicle, gathered my things from my desk and left the building, ignoring questions from my colleagues. Pearson was an asshole for firing me, but I didn't want to put the company in a negative light.

The strange thing was, when I got home, I didn't think about being unemployed or that my dream job was now gone. Griffin was my only thought, occupying my mind to a heart-wrenching degree. I couldn't stop reflecting on the time we shared, despite how short it was. I tried convincing myself that four days wasn't enough to fall in love, but the longer he stayed on my mind, more I ached for him, the harder it was to deny.

"I HOPE YOU'RE HUNGRY," Ashley announced as she breezed through the front door. "Get ready for a feast." She dropped the bag on the center table and shrugged from her jacket.

"What's this?" I asked, curiously peering into the bag.

"Just a little reward for sticking it to Pearson. I stopped by that Caribbean restaurant across from the hospital. Their jerk chicken pasta is to die for—or so I've heard." She brushed me aside and unpacked the small bag. "I'll go get us some juice from the fridge. Coke?"

"Yeah sure," I called after her.

I opened the lid and was welcomed with the sweet, mouthwatering aroma that filled my nostrils, making me realize how hungry I was. I'd barely touched food for a few days now. A stomach bug had taken my appetite.

The pasta looked divine, but it reminded me of when Griffin cooked for us and how amazing it was. How wonderful the entire day had turned out. I couldn't help the tears that pricked my eyes from missing him so much. If only I'd been honest from the start. If only he'd forgive me.

Ashley returned, sitting beside me with a deep sigh. "You need to go see him."

I scoffed, shaking my head. "What I need is a job, Ash, not a man."

"You've sent out applications, right?"

"Yeah, but it's been two weeks—almost."

"I'm sure you'll be flooded with calls soon. Just be patient," she smiled, handing me my drink. "For now, enjoy your well-deserved break."

"I'm trying, Ash. Really."

Ashley pursed her lips, the way she usually did when she debated on saying something. "Why don't you use the break to go see Griffin?" she finally said. "The fight has been ripping you apart."

I cleared my throat. "I'm fine Ash." With my appetite fading, I twirled my fork in the food.

"You are far from fine. You're in love with Griffin and you don't want to admit it."

"What good will it do, anyway? Love is just for a time. There's never a happy ending; the story just ends at the good part."

She shook her head. "I don't believe that for a second. I'm not saying that love isn't complicated, but I'd take the risk if it meant being happy."

I sighed. "Griffin doesn't want anything to do with me, anyway. He's probably relieved that I'm gone. At least now he'll have his peace."

"Vicky–"

"Can we not talk about it ever again, please?"

Ashley pursed her lips, then released a conceding sigh. "Okay."

But her expression told she wasn't okay with letting it go.

ASHLEY RESPECTED MY request for another week, but it didn't help with my obsession with Griffin. I scoured the internet, hoping there was some news about him emerging from obscurity, but there was nothing on him. I figured he was still in Anchorage, shutting out the world – even more now after what I'd done.

By now he must have known I didn't break the story, but I guessed he still felt betrayed. I wanted to fix that. I needed to see him. I craved his touch, his lips. The longing for him inside me was almost unbearable sometimes. After three weeks, I was a far cry from being over him.

I curled into my blanket, wishing I could smell Griffin on it, but it was just me.

A wave of nausea covered me, prompting me sit up and reach for the cup of peppermint tea. The stomach flu had gotten worse. Ashley's over-the-counter suggestions did not help at all. She advised me about visiting the emergency room if the symptoms persisted, but I prayed they would clear up in a few days. The thought of sitting in a medicine-scented room for hours, listening to the sounds of sickness didn't sit well with me.

I drank all the tea then curled up in bed once more, again thinking of Griffin. I loved him. It wasn't a declaration I wanted to admit to anyone, at least, not yet, but in the privacy of my room, I felt comfortable confessing it. I had no idea if Griffin shared my feelings. A part of me wanted to find out. Despite how scary it was, I had to give it a shot.

I couldn't continue to torture myself. Maybe I should visit Griffin and apologize. What was the worst that could happen, him turning me away? He'd already done that, didn't he? There was no way his actions could hurt me any more than before.

Right?

No matter the outcome, I had to try. My conscience wouldn't let me up until I made that move.

Amid my thoughts, my phone rang, and I took it up, seeing Jimmy's name on the screen. I wasn't in the mood for a conversation, but Jimmy had been good to me.

"Hey, you. What's up?" I answered.

"Hey, beautiful. I haven't heard from you in a while—not that I'm not used to it," he joked. "But I thought you'd get back to me about that lead I gave you."

"I'm sorry, Jimmy. There's been a lot going on."

"Well, I haven't seen your story in print, so I'm figuring it's something else, right?"

I scratched my head. "Kind of and not really, but the story was a bust and I lost my job," I informed him.

"Ah dang, sorry to hear about that Vic," he said, the genuineness clear in his voice.

"Thanks, Jimmy, but I'll be fine. You know me; I always bounce back."

"So... to the reason I really called," he began, and I pushed to a sitting position. I'd never heard him sound so doubtful before.

"I'm listening," I replied.

"About that dinner we talked about; are you still up for it?" he asked.

I fiddled with the edge of the blanket, pondering. It had been a minute since I last went out. A date with my good friend was probably what I needed to get out of this funk. "Sounds great. When?" I asked.

"How about seven tomorrow? There's an Italian restaurant in the new strip mall I'd want us to try."

"Ok, sounds good. I'll see you then." I ended the call and bit my lips, guilt digging at my insides. Why did it feel wrong to say yes to Jimmy? Griffin and I weren't together – we were far from it – which meant I could see whomever I wanted.

But as I placed the phone on the night table, the image of Griffin with another woman flashed through my head. White-hot jealously filled me. The thought of Griffin moving on cut me deep. I didn't want him with someone else. I wanted him to be mine, which means I had some serious groveling to do.

Chapter 15

Griffin

Watching Victoria leave was the hardest thing I ever experienced in my life. Not even when I discovered Rachel's treachery did it hurt like this. I'd watched through my window as she had climbed into that truck and for every day after that, I'd thought about it, the memory like a plague. Deep down, I knew I hadn't done the right thing, but I couldn't accept that — not when I felt so much pain because of what she had done.

Blinded by anger, I'd acted brashly, cursing myself for being so stupid. I should have seen through her façade, but like a fool, I'd allowed her beauty—and her body— to get to me. To think I would have learned from what Rachel did to me. In my heart, I knew Victoria was nothing like my ex-wife, but her betrayal hurt me. She'd worked her way into my life under false pretenses and had gotten what she came for. How could I even forgive that?

With her gone, the days felt longer and more meaningless. I wanted her by my side again, but I was too stubborn to admit it. As the weeks passed, I realized there was no story about me — I'd checked every article online and to my surprise, there was nothing. Victoria didn't print the story. At least she'd been honest about that.

I considered everything else she'd said. Did she sleep with me because she had feelings for me, or was it a strategy to make me open up? People got more vulnerable after sex, didn't they? Did she think I was that guy?

Turned out I was. Like an idiot, spilled my life story because she opened her legs.

I shook my head at my reflection in the mirror, raking my fingers through my hair that had grown longer over the weeks – my bushy beard brushing my chest. I looked terrible. Heartbreak had done a number on me.

Although Victoria had trampled on my heart, it still beat for her. Still fucking ached for her. Despite what she'd done, there was no denying I was in love with her. It was crazy to admit, but I fell in love with her from the day she stormed out of the house and almost froze in the snowstorm. There was little I knew about her – little I knew to be true, but I had to feel this way for some reason. Surely she was the woman for me.

Right?

I reached for the scissors, trimmed a few layers off my beard before I used the shear, and cut it low– the lowest it had ever been in a while. After washing my hair and styling it in a ponytail,

I booked a flight to Los Angeles. I'd vowed never to return to the city, but I was willing to break the vow for her. I wanted the truth. Did she feel anything for me?

My phone rang as I finished and I rushed to it, hoping by some miracle Victoria had gotten my number. I pursed my lips when I saw Kourtney's image on the screen. I pressed the answer button, placing the phone to my ear.

"Hey sis," I answered.

"Hey yourself. How are you?"

"I'm fine, just packing my things for the next flight out," I replied.

"The next flight out to where?" she asked, her voice filled with hope.

"LA," I said simply.

"You're coming to LA? Seriously?"

I couldn't help my smile. "Correct."

She choked a laugh. "Are you the same Griffin who vowed never to set foot in LA again? What changed?"

I shrugged. "I've been here long enough; I need to feel the sun on my skin again."

"Mhmm. I doubt that's the reason, but I'll take it. I've missed you so much."

Kourtney knew me too well, but I wasn't ready to tell her about Victoria, especially with all the complications involved. "I've missed you too."

She giggled. "You sound happy."

I sighed. "Not quite, but I'll get there. Hopefully soon."

"Oh, you will. Just one step at a time."

There was a short pause, then she continued. "So grandma called this morning. Wanted to know if I had a baby on the way."

"Typical Grandma," I replied with a snort. "Always with those baby questions. Isn't ten great-grandkids enough?

"Obviously not. It's different this time, though. She dreamt about catching fish last night."

I smirked, remembering the superstition. If there was a dream about fish, it meant there was a baby on the way. "So, is she right?"

Kourtney scoffed. "Right my ass, you know I'm into girls."

"Occasionally," I put in and she laughed heartily. I hadn't heard Kourtney laugh like that in such a long time and I realized it was because she always worried about me.

"But you know her dreams are always on point."

"Yeah, usually," I replied, pulling an overnight bag from the closet.

"So... I was thinking maybe it was meant for you instead."

I snorted right away. "Yeah, right."

"Oh, come on, Griff. You're my brother, but even I can admit you're a good-looking guy. I'm sure the ladies in Anchorage—"

"Kourtney, those dreams mean nothing, and they certainly aren't meant for me," I cut in, though despite my words, I couldn't help wondering it was true. Victoria and I didn't use protection—in hindsight, not the best decision—but that made it possible, right?

Kourtney giggled. "I'm just saying; it's more likely for you than me."

Rubbing the nape of my neck, I sighed. "I hear you loud and clear. Well, if there's an off chance that you'll become an aunt, you'll be the first to know."

"Oh I already know," she teased.

I rolled my eyes, though she couldn't see me. "If you say so. Listen, pick me up at five, tomorrow, okay? I've got some work to do."

That work involved packing the bag for my flight. It was a risk going to see Victoria, but one I had to take. Plus, Kourtney was right. Our grandmother's dreams were always true. Funny how she never dreamt of any fish when Rachel got pregnant.

Chapter 16

Griffin

The following day, I disembarked the flight at LAX, welcoming the weather that was a balmy contrast compared to Anchorage. It was around this exact time seven years ago when I left, vowing never to look back. Funny how my life had come full circle. The reason I came back wasn't a hilarious one, though.

Pulling in a breath, I exited the terminal, my eyes scanning the sea of people. Everyone wore bright smiles, their bodies bouncing with anticipation as they waited for their loved ones. The squeals were deafening, the smiles contagious as people reunited.

"Griff!" I heard a voice, my head snapping in the direction where I saw Kourtney's smile mimicking that of those around me. She wore a bright grin on her face as she rocked from side to side. I could tell she was just dying to hug me. I dropped my bags to the floor and opened my arms to her, watching as she ran to me, her head crashing against my chest as she hugged me tight. I chuckled and wrapped my arms around her, her body almost lost in the midst.

"Gosh, it's good to have you back," she croaked, followed by a sniffle.

I clenched my teeth, the emotions bubbling up inside me. "I missed you, Kourt."

"Not as much as I missed you," she said, easing from me and staring me up and down, her eyes pooling with tears. "You've gotten so... huge." She laughed and I joined in.

We spent the entire ride to her house trying to catch up—well, it was more talking on Kourtney's end. We stopped for gas, and as we pulled off the pump, she put the car in park and turned to me, a cheeky smile on her face.

"Okay. I'm done trying to be patient. Who is she?"

"Huh?" I said, surprised by her question.

She snorted. "Griff, don't act dumb. I know you love me, but you didn't return to LA for me."

I blew a sigh. "Fine. I came for Victoria, the journalist you gave my address."

Kourtney pumped the air with her fist. "I knew it! When you hung up after asking me about her, I figured that wasn't random. Does she know you're here?"

I shook my head. "We had a fight. A huge one. She lied about the reason she came to Anchorage."

"Oh, bummer," Kourtney said, staring at me with pity.

"I don't even know if I'm doing the right thing coming here. Can I look past that lie?"

"Nobody's perfect, Griff, and life's too short to not forgive, not to take risks... not to love."

"You saw where love got me the last time," I reminded her.

"Nothing's wrong with picking yourself up and trying again."

I sighed and leaned back in my seat, considering what she said.

"Do you even know where she is?"

I nodded. "I made a few calls while I waited for the flight. Remember Thomas, the PI who had a crush on you? He found her address."

She smiled. "Then what are you waiting for?"

"A shower and some sleep," I replied.

She rolled her eyes at me, changing gears. "Tomorrow isn't promised, Griff. I say you get there now and tell her how you feel."

My brows furrowed. "Where is all of this coming from, Kourt?"

"From you, Griff. From that sparkle in your eyes. I haven't seen you so..." she paused, slowing down to give another car passage. "So excited in a while."

I shook my head and gave her the address, trying to relax as she made the half hour drive to Victoria's apartment. I wouldn't admit it out loud, but she was right. Well, half right. This was more than excitement. Desperation was probably a better description of how I felt. The sooner I saw Victoria again, the quicker we could hash out our issues and be together again. I couldn't want to hold her in my arms.

Kourtney pulled into the driveway of Victoria's apartment building and parked the car. "Good luck, brother. Although, I doubt you'll need it. This mountain man vibe makes you dreamy. Like a meal; isn't that what the kids are saying these days?"

I reached for the handle, grinning. "I have no idea what the slangs mean these days."

The smile slowly faded when I saw Victoria coming down the steps. She wore her hair loose and she had a little makeup on – her skin glowing despite the cool air. A stylish coat covered her body, but I glimpsed a black dress underneath, one that hugged her tight and sat above her knees. I couldn't take my eyes off her. How beautiful she was and how much I'd missed her. All the emotions came back, overwhelming me. If I was ever unsure of my feelings for her, that moment made them very clear.

"That's her alright," Kourtney whispered, and I almost jumped out my seat, forgetting she was beside me.

As my hands moved to pull the handle, I paused, my teeth clenching tight when a tall, brown-skin man stepped out of a car and approached her. He smiled at her, and the blood draining from my face when he kissed her cheeks. I gripped the handle when they hugged. From where I sat, I could see the blush on Victoria's face.

My body heated with anger, the air in the car hot as a series of emotions passed through me. My chest rose and fell, and I swore I saw red as I tore my gaze away and grounded my teeth so hard, I thought they'd shatter in my mouth.

I snarled, pulling the car handle when I heard a click. I flashed my head towards Kourtney who swallowed visibly, concern on her face.

"Open the door, Kourt," I bit out.

"Griff, I need you to calm down before you do something stupid," she said.

"Open the damned door!" I growled and she flinched a bit.

She shook her head. "Not when you're this angry."

I huffed, watching as the guy opened the car door and guided Victoria inside. I wanted to wipe the stupid smile off his face with my fist. I dropped my head against the seat as his engine revved to life and the car sped off, disappearing within seconds.

I slammed my hands against the dashboard, muttering a curse before I glanced at Kourtney. "Take me back to the airport," I mumbled.

"What?"

"Coming here was a mistake. It was stupid of me to believe this would lead to anything good."

"Come on Griff. She's probably having dinner with a friend. Give her a chance to explain."

"No. She's clearly moved on. Heck, for all I know, she's been with him all this time!"

"Or, he might be a friend like I said—"

"Take me back to the airport, Kourtney," I cut in.

"Griff—"

"Take me back, or I'll call a cab."

With a sigh, Kourtney spun the car around and returned in the direction we came in. The drive was mostly silent until we got to the airport. She parked and bit her lips as she glanced at me.

"I just think you're making a huge mistake," she said softly.

"The mistake was in coming here," I replied, shoving the door open. "I'll call you when I get back home."

I heard her sniffs as I left the car, but I was too angry to look back. Too angry at myself. Besides, I didn't want to linger in LA any longer that I needed to. I entered the huge building, checking for an available flight. It turned out I had to wait a few hours, but it gave me enough time to reflect on how stupid I'd been for coming here. Victoria's lies were red flags I'd ignored because I assumed she was different, but she was just like my ex. A liar. As I sat in the departure lounge wrapped in anger and sorrow, I swore that when I locked out the world this time, it would be for good.

Chapter 17

Victoria

That date with Jimmy only confirmed what I already knew deep inside, that the only man I wanted in my life – the only man I wanted to get dolled up for, the only man I wanted to open my door and slip his hand around the small of my back, the only man I wanted to take me to an amazing dinner, was Griffin. For the first time since we met in college, I struggled to engage with Jimmy. Griffin occupied every inch of my thoughts.

Sure enough, Jimmy made the night fun, complimenting me on my outfit, entertaining me with stories about this job, prompting me to order the most expensive items on the menu, but he would never be the man for me. Not when Griffin was out there. When I returned home from dinner that night, I was even more desperate to see him – more tempted to book a flight to Anchorage just to be with him.

Christmas was a day away. I'd never spent the holiday without Ashley since my mom died a few years ago, but I had to do this. Time was against me—at least, that was how I felt. The sooner I booked that flight, the better. I didn't want to be apart from the man I loved during my favorite time of year, so I packed my bags, Ashley cheering me on as I prepared myself to do the wildest thing ever.

"Gosh, this feels like those Hallmark movies we usually watched on Christmas Eve," she said with a squealed. I shook my head at her enthusiasm, my nerves getting a hold of me.

"I'm doing the right thing, right?" I asked, pausing with a sweater in my hand.

"Of course you are, sweetie! Come here!" she said, opening her arms for a hug.

I grinned, moving to her. A sudden bout of dizziness made me sway, and I sat down instead.

"Are you okay?" Ashley asked, her voice laced with concern.

I rubbed my forehead. "Yeah, just a little dizzy, I guess. It's fine – it rarely lasts," I reassured with a smile.

Ashley's forehead wrinkled. "Still? I thought you were getting better."

I shrugged. "It's been on and off for a few days now, but I just figured I needed to rest."

"Hmm." Ashley came up to me, pressing the back of her hand to my forehead and examining my skin. "Your face looks a little yellow. Your blood count might be a bit low." She stood there puzzled, as if trying to solve a math problem. "When's the last time you had your period?" she asked, and I froze.

"What?"

"Your period; last time?" she hastened, flicking her fingers at me.

I swallowed hard. "Er, last month?" I guessed.

"What date last month?"

I reached for my phone, opening the period app I used to track my cycle. "Oh. It's three weeks late," I announced, glancing up at her.

"Well, that's no cause for alarm. Your periods have always been irregular. You used protection with Griffin, right?"

My stomach dropped, and my hands instantly became sweaty. "I...huh, Ash..." my hands shook.

Ashley's mouth flew open. She gaped at me before slapping the side of her head then dashing out the room. I sat there, staring in the spot she'd occupied until she returned, handing me a small box. I took it and read the label, realizing it was a pregnancy test.

I gasped, a lump forming in my throat as I imagined the prospect of carrying Griffin's child. "I'm not pregnant," I whispered, my voice too weak. "I can't be."

"One way to find out, Vicky," Ashley replied, her expression as somber as I felt.

I swallowed the huge lump in my throat and blinked back the blurriness from my eyes as I moved to the bathroom, Ashley right behind me, standing at the door.

I peed on the stick and pulled my pants up, waiting desperately for the results. Ashely chewed on her nails, clearly nervous, but I was feeling so many emotions, it was hard to pinpoint one. My hand shook as I lifted the stick peered at the blankness. Nothing had appeared yet, but it felt like I'd been waiting forever.

"Damn it, why is this taking so long?" Ashley muttered.

I ushered her out the bathroom because she made me extra nervous, then I sat on the floor, waiting for the beep on the timer. When it sounded, I got up, unable to control my shaking hands and the sweat that washed me as the results popped up on screen.

Pregnant.

A single tear fell on the stick, blurring the results on the small screen. The door opened and Ashley stepped in. I broke out in tears and she reached for me.

"What am I going to do, Ash?" I sobbed. "What if Griffin wants nothing to do with a baby? Or me?"

"Listen, Vicky. Griffin or no Griffin, you'll be a great mom plus, you have me."

That made me smile, but I still felt like shitting my pants. Ashley was right; I'd be a great parent, but I still wanted Griffin to be a part of our lives. As I calmed myself and considered how good this could be, I couldn't help the happiness that fluttered in my stomach.

"I have a feeling he'll welcome the news. Don't tell me how I know. I just do." Ashley wipe my face. "This is an even greater sign that you need to go see him."

Her response made me anxious, yet excited, ready to surprise Griffin with the ultimate Christmas gift.

Chapter 18

Griffin

Twenty-four hours had already passed since I returned home, and I was still moping – wallowing in self-pity and hating myself for not even hating Victoria like I should. It was Christmas Eve, and I was the most pathetic man in the world—in the top five, at least, pining over a woman who was having the time of her life with another man. I was just the guy she fucked as a means to an end – the guy she fucked up even more than he was. I meant nothing to her. It angered and hurt me to the very core.

In an attempt to get out of my funk, I made coffee, intending to write. There was nothing like pouring myself on a few blank pages, the perfect purge. Yes, exactly what I needed.

As I poured the coffee in my cup, I heard a knock on the front door. I frowned, wondering if Alan had taken my dinner invite seriously. I wasn't in the mood for company. Not tonight.

I walked to the door and pulled it open, my heart racing in my chest when I saw Victoria standing there, two bags at her feet. A thick coat covered her body, her loose hair framing her face. Fuck, I'd never seen her more beautiful. I'd never been more in love until that moment.

She swallowed hard, her cheeks reddening as her eyes ran over my face. "H– hi."

My heart danced from seeing her again, but I refused to let it show. "What are you doing here?" I asked, the image of her and that guy flashing through my head.

"Can I come in?"

I hesitated, my hand curling around the edge of the door. Her long eyelashes fluttered as she waited, the hope on her face melting my heart. I stepped aside, allowing her to pass. Her familiar scent filled me with longing, tempting me to pull her close and breathe her in. I kept my hands to myself as we made our way to the living room.

Victoria turned to me, clasping her hands together. She seemed cold, and I wanted nothing more than to warm her up. But as I stared at her, I could still see her in that man's arms – the pleasant smile on her face. My jaw tightened from the memory. I rolled my fingers into fists as anger bubbled up inside me.

"How have you been?" she asked softly.

I shrugged. "I've been better. You?"

"Totally miserable. I missed you."

I scoffed, pushing my hands in the pocket of my pants.

"I'm serious, Griffin," she replied, a plea on her face. "I know I hurt you and I'm so very sorry. I didn't mean to, but I was so desperate when I got here. It was either your story or lose my job. But when we got together, none of it mattered. I only wanted you."

She reached for me, but I stepped back. "I should've told you who I was the second I woke up. I'm still kicking myself for not doing that. Please believe me, Griffin. I didn't mean to hurt you."

I continued to stare at her, my frown still in place. She glanced up at me and visibly swallowed before rubbing her hands together and clearing her throat. "If it's any consolation, I didn't print the story. I couldn't."

I scoffed again. What was she expecting, a reward?

She bit her lips after getting nothing but a cold stare from me. "I also quit my job."

"Why?" I was curious to know.

She looked up at me again, her expression brightening at the single word from my lips. "My boss told me I could keep my job if we dated, so I quit," she said, rolling her eyes.

I breathed a harsh sigh, unable to believe she was lying right in front of my face... again. "Just leave, Victoria," I grumbled.

Her eyes widened and she looked confused. "What?"

I blew out another breath to calm myself. "You're standing here lying to my face again!" I roared, and tears settled in her eyes.

"What else did I lie about, Griffin?"

I raked my fingers through my hair, suppressing the anger. "I went to LA, Victoria. Like a fool, I felt guilty for the way I treated you when you left and I believed we stood a chance," I informed her, shaking my head.

"You visited LA?" It was almost a whisper. "Why didn't you try to find me?" Hurt filled her face, the words fragile and broken.

"I did find you," I replied through gritted teeth. "I was right in the parking lot of your apartment building when I saw you coming down the steps, dressed up, a smile on your face. I watched as some other man pulled you in his arms... kissed you."

Her face paled and she palmed her throat. "Jimmy kissed me on the cheek, not my mouth."

For some reason, her defense angered me even more. "Does that make it okay?"

"It meant nothing, Griffin."

"Don't lie to me, Victoria," I snarled. "I'm sick of it. The way he looked at you, that wasn't nothing—"

"Can you just listen to me?" she shouted, her big brown eyes glistening.

I paused, staring at her, surprised by the outburst. "That man you saw was my friend. He wasn't my boss. Jimmy and I knew each other since college. I owed him dinner for his help with finding you. That was all it was."

I processed the words. "And you expect me to believe you?"

"Yes," she said firmly. "It's the truth, Griffin."

A long beat passed as I battled with thc urge to believe her and the insecurities that plagued me. I wanted to believe she wouldn't hurt me again, but did I want to take that chance?

"I've need you, Griffin," she breathed, and my gaze shot up to hers, my heart soaring. How could I even hold back after hearing that?

"I'll never lie to you again, I promise." She moved closer, smiling when I didn't back away this time. "I love you so much."

Hell. I swallowed the lump in my throat as the walls crumbled around me. Hearing the words were all it took for me to concede. I had no doubt she was telling the truth. Not when her eyes didn't leave mine as she spoke – not when I could feel the genuineness radiating from her.

"I missed you too," I confessed. "And I'm sorry for how I treated you the day you left. Despite what happened, you didn't deserve that. Forgive me?"

She smiled, her eyes glistening. "Already done."

I approached her and she met me halfway. A gentle sigh left her lips as I brushed the hair from her face. "I missed your touch," she whispered.

"That's putting it mildly, at least for me," I replied. "I've never ached for anyone this much."

She gasped. "Oh, Griffin. You have no idea how happy you just made me."

I couldn't help my grin. "Well, you can show me how much..."

Victoria chuckled, giving me a gentle nudge in my side. I tackled her to the floor, and she laughed out loud, the sound like music to my ears. I wrapped my arms around her, breathing her sweet scent like I wanted to when she got here. She pulled back, staring at my face with the love that ran through me, too.

"Do over?" she said, and I nodded.

"Do over."

I helped her off the floor, her smile fading as she straightened. As I released her, she swayed, then grabbed onto the sofa to steady herself. Her ashen face left me concerned.

"Are you okay?" I asked, searching her face.

She nodded, sitting gingerly on the couch. "There's something I need to tell you, Griffin."

"Okay..." I sat beside her, taking her hand. "Whatever it is, I can handle it, okay?"

"Okay." She placed her hand over mine, breathing deeply. "I didn't just come for your forgiveness. We're having a baby."

My eyes widened, my heart rate running a mile a second I processed her words.

"Look, I understand if you need some time to process this. It's not like we planned it—"

I laughed, my vision blurring with tears. Kourtney was right! My grandmother was right!

Victoria gasped when I swept her in my arms, kissing her briefly before I hugged her tight and basked in the feeling of having her here with me again, with the most beautiful gift.

"You have no idea how happy you've made me, and I'm sorry it took our fight to realize, but I love you Victoria."

I clamped my mouth to hers, replenishing myself with what I'd missed so much these past weeks. Victoria was back in my arms and I was the luckiest man alive. She was my soulmate and I could feel that in her touch – how she fitted against me perfectly. I wanted her so much – had craved for her like I've never craved for anything and now, after what seemed like a lifetime later, I finally had her again.

I lifted her into my arms and carried her to my bedroom where I gently placed her small body on the bed, watching as she peeled off her clothes while I removed mine. My gaze went to her still-flat stomach and happiness washed through me as I envisioned her with my baby in her arms. She would be the perfect mother, I just knew it.

Victoria caught me staring and she stroked her stomach with a smile. "Are you truly happy about it?" she asked timidly.

"Happier than a man could ever be," I replied with a smile.

She grinned, pushing up on her knees and reaching for me, the longing obvious in her eyes. Her warm body pressed to mine. My cock hardened as she rolled against me. I kissed every inch of her body – lingering at her stomach, love rushing through me when I thought of the baby inside. My lips moved down to the flesh between her thighs. Victoria gasped, her body inching up when I lashed her with my tongue.

"God, I missed this," she moaned, her body writhing as I delivered hard licks to her clit. Her orgasm came swiftly, and from the violent way she gripped my hair, it was fucking intense.

Before she recovered, I eased up, settling between her thighs. She wrapped her legs around my waist and pinned her arms around my neck, trapping me in place, her warm body the perfect fit beneath mine. My breath paused as I sunk my cock inside her, emotions running from head to toe. A sweet moan left her lips as she gripped me tighter.

"Oh fuck, Victoria. You feel so fucking good around me," I whispered in her ear, my dick gliding through her warm flesh.

"You feel fucking good inside me, too," she said between moans, raising her hips to meet my thrusts. I went all the way, Victoria's legs pinning me in place as I explored her. It felt like heaven, her soft skin like velvet. I couldn't go another day without this woman by my side.

Her pussy pulsed around me, and I picked up the pace, knowing she was close.

"Oh yes! Harder, Griffin. Harder!" she begged, and I obliged, feeling her legs tightening around me.

I fucked her hard and deep, maintaining eye contact as I filled her with each thrust. Her small mouth fell open, a series of emotions played across her face while her pussy convulsed around me, trying to milk me dry.

"Yes, that's it, Victoria. Come for me," I ordered.

She exploded with a scream, her pussy holding me in a tight grip. Just like that, I came apart, filling her with deep long strokes until I emptied myself inside her.

Spent, I half rolled off her, careful not to crush her with my weight. "Merry Christmas, beautiful," I whispered. For the first time in seven years, I looked forward to the holiday, thrilled to share it with someone I loved.

Victoria smiled and wrapped her legs around me again, as if making sure I didn't go anywhere. "Merry Christmas, my mountain man," she whispered, arousal still on her face. She reached down and stroked me, and it took nothing for me to get hard again, ready for her. I groaned, already drunk from pleasure as she straddled me, sinking down on my cock.

Holy hell. This woman would be the death of me.

Epilogue

Victoria

6 months later

I breathed a sigh as I glanced at my watch and looked around the large studio. "Have you seen him?" I asked a crew member.

"No ma'am," she said with a tight smile before she walked away.

I headed to my office and took a seat, closing my eyes, happy to be off my feet. I glanced at my phone on the table and just as I was about to pick it up, my eyes caught the picture frame on my desk. It was my first day at the popular news studio and I had the biggest smile on my face. I remembered it like it was just yesterday.

Griffin and I had just disembarked the plane from Anchorage, and we were waiting for a cab ride to my apartment when my phone rang. Figuring it was Ashley telling me she'd gotten off work early, I dug through my bag and pulled it out. The unknown number on the screen made me hesitate. Usually I'd let it go to voicemail, but since I'd sent out my job applications a week ago, I'd hope this was the job offer I'd been waiting for.

"Hello," I answered.

"Hi, is this Victoria Danvers?" the female voice had asked.

"Yes this is she."

"I'm Jessica Hughes, calling from Premiere Communications. Ms Danvers, we've reviewed your application and did some research of our own. We'd like to schedule an interview with you..."

The joy that instantly bubbled in my chest was like no other. I hopped on my toes with a squeal, finding it hard to believe that it was true. Griffin raised a questioning brow at me, and I gave him a thumb-up sign, which meant nothing to him at the moment, but I would explain soon enough. Premiere was an even bigger news company than my previous job and I had only applied on a whim, doubting they would even call me.

I'd felt so lucky. Life was finally looking up. Griffin had decided to move back to LA. I'd landed the job of a lifetime. We had a precious baby on the way. There was nothing more I wanted. I was completely satisfied.

Little did I know, life still had a special reward for me.

The interview went so well that Jessica asked if I wanted my own show, which was beyond anything I could ever imagine. They wanted someone authentic and fresh and apparently, I fitted the bill. Saying yes took no effort. Now I was five months in, with my own producer, hairstylist, executive assistant... I even had a personal driver. Life couldn't get any better if it tried.

I smiled at the memory of my first day on the job and reached for my phone, dialing Griffin's number.

"Where are you?" I asked as the line opened.

"Right here," he replied. Hearing an echo, I spun in my chair to find him at my door, wearing a bright smile as he peeked around the edge.

A matching smile smeared my face as I got up from my desk and lurched towards him. He caught me and chuckled, placing a soft kiss on my lips.

"I thought you forgot."

He made a face. "I wouldn't miss this for the world."

I grinned and kissed him again. "I was starting to get worried."

He sighed. "I must admit, I'm a little nervous."

My fingers traced his low cut beard. "You'll be fine."

His gaze lowered to my stomach and he knelt on his knees to caress the round mound. "How's my little pea, doing?" he asked, large hands roaming the perimeter of my stomach.

I looked down, beaming as I watched him. "He was a little kicker today, but I think he's calmed down."

A flutter suddenly appeared in my stomach, causing Griffin's eyes to widen. "Guess someone's excited to see me."

I grinned. "We both are."

He kissed my stomach and then he rose to do the same thing to me. "You've given me the best gift ever; I don't know how I'll ever repay you."

"Oh, babe. Your love is always enough, you know that."

"Is it?" A wolfish grin appeared on his face as he gripped my ass. "If it's not, I could always make it up to you."

His hard pressed against my belly, letting me know exactly how he wanted to make it up to me. "Behave. We're about to go live."

He breathed a sigh, kissing me tenderly on the lips. Desire swept through my entire body as I kissed him back with just as much fervor.

A knock came at the door and we broke apart, both our gazes turned towards the door. "Mrs Holt, they're ready for you," the slender girl announced.

"Ok thanks Mandy, I'll be there in a sec." She nodded and then she disappeared around a corner.

I looked at Griffin who had a smirk on his face. "Mrs Holt. I like the sound of that."

"Of course you do," I said and he chuckled. "Let's go."

I went on set with Griffin by my side, my eyes trained on the space they'd decorated for me. The sofa neatly laid out, the contrasting colors, beautiful lighting. Everything was brilliant and lively and just how I liked it.

"Ok, Vic, we start in five," the crew manager announced, a makeup artist immediately stepping forward to retouch my makeup.

"Ok I'm all set." I glanced at Griffin who blinked as the makeup artist applied a little powered to his T-zone. "Babe?"

"I'm ready," he murmured.

We both moved towards the small set. I took a seat and glanced at the stack of books on the small coffee table in front. It was Griffin's newest title—another bestselling title – a romance inspired by our love. Pride bubbled in my chest as I glanced at him. He was neatly clad in a black suit with a blue tie that matched my dress.

Ashley came up behind him, waving at me with a huge smile on her face. I waved back, resting my hand against my stomach as I reflected on how lucky I was. I had everything I've ever wanted and more.

"Ok Vic, in three, two..." The producer gave a signal and I turned to the huge camera positioned in front of me.

"Good day America and welcome to Victoria's corner. Today I have a very special guest with me. Author of Save Me and a few other bestsellers, it's my pleasure to welcome Griffin Holt for the long awaited interview."

The small audience erupted in a series of cheers while I sat there smiling, watching as my man walked towards me, a smile on his face. I stood and accepted the small kiss he offered before he took a seat on a nearby single sofa.

Our gazes met. Bubbles of happiness filled my chest. I had no regrets going up that mountain in that snowstorm. I didn't regret falling for him. Griffin was my forever as I was his. I never believed in love, but with him, anything was possible.

MC Daddy Possessive Biker

Izzie Vee

Erotic & Forbidden[1]

IZZIE VEE[2]

1. https://www.amazon.com/s?k=izzie+vee&i=digital-text&crid=31LQJTEQYT2EE&sprefix=izzie+vee%2Cdigital-text%2C121&ref=nb_sb_noss
2. https://www.amazon.com/s?k=izzie+vee&i=digital-text&crid=31LQJTEQYT2EE&sprefix=izzie+vee%2Cdigital-text%2C121&ref=nb_sb_noss

Cover Design by Izzie Vee
Cover Photo by littlekzaka@gmail.com on Depositphotos.com

Table of Content

Chapter 1

Cassandra

I swallowed hard, watching the rain blasting against my bedroom window. That small, compliant and fearful part in my head told me it was a sign for me to stay, but I couldn't. Whether rain, sleet or snow, I had to get the hell out of there. I bit my lower lip, fearful of making a sound as I tiptoed across the creaky, hardwood floor. My hand tightened around the strap of my bagpack, and I moved toward my bedroom door, my heart thudding in my chest as I anticipated my escape.

As my hand curled around the rusting lock, I froze, a gasp almost escaping my lips as a sound echoed in the distance. Prying my room door open, I peeked through the small opening. Relief overcame me when I saw my daddy sprawled out on the worn sofa, a bottle of beer clutched to his chest as he snored, his round belly bouncing with every breath he took. Well, at least I knew what had made the noise. He was out cold, his gaping mouth glistening with drool at the corners.

I slowly pulled the door open and moved into the living room, where the TV provided the only light. My gaze moved to the corner where my big brother, Dean, lay stretched out on the double seater, fast asleep, his thick, dark hair covering his eyes. I glanced at the ashtray on the small wooden coffee table and saw a lit cigarette still positioned there, which meant Dean had just fallen asleep.

Swallowing the lump in my throat, I glanced to the kitchen where my eyes locked with a knife on the counter. I briefly glanced at my daddy and brother before I rushed to grab the small utensil, peanut butter still smeared across the blade. I clutched it tight and tiptoed into the living room, inching toward the coffee table where my father's car keys lay. I took a deep breath, reaching down between the pile of empty beer cans and pizza box. It seemed like time stood still as I carefully picked it up. My teeth clamped down on my lower lip, sweat dampening my forehead as I tried to keep quiet. My father shuffled on the sofa, a soft grunt leaving his lips, and I almost jumped out of my skin. Thankfully, I didn't scream, which would have turned things into a shit show. As I eased from in front of them, I glanced down the hall to the other room where my oldest brother, Johnny, slept. At least, I hoped he was still asleep, but I didn't have the time to find out.

As my sweaty palms clutched the knob to the front door, I checked the time on the clock right above the TV. It was a couple of minutes to midnight, and if I didn't act now, I might never get the chance to again.

The door creaked as I pulled it open. My breath paused in my throat. Chancing a glimpse behind me, I slipped through the small space, and a sudden clap of thunder had me gasping. I stiffened, staring at the pouring rain and the lightning flashing in the distance. It was a pitch-black night, not a hint of the moon in the sky. Fear crept up my spine, but I had to be braver than ever before. There was no way I'd survive living here much longer.

I looked to my father's old Lexus in the yard. Besides his two precious sons, this was his most favorite thing in the world. He wouldn't let anyone drive that thing, not even Johnny and Dean. I imagined the anger on his face when he woke up and discovered it was missing.

Too bad. This was a small price to pay for all the wrongs he and his sons had committed against me.

Just as I was about to make a run for it, a sudden voice had me gasping and whipping around. A tingle ran up my spine, the blood draining from my face when I saw Johnny sitting in the old wicker chair at the corner of the porch, a beer bottle in hand.

"Where do you think you're going this late?" he asked, his voice dangerously calm, but that was Johnny, a snake under the grass. He had the kindest face; bright blue eyes that sparkled when he smiled—he almost always smiled—, thin lips that spewed the sweetest compliments that made the ladies weak, a body many of them had fought over—Dad's front window was once a casualty in one of those fights. Underneath that façade was a cold-hearted woman-beater, and that woman was me. Staring at his hands, I imagined the pain from the beatings he often inflicted on me.

I swallowed hard as he stood and moved toward me. I wanted to run, but fear kept me paralyzed. It was as if my feet remained glued to the ground. My neck craned as I looked up at his face with his sly smile, that familiar sparkle now in his eyes.

"I uh... nowhere," I whispered, my body shaking with the rising fear.

Johnny scoffed as his gaze moved to my bagpack. "Nowhere, huh?" he said as he grabbed the bag and tore it from my shoulder. I gasped, pent-up tears fogging my eyes.

"Thinking of running away from your family, little Cass?" he jeered, his mouth twisting derisively.

My lips trembled as he grabbed my face with one hand, straining my neck, so I looked right in his eyes.

"You're fucking stuck with us forever, little sis. Now I want you to go back to your room, and we'll pretend like none of this ever happened. I'm sure you don't want Daddy finding out about your little move." He smiled, revealing buttered teeth with a single gold incisor.

At his words, tears streamed down my face, running down my chin to my chest. I tried to imagine being trapped here for the rest of my life, and the thought made me cry even more. This was no life to live. I was my family's prisoner, their housemaid and Johnny's punching bag. I had a fresh bruise on my stomach from when he'd hit me the day before, all because I didn't serve his lunch on time.

"Go on, now, before Daddy wakes up. I won't save your ass if he does," he said, shoving my shoulder.

Regardless of Johnny's words, I knew he would tell my father about my attempt to escape, thus making my life more hellish than it already was. I didn't have a cell phone or access to the internet. I was only allowed outside for an hour each day. With no neighbors for miles around, Daddy presumed it was safe. Even if I screamed, no one would hear me. I couldn't imagine my life getting worse, but he would find a way.

My lips tightened. No way could I endure any more of this. With my survival instinct kicking in, I knee'd Johnny. Directly in the groin. He screamed out and released me, grabbing his crotch with a deep-throated groan. My body quivered as I watched him hop around in pain, a single vein protruding from his forehead.

"You fucking bitch! I'll kill you!" he exclaimed, grabbing after me. I dodged him, and he fell to the ground. I made a run for his car, using the knife to stab the tires. The rain almost blinded my sight, and my shoes felt heavy in the muddy ground. Johnny had already gotten up, hobbling toward me. From his intense groans, he was still having severe pain from my knee in his groin.

"Shit!" I muttered, running to Daddy's truck, which I pulled open and locked the doors. I jammed the keys in the ignition and prayed this old piece of junk would operate fast enough this time. My eyes widened as the front door flew open, and Daddy and Dean stepped out, confusion on their faces.

"Shit, shit, shit!" I exclaimed as the car choked itself to life.

The engine turned over, filling me with relief, one that didn't last long. My scream pierced the air as Johnny slammed his hand against the window.

"Get the fuck out of the truck. Now!" he shouted.

I flipped my middle finger at him, pressed down on the gas, and the vehicle shot forward, spraying mud. Johnny stumbled back, and the corners of my lips curled into a smile as I sailed off the property. I glanced into the rearview mirror and saw the distorted images of all three of them, and I imagined the shock on their faces as I drove away.

I was still shaking like a leaf in the wind, but for the first time in two years, happiness bubbled in my chest. Until I realized I had nothing but the clothes on my back.

Shit.

I didn't get to retrieve my bag after Johnny grabbed it. All my clothes and cash I had managed to swipe from them over the months were left back there. I had nowhere to go, no way to survive without so much as an ID card, but my freedom was still better than all that.

With no plan in mind, I kept going, traveling for about five miles. By now, the rain had stopped, but the night was still pitch black. Come morning, reality would be clearer than now, which meant I needed to find a way out—fast. I had no friends, thanks to my family, scaring everyone away. Times like these, I wished Momma was still alive. She would've protected me from the bullshit. Daddy, Dean and Johnny would've been in prison by now.

Heck, she would be so proud of me for standing up to them. I imagined her cheering for me in heaven.

I was still basking in my bravery and freedom when I heard a loud pop. The car slowed, wobbling to each side.

"Fuck, fuck, fuck!" I exclaimed, slamming my palm against the steering wheel. I steered it to the corner of the road, the loud thumping confirming my worst fears.

Shoving the door open, I stepped out on the damp asphalt and glanced at the flat tire.

"Just my freaking luck!" I cursed, kicking the tire, frustration taking over as I raked my fingers through my wet hair. Huffing, I checked the back of the truck for a spare, surprised when I found none. This wasn't like Daddy. I couldn't recall him ever getting stranded. He was always prepared. Then again, he had been drinking more often than lately...

"This can't be happening," I muttered to myself, checking my environment for some sign of life. Daddy's truck was the only source of light on the long, empty stretch of road.

A chilly breeze wafted by. I wrapped my arms around my shivering body, which reminded me I didn't even have a blanket to keep warm. I had to get somewhere safe where I could hole up for the rest of the night. The nearest gas station was about fifteen minutes' drive away. To travel on foot would take more time.

An insurmountable dread washed over me as I reflected on my circumstances. Maybe I should have stayed home. Despite my family's terrible treatment, they made sure I got food and a place to stay. At least I wouldn't freeze to death back there.

I scanned the empty road, wishing rescue would come, but at this time of night, the chances of anyone coming this way was next to none.

Giving up, I returned to the dingy old Lexus, flopping down in the seat and mustering a sigh, wondering what my next move would be. I was happy about slashing Johnny's car tires because they'd come after me, and with this delay, they would've caught up to me by now.

I sat there for what seemed like hours, trying to work out a plan in my head. I could start walking, but the temperature had dropped even lower than when I started out. Besides, there was nothing but bushes for miles around. I couldn't take the chance, not knowing what danger lurked around me.

But if I stayed in the car until morning, Daddy and the boys would find me. The battle was only half won when I escaped. Total victory would only come when I left Alpine for good. While I had no clothes, no money, and definitely no plan, I couldn't go back home, no matter what.

With tears pricking my eyes, I locked the doors and pulled the lever to recline the seat. I needed rest for the journey tomorrow, wherever the road led. Better try to get some sleep.

As my eyes drifted shut, I heard the unmistakable sound of car engines in the distance. Hope blossomed within me. I uprighted the seat, glanced out the rearview mirror and saw a cluster of light approaching the truck. I smiled, whispering a thankful prayer that help had come at last.

But the closer the lights came, the more I realized they weren't cars, after all. The robust, throaty growls of the fleet of motorcycles sent my heart rate on an uncontrollable spike. This wasn't a rescue. Motorcycle clubs were nothing but trouble; at least, that's what I heard Daddy say.

"Motorcyclists are Satan's spawn," he'd grumble each time he had a run-in with one around town. "They are good-for-nothing, evil sons-of-bitches who want to wreck this country."

Well, considering that description fit Daddy to a T, I took his comment with a suppressed eye-roll. Hypocrite. He and my brothers had destroyed many lives with their drug-dealing ways.

The sudden roar of an engine made me jerk back to reality. I glanced out the rearview mirror again, my heart still racing in my chest. The group still lingered behind me, in no hurry to disembark. The band of motorcyclists weren't here to help, obviously. In fact, I suspected they were making plans to rob me.

Well, too bad, assholes. There's nothing to steal.

Another glance through the rearview mirror, and I tried to make them out. The night was too dark to see. I prayed to God it wasn't the Grimm Reapers from Phoenix. They were the most feared, with a reputation for being ruthless, robbing and killing without mercy. It had to be them. No other MC would dare ride these parts, especially this time of night.

Oh, God. I'm doomed.

I burst into a sob, fresh tears running down my cheeks.

The engines roared again, and they crawled closer, coming to a stop beside the truck. With sobs rocking my body, I reached for the knife I had thrown on the passenger's seat and gripped it tightly. My breath came out shaky and hitched as the motorcycle engines shut down. I squeezed my eyes shut as footsteps approached the car. My heart tilted in my chest when a knock came on my window.

I opened my eyes, and my body went numb when I saw the giant standing there. He wore a helmet, so I couldn't see his face, save for his thick beard that brushed his chest.

And his teeth. I could see his teeth.

Why was he smiling at me?

He gestured to the window, and I understood that he wanted me to roll it down. I hesitated, my hand curled around the knife. He mouthed something, and I shook my head. I didn't pick up what he said. He pursed his lips, then removed his helmet and leaned in, and my eyes dropped to his mouth.

I'm not going to hurt you, I read from his lips.

Yeah, right. Unless I'm stupid enough to open this door. Again, I shook my head at him.

He sighed, then glanced behind him, the smile still on his face when he looked back at me.

You have nothing to worry about, he mouthed.

For some reason, his smile won me over, giving me a reassurance that inched my guard down. Still gripping the knife, I wound the windows down an inch, allowing just a crack so we could speak.

"Everything alright here, young lady?" he asked, his clear blue eyes roaming over my face.

I nodded, summoning a smile. "Yeah, I'm fine, thank you."

He continued to stare at me, not looking all too convinced.

"Saw that you have a flat there. Maybe we could help you with that," he said, his face expanding into another smile.

"I don't have a spare or anything. It's useless, but thank you," I nodded, turning my gaze to the road, hoping he would take the hint and go away.

He didn't. There was a moment of silence, then he sighed. "Listen, young lady. We're not going to hurt you. Contrary to what you might believe, not every motorcycle club's violent. In fact, only a few are."

Yeah, I bet that's what they all say before luring you into their trap. I didn't believe a bunch of motorcyclists traveling past midnight were up to any good.

The middle-aged man slapped the front of his pants, and I sensed a slight frustration. "Ok, suit yourself. Have a good night, Miss," he said, raising his helmet to me and stepping away.

My brows furrowed as he walked to his motorcycle, where the gang of bikers waited for him. I gulped, looking behind me at the darkness, knowing I could either take a risk and accept help or stay here, where my family would find me. They were both scary options, but the former seemed more bearable.

With a prayer on my lips, I pushed the door open as the stocky man mounted his bike and adjusted his helmet.

"Okay," I quickly said, shivering as the cold air hugged my body again. Their lights were shining right at me; I blinked a few times, unable to see their faces, the silhouette of their huge bodies creeping me out a bit.

I swallowed hard. "Maybe I could get a ride into town," I said.

He glanced at the others and nodded. "No problem. We could get a spare in the morning. I'm sure you don't want to be without your ride—"

"No!" I blurted, then caught myself. "I mean, there's no need. That old piece of junk has more issues than a flat tire, anyway."

He nodded again. "Suit yourself." He glanced behind him. "Er, you can ride with Rodge—"

"Me," a low rumble came from my right. "She's riding with me."

"The hell she will," a whiny response came from the left. "Billy said she's riding with me."

Billy sighed. "Rodger, you've been overruled. Suck it up, and let's get out of here. Young lady, you're riding with Declan."

Rodger kept mumbling as Declan gestured to me. He seemed the biggest of the lot, the helmet hiding most of his face and covering thick, shoulder-length hair.

"Hop on, princess, your carriage awaits," someone teased from beside me. I rolled my eyes, and he laughed, causing soft chuckles to float around.

"You might wanna drop the knife, Kid," Declan murmured. My gaze wandered to the knife still tightly clutched in my hands, my knuckles pasty white.

I gritted my teeth. "I'm not a kid, and I'm keeping the knife," I replied.

A beat passed as he stared at me, then he shrugged, jerking his head to the back of the bike. "Suit yourself. Come on, we don't have all night."

I resisted the urge to answer, biting down on my lips as I approached the giant. He was even bigger up close, the size of the motorcycle reduced to nothing. His muscular arms were bare and covered with tattoos, his leather vest strapped over his broad shoulders.

He reached up and clutched his helmet before pulling it off. My breath caught in my throat when his face came into view. Well, what I could see of it. The light from the other bikes reflected on his sculptured face, his dark eyes almost glistening from the lights. A few strands of dark hair fell over his face, and he brushed it back with a sweep that was so sexy to me. I shook my head, pushing the ridiculous thought away. This man probably had more kills than a Navy Seal. There was nothing sexy about a gangster.

My eyes swept over his body again. Who was I kidding? I could hardly see much of him, but it was enough to confirm what a perfect specimen he was. It took me an instant to realize he was checking me out, too. A thrill ran up my spine, the cold completely forgotten based on how warm his scrutiny made me.

"So where to, Princess?" Billy asked, cutting into our moment.

"Anywhere but here," I replied.

Billy nodded, cranked up his motorcycle, then rode off.

I climbed on the back of the Harley FXR – only knowing the brand because Johnny had owned one a couple of years back. There I could see his straight hair that brushed his shoulders and his broad back, which had the motorcycle club patch inscribed on his leather jacket. It said 'Eagle Knights', hosting a crest in the middle with a majestic bird on each side. Declan cranked up his motorcycle, and I gasped, caught by surprise.

"Are you really going to leave this here?" he asked, cocking his head at the Lexus.

"I hope to never see it again," I muttered.

He glanced a little over his shoulder, a slight frown on his face. "Suit yourself. Hold on, Kid."

I gritted my teeth at him calling me a kid, with a pout on my face, I grabbed a helmet off the backseat, buckled it up and wrapped my arms around him. But the pout didn't last long because my stomach soon flooded with heat when I braced against his body, feeling the firmness and the warmth that came from him. He smelled divine, like a mix of leather and spice. I inhaled his scent, committing it to memory for some reason. I'd never been affected by a man like this, unless I counted the fictional boyfriends from the steamy novels I read. But as I curled myself around this big body of pure muscles, I realized they couldn't compare. No work of fiction had ever aroused me like this.

The icy night air whipped my damp body as we sailed down the narrow stretch of road. My teeth chattered inside the helmet, and I held onto Declan even tighter. He seemed unbothered by my grip as he rode in the cold like this was a usual thing.

A few minutes later, I saw lights, and a warmer air welcomed us. I released my grip around Declan, looking around to see where we were. We'd stopped in front of a rustic lodge with wooden columns and railing surrounding the porch. There were a few other buildings down the street; a small church, diner, gas station and a doctor's office among them.

Billy was the first to get off his motorcycle, followed by the others, who I now saw clearly under the lights. Except for Rodger, they were all huge, making me feel shorter than my five feet height.

"Well, this is where we stop for the night, Princess. Still don't have a destination in mind?" Billy asked, approaching me.

I hopped off Declan's motorcycle and hauled the helmet off my head. "This is fine, thanks," I said, offering a smile.

He nodded, still staring at me as if trying to figure me out. I quickly shifted my gaze and handed the helmet to Declan, who eyed me curiously, too. But I didn't care about his scrutiny. All that mattered was his handsome face, which I could clearly see now. He had the most intense pair of green eyes I'd ever seen, the low cut beard showing the cleft in his chin. His hair blew in the gentle wind, giving him the appearance of a mountain god. Or a Viking. Yes, definitely a sexy Viking.

"Thanks for the ride," I mumbled, watching as he reached out and took the helmet, his curt nod matching the tension in his eyes.

"Don't mention it," he replied, swinging his legs over his motorcycle and strapping the helmet to the handle. He towered over me and like the others, reduced my small frame to nothing. I took a deep breath and stepped back, overwhelmed by his presence in my space.

A flicker of amusement filled his eyes before it disappeared. I straightened, squaring my shoulders, pretending his powerful frame didn't intimidate me.

The wind picked up, reminding me of my predicament. I had nowhere to stay for the night. Most of the bikers had already entered the building, which made me relieved. At least they wouldn't witness me walking away to slump in the gas station until the following day.

Declan still stood there, watching me, probably waiting for me to go. I wished he wouldn't. I couldn't handle the embarrassment from him knowing what I'd planned to do.

I waved at him, backing away. "Well, I'll see you around, Big-Guy. Or maybe not."

A smirk lifted the corner of his lips as he watched me. I turned to leave, pausing almost immediately when I heard his voice.

"You don't have anywhere to go, do you, Kid?" he asked.

I whipped around, shooting him a glare. "I'm not a kid. Could you quit calling me that?"

"You ran away from home, didn't you?" he asked with a scoff, folding his arms, the action shifting my attention to his big chest.

"No, I didn't," I replied defiantly, lifting my chin.

Still wearing the smirk, he came closer. I swallowed but stood my ground. "Let's see," he murmured, his eyes slow-scanning my body. "It's the middle of the night, and you're alone on the road with just the clothes on your back. It's the typical description of a runaway, if you ask me."

"I am not a runaway," I bit out, pissed off by how close he hit the mark.

He cocked his head at me. "Fine. You're not a runaway. What are you doing out so late?"

"That's my business," I shot back. "I'm an adult, if you haven't noticed."

Again, his eyes slowly scanned my body, setting me aflame. "Oh, I noticed, believe me."

My cheeks were red hot, and even in the dim light, it showed. With a huff to mask how affected I was, I turned again to leave.

"Listen, this isn't a safe place for anyone, especially this time of night. Let me get you a room," he called after me.

I bit the inside of my lips and contemplated his suggestion. Declan was as much a stranger as anyone I'd ever meet tonight. He might have offered me a ride on his motorcycle, but I still couldn't trust him. Regardless of his gorgeousness, he was probably a troublemaker like all the other bikers I had heard about.

"I'll be fine, thanks," I replied, twisting to give him a forced smile.

"Are you sure?"

I didn't miss the trace of concern in his voice or the care in his expression. I wanted to lean into it because no one had looked at me that way since Momma died. Our eyes met, and it was as if time had stilled as we stood there. The swirling emotion in my belly reminded me of my earlier reaction to him. It wasn't a fluke. I was attracted to Declan.

Extremely attracted.

Which made no sense, considering I didn't know him at all. It couldn't be real, right?

Besides a few casual dates back in high school, I had no experience with men, and no way of knowing if these feelings were real. Maybe I was still on high from escaping. Yes, it wasn't an attraction; just an adrenaline rush.

Still, I hugged my shoulders to ease the emotions that consumed my body.

"Yes, I'm sure," I replied.

Declan stared at me for a beat as if he didn't believe me. "Okay, well, see you around," he finally said, turning to leave. I bit my lips, watching his large figure move farther away from me. The stillness of the town became even more pronounced. The road we'd just travelled was pitch black. Somehow, the entire scene reminded me of the setup for a horror movie.

"Hey!" I called, desperation filling me. Declan stopped and turned; his expression was stiff as he looked at me.

"Maybe that room wouldn't be so bad after all?" I said, rubbing my shoulders.

He smirked, his shoulders relaxing. "Come along, Shrimp."

I rolled my eyes and did a little run-walk to catch him up. We entered the small lobby of the motel, where a middle-aged woman sat behind a desk, a cigarette stuck between her lips while she scanned through a large book. Her matted grey hair covered half her face, but nothing could disguise her bright blue eyes. She looked up, blew out a cloud of smoke, and looked between me and Declan.

"Two rooms, or one?" she asked, her eyes still going back and forth.

Declan's eyes coasted to me as if he wanted me to answer. My cheeks flamed. He shook his head with a low chuckle.

"Two rooms, please," he replied, approaching the semicircular table and digging for his wallet.

She told Declan the price, which he paid before directing his eyes to me again. My stomach flipped as she handed him the keys. He gave one to me, a soft smile on his face.

"Up the stairs, last two rooms on your left," the woman instructed as Declan returned the wallet to his pocket. He nudged me ahead, his hand resting in the middle of my back, making my body even more awake.

We moved up the stairs, an awareness sending tingles up my spine. What did that earlier look mean? Did he consider sharing a room with me? Would I want him to?

Oh, no. I was too aroused to sleep in a room with a stranger. Despite how horny I was, Declan couldn't be my first.

"Have a good night, Shrimp," he said, bringing me back to reality.

With an eye roll at the irritating nickname, I flipped my middle finger at his back. My hands curled around the key in my hand as he moved into the room on the right. As his door closed with a soft click, I opened mine.

It was just as I expected for the price; outdated wallpapers, patterned sheets with matching curtains, and a stained grey carpet. But none of that mattered to me, as my home was much worse. I was too focused on the double bed more than anything else. The adrenaline rush had ceased. My aching body needed rest. Closing the door behind me, I dragged myself to the bed, flopping down on the soft mattress. It was too spongy for my taste but did enough to soothe my aches. My eyes stayed locked on the dusty ceiling fan above me, and I gave way to my consuming thoughts.

Tonight was the bravest move I'd ever made in my entire life; somehow, I still found it hard to believe I'd been courageous enough to escape my folks. It took months, during which I lost my nerve several times. Daddy and the boys wouldn't kill me if they caught me escaping, but Johnny would hurt me bad.

Growing up, I got little love from Daddy. Rumor had it, he wanted another son to put to work, and he lost his shit when Momma gave birth to me. Dean and Johnny were ten and twelve years old when I came into this world. They weren't pleased about having a baby sister, either, especially with how Momma doted on me. After a decade, they'd gotten used to having her to themselves. I was always the unwelcome outsider.

Throughout my childhood, they'd always been bullies, but they did nothing serious, just took away my toys, pulled my hair, pushed me from behind in the creek, that sort of thing.

Momma died when I turned eighteen. A semi on the highway took her life. It was my senior year in high school—a few weeks from graduation, actually, and it broke my heart when no one showed up to see me graduate. My plans for culinary school went down the drain. Momma had no life insurance; Daddy buried her with half her savings, then invested the rest in his farm. I refused to let that deter me. I had a goal to enroll in the Culinary Academy of Las Vegas, and I was hellbent on living that dream. I wanted to make Momma proud, too. She gave me my love for cooking, and I wanted to honor her by becoming the Michelin-star chef I promised to be. So, I got a job right out of high school, working part-time to save for my tuition.

All my plans came to a screeching halt when I found out that Daddy didn't reap the typical crops from his farm. He was a marijuana farmer. He and the boys sold the drugs from our basement. I stumbled on the stacks of compressed weed while searching for Momma's old mixing bowl one day. I should've been suspicious when seedy-looking guys kept coming around late at nights or when Johnny bought a new car months after the funeral. I tried to turn a blind eye, but it bothered me. I'd seen the effects of drugs. It wasn't cute. I tried to convince them to stop, but my pleas only made them zone in on me. To my dismay, they tried to force me to sell weed to my co-workers at the diner. Instead, I went to the cops.

Someone at the Sherriff's office tipped them off. The house was sparkly clean when the deputy showed up. The action almost cost my life. That night, Johnny beat the crap out of me, leaving me half-dead on the living room carpet. It took an entire day to pick myself up. Soaked in my urine, I crawled to my room. My phone and laptop lay in pieces on the floor. It took a week to walk again.

That was two years ago. For two years I'd been a prisoner. My friends thought I'd moved to France—which made no sense, considering I had no desire to leave the country. It was obvious they didn't know me enough to suspect Daddy had lied when they asked about me. I was a little too bitter to seek their help, but even if I wasn't, I didn't want to put them in danger. There was no telling what my family—especially Johnny—would do to them.

I had no one. No money, no way to survive. But I had my freedom.

Thank God for the motorcycle gang—the Eagle Knights—weird name, but for some reason, it suited them. If it hadn't been for them, I'd still be on the side of the road, plotting my next move in the pitch-black night. I couldn't thank Declan enough for getting me a room for the night, although my emotions were still running haywire since I met him, leaving my body in heat and my brain totally confused.

Why was I so affected by a stranger?

What was it about him that made me want to lose myself?

Groaning, I pulled myself up, deciding to take a shower since my clothes were still partially damp from the rain, and I hadn't taken a bath since that morning. I peeled my clothes off and entered the small bathroom with the mismatched tiles and stained toilet bowl. As I stepped into the small cubicle, I was happy to find that they had warm water.

I closed my eyes as the gentle blast hit my skin and sluiced down my body. It was like experiencing heaven on earth after the night I had.

Once done, I reentered the bedroom and threw my clothes over a single lounge chair in the corner of the room. Now completely naked, I welcomed the cool sheets on my body again and closed my eyes as a smile curled at the corners of my lips. I felt truly at peace – more than I'd felt in ages, and I didn't want to let the feeling go. In fact, I craved more of it.

My mind wandered to Declan again. Just knowing he was on the other side of this door, that with one knock, I could be in his room, showing him just how naked I was and inviting his huge hands to do whatever he wanted with me. The thought of him owning my body didn't make me fearful. Quite the opposite. My entire being craved for it. To have him inside me, taking my innocence, filling me with every inch of his cock—

I groaned, palming my hot face.

What the hell was I thinking? Maybe I was more exhausted than I thought.

But as I twisted in the sheets, warmth running from head to toe, I knew that wasn't the case. This wasn't exhaustion. It was raw, passionate need for the giant next door.

A tingling feeling ran up my thighs, lodging in the center, and filling me with the urge to touch myself. With Declan the source of my arousal, it meant he was the only one who could satiate me. My fingers were the next best thing.

As my hand moved between my thighs, my fingers teasing the seam, the breath hitched in my throat, and my heart thrummed in my chest. Despite getting turned on by steamy novels, I'd never masturbated before. I never had the urge. Now, with my ache for Declan rising to an unbearable degree, I wanted to try it. I needed release. I bit my lips, daring to probe further, gasping from the rush of pleasure when my fingers stroked my clit.

A sudden thud on the wall made me jerk my hand away. My cheeks instantly flamed, and embarrassment filled me. I fluffed the pillows and turned over on my stomach, closing my eyes with a deep sigh. Yep, masturbation wasn't for me.

Chapter 2

Cassandra

I woke the next morning to the growling of motorcycles and honking horns. It took me a moment to process; then it suddenly dawned on me. Declan and his club members were getting ready to leave.

A flurry of panic filled me, and I shot upright. Shit. I had nowhere to go, no money to get by. Maybe if I hitched another ride, I'd be far enough from my family. I'd get a job, somewhere to live and start anew.

It seemed easier said than done, but I had no alternative. I quickly shuffled out of bed and pulled on my dried clothes before grabbing the hair tie and binding my hair into a ponytail. The door banged as I slammed it shut on my way out. I hurried outside, finding Declan and Billy in a hushed conversation, one that paused when they saw me.

Billy smiled, but it wasn't as bright as the night before. Without a word to me, he headed to the diner across the road. I cleared my throat, feeling the color rise to my cheeks when I noticed Declan watching me, his gaze roaming over every inch of my body.

"You're finally up," he murmured. "I wanted to wake you, but I figured you needed the rest."

"Yeah... I did. Uh... what time is it?"

"Almost eight," he said, his eyes still locked on me.

I shifted my attention to the floor, feeling exposed from his head-to-toe assessment.

"The guys are grabbing breakfast; then we'll head home. Still haven't decided on where you want to go?" he asked.

I rubbed the back my neck. "Where's home?"

"Las Vegas."

My eyes flew up to him. "You live in Las Vegas?" Was this a strange coincidence, or was the Universe clearing the way for me?

He smiled. "Yep. Born and bred."

My gaze dropped to my dirt-stained converse shoes. "Er... if it's not any problem, could I get a ride there?" I asked, looking back at him.

His green eyes were still locked on me, assessing me as if trying to figure me out.

"Come on, let's get some food, then we can talk about it," he finally said, gesturing to the diner.

My stomach grumbled in reply, reminding me I hadn't eaten since last evening. I was famished. Timidly nodding, I followed behind Declan as he crossed the road. I couldn't take my eyes off him. In the daylight, he was even more gorgeous. But the sunshine revealed something I hadn't noticed the night before. He walked with a slight limp that was only obvious if you stared enough. It made me curious. In fact, I wanted to know everything about him.

As we entered the diner that was in full swing, his biker friends stopped eating to look at us. Some had smirks on their faces. I even caught a thick, bald-headed one nudging the tall, slender guy beside him, giving him a wink. I rolled my eyes. It was obvious they didn't know Declan and I had separate rooms. Did I care they thought we slept together? Absolutely not.

Declan gestured to an empty spot in the corner, and I followed, taking a seat on the opposite side of him.

As soon as we sat, a waitress with a warm smile on her face approached. "Hello, what can I get for you guys?" she asked, looking between us.

"Coffee with a stack of pancakes, bacon and eggs for me," Declan replied before gesturing to me.

"I'll have the same, please."

I ignored the surprise on Declan's face, thankful when he said nothing. The server nodded and then left, forcing me to contend with Declan and his intense gaze.

"Stop staring at me like that," I mumbled, unable to stop the words from leaving my mouth.

"Like what?" Declan asked, cocking a thick brow.

"Like..." I huffed, shifting my gaze to the salt and pepper shakers on the table. I reached for one, fiddling with it. "Like you are seeing right through me or something."

Declan chuckled; the low rumble so sexy in my ears. "Is there something you don't want me to see, Shrimp?"

"Stop calling me that."

"There's only one way to fix that, *Shrimp*." He emphasized the word with an obvious intention to rile me. "What's your name?"

I hesitated, not wanting to give too much of myself away. The least anyone knew about me, the harder for Daddy and the boys to find me. But it was the least I could do after what Declan had done for me. "Cass," I finally replied.

"Is that short for something?"

I nodded. "Cassandra."

"Ready to tell me what you're running from, Cassandra?"

"How about you tell me what your little posse is all about?" I countered. For some reason, I trusted Declan, but I needed to know who I'd been riding with since last night.

Again, Declan chuckled. "My brothers and I are the Eagle Knights. We're not a typical motorcycle club; besides riding for fun, our common goal is giving back to our community. We support small businesses, host fundraising activities, donate to food banks, volunteer at animal shelters... you name it, we've done it."

I glanced around the room, checking out the rough-looking, tattooed men who could rip someone in half without trying. "I find that hard to believe," I said.

"Ah. That's no surprise. People have judged us for our looks for years. It doesn't change the reality that we're decent guys." He looked over to the table where Rodger sat. "Well, most of us."

"Okay... how did you all meet?"

"We all served time in the military." He gestured with his head to the table beside us. "Billy was our staff sergeant back in Iraq. Rodge, Blue, Gear, Forger and I were a part of the same squad. The others and I met when I switched platoons."

I stared at him, impressed. "You were in the army?"

He nodded. "Twelve years, five tours. Got a leg injury as a keepsake, but no regrets."

"You're very brave," I breathed.

He shrugged. "That wasn't the case when I first got deployed. It was a means to an end for me."

"Meaning?"

He scoffed. "Think I've said enough, Cassandra. Your turn. What are you running from?"

"I um... I just wanted a new environment, that's all," I replied with a shrug.

His thick, arched brows furrowed. "With no money or clothes? Sounds like you were desperate to get out and ran the first chance you got." He leaned forward, his eyes narrowing at me. "Are you in trouble?"

My gaze met his. "What happened to Cass?"

"I never called you Cass."

I resisted the urge to roll my eyes. "About what I asked earlier...Would it be a problem?"

"What do you plan on doing once you get there? Las Vegas is no place for scared little girls," Declan said.

"I'll be twenty in two months' time. I'm not a little girl, and I'm definitely not scared," I snapped.

His gaze lowered to my chest, lingering. Heat flooded my core, spreading between my thighs. I locked my legs, trying to temper the throbbing down there. Declan opened his mouth to reply, then it clamped shut as the server arrived with our food. She placed them on the small table, my eyes following each movement before she walked away. I licked my lips, staring down at the food and the steaming cup of coffee beside it.

"What are you waiting for?" Declan asked. "Dig in."

I didn't hesitate, shoveling eggs down my throat as I ripped at the pancakes with my bare hands. I glanced up once to see Declan staring at me with amusement on his face as I scarfed down my food. My cheeks warmed with embarrassment, but I continued, too hungry to stop.

"I like a woman with a decent appetite," he said, forking a piece of pancake in his mouth.

"I thought you said I was a little girl," I replied around a mouthful of food.

His eyes sparkled with mischief like a dirty thought just crossed his mind. "In some ways, you're still a kid." His gaze dropped to my chest again. "In some ways, not."

I wanted to ask what he meant by that, but I suspected his answer would burn me up.

"I'll take you to Las Vegas, Shrimp," his voice cut into my thoughts.

I looked up to see him wiping his mouth with a paper towel. "You will?"

"Sure. So long as you have a solid plan."

"Of course, I do. Thank you," I said, my lips stretching into a smile I did not feel. I had no plan. After winging it this far, I leaned on faith. Things would work out. They had to.

Twenty minutes later, we finished, ready to hit the road again. The men got their things in order and shuffled out, mounting their motorcycles in unison.

"How about the princess rides with me this time?" the tall, slender man offered. Rodger. I remember his whining when Declan volunteered to take me last night.

I glanced at Declan, my mouth agape as I wondered if he'd agree. Truth was, I preferred riding with him, especially after the conversation we just had. I wouldn't be comfortable around anyone else.

"Like hell," Declan growled, and I whooshed a relieved breath. "She stays with me, Rodge."

Rodger smirked, glancing at the other guys. "I told you guys he hit it last night, didn't I?" He sniggered, and the others laughed. "Tell me something, Dec, is her pussy as sweet as her cute face?"

My cheeks flamed as more laughter sounded around me. Then, before I could blink, Declan had hauled Rodger off his motorcycle and slammed him against the wall.

"Watch your fucking mouth," he hissed.

"Or what, you're going to beat the shit out of me?" Rodger huffed, anger flashing in his eyes. "Fighting with me because I said something crude about your old lady won't bring Marie back."

I didn't know what Rodger's remark meant, but it ticked off Declan. His expression darkened, and he pounded Rodger's face with his fist. "Shut the fuck up!" he roared.

The other guys had watched in silent amusement until now. They all flew off their motorcycles, rushing forward.

"Guys. Cut it out!" Billy shouted. "Declan, let him the fuck go."

"He fucking overstepped," Declan grumbled, his grip tightening around Rodger's throat. I suspected it wasn't too tight, for Rodger still wore a smirk.

"Yes, he did. Rodger, apologize to Declan so we can go on our way," Billy said wearily. "This is not what this club's about; you know that."

Rodger sneered. "Sorry, man. It was all in fun, that's all."

"There's nothing about Marie that's remotely funny, asshole. Don't you ever mention her again."

"Declan, he apologized. Let him go," Billy cut in, sounding like an exhausted parent two steps away from emptying a bottle of alcohol down his throat.

Declan glared at Billy before he released Rodger, moving with purposeful strides towards his motorcycle, his mouth still set in a grim line as he handed me the helmet and got himself seated.

I took it and glanced over at Rodger, whose face was as red as an overripe tomato. He still wore a smirk, but I sensed he was embarrassed by Declan's beatdown. Something told me he was trouble, too. I hoped Declan kept an eye on him.

My eyes caught Billy staring at me, but I couldn't read his expression. When he noticed me looking, he gritted his teeth, then moved to his own ride.

I sighed and pulled on my helmet, climbing behind Declan who had already started his ride. In less than a minute, we were on our way with Billy leading the way.

I didn't think I'd ever get used to the feeling of riding with Declan, no matter how short-lived the experience would be. Exhilaration. Liberation. A feeling of insurmountable peace. We cruised down the highway, the wind caressing my body. As if compelled, I lowered my head to his back and clung to him tighter, once again feeling that invincibility with him by my side. This sensation was strange, but Declan made me the happiest I'd been in a long time.

Seven hours later, and after a few pitstops, we entered Las Vegas, where the entire city seemed to be alive. Except for what I watched on TV, I'd never seen such massive buildings before or so many people in one place. I'd been sleepy on the last leg of the journey, but as soon as my eyes caught sight of the skyscrapers, I became fully awake. My head swiveled back and forth as we rode the strip. There was not enough time to take everything in, but if I had my way, I'd have plenty of chances later.

We left the bustle of the city, and the motorcycles stopped at a huge bar on the outskirts with a sign that said 'Billy's' with some other motorcycles of the same brand parked outside. The other guys dismounted in a hurry, clearly wanting a drink after the long ride, but Declan took his time. He got off first, then helped me off, gently removing the helmet from my head. I looked around. This part of town wasn't as busy as the areas we'd passed earlier, but it seemed grander, the roads cleaner, the structure of the buildings luxurious.

It took me a moment to realize Declan still standing there, watching me with that direct stare. "So this is it. This is where the ride ends," he said, bouncing the helmet on his palm.

I nodded, managing a smile. "Thanks... for everything, Declan."

A brief flash of concern filled his eyes, his chest bouncing as he sighed. "Take care of yourself, will you?"

"Of course, I will." Our gazes held. I took a deep breath, overwhelmed by the emotions flowing through me. I didn't understand it. Not only had I never experienced anything so passionate, but I barely knew the man who triggered it. Unable to help myself, I closed the distance between us and wrapped my hands around his large body.

Declan stiffened, then his body softened. I almost moaned when he pressed himself to me. I didn't resist breathing in his scent. Safe. The first word that crossed my mind. His embrace made me feel safe. I didn't want to let go.

But after a short beat, he cleared his throat and pulled away. "Are you sure you'll be okay?" he asked.

"Positive," I replied, backing away in a hurry before he read the lie on my face. "Bye, Declan."

Tears pricked my eyes as I walked away. Why was this so hard? He was a rugged biker, clearly older than me, experienced, no doubt. I was an almost-twenty virgin who knew nothing about being alone in the world. Even if he were interested in me—which I doubted—it wouldn't work. We had nothing in common. I had nothing to offer. Heck, I didn't even have a place to sleep for the night.

I almost rounded the corner when I heard running footsteps behind me. "Hey!" Declan called.

With my heart soaring, I whipped around as he slowed down in front of me, his Adam's apple bobbing as he swallowed. "Uh... I have a spare room if you want to crash for a couple of days until you figure things out," he said.

My heart rate picked up pace at his words, the flutter in my stomach making me feel warm all over.

But I couldn't impose. After all that Declan had already done for me, could I accept more? Would it be too much?

"Declan, I appreciate your offer, but–"

"I won't take no for an answer. There's no way you can survive here alone with nothing to your name." He shot me a stare that locked me in place. "I don't know what you're running from, or who, but you need help. And I want to help you."

"But w– we don't know each other," I argued.

"That's an easy fix, *Cass*," he said, handing me the helmet.

I remained silent for a moment, weighing my options—who was I kidding? I had none. No money and nowhere to go. I would forever scold myself for not grabbing my bag from Johnny when I knee'd him, but then again, taking that chance wouldn't get me this far, either.

Declan being the good guy was still debatable. I saw his dark side when he collared Rodge; who knew what else lay beneath that firm exterior? What if he turned out worse than Daddy and the boys?

I looked into his eyes, seeing the concern there. He'd been good to me so far, and I couldn't deny how desperate I was. Desperation could lead to regret, but I only needed a few days to figure out my next move.

"Okay, just for a day or two, and I promise I'll be out of your hair," I conceded.

I didn't expect his bright smile. From how quickly it disappeared, I doubted he expected it, too. He cleared his throat and gestured for me to follow him. He made me wait outside the bar while he went in, but he was out in a minute. Without missing a beat, he climbed onto the motorcycle, beckoning me to follow suit.

I did so, assuming the position, my grip on him just as tight, although he only cruised on the road. We went uphill, passing a stunning golf course, tree-lined streets and lavish homes with swimming pools. It was like watching an HGTV program. My mouth stayed agape the entire time.

Declan finally rolled to a stop at the top of the hill, where the most luxurious house stood. I wet my dry lips, staring at his back in awe. Who was Declan, really? There was more to him than his rough exterior, obviously, but was that a good thing, or bad?

Taking his offer was probably the bravest thing I'd ever done or the stupidest. Time alone would tell.

Chapter 3

Declan

I'd done many impulsive things in my thirty-six years on this earth. Like the time I took Gear's baiting and bungee-jumped off a railroad bridge—something I'd never done before, the action fracturing my spine. Or when I took on a gang of twenty-somethings after I caught them harassing a teenage girl. Luckily for me, I'd never left my home unarmed. One flick of my wrist had them scattering in several directions.

Offering Cassandra a place to stay beat them both, though. I couldn't help it. Not after seeing her climb out of that busted truck like a damsel in distress, completely soaked with her shirt almost see-through. Not after she triggered the most passionate reaction I've had to a woman in five years. Definitely not after she stared up at me, the innocence in her bright eyes clashing with her delicious body. God, those curves, her tight little nipples pointing through the fabric, her thick, damp hair making me want to grab a fistful and take those full lips for a kiss to satisfy the hunger she erupted in me.

When Billy ordered Rodge to give her a ride, it moved something inside me. A wave of jealousy took over, and I pulled rank, staking my claim. I didn't want her arms around another man. I didn't want her body pressed against his back. Her touch was only for me.

What I felt was more than lust, though. There was an insane need to keep her safe. From her half-wet clothes, her frightened face and empty hands, I sensed she was in deep trouble. As she climbed on the back of my bike, I wanted to protect her with everything I had.

I could still feel her arms gripping my midsection, her long legs wrapped around mine, her breasts pressing against my back. The filthiest thoughts flooded my mind during that ride, half of which involved her nipples in my mouth. My reaction had nothing to do with not getting laid in a month. Even if I were, she would still evoke that response.

It was more than the fiery little temptress' beauty and body that drew me to her. Her bravery amazed me. I admired how she stood tall despite being shaken by whatever she tried to escape. I didn't miss the fading bruise on her cheek or the one on her arm. Something terrible had happened to her. I made it my duty to find out what it was.

No rush, of course. I didn't want to scare her away.

I'd give it time. She planned on leaving in two days, but I wouldn't let her. She wouldn't leave my side until I guaranteed she would be safe and sound. At the moment, it seemed only possible under my roof.

"You live here?" Cassandra asked as she climbed off the motorcycle, her wide eyes fixed on the two-story house in front of us.

"Yup," I replied, resting my helmet on the handlebar.

"It's... stunning," she breathed, looking at me. "Not what I expected."

I shrugged. It wasn't my first time being told this wasn't the typical house for a biker, but I fell in love with the property after a buddy of mine placed it on the market two years ago. I had just moved back from Fresno, looking for a fresh start. The custom-styled house with the two-story portico was the perfect home to raise a family.

I guided her up the steps and moved to the front door, pushing it open so she could enter first. There was an incredulity in her clear blue eyes as they skimmed over the high-ceilinged foyer with the cluster-glass chandelier. Without waiting for me, she walked down the ornate-marble hallway that led to the kitchen and the living room, turning left and taking a seat on the leather sofa.

"You have a really nice place," she said, her voice so soft, I could barely hear her.

"Yeah, it is. I fell in love with it when my friend put it on the market a few years ago."

"You don't seem like the type to like artwork and stuff, but you have plenty." She gestured to an abstract painting on the wall. "I like that one. It's beautiful."

My stomach flipped as I turned my gaze to the painting of the beautiful woman in the ballroom gown, holding an acoustic guitar. It wasn't the usual pain I experienced whenever someone mentioned anything connected to Marie. This time, the sensation was a pleasant one. It amazed me how she zoned in on the one Marie painted. Strange co-incidence, but I noted it as a good sign. "Yeah, it's my favorite," I replied.

She stared at me as if waiting for me to go on, but I wasn't yet ready to share that side of me. I cleared my throat, gesturing to the stairs. "Let me show you the spare room."

Her tiny footsteps followed me upstairs, and she bumped into me when I suddenly stopped outside the guest bedroom door. The redness on her face made me wonder about her innocence. She kept her eyes down as I opened the door and gestured for her to enter. Fascination filled her face as she checked out the king-sized bed, the seven-drawer dresser, the walk-in closet and the ceiling-to-floor glass doors that led to the balcony outside. When she was done admiring the place, she turned to look at me.

"Why are you doing this, Declan?" she asked, the sound of my name on her lips making my body come alive, leaving an urge to pull her in my arms and taste her mouth.

Instead, I jammed my hands in my pockets. "Because you need help."

"That's it? No ulterior motive?"

"Do you want me to have an ulterior motive, Cass?" I asked, my eyes narrowing at her.

I knew that my voice had dipped, and by the way she sucked in a breath, Cassandra was, too. I thanked God I'd opted for a pair of jeans and not my trademark leather pants, or the entire situation would be quite awkward by now.

"No, I don't," she whispered. "It's just that no one has ever offered me help before."

I wanted to ask her what that meant, but she turned her back on me, an obvious hint that she didn't want to continue the conversation. Remembering my decision not to push, I left her alone and fetched some fresh sheets for her bed. I returned to find her staring out the door with her arms crossed and a solemn expression on her face.

"Everything okay, Shrimp?"

She turned and smiled at the nickname this time. I thought it was only fitting considering her petite size. I imagined how easy it would be to throw her over my shoulder and—

"Yeah, everything's fine."

I moved farther into the room and handed her the sheets. "If you need to take a shower, the bathroom is right out there," I said, gesturing to the room on the other side of the open door. Pity this room didn't have an ensuite bathroom. I didn't look forward to her taking a shower so close to me.

She bit her lips, looking up at me with her big doe eyes that stirred something in me. "Do you have a shirt I could borrow? I'll have to wash these for another day," she said, looking down at her blouse and washed-out denim pants.

"Sure," I said. I left and returned with a cotton T-shirt that I handed her. She took it with a smile, her slender fingers brushing over mine. An instant thrill ran through me, sending blood rushing to my cock. My jeans pants weren't enough cover this time, and before I made her uncomfortable with my erection, I dashed from the room, slamming the door shut much harder than I intended.

Raking my fingers through my hair, I muttered a curse. Cassandra was only twenty years old, clearly innocent. Her blushing reactions were a clear sign. Not only was she too young for me, but I didn't want to take advantage of her vulnerability. Something told me she'd been hurt quite badly. She needed someone to trust. I wanted to be that man for her.

Yet, her presence was already driving me insane, and this was only day one. How long could I resist temptation? One more day? Two? I didn't want to scare her away. The last thing I wanted was for her to assume I only wanted to sleep with her.

I made my way to the living room and turned on the TV to my favorite crime drama series, hoping for a distraction. But soon after, I heard the shower running, and I couldn't help the filthy thoughts that filled my head. Her naked body under a warm spray of water that caressed every inch of her tiny body. I imagined how hard her pebble-like nipples were now, how water dripped from each peak. I licked my lips, imagining my tongue running over them and her soft moan when I nipped them with my teeth. With each thought, my cock hardened more in my pants.

Breathing a sigh, I refocused on the TV show until the shower stopped and the door to the bathroom creaked open. Temptation resurfaced, urging me to peek, but I wasn't a creep. I closed my eyes, balling my hands on my lap, only relaxing when her bedroom door clicked shut.

Some minutes later, she entered the living room wearing the T-shirt I gave her, which reached past her knees, the neck hole almost hanging down her shoulders. I couldn't help grinning, but there was something else that sparked within me seeing her in my clothes. It swallowed her up, but it was still the sexiest thing I had ever seen, especially when I realized she wore nothing beneath it.

Oh, fuck.

Forcing my eyes from her lower half, I took in her blonde hair tied in a messy bun on the top of her head, her fresh face fresh and the natural pout of her full lips. Breathtaking. She was absolutely breathtaking.

"I'll have to get you some clothes," I said, then paused, not understanding where the thought came from. It came as casually as saying hello.

She shook her head. "I won't be staying long, so that won't be necessary," she replied, ending with a meek smile.

"You can stay as long as you want, you know," I pointed out.

"I appreciate that, Declan, but I don't want to overstay my welcome. Besides, I'm sure your lady friends won't like me being here."

I scoffed. "Lady friends? What are you? Fifty?"

That earned me a laugh, the first one I'd seen since we met. With her head thrown back, her pearly whites gleaming, and that odd sparkle in her eyes, it was the most heartwarming thing I'd ever seen. I wanted her to laugh like that more often.

"Your girlfriends, Declan. I'm sure there are lots," she said when her laughing ceased.

"What makes you think so?"

Her face reddened as she gestured to me. "The way you look," she replied.

I knew what she meant, but I wanted to push her. I enjoyed seeing that blush on her face. "How do I look?" I asked.

I didn't think her blush could deepen, but it did. Her face resembled an overripe tomato. Her eyes latched onto her lap. "Hot," she muttered, the response so low I barely heard.

It was my turn to laugh. "Do you think I'm hot, Cass?"

She groaned, covering her face. "Can we change this conversation, please?"

Still chuckling, I rubbed the nape of my neck and decided to leave the topic for another day. "I'm thinking of ordering some food. Any suggestions?"

She slowly moved her hand from her face. "Er... not really. Anything is fine with me."

"How does Thai sound?"

"Yeah, sounds great."

I put through the order and changed the channel to a rom-com movie that Cassandra really enjoyed if the delight in her eyes was any sign. She curled herself up on the single sofa, her knees to her chest, the shirt covering her ankles, which somehow made it even sexier. She giggled occasionally, and I couldn't resist my smile, but as if caught doing something wrong, she placed her fingers on her lips and stopped herself.

The doorbell rang some minutes later, and figuring it was the food, I got up and made my way to the front door. As I swung it open, I saw Billy standing there, a frown on his face.

"Hey, everything okay?" I asked, stepping outside.

"I heard you brought the girl home," he said.

I immediately pulled the door close before stepping closer to him. "Yeah, I did."

"Have you lost your mind? You know nothing about her, Declan," he pointed out, his grey eyes intense.

"It doesn't matter. I couldn't leave her out there all alone. She had nothing. This is Vegas, Billy. We both know she would've been eaten alive."

He slowly shook his head, staring at me like I'd lost my mind. "What if she's running from something—someone— an ex-boyfriend, maybe?"

"And?"

"Nine chances out of ten, he's gonna come looking for her," he said, glancing over my shoulder. "You don't want that heat, brother."

"I can protect myself as well as her. You know that," I said, stiffly, offended. I could handle any son-of-a-bitch crazy enough to try stealing her from me.

Stealing her from me. I gave myself a mental slap. Cassandra wasn't my property. Her ex—or whoever it was—couldn't steal what didn't belong to me. But I vowed to use every ounce of my power to keep her safe if need be.

"No. What I know is you've been trying to prove yourself since Marie died, but this knight in shining shit is getting old, Dec," Billy chastised. "It wasn't your fault that we lost her. You don't need to rescue every troubled woman you meet."

My stomach churned. I crossed my arms on my chest, shooting Billy a glare. "That's not what I'm doing."

"Isn't it? If the shit hits the fan, just know I warned ya. This club's not into the mess, Dec, you know that."

I pulled in a breath. "I know that, Billy. You've made that clear countless times."

"Yet, I have to remind you over and over again. You have a thing for attracting trouble and getting yourself wrapped in it."

I sighed, giving Billy's shoulder a light tap. "The girl stays, and if the shit hits the fan, I will clean it myself."

Billy rolled his eyes and scratched his beard. "Just be careful. That's all I ask," he cautioned.

"That's a given, Billy, you know that."

He shook his head and muttered something about stubborn kids before hopping on his motorcycle and riding away. I watched him go, knowing he meant well. Billy had been like an older brother to me since I was first deployed at twenty years old. After serving for twenty-two years, he'd seen enough war to last him a lifetime. All he wanted now was peace.

I didn't blame him. Serving in the army made me fearless, but I didn't regret leaving the war zone behind. Running my business, riding with my brothers, and giving back to my community was the only life I wanted too.

The delivery guy came just as I was about to head inside. I collected, paid and went back in to find Cassandra still watching TV. When she saw the food in my hand, she perked up, her eyes almost glistening. But a slight frown filled her face when she peered up at me.

"Is everything okay?" she asked.

No. My mentor thinks you're trouble, that I should let you go before I get too deep. "Yeah, everything is fine," I replied, forcing a smile.

She didn't look too convinced, but I'm glad she didn't push it. "Come on, let's eat," I said, leading the way to the kitchen.

We settled around the dining table, Cassandra eating as urgently as she had done back at the diner. I figured she was either a food enthusiast or was always starving. She kept her head down as she dug in, only glancing up when only a few noodles remained in the box.

"Can I ask you a question?" she said, licking sauce from her lips.

I nodded. "Shoot."

"What do you guys do exactly? The club, I mean."

"We hang out, ride together. Like I mentioned before, we give back to charity when we can. It's like a brotherhood."

"And what do you do when you're not doing all that stuff?"

"We all run our own companies. You've seen Billy's bar. I own several auto shops in the state."

She raised her arched brows. "Several?"

I nodded. "I think it's only fair that I ask you some questions now, right?"

Her expression settled. She placed the glass of soda on the table. "Sure."

"What are you running from?"

"Nothing," she quickly mumbled.

"You'll have to do better than that. I'm not blind."

Her brows bunched together with a scowl. "What's the point of this, anyway? I'll be gone soon. You don't need to know anything about me."

For some reason, her response made my heart sink. "I'm not letting you leave without knowing you can survive out there alone," I replied, watching as her small lips tightened.

"It's not like you have a choice in the matter, do you?" she remarked, brows raised. "I'll leave whenever I want, and you can't stop me."

She attempted to rise from her seat, but I stopped her with a light grip on her wrist, desperation taking over. "How about I help you find a job, and you stay here?" I suggested.

"What makes you think I'd want to stay here?" she bit back.

"Where else can you go having nothing to your name?" I challenged.

"You might want to loosen the stick that's up your ass. It's starting to show. You're not better than me, Declan. I don't care how many businesses and fancy homes you own," she spat, rolling her eyes and leaving the table. I moved after her, reaching for her hand before she exited the room. She paused, her tiny body whipping around as she met my gaze.

"Look, I'm sorry. I didn't mean it to come off like that," I said, barely able to concentrate on my words when I had her in my grasp. I wanted to feel her body against mine so badly. The urge to wrap her in my arms was so great.

Cassandra's face softened as she looked at me, the fire in her eyes slowly dimming. Her cheeks lit up with a blush, but she quickly cleared her throat and pulled her hand away.

"Whatever, it's fine."

The silence dawdled for a beat until she managed the faintest smile, then walked off, heading upstairs. My eyes lingered on her legs, imagining them wrapped around my waist as I buried myself inside her, the curves of her ass cheeks fitting neatly in my palms. I'd go to hell for those filthy thoughts. I had no doubt.

"You're giving me that look again," Cassandra suddenly said, and I realized she caught me staring.

I raked my fingers through my hair and muttered a small curse as she smirked, continuing up the stairs. It would be a miracle if I lasted another day with her under my roof.

Chapter 4

Cassandra

As I curled in bed, I could smell him on me. He was everywhere. That strong masculine scent that stuck with you for hours on end, even when you were away from it. Declan was the type of man who could drive you crazy just from that intense stare. I couldn't imagine what a touch from him would do to me.

I wanted to run. Yet, I wanted to be curled up next to him, with his thick arms holding me tight. I'd never experienced this urge in my life. To have his hands all over me, him inside me, his mouth doing things to me that I'd only read in romance novels. Every second with Declan made my body ache. Right now, it was wound tighter than a string, screaming for release, longing for Declan to break down my door and have his way with me.

It was wishful thinking, quite stupid, honestly. Declan was way out of my league. It wasn't just the age gap. This man had money, lots of it, while I was just a high school graduate with nothing to my name. I'm sure he had women falling at his feet; women his age, his type, with their lives all figured out. Why would he want a girl like me?

I spent all night considering his offer to live with him while I found work. While it was a more than great deal, I couldn't impose so much on his life–not without giving something in return.

A solid plan formed in my head before I drifted to sleep, and I woke the next morning, ready to give Declan my answer. After showering and changing into my old clothes again, I left the bedroom, going in search of him. It took no time. I came to an abrupt halt the second I opened the door, almost bumping into Declan. He had just exited the bathroom across the hall, a towel wrapped around his narrow waist, his body still damp from his shower.

"Sorry," he said sheepishly. "My shower's broken. Hope I didn't hold you up."

"No... I, uh—" My brain turned to mush as I checked him out. "Um... I already showered..."

I backed against the wall, steadying myself, unable to stop my gaze from trailing up his solid figure. His shoulders were even broader-looking now, every inch of his torso ripped with muscles. And his abs... God, why did I want to run my tongue over his stomach so badly? I swallowed the saliva in my mouth as my eyes traveled to his face.

He had trimmed his beard, the cleft more obvious in his chin, his cheekbones sharper-looking. Water dripped from his thick hair, running down his chest, some settling in his belly button.

Christ.

"My eyes are up here," Declan said, his voice filled with amusement.

"Sorry," I blurted, my eyes flying up to meet his. "I didn't expect to bump into you—plus you're not wearing any clothes and—"

"Cass, I'm just messing with you," he said, a faint smile on his lips. "Don't worry about it."

I nodded, wondering if the sudden heat came from the temperature in the room or my embarrassment from being caught checking him out. When he flipped his hair, running his fingers through the damp strands, I realized it was my body's reaction to him that made it feel like I'd been trapped in a sauna. The familiar tingling peppered my skin, leaving goosebumps. The ache between my thighs made me want to do crazy things, like rip that towel from his body and climb him like a tree.

But Declan was a giant. From what the towel revealed, I didn't doubt how huge he was. Considering I'd never been with a man before, he would rip me in half if I ever gave in to temptation.

He waved his hands in front of my face, bringing me back. "You there?" he asked.

"Yeah, er... Were you serious about what we talked about last night?" I asked.

His brows slightly furrowed. "About what?"

"Me staying here long term."

"Of course. I wouldn't have offered if I didn't mean it, Cass."

"Good. Once I find a job, I'd pay you rent, then once I'm solid, I'll move out—"

"Cassandra, you don't have to pay me for anything." He moved to me, taking my shoulders, his touch making me shiver. As if he noticed, he instantly let me go. "You desperately need help, and I want to help you. No strings attached."

"Well, I *want to* pay you back. I'm not a charity case," I said, my response sounding a little snappier than I intended.

"No one said you were," he replied with a frown.

"'I desperately need help,' that's what you just said."

He rolled his eyes, his hand going to his towel. I bit my lip, half expecting him to remove it, disappointed when he just tightened it around him. "You read too much into what I said."

I didn't know why I was being so defensive, but I couldn't help myself. "Did I? I don't want your pity, Declan."

"Well, I don't need your money, nor will I take it."

"Forget it," he said, walking away.

Fire sparked within me at his rejection, and without even giving them any thought, hot words came flying from my mouth.

"Can you just quit being so Goddamn pigheaded?" I snapped.

He stopped in his tracks and slowly turned to look at me, a brow raised.

"Me? Pigheaded?" He scoffed, moving slowly toward me. "Have you seen yourself? It's only been a day, and you're already driving me nuts with how stubborn you are!"

"Well, if I'm so unbearable, I can just leave," I bit back.

"Goddammit, I didn't –" he cut himself short, and once again, he was right in front of me. "I don't want you to leave," he continued, his voice softening.

Our gazes met, and I couldn't look away. Declan was like a magnet, and I was a piece of steel that couldn't resist being connected to him. His shower-fresh scent washed over me, intoxicating me, muting my commonsense. The warning in my head went unnoticed. I didn't want to consider the repercussions of giving myself to a man I barely knew. For once, I didn't want to think. I only wanted to feel.

I pushed myself on my tiptoes, my eyes trained on his pink lips, and I anticipated tasting them. His eyes darkened, and he lowered his head, his forehead meeting mine. The rapid bounce of his chest, the harsh breaths from his mouth, his tight grip on my arms was a sure sign. My heart galloped in my chest, knowing he wanted me too.

"Are you sure about this?" he whispered, his voice softer than I'd heard since we met.

I nodded, hearing the loud gulp as I swallowed. "I'm sure."

I closed my eyes as our lips touched, electric waves running through my body. His warm tongue probed my mouth, and I slowly opened mine so I could experience my first real kiss, tasting his minty breath. It was like feather against feather, warmth radiating through me as our tongues made contact. If I died right now, heaven wouldn't be this good. My body was on fire, but the burn was an addiction. I moaned as pleasure coursed through every inch of me.

My panties were already soaked from this kiss. I couldn't imagine what making love to him would do to me. I wanted more than his tongue inside my mouth. I wanted him inside me. When he wrapped his thick arms around me, I was certain that would soon be the case. Lips still joined, I mimicked him, wrapping my arms around his waist. We stood so close, I could feel the coolness of his body, which contrasted the raging heat inside me.

As if sensing my inexperience, Declan led every step of the way, his tongue caressing mine, and I cautiously tried to replicate his movements. The longer we kissed, the more I craved him. When he sucked on my tongue, I moaned. When something hard poked my stomach, I froze on the spot.

I didn't need an anatomy class to tell me what that was. Declan's cock throbbed against me, swelling, scaring the shit out of me. My earlier guess about his size wasn't correct. He was huge.

Too huge. There was no way he'd fit inside me. Declan must have sensed my fear because he pulled away slightly and cupped my face in his large hands.

"Everything okay?" he asked, his voice so soft, almost chasing my fear away.

Almost. I licked my lips and swallowed the lump in my throat, wanting so much to continue, but I knew it would be a mistake for so many reasons.

I nodded, wiping my sweaty palms on my thighs. "Yeah, I er... I should probably get started on that job search, right?"

Declan still seemed confused, a slight frown on his face. Soon, he nodded. "You can use my laptop. It's in the office at the end of the hall."

I headed to where he gestured, but he called after me. "First, I'm making you breakfast. You can't job search on an empty stomach."

"That's totally unnecessary—"

"I thought you were done being stubborn," he interrupted, amusement dancing in his eyes.

I huffed, my shoulders slumping. "Fine. I'd like breakfast."

"That's better." He walked off, and I couldn't resist admiring how firm his ass looked in that towel. "Get comfortable in the living room. I'll be down soon."

I obeyed his instructions, settling on the couch and turning on the TV. On instinct, I scanned the news channels, half-expecting to see a missing report about me. I wouldn't put it past Daddy and the boys to flush me out—or at least try to. By now, they were probably shitting their pants, wondering if I'd gone to the cops.

Was I safe in Las Vegas? Was the seven-hour distance enough?

I hoped it was because I had no intention of leaving. The Culinary Academy was only a short distance away, which meant my dream was within arm's length. Once I got settled, I planned to apply. No one—not my daddy or my asshole brothers would stop me from achieving my goal.

A sudden thwack made me twist in my seat, eyes darting to the kitchen. I had been so lost in my thoughts; I didn't notice Declan had come down. He'd already gotten breakfast going, the scent of coffee and bacon soon filling the space.

With my chin resting on the back of the couch, I watched him work, his handsome face screwed with concentration. He'd changed into a pair of distressed jeans and a simple black T-shirt. His hair was done up in a messy man bun. Until then, I'd never seen anything so sexy. I hugged the seat, wondering what it would be like to have unlimited days like this; me sitting on the couch, watching him cook. Us sharing a home together. It was a crazy thing to want, but right then, I wished it was even remotely possible.

Breathing a sigh, I returned my attention to the TV. It was no use wishing for something I couldn't have. Declan was attracted to me, no doubt, but it would never work. We were from different worlds.

"Breakfast's ready," came his sudden rumble close to my ear, startling me. I turned to see him standing behind the couch, wearing a slight smirk.

"Not funny. You startled me," I reproached him.

He shrugged. "I kept calling you from the kitchen. You didn't answer."

"Sorry." I wiped my face. "My mind was elsewhere."

"I noticed that's a frequent thing. Where did you go?"

"Somewhere bleak." I caught the lingering question on his face and shook my head. "Something I'm not ready to talk about."

He nodded. "Yesterday, you didn't want to talk about it. Today, you're not ready. It's progress. I'll be patient. It's not like I'm going anywhere."

But I am, I thought sadly. As soon as I got on my feet, I'd leave. I couldn't afford to fall for Declan. Living under his roof long-term made it a guarantee.

We ate breakfast in silence. Well, not talking to each other. Declan's phone was already ringing off the hook, his clients booking their appointments. He was obviously late for work, but he insisted on washing the dishes, telling me to relax. His offer touched me, but I grew restless as the day went on. After doing a job search and coming up empty, I spent the afternoon cleaning up. Not that there was much to do. Declan's house was so neat and clean, definitely not what I expected. It made me admire him even more.

Boredom soon forced me to take a nap, though the opening front door soon woke me. Declan was home, a stark contrast to the clean, bubbly man who left this morning. His man bun was in disarray, tendrils framing his face. Grease spots kissed his jeans. His weary eyes looked me over as he dropped his bag on the floor.

"Rough day?"

"An understatement," he huffed, kicking off his shoes. He reached into his bag, pulling out a small shopping bag. "I brought you something."

Surprised, I gaped at the bag. He bounced it a little, urging me to take it. I opened it and looked in, my mouth falling open when I saw the contents. "You brought me clothes?"

He nodded calmly, like he didn't just blow my mind. "Just enough for one day. I figured you'd want to buy the rest yourself."

I closed my mouth, wetting my lips as I pulled out the pair of jeans. They were exactly my size. So was the shirt with the side split and the pair of silk panties. "Thank you. I... I'm blown away."

"You're welcome." Declan moved to the armchair and reached for his phone. "Are you hungry? Let me order some food."

"No." I was still in awe that he bought me clothes, now he completely knocked me over by thinking of my welfare, not himself. "I want to cook for you."

Something passed over his face, something resembling affection. He pulled back, shaking his head. "That's unnecessary, Cass."

"I've been at home all day with nothing to do. I want to cook for you," I repeated.

Again, that look, then he murmured. "No woman has ever offered to cook for me before."

I masked my surprise with a shrug. "Well, let me be the first."

"Sure." He got up and led the way to the kitchen, proceeding to show me where the ingredients were. He left to take a shower while I got busy making beef stroganoff, my momma's favorite dish. Declan reappeared when I was almost done, and he poured two glasses of wine, offering me one while joking about my age. The wine soon mellowed me out, and I talked loosely during dinner. My guard was totally down.

"This was a lovely meal, Cass," Declan said, placing his fork on the empty plate. "Where did you learn to cook like this?"

"My momma taught me. This was her favorite dish, actually."

His expression stilled. "Was?"

"Yeah." My heart lurched painfully, an automatic response to any mention of her. "She passed away a few years ago."

"I'm so sorry." He reached over and squeezed my hand. I nodded; my eyes locked to my plate.

"How about your dad? Is he still alive?" he asked.

I stiffed, pulling my hand away, placing it on my lap. "Yeah."

"Any siblings?"

"Can we change the subject?" I asked, looking up at him.

Confusion filled his face. He leaned back in his seat, giving me a slight nod. "Sure. What do you want to talk about?"

"Your girlfriend. Where is she?"

Declan's expression cleared, and he burst into a laugh. "What makes you think I have a girlfriend?"

"Didn't we already establish that?" I gestured to him again. "You're a good-looking guy. Tall. Totally hot. How come women aren't beating down your door?"

"Because of the wall," he said simply.

"Wall?" I stared at him, puzzled because I didn't recall seeing a fence when we got here. "You don't have a wall."

"Not a literal one, Cass. An emotional wall."

"Oh." I blinked at him. "Why?"

He shrugged. "I got tired of being used. And hurt."

"Now, that's shocking. I imagined it the other way around." At his wry stare, I brush him off. "Take a glance in the mirror, Declan. You have heartbreaker stamped all over you."

Again, he laughed. "It was the other way around, believe me." He suddenly leaned in, his eyes adapting a sudden intensity that stole my breath. "When I love, I love hard, Cass. I don't go in half-assed, and I take no one for granted."

I swallowed hard, nodding. "Got it."

He got up and cleared the dishes, and we got into a friendly fight over washing them. Eventually, he conceded and allowed me to dry. We settled into a comfortable silence as we worked, with nightfall approaching when we got done.

My head jerked back when he suddenly reached for me, running fingers through my curls. You have something in your hair," he explained, pulling out a piece of string.

"Thanks." I took the string, my fingers brushing with his.

"And you have something on your mouth," he mumbled, his thumb brushing across my lips.

I scoff when he pulled back. There was nothing on his thumb. "Liar. There's nothing on my mouth."

"Yes, there is. Mine," he whispered, capturing my lips, reducing me to a moaning mess with the hungry strokes of his tongue. I clung to him, trying to keep up, but he completely took over, eating my mouth like it was his last meal. Next thing I knew, I had my leg wrapped around his waist, grinding myself against his front. His cock nudged me, pressing against my clit. Caught up with the insane pleasure, I bit his lips. Declan growled, his hand going to my breast, gently kneading. I lost myself to the sweet sensation, desperate for more.

A sudden alarm went off in my head when he cupped my flesh. Once he got inside me, there was no going back. Was I really ready for this? Could I handle whatever came next?

I backed off with a harsh breath. "Sorry, I—I can't—we shouldn't do this."

"We're both adults, Cassandra. What are you afraid of?" Declan asked, and I didn't miss the frustration in his eyes. The bulge in his pants made it clear how aroused he was. I didn't want him to think I was a tease, arousing him twice in one day, then backing off.

"I'm not afraid, Declan," I replied. "Well, not really." I lifted my chin. "I'm a virgin."

His expression remained unchanged. "I see."

"And I don't want my first time to be a casual thing. It needs to mean something," I insisted.

He nodded. "I understand."

"So, yeah... goodnight, Declan," I mumbled, giving him a brief smile and dashing to my room, closing the door behind me, half-glad, half-disappointed when he didn't come after me.

A soft curse left my mouth as I leaned against the door, slowly sliding to the floor. I hugged my knees to my chest, groaning as I reflected on what had just happened.

Oh, how I wanted to give into Declan. I could still taste my need for him. Back there, I panicked, fleeing like a scared puppy. Now, as I sat, with the slickness of my arousal between my legs, all I wanted to do was get back out there and beg him to take me.

But I'd already rejected him twice. Would he even take me seriously if I did?

God, I was so turned on, my body so tight with tension, leaving me on the brink of bursting into pieces. I was tempted to satisfy myself, but it wouldn't be the same. I wanted Declan's fingers inside me, not my own.

Like the night before, I crawled into bed with Declan on my mind, but this time, the thoughts were hotter. Filthier. I tossed and turned until the ache grew so unbearable, forcing me to touch myself.

I pulled the sheet off, spreading my thighs, ignoring the rush of embarrassment. This was my body, so I was free to do whatever I wanted with it. Right now, I wanted to give it pleasure. I wanted to come.

A soft moan escaped as I teased my clit, the action sending a passionate thrill through me. I used the tip of my fingers to circle the nub, rolling my hips in beat to the motion. With my free hand, I slipped two fingers inside me, gently stroking, awed by how my aroused flesh tightened around them. The bed creaked as I picked up the pace, plunging deep, fucking myself to a climax. Sparks of bliss went off inside me. I moaned his name as my body tremored, welcoming the sweet release.

Sinking against the pillows again, my body damp from self-pleasure, it cleared my head a little, giving way to the memories of Declan making breakfast in the kitchen that morning, of him buying me clothes, and of the look in his eyes when I offered to cook for him. Declan was a decent guy; tattoos and motorcycle be damned. It would take nothing to fall for a guy like him.

Be careful, Cass.

Be careful.

I OVERSLEPT THE NEXT morning. After brushing my teeth and changing into Declan's T-shirt, I hurried downstairs to find him ending a phone call. My cheeks warmed when he looked at me, and the memories of our last kiss filled my head.

"I have some great news," he said, shoving his phone into his pocket.

My pulse tripped, excitement filling me. "What is it?"

"So I asked around, and it turns out, there's a vacancy in a store downtown," he said.

I gasped. "Really?"

"I told the owner about you, and she wants to meet as soon as possible. You could work there until you find something suited for you."

"Oh, my God. Thank you!" I said, my eyes filling with tears. "When can we go?"

His amused eyes traveled the length of me. "Maybe after you change that shirt. And put some panties on."

I looked down at myself, my body heating. Too late, I'd forgotten my underwear. "Holy crap."

His chuckling followed me back to my room, where I showered and got dressed in the outfit he had bought me. I let my hair down this time, loving how soft it was around my shoulders.

Declan was already by his motorcycle, his helmet in hand, as he waited for me. Once again, his gaze did a thorough inspection of me as I walked toward him.

Without saying a word, he climbed onto his ride and started the engine. It roared to life while I cautiously climbed on behind him. Touching his body after our kiss seemed more intense, and the need seemed worse, but for my safety, I clung onto him, taking in a lungful of his cologne, acknowledging how it made me even more aroused.

It was a beautiful morning, with just the right temperature for a motorcycle ride. A little sunshine peeked from the clouds, the cool air awesome against my skin as Declan cruised down the winding road. We passed Billy's bar, pulling up to a glass-structured clothes store minutes later. I hopped off and rubbed my sweaty palms against my jeans as I prepared to go in.

"Do you think they'll hire me looking like this?" I asked, turning to Declan.

I regretted the question right away. The way he stared at me was so hot. Too hot. I almost squirmed as his slow, deliberate gaze took in every inch of me, his eyes darkening as he did so.

"You're perfect. Of course, she will," he said with a tight smile.

Encouraged by his compliment, I confidently pushed the door open and entered the store. A brunette in her late thirties spotted us and instantly moved from around the counter. She wore a hundred-watt smile that made me feel welcomed at once.

Declan moved to her, and they hugged, the woman almost lost in his embrace. The smile waned from my face, though unintentional, but somehow their hug made me feel uncomfortable. I could be wrong, but I sensed a little chemistry between them.

"Grace, this is the young lady I told you about; Cassandra. Cassandra, this is Grace... an old friend."

Grace glanced at him with the smile still on her face, but I saw something else there I couldn't quite put my finger on. She turned to me, still pleasant as ever, as her gaze briskly ran over me before she stretched out a hand.

"Nice to meet you, Cassandra. I already know you'll do great with a pretty face like that. Everyone loves a pretty face. Right, Declan?" she asked, winking at him.

Declan grunted but said nothing. His expression remained unreadable.

I smiled. "Thank you. And please, call me Cass."

"Are you from around here, Cass?" she asked, her big brown eyes strained on my face.

"Er, no. I moved here recently."

She spread her arms. "If that's the case, welcome to Las Vegas! Come on, let me show you around."

Without waiting for my reply, she reached for my hand and took me around the store, Declan's eyes on us the entire time.

"We mostly cater to women, but we have a section for men's wear as well," she said, gesturing to the rack filled with men's jeans. "I've wanted an assistant for so long, but no one wants a boring job like this in Las Vegas. Not when there are dozens of casinos and clubs around." She chuckled. "My husband, Dan and I have been meaning to take a vacation, but I've never gotten the time. Now that you're here, it's perfect!"

I paused, gaping at her. "I–I'm hired?"

"Well, of course. I trust Declan, and that's how I know you're legit. He has a way of seeing the good in people," she said, turning and flashing him a wink.

I glanced at Declan, who was now smiling at the interaction, looking as delectable as ever.

"Thank you. When can I start?" I asked eagerly.

She looked between us. "Well, if you aren't busy now, I could get you acquainted with a few things so you could start tomorrow."

I shook my head, thinking of being stuck at home alone with nothing to do. "I'm definitely not busy, so yes, that'd be great."

"Awesome." She waved to a customer standing by the checkout counter. "Let me ring up that order, and we'll get started, okay?"

Declan came up to me as she moved off, and I couldn't resist hugging him. "Thank you."

He hugged me back, though briefly, then gestured to the exit. "Could I have a minute with you?"

I glanced at Grace, who was still busy attending to the customer, then I followed Declan out, curious to see what he wanted. We stepped outside, and I stood before him, his burly frame blocking the bit of sunlight.

"I'm heading to the shop, but I'll pick you up later when I'm done. Grace closes around the same time I do," he said before digging into his pockets and pulling out his wallet.

Confused, I stared at him and watched as he pulled out a few hundred dollar notes before handing them to me. "Get yourself some more clothes while you're at it and some breakfast, too."

I didn't expect all that, not after everything he'd already done for me. "Declan, I can't–"

"You can do whatever you want with it, Shrimp. You're going to need it," he said, his hands still outstretched with the notes.

My eyes stung with unshed tears. No matter what Declan's motive was, it still made me grateful. I couldn't have gotten this far without him. Unable to help myself, I flung myself into his arms once more, my head slamming against his hard chest as I hugged him tightly. He was warm and firm, and it made me feel so protected. I'd never experienced such safety in my life. After a beat, his hands curled around me, and I closed my eyes with a shuddering sigh.

I could remain wrapped in his embrace all day and not think anything of it. My heart raced a mile a second, but it wasn't from fear. A range of emotions coursed through my body, the strongest being desire.

"Thank you so much." I sniffed, breathing in his scent.

"Don't mention it," he whispered before easing from me, giving me a direct stare. "Everything will be fine."

He leaned in and kissed me on the forehead. My stomach fluttered, and my cheeks grew heated. He handed me the money again, and I took it this time, watching as his lips stretched into a smile.

Without saying another word, he moved to his motorcycle, climbed on and drove away. As I watched him leave, a feeling of dread came over me, and I didn't understand why. Chalking it up to a defense mechanism, I returned inside, ready to work.

The rest of the day was smooth sailing, with Grace's bubbly character remaining consistent, even in Declan's absence. After learning the rounds and assisting a few customers, I used the last hour of my workday to shop for clothes with the money Declan gave me. I bought a few pairs of jeans and comfortable, functional tops; then I moved to the underwear section.

A sexy lace lingerie caught my eye. My cheeks burned as I lifted it, my blush growing as I imagined wearing it for Declan, his expression hot for me as I danced for him.

I dropped the flimsy garment with a scoff. *Too many romance novels. It's not like I know how to dance.*

"Someone special in mind?" Grace suddenly asked, startling me. I didn't hear her approach.

I cleared my throat, knowing my face was probably deep red by now. "Er– I..." I stuttered, not knowing what to say.

"I think this color would do wonders against your skin," she said as she picked up a blood-red one-piece teddy.

"Er, no—I—" Damn it. *Why didn't I just walk past this section?* "I'm not looking for any lingerie, actually."

"Oh. I just assumed—" she flashed her hand. "Never mind." She dabbled with a few more pieces before glancing at me, a sly expression on her face. "Declan is a good one. He's loyal to a fault, and I trust him with my life."

"You know each other well?"

"We dated for a while in college, but it didn't work out." She shrugged, making a face.

Curious, I asked, "Why not?"

"Declan was a free spirit, and he didn't like the restrictions his father placed on him. In our second year of college, he suddenly quit and joined the army, with nothing but a simple goodbye. Back then, it devastated me. Now I realized it was for the best. If we hadn't broken up, I wouldn't have given Dan a chance."

I'd expected to feel jealousy like I did when they hugged, but I realized Grace was no threat. She didn't have feelings for Declan, not with that sparkle in her eyes when she mentioned her husband.

What did it matter, anyway? Declan and I would never be a thing.

"I can see that he likes you," she said.

"Huh?"

She nodded wisely. "I spent years wanting him to look at me like that, and he never did."

I lowered my gaze to the pile of lingerie, processing Grace's words. The thought of Declan liking me made me excited, but I knew better than to hope for love when there was a high chance I'd be disappointed in the end.

"He never looked at Marie that way, either," Grace added.

My head shot up, and I remembered the name being mentioned when Declan and Rodger got into the fight. "Who's Marie?"

Grace's expression shuttered, and she gave me a tight smile. "No one you should worry about." She held up the racy lingerie. "What do you say?"

I forced a smile, shaking my head. "Maybe some other time."

DECLAN PICKED ME UP around six, and we rode in silence until we arrived at his place. Throughout the journey, the question lingered in my head, and I itched to ask him. Who was Marie? It was obvious they had a thing, so where was she now?

I couldn't demand answers from him. It wasn't my place to ask. Plus, I wasn't quite open about who I was, nor was I ready to talk about my past. I tucked my curiosity away, tightening my grip around him and resting my cheek against his back.

"How was work?" he asked when we got inside.

"It was okay, I guess. I really like Grace," I replied, kicking off my shoes. The motorcycle ride made my body a little tense. I raised my arms, stretching out the stiffness. The action lifted the hem of my shirt, exposing my stomach. Declan's eyes darted there, lingering, the hunger there as raw as ever. My core tightened with need.

"Did you eat?"

It took me a moment to realize what he had said. "I had a bite around two, but I'm not hungry. I'm going to lie down for a bit."

I could feel his eyes on me as I left the room. If only he knew I was hungry alright but not for food. I couldn't be around him, not with such a strong ache for him. It was better to steer clear, and that was the aim, though I grew hornier with every step I took.

Although I had new clothes, I showered and changed into one of Declan's large T-shirts. There was something about sleeping in his clothes that brought me great comfort. I snuggled up in bed and sniffed his shirt, closing my eyes as his spicy scent overwhelmed me. I couldn't get enough; it was the closest thing to being with him.

I laid there thinking about my daddy and brothers and wondering if they were still looking for me or if they'd decided I wasn't worth chasing. They would probably leave me alone if I hadn't stolen daddy's truck and kicked Johnny in the groin, but they'd want their revenge. I imagined how much they'd make me suffer. A chill ran down my spine when I thought about seeing them again and the possible punishment Johnny had waiting for me.

To rid myself of the fearsome feeling, I switched my thoughts to Declan again, imagining a world where we were together despite our huge age gap and different lives.

I drifted off to sleep with him in mind and a smile on my face.

DECLAN'S TONGUE LICKED over my body as I lay in bed, heat consuming me. I was losing my mind, trying to concentrate on his tongue while his hands did wonders to my body.

My eyes popped open when he settled between my legs and spread them apart. I was soaking wet, ready for him to lick me dry. He looked up at me, his eyes burning with lust, my heart beating faster when he lowered his head again and lapped my clit. I quivered, screaming his name as I basked in my bliss.

His strong tongue kept lapping at my flesh, moving up and down, then circling my hardened clit. I gasped, my hips jutting upwards when he nipped the sensitive area with his teeth.

"Oh, yes!" I moaned, gripping his thick dark hair.

He licked down to the seam teasing my hole, moving to my clit again, gently sucking on it. I bit my lips when he repeated each motion, each one being more forceful than the last. Just when I was about to explode, he slipped a finger inside me, the action blinding me with sweet pleasure. I writhed beneath him, halfway to insanity from the slow, deliberate way he finger-fucked me.

"Declan, please, don't stop!" I screamed, my breath coming out in heavy pants.

He suddenly froze, staring at me with confusion on his face, then he called my name. The entire scene faded, making me realize this was only a dream.

My eyes snapped open, flickering to the door. Declan stood there, his eyes wide while emotions played across his face. I glanced down, seeing my hand between my thighs, feeling the moistness of my arousal on my fingers. It was a dream—at least, some of it was. I'd been touching myself for real.

And, oh God—Declan caught me. He'd seen me fucking myself!

I gasped and pushed to a sitting position, the embarrassment so strong I wanted to sink into the floor. Or hide my face. Gosh, I didn't know the first thing to say.

"I uh– I heard you... I heard you call my name. I thought it was urgent," Declan said, his gaze dark. "I'm sorry for barging in like this."

My heart fluttered painfully in my chest. I couldn't believe what was happening, and I was still speechless, my cheeks stinging as if I'd been slapped. My eyes lowered to his boxers, the bulge unmistakable in his grey sweats.

He was hard – for me.

I bit my lips, and our gazes locked, the energy in the room almost overwhelming. How much more of this could I bear?

"Please stay," I said, my voice barely above a whisper.

Declan's Adam's apple visibly bobbed. "Are you sure?" he asked.

I nodded. "Yes, please. I want you so badly, Declan."

His face softened, but the hunger remained. "Fuck, Cass. You have no idea how much those words are fucking with my head right now."

"I know, but I'm not sorry. I can't sleep without having you inside me."

"Fuck." He scrubbed his face with a groan. "Are you really sure about this?"

"Positive."

Declan sighed, backing away. My heart skipped a beat as he closed the door with a soft click and approached me. I was ready for him this time.

Chapter 5

Declan

For two days, I watched Cassandra struggle with her attraction to me. I saw the way her face reddened whenever we made contact. I witnessed the fire in her eyes after we kissed. She needed time. I planned on being patient. Never in a million years did I imagine getting my reward so soon.

I was about to go to bed when I heard her moan. It sounded low and inarticulate as if she suffered physical pain. I'd barged in only to find her safe and sound with her fingers between her thighs and my name on her lips.

Something primal ran through me. I wanted to cross the room and replace those fingers with my cock. I wanted to see the pleasure in her eyes as I filled her over and over until we got our fill. Instead, I'd remained silent, rooted on the spot, unable to take my eyes off the most beautiful thing I'd ever seen in my life.

Now that she'd given me permission to stay, I was as hard as steel, ready to feel exactly how wet and tight she was.

I couldn't get over how innocent she looked on that bed. So tiny, so pure with my shirt on and her hair in disarray falling down her shoulders. Every single inch of my body was now awake, ready to be caressed by Cassandra's soft hands.

I leaned in and kissed her irresistible lips that were full and as soft as they looked. She tasted sweet and supple, and I grew more aroused as my lips slid over hers and our tongues danced together.

My hand cupped her cheek, and as I pulled away, I ran my thumb over the soft flesh.

Staring right into her eyes, I said. "I want you to continue."

She looked confused, her brows wrinkling as she sought clarity. "Continue?" Her warm breath fanned against my face, and my cock stirred.

"To touch yourself," I explained, watching as her eyes widened and her cheeks reddened with a blush.

She licked her lips as her gaze faltered from mine and searched the covers as if they had the answers.

"I want to watch you pleasure yourself, Cass."

A small smile crept at the corners of her lips. "Okay," she said after a brief pause. Excited by the approval, I kissed her passionately before I shuffled to the end of the bed and pulled my shirt off, watching her assume the position.

She laid on her back and pulled the oversized T-shirt above her hips, exposing her naked bottom half, which had me adjusting the front of my pants, making room for my growing erection. I had seen many women naked, but this... her... it took my breath away. Light-brown hair feathered her pussy, but it wasn't too much to hide her pink slit that already glistened with her juices.

"You're so beautiful, Sweetheart," I said, my voice a little croaky.

She managed a shy smile as she spread her legs further apart and ran her slender fingers along them, moving further up to her flesh. I watched in anticipation, waiting for the moment when her delicate fingers would part her slit and sink into her warm honeysuckle.

But being the tease Cassandra proved herself to be, she lingered between her thighs, moaning softly as she stroked back and forth, her eyes fluttering from the pleasure.

"Show me how wet you are, Sweetheart," I said, and she complied by trailing her middle finger up her crease and slowly sinking it in. My cock hardened painfully as I watched her, my body on fire as I drank in everything with my hungry gaze.

She moaned as she ran that single finger up and down her flesh, spreading her juices, which lathered her fingers and her pussy. She was already soaking wet, and with every movement, I could hear the squishing sound of her soaked cunt being pleasured by her finger.

"Take the shirt off, Cass," I ordered, my voice thick with desire.

She stopped what she was doing, but my eyes didn't stop staring at the wetness between her legs. When she threw the shirt to the side, it drew my attention to her naked top half with nipples that stood out in her chest just like I imagined. Her tiny tits were firm, and I knew they would fit perfectly in my hands. Her nipples were like little peaks on top, begging to be caressed – to be sucked.

Her flat stomach rose and fell with her deep breaths as she found her pussy again, which welcomed her with a slick sound when she sunk her fingers inside.

She let out a sexy moan, caressing her clit, her legs falling further apart as the pleasure intensified. Her body jolted when she added another finger, then another. Fuck, I couldn't help but rub myself through my pants as more juices ran from her cunt. She was so wet, it was insane, and I couldn't believe it was all because of me.

As she fucked herself with two fingers, her back arched, and her moans got louder. Her blonde hair lay sprawled around her. She looked angelic lying there.

"What was I doing in your dreams, Cass?"

She slowed her pace, but her fingers still stroked her pussy. She sighed, then looked at me, her cheeks hot pink again. There was some hesitance, but her sweet lips parted, her next words surprising the shit out of me.

"You were going down on me," she whispered as her fingers left from inside her.

I swallowed the lump in my throat. "Do you want me to, right now?"

"I–if you want to."

I narrowed the distance between us, moving so close I could smell the sweet scent of her arousal. "Tell me what you want, Cass. Do you want me to eat your pussy like I was doing in your dreams?"

She swallowed and nodded. "Yes... please."

I smiled. "See how easy that was? Your wish is my command, sweet girl."

I moved between her legs and settled my face at eye level with her beautiful pussy. She was precious, so fucking pure, and that brought me the greatest pleasure. I didn't need to have my cock inside her to know she was mine. She willingly gave herself to me. That was a sure enough sign.

I used my thumb to caress her soft little quim that I just couldn't wait to sink my cock in. But I salivated as much to taste her on my lips. Her skin was smooth as velvet, and her cunt was as soft as silk. I smeared her juices against my thumb and eased up so she could see me. Then I sucked every drop of her from my finger and watched as her eyes widened with surprise.

She tasted sweeter than I imagined, though, in my imagination, she was the sweetest treat. Unable to wait a second longer, I lowered my head between her slender thighs and licked her from the bottom of her slit to the very top. She released a low moan that hardened me to an unbearable point.

Pushing aside the urge to bury myself inside her, I licked her dry, then stuck my tongue inside, moving in slow, teasing circles.

"Yes, yes, please..." she mewled, her voice as soft as every inch of her body.

She rocked her hips as my tongue slid into her, her tightened grip in my hair telling me she wasn't far from release. Pulling out, I sucked her clit, marveling at how it swelled beneath my tongue. Fuck, she was so aroused, dripping wet, trembling and screaming my name like she'd been doing when I'd barged into her room. Reality was far more rewarding because I did the job she wanted done.

Upping things a notch, I slipped a finger inside her, feeling her stretch around me. She was still tight. Too tight. As I drove my finger back and forth, I could feel the resistance, but she soon loosened up around me.

She gasped when I nipped her clit with my teeth. Her grip tightened around a handful of my hair. As I continued nipping, I curled my finger inside her, her sensitive walls eagerly squeezing me.

"Declan... oh, my God... that feels so good..."

I added a second finger, sinking deeper.

"Christ," she breathed.

Her pussy clenched around my fingers, the slickness more pronounced with each stroke. "Declan—" She made a loud, primal sound, her hips shooting upwards.

"Yes, Cass. That's it. Come for me," I rumbled.

Her head flew back as another loud cry pierced the air. She was coming, hard, her eyes rolling to the back of her head, the grip on my hair tighter than before. She bounced on my fingers, riding out her orgasm, her beautiful lips now whispering my name. It was the sweetest sound. She was the sweetest thing.

I withdrew my fingers as she sank down against the pillows, her chest heaving as she caught her breath. "That was awesome, Declan," she said, raking her fingers through her hair. "I've never had so much pleasure in my life."

"You might think differently once you feel my cock," I teased, crawling above her, staring down at her body glistening with sweat. She was perfect. Perfect for me. "Are you ready for me, sweet girl?"

Her eyes dropped to my front, then back at me, and I glimpsed the caution there. "Yes, I'm ready," she whispered. "Make love to me, Declan."

Without further delay, I peeled off my pants, my cock springing free. I didn't take my eyes off Cassandra, whose eyes widened as she stared at me.

"Do you think it will fit?" she asked, her voice carrying a slight tremble. She moaned as I stroked myself, her hips moving in a gentle circle.

"I'll be gentle for your first time, Sweetheart. I promise." I leaned in and kissed her softly on the lips, my cock brushing against her cunt.

She nodded, her lips parting to let me in. I ate her mouth, prepping her to take my length. When her body relaxed, I positioned myself on my knees and licked her, lubricating her enough to ease my entrance. Cassandra moaned when I groped her breast, kneading it firmly before driving my length slowly inside her. Her mouth flew open, her expression showing the discomfort that usually came with the first time.

My cockhead slipped in, and she gasped, looking up at me with wide eyes.

"Relax, baby. I won't hurt you," I assured her.

She nodded as I met the resistance. With one sharp thrust, her gasp filled the room, and I was deep inside her. I paused, allowing the pain to pass, my thumb caressing her clit. She pulsed around me, tight and warm, forcing me to remember I had to be gentle for her.

"How does my cock feel inside you?" I asked, my hips slowly rocking.

Her skin flushed pink. "Huge," she answered almost breathlessly. "But it feels amazing."

I smiled, inching deeper and deeper inside her.

"Soon enough, you'll get used to my cock. I'll fuck you every day until that's the case," I rumbled, squeezing her breast and driving further. She creamed and squeezed my cock so tightly I thought I'd bust inside her.

"Yes, Declan!" she exclaimed as I picked up the pace, watching as my length slid back and forth inside her, lubricated with her juices. "Don't stop fucking me like that."

My hands clawed at her soft skin as I pressed deeper, her moans increasing every time.

"How deep do you want me, Cass?" I grunted, hanging onto every bit of self-control, trying not to fuck her senseless.

"All the way," she mewled. "I want you to make me come."

I obliged and lowered myself onto her, driving my cock deeper. I kissed her open mouth, and she clung to me, her legs wrapped around my ass as she trapped me into her tightness. Sweat beaded our skins – more so me from holding back so much.

I moved inside her, completely sheathed by her warmth, completely awed by how perfect she was around me. She whispered my name, the sound so sexy as her sex pulsed around me.

My hips moved faster, the sounds of full length slamming into her wetness filled the room. She whimpered like a baby as she came, and as the last of her orgasm coursed through her, I stiffened, the pressure doubling in my balls before the biggest release of my life. I couldn't withdraw if I wanted to. The sensation was too amazing, unlike anything I'd experienced with anyone before.

I clung to her, filling her freshly ploughed pussy with my seed. The pleasurable thrill seemed to last forever until it finally stopped, and I pulled myself from her sweetness. I kissed her cheek before collapsing beside her, breathing heavily as I basked in the bliss that surrounded us.

"How do you feel, sweet girl?" I asked when I caught my breath, running my fingers down her arm.

She smiled, curling up to me, her face flushed and glowing like a woman truly satisfied. "There are not enough words to describe how awesome that was," she replied.

I grinned. "Not bad for your first time, right?"

"That's an understatement." She glanced down at my cock, a soft blush forming on her cheeks. "I could get addicted to this."

I brushed the hair from her face, tilting her chin to capture her gaze. "What if I told you I'm already addicted to you?"

Her brows shot up, and she scoffed. "Don't say things you don't mean, Declan."

"I never do." Again, I held her chin. "I'm serious. I'm addicted to you, Cass."

Making love to her had brought my guard down, making me crave more moments like this, with her wrapped in my arms, her soft, post-orgasm breaths filling my ears. I wanted to cuddle up to her and inhale the fresh scent of sex mixed with sweetness. I wanted her round little ass cushioned against me. Mornings and nights wouldn't be the same without her around.

"I want you in my life, Cass. Not as a temporary roommate, but as your lover and protector," I said.

She sighed, her fingers stroking my chest as she looked up, holding my gaze. "Declan–"

"I've never had this attraction for anyone, Cass, and I've been around the block."

"Not even Marie?" she asked.

I stared at her for a beat, too surprised to say anything at first. How did she know about Marie?

"In case you're wondering, I heard Rodger mention her name when you fought with him that morning. Grace did, too, but she didn't say much. Please don't tell her I told you," Cass said.

I shook my head, still lost for words.

"Are you going to say anything?"

"Marie is my past," I finally got out. "And I don't want to talk about her. My feelings for her have nothing to do with how I feel for you now."

She nodded. "I understand you don't want to talk about her, but what if she comes back? What if you decide to rekindle your relationship—?"

"I won't." My interruption came in a dead tone. "She's dead, Cassandra. She's not coming back."

Cassandra's mouth made a small O, and she palmed her cheeks. "I'm so sorry, Declan. I shouldn't have asked—"

"It's okay. You didn't know." I shot her a reassuring smile. "It happened five years ago, and I'm ready to move on."

Five years of finding myself again. Five years trying to find love, meeting women who weren't right for me, giving up on being in love and having casual relationships instead. Now, a renewed hope lay beside me, the attraction more intense than I'd ever experienced, even with Marie. I didn't want to let it go. I had no intention of letting her go. "Be with me, Cass. I want you here."

"You're saying that now, but soon you'll want your space, and I'll just be a nuisance—"

"Never." I clutched her chin, forcing her to meet my hard stare. "I'll never get tired of being with you, Cassandra."

She licked her lips and didn't say a word, which cut me deep. "Think about it?" I asked.

"Yes, I will." She ran her hand over my chest, my stomach, coming to rest near my cock. "I'll be sore in the morning, but I want you inside me again."

I drew back with amused surprise. "Did I unleash a sex fiend?"

"I warned you about my addiction, didn't I?" she said, giggling.

My hands trailed along her back, my cock hardening just from touching her. With a moan, she threw her leg over my hip, welcoming me inside her. Her gasp echoed in the room, heightening the arousal that was already rampant through me.

Chapter 6

Cassandra

Declan wasn't beside me the following morning when I woke up, but the evidence of him being with me was very much obvious. I gasped when I moved, the soreness between my legs more uncomfortable than I thought it would be. Everything smelled of him– even me, and I couldn't help my smile when I remembered last night. I missed having him next to me. If only we could lie in bed all day, but this was no fairytale. I had a job to show up for.

Speaking of my job...

I glanced at the clock, throwing off the covers when I saw it was already past seven. "Shit!"

After a quick shower, I went downstairs to find Declan dressed in his signature jeans and T-shirt with a cup of coffee in his hand and another steaming cup on the counter.

"Good morning," I greeted.

He turned to look at me, his gaze traveling down the length of my body, his eyes sparkling with interest.

"Good morning. You look... amazing." He whistled, shaking his head.

I glanced down at the flirty, sunflower-colored dress I'd bought at Grace's boutique. I'd spent a little extra time combing my hair and applying light makeup. The appreciation on his face made me glad I did. I smiled, happy he liked it. "Thank you."

He nodded, his gaze still fixed on me. "I made you coffee," he said, gesturing to the cup.

"Oh, thank you. I *need* this." I lifted it and took a sip while peering at Declan over the rim of my cup.

"Are you okay?" he asked.

I nodded. "Just a little sore. Last night was..." I took another sip to hide my blush. "Something else."

"I didn't hurt you, did I?"

The concern on his face made me vigorously shake my head to assure him. "No, I'm fine. I'm great, actually." I reached out and took his arm. "I hadn't slept that soundly in two years."

Declan cocked a brow. "How come?"

"No reason, really. Um... we should probably get going, right? I don't want to be late on my first official day at work."

He slowly nodded, and I sensed he wasn't pleased with my response. I heaved a sigh, watching as he placed his empty cup in the sink. I so badly wanted to tell him the truth, but the less he knew, about me, the better.

"Well, I'm ready when you are," he said. "Just let me grab my things."

When he returned, I was ready to go, my new crossbody bag strapped over my shoulder, a pair of sneakers on my feet. I climbed behind him on the motorcycle and wrapped my hands around his hard stomach when the engine gunned to life. The exhilaration would never get old as we cruised down the road, but today the thrill was more pronounced. I didn't want this moment to end. I wanted to be with him for a lifetime. Considering I hadn't known him for a full week, there was no way those feelings were real.

Right?

Last night, my heart screamed to tell him yes – that I would stay with him and never leave, but I couldn't make that promise when I didn't mean it. Maybe I was better off going through life alone. Throughout my life, people kept disappointing me; my mom when she died, my dad when he mistreated me instead of caring for me, and fate when it made me lose my bag after I knee'd Johnny in his groin— Declan would eventually do the same, I knew it. I would have loved to entrust myself to him, but I couldn't – not yet. Though my heart wanted to give in, my mind remained unyielding.

Declan's motor throttled, and I opened my eyes, realizing we'd arrived at Grace's store. He rolled toward a parking spot, and my heart suddenly dipped when I saw a car parked nearby.

"Declan, st– stop," I said, but realized my voice was barely above a whisper. "Stop! Declan, stop!" I exclaimed even louder as I slapped his shoulder, my gaze still fixed on the dark blue Subaru, its windows tinted dark black. Was that Johnny's car? Crap, I didn't even know his license plate number, but what were the odds it wasn't him? This was too much of a coincidence.

How the hell did they find me?

The motorcycle came to a halt, and he twisted to look at me, confusion etched on his face.

"What is it?" he asked, his eyes scanning my face. "Cass, you look like you've just seen a ghost. What's the matter?"

I heard his words, but I couldn't answer him. Not with my heart in my throat and my body shaking like a leaf. He frowned at me, then glanced at the source of my gaze before he looked at me again. When he realized, his expression changed; it was obvious he did. His hands tightened around the handlebars as he looked at the car again.

"Who is it, Cass?" His tone carried a hard edge, and so did his expression. "Who's in that car?"

"No one. Just take me home, please," I managed, my eyes foggy from the tears that settled there.

"Not yet," he growled, his body shifting as he slid off the motorcycle.

"Declan, no!" I didn't doubt he could handle himself, but I was almost positive Daddy and Dean were in the car, too. Declan wouldn't stand a chance with all three of them, no matter how big and strong he was.

He paused, looking down at me, fire dancing in his eyes. "I've never seen you so frightened, not since the night we found you. I'm going to tear in half whoever's making you shake like this."

"They're not worth it." Desperate, I grabbed his arm. "Please, Declan. Take me home."

He glanced at the car again, then heaved a sigh. Relief filled me when he finally nodded and climbed onto the motorcycle again.

Just as it revved to life, a couple stepped out from the pharmacy and moved toward the car. They were smiling at each other, obviously in love. Without missing a beat, they got in and drove away.

A harsh, shuddering sigh left my mouth. I gripped Declan's arm, the relief so great tears finally fell from my eyes. Seeing this, Declan got off the motorcycle and turned to me, cupping my face as I wept.

"Everything will be alright, my sweet girl," he said, grazing his thumb across my face, wiping at the tears. "You don't have to worry about a thing as long as I'm with you."

He pulled me into his arms, and I choked on my sobs, clinging to him, happy he was there with me. The tears couldn't seem to stop, and Declan didn't mind that I got his shirt wet. He held me until the last of my tears fell, and I was only left with hiccups.

"You're safe, Cass," he murmured. "I'll protect you as long as you're with me."

I closed my eyes as his lips lowered to mine, his soft lips comforting me, and I lost myself to a world where nothing and no one existed but us. My eyes flickered open when he pulled apart, and my gaze locked with his green eyes. I saw something there I hadn't noticed before, a deep affection that caused a flutter in my stomach.

"Ready to go home?"

Although I panicked for no reason, my body was still shaken up. I wanted nothing more than to go home and curl up in Declan's arms until calm returned. But, seeing it was my first official day on the job, I had to stay. I didn't want to give Grace a terrible impression of me.

I shook my head and smiled. "No. I'm better now. I don't want to miss out on work."

Declan seemed unconvinced. "Are you sure? I could talk to Grace and—"

"No. Please don't. I told you; I'll be fine."

He nodded, but from his expression, it seemed he still wanted to convince me. "Maybe I'm being overly protective, but I'd prefer if you take the day off. There's a terrible feeling in my gut."

"It's all my fault. I shouldn't have gone off like that. I promise you, Declan, everything is fine."

"Is it? Then why did you almost lose your shit like that?" His expression tightened with concern. "Cass, who are you running from?"

My peripheral vision caught Grace flipping the open sign, and I patted Declan's arm. "Later. I'll tell you everything later," I said.

It was time. If Declan wanted to judge me as trash based on my past, then so be it. The most he could do was tell me to leave. It would hurt like hell, but the truth would be out, at least. Right now, it weighed on me like a heavy blanket. I wanted to be free.

Declan nodded and kissed me on the forehead. "Ok then, later. I'll pick you up at six," he said, climbing onto his motorcycle and winking at me. I forced a smile, waving as he left, then I moved into the store, ready to forget this crazy morning.

I BATTLED WITH MY EMOTIONS throughout the day, anticipating going home with Declan. After my scare earlier, I was now sure I wanted to stay with him. He made me feel safe. There was nothing to fear once he was around. But would he still want me when he found out who I was? Would he want to settle down with a girl from the wrong side of the tracks?

God, I wished there was some way to see the future. I wanted to know how our conversation turned out before it even began. That way, I could brace myself for disappointment or look forward to satisfaction if he accepted me, terrible background and all.

It was a slow day. Grace spent most of her time on the phone with her best friend while I tried to keep busy, refolding T-shirts, rearranging shoes on the shelves, assisting the occasional customer—anything to keep my nerves from shattering. I kept praying tonight's conversation would go well. I didn't want to lose Declan. Not when my heart had already fallen for him.

I paused, clutching the T-shirt I'd begun folding for the third time. Yes. I was falling for Declan. I'd never been in love before, but from my racing pulse, the way my stomach flipped when I thought of him, the never-ending urge to be with him, I knew this was definitely love.

The day kept going at a snail's pace – seemingly unending as I checked the time nonstop. Some minutes after six, I expected to hear Declan's motorcycle, but nothing came.

Where was Declan? He promised to be on time.

I saw the way Grace occasionally checked her watch and sensed she wanted to leave. Bummed that I took up her time, I went over to her. "Hey, Grace. You can leave if you want. I'll just wait outside; I'm sure Declan will be here soon."

Grace managed a pitiful smile. "I'm sorry. I hate leaving you here alone, but Dan expects me home – we have a few things planned."

"Don't worry about it. I'm sure Declan will be here soon."

She took her purse from under the counter, dipping for her phone as she approached me. "I'll give Declan a call and see how far he is."

I leaned against the counter as she made the call, recalling the horrible feeling in my gut as he drove off that morning. Declan was okay. He had to be. There must be an explanation for his lateness.

When he answered, I almost sagged to the floor with relief. Grace's face lit up as they briefly spoke, then she hung up with a soft smile. "He's caught up with a customer, but he'll be here in fifteen minutes. I wish I could stay, sweetie, but I really gotta go," she said.

I smiled, seeing the distress on Grace's face. "Grace, I promise I'll be fine. Go."

She squeezed my shoulder before we exited the store and closed the door behind us, then she handed me the key. "Remember, you're on your own tomorrow. I trust you'll do well, but if there's anything you need, just call me."

I took the key from her and nodded. "I don't have a cellphone, but I'll figure out something if I ever need to call."

"Okay, great. Have a great evening, Cass. I'll see you in a couple of days."

"Have fun!" I called as she walked toward her car. She giggled and waved before she opened the door of her Jeep and slipped inside, leaving me standing alone on the sidewalk. It was still fairly light out, and the road was busy with constant traffic. I wasn't afraid, although the heaviness wouldn't go away.

I leaned against a wall and waited for Declan, getting anxious with each second. I had half a mind to start walking but figured I'd wait a bit longer until he came.

As I stood there, my hands crossed, I saw a van turn onto the street. It was an unfamiliar vehicle, so I thought nothing of it, but as it rolled closer toward me, alarm bells went off. With a pounding heart, I backed away, fear almost crippling every inch of my body. I still had no idea who it was, but my instincts told me there was trouble coming. As the side door slid open, bile rose in my throat.

Dean stepped out, a murky smile on his face as he stared at me. "Well, hello, little sis. You didn't take too long to find."

I gulped as Daddy stepped out on the other end, a scowl on his face as he sized me up with deadly grey eyes. "You little brat. Did you really think you could outrun us?"

The driver's door opened. Without waiting to see Johnny emerge, I broke into a run, already breathless from how fast my heart pounded in my chest.

I blinked back tears as I ran across the road, not caring about being hit. Most stores were closed by now, so there was no way to hide. I glanced behind me. They were coming, though moving slowly, as if they knew how slim my chance of escape was. My breaths came in a harsh rhythm as I ran. Sweat covered my skin, dampening my dress.

A gas station stood on the corner, the only sign of life, the only source of hope. My feet found a new gear, and I pressed forward, screaming for help. Glancing behind, I saw them pick up the pace. I mustered all my energy, my attention focused on my target. There were no cars at the pumps, but there must be an attendant inside, at least. I hoped to secure myself inside while they called the cops.

I was only a few feet away when I felt the rough grip on my hair. Seconds later, I flew face down on the ground, pain shooting through my body. It took me a second to realize Dean was on top of me, grabbing my hands behind my back as he pulled me up.

"I told Daddy you were more trouble than you're worth. Wish he'd fucking listened to me," he bit out, spittle flying at my face.

I gasped and tried to wriggle free, but he gripped me tightly with one hand and used the other to cover my mouth as he shoved me down the road. The tears trickled down my face as I scanned the road, hoping to see Declan's motorcycle appear, but there was no sign. I'd give anything to hear his engine or see his dark hair blowing in the wind.

Dean shoved me to the others. Daddy wore a satisfied smirk as he looked me over. Johnny leaned against the van, looking ready to kill.

"Do you really think you could run away and start a new life like nothing happened, Cass?" Daddy laughed, swiping his tongue over his yellow teeth.

Dean released his hold on my mouth. "Just let me go, please," I cried, still trying to wriggle from Dean, but he held me so tight I was sure it would leave a bruise later. "I won't tell anyone about the drugs, I promise."

Daddy's smile disappeared. "You won't tell anyone *else* about the drugs, you mean. Do you know how much trouble you've caused us? How business has been slow since you ran your fucking mouth?"

"I was only trying to get you straight. Daddy, there's more to life than dealing—"

"Shut the fuck up," he cut me off, his scowl darkening. "Dean, get her in the van."

"Let me go, Daddy. Please!" I begged, struggling against Dean's hold.

"Not after what you did!" Johnny spat, a drop of his saliva tainting the air. He used the back of his hand to wipe across his mouth.

"You left my truck on the side of the road like it was a fucking piece of junk. I can't get over that, baby Cass. You don't belong anywhere other than that fucking house I built for all of us. This is the thanks I get for taking care of you all those years!" Dad said, stomping his feet against the ground, his freckled face red.

"You call that taking care of me?" I cried. "I was practically a slave after Momma died. You treated me like shit every chance you got. That house is a piece of shit just as you are!"

Daddy charged at me, his fingers balled into a fist, but he didn't land a blow. Instead, he stared at me with deadly eyes, his lips drawn in a thin line as he worked up his mouth.

"You ungrateful bitch," he drawled, and I flinched from the smell of his nasty breath that was bad enough to linger. "Well, now, you have no choice, do you? You'll stay locked in that fucking house until you get old!"

"Not if I kill all three of you first," I bit back, so furious I couldn't stop myself.

They all chuckled dryly, probably thinking it was a joke, but if that's what it took to free myself of them, I'd gladly oblige.

Dean pushed me to the van, and I stumbled. "Where's your Prince Charming to save you now, little sis?" he whispered in my ear.

My heart paused. So did my body. Terror crawled up my spine. An acidic taste filled my mouth. "What did you say?"

Johnny caught the shock on my face and chuckled. "Yes, we know all about your big, bad biker boy, Cass. Pity you won't get to say your goodbyes, you little slut."

"What do you mean? What have you done to Declan?" I screamed.

"Let's just say that he'll never get to touch you again," Johnny replied with a smirk.

"Oh, my God. No. No!" Tears streamed down my face as I imagined Declan lying in a pool of blood, never to hold me again, never to hear me say how much I loved him. Why was life so cruel? What had I done to deserve this?

My loud sobs rang out as Dean pushed me into the back beside Johnny and slammed the door shut.

"Try anything, and you'll fucking regret it," Johnny warned, but I was too heartbroken to answer.

The van drove off, one I suspected they stole. It smelled like weed and musty shoes, but that was the air that always lingered around these three. My body tossed against Johnny's as Dean sped through town, no doubt in a hurry to leave before Declan's crew caught up to them.

"What did you do to Declan?" I asked, my voice shaky.

"Nothing to worry your pretty little head about," Johnny replied, sniggering.

His words brought a fresh round of tears. I threw my head against the back of the seat, crying my heart out.

"Aww, look at that. I think our little Cass has gone and fallen in love," Johnny teased.

Daddy scoffed. "Stupid, naïve bitch. He didn't fucking care about you. He wanted what all men want, and judging by the way you're reacting, I bet he already got it."

My lips trembled as I cried, watching the city shrink behind us as we drove back to that dreaded place.

I turned my face to the window and closed my eyes, using the memories I shared with Declan to bring me peace. It wasn't enough. There was no doubt in my mind. I'd never have peace again.

AFTER MIDNIGHT, WE arrived home, where everything remained the same as I left it. The stink from the garbage was the first thing that greeted me when Johnny shoved me inside the house. With me gone, the dirty dishes were still stuck in the sink. The floors were stained with dirty footprints, and the buzzing flies were like an annoying song.

"Welcome home, little Cass," Daddy said, closing the door behind him. "As you can see, there's plenty of work to do."

Fresh tears formed. I wrapped my arms around myself to stop the shivers. "Why did you hurt Declan? He did nothing to you."

"Except that he stole you from us," Dean snapped.

"He didn't—"

Daddy cut me off, waving his hand. "Dean, cut the shit." He looked at me. "We did nothing to your little boyfriend. We only saw him when he dropped you off this morning."

I plopped on the couch, relief making me dizzy. Gasping, I stared up at them. "Declan's alive?"

"For now. You try to run away again, and he gets a bullet in the head; you hear me?" Daddy pulled his shirt up, revealing the small gun strapped in the waistband of his pants. I shivered, my lips trembling.

"Do I make myself clear?" he spat.

I nodded after a second. "Yes."

"You're my fucking property. Not anyone else's. The sooner you learn that, the fucking better," he said, pulling me up and shoving me to my bedroom. "Get some rest. You'll need it for tomorrow."

I winced as he slammed the door shut. With a deep sigh, I flopped on the dingy bed and curled into a ball, wishing I had something of Declan's to bring me comfort. How I'd love to have his T-shirt balled into my fist, his scent all over it. Though what I wanted most was him, his strong arms wrapped around me.

It broke my heart that I'd never see him again. I'd never feel his lips on mine, his hands on my body, him inside me. A cruel fate. Didn't I deserve a break? Wasn't I good enough to have a decent life?

It seemed pointless to hope for a better life when all I knew was heartache and disappointment. I cried myself to sleep, wanting my Prince Charming to rescue me like in the movies, but I wasn't worth the trouble. Soon, Declan would see that too.

Chapter 7

Declan

"Rodger, what the fuck is this? There's nothing wrong with the car," I hissed, peeling the gloves from my hands and slapping them against a nearby table.

I palmed my hips, glaring at him. After a full hour thoroughly checking his car, something he insisted I do although I had a full staff—I found nothing wrong. The engine was in tip-top shape; oil and coolant levels were good, and there were no leaks. There were no tapping or pinging sounds when I started the car, and neither was there any smoke. It ran beautifully when I took it for a spin down the road. I was now pissed that he'd wasted my time.

"It made some weird noises earlier. I– I thought I'd check it out," Rodger said, shrugging.

"You don't even fucking drive this thing," I stated, my brows furrowing as I tried to see logic.

"I do when I pick up my son on weekends. I figured I'd give it a test run this morning, and that's when I heard the rattling noise."

I huffed in frustration. "There's nothing wrong with it. Now, if you don't mind getting out of my fucking shop and stop wasting my time," I said, grabbing my keys from the table.

Rodger smirked. "Can't wait to get home to that sweet little thing, huh?"

I flashed him a hard look and said nothing. Getting the gist, he hopped into his car. "I don't blame you man; I'd be hitting that nonstop. Take it while you can. We both know she'll be gone when she's done with you." He chuckled and slowly reversed out of the garage.

Rodger knew better than to say that to my face. If he'd remained in front of me, he'd be picking up his teeth off the ground by now. The asshole got on my nerves, and he knew exactly how much.

Without further delay, I bid the staff goodbye and went outside to my ride. I didn't want to keep Cassandra waiting any longer. Rodger's hold up had delayed me by about twenty minutes. I'd planned on stopping somewhere to get us some food but figured we could both go together once I picked her up.

The thought of seeing her and being with her again increased my mood by a hundred percent and after that interaction with Rodger, I needed it. Luckily Grace's place wasn't too far away from the shop, and I was there in a few minutes.

Based on my conversation with Grace, I'd expected to see Cassandra on the outside, but as I brought the motorcycle to a halt, I realized she was nowhere in sight. My forehead creased as I looked around the empty plaza to see if she was nearby, but there was no sign. Growing concerned, I wondered if Grace had decided to drop her home, but surely she would have called to say something?

After a minute, I fished my phone from my pocket when a gnawing feeling trickled up my spine. I couldn't shake the feeling that something was wrong, and a lump instantly formed in my throat. I dialed Grace's number and waited anxiously for her to pick up while I walked up the road, still scanning the place.

"Come on, Grace, pick up," I murmured after a couple of rings.

Just as I was about to cut the call, she answered, sounding breathless. "Hey, Declan. What's up?"

"Cassandra. Where is she?" I asked, getting straight to the point.

"Wh– I left her at the store, waiting for you to pick her up. Are you there yet? Is everything okay?" she asked, urgency filling her tone.

I clenched my teeth and raked my fingers through my hair, slowly losing a grip on the world. "Yeah, yeah, fine. I'm sorry for bothering you." I ended the call, not waiting for her to reply.

I moved around in circles, hoping Cassandra would appear in my line of sight, but there was nothing. "Maybe she took a cab home," I said to myself, feeling a slight tad of hope.

I hopped on my bike again and raced home, not caring that I'd broken the speed limit. The motorcycle came to a screeching halt in the driveway, and I quickly ran to the house before it hit me. Cassandra didn't even have a key to my house.

"Fuck!" I cursed, kicking the hard wooden door in frustration, losing my mind about where Cass could be. Why the hell didn't I think to buy her a cell phone?

I sat on the porch for ages, trying to figure out where she could have gone. Nothing made sense. We'd been fine. Making love to her last night was like a seal to our feelings for each other. There was no doubt in my mind she wanted me.

A sudden thought dawned on me, and I scrubbed my face with a groan. Did I scare her off with my offer last night?

What if she didn't want a commitment to me? She was young, beautiful... almost half my age. Doubt crept into my mind, convincing me that was the case. She ran the first chance she got, didn't she?

While waiting for me, she must've realized she didn't want to be with me. I didn't know a single thing about Cass. Heck, I didn't even know her last name. We were from two different worlds, and maybe mine had scared her a bit.

My heart sank at the thought, and I got up, feeling ten times heavier as I dragged myself inside the house. I did give her some money, after all. Maybe that had been enough to get her a cab to wherever she'd gone to. Back to whoever she'd been hiding from. My stomach curled with jealousy when I pictured her flying into the arms of a guy younger than me.

After forcing myself through my nightly routine, I went to bed, Cassandra stuck in my mind. It amazed me the difference a few days had made. A week ago, I'd been restless, disgruntled, just living for the heck of it. Since meeting her, I have looked forward to waking up each day. My life suddenly had meaning. I had someone to love, guide, protect...

Well, not anymore.

I soon drifted into a tortured sleep, one filled with dreams of Cassandra riding off on Rodger's bike in a white dress and a short veil. I chased after them, catching up when they stopped near a cliff. Rodger lifted her, and they kissed, and I almost lost my mind. She suddenly screamed, my body jolting as Rodger ran with her toward the edge of the cliff. I shot up from sleep, my body damp with sweat, a pounding headache making it hard to see. I didn't know what the dream meant, but Cassandra would plague my thoughts for a very long time. I wasn't about to forget her anytime soon.

The faint light against the curtains made me aware of the approaching daylight, so I got up, made my coffee as usual and took a shower, pausing at Cassandra's room with the opened door. I entered, half-expecting to see her in my T-shirt, her shapely legs curled under her as she slept. My heart hurt from seeing the empty bed, especially when I spotted the T-shirt I'd given her resting against the pillow.

Unable to help myself, I reached for the shirt, lifting it to my nose and taking a deep breath, inhaling all her scent. I could still smell myself on it, but it was mostly her. Sweet and subtle.

I could still see her in it. How it swallowed her up but emphasized her tight nipples when she moved. Or how it shimmied up when she lay curled up on the sofa, exposing her creamy skin.

Just the thought of her petite body beneath it made me hard. A body I had memorized in one night – my hands familiar with every inch of her curves. I cleared my head and got up with a raging boner, my gaze going to the lounge chair in the room's corner where some clothes were neatly folded. It took me a second to realize they were the clothes Cassandra had bought the day before. Why didn't she take them with her? I wondered, then I remembered it was a spur-of-the-moment thing.

But after I left the house that morning, the drive to the shop gave me time to think.

"Later. I'll tell you everything later."

Cassandra wanted to talk, so why run? We were good yesterday morning, so what had changed?

My earlier doubt faded as I gave it more thought. I reflected on the last morning we shared and how Cass had been frightened when she saw that car in the mall. She'd been scared stiff. Whoever that was, she wouldn't have gone back to them.

Not willingly.

Muttering a curse, I ran back to my motorcycle and headed to Billy's. My hands grew sweaty on the handle of the motorcycle as panic ran up my spine. I didn't want to think of a worst-case scenario, but I had to. What if someone had taken Cass? What if they had snatched her and left while I was wasting time with Rodger?

"Shit!" I exclaimed, driving at maximum speed until I pulled up to Billy's shop. I walked through the scanty bar and moved to the back, where his office was. It was still early, but I hoped Billy was already there.

But when I knocked, no answer came from inside.

"He hasn't come in yet," the red-headed bartender said as she wiped down the counter.

Fucking hell.

Fury swirled around me. I wanted to kick something. Or someone. Instead, I clenched my fist and headed out. I was almost at the door when Billy stepped in with Rodger and Gear behind him.

I sighed with relief and reached for Billy's shoulder, ushering him aside. "I need to talk to you," I said, looking over my shoulder at Rodger and Gear, who'd walked to the bar.

"Sure thing. What's going on? You seem on edge," he said, his bushy brows bunching.

I rubbed my nape. "You still have that friend down at the precinct, don't you?"

"Kenny? Yeah. What's going on?" he asked again, searching my face.

"I need to find Cassandra."

"Cassandra? As in that girl you had shacked up at your place? The girl I told you to let go?"

I knew where this was going, but I nodded anyway. "Yeah."

"What happened to her?"

"She's missing. Someone took her."

Billy glanced around the bar, lowering his voice as he spoke. "What do you mean someone took her?"

I threw my hands up, frustrated. "Can you quit with the twenty-one questions?"

Billy crossed his arms. "If I'm going to get Kenny involved, I need details, Dec. Who took her?"

I shrugged. "I don't know. She wanted to tell me everything, but we didn't get the chance." I kicked myself, wishing I'd pushed for more info that morning. I had nothing to start with. I didn't even know her last name.

"This is a fucking mess, Dec," Billy said.

I huffed out a breath. "Can you help me or not?"

Billy paced for a bit before he turned to me. "That girl is a runner. She's not missing. I bet my last dollar she's done this before," he said with a scoff.

"She didn't fucking run, Billy," I snapped.

He pulled in a breath and folded his lips. "What do you think happened to her?"

"She was running from someone. I think they got to her while she waited for me at Grace's store."

"Why do you think that?"

"Her clothes are still at my place. Besides, why would she run away from a job she just got?" I asked, searching his face for some understanding.

Billy pondered it for a second. "Maybe she went out to clear her head," he reasoned, shrugging.

I shook my head, pissed at him for taking my concern so lightly. "I'm telling you; something happened, Billy."

"So, what do you want me to do?"

"Talk to Kenny. See if he can pull up the CCTV cameras around here. Maybe they caught something. I hope."

"I doubt they are working, but we'll see. What's her full name?" he asked. "We need that information, at least."

I raked my fingers through my hair in frustration. "I only know her first name."

Billy gaped at me, then he sighed. "Do you have a picture of her?"

I shook my head, hopelessness taking over. Billy was about to give up on me. I could feel it.

He proved me right, sighing again. "You can't expect us to go off a first name alone, man. You don't know her full name or her address. You have nothing. Kenny is a decent cop, but he's not that good."

"Then ride with me back to where we picked her up that night. There were some houses a few miles down. Maybe that's where she lived," I urged him.

"She could have been traveling from anywhere, Dec. I love you, man, but you don't expect me to follow you on this wild goose chase, do you?"

My gaze shifted to Rodger in the bar, who was obviously trying to pick up every word from our conversation. When he realized I'd seen him, he quickly turned and went back to his phone. My attention zoned in on him, and I remembered last night when he came to the shop with the car he'd barely driven. I found nothing was wrong with it, which led me to suspect; did Rodger deliberately waste my time?

I charged over to the bar and kicked his chair, sending him flying on the floor with it. He shuffled backward, his eyes wide as he tried to collect himself.

"Did you have something to do with Cass missing?" I barked as he looked to Billy for help.

"What the fuck are you talking about, man?" he spat, scrambling to his feet.

"Declan, have you lost your fucking mind?" Billy exclaimed, grabbing my shoulder and spinning me around to face him. I pushed him away, charging at Rodger again, growling when Gear and Billy held me back.

"I swear to God, if I find out you have something to do with this, you're a dead man!" I threatened, pointing at him. I turned to leave, but Rodger's words had me coming to an abrupt halt.

"You don't wanna fucking mess with those loonies, Dec. Take my word for it; leave them the fuck alone."

"What did you say?" I asked, whipping around. His expression faltered as I shot toward him, my teeth clenched so tight I thought they might shatter in my mouth.

I grabbed Rodger before he ran and pinned him against the wall, my hand clasped around his throat. "What the fuck did you do, Rodger? How do you know all that?" I asked, squeezing a little.

"Declan, can you just calm the fuck down?" Billy exclaimed.

"Don't fucking tell me to calm down!" I spat, glancing at him before shifting back to Rodger, whose face was as red as my shirt.

"Listen," he said, grabbing my arm, wanting me to ease off on the pressure. "The motherfuckers showed up yesterday morning asking about your girl, looking like they'd cut my throat without a moment's thought."

"So you snitched?" I barked.

"Why the fuck wouldn't I? It's not like I had backup or anything. My piece was in my truck, and they were all strapped."

"I don't understand. Why did they approach you? It's not like you and I are close."

"How the fuck would I know? At a guess, they probably tracked us here. We're not exactly flying under the radar. Especially you, with a hot young thing on the back of your ride."

"What did you tell them?"

"They wanted to know where you lived. I didn't want them showing up to your house and – and that's when I thought about Grace's store. I suggested they snatch her there."

My grip tightened on his throat, and he gagged.

"Come on now, Declan. Don't do anything stupid," I heard Billy say.

My head whipped around to him. "Did you know about this?"

"Of course not! You're crazy for even asking me that," Billy replied.

"Look, I heard Billy on the phone with you. That's how I knew she got a job at Grace's. Billy had nothing to do with this," Rodger explained in a strained voice.

"You fucking sellout. You knew I'd be there to pick her up, so you came to distract me!" I rasped, squeezing down on his throat. "Where are they now?"

He clawed at my hands. "I–" he coughed. "I d– don't know. They came in a black van — that's all I know. Fucking hell, Dec..."

Gritting my teeth, I applied more pressure on his throat and slammed him into the wall, his head knocking against it before he collapsed on the floor. Billy rushed to his side and assessed the damage while Rodger touched his temple, wincing.

"Have you lost your Goddamn mind? You could have killed him!" Billy shouted.

"Do I look like I give a shit? He fucking betrayed me!" I shouted back.

He got up from the floor and stood in front of me. "You go charging into that place and stir up trouble, this club will be the first place they target. We aren't about that life, and you fucking know it."

"Then I'm out. Fuck this," I said, tearing off the patch from my chest and slapping it against Billy's chest. "Fuck all of you!"

Hopping on my motorcycle, I headed home, grabbed an extra gun, filled up my tank and then went back on the road, taking the same route I'd travelled that night. It would take hours before I got there, but I didn't intend to leave without Cass in my arms again.

Chapter 8

Cassandra

The nights were the most tolerable part about being back home. By ten Daddy and the boys had all drunk themselves to sleep, and it was quiet for once. It was then I allowed my mind to run free with the only thing that granted me peace. Declan. I kept thinking about him, wondering what he was up to. Was he looking for me, or did he assume I'd run away?

No. He wasn't looking for me. Considering my reaction the last night we were together, I knew it was the latter. I should've been honest from the start. If he'd known about Daddy and the boys, he would've connected the dots by now.

Still, I hoped he still thought about me even half as much as he crossed my mind. I hoped he knew our days together meant something to me, that I cherished the time we shared, although short.

Truth was, Declan was the best thing that had ever happened to me. He gave me hope. For the first time since Momma died, I saw beauty in the world, not the muck I'd experienced over the years. I had a purpose. My life wasn't bound to this pig sty. My dreams were finally within reach. It only required me to take them.

But that was two days ago. Now, I was back to square one, this time more confined. Daddy had secured the doors with an alarm only they had access to and bolted the windows so I couldn't escape like I'd done last time. I was a prisoner again, this time with a life sentence.

My father didn't love me. I wasn't the son he wanted or the daughter he could control, not like Dean and Johnny, the puppets who didn't act unless Daddy pulled the strings. I didn't want to conform to a life of dealing drugs. I didn't care how long they held me there; I would never give in.

But it was a living hell being confined like this. I had to figure out another escape route soon. I couldn't accept this life, not when the world had so much to offer. I wanted to make my way back to Declan again. That is, *if* he wanted me back.

I curled myself up in bed and tried to keep awake, knowing if I fell asleep, morning would come, and the cycle would continue again. Still, there was little I could do to stop the heaviness from weighing on my eyelids.

I WOKE UP THE FOLLOWING morning to chatter in the living room. Careful not to make a sound, I slowly padded to the door and pressed my cheek against it, listening.

"– gonna come looking for her?"

"Nobody's gonna come looking for her. She isn't worth it," Daddy said, scoffing.

"The last thing we wanna do is piss off a motorcycle club. You know how vicious they can be," Dean whined. "We should've just let her go."

"You must've lost your goddamn mind. Cass is my property. She doesn't belong to a bunch of gangsters," Daddy groused.

"Don't let the name fool you, Daddy. The Eagle Knights are just charity-giving pussies who use their motorcycles to hide how cowardly they are. They couldn't kill a bee if it pitched on their noses," Johnny corrected.

"Didn't you hear how that skinny one described Cass's little boyfriend?" Dean pressed. "Why do you think he discouraged us from going to his house? He's fucking dangerous. I don't want to mess with that."

Dad sucked his teeth. "What the fuck is wrong with you? If anybody comes wanting to rescue that little bitch, we're well prepared."

Laughter followed, and I shivered, remembering their gun collection. But Declan didn't know where I lived, so it was a waste of time worrying about his safety. He would never come for me.

As I moved back to the bed, a thought occurred to me, and I paused. "The skinny one?" I whispered, my brain going a mile a second.

Goosebumps filled my skin when I made the connection. It had to be Rodger. There was no other club member who fit that description. Why would he betray a fellow club member like that, though? I didn't understand.

A loud knock came on the door, halting my thoughts. "Rise and shine, princess. It's time to make us breakfast!" Daddy announced as he flung the door open, presenting himself on the other side.

Rolling my eyes, I got up and shoved past him, hearing his chuckle in the background.

"Soon, you'll realize this family is all you've got, little girl. No one's gonna have your back like we do."

I stopped, not bothering to turn around. "If this is your version of having my back, Daddy, I'd never want to be your enemy," I mumbled.

"Such an ungrateful bitch. I put a roof over your head, food in your stomach, clothes on your fucking back, and this is the thanks I get. Do you know how many kids would love to take your place?"

"Zero, Daddy!" I shouted, pivoting to face him. "No one in their right mind would want to live like this. You took my freedom, stole my dreams—this isn't living! I don't want this life!"

"Hey, hey. Easy with the fucking drama." He jutted his chin toward the kitchen. "Go make our fucking breakfast."

"Go fuck yourself," I murmured as I moved off.

"The hell was that?" Daddy asked, his footsteps coming up behind me.

"Nothing."

"That's what I thought." He scoffed. "You'll come around."

AROUND MIDDAY, DADDY allowed some porch time. Grateful for fresh air, I sat in the old wicker chair, watching Dean in the front yard washing off the van that was still a mystery to me, with the old Lexus parked to the side. I wondered how Daddy had reacted when he found it left like a piece of junk on the side of the road. I'm sure he would've been pissed because he loved that piece of junk, although it seemed the new van had taken its place.

"A beauty, isn't she, sis?" Dean asked when he saw me staring. "Perfect for our cross-state distribution. Did Daddy tell you the news?"

I didn't want to continue talking to him, but his question made me curious. "What news?"

"That we're expanding our business. We secured a contract with a dealer in Nevada, which means we'll be making frequent deliveries by next week." He sneered at me. "And you're coming along, FYI."

"Like hell I will!"

He chuckled. "You don't have a say in this, Cass. Consider it punishment for running away."

"Could be worse," Johnny added, stepping onto the porch with a cigarette between his lips. "I could've beaten the shit out of you." He took a seat beside me, blowing a cloud of smoke in my face. "Considering how much my balls hurt that night, I probably will, anyway."

With a cough, I fanned the smoke away, meeting his soulless gaze. "I'll never forget that. One slip-up, and I'll make sure I fulfill that promise."

The look in his eyes told me he was serious. I swallowed, casting my gaze from him when a sudden roar caught my attention. My heart flipped as a motorcycle appeared in the distance. I didn't need a second look to know it was Declan. The broad set of his shoulders, his thick, long hair blowing in the wind... yes, it was definitely him.

I shot to my feet with a gasp, happiness bubbling in my chest. Johnny quickly shoved me down, snarling at me. "Sit the fuck down!"

"Well, well, well. I assume that's your Prince Charming, right?" Dean asked, dropping the washcloth in the bucket. "Time to have some fun."

Declan rode up into the yard, stopping short of the van. I clutched the arms of the chair, the urge to run to him so strong. His eyes were on me, but he wore a helmet, so I couldn't read his expression. Still, there was no mistaking the tension in his body. His tight grip remained on the handlebars, the engine still running.

"You have someone who belongs with me," Declan rumbled, his deep tone rising above the engine. "Hand her over, and I promise there'll be no trouble."

Johnny scoffed. "You have a death wish, asshole? It's three against one. We'll fucking end you before you even make a move."

Declan shook his head, smirking. "You have ten seconds."

"This is a fucking joke," Dean said, chuckling. "Johnny, go get my gun."

"Nine," Declan said.

Johnny moved off, and I attempted to run off the porch, but he doubled back, holding me in place. "What the fuck are you doing, you little bitch?"

"Daddy!" Dean called. "We've got company! We need our guns!"

My lips quivered as Declan killed the engine and dismounted while pulling off his helmet, his dark hair falling over his shoulders.

My father ran out of the house, coming to an abrupt stop when he saw Declan. He clenched his teeth and moved closer. "Who are you, and what do you fucking want?" he asked, his hand resting on the handgun in his waist.

"I don't want any trouble. I just came for Cassandra," Declan said calmly. "Just hand her over, and I'll be on my way."

"Cassandra isn't yours to have," Daddy bit back.

"Look, I'm not interested in a debate. Give her to me. I'm not leaving here without her." Declan's face remained calm. Too calm. I remembered his demeanor before he beat the shit out of Rodger.

Johnny's grip on my hand tightened. Declan turned his attention to me, his eyes communicating what his lips couldn't say in that moment. The affection made my heart swell. I struggled against Johnny, so desperate to run into Declan's arms.

Declan's gaze lowered to Johnny's hand on me, and his jaw tightened, his eyes now gone cold. "Let her go. Now."

I tugged at Johnny's grip, but he held me painfully tight, causing me to wince. "Oh, she isn't going anywhere."

"Do me a favor, you piece of shit," Dad said, his tone carrying a dangerous edge. "Get the fuck off my property before Cass here is forced to clean your brains from the ground!"

He pulled out his gun and pointed it at Declan as Johnny said with a sneer, "You have ten seconds."

Declan moved so fast I'd barely blinked before he had Dean in his grasp, his gun pressed against my brother's temple. Daddy's throat bobbed as he swallowed. He didn't expect Declan's counter-attack.

"Ask about me, boy. I'm the best shot in this neck of the woods. You think this bullet won't reach your head before you hurt my son?" Daddy challenged.

"Do you want to give it a shot?" Declan pressed the nozzle against Dean's head. My brother tried to break free, but Declan had a height and weight advantage. It was like a mouse trying to escape the clutches of a tiger. "No pun intended, of course," he ended with a smirk.

Dean shifted on his feet, glaring at us on the porch. "Come on, Daddy. Just let him leave with the little bitch."

"No," came Daddy's hard reply.

My heart pounded even faster as I weighed Declan's options. If he managed to shoot one, the chances of getting all three down was slim. Daddy was right; he was the best shot around.

Desperation took over. I did something that was either incredibly stupid or smart. I stomped down on Johnny's foot so hard he yelped and released his hold on me. I made a run for it, charging as fast as I could to Declan's side. My dad cursed, his gun still pointed at Declan.

"You traitorous bitch," he growled at me.

Declan's eyes coasted from Daddy to Johnny, his grip still tight on Dean. "I'll let your son go if you promise not to do anything stupid," he said. "Now, lower your weapon slowly and kick it to me."

"Daddy, just shoot the bastard!" Johnny exclaimed.

"Shut the fuck up, boy. Don't you dare tell me what to do," Daddy snapped.

Dean's Adam's apple bobbed, the nozzle of the gun now making a dent in his temple. He stared at Daddy, his expression pleading. As if a block of ice had melted around his heart, Daddy's shoulders slumped, and his hand lowered with the gun.

"Fine, but if I see a scratch on my son, it's fucking war." Daddy placed the small weapon on the floor and then kicked it toward Declan. I ran for it, lifting it off the ground before he changed his mind.

"If you come after Cass, I'll kill you. No doubt about it," Declan threatened, shoving Dean to the ground. "Do I make myself clear?"

Daddy shot me a dirty glare, then spat on the ground. "I'm done wasting my time on this bitch. She's dead to me."

The sound of the safety being disabled on Declan's gun made my head shoot up. I gasped as he walked up to Daddy. "Say that again."

Daddy smirked. Declan was a ticking time bomb, and this was a house filled with ammunition. I sensed death, and it was my responsibility to stop it from happening.

I stepped between Daddy and Declan, spreading my arms. "Declan. Let's get out of here. Please."

"I'd listen to her if I were you, *Declan*," Daddy bit out. "For her sake, I'll let you leave in one piece. Consider it my parting gift."

Declan gritted his teeth and conceded with a curt nod, taking my hand. We backed away, my family watching with angry faces as I quickly climbed on the bike and tightened my grip around Declan. He kept Daddy's gun while holstering his; then he threw it in the bushes a short distance away. We rode in silence for half a mile before he slowed to a stop at a crossroads.

Before I realized his intention, he'd gotten off the motorcycle, clasping my face in his large hands. "I couldn't go any further without doing this," he breathed against my mouth before capturing my lips for a kiss. I leaned into him, letting him in, his rough strokes showing how much he missed me. His hands roamed over my body, grabbing, squeezing as if trying to confirm I was really in his arms.

"I can't believe you came," I whispered when we pulled back.

Declan chuckled. "Believe it, Shrimp. I'd go to the end of the earth for you." I giggled, and he kissed me again, briefly this time. "Come on, let's go home."

Home. That one simple word held such meaning, leaving me so thrilled, I wanted to burst inside. For the first time in years, I had a home. I had *love*. I climbed behind on the motorcycle, wrapping my hands around Declan, feeling the smile curve my lips as I pressed myself against him.

Maybe I was meant to be happy after all.

WE STOPPED AT THE SAME motel had Declan booked the night we met. This time, we didn't take separate rooms.

Declan reached for me the instant we entered the room. He cupped my jaw and grazed his thumb over the scratches on my cheeks from when Dean grabbed me at Grace's. "Did they hurt you?" he asked.

I shook my head. "It's fine. I'm fine now. I'm just glad you're here," I replied, giving him an assuring smile.

He kissed my forehead. I gripped his waist with a sigh, my love for him pouring out of me.

"I'm sorry I couldn't get there sooner. I –" he trailed off and swallowed. "For a while, I thought that you'd run away – that you didn't want to be with me."

I couldn't help my snigger. "That couldn't be further from the truth. I could never not want you."

"Weren't you ever concerned that I was too old for you?"

Moving closer, I held his sides. "Nope. I'm not concerned about our age gap. It was never an issue for me."

"Then why did you hesitate when I asked you to be with me?"

"The same reason I didn't tell you about my past. I'm not good enough for you, Declan. I'm young, with only a high school education, no job and no skills. Up to now, I've only lived in that four-bedroom slum you rescued me from. You're wealthy, educated, experienced... I didn't know what you saw in me. I thought you wanted a plaything, someone you'd let go once you got bored."

His thumb trailed along my cheek. "Not even close. You are everything to me, Cass. I've never felt this way about anyone, and it's scary, I know, but you're mine just as much as I'm yours."

I nodded as the tears pricked my eyes, a hot trail streaming down my face within seconds. "I thought you'd never come for me," I choked. "I was so scared and lonely..."

"Shh..." he comforted, trailing his thumbs across my wet cheeks. "I'm here now, sweet girl, and as long as I'm by your side, you won't ever feel alone or scared again; I promise."

I nodded and sniffed, believing every word. Declan was my person. I had no doubt he'd protect me with his life. He'd proved that just now.

He kissed me, awakening my desire for him. But I was filthy from all that running around. "Wait. I want to shower first."

I attempt to move off, but he tightened his hold around my waist. "And I want to have you pinned beneath me, moaning my name as I make you come."

Heat rose to my cheeks, and I sighed as he pressed his hard cock against my back. "Join me," I whispered, taking his hand.

"Now, that's better," he replied, pleased with my response.

I squealed when he suddenly lifted me, carrying me into the tiny stall. He put me down, making swift work of removing his clothes. His gaze trailed the length of me before he caught the hem of my blouse and pulled it over my head. Heat pooled between my thighs when he pinched my nipples. My back hit the cool tiles, a tortured groan leaving my lips as he nipped each erect bud with his teeth. I ran my fingers through his hair, welcoming the pleasure from his lips as he made a wet trail to my stomach. With a growl, he dragged my pants down, and I stepped from them, my knees almost buckling when he stroked me through my panties.

"Oh, yes," I whispered, rocking my hips.

He parted the seat of my panties and ran his fingers along the slit, groaning. "Fuck, you're dripping wet."

"Wet for you. I want you so much right now, Declan."

"I missed you so much. You have no idea," he said, pushing to stand, clamping his mouth to mine and kissing me passionately. I moaned against his soft lips and shivered when his prickly beard grazed my skin.

His hard erection pressed at my stomach, letting me know how ready he was for me. My walls tightened with anticipation. I'd craved for Declan so much, desperate to have him inside me. He picked me up, and I wrapped my legs around him as he pressed me against the foggy glass. I gasped in pleasure when he gripped my ass, pulling me against his erection.

I stiffened when he pressed against my entrance, knowing that with a little adjustment, he'd be inside me. But an impatient Declan couldn't wait for it to slide in. He reached beneath us and slipped it inside me. My flesh clenched, and a whimper left my lips as he filled me. He groaned, my arousal heightening as he stretched me; he's so huge that it took a few beats to adjust to his size.

I was stretched to the max with Declan inside me, my juices making it easier for him to slide back and forth.

He kissed me hungrily as we fucked, one hand on my ass while the other supported my back. The warm water flowed over our bodies as the slapping sounds from our contact filled the small space.

"Oh, yes, I missed having you inside me," I breathed, arching my neck, which Declan took as an opportunity to suckle on. My sopping core clenched repeatedly as pleasure flooded me. Declan was now deeper than he'd ever been inside me, touching every sensitive nerve.

The water made our bodies slippery, and he lost his grip on me. I almost fell to the floor, but he caught and steadied me, which made us giggle. Still, it didn't put a damper on the passion. I balanced on one leg while Declan raised the other in the air, slamming into me. My delighted scream echoed inside the room as he thrust deep inside.

He moved hard and fast, his cock thrusting like a well-oiled machine as he went deeper, deeper, pulling back out to the tip and slamming into me again.

The roughness was new to me, but I could see the hunger in Declan's eyes – feel it in his grip. I wrapped my hands around his neck and clung to him, breathlessly panting as he fucked me.

My orgasm came fast, rushing over me like a tidal wave. I screamed his name and dug my nails into his back as my release flooded me. I gripped him tight as I quivered. Declan didn't let up, still fucking me rough and raw as I came hard around his cock. He held me to him, pressed me to the wall and filled me with powerful thrusts. His warm seed filled me, his rough growls bathing my ear as he emptied himself inside me. When he pulled out, I could barely stand. My knees were too wobbly.

Declan wrapped me in a towel, carried me to the bedroom and placed me on the bed. I smiled in contentment as I lay there, watching as he dried himself. My gaze trailed down every inch of his body, but I paused, seeing the scar I hadn't noticed before on his leg.

I pushed up on my elbows, concern on my face. "What happened there?" I asked, looking at the pinched flesh.

His eyes moved toward my gaze before he joined me on the bed, snuggling with me.

"I got hit with an IED while I was overseas on duty. I was later discharged with an honorary Purple Heart," he said, using his fingers to brush the hair from my face.

"Oh, no... I'm sorry that happened to you. Truly."

He smiled, then kissed my cheek. "It's fine. It happened so long ago, I often forget it's even there."

I ran my fingers over it, seeing him shudder. "Do you miss active duty?"

He shrugged. "For a while, I did. Then my father died, and I took over the family auto business, which was a good distraction. Billy and I reunited a few years later, and we got the MC started."

His cell phone rang, and I wrapped myself in the sheet while he took the call. It was Billy, checking if Declan had found me. Declan brushed his apology aside, telling him he understood why Billy had been so hesitant to go searching for me.

"You weren't vested like I was, Billy. I hold no grudges. But I'm coming back for my patch, got that?" He chuckled at something Billy said, then hung up, coming back to join me.

"How did you find me?" I asked.

"I didn't know where you were, but I figured you hadn't been far from home when we found you that night. I drove around until I saw the old Lexus and the van parked in the yard."

"I think Rodger led them to me," I said.

Declan nodded. "He did. I gave him a beatdown for ratting us out." He caught the reproaching look I gave him and chuckled. "Don't worry. He's still alive. But if he fucks with me again, I can't guarantee he'll live next time."

"Declan—"

"I'll do anything for you, Cass. Remember that. He held my gaze and traced his thumb across my lips. "Because I'm falling in love with you."

Tears filled my eyes hearing his words. "You are?" I croaked.

"Yes. From the moment you climbed on my motorcycle that night. I just didn't realize it yet. I'm glad you came along for the ride."

I nodded and sniffed. "Yeah, so am I. And I'm falling in love with you, too."

Declan was the only one who cared about my welfare, the only man who'd ever fought for me. My heart was filled with love for him. I'd spend the rest of my life showing him my gratitude for rescuing me.

I was meant to be happy after all.

Epilogue

Declan

4 years later

I rubbed my sweaty palms against my shaking legs and tried to get comfortable on the hard, narrow chair. I raised my head, seeing if I could make out Cassandra, but she was lost in the sea of people who sat on the podium. Relaxing in the seat, I adjusted the lapels of my suit. I couldn't wait to take the jacket off but figured I'd endure the discomfort for a while longer. In half an hour, this would all be over.

"Are you alright, Declan?" Grace asked from beside me, concern on her face.

"Yeah. Just this damn suit," I grumbled, pulling at the collar.

She smiled. "I know it's not your thing, but I'm glad you got dressed up for her. You look great, by the way."

"Thanks."

"And nervous."

I huffed. "Maybe a little. She's wearing four-inch heels, for Christ's sake."

Grace chuckled softly. "She'll be fine. Look, it's almost her time," she reassured, and I smiled briefly at her before shifting my gaze to the stage.

"Cassandra Harrison!" the announcer called, and I immediately shot to my feet. Cass got up from the center and walked up the small steps, her blonde hair running down her back, her gown flowing around her ankles.

"You go, baby!" I shouted, causing a few heads to turn. Cassandra collected her degree and smiled, her cheeks pink as she gave me a tiny wave.

I watched in awe as she strolled across the stage, her baby bump showing. A series of applause rang out, her schoolmates standing as they clapped. A lump formed in my throat as I watched my baby girl gracefully take the steps again. I'd been worried about her walking in those high heels while pregnant, but she handled herself well.

Still, I wanted nothing more than to run to her and escort her back to her seat. I kept my composure, waiting for the ceremony to end.

The next half an hour went by in a blur, and as hats were thrown in the air, signaling the end of a chapter, I was the first to stand, making my way to the front where Cass was.

The crowd got to their feet, making it harder for me to maneuver through, but I took advantage of my size. People quickly moved to the side as I parted the sea with my outstretched hands.

I dropped out on a vacant area, where a few graduates stood talking to each other. I spotted Cass among them, a smile on her face as she chatted– an overall glow to her whole appearance. She had one hand protectively resting over her small bump. It was simply the most beautiful picture I had ever seen.

As if sensing my presence, she turned in my direction, and her face lit up. My heart warmed, seeing how happy she was to see me. Quickly dismissing the conversation, she moved to me, and I grabbed her, sweeping her off her feet for a moment. She giggled as I spun her in a small circle and then captured her lips. It felt as new as five years ago when we first kissed. Five years from now, the sensation would still be the same.

"Congratulations, baby. You looked perfect up there," I complimented.

She grinned, twisting the dummy degree. The actual certificate would be delivered in a few days. "You are looking at the new head chef of The Spice Factory!"

Cassandra had worked at Grace's for a few months before getting employed as a prep cook at the popular restaurant in the city. She worked her way up while going to college, and I'd been so proud of the progress she made. Her boss was so impressed by her performance that he promised her the team lead role once she finished her degree. "You deserve this," I tell her. "Enjoy every minute of it."

"Thank you for being my biggest supporter, honey," she replied, tiptoeing for a kiss.

My lips curled around hers briefly before I eased away. "Always." I dropped my attention to her bump, my hands running over the roundness. "How is my little guy behaving?"

"He's been kicking around as usual. I bet he's going to be just like his daddy, a bad ass." She winked, and I grinned.

Cassandra sighed contentedly when I took her hands, giving them a gentle squeeze. "Do you remember what you promised me?" I asked.

"I promised you a lot of things, Declan. You need to narrow it down."

"Do you remember when I asked you to marry me two years ago?"

She smiled. "When I told you I'd love nothing more, but I wanted to get my degree first. Of course, I remember. You haven't let me forget, have you?"

"I won't apologize for being impatient because I want more than anything else to make you my wife." I dropped to one knee with the diamond ring raised, Cassandra's face reddening from the sudden gasps around her. "There's no need to wait any longer. I'm crazy about you, Sweetheart, and I want to spend the rest of my life with you. So, what do you say? Ready to make an honest man out of me?"

Her thin brows lifted, amusement filling her face. "I thought you already were an honest man."

"Come on, don't leave me hanging. I'm sweating like a pig in this goddamn suit."

She grinned "It's a yes, of course! Yes, I'll marry you!"

Amid the clapping, I slipped the ring on and pushed to stand, taking Cassandra's lips for a kiss so hot it left me with an urge to bury myself inside her. Not willing to wait, I lifted her in my arms, the cheering crowd parting as we went. Contentment followed me out, along with a gratitude for the woman in my arms and the life we were about to share.

More than anything, I was truly grateful she'd come along for the ride the night I found her.

Big Brother's Quarterback Friend

Erotic & Forbidden

[1]

IZZIE VEE[2]

1. https://www.amazon.com/s?k=izzie+vee&i=digital-text&crid=31LQJTEQYT2EE&sprefix=izzie+vee%2Cdigital-text%2C121&ref=nb_sb_noss
2. https://www.amazon.com/s?k=izzie+vee&i=digital-text&crid=31LQJTEQYT2EE&sprefix=izzie+vee%2Cdigital-text%2C121&ref=nb_sb_noss

Cover Design by Izzie Vee
Cover Photo by Vishstudio on Depositphotos.com

Table of Content

Chapter 1

Lindsay

"Is college all you imagined, Linds?" my friend Amy asked from across our dorm room.

"We've only been here a month, Ames; there's still a lot to figure out and wrap my head around," I replied, moving from the window I'd been staring through for the last five minutes. For the first time in my life, I was far away from Colorado Springs; two thousand miles, in fact. It still felt surreal.

Amy sat up in bed, placing the book to her chest. "True, I'm just happy we get to be roommates," she said, flashing me a wide grin.

"Me too." I flopped down on the soft pillows, breathing out a sigh as I briefly reflected on the first day we entered college just a month ago. Amy's uncle Byron was a member of the school board, and his connection made it easy for Amy and me to room together. Of course, I was over the moon about her being my roommate. I'd rather have my best friend of over a decade than a complete stranger.

"I have a feeling college will be good to us," she continued.

I raised a curious brow. "What makes you think so? We aren't popular or anything like that."

I considered Amy quite average, not in her appearance, because she was a beautiful girl. Shoulder-length dark hair, a petite body with curves in all the right places, and eyes that changed from emerald to lime green, depending on her mood. As attractive as she was, Amy had never been a part of the popular crowd. I didn't understand why. She was the most fun-loving person I'd ever met.

As for me, it wouldn't take long to find the reason I didn't belong to that crowd. Not only did I consider myself socially awkward, but I didn't fit in with the perfect-looking cheerleader types, the former high-school jocks, the rich kids decked in outfits that cost an entire semester's tuition. My face was too round, my nose too big. I hated how thick my thighs were. My ass was another part of my body I couldn't stand. The only thing I loved was my hair, its silky, golden-blonde tresses brushing my butt.

If it weren't for Amy befriending me ten years ago back in elementary school, I might not have any friends at all.

Amy shrugged. "Yeah, you're right; we're not popular right now. Not for much longer, though."

"What does that even mean?" I ask her.

"There's something I've gotta tell you that slipped my mind. You probably don't care anyway, so–"

"What is it?" I cut in, suddenly too curious.

"Austin's getting transferred from New Hampshire," she replied, wiggling her shoulders.

I cocked my brow at her, wondering why she was so excited by her brother switching from the school he'd already spent two years. "So?"

"So, he'll be spending his junior and senior years here in Maine."

"Where in Maine?" I pushed, sitting up in bed.

"Our school, silly," she said so casually without the slightest idea of how her words suddenly affected me.

I froze in that spot, mobility completely gone from my limbs as I processed her words. My throat felt parched, and as I swallowed, it felt like a razor slipping down my throat.

"What?" I managed, my voice low, but somehow, Amy heard.

"Yeah, my dad thinks he can bring the Bruins to victory this season, plus our curriculum is way better than New Hampshire," she said, sitting up, her legs folded under her. "Not that I care about any of that. I just want him around."

"Bu– but... he's coming here?" My heart rate had doubled for sure, and I could feel the heat warming my cheeks. I prayed Amy didn't notice. The last thing I wanted her to see was how the news affected me.

"Yep, I can't wait! Maybe with him here, we can be on the popular radar for once," she scoffed.

I shook my head as if trying to clear it. "That's actually the last thing I want. Ames, we'll be just fine. We've been doing well without all that spotlight, anyway."

"I know that, but it doesn't hurt to have certain perks when my brother's the star player on the team. I'm so looking forward to that."

"When is he coming here?" I asked, with many more questions on my lips.

"He's back in Colorado Springs, sorting some stuff with Dad. He should be here tomorrow or so."

I cleared my throat, willing the panic inside to go away. "How long have you known he was coming?"

She shrugged. "From the end of summer, I think. Dad was a bit displeased with the negotiations, which is why Austin's starting so late. I guess everything is worked out now."

"Why didn't you tell me earlier?"

"Because... I didn't think you cared," she said, her brows bunching together with a frown. "Is something wrong?"

I shook my head. "No. It's just that... I'm a little worried about being around Austin, that's all."

Amy looked amused. "Why, because he used to bully you when we were kids? Come on, Linds, that was a lifetime ago. You're a little too old to carry that grudge."

Sure, Austin had been a jerk to me when we were kids, and I'd expressed how much I couldn't stand him, but that definitely wasn't why I didn't want him around. I couldn't confess the truth. Instead, I nodded with a scoff. "I can still feel him pulling on my pigtails. Asshole."

Amy laughed. "Remember that time he oiled the patio and called you out?"

"Oh, you mean when I slipped and almost busted my ass? Of course, I remember," I said dryly. My butt had been sore for an entire week.

"Oh, my God, I can't believe you fell for that trick, though. Did you really think Liam came to see you?" Amy said, guffawing.

Liam was a kid from our seventh-grade math class, a guy I really liked back then. Austin found out about my crush, then lied about Liam coming to see me. Of course, I got too excited to think straight because if I did, my commonsense would've spotted Austin's lie. "I shouldn't have since Liam never gave me the time of day. Austin's an even bigger asshole for playing with my feelings like that."

"He didn't mean any harm, Linds, you know that."

"What I do know is that I'm not completely over the crap he pulled on me."

"Don't worry; Austin has no time for pranks these days. He won't even notice you with all the girls that'll be fawning over him." Amy rolled her eyes. "Goddamn groupies."

My stomach tightened at her words, and I forced a smile. If I didn't get a grip of myself, I'd give too much away, which was the last thing I wanted. I had to control my reaction to keep my secret buried. My best friend could never know I'd fallen in love with her brother.

"Yeah, you're probably right. I probably won't even see him at all," I said.

"That's what I'm saying," she replied.

Still, there was a dip in my chest at the thought of not seeing him at all. I quickly dismissed the feeling with a deep sigh. "You must miss him – with him being away so long and all," I said, watching her.

Amy twisted her small mouth and drew a few stray locks of her dark hair behind her ear. "I mean, he's been in New Hampshire for two years, and even though we still saw each other on holidays, and we kept in touch through Facetime and text messaging, it wasn't enough. He was always like a cushion between me and my parents; you know that. When he wasn't around, it forced me to put up with being alone with them."

Amy's eyes glazed over, and I sensed she was having a terrible memory as she spoke. Her gaze grew distant, the cheeriness in her voice now gone, and I instantly regretted broaching the subject, especially when I remembered how hard it was for her.

Amy and Austin came from privilege. While my family lived comfortably, hers had a net worth that far outweighed every home on our street. The size of their house was a clear sign; two floors, five bedrooms, a swimming pool big enough to fit the entire Olympic swim team, and luxury cars that filled both driveways. One would think they lived a happy life, but I'd been friends with Amy long enough to know how miserable she was. Nothing Amy and Austin did was ever good enough for their dad. He was a 'dictator', or so Amy called him, and their mother was a spineless bystander most of the time.

Amy snapped out of her reverie and managed a smile, being the best friend I knew and loved. "Anyway, it's not like I've been completely alone since he left. You've been here with me, which is better than anything I could have ever asked for."

A huge grin brightened her face as she moved across the room and dropped beside me on the bed. "We should go get something to eat. It's a Saturday, and I'm a little sick of being cooped up in this room."

"Where do you have in mind?" I asked, turning to her.

She shrugged. "We could grab pizza at that new spot in the strip mall and a movie after. What do you think?"

"Okay, sounds good," I said. "I need to take a shower, though."

"I already did, so in the meantime, I'll pick something for us to wear."

I paused, eyeing her. "Nothing too sexy, K? You know how I feel about those booty shorts you wear."

"I wish you would let yourself go for once," she replied. "You have a gorgeous body. If only you would show it off."

"I'm good with leggings and a loose T-shirt," I told her. "Nothing with skin, please."

Without waiting for her reply, I grabbed my caddy and made my way to the bathroom I was still trying to get used to. As close as Amy and I were, it was still weird not having my own space.

I stepped into the stall and turned on the tap, our conversation coming back to the forefront of my thoughts. With the water pouring down my body, I processed what she told me. Never in a million years would I imagine Austin coming to Maine. In fact, I never thought I'd see him any time soon. Though the news knocked me off my feet a little, there was an undeniable swell of excitement bubbling in my chest, one that refused to go away.

It had been two years since I'd last seen him. Two years of holding on to a memory, using it as a crutch when life got hard. Two years of wondering if I would ever experience that moment again. It was also two years of suppressing guilt whenever I remembered that night, those stolen minutes at the back of the school with our bodies pressed together and our lips doing a sweet, sensual dance. The best five minutes of my life. Even now, the flash of remorse made me glance at the door, hoping my best friend wasn't a secret mind reader.

Austin probably wouldn't even remember that night. Back then, he was fresh out of high school, still high on the popularity from his days on the football team. Now, he was a college star, attracting women from every level. I was just the girl he kissed during a school dance because her date had gone to be with an 'easier' girl. Austin had no idea what that kiss meant to me and how comforting he'd been that night.

Yes, it would be silly of me to assume he still remembered that kiss – remembered me, especially when he'd changed so much. I wasn't afraid to admit I'd stalked his Instagram page, especially in the last year, and I was always awestruck with how gorgeous he'd become. His body was like a work of art; thick arms and thighs, muscled torso, a face the Greek Gods would envy, and a smile that would make a nun weak in the knees.

He had such a large following, fifty-two thousand to be exact. There was no doubt his DMs were always full, with many girls trying to get at him. He could easily have anyone he wanted. I really didn't stand a chance, even if I wanted it.

Which I didn't.

Being with Austin was definitely a no-no, not only because too many changes had happened since we'd last seen each other but because we were totally different people. As much as I spent countless nights fantasizing about being with him, he was completely off limits. Completely. In fact, what happened between us was a secret I'd gladly take to my grave.

HALF AN HOUR LATER, Amy and I began our walk. Though we had our cars, we wanted the exercise. Besides, the pizza shack wasn't that far away. She wore a smile that made me curious. Amy was always a happy person, but the way she buzzed with contagious joy was a sign there was something going on.

"What's got you smiling so hard?" I asked, my question tainted with humor.

Amy shrugged and skipped a little as she grabbed my hand. "Nothing... nothing at all."

"Amy," I warned. "Come on. Fess up, or I'll tickle the shit out of you."

She giggled and pulled away, pressing her arms to her sides, hiding her sensitive spots. "Don't even think about it."

"Then tell me," I pushed.

"It's nothing, honestly. I'm just really happy Austin's coming here, and we'll be hanging out on the same campus," she replied.

I managed a smile, although the thought of Austin being near gave me no great comfort. "Austin was an awful neighbor, but he's always been a good brother, hasn't he?"

"The best. You know, some people are always crappy to their siblings, but not us. The truth is, I don't know how I would have made it through my teenage years if it hadn't been for you two."

I smirked. "Well, we haven't completely made it through," I dragged. "We have a year left."

Amy scoffed. "Whatever. I just can't wait to be 21, so we can go to more than just house parties," she rolled her eyes. "I'm telling you, Linds, as soon as we hit 21, we're gonna to tear shit down. We're flying out to a Caribbean island, and we're gonna smoke weed and drink like there's no tomorrow!" she exclaimed.

I chuckled. "Okay, hold your horses just a second. You do realize we'll still be students, right? Broke students."

She snorted. "Speak for yourself, but as soon as I hit 21, I'm tapping into that inheritance my grandparents left for us before they died."

"Sure your dad's gonna allow that?" I raised a brow. Mr. Callaghan had always been a shrewd, calculating man. I didn't expect he'd want his kids to be exposed to anything that would pull them from under his controlling thumb.

Amy shrugged nonchalantly. "It's not like he has a choice. The paperwork really matters, and if he plays hardball, then I get a lawyer."

"Do you think it'll get to that?"

"It can; Dad likes to be in charge, and when things aren't in his control, he gets pissy – but not this time. I want what's mine."

A small silence passed between us, and I pictured the tall, dark-haired man who I'd never seen smile in the years I'd known him. Mr. Callaghan always wore a permanent scowl, his eyes always cold, his body always stiff with tension. Kudos to Austin and Amy for surviving living under his roof.

"Anyway," Amy continues, "Austin gets his money next year. We'll see if he puts up a fight then. I have a feeling he won't, though. Austin will do anything to please Dad."

"What's your mom gotta say about your dad's controlling ways?" I asked.

Amy rolled her eyes. "She's like an echo for my dad, so what'd you think?"

I made a face and rubbed her arm sympathetically. "Sorry, Ames."

"Nothing to be sorry about, bestie. Just be grateful you don't have parents like mine."

"Mine aren't perfect either, remember?"

"Anything is perfect compared to what I have, believe me," she replied with a scoff.

Another small silence fell between us, which was usually the case when the topic of Amy's family arose. There was always an awkwardness that filled the air as if giving us time to make it all sink in before we got back to our usual programming.

A couple approached us on the walkway, the guy with his arm around the girl's shoulders. He kissed her temple as they walked past us, and I spotted the disgust that filled Amy's face as she twisted and watched them go. She turned back with a deep scowl. "Can you freaking believe that?" she exclaimed.

"What?" I asked, oblivious.

"I think I just threw up a little in my mouth," she murmured, dramatically gagging.

I laughed, looking back to the couple, the guy's hand now squeezing the girl's butt. "Why?"

"That's Alexia Francis, Regina Davis' best friend," she informed.

"Okay..." The names didn't ring a bell, but I suspected this was a backstory to whatever made her gag.

"And the guy is Sean Davis," she went on. "Do you see where I'm going with this?" She gave me an expectant stare.

I shrug. "Um... Regina and Sean are siblings?" I guessed.

She slapped my shoulder with a grin. "You got it!"

"Did I?" I asked uncertainly, still trying to understand her reaction.

"Okay, slowpoke, let me spell it out. Alexia is dating her best friend's brother," she said, shaking her head.

My brows furrowed. "What's wrong with that?" I asked.

She stopped walking, staring at me as if I'd just committed a crime. "Do you even have to ask? Dating your best friend's brother is the master of off limits. I swear, it's the worst thing."

"Is it?" I asked, puzzled. I could think of many things worse than that. Like global warming, animal cruelty, white collar crime... it was an endless list.

"Of course it is! I don't know how some people do it. Like the awkwardness, the grossness! I mean, how do you even discuss men with your best friend when she's sleeping with your brother?" she exclaimed, mimicking that gagging again.

Oh, boy. I rubbed my hands on my sides, guilt consuming me. Austin and I hadn't taken things beyond that kiss, but I felt terrible anyhow.

"I'm so happy you and Austin are complete opposites. I'm glad that will never happen between you two because seriously, you and I could never work out."

"You don't need to worry about that, believe me," I assured her.

Amy beamed at me, and my cheeks burned as I remembered prom night and that steamy kiss, Austin's hand slipping under my dress, my leg wrapped around him, his fingers running up my thighs, going up, up, touching—

Holy shit. I resisted the urge to fan my face, the heat spreading to every inch of my body.

Amy still didn't know about our encounter. In her head, I considered Austin my gross and annoying neighbor. Guilt still consumed me, although what happened was years ago. Knowing I did something that would rip Amy to shreds if she found out still haunted me to this day.

In my defense, I didn't know Amy would hate me and Austin being together. Her outburst proved I'd been right not to say anything to her. It also proved I had to keep what happened a secret ... forever.

That is, if I didn't want to lose my best friend.

Chapter 2

Austin

I pressed my fist against my cheek, my elbows on the armrest of the chair as I stared at the two persons in front of me. Suppressing a sigh, I shook my legs under the table while checking the time and resisting the urge to roll my eyes.

"Austin, are you listening?" the woman – my mother – asked as she glanced at my father with her perfectly sculpted brows, furrowed.

One glare from my dad, and I sighed out loud, easing up in my chair with my back firmly pressed against it.

"I'm listening, Mom, though I've heard this speech a million times before."

"And you're going to hear it again," my dad said sharply, the signature scowl on his face. "We expect nothing but the best from you, and if I ever hear that your focus has shifted, you won't like the outcome."

"By that, he means girls," Mom clarifies. "It's time to get serious, Austin. The long line of women can wait. If you have plans on playing pro football, we expect nothing but unwavering dedication from you."

I opened my mouth to speak but clamped it back shut at once. There was no use arguing; it would only prolong the conversation, and all I wanted was to get the heck out of this room.

"Okay, I hear you, Mom; I hear both of you," I said with a tight smile, glancing from one to the other. "Now, I want to get settled in before it gets any later. Can we go?"

My mom glanced at Dad, who hesitated, and his eyes narrowed on me before he nodded. I perked up and pushed the chair back, which screeched against the board floors as I stood, pulling at my shirt.

Mom escaped—yes, escaped to the other room, leaving me with my dad, who slowly walked around my side of the table. I gritted my teeth, staring determinedly as he came up to me and slapped an arm around my shoulder, gripping me as he led us to the porch.

"Your mom and I are heading to back Colorado Springs, and I'm leaving you in charge of the house," he said. "I don't want you having any parties with your little girlfriends or your pals," he said gruffly.

I glanced back at the beachfront property, one of the many properties my parents owned. It stood on a quarter-acre of land, with a view of the beautiful coastline. A huge patio stood out back, along with a perfectly manicured lawn and an Olympic-sized swimming pool.

"Do I make myself clear?" dad asked.

I tightened my jaw. "Yes, sir." The words came out forced, though I wanted to point out I was twenty years old, perfectly capable of hosting a party with no damage. There was no use in arguing. Better not to stretch this out and endure more of Hunter Callaghan.

"I expect the house to be spotless when we return. Don't think we won't have an eye on you after we've left," he warned.

"I have no doubt," I murmured, sure that he had PIs on speed dial.

A second passed before he released me. "Let's get you settled," he said as he turned abruptly and headed back inside. I watched him go, muttering a curse under my breath.

MY PARENT'S BEACH HOUSE stood about twenty minutes away from the campus, but I wished the distance was shorter. They didn't make the best company, with my dad lecturing me all the way and Mom being silent, as usual. I kept my mind on reuniting with my sister Amy. Almost six months had passed since I'd last seen her in person, hugged her – experienced the feeling of home radiating through me.

Admittedly, Amy wasn't the only person I was excited to see, though my sister would castrate me if she read my thoughts. I couldn't stop them from surfacing no matter how many times I tried to keep them buried– no matter how much I thought the distance would make the feelings just ... distant.

I'd known Lindsay Peart since we were kids. The short, round-faced girl with the trademark pigtails had been a staple in my life, a target for my practical jokes. I'd never seen her as my little sister, just Amy's quiet friend, and I was so glad that was never the case. It would've made things quite awkward for me when I began noticing how much she'd changed.

Gone were the braces, the acne, the baby fat. At sixteen, Lindsay was a goddess, with a body that made everyone else fade around her. She was the center of attention in a sea of people wanting my attention, and she didn't even have to try.

I didn't understand why she made me feel so... alive. She wasn't like the typical girls I dated. I preferred my women bold and outgoing; Lindsay was the opposite. Maybe it was her innocence that made me crave her like I did. I could do nothing to stop my ache for her.

It was stupid of me to fall for my sister's best friend. Yes, I said it. I was in love with her. Weird, when all we'd shared was a stolen kiss at the back of the school auditorium. For some reason, she got under my skin. Two years had passed, and I still couldn't get her out of my head. If I overstepped, if I allowed my emotions to guide me, the outcome wouldn't be all sunshine and rainbows. It would be a thunderstorm with razors falling from the sky – aimed solely at me.

No matter how I craved Lindsay's soft lips again, her touch, her company... I couldn't have her. Not now. Maybe not ever.

The thought of never sharing another moment with her, of never having more caused a lump in my throat, which I quickly swallowed as I narrowed my gaze ahead. Luckily, we turned onto the campus just then. Small mercies. Ten minutes, and I'd be rid of my parents for a long time.

I sat up in my seat, staring through the heavily tinted window at the students walking around the campus, some scattered on the front lawns, their eyes locked on the luxury car as we rolled by. I bet no one had ever seen a Tesla Model S on campus before. I was already cringing at the thought of disembarking. Don't get me wrong, I enjoyed not having to worry about money, but I hated the attention that wealth brought. All I wanted was an inconspicuous life.

The desire may be odd coming from a guy with fifty thousand followers on Instagram, but I wanted no part of that. Sure, I'd done well. With some of the best touchdown throws last season, I was in high demand, with colleges falling over themselves to have me. If only they knew I had no desire to play. Football was never my dream.

I heard a few gasps when I made my way out of the car and opened the trunk to get my suitcases. With a sigh, I ignored the phones trained on me. Another day, another attempt to put up with the spotlight created for me, a spotlight I didn't want.

Mom's face suddenly brightened as she looked behind me. I turned, the tension draining from my body and my lips parting into a smile when I saw Amy speeding down the pathway, squealing, wearing an excited grin.

I laughed as she launched into my arms, almost knocking the air out of me. She wrapped her arms tightly around my neck, nearly cutting off my oxygen supply as she hugged me tightly.

"Gosh, I missed you," she exclaimed, and I smiled, swallowing her up with my arms.

"Not as much as I've missed you, I'm sure." I peeled her off me to take her in.

My chest tightened to see her so happy to see me – to be looking at her after so long. She suddenly launched back and punched me slightly in the gut, causing me to double over theatrically.

She grinned smugly, clearly thinking she'd done some damage. "That's for staying away for so long."

I quickly grabbed her in a headlock and rubbed my knuckles on top of her head while she struggled to break free. "This is for not calling me often enough," I said, laughing.

I released her to find her sporting a frown. "I call..." she struck my shoulder. "You're just always so busy."

I grinned. "Yeah, comes with the territory." I pulled her in for another hug, glancing at my parents, who stood stiffly watching us. One would think they were strangers observing siblings teasing each other.

My attention shifted down the path Amy came from, and my heart instantly skipped a beat. Lindsay Peart. I couldn't believe this was the same girl I'd kissed two years ago. Back then, she was cute; now she was beautiful – no, stunning. She still had that shy walk with her hands in front of her, her blonde hair like a curtain around her face and down her shoulders. Her intense blue eyes pulled me in, making her the only person who existed in that moment.

As she came closer, my heart rate sped up, and I struggled to breathe right. Her gaze held mine, and I swallowed hard as emotions swept over me. Joy, relief, tension, longing. They all took turns assaulting me.

Her cheeks slightly reddened, and she dipped her gaze, fiddling with her hands. My heart soared, happy to have gotten a reaction from her at least.

"Hey, Austin," she said, her voice like a pacifier.

"Lindsay...hi." For some reason, my voice didn't sound like my own, so I cleared my throat and tried again. "Hi."

I was aware of my parents and Amy standing there, but I couldn't help myself. I reached out to her, feeling her hesitance as I wrapped my arms around her tiny frame. No one would think anything of us hugging. I'd known Lindsay since we were kids.

There was a soft hiss as if she inhaled my scent. I swore I heard a slight moan as she melted into me, accepting the hug as the seconds passed. I didn't want to let her go, I wanted to stay pressed against her for much longer than this, but then she eased off and awkwardly looked to the ground before clearing her throat and managing a meek smile.

I glanced at Amy, who remained oblivious to what had passed between Lindsay and I just now. She wore a contagious smile as she soaked up our reunion.

"You guys look great," I said with a nod, glancing at Amy, too, so she wouldn't catch on to me staring unabashedly at her best friend. "College life agrees with you, huh?"

"Thanks, you don't look too bad yourself," Amy complimented, striking me in the gut again.

"Amy, stop abusing your brother," Mom scolds, a half-hearted attempt at parenting.

Amy and I ignored her. I nudged my sister's side, then pointed to the suitcases at my feet. "Now, who's gonna help me get this luggage to my room?"

Amy scoffed. "What do you have those huge muscles for?"

I flexed my arm, and Amy rolled her eyes. "These bad boys are for one thing only," I said.

"Yeah, we know," Amy drawled, looking bored. "The ladies already have their panties in a bunch, and you just got here—look."

I glanced around me, earning a few excited screams and waves, the clicks from photos being taken making me want to grind my teeth. A group of girls passed right by us, little giggles erupting when I forced a smile at them– their cheeks gone red.

I couldn't care less about them. There was only one person I wanted to notice me. She was already standing in front of me, looking everywhere but at me. Did I read the signs wrong? I'm sure I didn't.

I sighed, clutching the handle of my suitcase and throwing the duffel at Amy, who stumbled and gasped as she caught it. I laughed and quickly grabbed it from her before she fell, wheeling a suitcase toward her instead.

"Come on, the least you could do is follow me to my room," I said.

Amy rolled her eyes as we moved on, with her on one side of me and Lindsay on the other. I tried my best to concentrate on walking while listening to Amy's constant yapping, but it was a struggle with Lindsay being so close — her sweet perfume wafting past my nostrils, making me want to bury my face in her neck.

"Are you getting a single or a roommate?" Amy asked as we entered the lift.

"A roommate," I replied.

"Oh, wow. I thought the star quarterback would get his own room," she teased.

I smiled. "You know I don't care for the star treatment, Ames. Besides, my roommate plays football too. I'm looking forward to making a new friend."

I held the elevator doors for Mom and Dad, who lagged behind, but they waved us off, pointing to the next lift. Relief flooded me as the doors closed.

"So, Mom and Dad left you in charge of the beach house," Amy said.

It wasn't a question, but I nodded anyway. "Right you are."

"Hmm. I can imagine those parties you're already planning in your head, those girls who'll be lining up outside your bedroom door."

I caught the heavy blush on Lindsay's cheek, and I scoffed at Amy. "Why do you assume I'm some man whore?" I glanced at her to see the amusement on her face.

"Maybe because you are."

I laughed and shook my head. "Not even close. I only had two girlfriends after leaving high school. You know that."

"Yeah, but how many one-night stands?" she threw back, and I wanted to palm my face. I didn't want to have a conversation about my promiscuous life with Lindsay standing right there.

Lindsay cleared her throat, her entire face red now. "Hey, Ames, I just remembered about heading to the library for some research. I should get going."

Amy and I both paused. "Okay. Wait for me, though. We won't be long. We're just getting this ogre settled; then we can go together," she said.

"I–"

"I promise we won't be long. Pretty please; if you leave, I won't have anyone to walk back with me," she said, pouting, an action that usually melted my heart when we were kids.

Lindsay pondered her decision while biting her lower lip. My attention latched onto her rosy mouth, and I ached for a taste.

Just one taste.

"Ok, fine," Lindsay finally said. "I'll wait for you."

Amy grinned, and we continued our walk to my wing, a conversation in full effect again with Amy as the instigator.

"So, won't you like, miss your friends back in New Hampshire?" she asked me.

I shrugged. "I guess, but it's not like we won't ever get to see each other again. It's the age of technology, remember?" I winked.

"Well, I'm sure the ladies will be missing you." She gave me a nudge in my side. "Remember that girl you found in your bed after that party?"

"Ugh. Don't remind me." It took an entire hour and the threat of calling the cops to get her out of the apartment I shared with a friend. Since then, I ensured to keep my bedroom locked whenever we had a party going on.

I glanced at Lindsay, the discomfort on her face making me flinch. The last thing I wanted was the misconception that I was a player who only wanted one thing. Sure, I had my man-whore moments, but those days were all behind me.

We arrived at my wing, all eyes on us — well, me mostly, since I was a head taller than most people in the building and, of course, being a renowned football player and all. The cell phones were out, people whispering, the same old spotlight that I didn't want.

"Callaghan," a guy greeted as he stepped in front of me. "We heard the news you were being transferred here. Welcome, man."

"Thanks, dude." I shook his firm handshake and nodded to some other guys observing in a corner.

"So, think you can bring the championship to Maine? It's been twenty years since the last win," the guy continued.

"I'll do my best," was the only answer I had.

He patted my shoulder as I moved off. "Well, we're counting on you, man."

No pressure. I shot him a smile I hoped didn't show how annoyed I was. Imagine carrying a burden you didn't want. I hated the responsibility Dad placed on my shoulders, and for what? So he could live vicariously through me?

Pushing my irritation aside, I paused at my dorm door and turned to Lindsay and Amy. "Well, this is it."

"Open the door," Amy ordered. "I want to see if they gave you a gold-plated bedframe or something."

A loud snicker left my mouth. If there was one thing I could count on Amy for, it was her ability to make me feel better without even trying. I reached for the door handle, but the door opened before I could turn the knob. A guy as tall as me stood on the other side, his unruly jet-black hair and green eyes giving him a mischievous look.

"You must be my roommate, Carter, right?" I said in greeting.

A tiny smirk lifted the corner of his mouth. "That's right, Callaghan. Pleasure to meet you," he said, sticking out his hand.

We exchanged a firm handshake before his eyes drifted to Amy, then lingered on Lindsay. His gaze roamed the length of her. I could see it in his eyes that he found her attractive – I mean, who wouldn't? Even so, I could feel my jaw tighten, my hands gripping the suitcase even tighter.

I cleared my throat when he looked at me expectantly. "This is my sister Amy and Amy's best friend, Lindsay," I said, my voice firm.

Carter looked between them and smiled, his attention staying on Lindsay. "Nice to meet you, ladies." He reached out and took her hand, giving it a quick shake before kissing the back. Fury rose within me, and I swallowed to temper it. He shook Amy's hand, and I waited for him to kiss the back of hers, but he didn't.

Ok, dude. I see what you're doing.

"Thanks for the company, guys," I said, turning to the girls. "Once I get settled, dinner or lunch is on me."

Amy grinned, being the foodie she was. "Dinner *and* lunch are on you, bro! See you later, punk."

I chuckled, glancing at Lindsay who wore a smile on her face. Her eyes shifted to me, and our gazes held for a second before she nodded, whipping around to follow Amy.

I watched her go, noting how those jeans hugged her round ass and how her hair brushed the curve of her back as she walked, her hips swaying with each step.

Sweet mother of God, help me.

I vividly remembered the night we kissed, the night I found her crying behind the school after her date had left the dance with someone else. When I pulled her into my arms, my only thought was to comfort her. I didn't expect the magnetism that made our eyes lock, breaths paused, heart rates going at the speed of light. Back then, my only thought was to taste her lips for a second, just to see if the emotions swirling inside me were real. When our lips touched, it confirmed what I'd suspected all along; this wasn't just a crush on my sister's best friend. Lindsay Peart was made for me.

I'd masked my surprise when she pushed me away with a gasp, her eyes wild with shock. There was no doubt in my mind she wanted me. I felt the slickness between her pussy lips when I touched her there, heard her soft moan when I rubbed my hard cock against her. It was obviously bad timing. Lindsay wasn't ready for me back then. Two years had passed, and my desire for her hadn't waned one bit. In fact, it burned even brighter, fueled by our proximity to each other.

I let her go back then, convinced it wasn't the right time. Now, I had no intention of walking away again.

Buckle up, Lindsay because I'm coming for you.

Chapter 3

Lindsay

THAT NIGHT, I LAY CURLED up in bed with one thing on my mind. Well, one person. Austin. Every cell in my body was now aware of Austin's return, of him being more gorgeous and chiseled than before. Sure, I had stalked his Instagram page multiple times, but seeing him in person was just so ... surreal.

I'd missed that cocky smile, that thick, silky hair that made me want to run my fingers through it before stroking his hard jawline, looking into those deep brown eyes that turned my insides to mush on prom night. I noticed the way he stared at me earlier, the look of longing that made me confused and fuzzy. Maybe Austin had a thing for me a few years ago, but I figured with him moving on, those feelings would eventually fade. But the longing was still there; I saw it in the stare that made me feel exposed, like I was being stripped of every article of clothing I wore.

I wanted to believe I still had that effect on him, but it was probably a side effect from the shock of seeing him again and my raging hormones. Who was I kidding? Austin was a charmer. A player. That was his way of flirting, something he did very subtly, yet very well. I was nothing special. Was I ever?

The thoughts left me uneasy. It was silly to think of a budding relationship between Austin and me, especially after what Amy revealed earlier. It would never be possible. Ever. I cherished my friendship with Amy more than anything and to ruin that would be an unforgivable sin.

Austin was a fantasy and that was all he would be. We were like fire and gas. Us coming together would be complete destruction.

I uncurled, laying on my back and staring at the ceiling. I'd been a good girl all my life. Gotten good grades, helped around the house, kept away from boys. Heck, at eighteen years old, I was still a virgin. Not saving myself for marriage or anything, just waiting for someone who made me feel that spark. I'd been walking on the straight and narrow for a long time. Was it wrong to want to cross over to the bad side for a while?

Just once?

AMY'S SLEEPY GROAN woke me the next morning. I kept the covers over my head, listening as she got out of bed and moved around our studio. My eyes still burned from not sleeping too well. Thoughts of Austin had kept me up for most of the night. I kept debating on whether he still wanted me, if I imagined that look he gave me. Then I scolded myself. It didn't matter. Austin was off limits. It was either him or my best friend.

I couldn't lose Amy. She was the only friend I had. Considering it took us years to form our bond, I couldn't throw that away for another steamy encounter with Austin.

Especially since he wasn't the settling down type.

"I was wondering when you'd be up," Amy said when I finally hauled the sheet off my head. She smiled, struggling to get a pair of jeans over her hips.

"What time is it?" I asked groggily, rubbing at my eyes.

"Almost eight. I have a class in half an hour. You have a class at nine, which means you should be up and getting ready."

I eased up on the bed with a sigh. "Yes, Mother."

She cut me a stern look, then burst out laughing. "By the way, Austin will be on the field today for practice. I want to stop by in the evening to see him in action."

I swallowed, hoping my face didn't show my emotion. "Oh, that's cool."

"Of course, I want you to come with me," she said casually.

I shook my head. "Ames, you know I'm not really into football–"

"Neither am I, but this is Austin we're talking about. I'm sure he'd appreciate the support."

I pulled in a breath and scratched my head. Being around Austin wasn't safe right now. Not until I learned to control my reaction to him. I didn't want Amy to notice how attracted to her brother I was.

"Come on, Linds, it's not like we have anything better to do after school. We don't have exams for a while, and we're always stuck in our room, anyway," she went on.

Not wanting to arouse her suspicion, I finally nodded. "I guess you're right."

She grinned. "Of course I am. Anyway, I'll meet you there at three thirty. Don't be late. I want Austin to know he has our full support.

I smiled. "I'll be there, don't worry." *Even if it means wearing the heck out of my emotional mask.*

Amy blew me a kiss, grabbed her knapsack and then moved toward the door. "Sweet, see you then, love ya," she called, slamming the door behind her.

I moaned and flopped back on the bed, just about ready for another round of sleep since I'd spent last night thinking about a man who could never be mine, depriving myself of much-needed rest.

Time would not allow me, though. With only an hour left for class, I dragged myself out of bed, yawning all the way to the bathroom. There, I took a quick shower, returned to my room and got dressed in leggings and a loose-fitted sweater.

Sitting through math class was torture, but at the end of it, I'd meet up with Amy, who'd texted me earlier about lunch at our favorite little cafeteria on campus.

I made my way there with a smile on my face, spotting her seated in the far corner, texting away on her phone with two trays in front of her containing our food. Eyes turned to me as I entered the room. I swallowed hard as I made my way through the noisy batches of college students, my cheeks flaming from the attention on me. I lowered my head, the walk to Amy eternal.

A sigh of relief escaped my lips when I slid onto a chair opposite Amy, who placed her phone on the table, giving me her full attention.

"Gosh, I was wondering when you'd get here, I'm starving," she said, unwrapping her sandwich and immediately taking a bite.

"Math was a bitch," I grumbled, peeling the wrapping off my chicken salad.

Amy smiled. "When is it never?" she said with a packed mouth.

"Good point. Some days, I wonder why I even picked Econ."

"Because as much as you complain, this is what you love, and you'd like to run your own business someday. This is just a step up the ladder you have to climb," she said with a wink.

She had a point, but I still groaned. Not that I hated doing hard work, but my life contained nothing more. School, back to the dorm to study, sleep, school, assignments—the cycle continued. I wanted more out of life.

"You remember later, right?" Amy asked.

How could I forget the two-hour self-inflicted torture? Watching Austin's practice game would be nothing less than torment. "Of course, I remember." I gestured to my outfit. "See, I even dressed the part."

"Great. Maybe we can meet a few of Austin's hot team members." She winked while taking a sip of her juice.

"Yeah, I don't think so," I immediately blurted.

Amy grinned, mischief lighting up her eyes. "I saw the way Austin's roomie looked at you yesterday. He might be into you."

I scoffed as I shook my head. "Please, you're either blind or clueless. He definitely wasn't."

She raised a brow. "You should give yourself more credit, Lindsay. You can have anybody you want right now."

"I'm flattered that you think so highly of me, Ames, but I'm certain I'm not the majority of these guys' type. Not that I'd want to be anyway," I said with a slight scowl.

Amy paused amid unwrapping the other half of her sandwich, her eyes squinting as if trying to figure out something. "If you're into girls, you can tell me. I'd definitely be fine with it."

I snorted. "I'm not... it's just that college boys only want to party and have sex with random girls, and I'm not at all up for that."

"Nothing is wrong with random sex, y'know."

"Well I don't want a high body count at the end of college," I quipped.

She laughed. "Spoken like a true virgin!"

"Who's a true virgin?" a voice behind me asked, and my entire body heated when I recognized the voice. Austin made an appearance seconds after with a curious smile as he looked between us. I immediately wanted to sink through the floor.

"Not that it's any of your business, but my best friend and I were having a conversation about boys, and Lindsay here doesn't want the whole college experience. I, however, am up for it one hundred percent."

Austin's thick brows slightly lifted as he assessed my face, staring as if trying to read my mind. I wanted to run from his intense stare, but I couldn't move if I wanted to, so captivated I was by him. Instead, I shifted my gaze to the salad in front of me, using the fork to play around in it.

"Well, Lindsay is being the smart one. You don't want to leave this place with regrets," Austin finally said.

"Who said anything about regrets?" Amy chipped in. "We only live once, baby!"

"And life can suck when you make stupid choices," he countered.

"Who died and made you the great philosopher?" Amy scoffed.

Austin stuck his tongue out at her. "We learn from experience, punk."

Amy rolled her eyes and took a sip of her drink before she pushed back her chair and got up. "Well, you can stay here and advise Lindsay. I need to pee."

My mouth flew open as Amy walked away, and I searched for an excuse to go with her, but none came fast enough. I was stuck in Austin's presence, subjected to having our first private conversation in two years. Austin sat there, staring at me unabashedly, pinning me even further in place.

He folded his lips and glanced in the direction Amy had gone, then turned his gaze back to me. "It's nice seeing you again, Lindsay."

I cleared my throat, my cheeks warming. "It's nice seeing you too."

I scratched the back of my neck and looked around the busy cafeteria with everyone minding their business, yet with Austin here, it felt like all attention was on me.

"You look beautiful... as always."

I bit my bottom lip. "Austin..."

"And I've missed you," he added as his fingers crept toward mine on the table.

I quickly pulled my hand away before he touched it, my heart racing in my chest. "Don't," I whispered, looking around to see if anyone had noticed. "We can't."

Austin eased back in his chair, eyes still steadily fixed on me. "Why not?"

"I think we both know why," I replied, my voice a little higher than before. I lowered it, leaning forward. "I made it clear that night, didn't I?"

Back then, my decision not to move past second base only relied on the fear Austin wanted nothing more than sex. I knew his track record. For years, I'd seen the girls climbing up the fire escape to his room. Austin was a player; why would I assume there was something special between us?

"Of course you did," he said firmly, and I pressed my lips together and looked to the exit again.

"But like I told you back then, your assumptions weren't fair. I wanted more than your body, Lindsay."

His words sent tingles through me, and I squeezed my thighs together as an ache settled between them. "I'm not having this conversation, Austin."

He grabbed my hand as I tried to rise. Not wanting to draw attention to me, I quickly sat back down. "I know that kiss meant something to you like it did to me," he said. "I haven't forgotten."

"Is that why you haven't called me in two years?" I shot back, satisfied when he flinched. "Not even a text message, Austin. Nothing."

"You asked for space, so I gave it to you," he defended.

He made a valid point, so I searched for another angle. "There can't be anything between us, anyway. Amy disapproves."

"And?"

I glared in disbelief. "Amy is my best friend, and I'll be damned if I let anything or anyone impede our friendship."

Austin stared at me for a beat, his expression hard to read. "I hear you loud and clear, Lindsay," he finally said, my name sounding like a caress on his lips. Lips that were so damn attractive. Lips I wanted to feel against mine.

Damn it. What's wrong with me? I literally just told him to beat it. Now, I'm fantasizing about kissing him. Pick a struggle, Lindsay.

I breathed a sigh and looked around again, relieved when I saw no one looking at us. Just then, I spotted Amy coming back, a smile on her face, one I quickly replicated as I eased back in my chair.

"I don't want to talk about this ever again, Austin. Nothing can ever happen between us, got that?" I mumbled.

Austin didn't reply, but his clenched jaw told me how he felt. When Amy arrived at the table, he stood and kissed her forehead. "I'll see you later, sis."

Amy frowned as Austin walked away without saying goodbye to me. "What was that about?"

I shrugged. "Beats me."

Amy continued talking, but I hardly heard a word. My thoughts were too wrapped up with my conversation with Austin. I still reeled over his confession that he missed me. The honesty in his eyes confirmed I wasn't the only one with such feelings. My heart soared, then fell flat when I thought of Amy and how devastated she would be.

As great as the words were to hear, the depressing truth remained. Austin and I would never be a thing, despite how much I craved for it. There was no use longing for something I would never have.

Something that would make me happy.

Something that would make me feel alive.

My friendship with Amy was more important than being with the guy who'd stolen my heart two years ago.

Chapter 4

Austin

I'd only been here for a day, but I was already the center of attention. It wasn't all positive, though. I caught the malicious attitudes from the senior guys on the field. Not that it surprised me, nor did I blame them. The fanfare placed on my transfer must've left them feeling inadequate. I would be offended, too, if the entire coaching staff placed the team's future in the new guy's hands. There was nothing I could do about that except show them I wasn't the enemy. We were all playing for the same goal.

It also killed the team that girls were already throwing themselves at me like I was a treasure they'd just discovered. Now, there was nothing I could do about *that*.

While the girls on campus were mostly hot, none held a candle to Lindsay, who was simply the most beautiful human there was. Just my bad luck; the woman I wanted the most was the one I couldn't have. She'd made it clear on her prom night, yet I bided my time, hoping the years would change her mind. So when Dad announced my transfer to Maine, my first thought was that I'd be near Lindsay again, and I hoped we could pick up where we left off.

I should have known not to hope. Lindsay was loyal and kindhearted, and even if it meant sacrificing her own happiness, she wouldn't do anything to jeopardize her friendship with Amy.

Truth was, I should take a page from her book. Amy was my sister, and staying away from Lindsay would keep our relationship intact. I'd hate for my sister and I to be at odds.

"Hey, Callaghan, quit daydreaming and let's get to practice." Coach Johnson's deep voice pulled me from my thoughts. I winced as he gave me a hearty slap on my shoulder. "No time for goofing around. The team is depending on you."

I sighed, reaching for a towel to wipe my face before jogging behind the others onto the field.

"Two laps!" Coach Johnson shouted.

The warm sun welcomed me, and I squinted my eyes as my gaze traveled to the stands in search of Amy since she promised she'd be here. There was a high chance Lindsay would be there, too. My main reason for checking out the crowd.

I got knocked from my stance when someone bumped into me. With a frown, I turned to see who it was and met a deep smirk.

"Head in the game, Quarterback," Lance Adams, the linebacker quipped, flipping his middle finger at me.

I was just about to rush him when Carter, the team's wide receiver and my roommate came into view. "Don't pay him any mind, he just always wants to be the center of attention around here, and with a face like that, I guess that has never happened."

I smiled. "Well, if he keeps it up, he'll eventually know my right hook."

Carter grinned back. "I did my homework on you, Callaghan, and I believe you can really give us a win this year. You just gotta stay as sharp as you did back in New Hampshire."

"Yeah, well, that's the aim, right?"

He nodded. "Damn right."

Later, we did a couple of drills and warmed up for actual practice. I looked to the stands again and caught sight of Amy, who waved at me, a huge smile on her face. I waved back and smiled, my eyes shifting to Lindsay, who sat right beside her. Carter saw me staring and came up to me, peering at the stands, too.

"Hey, I've been meaning to ask; what's up with that Lindsay girl?"

My head snapped towards his so fast I swear I got whiplash. My brows furrowed. "What do you mean?"

"She's cool, right? I wanna shoot my shot, but she seems a little standoffish," he replied, not taking his eyes off her.

I clenched my teeth, willing my expression to remain casual. "Yeah, er – she's... last time I heard she's taken."

Carter made a face. "Crap, that sucks. She's definitely my type: pretty and shy, but you know how those innocent-looking girls are in bed, am I right?" He chuckled, nudging my side, waiting for me to join on in.

The very thought of Carter touching Lindsay filled me with an anger I didn't know I possessed. My jaw tightened as I gripped my helmet and moved off without a word, heading farther onto the field before I did something I'd regret. I glanced back to the stands and saw Lindsay and Amy in the same spot, talking and laughing.

The anger slowly faded as I stared at Lindsay, soothed by that big smile that could light up any dark room. If only she did it more often. If only she would smile for me.

"Callaghan!" Coach Johnson called, snatching me from my thoughts once more.

I looked to the sidelines to see him waving me over. I sighed, slowly jogging to confront him.

"What's up, coach?"

"Eyes on the field and nowhere else, Callaghan," he said, brushing his thumb over his nose and placing his other hand on my shoulder. "Hey, I get it. You're a star player and a darn good-looking one at that. You've got a loaded family. Girls are gonna throw themselves at you, and being the young blood you are, you're gonna want it all and more..."

"That's not–" I began before he cut me off.

"Listen, your old man told me to keep an eye out, and that's what I'm doing. Everyone is depending on you this season, and hey, I've seen your work, I know you can do it..." He paused, his clear blue eyes searching my face.

I wanted to roll my eyes, but I didn't. I was so pissed at my Dad. He just had to get his hook into everyone, didn't he?

"I know what I'm here to do, Coach. Trust me, I won't let you or anyone else down," I said, knowing that I'd keep my word but already so exhausted with everything.

Coach Johnson's grip tightened on my shoulder as his thin lips stretched into a smile. "That's the spirit. Now you go out there and show them what you're made of!"

I pulled in a breath as I anchored the helmet on my head and jogged back onto the field. The next hour seemed never-ending, and when I looked to the stands again, Lindsay and Amy were already leaving.

With a sigh, I walked to the locker once practice was done and took a quick shower before I grabbed my things and left before I bumped into Carter. The last thing I wanted to do was buddy up with someone who had his eyes on Lindsay – roommate or not.

AFTER FRESHENING UP and packing my gear, I drove down to the beach house, totally not meant to host any girls as I promised Dad, but I wanted somewhere to clear my head. This was the only place I could think of, the only place that guaranteed total privacy.

I reversed into the driveway, then got out and grabbed my bag from the backseat. I needed a shower again– never having been a fan of locker rooms and public showers, but the beautiful sunset gave me reason to make it wait.

Heading to the balcony, a perfect view of the ocean welcomed me, although the weather was a little frosty. It shaped up to be a chilly night. My favorite kind of night.

Smiling, I dug into the shopping bag and popped out my easel and my painting supplies. I didn't waste any time; I got everything set up and painted colorful lines across the canvas while my gaze traveled to and from the dying sunset.

The exhaustion I'd felt earlier faded like the sunshine in front of me. For a few minutes, nothing else mattered but getting a perfect painting.

Lindsay soon popped up in my mind, leaving me focusing on two things, struggling with figuring out which was the most beautiful.

I was obsessed with her, and although I couldn't admit it out loud, I had no problem confessing it to myself just now. I hadn't stopped thinking about her for the entire two years we'd been apart. Being with other girls felt so wrong, which made me stop sleeping around. No one knew this, but I hadn't been with another girl in a year. Celibacy seemed stupid since the only thing Lindsay and I had ever shared was a kiss, but it made an impact – an everlasting one.

As long as we were only a few buildings apart, I'd never stop thinking of having her and fantasizing that someday I could.

TWO HOURS LATER, I applied the finishing touches to my piece, gave it a lengthy stare, contentment rushing through me. Some people got massages, drank alcohol or took vacations when they were stressed. I painted. It was the only escape that balanced my equilibrium. It was also the only escape that no one knew about.

I started packing up my stuff, then searched the house for a spot to hide them since my parents could pop up. I hid them in a closet behind some boxes, pleased with my hideaway spot.

I'd do anything in my power not to let them control this one thing.

Chapter 5

Lindsay

"I've got a date!" Amy announced as she sailed into the room with a proud smile.

I bounded from the bed, my eyes wide as I stared at her. "What?"

"Told you, the perks of having Austin as my brother," she said.

"Who's the date?"

"His name is Jason. He's a linebacker or something like that. I met him at football practice," she replied.

"How come you didn't tell me you were going?" I voiced in disbelief.

"Come on, Linds, I saw your face the last time. You didn't seem interested in a single thing that happened on that field."

Oh, I definitely was. Amy just couldn't know. "I still didn't mind being there for you ... and Austin." I could feel my cheeks warming at the memory of Austin in those tights.

Amy made a face. "That's sweet of you, but don't worry about it. My dear ol' brother has all the little groupies for support, and as for me, I'm okay sitting alone. Besides, I know you have an exam in the next two years to study for," she said with a laugh.

I rolled my eyes. "When's the date?"

"Tomorrow," she said, falling backward on her bed and reaching for her phone.

"Wow, okay. Are you sure about this, Ames? I mean, you barely know the guy."

"Well, that's usually the point of dating, isn't it, Linds? ... where you get to know each other..." she dragged on slowly as if I were dense.

"You're a freshman; these guys only want one thing," I argued.

Amy groaned, annoyance filling her face. "OMG, Lindsay. Don't be like my mom. I'm going on this date, and even if Jason wants sex, I'm sure it'll be consensual. I'm not a virgin, y'know."

"How can I forget?" I snapped defensively. I couldn't help feeling that was an intentional jab at me. "You've made zero efforts in trying to keep it a secret."

Her mouth fell open. "And why should I? This isn't the Middle Ages where I'll be shunned and scorned if word gets out," she scoffed. "You should live a little!"

"Oh, if this is your idea of living, then count me out. I live fine knowing I'm not at risk of contracting something nasty from these man whores."

Amy stared at me in disbelief. "Maybe some sex is exactly what you need to blow some steam off. It will probably loosen that stick up your ass!" she exclaimed before bouncing off the bed and leaving the room, sealing the door behind her with a hard slam that made me wince.

How the hell did we get from zero to one hundred so quickly?

Blowing out a sigh, I flopped back onto the bed, considering a thousand ways that conversation could've gone without ending in a fight, but I just couldn't help the words that left my lips. I was just looking out for Amy, and even though she thought she had it all figured out, it could come back to bite her in the ass. Football players were for the streets. Heartbreakers. I didn't want her to get hurt.

Thinking I needed some time away from the dorm room, I brushed my hair and pulled on a sweater before heading out, not having a destination in mind but walking alone was nice, regardless.

Austin had been here almost a week, and I'd only seen him about two days in the beginning. The last time was at practice, and I never saw him afterwards. It made me reflect on the last conversation we had and what I'd said. Maybe that was the reason he'd stayed away. Maybe he'd finally settled in and had too many distractions to even think about me. Though the thought made my stomach tighten, I couldn't really blame him, could I? I'd made it quite clear nothing could happen between us.

I stopped at a nearby café and ordered a slice of cheesecake and coffee before I sat and scrolled through my dormant Instagram account, curious to see if Austin had posted anything since the last time. Just as I was about to click on his page, a shadow appeared in front of me.

I looked up, meeting Carter's smile. He looked even more attractive than when I last saw him, dressed in a snug pair of jeans and a sweater that hugged his bulky torso, a milkshake in his huge hand.

"Hey, Lindsay, right?" he said.

I cleared my throat. "Yeah, hi."

Carter glanced at the empty chair in front of me, and I prayed this wouldn't go in the direction I was thinking. "Mind if I take a seat?"

"Er... yeah, no." I managed a smile despite myself.

He slid gracefully into the seat, which surprised me considering how huge he was, that charming smile still plastered on his face. "I really like you, Lindsay."

I froze as my mind processed his confession. *He certainly doesn't beat around the bush, does he?*

"Are you going to say something?" he asked, making me realize I'd been staring at him with my mouth half-opened.

My forehead wrinkled as I frowned at him. "You don't even know me," I said.

He shrugged. "You're beautiful; that's all I need to know."

I scoffed, shaking my head. "That's pretty weak. And shallow. If you're expecting me to swoon at your feet, I'm sorry." I couldn't help my laugh as I tucked my hair behind my ear.

He threw his head back and laughed at that, surprise in his green eyes as he looked at me. "You know, I underestimated you, Lindsay..."

"Really?" came my dry response.

"Yeah, I kinda thought you were the shy girl who barely said a word."

I shifted in my chair. "And that's your type?"

He shrugged and licked his lips. "Usually."

"I'm sorry to disappoint you," I cut in sarcastically.

"You haven't. I'd still like to get to know you."

I sighed. "Carter I –"

"You have a boyfriend, right. I know," he said, disappointment in his tone.

"What? I don't, but–"

He raised a thick brow. "Really, Callaghan said you did, but I still thought I'd shoot my shot—"

"Wait, Austin said that?" I asked, crossing my arms on my chest.

"Yeah, he said you were taken."

My mind spiraled as I considered why Austin would say such a thing. We'd never had a conversation regarding that before, but I figured it was Austin's way of discouraging Carter from asking me out. Which I still found puzzling. He still wanted me, had basically said it, but I still couldn't fathom why. He was a freaking superstar, for crying out loud, while ninety-nine percent of the school didn't even know my name. We were complete opposites. Even without Amy being an obstacle, we wouldn't have worked out, anyway.

"I'm sorry, Carter, I've got to go," I said, needing some time to clear my head. I just wished things were simpler, but they weren't. If I hadn't been so hung up on Austin, I'd probably give Carter a shot. Or not. He wasn't my type, although, according to him, I was his. I knew why, though. He was a typical footballer who wanted to break in the shy, innocent girl. Too bad he wouldn't get to first base with me.

I got up from the table, Carter's puzzled face the last thing I saw before I headed to the exit, regretting that I'd left the dorm for 'fresh air'.

Just as I bolted through the exit, I collided with a hard body, my face hitting the center of his torso. His scent washed over me as I pulled back, knowing who it was before I even peered into his face.

"Hey there, slow your horses," Austin said, an amused smile on his face as he stared down at me, his brown eyes darker than usual.

I could get lost in them, and for a second, our gazes remained locked together while my skin sizzled from his touch. It seemed he'd just left the gym, dressed in a pair of jogger pants and a tank top, a pair of black sneakers covering his feet. His tousled hair hung in damp waves, a few strands brushing his eyes. God, he was so good-looking, making it hard to look away, but then I remembered the conversation with Carter.

Shrugging myself out of Austin's hold, I pushed past him to leave.

"Hey, did I do something wrong?" Austin called as he followed me, easily catching up.

"Leave me alone, Austin."

He moved in front of me, blocking my path and forcing me to stop. I swallowed hard and crossed my arms, flashing him a hard stare.

"What did I do?"

"What right do you have going around telling people I'm taken?" I snapped.

He seemed confused until realization dawned on his face, his jaw hardening. "You spoke to Carter."

"Yes." I poked his chest, my fury rising. "Why did you do that?"

"Because Carter isn't the guy for you. I wanted to save you the trouble," he replied.

I balked at him in complete disbelief. "You had no right. What I do and who I date isn't any of your business!" I exclaimed.

A bunch of kids walked by, staring at me oddly. I took a deep breath, now pissed at myself for losing control like this. "You had no right, Austin," I repeated in a lower tone.

His Adam's apple visibly bobbed as he swallowed. "You're right. I overstepped, and I'm sorry, but I'm sure you understand how hard it was for me, hearing him talk about how much he wanted you – seeing the way he looked at you."

My heart rate spiked, and I felt breathless even while standing still.

"Why are you doing this?" I asked, my voice barely above a whisper.

"You know why, Lindsay," he murmured, inching closer.

I sucked in a breath. "Austin, we can't do this–"

"Yes, you've made that clear, but why is it that I still want to be with you despite the risk? I can't stop thinking about you, Lindsay. Can't stop wanting you."

I gasped when his fingers laced through mine. I swallowed hard, the sudden tension in my body almost unbearable. "You left for two years and didn't even try contacting me. We can't just pick up where we left off."

"You made it clear from the moment we kissed that it couldn't happen again. I thought the distance would be just what you wanted, so I did as you asked. I left you alone, but coming back, seeing you again – I can't stay away anymore," he said.

My chest rose and fell, and with his hands holding mine, I wasn't sure there was a way to calm my racing heart. "Amy," I said. It was my safe word, the only word that kept me from falling into his arms.

"We can go tell her right now if you wish," he was quick to say.

"I can't do that. It would rip her to shreds," I replied, my eyes pricking with tears. I wanted him so much it hurt.

A soft gasp left my mouth when he pulled me around the corner of the coffee shop, pressing my back firmly against the wall, towering over me.

"What are you doing?" I hissed, pushing at his shoulder. If someone should pass by and see us...

"I can't stop thinking about you, Lindsay. Tell me you don't feel the same way." His hand found my cheek, and I held my breath, a shiver running through my body when his fingers grazed my skin, capturing a few stray strands of my hair and tucking them behind my ear.

My body was on fire, the flesh between my legs thrumming wildly. My panties were already wet, so aroused I was for him. Austin's scent didn't help, either; that combination of sweat and sandalwood making me want to lose myself.

I licked my lips and met his gaze again, seeing the lust that filled his eyes, over the moon that I still had such an effect on him.

"I do feel the same way, Austin, it's just–" My words were cut short when his lips met mine. Shocked, I froze, allowing myself to get accustomed to the feel of his warm lips again. Then, like an ice cube in the sun, I melted into him, my lips moving over his as our tongues met.

Austin's hand found the small of my back as he pulled me closer to him and deepened the kiss. I could feel the eagerness and the passion– similar to what we'd shared years ago, but this time, it was much more intense. Almost greedy. A moan escaped my lips as I wrapped my arms around his neck, moving against him. My nipples tightened, my core pooling with more heat as we kissed.

I wanted him so much. I didn't want to let go, but commonsense popped up and reminded me where I was. It was dark out, but if someone passed by, they could clearly see who we were and what was happening.

With a moan, I pulled away, my cheeks blazing hot as I stared up at Austin, whose eyes were dark with desire, his lips still slightly parted.

I touched the spot where he kissed, more heat assaulting my body. "I'm sorry Austin, but this can't go on," I choked, backing away.

"Lindsay, let's talk about this."

"There's nothing to talk about. I meant it when I told you to leave me alone."

"Really?" he cocked his head, giving me a quizzical stare. "Then why did you kiss me like that just now?"

I had no sensible reply, not when my body still craved more of that kiss, more of his fingers stroking my back, more of his hard cock pressed against my stomach. More of everything. I wanted to get lost in Austin so badly. "I have to go," was all I could say.

"Lindsay," he called, reaching for me. I eased back, taking off before I found myself trapped in his arms again.

To my surprise, he didn't follow, and during my brisk walk back to the dorm, I debated on whether it made me relieved or sad. It wasn't until I closed the door behind me that it occurred; I wasn't relieved or sad. The only emotion that ran through me was utter devastation.

Chapter 6

Austin

I never thought I'd have it this bad for a girl, but here I was, losing my mind over my sister's best friend. When Lindsay ran off, I wanted to chase after her and make her see that whatever her fears were, we'd get through them together, but I didn't want to push her further away, so I gave her space.

Wanting to clear my head, I drove down to the beach house, going out to the front patio and getting comfortable on the modular wicker couch. I tried to enjoy the view of the full moon that cast a silver sheen on the ocean, but Lindsay was my only focus. The kiss we'd just shared was like gasoline on a fire. I wanted her even more now, which seemed impossible since my body had always yearned for her.

I reached down and massaged the erection in my pants, uttering a groan as pleasure surged through me. I needed release. Another girl would never be enough. Since I couldn't have Lindsay—yet, I told myself—then self-pleasure was my only option. I pulled my zipper down and pulled out my cock, stroking it while filling my thoughts with Lindsay and the possibilities if that kiss had lasted a little longer — if we were somewhere private.

Every inch of her body was just as soft as her lips. I didn't need to explore Lindsay to know that. My cock grew more rigid as I imagined myself sinking deep into her body, her warm flesh hugging me tight.

My hands moved faster as I massaged my cock to the thought of her spread wide for me, taking every inch of me. The pleasure built with each passing second. I envisioned her sweet mouth opening up whenever I hit a sweet spot, her flesh pulsing around me as she neared her release.

My eyes fluttered, sharp tingles pricking my skin when I pictured Lindsay now on top of me, her back arched as she rode my length. I wanted to rub my thumbs over her hard nipples, and feel every inch of her flesh as I moved inside her. I wanted my name on her lips as she begged for her release, and once she had it, I wanted her to shout my name to the sky as she hugged me tightly.

I stiffened on the seat, a grunt leaving my lips as cum spurted from my cock, flying to the floor. "Fuck," I exclaimed, wishing Lindsay was here to collect every drop in her mouth. I cursed again, the image of her swallowing and licking her lips almost driving me up the wall.

That night, I went to sleep with a smile on my face, knowing my dreams would soon become a reality. I didn't know how or when, but I wouldn't stop until it did.

BEFORE MY CLASSES BEGAN the following day, I tried to contact Lindsay. It didn't occur to me that I didn't have her cell phone number anymore. I couldn't ask Amy since she'd find it weird, and I didn't want to raise her suspicions. Instead, I found Amy's Instagram page and scrolled through her followers, happy when I found Lindsay's name at the very bottom.

I clicked on her page and noticed she hadn't posted updates to her feed but instead to her stories. There were mainly photos of her and Amy doing random stuff, that smile always on her face, her blue eyes twinkling with happiness. Some were of sunsets, with her silhouette in the foreground and some with her and Amy.

For as long as I remembered, it had always been Lindsay and Amy. I understood their friendship and somehow felt guilty for being a threat. Amy was my sister, and I had no intentions of hurting her, but fuck, the ache I had for Lindsay magnified with each day of not having her. I didn't have the self-control to ignore it. I didn't want to, either.

Acknowledging what a selfish prick I was, I followed her account, intending to text her later. Until then, I got dressed and headed to school where I endured sociology and calculus classes before I made it to the gym for a workout session. Tonight would be the first game with me on the team, and I didn't want to mess it up.

In the middle of pumping weights with a teammate spotting me, Carter appeared, the trademark smirk on his face. With a jerk of his head, he told the other guy to get lost. I continued working, baring my teeth as I lifted twenty-five kilos.

"I see you're getting pumped for tonight," he observed.

"I imagine everyone is," I replied between breaths.

Carter nodded. "Got that right, but I bet *you* can't wait to dominate the field."

He assisted me with putting down the weights, and I got up. "It's whatever, I'm just gonna do my best." I reached for a towel to wipe my face.

He scoffed. "You know, for a man who's got all eyes on him, you don't seem to dig the attention." He searched my face as if looking for the reason there.

"Why? Because I'm not running around beating my chest with my fists? I asked.

"Not really. It's just that I've never seen you giving these girls the time of day," he said.

I frowned. "What are you saying, man?"

He shrugged and twisted his mouth. "Maybe you're hung up on someone."

"And maybe it's none of your business," I put in firmly. *Who the fuck does this guy think he is?*

Carter raised his hands in surrender. "Hey, I'm not tryna offend you or anything like that, but I've seen the vibe between you and Lindsay. I saw the way you looked up at her in the stands the other day."

My jaw tightened. "*What are you saying, Carter*?"

"That you've got a thing for your sister's best friend. I ran into her the other day, mentioned her boyfriend, and she seemed shocked. Looks like she isn't taken after all," he said.

"I've known Lindsay for years. I was only looking out for her," I defended.

"Okay, but wouldn't I be a good guy for her, Callaghan?" He raised a thick, challenging brow.

"We might be roommates, but I don't know you enough," I admitted firmly.

"Fair enough, but now that I know she's single, I'll shoot my shot again and again until I have her. You don't have a problem with that, right?"

Carter smirked, and my anger raised tenfold. I got up from the bench and stood, just as he did. Carter was a big guy, but I had the height and weight advantage. At this moment, nothing would've given me greater satisfaction than to beat the shit out of him.

"I don't want any trouble. Stay away from Lindsay," I warned.

Carter choked out a laugh and stroked his jaw, straightening his shoulders and sneering at me. "You just made the chase so much more interesting. See you on the field, roomie," he said, walking away.

I watched as he left the room, my anger still coursing through me, my hands balled into fists. Next time, I wouldn't be so lenient with him. Another talk about Lindsay, and I'd guarantee him a visit to the dentist.

"Everything okay, Austin?" a fellow team member asked in passing, a towel thrown over his head.

I managed a stiff nod. "Just fine, Cameron."

The slender guy nodded and was about to walk away when I called out to him. "What do you know about Carter?"

He turned back to look at me, then glanced in the direction Carter had gone. "Guy's a snake who loves being on top. He acts nice at first, and then his fangs start to show."

I nodded, realizing how right he was. Carter had been the perfect roommate for the first couple of days, and then he changed into someone else completely. He proved to be an asshole with each passing day, and after today, I had a feeling he would get worse.

"He gets pissier every year when Coach appoints someone else as Captain. It's his dream to lead the team, and I imagine with you here; he sees you as another threat."

I scoffed. "Mathews is a great captain, and I'm not the least bit interested in that role." If only they knew I wasn't even interested in football anymore.

Cameron shrugged. "In other news, there's a party at my place tonight if we win. I'll text you the address."

I nodded. "Sure thing." We bumped fists; then he left me to my thoughts.

I never thought my biggest threat would be my roommate, but here I was, faced with being on defense. I didn't mind Carter on the field; I just didn't want him near Lindsay. She was mine. Only mine. If he didn't want to back off, I'd make him regret the day he set eyes on her.

Chapter 7

Lindsay

FROM MY SEAT IN THE cafeteria during lunch, I saw Amy approaching, her lips set in a grim line as she came toward me. Things were still a little tense from our last argument, but we were still on speaking terms.

She slid onto a chair and dropped her food on the table. "Can we please get back to normal? I miss being able to talk to you about every little thing, and that hasn't been the case lately."

I smiled. "Of course. I miss that too, Ames."

Amy sighed heavily. "Good, 'cause there's a game tonight, and I want you there with me."

"I know. I was wondering when you'd ask," I smirked.

Amy's brows raised at me. "Since when you were interested in football?"

I grinned. "I mean, I'm not deaf or blind. Everyone's talking about the big game, plus the flyers are all over social media with Austin's face plastered on the front."

"True. So it starts at six—"

"I know that," I interrupted with another smirk.

She rolled her eyes at me, then continued. "And there's a party afterwards that you're totally coming to."

I opened my mouth, but before I spoke, Amy cut me off. "Before you say no, we'll be in good hands. Austin will be there, and so will Jason," she said, referring to her new boyfriend.

"No. I won't be a third wheel," I replied, shaking my head vigorously.

Amy clasped her hands in a prayer pose. "Come on, Linds, pleaaasseee!"

I mustered a sigh. As always, her puppy-dog stare did me in. "Ok, fine."

"I don't mean to sound like a broken record, but you need to come out of your shell. We only live once, and we won't get this experience ever again," she advised.

"True, but I'm quite happy as is," I said.

"Nothing wrong with being happier." She winked, and I smiled.

"Speaking of which, Jason says Carter, Austin's roommate has a thing for you," she grinned.

I rolled my eyes. "He made that clear in the cringiest way possible."

Amy's mouth fell open. "Really? When?"

"After our fight, I went to the café on campus and bumped into him. Turns out he liked me without even knowing a single thing about me," I said, suppressing an eye-roll.

Amy laughed. "You know how shallow guys are, Linds, but Carter is a hottie. I say you give him a chance."

"Not a chance in hell. Carter isn't really my type."

Amy raised a brow and eased back in her chair, surprise etched on her face. "So you do have a type. Do tell."

I immediately regretted saying anything. I shrugged and cleared my throat. "I guess I like them taller."

"Ooh. Well, he's a little on the short side isn't he?" she said as she placed her hand over her mouth and laughed. I joined in.

AMY AND I CHATTED FOR a bit until she left for a class. I was on my way back to the dorm when my phone rang. Seeing my mom's name on the screen triggered a swift intake of breath. I answered with a quick press of the answer button.

"Hey, Mom."

"Hey, Sweetheart, how are you?" Mom's weary voice greeted me.

"I'm good, Mom. Is everything okay?"

There was a small silence. "Yes, honey, how's school?"

I sidestepped two cheerleaders barreling down the corridor. "It's going great. I have Amy here, so it's not all bad."

"That's great. How's she?"

"She's okay. You know Amy. Where's Dad?" I asked, observing her quiet background.

"Beats me." She sighed. "He's probably doing what he does best; cheat." She laughed casually as if it didn't bother her, but it tugged at my heartstrings, bringing tears to my eyes.

For years, I thought my parents were the most perfect couple in the world. Dad was always home for dinner, we took family vacations together, holidays were always a great celebration. Until I stopped by his office after school one day. I was thirteen years old back then, but I still realized there was something wrong with Dad's assistant pulling down her skirt and Dad doing his zipper when I entered his office. He took me out to a jewelry store that afternoon, and I was so excited about the mood bracelet I'd always wanted I thought little about his warning not to tell Mom what I'd seen. I didn't need to tell her anything, though. I overheard her on a phone call a few months later, telling Amy's mom about makeup she found on Dad's clothes and the private investigator who discovered Dad's many affairs.

Mom took to alcohol instead of kicking Dad out. The family traditions continued until they slowly faded. Now, we were three strangers living in a huge house.

"Mom, why don't you guys just get a divorce?" I asked, my voice cracking. "This isn't healthy."

She sighed. "I've gotten used to his cheating, honey. We don't love each other anymore, and we've both accepted that, but it's better to stay married than apart. There are certain perks I don't want to give up, and Derek knows that too."

I swallowed the lump in my throat and blinked back the tears, not understanding her actions one bit. I'd rather live alone than endure such a miserable life.

"Just keep focused, Lindsay. These college guys will cross your path, and you might even think you're in love, but it's not really love. Next thing you know, you're married to an asshole with a kid who doesn't deserve the misery."

"Mom, I'm just fine," I whispered, almost biting my tongue with the lie.

She sniffed on the other end. "I'm sorry – I've completely ruined your day, but sometimes, I have no one to talk to, and I'm just surrounded by all these...fake people." She sighed heavily. "Sometimes, I'm tired of keeping up appearances, y'know."

"I'm sorry, Mom. I wish I was home so we could talk and go out for dinner or something..."

"Oh, honey, I know, and it's fine... I'm just a mess right now." She inhaled deeply. "But listen to me, okay? Don't make the same mistake I did. Don't fall in love until you've lived a little. Men will distract you, and for some, you'll always be inferior. The last thing I'd want for you is to live in someone's shadows like I did." She choked a sob, and the tears finally fell from my eyes. I quickly brushed them away, clearing my vision as I climbed the stairs.

"Okay, Mom," I muttered shakily.

She cleared her throat. "Oh, sweetie, you must think I'm a mess."

I shook my head, even though she couldn't see me. "I think you're the strongest person I know, and I admire you for it," I croaked.

She choked on a sob on the other end. "I love you so much. I don't know what I'd do without you," she cried.

"I love you too, Mom." It took great effort not to cry with her. Someone needed to show strength in that moment.

"I'll talk to you later, honey. I don't want to keep you any longer, and I'm sorry for piling this on you."

It's okay, Mom, just... take care of yourself, okay?"

"Okay, sweetie."

I ended the call and pulled in a shaky breath, trying my hardest to collect myself. From the moment I saw her name on the screen, I knew it would break us down – her, mostly. Mom and Dad had been together for ages. They met in college where he was the popular kid, and she was the shy bookworm. He chased her hard, and she gave in. A year after graduation, they had me. We enjoyed a few decent years until things went downhill, then I watched as the love faded from their eyes.

Only a fool would dismiss the similarities with me and Austin. It was a huge reg flag, a writing on the wall I couldn't ignore.

That evening, I struggled to find something to wear to the party, majorly because there was a high chance that I'd see Austin, and I wanted to look my best. I shouldn't be trying to impress him, but I couldn't help myself. Not after that kiss that had filled me with longing ever since.

I wanted him. There was no doubt how much I craved him. I hated the obstacles in our way. All that logic that I'd mustered was now gone with the wind. Austin was everything I shouldn't want in a guy, yet he was everything I craved.

Huffing a sigh, I dug through my closet and pulled out a pair of denim shorts and a crop top I'd bought on impulse—and with Amy's prodding— months ago. I bit my lips as I inspected each piece. Wearing this would turn heads for sure, but I didn't want the attention. Only Austin's.

The doorknob suddenly rattled, and in the next second, Amy stepped inside. Her gaze immediately moved to the clothes in my hand, and I moaned mentally, bracing myself for her pushing.

Her face lit up as she moved toward me. "OMG, seems like that talk we had earlier worked. You're definitely wearing this!"

"Yeah, I don't think so," I said, throwing them to the side.

Amy picked up the shorts as soon as they left my hands. "You sure are! These shorts are sexy, perfect for the after party."

I sighed. "I swear, after tonight, I'll be sleeping for a whole week."

She laughed. "True, but I'm so very excited, you can't imagine."

"I wonder why?" I quipped.

"Well, for one, this is Austin's first game. Also, this will officially be our first college party."

"Ugh. Don't remind me."

"Don't be a Debbie Downer. I'm gonna take a shower, and then we can leave after." She dropped the shorts on my bed. "Don't even think about picking out anything else."

"Yes, Mother."

Amy giggled in response, and I managed a smile, keeping my fingers crossed that tonight wouldn't be a complete disaster.

AN HOUR LATER, AMY and I headed to the stadium in matching outfits, although I'd slung a jacket over mine, feeling self-conscious as soon as I pulled it on. Scores of fans had already arrived, their respective flags high as they chatted and cheered. I pulled my jacket closer, leaving only my legs exposed.

Once inside, I squinted, taking in the bright lights and the hum of noises that surrounded me. Most of the stands were full, and I anxiously searched for a spot for me and Amy.

"Come on, Austin reserved some seats for us," Amy said, pulling at my hand and leading us down the steps toward the front.

The players were already in their respective areas, and I could see the Bruins gathered right in front of us.

Jason spotted Amy and waved as he ran up to the fence. "Hey babe," he greeted Amy. I smiled when he waved to me.

"To the side," he said, referring to our reserved spot. He pointed to confirm.

"Thanks, babe," Amy said, blushing as Jason smiled and ran back to his team.

"Already calling each other babe, huh?" I teased as we made our way to the seats.

She giggled. "What can I say; we're on the same page."

We got settled in, my eyes searching the field for Austin, but he couldn't be missed. He was the tallest, commanding everyone's attention as they huddled around him, listening to what he had to say. My heart picked up pace for some strange reason I couldn't quite comprehend. I narrowed it down to the 'Austin effect.'

I wished things weren't so complicated, but I just couldn't see where it would work out for us.

Just then, he looked up to the crowd, his gaze searching the space before our eyes locked, and I held my breath. The tiniest smile lifted the corners of his lips, and he raised his hand, giving me a huge wave. Timidly, I managed a smile and waved back, watching the way his grin broadened.

A team member touched him, and his attention returned to the field. I still wore a smile when my gaze shifted and met with Carter's. His expression told me he'd witnessed the exchange between Austin and I – the blush on my face – but then a smile popped up on his face, and he waved at me as well.

With a bit of hesitance, I waved back, sinking further into my chair and glancing back at Austin, whose jaw visibly clenched as he glared at Carter.

Oh, boy.

I glanced at Amy to see if she'd noticed, but she was busy chatting with a group of girls sitting on her side. *Whew!*

"I swear, your brother is such a hottie. What I wouldn't do to climb that stallion," the girl right beside her giggled. My brows furrowed as I leaned to inspect her, then swallowed the sudden lump in my throat.

She was stunning. Long, dark hair, clear brown eyes, and clothes that barely covered her private parts but showed her gorgeous body. Would Austin go for someone like her? I couldn't help but wonder. Someone so stunning, sexy and confident. She was exactly his type, right?

"I mean, he's single. Nothing wrong in shooting your shot," Amy replied. Her response felt like betrayal, although I knew it was all in my head. Amy had no idea I had a thing for her brother.

"I hear there's a party tonight. Maybe I can approach him there."

"You should, but get there early. I have feeling there will be a long line," Amy advised.

I never thought I'd experience jealousy, but the emotion that coursed through me was exactly that. It had to be. It was coupled with anger and sadness, and I wanted to sit and pout for the rest of the game.

But as soon as the game started, I perked up in my seat, attentive as ever, my eyes never leaving Austin, who I knew was the most pressured on the team. I knew little about the sport, but I knew the basics.

As it boiled down to the end, the Bruins had a lead of five points, and a deep tension filled the entire stadium. Austin had the ball, and though he had a clear path to hand it over to Carter, he didn't. I glanced at Amy, who seemed just as confused as I was, then I turned my attention to the field again, where Austin was running at high speed, knocking guys out of his way and dodging some while others were at his tail, grabbing after him.

I held my breath and bit my lips on the edge of my seat as I watched with a bouncing heart. The stadium exploded into cheers when he ran over the opponent's end zone with the ball clutched in his hand.

I bolted from my chair and shouted, my hands stinging as I clapped. Amy hugged me, and we both jumped around with the rest of the stadium doing the same.

I thought the grin wouldn't leave my face, but as the game ended and the celebrations died down, I saw Carter punch Austin's shoulder, making him stumble.

I gasped, my hands over my mouth as I watched the scene that caught everyone's attention. Austin advanced on him, about to strike when a few team members intercepted. Austin shrugged them off, peeled off his helmet and flung it to the ground before storming off the field with his teammates behind him.

"What the fuck is Carter's problem?" Amy hissed. "He really doesn't want to get on Austin's bad side."

I sighed, hoping their fight had nothing to do with me.

Chapter 8

Austin

I gritted my teeth so hard, I thought they'd shatter in my mouth as fire coursed through my veins. My body ran hot, my heart racing in my chest. It wasn't adrenaline from winning; it was from wanting Carter's head on a stake.

I slammed my fist into the locker, causing a slight dent and wishing it was Carter's face instead. The coach and a few others on the team came in, and then Carter followed behind. I immediately lunged at him again, but two tight ends stopped me.

"What's the fucking problem, guys?" Coach Johnson demanded gruffly.

Carter scoffed. "Were you blind, Coach? That asshole could have cost us the game!" he exclaimed.

"If it weren't for me, you'd all have your tails between your asses right now. Try another fucking stunt like that again, and I'll make sure it's your last!" I growled, still attempting to reach him despite being restrained.

"I thought we were a team, but this guy abandoned the playbook and decided to make it a one-man show," Carter spat, his hands curled into fists. I fucking wished he'd try.

"A win is a win," a wide receiver said. "We haven't had that in a while, Carter."

"Are we going to turn a blind to his bullshit because he gave us a win? No way in hell!" Carter exclaimed, banging his fist against the locker.

"Can you all calm the fuck down?" Coach Johnson thundered. "The only thing we should be doing is celebrating, not fighting. Carter is right, we're all one team, and we should play like it. Callaghan, a reporter is outside to see you; you should get going."

I tugged myself out of my teammates' grip and moved past Carter, hanging on to all the restraint I had.

"Tell Lindsay I'll see her at the party," he teased, and unable to help myself, I spun around, swinging my fist, which instantly connected with his jaw. He stumbled before falling to the floor, his hand covering the gnash on his lip.

"Say her name in your filthy mouth again, and you'll regret it," I warned before I turned and left, ignoring the murmurs behind me.

My hatred towards Carter stemmed solely off him having his eyes on Lindsay. She was my woman, whether or not she realized it. I'd be damned if I let that slimy little snake get near her.

After talking to several reporters, I drove to the beach house and quickly showered and changed before heading to Cameron's party. Of course, Carter would be there, and I'm sure he'd try to make a move on Lindsay, especially since he realized I had a thing for her. Spiteful bastard.

I entered the mansion, pushing through the enthusiastic crowd. They parted like the Red Sea when they saw me. Whistles and squeals greeted me, and I stopped to take a few photos with the ladies before making my way through the rest of the crowd, searching for Lindsay.

Finally, I spotted her on the stairs nursing a drink as she hugged her shoulder with one hand. I paused to gape at her, unable to believe my own eyes. She wore a crop top that clung to her like a second skin, exposing her flat tummy and hinting at the flare of her hips that flowed gracefully into ripped denims that barely covered her ass. Her long slender legs were exposed, sinfully tempting, and the thought of trailing my hands along them caused a stirring in my groin.

She wore her hair down, golden as the sunshine, the lighting above her casting an angelic glow over her head that left me speechless. I was just about to head over when I noticed Amy sitting on the other end, and I realized they were having a conversation. I decided to hang back for a while, moving to a table in the center of the room to pour myself a drink.

"Congrats on the game, Austin," a soft feminine voice said behind me.

I turned to find a pretty brunette with a seductive smile on her lips, her sultry brown eyes traveling the length of me.

"Thanks," I replied, taking in her tight leather top that almost pushed her boobs out her chest.

"I'm Stella, by the way," she said, pushing out her hand.

I hesitated before I took it in mine and offered a smile. "Nice to meet you."

"The pleasure is all mine," she mused, shimmying closer to me.

I cleared my throat, glancing up the stairs where Lindsay was. My gaze met hers, but she quickly turned her attention back to the conversation with Amy.

"So... I've been meaning to talk to you for a minute," Stella continued, her long eyelashes fluttering. "You're quite a busy one, aren't you?"

"Comes with the territory, doesn't it?" I replied, and she giggled.

"Must be nice, being such a superstar." She ran her fingers up my arm, the action making me cringe. It spoke volumes of how much I'd changed, especially within the last year. The old Austin wouldn't hesitate to take her up on the subliminal offer she'd been giving me. I recognized the signs of an easy woman. One jerk of my head, and we'd be heading to a bedroom upstairs.

But that was the old me. New Austin only had eyes for one girl.

Stella pulled her phone and typed something in it. "I just followed you on Instagram. You don't mind if I text, do you?"

I looked back to the stairs and saw Amy leaving with Jason. Lindsay still stood there, hugging her shoulder while taking a sip of her drink. She caught my stare, cut her eyes at me, then descended the stairs and headed outside.

I turned to Stella. "Er, I'm sorry, I've got to go."

"But you didn't follow me back!" she exclaimed as I made a quick escape.

Once outside, I searched the grounds for Lindsay but couldn't see her anywhere with the crowd that surrounded me. I moved farther outside and saw her walking toward the gate, and relief overcame me. As I headed in her direction, a guy stopped in front of her, his gaze trailing along every inch of her.

Oh, hell to the fucking no.

Gritting my teeth, I approached with quick strides and reached for Lindsay's hand, pulling her away. The asshole glared at me, but he knew better than to try me. I uncurled my fist when he gave me a curt nod and went on his way.

"What the hell is your problem?" Lindsay snapped, tugging her hand loose.

"*What the hell* are you wearing?" I asked, taking in her outfit, trapped between the desire to cover her up with a sheet or rip that pair of sexy shorts off her.

"Excuse me? I wear whatever the hell I want to!" she exclaimed.

"You're only attracting assholes. Have you seen the way they've been looking at you?"

"Clearly," she snapped back as she raised a brow and crossed her arms. "You can have girls throwing themselves at you, but I can't talk to guys?"

"That girl back there was just congratulating me on the game," I defended.

"I bet she was. You usually give your number to everyone who congratulates you?"

I couldn't help my smile. "Are you jealous, Lindsay?"

She rolled her eyes and moved off. "Don't flatter yourself."

I ran up behind her, grabbing her arm and forcing her to stop. "Let's go somewhere private," I suggested.

Lindsay's brows furrowed. "Are you for real right now?"

"Yes, I am."

She sighed. "Austin—"

"Yes, it's a risk, but it's one I'm willing to take. I need you, Lindsay." I took her other arm, pulling her close to me. Lindsay took a deep, shuddering breath, but she didn't ease away. "Tell me you don't want me too."

"God, Austin..."

"Just say the words, Lindsay, and I'll walk away."

She licked her lips, making me more eager to have her. "Just allow us this one chance." I didn't care how desperate it made me. I'd gladly drop to my knees and beg if it meant being in Lindsay's life.

Another sigh from her and she threw her head back, exposing her beautiful throat. I suppressed the urge to run my tongue along that spot, kissing her jaw, her cheeks, my hands gripping her ass—

Lindsay gently squeezed my hand, cutting the filthy thoughts from going any further. I almost punched the air in triumph when she whispered, "Okay."

Chapter 9

Lindsay

When Amy and Jason left the party early, my only plan was to return to the dorm and go to bed. I couldn't stand being in the same room with Austin and the women throwing themselves at him.

Especially that bimbo, Stella.

From my spot on the stairs, I tried not to stare as they talked. Well, Stella mostly talked. I bit back my fury when she ran her fingers up his arm and moved closer to him. A flood of jealousy filled me when she pulled out her cell phone.

Taking a final sip from my cup, I dropped it in the trash can, then moved off, an ache in my stomach. I didn't expect Austin to chase me. His grip on my arm took me by surprise. I turned around, and he stood there, eyes filled with the same fury I'd felt earlier. He shot a glare at Troy, the guy who approached me earlier, asking for a date. Troy took the hint at once, and from the corner of my eye, I watched as he moved to another girl.

Ugh. Guys.

Austin's comment on my outfit should have pissed me off; instead, it made me hot all the way to my toes, especially from how intensely he stared at me. I shouldn't have said yes to being alone with him, but who was I kidding? I didn't have it in me to say no to Austin. At least, not for long.

Whenever he came around, he triggered emotions I couldn't quite explain. Emotions that stripped my character, transforming me into a horny, confused mess. His touch always did me in; it was like something sparked when my skin met his, forming an entire force field around me.

He was my best friend's brother – completely off limits – but my body wanted him so badly, my mind and soul craved for him. I didn't have the self-control to resist him.

So, I took his hand, and we walked to his car. I was either too tipsy to care if anyone saw us or just too brave. Excitement coursed through me as I slid onto the leather seat in his car when he opened the door for me. I didn't know our destination, but it didn't matter. All I cared about was being with him. The consequences could wait.

We silently drove for a few minutes. There was a slight sexual tension that followed us along the coastline and into a gated beach community. Awareness filled my head when he reversed parked in front of the first house on the avenue. I recognized the family beach house right away from the photos Amy showed me. It was even more beautiful in real life, and it wasn't even daylight.

Austin got out and quickly walked around to my side, opening the door with a huge smile on his face. I couldn't help my own as I placed my hand into his outstretched one and got out.

"Welcome to my humble abode," he said, smirking.

I glanced at the two-story contemporary dwelling, complete with four bedrooms, five bathrooms, a giant living room and a view to die for. At least, that's how I remembered it from Amy's photos. "This is anything but humble," I replied, chuckling.

We headed inside, where the furniture was either pure white or made of glass. The only thing of color was the two-toned wood flooring and the oil paintings on the wall that created a bit of contrast.

"I didn't know you had access to this place," I said, looking around. Amy once told me her parents kept the keys to the beach house wherever they went.

"Yeah, surprisingly, my dad felt generous enough to leave me the keys, though he did make me promise not to host any parties here."

"Do you plan on staying here now that you and Carter aren't on good terms?" I asked, turning to look up at him.

His brows shot up. "How did you know about me and Carter?"

"That little fight after the football game. Remember?"

Austin groaned. "God. I can't believe you saw that."

"Everyone did. What was that all about?"

"He was pissed about something I did during the game," Austin said casually, but from the tension in his shoulders, I suspected that wasn't the entire truth. "Can I get you something to drink?"

It was a deliberate attempt to change the subject, but I shook my head. "I'm good. Can we head down to the beach?"

Surprise etched his features, and his face broke into a smile. "Oh, I like the sound of that. We can make a bonfire and get cozy," he suggested.

"Yeah, I can definitely use cozy right now," I replied. The thought of lying curled up next to him sounded like heaven to me.

Austin winked, and I just couldn't help my smile. My heart bubbled with happiness when he leaned in to kiss my cheek. He headed to the storeroom to grab logs while I carried a basket with blankets and a few cushions. We stopped a few yards from the shore, where it was dark, the only light coming from the house. Austin hastily stocked the logs, occasionally flashing me grins as he prepared the fire.

I clapped dramatically when he finally got the fire going and spread the huge blanket, which I sat on right away. Austin stood in front of me, a smile on his face as he reached down and grabbed the hem of his shirt before pulling it over his head. My mouth hung open, and my heart fluttered as I feasted my eyes on his toned chest, each ab carved to perfection with meaty, toned pecs.

"What are you doing?" I asked, though it was obvious.

"What does it look like, beautiful?" he said, hooking his hands into his waistband and pulling down his jeans. My heart hammered even faster, and I held my breath, watching unabashedly as he stripped down.

My cheeks burned when only his pair of boxers remained, the bulge in the front telling me he was just as excited about the impromptu strip tease as I was.

"I'm going for a swim, join me," he said.

I swallowed to soothe my parched throat. "You're crazy! That water must be freezing cold."

Austin shrugged, raking his fingers through his sandy blonde hair. "One way to find out," he said and, without another word, went running into the darkness. A huge splash echoed in the distance as he dove in, and I stood, wanting to see it all. He came up after a few seconds, his pearly whites glistening in the distance.

"Come on!" he shouted.

I bit my lips and analyzed the risks with my fingers on the waistband of my shorts. At the very least, I could get hypothermia. At the most, I could probably drown if the currents were too heavy.

You live only once, said the voice in my head, one that sounded ridiculously like Amy.

Damning it all to hell, I quickly pulled off my shorts, conscious of my cotton panties, wishing I'd worn something sexier. But the lust in Austin's eyes canceled my insecurity. Something powerful ran through me as he stared, drinking in every inch of me. I didn't lose my top because I wasn't wearing a bra, but it was light enough for the ocean.

Austin laughed when I screamed as my body contacted the ice-cold water. "Oh, my God, it's freezing!" I screeched.

"Just breathe," Austin said, pulling me closer to him.

The breath hitched in my throat as he circled his hands around the small of my waist, my body pressed against his. It felt so good, so right being in his arms. I didn't want to leave this place. I never wanted to let go.

Though the water was cold, Austin's touch soon warmed me up. We bounced in the water, our bodies stuck together like glue, the mist from our breaths mixing. I licked my lips, and Austin's eyes dropped there. I wanted him to kiss me, but it was obvious he wanted the green light. Ready to make the first move, I tipped sand between my toes and pressed my lips against his. They were a little cold upon contact, but they soon got warmer, especially when his tongue probed my mouth, his deep groan telling me how much he ached for this, too. The alcohol on his breath mixed with a minty flavor that made the kiss so delicious, and I didn't want it to end, especially when he deepened the strokes, gripping my ass, pressing me against his hard front.

I moaned, surprising myself by throwing my leg over his thigh. The action placed my pussy directly against his cock. Austin cursed as I dry-humped him, desire sending sparks running through me.

"I want you so fucking much, Lindsay," he said, voice husky with the same lust that burned me.

I swallowed hard hearing the words, already on cloud nine. "I want you, too," I confessed, pressing my lips against his once again for a mind-reeling kiss.

I gasped when Austin swept me off my feet and carried me out of the water. The wind pinched my skin, and I shivered, staring at his perfect face as he smiled down at me. He placed me on the blanket, and I reached for a towel to dry myself while Austin did the same. I grew nervous, but I didn't let it show. I wanted this. I needed him.

Austin joined me, taking my lips for another heated kiss that erased every nervousness and doubt. He propped me on his lap, my legs straddled around him with my pussy sitting right at his crotch. The fire cracked, and my sighs penetrated the silence as Austin kissed me with his large hands trailing down my back.

The longer we kissed, the hotter we became. One would not believe there was seventy-degree weather because of how sweaty we'd gotten. Austin's boner was in full effect, my panties soaked with my arousal for him. He adjusted a little, wrapped his hand around my waist and pressed me further against him. I moaned, my entire body tingling as I rolled myself against him.

"Use your words, Lindsay," Austin whispered. "Tell me what you want."

Heat filled my cheeks. This wasn't the time or place for shyness, but I couldn't help myself. "Austin..."

He chuckled. "I'm going to need more than that, babe. Tell me." He jerked against me, his crotch brushing my clit. I dug my nails into his shoulder with a moan. "Come on. Tell me."

"I want your cock, Austin," I breathed, wanting to hide my face in his shoulder.

He tipped my chin, forcing me to meet his eyes. "How deep do you want it?"

I searched his face, seeing the confidence there, yet something else stood out. Austin wanted me. He was just as desperate as I was, just as anxious. Knowing that, it gave me a boldness that made me say, "I want every single inch."

Austin let out a strangled breath, then muttered, "Fuck," before kissing me so hard I lost every coherent thought.

He flipped me onto my back, my chest rising and falling hard, my nipples poking through the clinging crop top. Austin's Adam's apple visibly bobbed as he stared down at me, propped on his knees with beads of water still trailing down his body. I didn't need to ask what his thoughts were because his eyes told me everything. It still amazed me that a guy like Austin wanted me.

Wordlessly, he got up and removed his boxers, and I watched with bated breath as his cock sprang out, bobbing a few times before it settled, pointing at me. I licked my lips, my heart racing so fast I feared I'd pass out. Never once did I consider his size, but it amazed me that he was so huge. Would he even fit?

He lowered himself to his knees again and hooked his fingers in the waistband of my panties before pulling them down my legs. Feeling a little self-conscious, I snapped my legs shut.

"Relax, Lindsay. There's nothing to be afraid of. You're simply the most beautiful thing I've ever seen. I'm going to make this good for you."

Believing his promise, I nodded and tried to relax. Austin slowly pried my legs apart and swallowed visibly as he stared between my thighs. My face burned from his scrutiny, and I thanked the stars I'd shaved a few days ago.

"Yeah, you really are fucking beautiful," he mumbled. "Every inch of you."

Austin positioned himself between my legs and trailed his hand along each slender column, then up my hips and toward my stomach. I released a shuddering breath when he ran his thumb over my clothed nipple. A shiver ran through me as he continued to rub them both into circles.

"Austin..." I managed, almost breathlessly. Tension rose, leaving my body right, desperate for release.

"I want to make every inch of you feel good, Lindsay. Let me."

I nodded timidly and moaned as he continued, my pussy clenching when he pinched each nipple. He rolled the top over my breasts and tucked it, so it stayed in place. His eyes traveled from one mound to the other, incredulity in his eyes as he inspected each with equal fascination.

"You're perfect, baby," he said, his voice low as he took both into his hands and gently massaged each, pulling gently at my nipples.

I moaned and arched my back, succumbing to the pleasure, every inch of me so incredibly sensitive, his touch sending me closer to the edge. He dipped his head and latched his mouth to the right breast while his hand massaged the other. A gasp left my lips as his warm mouth covered the nipple, suckling hard, then slowly circling, moving back and forth between each method.

My loud whimpers cut into the air when he bit my nipple, the pleasure-pain running up my spine. I writhed on the blanket, lost to the sensation, staring at the stars in the pitch-black night but not really focused on them. Nothing else mattered but the guy settled between my legs, his mouth doing things to my nipples I never imagined. My fingers raked through Austin's damp hair, gripping a handful when he suddenly slipped a finger into my warmth.

"Oh, God..." My hips jerked upwards, the pleasure increasing tenfold. It amazed me that a single finger could do so much. "Austin, that feels good."

"I can tell. You're so wet for me, baby," he growled, gently moving his finger back and forth. He didn't need to tell me how wet I was – I could hear it as his finger moved inside me.

"Oh, yes," I mewled when he added another that made me feel fuller than I'd ever been. With a few strokes, he easily left a wet trail of my arousal trail to my ass.

His pace grew faster, my pussy more welcoming with each stroke. Austin eased up from my breast and met my gaze. My cheeks burned as he looked at me while his fingers worked inside of me.

"I'm ready for you, Austin," I murmured, unable to bear the tension any longer. I want you inside me now."

Austin shook his head, still pumping me with his fingers. "Not yet, my love," he murmured back. "Almost."

My love. Those two words bowled me over for a moment, then I caught myself. *He's just aroused. There's no way he meant what I thought.*

The momentum built as he worked inside me, twisting his fingers, then gently stroking, going hard, then slowing down, all done with such precision that left my vision blurry and my body bucking as pleasure increased, spreading to every inch of me.

I grabbed Austin's arms, fucking his fingers. He kissed me hard on the lips as he moved within me. I squealed; my lips still stuck to his as my pussy tightened around his fingers. My body jolted and slammed against the blanket, my orgasm crashing through me like a hurricane.

"Austin!" I cried, unable to hold back.

"Yes, that's it, baby. Call my name," Austin ordered.

I'd never seen him so wild, so primal. The hunger in his eyes made me want to run out of fear he would destroy me with just a single stroke from his cock. Yet, I wanted to bury myself in him. I wanted him to possess me. To put his stamp on me.

I moaned against his lips and clutched him tight as his fingers gently slowed before slipping from inside me. A second later, Austin lifted them to my gaze, his two digits so drenched, they were dripping.

"*Now* you're ready," he said.

He pulled me up and hauled my top over my head, both of us now completely naked. My back hit the ground as he laid me down again, spreading my legs, readying me to take his length. I gasped as he rubbed the head against my entrance. His fingers didn't compare to his cock—David and Goliath, in this case. My body shivered as it glided over my clitoris. *Would it really fit?*

Austin suddenly stopped, throwing his head back with a loud groan, triggering a flare of panic inside me.

"Something wrong?" I asked.

"I forgot condoms," he replied, disappointment clear on his face.

I reached for the hand, giving him an assuring squeeze. "Don't worry; I want to feel all of you."

"Are you sure?" he asked.

I nodded. "Yes."

He huffed a slow breath, teasing my entrance with the tip of his cock. I can't promise it won't hurt at first, Lindsay, but I'll make it up to you," he said softly.

Tears filled my eyes at how sweet he was. I nodded, spreading my legs wider before Austin pressed himself inside me. I gasped from a sharp pain that shot through me. He paused, kissing my forehead and trailing his hand along my thigh, allowing me to get accustomed to his size.

"I feel so honored for this gift, Lindsay. I promise to make it worth your while," he said, kissing my mouth. I moaned as he moved inside me, filling me completely, my walls tight around him. Knowing he was inside me, that we had this connection at last, soothed every ache.

I wrapped my arms around his neck, meeting his lips as he gently resumed the pace, loosening my walls that clenched with each stroke.

Austin's breathing grew labored, and I could see him trying to restrain himself. I wanted to be brave enough to tell him to go faster, but I was still becoming accustomed to him inside of me. He eased up and pulled out, prying my legs further apart. His cock trailed down my pussy, scooping up every bit of wetness before he entered me again.

"Ohh, Austin... oh my God," I murmured, realizing he'd gone deeper but still not filling me. The pain faded, my pussy hugging him as he smoothly slid back and forth inside me. The squelching from his cock in my pussy made me blush, but it added to the appeal.

Soon, I relaxed, growing more confident with taking him, desire bubbling up inside me yet again. He moved faster now, making me spiral as his sweet cock hit my sensitive spots.

"I want all of you," I challenged breathlessly, and without another word, he sunk himself to the hilt.

I screamed, my nails digging into his muscular back, my walls convulsing as he hit a spot that sent sparks flying. Desperate to feel it again, my hands gripped his ass, and I pressed him deeper inside me, moaning when his cock rubbed that very sweet spot again.

My mouth fell open, and I looked to the stars again, but Austin took that as an opportunity to kiss me while he remained buried deep inside me.

"Ohh, this feels so good. You feel so good!" I exclaimed. He cupped my head with both hands and nibbled my lips, pulling back and filling me with a sharp thrust that knocked the wind out of me.

"You're perfect. So very perfect, Lindsay," Austin breathed, his hard, purposeful strokes making my head reel.

My nipples rubbed against his chest, sending more pleasure rupturing through me. Our bodies slid against each other like we were coated in butter, and my creamy pussy against his cock was the perfect cherry on top.

My legs grew numb, and I opened them wider, wanting every inch of Austin. "Faster," I begged, my breath jagged.

He complied but maintained the same hard strokes that made my eyes water.

"Fuck, I love the way you feel around me," Austin growled, digging deep, pushing me over the edge. My body quivered as another climax took over, my screams echoing on the empty beach.

Austin muttered a curse, his body stiffening. A few rough strokes, and he pulled out with a sexy grunt. My core squeezed at the emptiness, my body already missing his hard length. His eyes rolled back, his hips rocking as he emptied himself on my stomach. I sighed, feeling like I'd just won the lottery. This was simply the best day of my life.

Chapter 10

Austin

A flood of contentment filled me as I gazed down at Lindsay's sleeping body, a towel draped over her midsection, but the rest of her left completely naked. She was truly a work of art, and I smiled as a sudden thought came to me.

Lifting her in my arms, I carried her to the house, unable to take my eyes off her. She wore a peaceful countenance, and it pleased me that I was the reason she looked like that.

I'd had great sex before, but with Lindsay, our encounter stood out of this world. The connection between us made everything so much more intense, more pleasurable. I couldn't get enough.

After entering the bedroom, I placed her on the bed and rushed to the bathroom to get a warm washcloth. There, I wiped my essence from her, my hand running over every mouth-watering curve on her body.

It still amazed me how I had so much energy after fucking so hard and long, but I was fully awake, fully charged. Despite being so fulfilled minutes ago, I still ached for Lindsay, but she needed rest. This was her first time, and I wanted to go easy on her. I draped a blanket over her legs, leaving the rest of her exposed for my eyes only. The heat was on in the house, so she wouldn't be cold.

Pulling on a shirt, I made my way to the closet and retrieved my art supplies. I returned to find her shifting in bed, her eyes fluttering open. I stopped at the door, the supplies tucked behind me. I didn't want her to see them. Not right now.

I backed out of the room and placed them on a small table outside the door, then I rushed inside and climbed into bed with her.

"Austin," she muttered, her blue eyes sheltered by long, droopy lashes.

"I'm here; go back to sleep, baby," I whispered, kissing her lightly on the lips. She smiled as her eyes closed, sleep once again taking over.

When her breathing got steady, I hurried to get everything set up and positioned myself to the side of the bed, taking a photo before tracing her outline.

I spent three hours perfecting every curve, every perfect feature that Lindsay possessed until I grew weary. Deciding to call it a night, I joined her back in the bed and snuggled up to her, sweeping her in my arms while acknowledging how surreal this was.

It was around five am the following morning when Lindsay's shuffling woke me up. My eyes opened to see her walking away from the bed, heading to the bathroom, her slender hips swaying.

I smiled and waited for her to return. She soon did, a soft blush covering her cheeks when she saw me staring.

"Come here," I said, and she came over and nestled her warm body against me with a contented sigh. "Did you sleep well?"

"The best sleep I've had in a long time," she replied, and I couldn't help my grin. *Another point for me*. "How did you sleep?"

"I stayed up half the night watching *you* sleep."

Lindsay groaned and covered her face. "What? That's so embarrassing! I hope I didn't drool."

"You were perfect."

She leaned in to kiss me softly. "I'm glad last night happened."

"Me too."

Her cheeks reddened again, and she covered them with her hand, biting her lower lip. "I want to do it again," she said.

I grinned, covering her hand with mine and kissing her tenderly. "You don't have to say that twice," I replied, happy she was still naked. Easy access.

"I want to be on top," she whispered, her eyes dipping. I raised my brow, another part of my body also raising at the request.

"I have no complaints, babe. Do your thing."

I rolled over on my back, watching as Lindsay straddled me. She poised right above my throbbing dick, then slowly lowered herself onto it, moaning as her flesh captured every inch.

I clenched my teeth and reached for her firm breasts, squeezing them while Lindsay rode me. Her tight cunt massaged me, the nub of her clitoris occasionally running over my sensitive tip and making me moan.

Lindsay's eyes flew shut as she continued to pleasure us both, her pace getting faster as her juices lathered my cock. She leaned in to kiss me, a gasp escaping her lips just in time and allowing me to catch the sweetness of her breath.

"That's it, baby, fuck me," I grunted, my hips rising to match her strokes. I captured her lips again. She slowed on my cock while we sparred with our tongues, the arousal still raging rampantly inside me.

Lindsay flipped her shiny hair over her shoulders and raised her body to the tip of my cock, hovering, then slowly lowered herself on me again. Heat engulfed my entire body as my cock reunited with her magical pussy. Every second was sweet agony as her body consumed inch after inch, her pussy stretching even further to accept my girth.

Halfway, she paused and threw her head back, bouncing, her eyes closed, her tightness expanding for me. I lay back, watching my cock drilling her, disappearing and reappearing, coated with her juices, her pussy lips fluttering back and forth. Lindsay was a fucking champion for taking my monstrous cock like this.

I trailed my hand along her chest, and she shuddered, moving an inch further. I sighed heavily and reached for her hips, slowly pulling her down to take all of me in.

Lindsay looked down between us, her mouth agape as her pussy swallowed my length all the way to the base. My hands moved to her ass cheeks, and I squeezed hard just as she leaned over to kiss me. She moved again, my cock still buried to the hilt as she rotated her hips, bouncing faster with each second.

"You feel so good inside me," she said, her voice low and sultry.

I couldn't find the words to respond. I was too overwhelmed by the pleasure barreling through me. Lindsay rode harder, faster, my entire length escaping inside her over and over again. The smacks were loud in the room as she moved, her actions getting more chaotic – a mix of bouncing and rotating. Her release was on its way; I could feel how her pussy clenched each time my cock hit the back of her channel.

I gripped her hips and slightly raised her body while thrusting upward, filling her. The smacks grew even louder, and so did Lindsay's moans as her tight pussy clung to me. With one hard thrust, I buried myself completely and gripped onto Lindsay, holding her in place. Her scream came just as my growl echoed through the room.

As her walls hugged me, my cock swelled, releasing my cum deep inside her. She collapsed on top of me, our heavy breaths mixing as we tried to catch our breaths, basking in our release. After several minutes, my sodden cock slipped from her in a plop, followed by a dollop of my cum.

I kissed her clammy shoulders and held her tightly against me, never wanting to let her go. Ever.

Chapter 11

Lindsay

After recovering from that toe-curling encounter, I reached for my phone and checked to see if I'd gotten any messages. Luckily, there was none from Amy, but the time told me I had to get a move on.

"I should get going," I said, propping myself on my elbow and staring down at Austin's handsome face.

Austin reached for me, pulling me into his bulky arms. "I wish we could stay like this forever," he groaned.

I smiled. "Me too, but now it's back to reality," I reminded.

He gave a pout before easing himself up in the bed. "Speaking of reality, where do we go from here?" he asked, and my heart dipped.

If only I could ignore the complications and forget everything else but Austin. That was impossible, not worth imagining. Facing the truth hurt, but better to handle it now before we got too deep.

"I want to be with you, Lindsay. I want to make this official," Austin said, and my heart dropped to the floor of my stomach.

"Austin... we can't. Last night was amazing, but we can't make anything official. This can only stay between us. I'm sorry."

He nodded slowly as if processing the information. "Okay, but will it be that way forever?"

I swallowed. "We don't have to think about that for now. We can just take things one step at a time until we figure out where to go from here," I said, forcing a smile. I wanted to be with him more than anything, but deep down, I knew this could never happen again.

"Lindsay, I already know where I want this to go," he said. "I want to be with you."

"Austin, don't make this more difficult than it is, please..."

He sighed heavily. "Okay, fine. Sure, this can be our little secret." He smiled, but this time it didn't reach his eyes.

I leaned in and kissed him, then pressed my forehead against his. "Just give me some time, okay?"

He nodded before capturing my lips again. "Okay, what do you say about tonight at six?"

I grinned. "I'll text you."

"You don't have my number!" he exclaimed as I slid off the bed and grabbed my clothes.

"I have your Instagram," I reminded as I pulled on my shorts and my crop top. I pulled my hair in a messy bun on the top of my head before I went over to Austin and kissed him one last time.

"I could drive you back to campus," he smirked.

I rolled my eyes. "You're not funny." The last thing I wanted was for Amy to see him dropping me off. "I already ordered an Uber."

As if on cue, a sudden horn sounded in the driveway. Austin pouted, then pulled me in for a quick peck. "I miss you already."

The sincerity in his eyes made me want to pinch myself. This was a dream, right? It had to be.

REALITY HIT ME AS THE car sped away from the beach house. It was like being transported into another world, one that didn't feel as glorious. There was no happiness, no satisfaction, nothing but the startling fact that I had to face my best friend again, knowing I'd betrayed her. Bile rose at the back of my throat, but I quickly swallowed and pulled in a breath to collect myself.

Austin was an amazing guy, superb in bed. I didn't want to walk away from him, but Amy meant much more to me. I just couldn't fathom the thought of losing her. In fact, I couldn't lose either of them. Like I'd told Austin, last night would remain a secret between us until I figured out a way to find a balance. For now, I wanted to keep making careful moves.

I returned to an empty dorm. Seeing Amy's neatly made bed left me relieved. She'd obviously spent the night with Jason, and I was happy about not having to explain where I was last night. Quite frankly, I didn't have the slightest clue how I'd respond.

I used the opportunity to take a quick shower, inspecting myself in the mirror for any love bites. I was happy when I found none but felt myself blush when it triggered memories of the previous night. Austin's skilled fingers on my body, his cock inside me, those sexy sounds that left his mouth...

It was just one taste, and I was already addicted. Staying away would be much harder than I thought. No, totally impossible. I needed to be with him again.

After leaving the bathroom stall, I quickly got dressed while planning the rest of my day. A sudden rattling at the door made me jump, and in the next second, it flew open, and Amy sailed inside.

"Hey, Babycakes!" she greeted me, throwing her coat over a chair.

"Hey yourself." My eyes narrowed at her, taking in her flushed cheeks and messy hair. "Someone had a good night, didn't they?"

Amy stretched, a Cheshire-cat grin on her face. "The best. Jason wore me out last night!"

"Ok. TMI. Say no more," I said, reaching for my hairbrush.

"Hey, where are you off to?" she asked, meeting my eyes in the mirror.

"The library. Thought I'd get some studying done."

"Good for you." She wrapped her arms around me from behind, giving me a gentle squeeze. "I'm sorry I ditched you last night. I was afraid you'd be mad."

"It's fine," I said as I returned my gaze to the mirror. "I'm happy you had fun."

"'Fun' is an understatement. Her face lit up with another grin. "Jason is a beast. I'm amazed that I'm walking right now."

"TMI!" I called out, and she laughed.

"Linds, I swear, you don't know what you're missing."

Oh, if only you knew, Ames, I thought.

"It's time to hop off that virgin train," she continued.

Already off, my friend.

Through the mirror, I watched as she stared at my bed with a sudden frown on her face. "You came home last night, right?"

I swallowed hard as guilt and nervousness took over. "Er, yeah... why would you ask me that?"

She gestured to my bed. "I've never seen you make your bed so soon after getting up. It looks just like it did before we left last night."

Oh, shit. Amy was always an observant one. "I don't know what you mean. I literally made the bed half an hour ago. Besides, if I didn't sleep here, where else would I have been? It's like I have any other friends."

Amy nodded. "I see what you mean."

Guilt left a terrible taste in my mouth as I resumed brushing my hair. If Amy ever found out I lied to her, our friendship would never be the same.

Well, she won't find out, I told myself. *Austin and I made a vow, and we won't break it. I hope.*

"So... Jason told me the weirdest thing last night," Amy began.

I placed the brush down and turned to face her. "Yeah?"

"Yeah, so apparently, the whole Austin-and-Carter feud got extended to the locker room the other day. Austin punched Carter when he made a comment about you," she said, her forehead wrinkling.

My heart bounced. "Me? What comment?"

"That he'd see you at the party or something like that," She shook her head as if trying to summon more information. "Anyway, Jason said Carter's an ass and that's why I think Austin got all protective ..."

I swallowed the lump in my throat. "Yeah, er, I guess so–"

"It's kinda sweet isn't it? Knowing we have a big brother looking out for us," she said with a smile.

Oh, boy. I don't know how to tell you this, Ames, but I don't see Austin as a big brother. Not even close.

"It is," I said out loud, moving toward my bed and grabbing my bag. "Listen, I should get going. Maybe we could catch up later?"

"Oh, um... Jason wants to take me out tonight, so I might not be here," she said, making an apologetic face.

Her response would have upset me if I hadn't been planning on seeing Austin later, but this was the perfect opportunity, though I felt like crap for being excited over it.

"Oh, okay. Have fun," I replied, my voice slightly squeaky.

Amy narrowed her eyes at me. "I kinda expected you'd be upset," she said. "Why aren't you?"

I pulled in a breath. "I don't want to rain on your parade or ruin any of your 'college experience,'" I made air quotes, and she scoffed. "I still trust you'll make great choices, regardless."

She relaxed visibly. "Well, thank you, sweetie. I appreciate you."

"Right back at you, hon. Gotta run," I said, kissing her cheeks, then grabbed my keys and left the room.

The door closed behind me, and I could breathe again, some of the guilt easing from my shoulders. I tried not to think about my sin and planned on doing the very thing I told Austin I'd do: take it one step at a time.

Which reminded me of what Amy said earlier about Austin and Carter. Austin didn't mention a fight that involved me, and while Amy only saw it as him being protective, others might not see it that way. All it required was one suspicious person, and our secret would exist no more.

My phone beeped with an incoming text message. Speak of the devil.

I miss you already, Austin's text read. *I hope we're on for later.*

I bit my lips as my fingers hovered over the keyboard. *Yeah, we are,* I texted back.

Can't wait, came his response. *I can already feel my lips on your soft skin.*

I groaned as I read his words, the visual already arousing me. Not knowing how to respond, I tucked the phone in my bag and made my way to the library, where I spent the next two hours trying to focus on my assignment. A huge feat, considering my constant thoughts involved riding Austin, pleasure bubbling up inside me as his cock filled me.

By some miracle, I got my work done, then headed back to my dorm, getting ready to see Austin. My phone rang as I slipped on a cute maxi dress with thin straps. It was Mom. I sucked in a weary breath and cleared my throat before I answered.

"Hey, Mom," I greeted, trying to sound perky for her.

"Hey, sweetie, how are you?"

"I'm good, I guess. Just getting ready to head out."

"Listen, sweetheart, I was wondering if you could come home on the weekend. I really miss you. You're the only one who truly understands what's going on with me."

I raked my fingers through my hair, knowing how depressing the weekend would be if I said yes. "I don't know, Mom.... er, I have several upcoming assignments and–"

"Please. I'm just so lonely here," she said softly, then choked on a sob.

I gave in with a face palm, bracing myself for an unpleasant weekend. "Ok, ok, Mom, I'll be there."

"Thank you, sweetie. I love you so much."

"I love you too, Mom."

The call ended a minute later, and I swallowed the lump in my throat, willing myself not to cry. I had no problem visiting Mom, I just knew it wouldn't go well. I didn't want to spend my weekend listening to her gripe about Dad coming home late or not answering his phone when she called. I didn't want to hear about the new woman he'd been seen with. Mom would rather live a miserable life than get a divorce, and I didn't understand it. What did she have to lose?

Sweeping the gloomy thoughts aside, I resumed getting ready. Knowing I'd see Austin in half an hour cheered me up a whole lot. I smiled to myself, slipping on a pair of strappy sandals before heading to the beach house, ready for another fix.

Chapter 12

Austin

Ever since Lindsay left earlier, I'd been working on the painting I started the night before. A couple of long hours later, I was finally finished and had just barely managed to shower and get a few things in order before she arrived.

At approximately 6 pm, I heard a car pull up in the driveway and knew it had to be her. I checked my reflection in the mirror on my bedroom wall, tugging at the hem of my shirt. I mussed up my hair a little as a knock came at the door.

I went to open up, my heart doing a little flip when I saw her. I couldn't get over how beautiful she'd become with the most commanding set of blue eyes I'd ever seen. Her body seemed curvier and sexier each time I saw her.

"Hey, you," she said, a shy smile on her face.

It was then I realized how nervous I'd been, wondering if she'd come back. I didn't miss the tentativeness in her eyes that morning. She was on the fence, and I didn't blame her. "I'm glad you came," I said.

"Me too," was her simple reply.

Our gazes held for a second before I quickly moved to the side to allow her entry. She stepped inside, and I closed the door behind her before doing the one thing I'd been dreaming of since she left. I kissed her like a man starved, my tongue tangling with hers as she kissed me back with the same desperate response.

"I hope you're hungry," I said once I slightly withdrew from her.

"For what exactly?" She smiled, and my cock stirred.

"Actual food now, but definitely dessert later." My eyes dropped to her front.

She blushed, pushing at my shoulder. "You're something else, you know that?"

I chuckled, resting my hand on the small of her back as I directed her to the porch out back where I'd set up a candlelit dinner. Lindsay's mouth fell open as she gazed over the display.

"This is... wow," she breathed.

"I remembered that you liked Chinese food, so I ordered your favorite and er – hot wings – everybody likes hot wings. And..." I lifted a bottle of sweet red. "Wine. This is my mom's favorite, so I figured maybe you'd like it, but I also got coke just in case you don't." I rattled on, suddenly so nervous about her response. All that mattered was getting it right. I wanted to please her in every way.

She giggled. "Austin, this is perfect." She leaned in and kissed me softly on the lips, filling me with relief.

I pulled out her chair, and she sat, then waited for me to fill our plates before saying another word. "It didn't occur to me before now, but don't you have practice today?"

"Coach gave us a day off since we won yesterday," I replied, taking up a forkful of food.

"Great. I don't want you missing practice on my behalf. Also, I don't remember telling you congrats on winning the game. You did well."

I couldn't contain my proud grin. I hated playing, but knowing Lindsay was in the stands made it much more bearable. "Thanks."

"I have a feeling you'll have no problem getting drafted to the NFL," she said with pride in her eyes.

I scoffed. "I hope not."

Her head drew back as she frowned. "What do you mean?"

"I don't plan on playing football for the rest of my life, Lindsay," I confessed.

Her brows furrowed. "I thought you loved the game."

I shrugged. "To a degree. It's really my dad's dream to play professionally, not mine. I'm the biggest cliché there is." I choked out a laugh. "My dad missed the opportunity back in his day, and now he wants to live vicariously through me." I shook my head.

"Wow, I didn't know that. I'm sorry, Austin."

I reached for her hand and gave it a gentle squeeze. "Nothing to be sorry about. I'm just trying to muster enough courage to tell him I don't want to do this for much longer."

"Just tell him. What's the worst that could happen?"

I shook my head. "It's not that simple. My dad's an asshole and a monster rolled in one. There's no limit to what he could do."

She ran her thumb over my hand and sighed. "I'm sorry this is happening to you. No one wants to be stuck doing something they don't love."

"I wish my dad could understand that. He's selfish and controlling and –"

"You're an adult now," she cut in. "You're not the kid who started doing this to please your dad."

I smiled and nodded, squeezing her hand a tad harder. "True, and you're right; I'm not a kid anymore – definitely not the scared one."

"Good, because you've got this, and I'll be here for you no matter what."

I smiled; my heart just about ready to burst in my chest with all the emotions swirling inside me. "You have no idea what those words mean to me."

Lindsay smiled back, lifting my hand and kissing my knuckles. "I have a tiny guess."

A comfortable silence settled between us as we resumed eating. Being with Lindsay felt so good, so natural. I couldn't imagine being anywhere else.

"So, what are your plans for next weekend?" I asked, taking a sip of my wine.

Lindsay paused eating, her eyes still on her plate. "I'm taking a trip home."

"Missed your folks already?" I joked.

She shrugged. "Something like that."

"You must be grateful for your parents. I had always envied how perfect your family was."

"My parents are eons away from perfect," she scoffed.

"Wh– I thought–"

"They do a good job at keeping up appearances, but they hate each other. My mom's always sad and miserable, and I haven't even heard from my dad since I got here." She shook her head. "He's barely around. Everything's just a whole mess."

"Damn. I didn't know that."

She cleared her throat. "No one knows, really. I haven't even told Amy. Like you, she thinks they're perfect, and I just can't find it in me to tell her they're worse than yours."

I watched as a series of emotions played across her face before she continued. "My dad has been cheating on Mom since I was thirteen years old."

"Holy shit." I stared at her, shocked to my core. The Pearts were the epitome of a perfect family back in Colorado Springs. At least, back in the day. What happened? If Lindsay hadn't told me, I wouldn't have believed it.

"Yup," Lindsay replied, bitterness lining her voice. "Because of how he treats her, Mom constantly reminds me never to rush falling in love. She warns me about being sure before giving my heart to anyone."

I shifted in my chair, not sure about her direction, but not liking how nervous it made me feel. "Her story isn't yours, Lindsay."

She sighed lightly. "I know that, I just..." she shrugged her shoulders and forced a smile. "Can we talk about something else?"

I nodded at once. "Sure. As a matter of fact, I've got something for you."

"A surprise?" she asked, her face lighting up.

"Something like that." I got up from the table and moved to the living room, retrieving the painting of her and taking a deep breath, hoping she'd like it.

I returned to find her sipping a glass of wine, grinning coyly. "This is good," she said, twirling the glass.

"I'm glad you like it, and I hope you like *this*," I said, handing the canvas to her. Her brows dipped as she took it, and there was a small smile on her face as she gently ripped the wrapping.

My heart raced a mile a second as I awaited her reaction. As the painting became visible, she gasped, her eyes roving over the perimeter before she looked up at me, eyes glistening.

"Austin, what – how—when?" She looked back to the medium, her eyes searching, her lips slightly agape. My heart soared. "Did you do this?"

I nodded. "Yeah, last night when you were asleep. I finished this morning."

Her hand flew to her mouth, a single tear drop falling from her eyes. "It's beautiful," she said, managing a shaky laugh.

It was like being twelve again, giving my first crush her Valentine's Day gift. "You inspired it, after all."

Lindsay smiled and stood, reaching out her hands for a hug. "I can't believe you did this. This is actual talent," she said as she hugged me.

"I appreciate that, Lindsay."

"Is this what you're studying?" she asked as she withdrew to study the painting again.

I laughed. "Nah, this is just a hobby."

"What? You can make actual money from this. *A lot*, Austin. You're really good!"

I traced my hand along the curve of her jaw. "You're the only person who knows now."

Her eyes widened. "Not even Amy?"

I shook my head.

She swallowed. "Is this something you love?"

"Definitely. It usually clears my head."

"I'm so honored; thank you."

I kissed her tenderly, tasting the wine she had just drank, sweet and sultry, as her soft lips moved against mine. My need for her grew more intense, and within seconds I was sporting a boner only meant for her.

When I pressed it against her stomach, she moaned into my mouth and rested the painting on the chair before wrapping her arms around me, clinging tightly.

We stumbled inside, and I kicked the door shut while tugging at her dress. Lindsay's hands were at my crotch, massaging my hardness while the kiss deepened, the temperature in the room rising to a scorching degree.

Thinking I couldn't make it to the bedroom, I spun her around in the living room, my hands groping her tits while I sucked on her neck. She threw her head back, allowing me easier access while her warm hands directed my every caress.

"Austin, please... don't keep me waiting," she moaned, her panting loud as she writhed her body against me.

My hands moved quickly as I positioned her on a small table close to the wall and peeled off her dress. To my surprise, Lindsay wasn't wearing any bra, only lacy panties that hugged her round ass. I ran my hands down her body, feeling her tits that were firm yet soft in my palms, fuller than my hands could hold.

My cock twitched, eager to have her again – every inch of my body basking in her perfection.

Lindsay peeled off her panties before doing something that made me harder than steel. She turned her back to me, propping one leg on the table and glancing over her shoulders at me, her ass like an offering.

I groaned, trailing my fingers along her slit, loving how her entire body shivered in response, a soft gasp leaving her mouth. It amazed me how drenched she could get so quickly. I could feel her slickness on my fingers before I dipped two of them inside to test her readiness. She was still tight as fuck, but unlike last night, I could go all the way without feeling any resistance. As I sank my hard digits inside her, her flesh parted for me, my fingers sliding along the wetness of her walls.

"Fuck, Austin," she breathed, her hips slowly circling.

Wanting to push her even closer to the edge, I dropped to my knees and licked her soaking flesh, my cock hardening even more with her sexy groan. Lindsay jutted her ass as if begging for more and finding the perfect angle, I lapped up her juices, gulping hard as I indulged in her sweetness.

"God, yes... that's it," she whispered.

My tongue moved in circles around her clit while my fingers worked her pussy. She bucked against my mouth, her breaths quickening. Just as her moans heightened, I eased away and stood, licking at my mouth and wiping at my chin.

Lindsay spun around and kissed me hard, tasting herself on me. It was the sexiest thing. The most arousing thing. If I waited a second longer, I'd come just from this kiss we'd shared.

I flipped her around, and she repositioned herself, leg hoisted as she leaned forward. I took my cock in hand and rubbed it against her soaking entrance, muttering a curse under my breath before I plunged into her.

Lindsay cried out, but from the tone of her voice, I knew it was one of pure pleasure. I clenched my teeth and shifted slightly in my spot before pressing further in. Her fingers whitened on the edge of the table as she gripped it hard and moaned throatily.

I pulled back a little, spreading her perfect ass cheeks, watching my cock moving back and forth inside of her. It was the hottest thing I'd ever seen. She was so fucking wet, my cock collecting the cream from her pink flesh.

"Yes, Austin, don't stop. Please, don't stop," she moaned.

She didn't need to tell me twice. I grunted as I gripped her hips and slammed into her. She screamed, her flesh clenching around me with each stroke. Gritting my teeth, I continued to plough her, using all the restraint I could muster not to burst into a million pieces like I wanted to. Lindsay's body hugged me so tight. Too right. Simply driving me insane.

"Fuck, I don't think I have much longer," I gritted out, slowing my pace.

Lindsay pulled herself off, and before I could fathom what was happening, she sank to her knees in front of me. She looked up at me with those seductive eyes and held my cock, fisting it before taking it into her mouth.

"Oh, fuck!" I exclaimed, closing my eyes as heat encased me. She slid her mouth down my length, only going halfway before coming back up and repeating the same motion.

It was obvious this was her first time by how awkward her movements were, but for some reason, it turned me on even more. When she tentatively brushed her tongue over the tip, I completely lost it.

"I'm gonna come, baby," I grunted, barely recognizing my own voice as I thrust inside her mouth.

Lindsay didn't let up after hearing me. She gripped my ass, her mouth moving faster along the base. Realizing she wanted my cum in her mouth made me bust right away.

Cum spewed to the back of her throat. The force must have caught her by surprise because she drew back a little, but like the trooper she was, she didn't let up. I emptied myself in her mouth, watching as she looked up at me, those pretty lips stretched by my cock.

A creamy white trail seeped from the corners of her mouth as I finished, and she swept it back into her mouth. I watched in amazement, completely dumbstruck and beyond fascinated.

"You're amazing, you know that?" I asked as I pulled her up from the floor and wrapped my arms around her. I kissed her hard, tasting myself on her just as she had tasted herself on me earlier.

In that moment, there wasn't a fucking thing I wouldn't do for this girl.

I was in love.

Chapter 13

Lindsay

I smiled with contentment, rolling onto my side, staring at Austin, fast asleep in bed. He seemed so peaceful, his eyelashes fanning his cheeks, the hint of a smile on his lips. I chuckled to myself as I imagined him dreaming of our encounter. The memory of swallowing his cum only half an hour ago made me blush. I didn't know what got into me, but I wanted to give him as much pleasure as he gave me. It was an experience having his cock in my mouth, and I didn't regret it one bit.

Leaving the bed, I pulled on his robe, tied the belt around me, then walked to the porch where I'd left the painting. It had already gotten dark and windy, the sound of the waves hurtling back and forth.

I picked up the painting and was amazed all over again as I analyzed the details. It was definitely me, and anyone could see that. Austin had captured every single tone, the lights, the colors, the curves. I was totally naked, but he'd captured me with the sheets slightly draped over my hips, leaving my belly button exposed. My breasts were hidden by my arm, and my dark hair cascaded behind me like a waterfall.

My eyes teared up as I took in the beauty of the art piece, my heart filled with gratefulness and pride for Austin. He had an undeniable talent, and the thought behind it meant more to me than words could explain.

My phone buzzed from where I'd left it on the table. I picked it up, and my heart skipped a beat when I saw Amy's name there.

Where are you? Her text message read.

I bit at my nail before I finally replied. *Grabbing something to eat, will be there shortly.*

Ok, if you're at that café we love, grab me a cheese Danish. Thanks xx

Ok, no probs. See you soon.

I sighed heavily before scurrying back inside and picking up my discarded clothes, fully dressed when I got back to the bedroom with Austin still in deep sleep.

I hated to wake him, but I couldn't leave without saying goodbye. I gently shook him. "Austin."

But he was out cold.

"Babe," I tried again, and he shuffled. I continued to rouse him until he opened his eyes and smiled at me. My stomach fluttered from the emotion I saw there.

"Hey, beautiful," he murmured, stretching.

"I gotta go," I softly said.

My response brought him fully awake, his brows furrowing. "What? It's not even that late," he said, reaching for his watch on the bedside table to check the time.

"I know, but Amy just texted, and she'll be expecting me home soon."

He sighed. "Lindsay, please, why can't we just tell her?"

I huffed as I moved away. "Austin, we've been over this already."

"I know, but it'd be better if we break the news from early–"

"No. I'm not ready to lose my best friend!" I exclaimed.

He frowned. "So what are we doing here, Lindsay? Are you just waiting to get tired of me to end this?"

I gawked at him. "What, no!"

"If we plan on being serious, Amy will have to know, eventually. Unless you aren't. Unless this is just plain ol' fun for you."

"How could you say that?" I asked.

Austin sat up in bed, fixing me with a direct stare. "I'm really into you, Lindsay, and I'd love for this to be more than just a casual fuck."

"I don't want this to be a casual fuck, either, Austin, but we both promised to keep this on the down low."

"That was a stupid promise," he grumbled.

"I thought you understood," I replied. "No one can know about us, Austin. Not yet."

"This is ridiculous. I can't believe this is now my fucking life."

"What do you mean?"

He sighed, throwing the sheet back. "I could have any girl I wanted, Lindsay. You're asking me to settle for being a secret, and that's not fair—" He caught my widened eyes and sighed. "Fuck."

"Thank you for showing me your true colors, you prick. Thank you for letting me realize this was a huge mistake." My voice broke in the end, and I swallowed to keep the tears at bay.

Austin moved toward me. "Lindsay, please. I didn't mean it like that—"

"Stop." I raised my hand at him. "Don't come any further."

He paused, giving me a pleading stare. "I'm sorry. That was fucked up."

"Yes, it was," I agreed, grabbing my bag. "I can't do this, Austin. Just... forget this ever happened."

I quickly fled the room, hearing Austin repeatedly call my name in the background. I choked a sob once I got outside and allowed the tears to trail from my eyes, glad that he didn't chase me. Our fight had left me conflicted. I was mad at him for what he said, but it was the truth. Austin had no problems getting women. Asking him to sneak around with me was too unfair. I was scared of the outcome if Amy ever found out, but I was even more terrified to lose him. Whatever I decided, I needed space.

I cried all the way to the café, stopping only to order the cheese Danish for Amy. My sniffs were still constant as I made my way back to the dorm, but I got a grip on myself before entering the room I shared with my best friend.

She perked up when she saw me, rubbing her hands together as I raised the paper bag in my hand.

"Eek! Thank you, I'm starving!" she said, grabbing it from me and taking a big bite of the sweet pastry.

I laughed. "I thought you went on a date. Why are you so hungry?"

She rolled her eyes. "I did, but you know how stupid we get trying not to eat around boys while our tummies are growling in anger."

"Speak for yourself. I have no problem eating on a date."

A brow instantly perked up. "What would you know about eating on a date? Have you been on any?"

I stiffened, realizing what I'd just walked into. As far as Amy knew, I'd dated no one.

"Er, I meant *if* I went on an actual date, I don't think I'd starve myself," I said, making my way over to my bed.

"Hmm, well, you never really know until you're in the situation." Her head tilted as she paused and observed my face. "Are you okay?"

"Yeah, why?" I asked.

"Your eyes seem a little puffy – like you've been crying."

I cleared my throat and rubbed the back of my neck. "My allergies have been acting up is all. I'm fine," I said, managing a smile.

Amy didn't seem convinced, but she nodded. "Did you take your meds?"

"It's not that serious. A decent night's rest and I'll be good as new."

"Okay... if you're sure."

I changed into my PJs and pulled the covers from the bed, glancing over at Amy who was now on her phone. "Good night, Ames."

"Good night, sweetie. I hope you feel better tomorrow."

As soon as my head hit the pillows, my face to the wall, the tears came. Not only did I feel like crap for lying to my best friend, but I also didn't like the way I'd left things with Austin. There must be a way to fix what had quickly turned into my miserable life.

My phone buzzed, and as I picked it up, I realized it was an Instagram text from him.

I'm sorry I made you upset. You're right. We're new, and we don't have to rush this. I just don't want to lose you. Please disregard what I said.

My lower lip trembled, and I clamped down on it hard, trying to stop myself from bursting into tears. Our fight only renewed my insecurity about being out of Austin's league. What did he see in me? Why did he want to be with me?

I'm sorry, too, were the words I felt, but the ones I didn't send.

Chapter 14

Austin

I kept checking my phone every chance I got, hoping to hear from Lindsay, but nothing came. It had been days since she last fled the beach house, and since that time, I hadn't seen or spoken to her.

I contemplated going by her dorm room to talk to Amy just so I could see her, but I stopped myself. What we had wasn't a mistake, but I didn't know where she stood. Maybe our attraction was a mutual one, but the feelings were one-sided. She wasn't in love with me. Not even close.

"Hey, Callaghan; heads up!"

I turned to see a football blasting towards me. It was mere inches away from my face when I caught it.

Jason ran up to me with a grin on his face. "Yo man, what's up with Stella? You hit that, didn't you?"

I frowned. "Wha– who?"

He jerked his head toward the stands, where a brunette held a card with my name on it. She waved rigorously when she saw me. Recognition dawned, and I realized she was the girl I'd met at the party whose DMs I hadn't replied to.

"Oh. Nah, I barely know her."

"Well, it's obvious she's your number one supporter. She's been here all week, cheering you on like she's getting paid." He laughed. "Weird that you're just noticing."

"I've had other things on my mind," I mumbled.

"Like what, dude? She's pretty hot, and you're single. Are you blind?"

I was about to reply when I saw my uncle on the sideline, dressed in a suit—despite the eighty-degree weather— and looking like the older version of my dad. He waved me over, and I sighed before jogging to him.

He greeted me with a smile and slammed his hand against my shoulder. "Looking good, son."

"Thanks, Uncle Ben."

He smiled, nodding proudly. "Listen, I pulled some strings and scored a meeting for you with a recruiter. If it goes well, we could have you getting drafted by next year."

I rubbed the back of my neck and pulled in a breath. "Er, that's awesome."

"Your father will be flying down to join us. He's a charmer; we can definitely get a deal with his influence."

I nodded, my eyes shifting to the stands, catching Stella's eye. She waved at me, then blew me a kiss.

"I'm just giving you a heads up, so you can be prepared," Ben nodded curtly, obviously displeased with my distraction.

I cleared my throat, giving him my full attention. "Yeah, I appreciate it, Uncle Ben."

He gave me one last pat on the shoulder before he left, and I headed to the lockers to change. Once done, I returned outside to find Stella on the field, her little poster in her hand while she stood there.

I was about to make a quick escape, she spotted me, a grin on her face as she ran up to me.

"Austin, hey."

I managed a tight smile and met her halfway. "Hey."

"You remember me, right? I've been texting you on Instagram, but you haven't replied." She bit her lip, making a pout I would normally find cute, but since Lindsay, it did nothing for me.

I scratched the back of my head. "Yeah, been crazy busy; you know how it is."

"Yeah, yeah... I understand – quarterback duties," she laughed.

"That's about right." I jerked my thumb at the exit. "I should get going..."

"Maybe I could walk with you?" she suggested.

My mind said no at once, but when I opened my mouth, I said, "Sure, why not?"

It was just a simple walk. Totally innocent.

Right?

I moved off, and Stella jogged to keep up with me, her short legs no match for my long strides. Despite trying to create a little distance between us, Stella remained right at my hip.

"I was thinking maybe we could hang out when you're not so busy..." she said.

A soft sigh left my mouth, and I stopped abruptly. "Listen, Stella, you're a beautiful girl, but–"

"You've got a girlfriend already," Stella cut in. "Of course you do, you're Austin Callaghan." She moved closer, running her fingers down my chest. "I don't mind sharing, you know."

I opened my mouth to reply when I saw Amy moving toward us. My heart skipped a beat as I spotted Lindsay beside her. I could feel the blood drain from my face.

"Hey, big brother!" Amy exclaimed, lunging into my arms.

I wrapped my arms around her, staring at Lindsay over her head. Lindsay glanced from me to Stella, her brow raising just a tad before she cut her eyes at me.

Shit.

Amy drew back and spotted Stella, who she gave a sly grin. "Ooh... I see you followed my advice and shoot your shot."

My forehead wrinkled as Stella scoffed. "Oh, I'm trying to, but your brother's putting up a fight," she replied.

Amy's brows lifted at me. "Are you kidding me? Do you not see all that?" She ran her hand along Stella's body. "She's totally your type."

I scratched the back of my neck, trying to find an excuse to get the hell out of there. I'd never felt so awkward in my life.

"Seems Mr. Handsome here is already taken," Stella said.

"By who?" Amy was quick to ask, giving me a questioning look.

I glanced at Lindsay, whose eyes were locked on the book in her hand, an unreadable expression on her face. Did she even care that her best friend wanted to hook me up with another girl? It didn't seem that way.

"Have you been holding out on me, Austin?" Amy asked, nudging my shoulder. "Who are you seeing?"

"No one," I blurted, the words flying out so fast, I couldn't stop them. My body went rigid. I glanced over and Lindsay, and the look on her face...

Fuck.

Utter devastation.

She recovered quickly, forcing a smile, one that made me feel like an even bigger asshole.

"Okay then, if you're not seeing anyone, what's the problem?" Amy asked.

Lindsay cut in by clearing her throat—a saving grace, stopping from digging a bigger hole. "Come on, Ames, we're gonna be late," she said, taking Amy's arm.

Amy checked her watch and gasped. "Oh crap, we do need to go. I'll see you lovebirds around – hopefully, we can double date soon!" she said, winking.

Oh, fuck my life.

I managed a tight smile as I watched them leave, my eyes on Lindsay the entire time.

"I get it now."

My gaze snapped to Stella. "Huh?"

"You've got a thing for your sister's friend," she said, giving me a smirk mixed with a pissed off attitude.

"What are you talking about?" I asked.

"I saw the way you looked at her – it's pretty obvious, Austin." She came closer, the smirk deepening. "Although, I have a feeling your sister has no clue."

Stella ran her fingers down my chest, and I caught her hand. "That's none of your business–"

"Isn't it?" She cocked her head. "I bet sister dearest wouldn't be so pleased if she found out, would she? I'm sure you wouldn't want to ruin the relationship with your only sibling."

"What do you want?" I asked, getting to the point.

"For you to claim me as your girl," she replied simply.

"Why? It's obvious I'm not into you."

A hurt look crossed her features; then she managed a smile. "I need an influencer status, and you're my key." She shrugged. "Besides, you can't deny how great we look together. Think of the eyes that would turn whenever we entered a room."

"Contrary to what social media makes you believe, I'm not a superficial guy, Stella. I could give two fucks about the spotlight."

Stella sneered. "Stop lying. I've seen the way you carry yourself, with that big dick energy everyone can't help but notice. You love being seen. Everyone does."

I didn't need to keep arguing with this girl. "Think whatever you want, Stella. It won't change the truth."

"Think about my offer, will you? That way, I won't tell Amy about your little crush." With a chuckle, she walked away, her hips swinging with more rhythm than usual.

I raked a hand through my hair. "Fuck."

Did anyone else notice how into Lindsay I was? Carter had picked up on it, and now, so did Stella. Was I so transparent with my feelings for my sister's best friend? If so, why couldn't Lindsay see it?

Stella's threat didn't scare me. In fact, I wished she would tell Amy about what she suspected. Who knew? It would probably force Lindsay to face her feelings for me out in the open. Which is exactly what I wanted.

Until then, I had damage control on my hands. After the stunt Amy pulled earlier, I didn't want Lindsay getting any ideas about me and Stella. I had to see her and clear the air before it was too late.

Chapter 15

Lindsay

I should have listened to my mom when she told me to guard my heart against boys. She'd been pounding the same message in my head since I was sixteen, and guys had started hanging around. Men lied, they cheated, they couldn't be trusted, and they would break your heart without a care in the world.

At first, I took her advice, but ever since Austin and I kissed on prom night, I'd buried it at the back of my head. Now, when I realized how right she was, it was already too late to guard my heart. It was already in shambles, destroyed by the one guy I thought wouldn't hurt me.

Our fight was only a few days ago, yet he was already hooking up with someone else. Someone hotter, someone in his league, a girl who'd look much better on his arm than I did. A painful lump formed in my throat. If I weren't in Amy's company, I'd be crying my eyes out.

Amy didn't make the situation any better, either. She kept going on about Austin and Stella, how hot they were and what a great couple they'd make. I wanted to shout at her to shut up, but Amy didn't deserve my anger. She was oblivious to everything going on.

My phone beeped with an incoming message. I reached for it, frowning when I saw Austin's name on the screen.

I need to see you, his text read.

My heart flipped with happiness, but I forced the joy away, hardening it with the memory of him and Stella. *Funny, I thought you were already seeing Stella*, I texted back.

Stella and I aren't together, Lindsay.

Bullshit. I was there when Amy set you up, remember?

There was a slight pause; then he started typing back. My breath paused as I waited.

I don't want to do this over the phone. Come by the beach house at around 7, please.

I started to write a reply but cleared it off immediately.

"Who are you texting with that intense look on your face?" Amy asked.

I almost dropped the phone, and I hoped she didn't read the guilt on my face. "Er – no one."

She shrugged it off and went on to a different topic while I sat there pondering over the text messages. The responsible action was an obvious one; leave Austin alone, forget that we even happened. But that was impossible. As long as he was around, I couldn't stay away.

I was still angry, but I wanted clarity more than anything, so even though I didn't tell him I'd stop by, I knew I would.

That evening, I hoped Amy would head out to see Jason, but when she stayed, I searched my mind for a reasonable excuse to leave. I'd already showered and changed, waiting on the answer to come to me.

When nothing creative came to mind, I muttered, "Fuck it," then grabbed my bag. "Hey, Ames, I'm going to get some fresh air; I'll be back soon."

Her brows bunched together as she sat up in bed. "Everything okay?"

"Yeah, everything's fine." I managed a smile.

"Want some company?"

"Er, no, I'm good. I won't be long."

She laid back down, reaching for the book she'd been reading. "Okie."

I grabbed my phone and walked slowly out of the room. When the door closed, I made a dash down the stairs. Not wanting to drive with my mind in such a mess, the Uber I'd called was already waiting, and in no time, it pulled up at the beach house. I glanced down at my fitted jeans and T-shirt as I knocked and waited for Austin to open up. A casual yet sexy outfit, not screaming desperate. I didn't want Austin to get any ideas since I only came to talk.

In less than a minute, the door swung open, and there he was, looking so yummy in a light pink T-shirt that hugged his torso, his hair golden under the lights.

His Adam's apple bobbed as his gaze ran over me, triggering a longing that spread from head to toe. "I'm glad you could make it," he said.

I hugged my shoulders. "Yeah, you said you wanted to talk, so here I am."

"Come in," he said, moving to the side.

Being here again brought back all the memories. From where I was, I could see the table where we made love the last time, and I couldn't help the heat that instantly warmed my cheeks.

"Can I get you something to drink?" he offered.

"No, I won't be here long. I've gotta get back before Amy gets suspicious."

An annoyed look flashed across his face so fast, I wondered if I'd imagined it, then he nodded and approached me. "I missed you, Lindsay."

I crossed my arms protectively on my chest. "Didn't seem like it. You and Stella seemed so cozy today."

He scoffed and rolled his eyes. "There's nothing going on between me and Stella. You know that."

"Actually, I don't know, Austin. That's the thing, we barely know shit about each other."

"And all I'm asking for is a chance to change that. I want to be with you. I want to know everything about you."

I rubbed at my temples. "I can't be with you."

"Why?" he snapped, his jaw tightening. "Don't give me that bullshit about Amy. If you really wanted to be with me, you wouldn't be scared to tell her the truth."

"How could you say that?" I spat. "Amy's my friend—my only friend. You know that. I can't lose her, Austin."

"You won't. Sure, Amy will be mad at first, but she'll eventually see reason."

"I don't see that happening."

"Then what, Lindsay? We're over, just like that?"

I remained silent as tears stung my eyes, unable to find the right words to say.

"I know you want me as much as I fucking want you," he said, moving closer to me. My heart flipped in my chest, every inch of my body alert in his presence.

"Tell me you don't miss this — us being together, my hands touching you." His fingers trailed down my skin, making me moan. "Me being inside you." His breath fanned my ear, and a shiver ran through me.

I pulled in a jagged breath. "Austin..."

"I love you, Lindsay – there I said it – I think I've been in love with you from the very moment we kissed two years ago, and heck, I might not know everything about you, but I'd like that chance. I want you. Only you."

I froze, feeling breathless despite standing still. I wasn't expecting those words. My heart rejoiced, happiness running through me in waves. Tears of joy sprang from my eyes because it was too much to keep in.

I opened my mouth to replicate those three magical words because I felt the same way. But Austin pressed a finger against my lips, forcing them back down my throat.

"Shh, you don't have to say anything. Just let me love you for tonight and always."

I closed my eyes, throwing my head back as his lips found my throat, his fingers working to loosen the buttons on my pants.

My fingers raked through his silky soft hair, my body in shambles as each touch aroused me even more. I kissed him, the feeling almost brand new yet so familiar. I missed this, I missed him, and like the compliant girl I was, I caved in.

We kissed hard with such urgency that made my knees buckle. My hands found the hem of his shirt, and I hauled it over his head, desperately needing to feel him against me – inside me.

When we were both completely naked, he lifted me, and I wrapped my legs around him, his cock grazing my entrance. He anchored me against the wall, and I gasped as my skin met contact with the coolness that clashed with my burning skin.

Austin nibbled my neck, his hands supporting my legs as our bodies ground against each other.

"Now," I managed, my eyes fluttering as I tried to make sense of the pleasure coursing through me.

Austin plunged into me, his cock immediately hitting a sweet spot that had me moaning aloud. I clung to him, my body humming as he thrust into me over and over, each stroke getting deeper. My hands found his buttocks, and I dragged my fingers along his flesh, admiring how effortlessly he pleasured me. Every toned muscle was emphasized and in perfect glory as he moved inside me. I gasped with each stroke, arching my neck, never wanting this insane pleasure to end.

Just as the pressure started to increase, Austin pulled out and put me down. I only had time to glimpse his lust-filled eyes before he spun me around and entered me from behind. My body shivered, and my knees buckled as he grabbed my breast, fucking me hard, my ass smacking against him.

His other hand found my clit, and I gasped, my mind reeling from the ecstasy surging through me. He knew exactly where to touch, and when he circled the most sensitive spot on my clit, I fell apart. With one sharp thrust, my limbs grew weak, and my knees buckled. My orgasm moved through me like a tidal wave, the screams frozen on my lips, leaving my mouth hanging open.

With a deep thrust and a loud grunt, Austin squeezed my tits, and once again, I experienced the warmth of his cum inside me. He held me up while tremors racked my body, my limbs turning to mush as I reveled in my release.

I SHOULD'VE PASSED out from that mind-blowing orgasm, but arousal still rushed through me, triggered by Austin's love for me and knowing I truly loved him. Yes, it was the perfect way to describe what I felt for him. Love. I didn't realize how truly in love with him I was until he confessed it.

"Oh, my God," I exclaimed as Austin pulled me back onto his cock, my back slightly raised off the bed as he tightly gripped my hips.

My tits bounced back and forth in my chest from his swift movements. I reached for them, massaging them with my hands, moaning as I pinched my sensitive nipples, my pussy tightening around Austin's cock.

He moaned as he lowered me and leaned forward, still stroking me while sweat glistened on every inch of his toned skin. He pushed my legs back to my tits, my pussy completely exposed to him with his gaze fastened there.

Austin groaned as he pressed inside me, sinking deep, lingering there for a second as he muttered a curse. My gasps pierced the room as he picked up the pace, fucking me so hard my vision blurred. Just when I thought he'd come, he pulled out and slapped his cock against my pussy. I trembled, my legs almost snapping shut as I saw stars. Austin pried them open again before he entered me once more with a soft pop.

I closed my eyes and bit my lips, enjoying the way he slid in and out of me effortlessly – the perfect fit.

"Touch yourself," he grunted, and my eyes opened to find his dark eyes on me, his face serious and demanding, making my pussy clench.

With a bit of hesitance, I slid my hands along my sweaty body and found my clit with my middle finger. My body jolted as I circled it, and I saw the smirk on Austin's face as he moved slowly inside me.

My fingers glided over the slippery nub, more pleasure erupting inside me as my juices lubricated Austin's cock.

My eyes rolled back in my head, my pussy clenching as I rubbed myself even faster. I didn't want the pleasure to end, so each time the climax beat at my gate, I pulled back, and Austin pulled out. My pussy was only empty for a few seconds before he went back in, moaning loudly as he slid his hands up and down my legs.

"Oh, shit," he exclaimed, pulling out just enough, leaving only the tip inside me. My body shivered as he dispensed his cum inside, then pulled out. A thick, creamy trail seeped out from my entrance. Austin shoved his solid length inside me again, taking me by surprise.

His hands trembled as he forced his sensitive cock in, forcing his cum back inside me. He sighed heavily when he inched his length inside, immediately moving back and forth. Five deep thrusts later left me shivering from ecstasy, my eyes rolling over as I grabbed his thick arms.

I screamed, and he gripped my legs tightly as he emptied himself inside me yet again. This time, as soon as we recovered from our climax, he pulled out, falling beside me on the bed.

"You're one in a million, baby girl," he said breathlessly, kissing me on the cheek.

I smiled, trying to catch my breath, wanting to cuddle up against him, but the slickness between my thighs left me uncomfortable. Deciding to shower before I returned to the dorm, I left the bed, not realizing how sore I was until I started to move.

As soon as the warm blast of water hit my skin, Austin appeared at the door with a wicked grin on his face. He stepped into the stall and pulled me in for a kiss, our wet bodies grinding against each other. Instead of taking me again like I expected, Austin took his time to wash every inch of me until I was squeaky clean.

"I think there's a blow dryer somewhere around that you could use," he said as we stepped out. He immediately started searching the cupboards, a smile lighting up his face when he found it.

I smiled and kissed him. "Perfect."

I was about to switch it on when a pounding came from the front door. My head snapped to Austin, who looked just as confused as me.

"Who could that be?" I whisper, alarm bells ringing. I didn't want our cover blown. Not until I figured out a way to confess to my best friend.

The knocking at the door came again, and my heart pounded in my chest. "Stay here, I'll go check," Austin said, tension tightening his face.

I plugged out the dryer and put my clothes on. A gnawing feeling settled in my stomach. It wasn't a good sign. Shit was about to hit the fan.

Chapter 16

Lindsay

MY BLOOD RAN COLD WHEN I heard Amy's loud voice in the living room. My heart fell on the floor on my stomach, the pulse beating loudly in my ear. Taking a deep breath, I turned the handle of the bathroom door, ready to face the music.

"Where is she?" Amy shouted, and the tears instantly pooled in my eyes.

"Can you calm down?" I heard Austin say. "I'm not letting you near her until you do."

Too late. His response came as I stepped into the living room, gasping when I saw Carter there as well, a smirk on his face.

"Gotcha," he said with a snicker.

Amy twisted to face me, her body trembling with rage, tears pouring down her face. I saw the disappointment in her eyes and immediately wanted to sink through the floor.

"You fucking bitch! How could you?" she shouted, spit flying. I flinched.

"Hey, Amy, chill," Austin intervened, reaching for his sister.

"Don't touch me, you asshole!" she snapped, glaring at him for a split second before her gaze returned to me. I could only cry in response, my world crumbling around me.

"Carter came to me that night at the party," she said, hands shaking. "He told me Austin had a thing for you, and I didn't want to believe him." She paused, then sniffled. "He told me to look out for the signs, and I did, but I still didn't want to believe it."

"Amy," I managed, my voice quivering.

"I caught onto your silly little excuses, I saw the way you both looked at each other, I – I saw how you reacted whenever I mentioned Austin or even when he was close by. I fucking saw it all, Lindsay. Yet, all this time you've been lying to my fucking face!" she cried.

I sniffed. "Amy, I never meant to hurt you–"

A slap to my face silenced me and brought more tears to my eyes. "I don't want to hear a fucking word! You knew my take on relationships like this, and you went behind my back and fucked my brother, anyway."

Austin tried to reach for her again, but she tugged herself from his hold. "All this time, you've been acting holier than thou, giving me lectures about not being a slut in college while you've been the biggest one this entire time."

I flinched at her words.

"That's enough, Amy!" Austin exclaimed.

She slowly turned to him. "And you, I thought you were my brother. I looked up to you. Now, you mean nothing to me, I swear."

Austin visibly swallowed. "Be angry at me all you want, I can take it, but don't be mad at Lindsay. She's felt like crap this entire time. The last thing she wanted to do was hurt you."

Amy scoffed. "And yet she continued to fuck you. I bet my feelings were the furthest thing from her mind," she snarled.

"See, all this could've been avoided if you'd gone out with me instead," Carter chipped in with a smirk.

Austin's expression hardened as he marched over and collared him. "Get the hell out of my house!" he roared.

"No!" Amy cut in. "This is my place as much as yours. Carter stays. If it hadn't been for him, I would be living in the dark, not knowing the two people I loved the most betrayed me."

My heart broke into a dozen pieces. "I'm sorry, Amy."

"Your apologies mean nothing to me now, Lindsay!" she snapped, her eyes wide and blank.

Austin raked his fingers through his hair. "I never wanted to hurt you – none of us did – but I've been in love with Lindsay for years, and I've kept it a secret just as long, but after being here and seeing her again after such a long time, I couldn't stay away."

Amy blinked, and I squeezed my eyes shut, wanting to strangle Austin.

Amy choked a dry laugh. "Love?" She looked at me as if searching for confirmation, and when I didn't respond, she scoffed. "You know what, I'm done with this."

She turned to leave, and I reached for her hand, only for her to slap it away. With an index finger pointed at my face, she said, "you fucking stay away from me! You're dead to me!" She glanced at Austin. "Both of you."

She walked away with Carter following behind, sealing the door with a hard slam. A sob broke free from my lips, and I broke down, tears running like a river down my cheeks. Austin rushed to my side, wrapping his arms around me, but after what just happened, the last thing I wanted was for him to touch me.

"Don't," I said, taking a step back. "You've only made things worse."

"Amy already knew the truth, Lindsay. I was only coming clean with everything," he said, confusion filling his face. "I don't get why you're mad at me."

"This is what you wanted all along, wasn't it?" I accused.

"Not like this!" he exclaimed. "I didn't want this shit show, believe me."

I wrapped my arms around myself, sobbing. "I knew this would happen. I knew she would be angry, and I knew she'd hate us."

"Amy just needs some time to cool off. She'll come around," Austin assured.

I shook my head, totally not convinced. "I gotta do damage control."

He held my hand. "Stay here; give her some time."

"I can't," I cried. "Maybe I was right the first time, Austin. Maybe this was a huge mistake."

He swallowed, his dark blue eyes strained on me. "Don't say that. Loving you can never be a mistake, I know that."

I tugged my hand from his and moved toward the front door, wiping the tears from my face.

"Lindsay, don't do this. Don't walk away," Austin called, but I was already outside, taking one last glance at his sad face before I closed the door behind me.

I sobbed all the way back to my dorm, dreading a further confrontation with Amy. I understood her words, I knew they came from a place of hurt, and I hated myself for being the reason. I'd promised not to get involved with Austin, but I did the opposite, knowing the truth would eventually come out. I just never expected it would be so soon.

I pulled in a breath when I arrived at my dorm, bracing for the onslaught. With a bit of hesitance, I pushed the door open and opened my mind to a few possibilities of how this would turn out. To my surprise, the room was empty – Amy wasn't back as yet, or she probably went to Jason's to cool off.

Relief filled me as I walked over to my side of the room and curled under the blankets, crying simply because I couldn't stop the tears. There was too much to think about, too much to process. In just a few hours, Austin had confessed his love for me, and in another split second, my world had crumbled around me. I didn't know what to do or how to make this better.

Everything was completely ruined.

Chapter 17

Lindsay

I might have gotten two hours of sleep after staying up all night, replaying the scenes in my head and crying over them. I woke up to shuffling, my heart pounding when I saw Amy on her side of the room, packing her knapsack.

I swallowed hard and carefully eased up as I looked over at her. Her back faced me, and my lips parted to speak, but then I clamped them back shut, not knowing exactly what to say.

"Amy, I'm sorry I didn't tell you the truth earlier," I finally blurted, watching as she stiffened and paused for a split second before she returned to packing.

"I knew you'd be upset, and that's why I said nothing, but I really love Austin. I'm not sure when it happened, but it did, and I'm so sorry I hurt you," I continued.

She finally turned to me with a scowl on her face, but I could see the tears in her eyes. "I'm gonna ask my uncle for a transfer to another room. Maybe when I'm gone, you and Austin can shack up together," she said before pulling her bag from the bed and storming out the door.

My lips trembled as the door closed with a hard slam that made me flinch. This was probably the end of our friendship – I could feel it. Amy wasn't a forgiving person. and what I did was heavy duty. There was no way she would look past it. Our lives would never be normal again. The thought of our friendship ending broke me more than anything could.

The buzzing phone on the bed pulled my attention. Checking the screen, I realized it was Austin, and my heart swelled in my chest.

Are you okay? his text read.

I contemplated not answering, but he didn't deserve that after being so sweet this entire time.

She's still not talking to me, I replied.

Don't worry about it. Amy will come around, trust me.

I pulled in a breath and put the phone down. She was his sister, which meant he'd known her longer than me, but Amy and I were much closer. She would never get over this. Ever.

I went through classes like a zombie, my mind trying to form a plan to win my best friend back. Amy wasn't giving me the time of day, no matter how many texts I sent out.

IT WAS THE WEEKEND, and the Bruins had another game. I wanted to support Austin, but I figured my presence would only add fire to fuel if Amy saw me there. Besides, it was the perfect time to visit my mom.

That afternoon, as I packed a bag, Amy came in, a frown on her face as she moved to her side of the room. I bit my lips, waiting for her to greet me, but she didn't. "I'm visiting my parents for the weekend," I said.

No response.

"I'll be back on Sunday."

Amy pulled in a breath. "I'll let you know when I give a fuck," she said as she cut her eyes at me.

It hurt to hear those words, but I reminded myself that this was my fault. This wouldn't be happening if I hadn't gone behind my best friend's back. Wordlessly, I finished packing my bags and left the dorm room with a single goodbye that Amy didn't respond to.

I put my phone on Do Not Disturb and prepared myself for the journey ahead. I doubt heading to Colorado would clear my mind or make me feel better about anything, but with my mom's never-ending list of problems, I'd be a bit distracted from my crumbling life.

The five-hour flight gave me time to think, and I loathed myself for still having Austin on my mind throughout this ordeal. Amy should be my priority, yet as I watched the clouds pass around me, it reminded me of times with Austin when I felt like I'd been on Cloud 9. He made me happy, and that was the hard part. My life would be better with him in it. Reality sucked because everything I hoped and dreamed between us was just fiction in the real world.

As long as he was Amy's brother, we couldn't be together. I couldn't be with Austin, knowing Amy hated me, knowing I'd ended years of friendship because of a guy. Her brother.

What if Austin broke my heart? What if he woke up tomorrow and realized his feelings for me weren't real? I'd have no one. The two persons I truly cared about would be gone.

This was a no-win situation. I'd always end up the loser.

THE CAB DROPPED ME off, and I pulled my small carryon along, pausing as I stared at the two-story house that I'd spent my entire life living in, with Amy just across the road. Dad's truck wasn't in the driveway, but Mom's SUV was. No surprise. Dad was never home when it mattered.

I pulled in a breath and walked up the driveway, my steps heavy. I knocked as soon as I reached the large front door and braced myself to see my mom. When she opened up, a glass of wine in hand, her blue eyes widened, and her lips trembled. In the next second, she had me in her arms, sobbing, and I just couldn't help my own tears.

When we finally parted, she brushed at her cheeks and smiled at me. "Why didn't you tell me you were coming today?" she asked, sniffing.

"I wanted to surprise you."

"Oh, you shouldn't have. I would have looked more presentable," she said, pulling at her satin robe.

I snickered. "Mom, I've seen you like this a thousand times before."

She smiled as she reached for my bag and ushered me inside. "I hope your flight was good."

"Yeah, except for my neighbor almost boring me to death with his constant yapping, it wasn't half bad," I said, following her to the living room. "Where's Dad?"

Mom rolled her eyes and took a sip of her wine. "Who knows at this point," she scoffed.

I peered at her closely, taking in the dark circles around her eyes. "Are you okay, Mom?"

She smiled briefly, raking her fingers through her dark hair. "You're here now; of course I am. We have a lot to catch up on." She pinched my chin and made her way to the kitchen. "Take your bags to your room honey, I'll be down here."

I nodded and moved upstairs to my bedroom, which held so many memories of my childhood. The sheets had been changed, but everything else remained the same. From my window, I could see the Callaghan's house, the biggest in the neighborhood. I remembered when Amy would sneak over or vice versa, our nights filled with endless giggles as we played games and stalked the Instagram pages of the popular girls at school. Austin was mostly at his friends' houses or chasing skirts, but every time he came home, I'd hear his truck entering the street and rush to the windows to see him.

Sometimes, he snuck in girls, and other times, he tried to sneak himself in after breaking curfew. The sneaky watching continued for some time until he noticed and turned to smile and wave each time.

Funny how things could change so drastically over time. I no longer lusted after my crush because I finally had him– only for him to slip through my fingers again.

"Honey, is everything okay?" I heard my mom ask, jolting me from my thoughts.

I didn't even know how long I'd been standing there, but Mom wore a concerned look as she slowly entered the room and sat on the bed.

"Aren't the Callaghan's home?" I inquired about Austin's parents.

"No, they drove out early today. Jessica mentioned Austin had a big game that they didn't want to miss."

I tore my gaze away and nodded. "Yeah."

"I thought you'd be there – for Amy's sake, at least. You know she always liked your company."

I cleared my throat. "Amy and I aren't really on speaking terms, Mom."

Her green eyes widened. "Oh, honey, is everything okay?"

My lips trembled, and the dam I'd held back for so long broke free. Without waiting for a single word, Mom rushed toward me and pulled me in her arms. I cried even harder.

Chapter 18

Austin

"You call that a fucking game?" My father exclaimed from behind me, his tone heavy with fury.

From the center of the living room of the beach house, I bit my lip, holding back an angry retort. The game was a shit show, and I felt awful that we lost. I didn't need Dad's crap on top of it.

"I could have gone out there and done better!" he roared.

With teeth clenched, I turned on my heels, then stopped dead. He almost bumped into me, his angular jaw rigid as he stared me down.

"Then why didn't you?" I snapped.

Amy and my mom stood at the other end of the room, staring at us, while my dad and I stood face to face in a challenge.

His jaw clenched. "There were recruiters there, Austin, plus friends I invited to see you perform, and all you did was embarrass me!"

"Sucks to have your expectations so high. You know what they say," I shrugged as I turned to walk away.

My body halted when he grabbed my shoulders and spun me around. "Don't fucking tempt me, Austin. You know what I can do."

I met his icy gaze. "And here I am, not giving a fuck. Your macho act doesn't scare me, Dad. I'm not a kid anymore."

His nostrils flared, and the muscles in his jaw flexed as he glared at me. I did the same, not backing down for even a second. I was in a piss-poor mood after not hearing from Lindsay and not understanding where she was. Amy was still being a bitch, shutting me out, too. I was slowly losing my mind. I tried my very best at winning, but there was only so much I could do. I gave one hundred percent to a game I didn't even give a fuck about, and there was still no appreciation. What was the fucking point?

"Can you guys just calm down, please? Hunter, honey, I'm sure Austin did his best," my mom intervened.

One glare from my dad had her backing away, her lips sealed. No surprise there.

"Austin's just in a shitty mood cause his girlfriend dumped him," Amy said, rolling her eyes and crossing her arms.

"And what a fucking friend you are. Lindsay's missing, and you can't even put aside being a bitch for one second to find out if she's okay."

"Lindsay's missing?" my mom asked, gasping. "Does Althea and Derek know about this?"

Amy's face went red as a beet. "She isn't missing, you asshole!" she shouted at me.

"Then where the hell is she?" I exclaimed. She hadn't answered my texts or phone calls. I searched for her in the stands. She wasn't there.

"Did you ever think she just doesn't want you to find her?" Amy asked.

"Wait, what's happening here?" my mom said, her forehead creasing.

"My ex-best friend and my brother have been screwing behind my back this whole time!" she exclaimed. Mom turned reproachful eyes on me, intensifying my anger.

"I don't get why you're so butt-hurt. I'd assume that as long as we're both happy, then nothing else matters, but you're so selfish, Amy, that our feelings didn't even cross your mind. You'd rather have Lindsay behind you like a fucking lapdog, doing as you say, doing God knows what for your benefit. It's always about you, isn't it, Amy?" I exclaimed, and tears pooled in Amy's eyes.

"I trusted you two!" she said, her voice breaking. "How could you betray me like this?"

"How did we betray you? Lindsay has done nothing but put you first, and you couldn't even be understanding. You didn't even give her a chance!"

Amy's chest rose and fell as she breathed, and I watched a calm return to her face. Without another word, she grabbed her bag and stormed out, leaving me still at a hundred. There wasn't any calming me anytime soon.

I raked my hand through my hair and looked at my parents. Dad stood over by the liquor cabinet, filling his tumbler with scotch. Mom massaged her temples, stress lining her face.

"I'm quitting football," I announced.

Mom and Dad turned to me at once, both wearing matching expressions of shock. "What?" They exclaimed in unison.

I smiled, feeling how good it was to get the news off my chest. "After this season, I'm done. I don't want to play anymore. Being with Lindsay made me realize that more than ever."

"Have you lost your mind?" my dad raged, slamming his tumbler on the counter.

I stared at him calmly, unfazed by his outburst. "Quite the opposite; I've never felt this sane."

"Okay, honey, maybe you just need some time to cool off," Mom suggested.

"I'm fine, Mom," I said, laughing. "This was never my dream; it was Dad's, but now I'm done living for him."

I was halfway up the stairs when his voice stopped me. "If you quit, I'll cut you off – you'll lose everything, Austin."

I shrugged. "Okay. Do your worst, Dad."

Silence followed me as I continued to my room.

A DAY LATER, WHEN THE dust had somewhat settled, I made my way down to the beach. The fresh air, the sun on my skin would all be perfect if I had Lindsay by my side to share the moment with me. I retrieved my phone from my pocket again, checking if she'd replied to the messages I'd sent, but there was still nothing. I figured she needed her space, but all I needed was a sign to know she was okay.

As I gazed upon the roaring sea, I couldn't help smiling when I remembered Lindsay's first night here. The shock on her face when she ran into the ice-cold water and realized how cold it was, the feel of her soft skin, her bliss on her face as I'd made love to her. It was probably the best night of my entire life, and every other time I spent with Lindsay was close seconds.

I was in love with her; I could feel it in every fiber of my being. Not being able to have her now felt like something inside me was missing.

A shadow appeared in my vision, and my heart raced for a moment, thinking it was Lindsay, but the familiar scent of cherry blossom perfume told me it wasn't her.

"Lindsay will be back tomorrow," Amy assured me.

I whipped around to look at her. "Where is she?"

"She's visiting her mom," she said after a second.

Relief consumed me, and I couldn't help the brief smile that played at my lips. "Thanks for telling me."

Amy nodded. An awkward silence settled between us, battling with the guilt that filled me. "Hey, Ames, about what I said –"

"You were right," she cut in. "I didn't consider you being happy together, and I should have. My opinion shouldn't have mattered as long as you guys wanted to be together."

I nodded. "Still… I said some ugly things."

She forced a smile. "None that wasn't true, and hey, I said some pretty nasty things about you guys the other day, too, and I'm sorry for that."

I smiled as I stood, dusting sand from my shorts. "You should know we didn't mean to hurt you. Everything happened so fast, and we… we just went with the flow, Ames."

She nodded, smiling. "You really love her?"

I nodded, my stomach fluttering at the thought. "With all my heart."

"Lindsay loves you too. She isn't the most open, but she does."

"How do you even know that?" I ask.

"Because she risked our friendship to be with you," she said simply.

I grinned and ruffled my hair. "God, this is insane."

"It is, and so is you quitting football," she said, her expression shifting to sternness. "Mom told me about your announcement yesterday."

I pulled in a breath. "I want to follow my own path, Ames."

"I know, and I'm proud of you, but are you sure, Austin? I don't think Dad was joking about cutting you off."

"I know he wasn't, but I don't care. I've never been so sure about anything in my life."

She sighed. "Buckle up, bro. It's going to be a bumpy ride."

"I'll be fine, sis," I said, pulling her in for a hug.

Chapter 19

Lindsay

"Sweetheart, you don't have to live your life fearing the same thing that happened between me and your dad will happen to you," my mom said with a smile as she placed her hand atop of mine.

"Mom..."

"I said some crazy things to you – some I'll never forgive myself for, but love exists, Honey. If you think Austin is the right one, then go for it."

I looked down at my pancakes, still feeling a bit awkward from this conversation with my mom. We'd talked about boys, but nothing specific. I'd never had a boyfriend issue before.

"It isn't so easy, Mom. There's Amy..."

She scoffed and fanned me off playfully. "Amy is your best friend; she'll come around. She might be hurting now, but a true friend will eventually see reason."

"I don't know... you should've seen the look on her face, heard the things she said... I don't think we'll come back from this."

"Listen to me, sweetheart. Not everyone gets lucky enough to find love — it sucks that I wasn't among them— but I've realized there's still time if I truly want to. Austin has done nothing wrong, and that boy has always been a polite and smart kid – if he says he loves you, I believe it," she nodded as if that was final.

"This isn't just about his feelings for me. I can't be with Austin knowing Amy doesn't approve," I said.

"Aim to please yourself, darling, not people. I just discovered that last night," she giggled.

"Mom..." I scolded.

"What?" she dragged. "It might seem selfish, especially in your situation, but you don't want to live with regrets. One person can make you happy for the rest of your life, or it can be the opposite. You just have to choose wisely."

"But what if Austin and I are just in the honeymoon phase, and it fizzles after a time?"

Her forehead wrinkled as she gave it thought. "Well... that's a very good question, but you just have to trust your gut."

"Didn't you trust your gut with Dad?"

She sighed heavily. "In retrospect, I don't think your dad and I were ever in love. The chemistry was great, and we were compatible in bed. He was a popular guy, and I made it a goal to be with him because I wanted the spotlight, too. When we finally got together, it worked because we were both so outgoing and spontaneous, but then I got pregnant, and reality hit hard."

I swallowed. Mom must have seen the look on my face because she was quick to continue.

"Honey, don't get me wrong; we both love you, I just think your father is all types of fucked up. Having you was the best thing that ever happened to me. I haven't exactly been mother of the decade, but you're the only thing that ever truly made me happy."

I smiled. "Thanks, Mom."

She patted my hand. "You can't imagine how much it means to me to see you opening up to me like this," her voice broke. "To be talking about boys..." She laughed, and I couldn't help but join in. "I'm really grateful, sweetie."

I got up to hug her. "I love you, Mom, and I'm glad I came."

She dabbed at her eyes, her smile contagious. "I just feel so horrible for everything I said to you about boys and love. It's just that, from my own experience, I didn't want the same thing to happen to you, but you being here and telling me about Austin, I've had some time to reflect, and I'm so sorry if I made you believe there was no love at your age," she sniffed.

"Mom.."

"Your dad and I got together for the wrong reasons. It doesn't mean you will, too. I see the look on your face and hear the words from your mouth, which confirms you're in love with Austin. Sweetheart, take the risk and be happy. Life is too short."

I sniffed as I reached for her hand and gave it a gentle squeeze.

AROUND MIDDAY, I WAS getting ready to leave for the airport when I heard the doorbell ring downstairs. I continued to pack, then pulled my bag downstairs once I was done.

I would never have thought otherwise, but coming here was exactly what I needed. My mom and I had never spoken about anything so intimate in my entire life, but she put things into perspective for me. I believed Austin was the one; I could feel it in my gut, my heart – in every inch of me. I just had to make Amy see that as well.

I found Mom in the kitchen, pouring herself a glass of wine. When she saw me, she smiled and raised the glass.

"Isn't it too early for that?" I asked.

"It's five o'clock somewhere," she simply replied, taking a drink.

"Did someone stop by?"

"Oh, just Jessica; she and Hunter are back, and apparently, Austin lost his game." She made a sad face.

I held back a gasp, feeling guilty for missing it. Austin was probably depressed right now. I wanted to comfort him – be there in his victories and defeats.

"I'm ordering an Uber," I said, reaching for my phone.

"Nonsense, honey, I'll drive you to the airport."

I gave her a skeptical stare, then pointed at the glass. "Are you sure about that?"

She grinned, pouring the entire contents of the glass down the drain. "I only took one sip... are you ready?"

"Yeah, just about."

I looked around to ensure I had everything with me. My gaze landed on a brochure on the counter. With the attractive cover, I picked it up and mouthed the words *'Sip n Paint'.*

"What's this?" I asked, scanning the first page.

"Oh, my Pilates instructor introduced me to it. It's this thing where you drink wine and learn to paint."

I raised a brow. "I never knew you liked to paint."

"I'm mostly there for the free wine, but I find the painting to be therapeutic, too," she smiled. "I suck at it, though."

My mind drifted back to Austin and how good he was at it. I wanted to tell my mom how talented he was, but I held back. I didn't want her mentioning it to Jessica Callaghan because then Austin's secret would be out, and I didn't want to be the one to ruin his dream.

"The moderator owns an art gallery too. You should check it out when you come back. Anyway, we should get going; I don't want you getting back too late." She grabbed her car keys before running upstairs. "I'm gonna get a coat!"

"Okay!" I replied, slipping the brochure into my pocket.

I headed outside with my luggage in tow, pulling in a breath of fresh air. Heavy footsteps made me look to the right, and I stopped when I saw Hunter Callaghan crossing the street, heading toward me with his face as sour as vinegar.

I gulped, tightening my fingers around the strap of my bag, conjuring a smile.

"Mr. Callaghan."

He stopped in front of me, giving me a quick once-over. "Lindsay, I'll be quick."

I stiffened at his tone. "Austin seems to have this crazy notion that football is no longer what he desires, and I know he made that decision with your influence."

I gasped and took a step back, realizing the Callaghans now knew about me and Austin's relationship and that I'd been made a villain by them, too.

I straightened my posture. "With all due respect, sir, Austin made that decision all by himself long before we got together."

He shifted in his spot. "Austin loses focus when he sets his sights on a pretty face. If you really care about him, then you'll convince him to keep playing."

"I won't do that, Mr. Callaghan. Football has never been Austin's dream. It has always been yours," I argued, watching as a muscle ticked in his face.

He scoffed. "Listen to me, Lindsay; you either break up with Austin, or I cut your little boyfriend off forever," he smirked. "With you out of the picture, I bet he'll start to see reason soon enough."

The blood drained from my face as I stood there, taking in the triumphant look on his face before he turned and left. Mom came out, and I gasped as soon as she touched me, the tears threatening to spill.

"Sweetie, is everything okay?" she asked, looking over to Mr. Callaghan, who was already at his doorstep.

I nodded, my gaze shifting to Mom. "Yeah, er, let's go."

THE DRIVE TO THE AIRPORT was mostly silent as I pondered what Hunter Callaghan said to me. After my mom's advice, I had a plan, but my conversation with Austin's dad brought me back to square one.

I believed him when he said he'd cut Austin off, and I couldn't risk that. I couldn't be the reason Austin had nothing to his name. The tears threatened to spill, but I held them back, desperate not to arouse suspicion from my mom.

When we finally arrived at the departure terminal, she smiled and turned to me. "This is it, baby."

"Thanks, Mom, for everything," I said, pushing the car door open.

"Call me when you get there," she smiled. "I love you, honey."

"I love you too, Mom and some advice..." I said, watching as she perked up. "Get a divorce."

She gave me a surprised laugh in response, blowing me kisses as a sendoff. I got out and waved as I entered the huge building.

Time to face my ugly reality.

Chapter 20

Austin

Is she back yet? I texted Amy.

Not yet.

I released a heavy sigh and flopped down on the sofa as I glanced at the time. It was almost seven; what was taking her so long? I couldn't wait to tell Lindsay that because of her, I'd stood up to my dad for the first time in my life. Because of her, the weight of Dad's expectations had been lifted off my shoulders, which made me realize how in love with her I was.

Dad might have believed I only needed cooling down – that I wasn't serious – but I was, even with his threats. I wanted to explore the world with Lindsay by my side, and nothing would stop that.

She just came in. Hold your horses. Maybe you could talk to her tomorrow, Amy texted.

I rubbed the back of my neck and replied with a hesitant, *Okay.*

My night was a restless one, filled with anticipation for the next morning. I had no idea what the outcome would be, but I would fight like hell to convince Lindsay we would be great together. Amy had been the only stumbling block between us, but now that she was on board with our relationship, there was nothing standing in our way.

I rose at the crack of dawn, willing the day to be over soon enough, but it was like an extra hour got added each time it drew closer to the time I'd see Lindsay. Luckily for me, Coach had given us the day off from practice. When I knew Lindsay's classes were done for the day, I made my way to her.

As I walked down the hallway to her dorm room, I spotted Amy coming toward me, her face tight with tension.

My stomach dropped as I stopped in front of her. "Don't tell me you guys had another fight. Please."

"No, we're fine. Just... talk to her." She smiled tightly, patting my shoulder before heading in the opposite direction.

With a prayer on my lips, I knocked on the door, then did a quick scan of my denim shorts and snug black T-shirt. I sniffed my arms a little and popped back my head quickly when the door opened. The breath hitched in my throat when I saw Lindsay standing on the other side, stunning as ever, with her dark hair bound in a messy top bun, a few loose tendrils falling around her face.

Her eyes widened when she saw me standing there. She hugged her shoulders, drawing my attention to the tank top and cotton shorts that left her creamy skin exposed.

"Hi."

"Hey, Austin. What are you doing here?" she asked, her voice a little husky.

"Can we talk?"

She hesitated, her hand on the door. For a second, I thought she'd say no, but then she opened the door wider and stood aside, waiting for me to enter. This was my first time being inside their room, which made me notice how she and Amy differed in style.

She decorated her side with subtle earth tones that complemented every individual piece. Meanwhile, Amy's side contained a chaotic burst of colors, making it hard to concentrate on one thing.

The soft click of the door pulled me from my thoughts and brought my attention back to Lindsay. She stood before me, overwhelming my senses with her, sweet, warm scent.

"What's up?" she asked, so casually it made me frown.

"Is that a trick question?" I asked. "You haven't been answering my calls, Lindsay. I was worried sick until I heard you'd gone to visit your parents."

"Sorry about that. I needed some time to clear my head," she replied.

I slowly nodded. "And did you?"

She swallowed, bringing my attention to her slender neck that I'd laced with kisses countless times.

"I did."

"And? What did you decide?" I prodded.

She moved to her bed and took a seat on the edge, uncertainty bathing her face. "Austin..."

It wasn't a good sign when she said my name like that. I raced to say something else before she shot me down.

"Amy and I spoke over the weekend. We've cleared things up," I blurted.

"She told me. We talked long and hard last night, and I'm happy she's no longer mad, but... I don't think you and I will work."

I moved toward her, not opposed to falling on my knees. "Lindsay, don't do this, please."

Her eyes glistened with tears. "I'm sorry."

"You know we're good together. Amy was the only reason standing between us, and now that she's okay with it, I don't see the problem," I argued.

She didn't say a word, just sat there as her face reddened and more tears pooled in her eyes.

"Is this because of your parents?" She looked at me then, her eyes a sea of blue. "Lindsay, we're not them – we won't be. I love you."

"I just can't be with you," she said, her voice shaky as she got up from the bed.

"Why not?" My frustration grew.

No response.

"I thought Amy was the issue, but apparently, she wasn't. You got what you wanted from me, now you're ready to move on. Did you even mean it when you said you loved me?" I asked, a painful lump forming in my throat.

Tears streamed down Lindsay's face, but she said nothing, which made me wonder if I'd hit the nail on the head. She lied, didn't she? The tables had turned. I was no longer the heartbreaker but the schmuck who'd been taken for a ride by the last person I expected to do me wrong. Taken aback by disbelief, I blinked away the stinging in my eyes and stormed towards the door.

"Austin, wait!" Her quivering voice called after me, and I paused abruptly, slowly turning to face her.

"I do love you," she cried.

I rushed to her, gripping her shoulders. "Then what's the issue, Lindsay, tell me," I begged.

Her lips trembled. "Your dad," she muttered, and my eyes widened. "He said if I didn't break up with you, he'd cut you off."

My jaw clenched as anger raged through me at my father's audacity. But I didn't care for him at the moment – not with Lindsay here with me.

I shook my head. "He threatened to cut me off if I gave up football, but I told him I didn't care."

Her forehead wrinkled. "You did what?"

"I don't care if he cuts me off, Lindsay. Heck, I don't care if he disowns me. Once I have you, I know everything will be okay."

She sniffed. "But how will you survive?"

"My tuition had already been settled for the year. In a few months, I'll be old enough to get my grandfather's inheritance, which will have me set for a long time," I assured her, using my thumb to brush away her tears.

"But..."

"There are no buts; I love you Lindsay, and that's all that matters to me right now..."

She smiled and nodded. "I love you too."

With that, I kissed her long and hard, feeling like a man who had been deprived his entire life. With Lindsay, I felt whole, confident that when the storms came, I had nothing to worry about. She was *home*. I'd found my place with her.

Just as my cock hardened against her, she pulled away and smiled. "Wait, I have something to show you." She retrieved her bag on the floor and pulled out a paper, handing it to me.

"Sip n paint?" I asked, confused. "What is this?"

"It's an art class my mom attends once a week. The moderator owns an art gallery, and I did some research — turns out there's one here as well." She grinned. "I figured maybe you could go, check it out – show him a few of your pieces."

I flipped over the paper and scanned the back. "This definitely sounds interesting. I'll check it out. Will you come with me?"

"You don't need to ask twice, Austin Callaghan," she said sweetly, her body brushing against mine. "Of course, I'll go with you."

I kissed her again, but this time, it didn't stop there.

Epilogue

Lindsay

5 years later

"I CAN'T BELIEVE WE'RE here." I smiled at Austin, my arms looped around his neck as we waded through the warm Caribbean sea.

"Better than we imagined, right?" Austin asked, kissing me lightly on the lips.

"So much better. This is the best summer yet," I replied as my gaze shifted to the shore. "Me and Amy always talked about it, but I never believed it would happen this soon, I guess."

"Well, I promised to give you everything you wanted and more, didn't I?" Austin raised a brow, and I blushed at the memory. "That was the vow I made to you on our wedding day."

My heart fluttered at the mention of our wedding day, the best day of my life. Austin proposed to me the night of graduation night, and one year later, we sealed the deal. My life had been golden ever since. No complaints. Hands down, I was the happiest woman alive.

"You did, and I love you so much for that," I whispered, unable to resist his incoming kiss.

"Hey, guys! Your phones!" a voice called, causing us to pull apart. We looked to the shore, where Amy stood, waving at us with her shades on and our cellphones in her hands.

We waded from the water, and I took mine, a smile on my face when I realized it was my mom. I glanced at Austin as he got his and walked farther away on the shore.

"Hey, Mom," I said, taking a seat on one of the lounge chairs. My gaze shifted to Amy and Jason curled up on a chair together, giggling.

"Hey, sweetie, how is your trip?" Mom asked.

"It's the best; I truly couldn't ask for more," I replied.

"I'm happy to hear that; you deserve it, honey."

"Thanks, Mom. How's the condo hunting going?" I asked.

"Oh, it's good, I guess. There are just so many options," she moaned. "But I wanted something close to you, so I'll just settle on something in that bracket."

"Okay, did you see Dad?"

"Yeah, he's still pissed about our divorce for some reason, but he did promise a few connections to start up our consulting business."

I smiled. "That's great!"

"I'm so excited – you and me side by side like the boss ladies we are," she laughed.

I grinned. "I can't wait."

"Likewise, honey...You should talk to your Dad when you get back from your trip," she said.

A soft groan left my mouth. Dad and I weren't on speaking terms after I gave him a piece of my mind when Mom filed for divorce. Now, I no longer harbored any anger, just wanted everyone to get along. "I will, definitely."

"Okay, sweetheart, I don't want to keep you. Enjoy your trip, and tell Austin and the others hi for me."

"I will, Mom. I love you."

"I love you too, honey. I'll catch you later."

I had a smile on my face as I ended the call and turned to find Austin walking toward me, a beautiful specimen of a man with his muscles on full display – carved to perfection. It was all mine – he was all mine, and I counted my blessings every day.

"Is everything okay?" he asked, wrapping his hands around me and pulling me close.

"Yeah, everything is fine; that was Mom. She said hi."

"Did she finally find a condo?"

"Not yet, but she's close to finding one."

"Mmm..." He rocked with me; his head turned up to the sky. "So I just got off the phone with the art dealer from New York, and I have an exhibition next week," he said with a smile.

My eyes widened. "OMG, babe, that's amazing!" I exclaimed as I hugged him, smiling hard in his embrace. I knew how much this meant for Austin because the transition into his career hadn't been the easiest. But he'd worked really hard, and it was now paying off.

"I know. All my dreams are coming true, and that's because I have you." He looked down on me. "All I need now is a mini you—or me," he placed his hand on my stomach, grinning.

"How about we start trying now?" I whispered in his ear.

His eyes widened before he looked toward Amy and Jason. "You think these two will notice if we slip away?" he asked, humor in his voice.

I glanced over at our friends who were busy making out. "Not a chance." I giggled. "Let's go." I pulled his hand and raced to our hotel room.

This wasn't the first time we'd left Amy and Jason, but they never seemed to mind since they always enjoyed the privacy, too. We'd been on vacation for a few days now, and although we'd just decided to start trying for a baby, there was a high chance one was already growing inside me. We were always on each other every chance we got and that hadn't changed since college. I doubt it ever would.

Austin lifted me the instant we entered the hotel room, taking my lips for a kiss that left me breathless. I wrapped my legs around him as he made his way to the bedroom, where we spent the entire afternoon reaffirming our love for each other.

Night had already fallen when Austin finally rolled from my sweat-drenched body, his labored breathing matching mine. "You're amazing Mrs. Callaghan," he whispered, nuzzling my neck. "I can't believe I get to spend the rest of my life with you."

"Right back at you, Mr. Callaghan," I whispered back, happiness bubbling in my chest, excitement filling me at the thought of our future together.

I couldn't wait for our next adventure.

Pssst ... Do you enjoy reading full length *steamy* novels? If yes, then I have some great '*insiders' info'* just for you, but keep this on the hush. This deal is only for readers who have at least read one of my books to the end, ok? Did you know you can have 8 full-length novels for just **$2.99** or ***download it for free*** if you are a Kindle Unlimited or Prime Member? This amazing deal is ***over 2,100 pages***. Don't miss out ^_^

[1]

CLICK HERE TO GET THE DEAL[2]

1. https://www.amazon.com/dp/B0B1YTNCKQ

A HOT, STEAMY COLLECTION OF AGE-GAP ROMANCE NOVELS.

List of novels inside are:

Heating Up the Kitchen - a reverse harem romance

Just Can't Behave - a forbidden, age-gap romance

Protection Details - a bodyguard, forbidden, age-gap romance

Getting Through the Seasons - a stepbrother's best friend, enemies to lovers

Getting Through the Seasons 2

Getting Through the Seasons 3

A Dose of Sunshine - a rockstar, enemies to lovers romance

Mr. Grumpy's Fake Ex-wife - a boss, stalker, enemies to lovers romance

A Bonus Novella - My Roommate's Daddy - an instalove, OTT, age-gap romance

All are standalones, contain no cheating and have happy-ever-after endings ♡

Don't miss out on this fantastic offer, grab your copy today.

That's a completed 3 books series, 5 full length novels and a novella inside. **CLICK HERE**[3] to download and enjoy!

Let's connect.

Get this book for **FREE**[4] when you sign up for our newsletter.

WICKEDLY STEAMY & FILTHY!

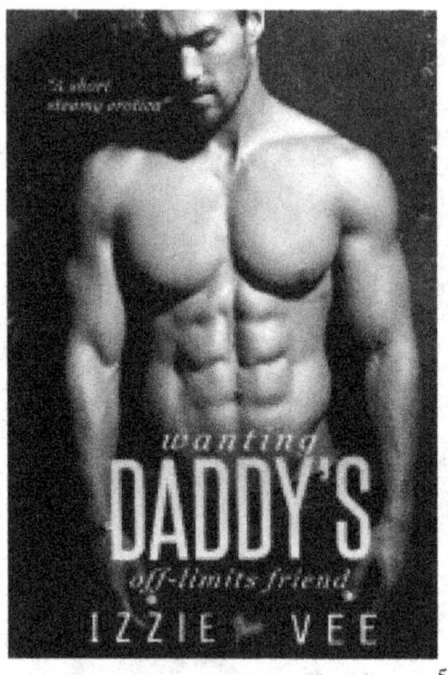

5

2. https://www.amazon.com/dp/B0B1YTNCKQ

3. https://www.amazon.com/dp/B0B1YTNCKQ

4. https://dl.bookfunnel.com/51j08erf93

5. https://dl.bookfunnel.com/51j08erf93

CLICK HERE TO GET FOR FREE[6]

SAMPLE

I COULDN'T BELIEVE that I was about to head off to college and never had a sexual experience in my life. The person I considered my boyfriend in my senior years of high school was initially the person I thought I would take the big step with but later found that he only had one intention in mind, and that was to fuck the only girl in our year who was rumored to still be a virgin – me. It had hurt, and I had broken off the relationship with a few heated words thrown at him but later realized there wasn't much I wanted out of the relationship either rather than sex.

I didn't want to be a virgin anymore, so I picked the boy that had given me the most attention and decided that he was the one. Unfortunately, he wasn't and here I was, about to head off to college with my hymen intact.

If it were only based on desire alone, then my dream guy would be the one who came over to my house every now and then with all his charm and kindness. He was the first crush I ever had, but I knew there was nothing I could make of the relationship considering he was my father's best friend.

Connor was everything I wanted in a man; he was sweet, kind, caring, incredibly handsome, and packing for his age. He taught gym at the college that I was accepted into, which made my excitement all the more profound. Dad said that Connor would be there to look out for me as he had always done, and I ... ***To continue reading get your FREE DOWNLOAD HERE[7].***

6. https://dl.bookfunnel.com/51j08erf93

*7. **https://dl.bookfunnel.com/51j08erf93***

Made in the USA
Monee, IL
13 December 2023

49132335R00393